Western Political Thought

(From Plato to Burke)

Western Political Thought

(From Plato to Burke)

Volume I

S.K. Sharma
Urmila Sharma

Published by

ATLANTIC

PUBLISHERS & DISTRIBUTORS (P) LTD

7/22, Ansari Road, Darya Ganj, New Delhi-110002
Phones : +91-11-40775252, 40775214, 23273880, 23275880
Fax: +91-11-23285873
Web: www.atlanticbooks.com
E-mail: orders@atlanticbooks.com

Reprint 2003, 2006, 2013, 2017, 2020, 2021, 2022, 2023

Printed & bound in India by Atlantic Print Services

Preface

This book on Western Political Thought covers political thought from Greek philosophers to Edmund Burke. Among dozens of books on this subject, this book is to the point, concise and covering syllabi of all the universities. Analytic in presentation, matter has been presented under central, side and running headings to make the readers easily understand and remember the subject matter. While matter has been drawn from authentic originals and books written by Western authors, care has been taken to avoid unnecessary details. Criticisms have been given along with description. An integral approach has been taken in all controversial matters. Questions actually asked at the various university examinations have been given at the end of each chapter so that the students may prepare for examination. Thus, this book has been planned as an ideal textbook for the students and a reference book for the teachers.

Today, Political Thought is being taught to all the students of political science in India. This book has been written in an easy style and simple language. However, suggestions are invited for improvement of further editions.

S.K. SHARMA
URMILA SHARMA

Contents

Page Nos.

Preface v

1. Introductory 1

PART I — ANCIENT POLITICAL THOUGHT

2. Ancient Greek Political Thought 7
3. Sophist Political Thought 18
4. Political Thought of Socrates 23
5. Political Philosophy of Cynics and Cyrenaics 32
6. Plato (427 B.C. — 347 B.C.) 34
7. Aristotle (384 B.C. — 322 B.C.) 124
8. Epicuream and Stoic Political Thought 189
9. Roman Political Thought 195
10. Christian Political Thought 220

PART II — MEDIEVAL POLITICAL THOUGHT

11. Political Thought of Middle Ages 229
12. Power Controversy Between State and Church 246
13. Papalist Thinkers of Medieval Age 251
14. Thomas Aquinas (1227 — 1274 A.D.) 257
15. Sacerdotal Thinkers of Middle Ages 278
16. Marsiglio of Padua (1270 — 1340 A.D.) 285
17. End of Medieval Period : Conciliar Movement 305

PART III — MODERN POLITICAL THOUGHT

18. Niccolo Machiavelli (1469 — 1527 A.D.) 317
19. Reformation Movement and its Thinkers 344
20. Jean Bodin (1530 — 1596 A.D.) 348

21. Hugo Grotius (1583 — 1645 A.D.) 372
22. Seventeenth Century Political Thought 378
23. Thomas Hobbes (1588 — 1679 A.D.) 384
24. John Locke (1632 — 1704 A.D.) 416
25. Baron De-Montesquieu (1689 — 1755 A.D.) 443
26. Jean Jacques Rousseau (1712 — 1770 A.D.) 461
27. David Hume (1741 — 1778 A.D.) 481
28. Edmund Burke (1729 — 1796 A.D.) 489
Bibliography 509

1

Introductory

Man is a social animal, he is unable to lead a solitary life. But he is not satisfied only by living in a society because his rational faculty impels him to know about himself and the phenomena and surroundings which influence him most. Nature has endowed him with curiosity and desire to know about his social surroundings and natural environment. From the very beginning he attempted to know something about natural phenomena.

Nature of Political Thought

Thus came into existence various sciences like Botany, Zoology, Physics and Chemistry etc. His natural desire to understand himself and the social surroundings in which his life is passed gave rise to social sciences like History, Politics, Economics, Sociology and Psychology, etc. His desire to know something about a creator and universe gave rise to philosophy, religion and astronomy etc.

Thus, *human beings began to study various subjects to satisfy their curiosity.* Man made all round progress and divided his knowledge into many sciences. The vast progress that man has made is not the work of one race or of one country. Various countries in different epochs contributed towards its progress. Thus, a subject had to be studied without dividing it into water tight compartments. As knowledge is so vast that none can gain mastery of a single subject, even of a single country, we have to study only that material which may be useful for our purpose and study of the present set up of society. As the political thought of modern world is based on the western political thought so we have to begin our study of political thought with the western thought useful to modern set up.

SUBJECT MATTER OF POLITICAL THOUGHT

1. The State. Political science may be defined as the study of state and Government. *It studies the process in which man attempts to govern himself* and his social surroundings. The state and its institutions, particularly the Government, constitute a very important part of social set up. Today with the emergence of social welfare states each and every activity of a man living in society is controlled by the Government. Political power is more vital than the physical and biological forces of the world. Though the state has been the subject of human speculation from the dawn of human reflection but now it is all pervading. It is necessary to study about it most thoroughly.

2. The Government. The people of all countries and of all ages have speculated about the Government, its nature, function and organisation. They have tried to understand the manner in which through the various institutions the Government achieves its purpose and on which these should be organized, if they are to work better. Such speculation gave rise to political thinking which is as old as the recorded history.

3. Human Nature and Its Relation with the Universe. Political thinking does not restrict itself to the state and government, it has gone beyond them. It is interested in the very nature of man and his relation to universe. According, to Phylis Doyle there are three main subjects that constitute the substance of political thought. "The nature and function of man: his relation to the rest of universe which involves a consideration of the meaning of life as a whole: emerging from the interaction of these two the problem of the relation of man to his fellow men." The latter is the main concern of political theory in the narrowest sense. It involves a discussion on the nature, purpose and function of the state. In politics man learns to govern himself, to acquire power and to work according to circumstances.

The great political thinkers like Plato, Aristotle, St. Thomas Acquinas, Marx, Hegel and Green have illustrated the comprehensive scope of political thought. In India, in ancient ages, Chanakya, Brahaspati etc. provided a good example. So intimate is the relation of the man and goal of his life that there is no use to try to understand the later without knowing the former. As such ethical, metaphysical and philosophical views of a writer are bound to colour and determine its philosophy. However, the primary concern of political thought is state. Political thinkers devote more time and attention to the discussion of its nature, origin, purpose, functions, organisations etc. than to speculation about the nature of man and his place in the universe.

IMPORTANCE OF WESTERN POLITICAL THOUGHT

It is generally asked that why should Indian students begin their study of Political Thought with Greek political thought and not with the political thought of ancient Indians, Egyptians, Babylonians, Chinese, Syrians and Persians etc. though these people did develop their own political thought. According to Binoy Kumar Sarkar, the Hindu counterparts of Pericles, Caesars, Justinians, Charlemagnes and Fredric Barbarosas could easily come out in flying colours in comparison with their western underscore peers on their own terms. In ancient time Indians produced political thinkers like Vidur, Chanakya, Brahaspati and Sukra and law givers like Manu, who can challenge their European counterparts. Jews and Chinese produced their own political thinkers and law givers. This contention of some writers that these early civilizations were unpolitical cannot be sustained.

Why start with Greek Political Thought? Two different reasons are given as to why we begin our study with Greek political thought. Firstly, the ideas developed by other ancient countries did not become parts of the European civilization as those of ancient Greeks did. Secondly, the results of their speculation of political problems were not exclusively contained in separate and independent treatises as was the case in Greece. They formed part of literature which was predominantly religious and ethical. This is particularly true about India where political thought is to be found in Ramayana, Mahabharat and Buddhist Jataks which are predominantly religious and ethical books. In Kautilya's Arthshastra also, one finds mixture of religious and metaphysical thought. In modern age even M.K. Gandhi did not embody his reflections on political phenomena in the form of a systematic treatise, his thoughts lie scattered in his speeches and articles. His political thought is coloured by religious and ethical outlook.

Thus one has to begin his study with Western or European political thought and its development from its beginnings in the speculations of the early Greeks.

Political thought does not develop or grow from simple to complex. Political problems present themselves in different ways under different circumstances. These are discussed in terms of different assumptions. Generally they remain same in essence. Answers to them though, different in detail, reveal some common elements, at least in the basic point of view from which they are approached. Sometimes it happens that an idea which held the field for a long time in one age, completely disappears for a few centuries and is revived again when circumstances favour its revival.

DIVISIONS OF POLITICAL THOUGHT

Political thought can be divided in four periods:

1. Ancient political thought.
2. Medieval political thought.
3. Modern political thought.
4. Contemporary political thought.

According to Gettle, ancient political thought is the basic foundation of modern political thought. To quote Gettle, "The problems of present have grown up out of the conditions in the past and the political principles that are now being applied are the result of evolution of past political thought." But it must always be kept in mind that all political thoughts have been influenced from different social environment and different political outlook of different persons.

Political thinkers have generally dealt with the following political problems:

1. The origin of state and its nature.
2. Relation of political science with religion and ethics or the controversy between the church and state.
3. The functions of the state.
4. The organisation of the state and government.
5. Sovereignty.

6. Law.
7. Justice.
8. Classifications of the government.
9. Utility or justification of the state.
10. Relation of political science with other physical and social sciences.

According to Will Durant, "To devise a method of barring incompetence and knowing from Public office and of selecting the best to rule for the common good is the problem of political philosophy. Politics is practical participation in political affairs or matters but in political science we confine ourselves to theoretical study. Political philosophy speculates about political problems and the idealistic view of the state or as the state ought to be."

Scope of political thinking can be divided in three parts:

1. Politics or Political Act.
2. Political Science.
3. Political thought or philosophy.

SOURCES OF POLITICAL THOUGHT

1. Geographical conditions.
2. Contemporary conditions and social set up or social environments.
3. Individual circumstances and experiences.
4. Great philosophers and their works.
5. Official documents.

1. Geographical Conditions. Montesquieu placed much emphasis on geographical factor. To some extent he was right, as no political thought has been developed by Eskimos in Tundra. However, geographical barriers are no longer important today as these were before city states developed in Greece as geographical factors suited for their growth but now same political thought may hold sway in England, India and U.S.A. etc. in spite of the differences of climate, environment and other geographical factors. With the development of science and means of communication geographical factors play a minor role. Marx may have been born in Germany and may have written in England but he influenced leaders of Russia, Cuba, India and China while he failed to have his sway in Britain and Germany. Thus geographical factors play a minor role.

2. Contemporary Conditions. Social environments affect a thinker. No thinker can remain uninfluenced by his contemporary social surroundings and problems. Aristotle defended slavery because he found it a common feature and was unable to think as to how citizens can get leisure to devote their time to solve the political problems and actual participation in states affairs. Similarly, contemporary controversy of church and the state affected all political thinkers of medieval period. With the development of individualistic political thought when man was free to think, psychological school of thought came into existence.

With the emergence of omnipotent states which shaped the destiny of individuals and moulded their life, thinkers like Hegel came into existence, who supported the power of state and called it, a march of God on earth. As economic forces became all pervading, economic surroundings began to colour the thought of political philosophers. Modern political thinking is influenced by economic considerations. U.S.A., Japan, Germany etc. being the richest countries on earth have supported capitalism while China being one of the poorest country supported communism. Now-a-days not the public, but rulers or persons in power influence most. If Chiang Kai-Sheik might have been in power in China, he would have supported capitalism, in spite of the poverty of the country. It has to be admitted that today economic factors play an overwhelming part and dominant role. In England which contains labour majority even conservative and liberal forces were unable to check it in gaining control over the Government in spite of the dominating personality of Mr. Churchil. Similarly, with the advent of prosperity and plenty, U.S.S.R. lost its old vitality and force for communism. Thus, economic factors shape our political thinking and set-up as recent events of Russia and Europe have shown.

3. Individual Experience. Man is the creature of circumstances. Not only social environments but individual circumstances and experiences also colour his thinking. It is said that Plato never lost the image of his teacher Socrates and never supported democracy under which his teacher Socrates was poisoned. Similarly "fear" which Hobbes experienced haunted all his political thoughts. The poverty which Karl Marx experienced and the inhuman treatment, which he experienced by the governments of different countries never lost profound impact upon the thinking of Marx. Appalling poverty and deportation by the various Governments were responsible to impress his thinking of stateless and classless society. Similarly, in spite of the fact that Britain had best administration, Mahatma Gandhi along with his followers had to personally suffer ruthless suppression and merciless suppression which forced him to say that man has a soul but state is a soulless machine and can never be separated from violence. Thus, personal experiences colour the thinking of the greatest political philosophers which the world has ever produced.

4. Great Philosophers and Their Works. Great political philosophers mould and influence the thought of future generation. Karl Marx borrowed from Plato though disagreed with Plato in many respects. According to Gettel, this source gives a history of political literature rather than of political thought. "Political philosophers are often too much removed from practical political life...." to make any attempt to view political thought in connection with the history, institutions and general intellectual background of its time. This source must therefore be supplemented by others.

5. Official Documents. Official documents are very important for the history of political thought. To quote Gettel, "The official documents of states furnish a most valuable source of political thought. These include written constitutions, treaties, diplomatic correspondence, state papers and the like."

IMPORTANCE OF POLITICAL THOUGHT

According to Gettel, "The study of political thought, therefore has practical value in that, it aids the formation of habits of more thorough and candid examination of the meaning and tendency of our political understanding." Political thought has always held an important status since the creation of state but now-a-days it occupies a most honourable place due to international circumstances. Now-a-days when social evolution is taking place with leaps and bounds, political thought is doubly important. The task of understanding the deeper implications of the present situation and the future planning can be assisted by a careful study of political thought of the ages. Study of Political thought in the historical perspective trains the mind to think, to criticise and to construct. It leads to mature thinking and enables a politician to solve contemporary problems in a better way.

QUESTIONS FOR EXERCISE

1. Give a brief introduction of Political Thought.
2. State the subject matter of Political Thought.
3. What is the importance of Western Political Thought to an Indian student and why is it taught in Indian Universities?
4. Describe the usual division of the history of Western Political Thought and discuss its problems and sources.

PART I — ANCIENT POLITICAL THOUGHT

2

Ancient Greek Political Thought

According to Barker "Political thought begins with the Greeks. Its origin is connected with the calm and clear rationalisation of Greek mind." However, the recent researches of historians and of archaeologists show that the people of ancient India, Egypt, Babylonia, Persia and China had developed political thought. According to Maxey, Egypt has the story of civilization lasting more than three thousand years. According to the same writer "The great thinkers of China did not neglect political thought, nor were political ideas alien to the Chinese people." Similarly, political motivation was an unconquerable element in Hebrew psychology. Maxey further observes, "It cannot be said about Hindu political thought, but the extent of their influence upon the past and present, and possibly upon the future, political life of India, no western mind is wholly competent to measure."

According to Mayer, "It is not possible to make any progress in our political thought, as without Greek Political thought the categories of European thought and approach to their understanding of life have been permanently moulded by the Greeks from the very beginning." As H.G. Wells said, "The Greek philosophers began an enquiry, and they arrived at no solutions. We cannot pretend today that we have arrived at solutions to most of the questions they asked."[1] According to George Wilhelm Friedrich Hegel, "The Greek spirit, on the whole...is free from superstition, since it changes the sensuous into the sensible — the Intellectual — so that oracular decisions are derived from Spirit."[2] To quote Bertrand Russell, "They invented mathematics and science and philosophy; they first wrote history as opposed to mere annals; they speculated freely about the nature of the world and the ends of life, without being bound in the fetters any inherited orthodoxy."[3] Man in ancient Greece was neither a worshipper of gods nor a seeker of utility in the economic sense of the term. He was a political man, as *zoon politikon*. The Greek thought centres round man *qua* man. It is a thought concerning neither *civitas dei*, nor

1. H.G. Wells, *The Outline of History* (1951), p. 335.
2. George Wilhelm Friedrich Hegel, *The Philosophy of History*, p. 237.
3. Bertrand Russell, *A History of Western Philosophy*, p. 21.

civitas terrena but civitas humana. The Greeks adored freedom and self-assertion. They were human *par excellence*. "The world is", says Sophocles, "full of wonders but nothing is more wonderful than man". "It is the unexhausted vitality, the permanent inspiration, the eternal humanity of Greek political ideas which gives them their claim to be re-studied and restated in our time". "Religion and worship", says McIlwain, "did not draw the Greek citizen away from the affairs of his city." They stood for the ideal that "government rests in the last resort upon conviction and not on force, and that its institutions existed to convince and not to coerce." Freedom, consisted in the rational capacity of the citizen to convince and to be convinced in free and untrammelled intercourse with his fellows.

Laboratory of Political Experiment

Greece has been called "a laboratory of political experiment", due to the following reasons:

1. Greece abounded with city states. Aristotle found as many as one hundred and fifty-eight city states with full-fledged constitutions and governments to many of which he refers in his *Politics*. The existence of so many states so near to each other naturally invited comparison and postulated detachment as a condition of their examination.

2. Ancient Greece presented a picture of flux. Constitutions changed in a quick succession. Instability was the nature of the Greek cities. It called for an attempt to determine what could be the best or the most excellent of the constitutions.

3. Greek outlook was rational. They tried to understand nature and the world in terms of reason. By reason they could make an objective study of the nature and problems of the cities. As Pericles proudly stated that by being rational, they developed the culture of reflection before action, which enabled them to be the builders of the science of politics.

THE SCOPE OF GREEK POLITICAL THOUGHT

Greek thinkers approached the political thought in the scientific spirit of examining the facts without any mental presuppositions and formulating generalisations to explain them. They devoted their attention mainly to the nature of the state and to man as a political animal. They came to the conclusion that man is a political animal. This is their main contribution to political thought. Being a political animal, man can realise himself only in and through membership of state. As such state naturally became the centre of Greek political thinking.

Greek thinkers discussed about the origin of the state and its end or purpose. They named the various forms of Government as Monarchy, Aristocracy, Democracy, Oligarchy and Tyranny etc. They were profoundly impressed by the fact that forms of government are subject to change. They tried to find out the reasons of changes, as well as the laws governing them. They discussed liberty, education and fundamental questions of political obligations and revolution etc. They examined carefully the various grounds on which different social classes based their claims to political authority. They also tried to find out the ways by which government can be stable. These topics are of permanent interest and of considerable value to a student of political thought.

As a thinker is influenced by his environment, so the thoughts of Greek thinkers were influenced by the nature of city state. It constituted the background of their thinking and furnished data for it. As such, a cursory glance about the city state is indispensable and useful.

THE CITY STATE

Nature of City State

About 1500 B.C., Aryan nomads conquered the region of Aegean. As military masters, the Aryan raiders settled down upon this pre-Hellenic social order. Each conquering hand succeeded in erecting an independent city state. The rivalry of kinsmen did not encourage voluntary unification. Hence, separation became the very keynote of their behaviour. Greek city state was a community, a true commonwealth or republic.

Common Life

A modern city like Calcutta, Bombay, Delhi or Madras or New York is a huge congregation of men living in a given area brought together mainly due to economic needs. In such cities persons living in the same building do not know one another. But in a Greek city state citizens used to share a common life or purpose. As Barker said, "It was the place of a common life and the home of union of classes. Life within common walls drew men together in a natural intimacy. If it did not abolish prestige of wealth and birth and culture, it established a tradition of easy intercourse between all classes. Like a college they walked, talked, played and met together in Assembly for deliberations to discuss or settle their matters."

Institution of Slaves

After the completion of conquest, Aryan conquerors became free citizens, while the conquered aboriginal population was reduced to the status of serfdom or slavery. No slave, no resident alien could take part in public assemblies, cast a vote, hold an office, appear in a court of law or enjoy any of the privileges of membership in the body politic.

Slave labour gave the citizens the leisure which they needed for the performance of civic functions. Slavery was an essential feature of Greek civilization. It was the basis of the political life of the state. Aristotle explicitly justifies slavery as a necessary institution. Plato nowhere condemned it. As Greek philosophers generally exhibited a pronounced contempt for manual labour, it was performed by slaves. However, this did not mean that nobody worked there as a manual labourer. In Athens there were 40 thousand citizens and 80 thousand slaves. While some slaves used to work in silver mines, others were owned by wealthy persons. The average artisan and farmer had no slaves.

He depended on his own labour for livelihood. Adequate payment enabled them to devote their leisure time for political matters and for participation in civic duties. Therefore, all Greek citizens participated in civic affairs.

The States of Athens

Athens and Sparta were the two most powerful and prominent states. These influenced the political thought of Plato and Aristotle etc. Plato was a full-fledged Athenian. The citizens were generally allotted one plot of land outside the city and one building within the city. The city states were even smaller than the districts of U.P. Plato imagined population of 5040 citizens enough for the ideal city state. If one includes women, dependents, children and alien, city population comes to about 20 or 25 thousand in all. Thus city states were very small in size and population. They included and absorbed the entire collective activities of the citizens. They played the same role in the life of citizens which society plays in the life of modern man. Hence Aristotle said that man is a political animal as we today say that man is a social animal. This city was small in size, possessed a corporate or communal character. It was the combination of urban and rural elements. Above all it was self-sufficing. Aristotle defined the state, as a union of families and villages, having for its end or purpose, a happy and self-sufficing life. Individual and state were so much identified that the idea of individual state would have appeared meaningless to the ancient Greek. Athens was a closed communion in which only citizens were allowed to participate. According to H.G. Wells, patriotism of these privileged people (citizens) took an intense and narrow form. A man's love for his country was reinforced by his love for his native town, his religion, and his home, for these were all one. Gods of Greeks were little more than human beings of heroic world, so their political ideas were undefined by religious heads. Priestly class was small and inconsequential. Economically there was no landed aristocracy in Greek society particularly in Athens. Diligent artisans, clever tradesmen and even slaves made fortunes and so it was involved in every class of economic forces.

Athenian Government

The active management of Athenian state was in the hands of citizens. Every adult male citizen was *ipso facto* a member of general assembly of citizens which possessed supreme authority. In addition to it, a citizen may also be called upon for service in courts. In Athens there were the archons, a board of magistrates, generals (ministers) and a council of five hundred whose function was preconsidering, proposing and supervising body elected by the citizens.

State of Sparta

Sparta was an agricultural state with a monarchical form of government dominated by military junta. It had a most rigid system of athletics, military exercise, diet and education. The Spartan boy was trained for warfare and government. Girls were trained for motherhood. Only strong children were allowed to survive. Perioikai had civil but no political rights and helots or agriculturists possessed no rights at all. There was a popular assembly. Though nominally it was supreme but it delegated most of its powers to five officers. The senate was the judicial body.

Charmed by the martial organization, repressive discipline, standardised education, social, regimentative and concentrated authority of the Spartan state, Athenian thinker considered these qualities essential for polity.

Athenians defeated Persians at the battle of Marathan in 490 B.C. The imperial age began under the leadership of Thermistocles. It reached its climax under the Pericles. Athens became the leader of maritime states and Sparta of the land states. A clash took place between these two states which lasted about eighty years in which Athens was defeated. This gave a setback to Greek city states.

CHARACTERISTICS OF GREEK POLITICAL THOUGHT

1. Political Science as Triology. The everlasting political philosophies of Athens produced immortal thinkers like Socrates, Plato and Aristotle and historians like Herodotus and poets like Homer. To a Greek thinker state was an enlarged and sublimated family, fusing the individual and the community into a harmonious and perfect whole. Citizens were duty bound to conform their behaviour with patterns prescribed by states. To them law was common sense and right reason in the form of specific rules of human action. They approached political thought with a moral point of view. Political science in their hands became an ethics of whole society. Republic of Plato is as much a treatise on politics as on ethics. For Aristotle ethics was an introduction to politics. In the words of Barker "Political Science is a Triology. It is a theory of the state; but it is also theory of morals and theory of love. It contains two subjects which have since been removed from its scope and treated as separate spheres. Greek political thought was connected with municipal or parochial character of the city state. There was conflict among the states as well as between rich and poor within the states. Political philosophy deals with practical political problems."

2. Importance of reason. Political thinking was born when men directed reason to the political life. The Greek thinkers considered reason as the highest faculty in human beings. Therefore, they raised a rational enquiry into the merits and demerits of different forms of government.

3. Practical nature. The Greek political thought was pragmatic. Greek thinkers aimed at the establishment of an ideal state in practice. Even in the thinking of Plato, while *The Republic* was a bit utopian, *Statesman* and *The Laws* were more pragmatic. *Politics* of Aristotle was solely based upon a pragmatic attitude in political science. It was due to this pragmatic approach that the Greek political thought had been giving valuable guidance to political scientists in the West.

4. Influence of Geographical conditions. Like thought in any other country, the Greek political thought too was influenced by the geographical conditions of Greece. Greeks faced few attacks from outside and therefore they could develop independent thinking. While the civilizations of ancient China and India were the result of Nature's bounty, the civilization of Greece was developed by the Greek power of reason.

5. Value of the individual. Though ancient Greek political thought prescribed wide rights for the state, it centralised upon the individual since the moral aim was the most important objective of the state. Ancient Greeks loved freedom. As the size of the state was small, each individual used to take part in almost every state activity. The citizens had a sense of responsibility, political consciousness and deep awareness. Therefore, the ideals cherished by the ancient Greek citizens can still be the guidelines of the citizens of the modern states.

6 Faith in political life. The most important characteristic of ancient Greek political thought was its faith in political life. The Greek thinkers did not distinguish between the political life and the moral life. Both in the political as well as in the moral fields the only aim was the evolution of the individual and providing him happiness. Man, according to the Greek thinkers, is a social animal. Therefore, the state and the community cannot be distinguished. The social development of man was carried on within the state. The state aimed at individual welfare. It gave sanction to all the religions. There was hardly any distinction between political and social life.

7. Quest for the ideal state. The Greek thinkers reflected upon the ideal state. They tried to determine its characteristics. In this connection the ideas of Plato and Aristotle have been found to be most valuable. The Greek concept of the ideal state can be a model even for the present day political thinkers because in Greek thought the ideal state was that which could realise the maximum welfare of the maximum number of citizens.

8. Faith in laws. The Greek political thinkers had faith in the law. According to Aristotle, the prescription of law is the highest principle to be followed in a state. The sovereignty of the law makes the state secular. The importance of law in the modern state given by the political scientists is the contribution of the ancient Greek thinkers.

9. Sentiments of Communal Welfare. The Greek thinkers did not distinguish between the society and the state, communal life and the political life. Therefore, communal welfare was the aim of the state. It is on the basis of this idea that modern political science has developed the concept of welfare state.

10. Unity in diversity. Unity in diversity is the basis of communal life. In the modern democratic states the citizens have to maintain communal unity while keeping intact their individual multiplicity. This principle has been borrowed from ancient Greek thought. In Greek city states an effort was made to establish unity among the citizens belonging to different classes and levels. The idea of unity in diversity is particularly important in the political thinking of Aristotle.

11. Ideal of civic life. The ideal of civic life, according to Greek political thinkers, was universal welfare. The theory of the state, the principle of law and the moral theory were considered identical. Aristotle maintained that constitution is the state and this constitution is not the system of the organization of the state but a moral life.

12. Identity of the society and the state. The Greek thinkers identified the society and the state. Plato suggested the theory of communism of property and women. In order to balance social forces, Aristotle suggested that the power of the state should be vested in the hands of the middle class so that there will be order and balance between contradictory classes of society.

13. Secularism. Greek thinking was secular while medieval thinking was religious. They thought about body and soul, i.e. about worldly affairs to be guided by the state and spiritual affairs by the church.

14. Humanising. Greek thinkers believed that man is the measure of all things. As such they were individualistic while medieval thinkers gave prominence to state and the church and man was bound to obey both king and the Pope.

15. State as Means of Good Life. According to Socrates, Plato and Aristotle etc., state is the means of good life and highest development while medieval thinkers were of the opinion that state came into existence due to sin of man and they considered the state based on violence and for punishment of sin. Epicurians, Sophists and Cynics did not give high place to state but they also did not support church while medieval thinkers gave prominence to church in their political thinking.

COMPARISON WITH MODERN THOUGHT

Similarities

Like modern thinking, Greek thinking was intellectual, secular and rationalistic. In the words of Mayer, "The categories of European thought and approach to the understanding of life have been permanently moulded by the Greek from the very beginning so long as the European thinker continues in his endeavour to know the historical world, it is adoption of Greek ideas and concepts which make this knowledge at all possible."

Distinctions

Modern thinking centres around national states as Greek thinking round city states but now with the emergence of world organisations like League of Nations and U.N.O. Universalism is also gaining ground. In modern age, biological, psychological, sociological, humanistic, pragmatistic and economical schools of thought have emerged which were unknown to Greek thinkers and were not prominent in medieval world. We should examine the ideas of the predecessors of Plato and Aristotle for three reasons :

1. Some of the predecessors are equally original and fertile in their thought, and should be studied in their own right.

2. The ideas enunciated by and the issues engaging the minds of the predecessors, go to some extent, to determine the thought of Plato and Aristotle, and, therefore, their study will facilitate the understanding of the latter."

3. They also deserve to be studied because, as J.W. Allen points out, the political thought of a period is to be found rather in the writings of obscure or anonymous persons than in the works of writers whose real distinction and originality makes them untypical.[4]

HOMER

An account of the predecessors of Plato must begin with Homer, who may be held as the first spiritual father of the western civilization. In Homer man was essentially proud and free, on happy terms with himself, with the world and with Olympus. The gods were his friends and partners, and are very human. The king to him was no eastern despot, speech was free. In certain broad particulars his outlook on the world, to quote Fisher, was also ours, "The joy of life, a sense of dignity of man, the eager desire for personal eminence, the cheerfulness, curiosity and love of adventure, which are characteristics of the Greek genius and were destined to make the fortunes of Europe are to be found in Homer."[5] Again, the rudiments of the Greek political organisation made their appearance first in Homer. The earliest Greeks made their first acquaintance with political terminology and political history, and learned the rudiments of their religion in the poems of Homer. Homer and Hesiod teach that the right way of doing things is not the way of violence. They contrast violence and lawlessness with "dike" (justice) which is the "way", "habit" or "custom" of a person. When "dike" has a divine content, it is called "themis". Homer personified "themis" into a goddess. He considered attainment of excellence as the value of life. If Homer was known for his *Illiad* and *Odyssey*, Hesiod was famous for his *Works and Day* and *Theogony* which contain the "earliest written record of the conscious application of human thinking to the problems of living together". Hesiod exalted "dike" to the status enjoyed by "themis" in Homer and brought it into association with the "polis". He underlined the divine origin and nature of *eunomia* good order and *eirene* (peace) as well as "dike" and announces all the three to be the principles of human society.

SOLON

Thus Solon made "good order" the theme of his poems. Solon was more famous as a law-giver. He was the founder of Athenian democracy. He valued justice, order, equality and condemned violence. He stood for a balanced social equality. He said, "I gave the people such power as sufficed, neither taking from their due honour nor giving yet more than was due. I have heard that men who had influence and were famous for their wealth should suffer nothing

4. J.H. Allen, *A History of Political Thought in the 16th Century*, p. xviii.

5. H.A.L. Fisher, *A History of Europe*, Vol I.

unseemly. I stood with my shield aloft to guard both the rich and the poor nor did I permit either triumph wrongfully."[6]

Solon believed in the sovereignty of law. He upheld people's right over the state. He stood for mixed constitution and a neutral state as a way out of the strife between the rich and the poor. Right order was the very life of the state and depended on justice. He abhored tyranny and advocated freedom, that is, freedom from subjection to a tyrant and freedom from debt or from subjection to the land-owning class. He was against large estates. He rescued the free labourer from bondage. He looked to trade to improve the general economy of Athens. In the Athenian constitution he retained the old gradation of the people in classes according to property. He added the *Thetes* as a fourth class and gave it certain political rights. The fourth class could hold no office but participate in the meetings of the *Ecclesia*, and have a voice in the election of the magistrates. He established courts consisting of all the citizens including the *Thetes*. Through these courts the people exercised great control over administration. He provided for the use of lots for the purpose of appointing public officers.

SIXTH CENTURY B.C.

The sixth century B.C. constituted a glorious era in the history of ancient Greece. The Greeks of this century invented mathematics, science and philosophy. They for the first time wrote "history" as opposed to mere annals. They speculated freely about the nature of the world and the ends of life."[7] They studied nature, but conclusions with regard to the elements of physical nature and their mutual relations involved similar conclusions about the elements of man's moral nature and the connection of those elements about the elements of the state and the scheme by which they were united.[8] If they saw growth in nature, they began to read it in man and his society. If they considered "harmony" or measure to be a principle of nature, harmony came to acquire importance in music and politics.

Among the philosophers who flourished in this period were Thales, the first man of science and the first philosopher, who held the primal substance to be water, Anaximander considered that substance is something infinite, eternal and ageless. He displayed a remarkable measure of scientific curiosity. Anaximenes held the fundamental substance to be 'air'.

PYTHAGORAS

These Milesian philosophers were followed by the Orphics led by Pythagoras about whom it has been contended that no other man has been more influential in the sphere of thought because "what appears as Platonism is, when analysed, found to be in essence Pythagoreanism". "The whole conception of an eternal world, revealed to the intellect but not to the senses is derived from him. It is

6. Quoted by Earnest Barker, *Greek Political Theory*, p. 50.
7. Bertrand Russell, *A History of Western Philosophy*, p. 21
8. Earnest Barker, *op. cit.*, p. 503.

also held that but for him Christians would not have thought of Christ as the 'World', and theologians would not have sought logical proofs of God and immortality."[9]

HERACLITUS

Heraclitus (500 B.C.) was an intellectualist, an individualist, and a mystic. He held that man's nature is a microcosm of the entire nature, that intelligence is common to all men. Fire was the primordial element out of which everything arises. Everything is in a state of flux so that "you cannot step twice into the same river", and that "war is the father of all". All things, come into being and pass away through strife. But there is a harmony of opposites. Man must be self-controlled and not give way to pleasure. There is nothing so inimical to intelligence as self-indulgence which causes the mind to become wet and flabby instead of firm and dry. The individual is responsible for his action; he cannot blame God for the defects of his own character. Law is a universal principle of divine origin just as strife and intelligence. It is to the polis what intelligence is to man.

PERICLES

Pericles's ideal for Athens was one of free citizenship in a free state. He said, "The citizen's freedom is his freedom to understand, to discuss and to contribute not according to his rank or wealth, but according to his innate capacity and his merit. The end of the whole is to bring into being life in common, for the individual the finest training school for his natural powers, for the community the amenities of a civilised life with its treasures of material comfort, art, religion and free intellectual development. In such a common life the supreme value for the individual lies just in his ability and his freedom to contribute significantly, to fill a place however humble in the common enterprise of civil life."[10]

His principles of politics may be summed up as follows: Everyman in his turn should be modified by the proper recognition of merit. The city should have an easy social atmosphere, and not one that is rigid and hide-bound. There must be proper submission to law, to authority and to the accepted code of behaviour. The state must be rich and powerful. It is the quality of the citizens that counts, and their training is all important. There must be no softness.

In the age of Pericles there flourished great poets and intellectual figures, namely Thucydides, the historian, Aeschylus, Sophocles, Euripides and Aristophanes, all of whom represented a new, dynamic human spirit and produced works of abiding importance. Equally important were the sophists who were, by and large, rationalist and individualist in their attitude. Gorgias, Protagoras, Prodicus, Hippias and others, discussed occasional topics, criticised political affairs and diffused ideas. Though varying in their views and doctrines,

---

9. Bertrand Russell, *op. cit.*, p. 50.

10. G.H. Sabine, *A History of Political Theory*, p. 30.

they were all agencies of enlightenment. The greatest of them was, Protagoras who maintained that man is the measure of all things (*homo mensura*). The state, according to him, depends upon a contract by which the individuals surrender the liberties for the sake of their mutual protection.

QUESTIONS FOR EXERCISE

1. "The Greeks began the political thought the first time." How far do you agree with this statement? Give reasons for the origin of political thought in Greece.
2. "The political thought begins with Greeks. Its origin is connected with calm and clear rationalism of Greek mind." (Barker) Comment on this statement.
3. "Before Greeks there were Government and its subjects hut not the politics." (Prof. Wayper) Discuss.

3

Sophist Political Thought

The 5th century B.C. was a period of great economic and political disturbances in Greece. The country faced with the great Persian war, in which Greeks were victorious. The fund of anthropological lore embodied by Herodotus in his history proves that the Greeks of the 5th century had formed a timely curiosity about the facts. An active and violent link between rival institutions of Persian absolutism and Greek autonomy and between Spartan oligrachy and Anthenian democracy presented a scene which provide much food for speculation to the keen intellect of the Greeks. They discussed that the monarch tends to degenerate into a tyrant, while democracy makes all men equal before law. But democracy follows mob rule and the government by the best person is certainly preferable. Perhaps rule by the best men is best of all. This period was characterized by great intellectual activity and freedom of thought. Political philosophy became one of the favourite subjects of study. This gave rise to a class of teachers who discussed and lectured on politics and taught the eloquence, dispution etc. They were called Sophists.

According to Barker, "The Sophists have been called half professors and half journalists, half teachers and half thinkers, half disseminators of things new, strange, paradoxical and astonishing, which could catch the ear. with something of the charlatan they combined something of philosophy."

To quote Sabine, "so tar as the Sophists were concerned they had no philosophy they thought what will-to-do students are willing to pay for."

SOPHIST PHILOSOPHY

Sophists had no systematic philosophy. They taught what well to do students were willing to pay for. They represented a transitional period rather than any particular system of thought in the growth of Greek philosophy. Their teaching of philosophy was characterized by a common method of approach and common point of view rather than by any community of thought. As they taught everything, this led them to systematize different subjects of knowledge. Humanism was the positive side of their thought. To the sophists abstract notions about universal truth and justice meant nothing. They believed that knowledge is the creation of senses and other human faculties and so it is a strictly human enterprise. To them "Man is the measure of all things." They propounded that "the proper study of mankind is man." An individual himself was to be the judge of whether his action was good or bad. This resulted in upsetting old ethical and legal code of conduct and pointed to individualism.

The Sophist did not believe in the natural origin of laws, the state and other associations. As evidenced by the fact that there was an endless variety of laws, the laws were not natural but conventional. If laws were natural, they would have been characterized by uniformity rather than by variety. To the sophists the laws were often based on political expediency. They were divorced from morality. Therefore, obedience to law was a question of personal interest. Sophists believed in the selfishness of human nature. They held that power, i.e. political authority was based on force. Even rebellion was defended in the name of a higher law, against the standing convention and the existing laws of society. In Antigone of Sophocles an artist exploited the conflict between duty to human law and a duty to the God. Antigone defended herself in the name of law of God when she was charged with having broken a law by performing funeral rites of her brother. She replied "Justice enacted not these human laws." Euripides denied the validity of social distinction based on birth. He opposed slavery and said that like freeman the slave hears an upright soul. Honest man is nature's noblemen. Thus according to Maxey, sophists were not a body of philosophers united by devotion to common principles but were sharp fellows who made a good living by acting as private tutors in rhetorics, argumentation, eloquence and other subjects.

TEACHINGS OF IMPORTANT SOPHISTS

The word 'sophist' has been formed from sophistes which means to be wise and learned. The fundamental idea of sophists was harmony of a life shared in common by all its members. Solon commended his legislation as producing a harmony or a balance between the rich and the poor. Anaximander tried to picture a system of opposite properties which are divided off from an underlying neutral substance. Harmony or proportion or if one prefers 'Justice' is an ultimate principle. The pythagorian philosophy specially regarded harmony or proportion as a basic principle in music, in medicine, in physics and in politics. In English, justice is still regarded as square number.

Alcidamas was of the opinion "God made all men tree, nature has made no man a slave." Sophist Antiphon denied that there was "naturally" any difference between a Greek and a Barbarian. In his book *On Truth* Antiphon wrote that law is merely conventional and hence contrary to nature. The advantageous way is to hold the law in public but to consult one's own advantage when one is not observed. For Antiphon, 'nature' is simply egoism or self-interest. Legal justice is of no use to those who follow it.

Thrasymachus said that justice is only the interest of the stronger, since in every state the ruling class makes those laws which it deems most conducive to its own advantage. Nature is not a rule of right but a rule of strength. Callicles observes that natural justice is the right of the strong man. Similarly, ambassador Melos said the Gods, we believe, and of men we know, that by necessary law of their own nature, they rule whenever they can.

TWO VIEWS

It seems that two views developed among sophists. One view was that nature is non-moral and human beings are motivated by self-assertion or egoism, the desire for pleasure or power. If interpreted moderately it comes near to utilitarian theory but it may also be taken to support anti-social theories. Other view was that nature as a law of justice is inherent in human beings and in the world. It is intelligent and beneficent, consequently moral and in the last resort religious.

IMPORTANCE OF SOPHISTS

According to Will Durant, "Sophists invented grammar and logic for Europe, they developed dialectic, analysed the forms of argument and taught man how to detect and practice fallacies." Knowledge before the sophists was unsystematic and indefinite. Led by necessity of teaching, the sophists systematized knowledge and thus rendered an inestimable service to humanity. On account of this, systematization of human speculation could be more definite and accurate in future. It was again Sophists, who made political science a practical study. Plato borrowed many of his ideas from the sophists. In Book II of *The Republic* Glaucon developed the idea of nature with egoism in a kind of social contract, of not to do injuries so that they may escape from the injuries of others, a kind of enlightened self-interest.

The sophists represented a sceptical time. Their scepticism and subjectivism led later on to the idealising of a man like Plato and others. General teachings of sophists and their individualism gave birth to the philosophy of Socrates. Their main contribution was that they looked upon the individual reason being the sole criterion of truth. Epicurian philosophy was based on lust for pleasure based on sophist philosophy. Aristotle was also influenced by their teaching. The view that Law of God or conscience is higher than man made laws was supported by Tilak and Gandhi, who opposed unjust laws which were against their conscience. Sophists gave political shape to political ideas. They accepted Reason as measure of truth.

Socrates used to say "I am following the occupation of my mother in as much as I bring about the birth of new ideas." Barker remarks, "A steady discharge of civic duties, and a steady refusal to go outside the bonds of civic law," are thus, two features, which mark his life as a true citizen of Athens. There was definite method and the rules for the relevant answering of question.

Man must be guided by true knowledge, which penetrated the surface of things irrespective of the motives and interests of passing periods and personalities and arrives at truth that is universal and eternal. Like other Greek thinkers, he believed that man is a political animal but he opposed the set up of the Athenian Government, which was based on equality and believed that all citizens are not equally qualified to participate in governmental activities and offices. He opposed the idea of equality and supported the view that only virtuous and wise persons should be entrusted with the administration of Government. This was too much for the Government which was based on equality to suffer, and Socrates was prosecuted and condemned to death for irreligious ideals.

In the words of Barker, "Yet he always and never more than in his death, was a loyal son of Athens. He had served in her army, he had been member of her council, her laws were to him only less sacred than the commands of God, and not to be disobeyed except for righteousness sake nor would he leave the prison where be lay doomed for ever when escape was easy, lest the laws should rebuke his life." As per Maxey, "His death by the cup of hemlock, subsequent ages have made a symbol of fallacy of trying to exterminate ideas by killing the man who advocated them."

SOCRATES AND SOPHIST THINKING

Socrates was heir to Sophists. He supported their contention that "conceptions of right must be subjected to the scrutiny of individual and not rest upon religion or traditional custom." According to Will Durant, "He was rich in crafty dodges and argumentive tricks, slyly changed the scope or meaning of terms, drowned the problem of loose analogies, quibbled like a school boy, and beat the wind bravely by studies. But he was not a sophist as he refuted their theories and aimed in reforming moral nature of man. He was more a prophet than a philosopher. To Socrates, "knowledge was virtue" but his knowledge was related with character. "Know thyself" was his motto. Against the ideas of equality, he was in favour of wisdom and not of birth or equality. He was for creating a professional class of moral and political leaders representing an aristocracy of intellect. There was in him and anti-democratic touch due to which he considered democracy an impossible form of Government and favoured aristocracy of talents.

Points of Differences

1. Validity of Social Laws. Sophists used anti-thesis between nature and convention to deny the validity of social laws and customs but Socrates held that these must be observed. He taught that virtue is knowledge and vice is ignorance.

2. Mechanical v/s Teleological Method. Ionians confined themselves to mechanical explanation of things; they tried to find out how things are made but Socrates enquired into their purpose or final cause. In brief Ionians method was mechanical but method of Socrates was teleological which was further developed by Plato and Aristotle.

3. Nature of Goodness. Sophists maintained that goodness was special art, which could be mastered by attainment of a special knowledge but Socrates believed goodness was general capacity and thus unique. Goodness according to him was the knowledge of nature of things of ultimate reality.

4. Independence of Spirit. Socrates taught without taking fees and showed a greater independence of spirit than the Sophists.

5. Law and State. Whereas the sophists did not believe in any abstract notions of right and justice, Socrates believed that out of the general mass of laws, conventions and customs, a general code of ethics could be prepared to guide mankind. He entertained a great respect for laws and could conceive no natural justice outside laws. Law was to him sovereign both for ruler and ruled. It was "the written agreement of the citizens, defining what should be done and what should not be done."

QUESTIONS FOR EXERCISE

1. Give a brief account of the Political Thought of Sophists.
2. Give main teachings of important sophists and point out their importance.

4

Political Thought of Socrates

Born in Athens in 469 B.C., Socrates was the son of poor parents. His father was a sculptor and mother a mid-wife. Nothing is known about the early education of Socrates but so many stories are current concerning his love for learning right from his childhood. He grew as an adult very much unnoticed by the people around him and took up the occupation of his father. But soon, Socrates felt a divine vocation to examine himself by questioning other men. Thus he used to visit people in the streets, in the market places, in the gymnasia, and at other places and engaged them in discussions concerning war, politics, marriage, love, house-keeping, friendship, arts and trades, poetry, science, religion etc. His main topics of discussion were the moral aims and ideals and virtues. His range of knowledge and discussion covered almost the entire life, theoretical as well as practical. He was not interested in the physical world. The subjects of his enquiries were the human life itself particularly the life of reason. He gave so many examples of great physical and moral courage. This was seen in his performance in war time. He was kind and gentle and had a great sense of humour. He was, however, keenly interested in exposing the quacks and humbugs of the society around him and show them how ignorant they were. This gradually increased the number of his enemies. The prediction of the oracle of Delphi that Socrates was the wisest man of Athens also caused the growth of so many enemies around him. The people around him, gradually started talking against him. As the number of his admirers grew so also grew the number of his enemies.

Ultimately, a complaint was lodged with the stale that Socrates was corrupting the youth and propagating atheism. He was tried in the court and so many witnesses were produced. In this trial the words of Socrates concerning death, virtue and so many other important things have become historical. However, he was condemned to death. In jail, his friends tried to persuade him to escape. He, however, refused and pointed out that everyone must obey the laws of the state even at the cost of his death. He was given hemlock which he drank cheerfully and embraced death.

In the whole history of humanity there had been no greater humanist, philosopher and lover of wisdom than Socrates. This short, stocky, stout, blear-eyed and snub-nosed man, with a large mouth and thick lips, careless in his dress, clumsy and uncouth, was perhaps the most beloved teacher of his disciples. This is amply clear by the writings of his main disciple Plato. Socrates himself did not write much. We, however, know about him from so many works some of which are: Xenophon, Memorabila, in *Works of Xenophon*, Vol. III, trans. by H.G. Dakyns, 1890-97; Plato's *Dialogues*, especially *Protagoras, Apology, Crito, Phaedo, Symposium, Theaetetus*, trans. by Jowett, 3rd ed., 1892; Aristotle, *Metaphysics* (1, 6; XIII, 4). trans. in Bohn Library, also by W.D. Ross; Aristotle, *Ethics*, trans. by J.E.C. Welldon, 1892; E. Zeller, *Socrates and the Socratic Schools*, trans. by O.J. Reichel, 1885; J.T. Forbes, *Socrates*, 1905; A.E. Taylor, *Varia Socratica*, 1911; E. Pfleiderer, *Socrates, Plato und ihre Schuler*, 1896; M.M. Dawson, *The Ethics of Socrates*, 1924; A.K. Rogers, *The Socratic Problem*, 1933; A.D. Winspear and T. Silverberg, *Who was Socrates*? 1939.

THE AIM OF PHILOSOPHY

About the words of Socrates, Plato said, "You will find his words first full of sense, as no others are; next, most divine and containing the finest images of virtue, and reaching farthest, in fact reaching to everything which it profits a man to study who is to become noble and good."[1]

Unlike most philosophers, Socrates did not wish to influence others by his views; he did not wish to convince them about the validity and correctness of his views. Rather he wanted that everybody should be his own philosopher; should be critical and think for himself. He was convinced that every person had in him the germ for rational thought and the aim of philosophy was to bring rational thought to full blossom in everyone. The tendency among philosophers to persuade others to believe that their views are more valid gives rise to schools and controversies in philosophy. Socrates, on the contrary, did not wish to convert others to his views nor did he wish to propagate a set of philosophical views. He only wanted to draw the attention of others to the crucial significance of philosophy for life and inculcate in them a love for philosophy, that is, love of wisdom. The approach of Socrates to philosophy is known as mimetic approach, that is intellectual midwifery. As a midwife delivers a child of a pregnant woman, Socrates wanted to bring to surface the germ of rational thought and critical inquiry. The whole approach of Socrates in philosophy is summed up in two words — Dialectical Method. Now we turn to a detailed examination of this method.

THE DIALECTICAL METHOD

Socrates was fully conscious of the value of knowledge. According to him, "*Knowledge is virtue*". Knowledge for Socrates was vision of universal truths. To discover this knowledge he made use of dialectical method. Though Socrates invented and used dialectical method he was nowhere given a systematic description of this method. As remarked earlier, Socrates did not commit his

1. Warmington, E.H. and Philip G. Rouse (Ed.), *Great Dialogues of Plato*, Trans. by W.H.D. Rouse, Mentor, New York, 1956, p. 115.

ideas to writing. His style of developing philosophical ideas was unique. He was used to go down the market place and would draw philosophically inclined persons to discuss with him the real and objective meaning of such simple concepts as friendship, love, courage, virtue etc. In the course of his dialogue he would let people know that what he was interested in was not the conventional meaning but the real and objective meaning of the concepts. Thus he would direct the course of conversation. This method was dialectical because to all proposed meanings and definitions of concepts, Socrates would bring out the defects in them and thus persuade his interlocutor to modify his definition to rectify the defects pointed. This procedure of point and counterpoint would go on till a really satisfactory definition was found.

Thus we find that in the hands of Socrates dialectic was a means of discovery of objective and valid definitions of concepts familiarly used in daily life. It is not the condition of a dialectical argument that the domain of the argument should be confined to the concept being discussed. It is indeed considered desirable to examine the allied and other concepts if clarification of the concept in question calls for such a discussion.

IMPORTANCE IN POLITICAL THOUGHT

Socrates is important to humanity for all time to come because his thought goes into the making of what has been termed as the perennial philosophy. He is particularly relevant to the modern world which stands in a dire need of listening to his words that have become classics in the annals of mankind. He might as well be considered as a living influence. His spirit, in its critical aspect, embodies itself in the thought of Rousseau. To a student of political thought he is particularly important as the teacher of Plato, the greatest philosopher of the West. It was on the foundations laid down by him that Plato erected his splendid mansion of thought and philosophy.

In the whole history of civilization, the personality of Socrates as well as his outlook remains unique. He was considered to be "the best, justest and wisest man of ancient Greece." He was the man who defined knowledge as an awareness of one's ignorance. If truth is what matters most in life, Socrates was its indefatigable champion. If freedom is what constitutes the essence of manhood, he was its messenger *par excellence*. While he stood for truth and spiritual freedom, he was no advocate of renunciation. He excelled all his contemporaries in his duties towards the state. If there was a higher court than the highest in the land, it was stationed, he said, in the conscience, in the inner voice or the daemon of man.

IMPACT ON GREECE

Socrates left his impact upon the age and the posterity first in the manner of his conduct, secondly by his sayings and thirdly by his death. In the dualism of the heavenly soul and the earthly body he is said to have acquired complete mastery of the spirit over the flesh. His indifference to death is the final proof of this mastery. He anticipated both the Stoics and the Cynics. Like the former he held that the supreme good is virtue, and that man cannot be deprived of virtue and therefore of happiness by outside causes. Like the latter he despised worldly goods and went barefoot and ill-clad.

HUMANISM

Socrates was interested more in man *qua* man than in the institutions of society. In *The Apology* he describes his mission thus: "I have no other business but to go about persuading you all, both young and the old to take care less for your bodies and your wealth than for the perfection of your soul, and telling you that goodness does not come from wealth but it is goodness that makes wealth or anything else in public or private life a good thing for man."

PHILOSOPHY AS A WAY OF LIFE

Influenced by the orphism of Pythagoras, Socrates looked at philosophy as a way of escape from the wheel. Once a man understands what is "right", his nature, Pythagoras held, makes him act in the light of that understanding. Intelligence, therefore, must not be separated from will: the test of knowledge must be a proved capacity of action. Knowledge thus not only imparts perception of truth but also inspires action in correspondence to the same.

MYSTICISM

A mystic, a man possessed by the daemon, Socrates often fell into trances. He remained in that state for hours and days together, and he used to hear the inner voice, the daemon speaking from within. One fine morning, as Plato writes in the Symposium, Socrates was thinking about something which he could not resolve; he would not give it up and continue thinking from early dawn until noon, fixed in thought. At noon his attention was drawn to the rumour spread through the wandering crowd that Socrates had been standing and thinking about something ever since the break of the day. At last in the evening after supper some Ionians out of curiosity brought out their mats and slept in the open air that they might watch him and see whether he would stand all night. There he stood until the following morning, and with the return of light he offered up a prayer to the sun and went his way. This sort of experience was a usual feature of Socrates. Thus, again at the beginning of a symposium Socrates and Aristotle go together to the banquet but Socrates drops in a fit of abstraction or trance. Little wonder that Socrates had faith in the mysterious daemon. The latter often spoke to him in its typical way and prompted him to do or not to do a thing when he wanted to. It was probably on account of his faith in the daemon that he was accused of introducing new gods or daemons in the Athenian society. As the daemon was made of a stuff that was mystical, he would not explain it in rational terms as he could not. The daemon is not within and at the disposal of a person but is received from a larger sphere external to him and acknowledged with reverence and awe. He who listens to the daemon enhances his character for he has a divine guide to lead his steps in life.

THE DAEMON

The daemon, as Plato writes in *The Timaeus*, is given by God to everybody as part of his soul. Its seat is the head which is akin to heaven, and therefore, raised towards it. The daemon is a divine element which must be cultivated so that man becomes 'eudaemonic'. Before Socrates it was taken to be an element that remained constant throughout all the flux and fluctuations of life, and made any action of an individual his characteristic action. As Heraclitus said, man's character is daemon, and it is not confined to his earthly life but follows him across the threshold of birth from a previous existence, or accompanies him in all the lives that his soul lives. The daemon is a bond inexorable and mysterious between the human life and divine. It is the idea of the daemonic as a realm intermediate between the human sphere and the divine which unites the cosmos with the world by virtue of its intermediate position.

RATIONALISM

The way you gain knowledge, holds Socrates, is more important than knowledge itself. The right way of acquiring knowledge of old things matters more than the knowledge of new things. He views Reason as a court from which there can be no appeal, and after which a man must fashion his life. Tradition or prescription should never be allowed to stand between man and Reason which he must follow to its extremest end. Knowledge and veracity, sovereignty of wisdom and loyalty to the daemon are the ideals, which one must follow regardless of the consequences and prejudices concerning the family and the state.

KNOWLEDGE IS VIRTUE

That knowledge is virtue is the most significant teaching of Socrates. What he means by it is that real knowledge must be a matter of realisation in life. It must be a power that brings about the transformation of personality. Knowledge is an insight gained by the soul. It is lived by him from the depth of his being. When man has knowledge he has it not as possession but as qualification or excellence of the soul which results in action marked by that excellence. The excellent state of the soul is the highest happiness which a wise man attains. The term virtue here indicates not any moral quality as such but the excellent working of the soul of which the moral quality may be an aspect.

ART OF DIALECTIC

Socrates is the inventor of the art of dialectic-discussion through question and answer. In dialectic, definition is the essential point. When we make a judgement we compare two ideas, and in order to do so correctly we must see that the ideas are very clear, for error comes from comparing vague and undefined ideas. Truth can be reached only through discussion in which there must take place a clash between two opposite points of view. The procedure of dialectic is governed by strict logical rules. The answer required in reply to the question must be in the fewest clearest possible words, and both answer and question must be precise on every point. Socrates, however, is said to have learned it from Zeno.

POLITICAL PHILOSOPHY

The following are the most important views of Socrates concerning political issues —

1. The Laws and the State. According to Socrates laws should be based upon the moral principles so that they may guide the citizens who, in their term, may respect them. Therefore law, according to Socrates, is above both the ruler and the ruled. It points out what a citizen should do and what he ought not to do. Man is a social being and therefore the institution of the State is necessary and beneficial for him.

2. Theory of knowledge. Man's aim in the field of knowledge is to know himself. Knowledge is of two types—based upon common sense and based upon philosophic goodness. Knowledge, cherished by the Sophists, was based upon common goodness. Socrates aimed at universal knowledge, a knowledge of virtue since, according to him, virtue is knowledge and knowlege is virtue.

3. Theory of State. Politics, according to Socrates, is not a profession but an art. The ruler should be well versed in the art of politics. The state is a natural institution. It is prior to the individual and the community and aims at general welfare. Only a person well versed in the art of politics may be appointed a ruler. The ideal state is that where intellect and reason are utilised in state craft.

4. Human nature. Man, according to Socrates, has both selfishness as well as the urge to welfare. While the former is injurious, the latter is useful. The latter nature is the primary human nature.

5. Means of knowledge. Socrates adopted the dialectical method for the achievement of knowledge. In this method he used to visit the so-called scholars and political thinkers of Athens and discuss with them different issues. As they could not give satisfactory answers he used to argue and prove that they are ignorant though he never claimed any knowledge for himself. The utilisation of this dialectical method turned almost all the contemporary scholars against Socrates. He was charged and presented in the court as a result of which he was sentenced to death by drinking poison. His death, however, resulted in a wide and fast circulation of his ideas. The most important role in this process was performed by his eminent disciple Plato. His contemporary Athenians considered him as a Sophist as his criteria was also humanist and yet his thinking was different from that of the Sophists on the following counts:

(i) While according to Sophists the world is mechanical, Socrates considered it as purposive.

(ii) According to Sophists goodness is an art which can be achieved by specialised knowledge. According to Socrates, on the other hand, goodness is not an art but an innate power of man.

(iii) While according to Sophists man is the measure of all things, according to Socrates the criteria of different things are established according to their different purposes.

(iv) The theory of knowledge presented by Socrates was very much different from that of the Sophists.

(v) According to Sophists the social rules are not based upon the nature and the traditions but they are man-made. According to Socrates the traditional laws are above man. It is hence that he embraced death while following the law.

The above distinctions between the thought of Sophists and that of Socrates show that they had real differences. While Socrates was a citizen of Athens, the Sophists were foreigners. While Socrates did not charge anything as his fee for education, the Sophists used to make charges. Socrates, therefore, was not a Sophist. At the age of 70 he was charged and sentenced to death. His death shocked his disciple Plato. It influenced thinking men everywhere. It encouraged enquiry into freedom of thought. Socrates laid emphasis upon reflective thinking. He preached that man should himself decide about the true and the false and follow the path directed by his soul. Besides having individual decisions the individual should follow the laws of the state which are obligatory upon him. The greatest contribution of Socrates is his dialectical method which was later on utilised by his eminent disciple Plato.

SELECTIONS FROM THE APOLOGY

The Socratic Enquiry

"Those who had the highest reputation seemed to me nearly the most wanting, when I tried to find out in the god's way, but others who were thought inferior seemed to be more capable men as to common sense."[2]

The Criteria of Good Life

Well, gentlemen, I am no criminal according to Meletos's indictment, that needs no long defence from me to prove, but this is enough. However, when I said some time ago that I was heartily disliked by many, you may be sure that it is quite true. And this is what will convict me, if anything does, not Meletos or Anytos but the prejudice and dislike of so many people. The same thing has convicted many other good men, and I think will do so again; there is no fear it will stop with me. But perhaps someone may say: Are you not ashamed then, Socrates, at having following such a practice that vou now run a risk of a sentence of death? I would answer such a one fairly: *You are wrong, my friend, if you think a man with a spark of decency in him ought to calculate life or death; the only thing he ought to consider, if he does anything, is whether he does right or wrong, whether it is what a good man does or a bad man.*"[3]

2 Warmington E.H. and Philip G. Rouse (Ed.), *Great Dialogues of Plato*, trans. by W.H.D. Rouse, Mentor, New York, 1956, p. 428.

3 *Ibid.*, p. 434.

No Fear of Death

For to fear death, gentlemen, is only to think you are wise when you are not; for it is to think you know what you don't know. No one knows whether death is really the greatest blessing a man can have, but they fear it is the greatest curse, as if they knew well."[4]

Follow God's Commands

Many thanks indeed for your kindness, gentlemen, but I will obey the god rather than you, and as long as I have breath in me, and remain able to do it, I will never cease being a philosopher, and exhorting you, and showing what is in me to any one of you I may meet, by speaking to him in my usual way: excellent friend, you are an Athenian, a citizen of this great city, so famous for wisdom and strength, and you take every care to be as well off as possible in money, reputation and place — then are you not ashamed not to take every care and thought for understanding, for truth, and for the soul, so that it may be perfect ? And if any of you argues the point and says he does take every care, I will not at once let him go and depart myself; hut I will question and cross-examine and test him, and if I think he does not possess virtue but only says so, I will show that he sets very little value on things most precious, and sets more value on meaner things, and I will put him to shame. This I will do for everyone I meet, young or old, native or foreigner, but more for my fellow-citizens as you are nearer to me in race. "*For this is what God commands me, make no mistake, and I think there is no greater good for you in the city in any way than my service to God.*"[5]

Value of Virtue

"All I do is to go about and try to persuade you, both young and old, not to care for your bodies or your monies first, and to care more exceedingly for the soul, to make it as good as possible; and I tell you that *virtue comes not from money, but from virtue comes both money and all other good things for mankind both in private and in public*. If, then, by saying these things I corrupt the young, these things must be mischievous; but if anyone says I say anything else than these, he talks nonsense. In view of all this, I would say, gentlemen, either obey Anytos or do not obey him, either let me go free or do not let me go free; but I will never do anything else, even if I am to die many deaths."[6]

Freedom of Speech

"For if you put me to death, you will not easily find such another, really like something stuck on the state by the god, though it is rather laughable to say so; for the state is like a big thorough-bred horse, so big that he is a bit slow and heavy, and wants a gadfly to wake him up. I think the god put me

4. *Ibid.*, p. 435.

5. *Ibid.*, pp. 435-36.

6. *Ibid.*, p. 436.

on the state something like that, to wake you up and persuade you and reproach you every one, as I keep settling on you everywhere all day long."[7]

"Do not be annoyed at my telling the truth; the fact is that no man in the world will come off safe who honestly opposes either you or any other multitude, and tries to hinder the many unjust and illegal doings in a state. It is necessary that one who really and truly fights for the right, if he is to survive even for a short time, shall act as a private man, not as a public man."[8]

"But you also, judges of the court, must have good hopes towards death, and this one thing you must take as true — no evil can happen to a good man either living or dead, and his business is not neglected by the gods; nor has my business now come about of itself, but it is plain to me that to die now and to be free from trouble was better for me. That is why my signal did not warm me off, and why I am not at all angry with those who condemned me, or with my accusers. Yet this was not their notion when they condemned and accused me; they thought they were hurting me, and that deserves blame in them. However, one thing I ask them: *Punish my sons, gentlemen, when they grow up; give them this same pain I gave you, if you think they care for money or anything else before virtue; and if they have the reputation of being something when they are nothing, reproach them, as I reproach you, that they do not take care for what they should, and think they are something when they are worth nothing.* And if you do this, we shall have been justly dealt with by you, both I and my sons. And now it is time to go, I to die, and you to live; but which of us goes to a better thing is unknown to all but God."[9]

QUESTIONS FOR EXERCISE

1. Describe the ethical and political ideas of Socrates.
2. Show how the Socratic doctrine of the sovereignty of knowledge might, as Barker points out, easily become, in its political application, a doctrine of enlightened despotism.

7. *Ibid.*, pp. 436-37.
8. *Ibid.*, p. 437.
9. *Ibid.*, p. 446 last paragraph.

5
Political Philosophy of Cynics and Cyrenaics

The preaching and unprecedented sacrifice of Socrates gave birth to a new ideology in Greece known as Cynicism. Its originator was Antisthenes. Along with it was born another ideology known as cynicism. The pioneer of Cyranaics ideology, was Aristeppus who resided at Cynics on the sea cost of Africa. Hence, the title Cyrenaics.

CYNIC IDEOLOGY

The cynics tried to extend Socratic wisdom applying it to all the world instead of confining it to Greek city states. This attempt was against, the traditions as well as against Political constitution of Greek city states. Cynics pleaded for world citizenship in place of citizenship of Greek city state.

Taking clue from Socratic plainness and his simplicity cynicism supported indifference and the detached attitude of a beggar as an ideal life. They criticised the worldly things including the political life and preached for its rejection. They were against all human institutions, *viz.* family, marriage and state. They advocated good news to all and everywhere. They gave a spiritual meaning to the famous Socratic dictum: Virtue is knowledge. They believed that worldly things is knowledge. They believed that worldly things are an impediment to attaining spiritual goods.

Antisthenes supported complete freedom of thought and expression. He remarked, "Against the current of his baneful stream of political ideology, Socrates set himself like a stubborn bastion." Cynics supported complete renunciation to achieve perfection. The whole world is one state and man is a citizen of this universal state. Plutarch ridiculed this idea of universal citizenship by saying that Alexander, the great, planned for the conquest of the world, giving a political shape to cynic ideology.

Antisthenes was a contemporary of Plato. He wrote *Concerning Law* and *Cyrus or Concerning Monarchy*.

He gave the slogan "Back to Nature," In Greek, cynic means a dog. This level was given to this ideology by those who hated and opposed it.

CONTRIBUTION TO POLITICAL THOUGHT

1. Individualism. Cynics gave birth to individualism in political thought. They believed that man is perfect is himself. Self-knowledge leads to human liberation; society or state is not required for it. This individualist attitude of cynic gave lead to political ideology of individualism.

2. Return to Nature. Cynics gave the slogan: Back to Nature. They supported living in the lap of Nature away from the artificiality of society and state. Later on Rousseau supported this cynic slogan in education.

3. Cosmopolitanism. Away from the Greek city states, cynics supported cosmopolitanism and world citizenship. This was against the political ideology of both Plato and Aristotle. Cynics were very much against the theory of city states.

4. Idea of World State. According to cynics, we are citizens of a world state. This idea was pioneered by Diogenes, according to whom all of us are citizens of a universal world state.

5. World Brotherhood. Cynics propagated world or universal brotherhood. They preached that the whole world is one family, one state and one should fulfil his duties accordingly. Irrespective of different races, colours, creeds and state, all are brothers. Intelligence and knowledge are not monopoly of Greece. An African is as much capable of attaining knowledge and wisdom as a Greek. This ideology of universal brotherhood had a wide impact on political thought.

CYRANAIC POLITICAL IDEOLOGY

1. Attaining of Self Knowledge. Man should aspire after liberation from worldly bondage. Self-knowledge alone can lead to it. Man can attain liberation by following Socratic dictum 'know thyself'.

2. Present is an Ultimate Truth. According to Cyrenaics achievement of pleasure is the ultimate aim of man. To attain maximum pleasure, man should live only in the present. He should not think of past or future because the present is the ultimate truth.

3. Custom as Law. Custom is not natural but based on traditions. Following the custom depends on human aspiration and circumstances.

4. Opposition of Artificiality. Cyrenaics were seriously opposed and contemptuous of artificiality. The state and its laws create impediments in man's developments. They are artificial. Man should attain self knowledge and seek perfection. Law and state are not required.

QUESTIONS FOR EXERCISE

1. Critically discuss the political philosophy of Cynics.
2. Write short note on 'Cyrenaic Political Theory'.

6

Plato (427 B.C. — 347 B.C.)

Plato was born in 427 B.C., the son of a noble parents. According to tradition he first studied music, poetry, painting, and philosophy with other masters and became a pupil of Socrates in 407 B.C., remaining with him until the latter's death (399 B.C.), when he accompanied the sorrowing Socrates to Megara. He is said to have travelled in Egypt and Asia Minor, to have visited Italy and the Pythagorcans (388 B.C.), and to have lived for a time at the court of Dionysius I, the tyrant of Syracuse, who became his enemy and sold him into slavery as a prisoner of war: but all of these stories have been denied. He founded a school in the groves of Academus, the Academy, where he taught mathematics and the different branches of philosophy, by means of connected lectures and the dialogue. The story goes that he interrupted his work on two occasions (367 B.C. and 361 B.C.), by further visits to Syracuse, presumably in the hope of assisting in the realization of his ideal State, and that he was disappointed in this hope. His death occurred in 347 B.C.

"Plato was a poet and mystic, as well as a philosopher and dialectician; he combined, in a rare degree, great powers of logical analysis and abstract thought with flights of poetic imagination and deep mystical feeling. His character was noble : he was an aristocrat by birth and by temperament, an uncompromising idealist, hostile to everything base and vulgar."[1]

The life of Plato can be divided into three ages. In the first age, he received the education from his great master Socrates besides some other minor Teachers. He lived with Socrates for eight years and received instructions and ideas in different fields of human thought. After the death of Socrates, perturbed as he was, Plato went on his journey through Egypt, Cyrene, Italy and Cicley etc. For ten years he was roaming in different countries, observing their ways of life, social and political structures and institutions and discussing with scholars of different countries. It was in this age that he planned his important dialogues. During this period Plato's thinking was generally centred around ideas, the universals. The dialogues written during this period do not exhibit much literary excellence. The important dialogues written during this period were *Gorgias, Theaetetus, Sophistes, Statesman and Parmenides.*

---

1. Frank Thilly, *A History of Philosophy*, Central Book Depot, Alld. p. 74.

After ten years of journey in different countries Plato's mind was almost settled. He now returned to Athens and started third and the most important age of his life. He established an institution known as Academy or Gymnasium. Here he started to live as a teacher, a mathematician and a philosopher. For 40 years he educated hundreds of illustrious desciples and created dozens of dialogues upto his death at the age of 82.

WORKS OF PLATO

It seems unlikely that all of Plato's works have come down to us. Of the writings transmitted under his name (35 Dialogues, 13 Letters), most of the Letters and all of the Dèfinitions are considered to be spurious, although it seems likely that several of the Letters including the philosophically important seventh letter, are genuine.

Chronological Order of Works

Attempts have been made by many scholars to arrange the dialogues in chronological order. One method of ordering them employs the criterion of relative maturity of philosophical doctrine, but this method has produced very different orderings by different scholars. A method which has in recent years proven very useful is the ordering of the dialogues in accordance with stylometric considerations, adopting as a standard the style and vocabulary of the laws, which is universally accepted as the latest of the dialogues. Sir David Ross, after summarizing the results of these stylistic and linguistic investigations suggests the following probable order of the Platonic dialogues:

(1) **First Period** (before 389-388 B.C.): *Charmides, Laches, Enthyphro, Hippias Major, and Meno.*

(2) **Second Period** (between 389-388 B.C. and 361-366 B.C.): *Cratylus* (date doubtful). *Symposium* (385 B.C. or later), *Phaedo, Republic Phaedrus, Parmenides, Theaetetus* (369 B.C. or later).

(3) **Third Period** (between 367-366 B.C. and 361-360 B.C.): *Sophistes, Politicus.*

(4) **Fourth Period** (after 361-360 B.C.) : *Timaeus, Critias, Philebus, Seventh Letter* (353-352 B.C.), *Laws,* (Plato's Theory of Ideas, Ch. I).

This list does not include those of the earlier dialogues which throw little or no light on Plato's Theory of ideas : *the Apology, Crito, Lysis, Protagoras, Gorgias* and *Euthydemus.*

Spurious Dialogues

Among the thirty-five dialogues the following are now generally rejected as spurious : *Alcibiades* I and *Alcibiades II, Epinomis, Anteras, Hippachus, Theages, Minos, Cleitophro,* and *Menexenus.* Many scholars have questioned the genuineness of *Hippias Major.*

Important Translations

(1) *The Dialogues of Plato,* trans. by B. Jowett, 3rd ed. 5 vols., 1892;

(2) Jowett trans. of *The dialogues of Plato* with an Introduction by R. Demos, 2 vols., 1937;
(3) *Thirteen Epistles,* trans. by L.A. Post (1925);
(4) A.E. Taylor, *Plato: Timaeus, and Critias,* (1929) and *The Laws of Plato,* (1934);
(5) J. Howard, *The Platonic Epistles,* 1932;
(6) F.M. Cornford, *Plato and Parmenides,* 1939;
(7) R. Hackforth Plato's Examination of Pleasure: A Translation of the *Philebus,* 1945, and Plato's *Phaedrus,* 1952;
(8) *Republic,* trans. by F.M. Cornford, 1942;
(9) J.B. Skemp, *Plato's Statesman,* 1952;
(10) R.S. Bluck, *Plato's Phaedo,* 1955;

Important Commentaries

(1) G.R. Morrow, *Studies in the Platonic Epistles,* 1935;
(2) A.E. Taylor, *Commentary on Plato's Timaeus,* 1928;
(3) G. Grote, *Plato,* 1865;
(4) E. Zeller, *Plato and the Older Academy,* trans. by S.F. Alleyne and A. Goodwin, 1888;
(5) B. Bosanquet, *A Companion to Plato's "Republic",* 1895;
(6) T.G. Ritchie, *Plato,* 1902;
(7) T. Comperz, *Greek Thinkers,* Vols. II and III, 1905;
(8) J.A. Stewart, *The Myths of Plato,* 1905;
(9) W. Lutolawski, *Origin and Growth of Plato's Logic,* 1905;
(10) E. Barker, *Political Theory of Plato and Aristotle,* 1906;
(11) J.A. Stewart, *Plato's Doctrine of Ideas,* 1909;
(12) R.L. Nettleship, *Lectures on the "Republic" of Plato,* 1914.
(13) J. Burnet, *The Socratic Doctrine of the Soul,* 1916;
(14) P.E. Moore, *Platonism,* 1917, and *The Religion of Plato,* 1921;
(15) E. Barker, *Greek Political Theory : Plato and His Predecessors,* 1918;
(16) E. Rohde, *Psyche,* 1894, 1925;
(17) A.E. Taylor, *Plato : The Man and His Work, 1926;*
(18) A.E. Taylor, *Platonism and Its influence,* 1927;
(19) G. Santayana, *Platonism and the Spiritual Life,* 1927;
(20) J. Burnet, *Platonism,* 1928;
(21) G.C. Field, *Plato and His Contemporaries : A Study in Fourth Century Life and Thought,* 1930;
(22) F.M. Cornford, *Before and after Socrates,* 1932;
(23) C. Ritter, *The Essence of Plato's Philosophy,* trans. by A Allan, 1933;

(24) P. Shorey, *What Plato said*, 1933, and *Platonism Ancient and Modern*, 1938;

(25) F.H. Anderson, *The Argument of Plato*, 1934;

(26) R.L. Nettleship, *Theory of Education in Plato's Republic*, 1935;

(27) F.M. Cornford, *Plato's Theory of Knowledge*, 1935;

(28) G.M.A. Grube, *Plato's Thought*, 1935;

(29) L. Robin, *Plato*, 1935;

(30) W.A. Hardie, *Study in Plato*, 1936;

(31) R. Demos, *The Philosophy of Plato*, 1939;

(32) J. Stenzel, *Plato's Method of Dialectic*, 1940;

(33) P. Leon, *Plato*, 1940;

(34) R. Robinson, *Plato's Early Dialectic*, 1941, 2nd ed., 1953;

(35) F. Solmsen, *Plato's Theology*, 1942;

(36) W. Jaeger, *Paideia*, Vol. III; *The Conflict of Cultural Ideals in the Age of Plato*, 1945;

(37) A. Koyre, *Discovering Plato*, 1945;

(38) H.F. Cherniss, *Aristotle's Criticism of Plato and the Academy*, 1944, and *The Riddle of the Early Academy*, 1945;

(39) J. Wild, *Plato's Theory of Man*, 1946;

(40) R.S. Bluck, *Plato's Life and Thought*, 1949;

(41) W.D. Ross, *Plato's Theory of Ideas*, 1951.

The Dialogues of Plato

A study of the different dialogues of Plato reveals him as a prophet of the light divine. We come across in his writings the inspiration of an exalted poet, the insight of seer with his eyes turned inward, the vision of a prophet probing into the galaxies, and the depth and fire of a mystic possessed by the Ideas. A philosopher of Himalayan heights, Plato was also a prolific writer, and at least twenty-eight dialogues produced by him are available till today, all of which have been translated by Jowett, the doyen of writers on the Plato's early dialogues centre around the life and thought of Socrates, viz. *The Apology, The Crito, The Charmides, The Laches*, and *Euthedemus*. *The Meno, Protagoras*, and *Gorgias* are also Socratic dialogues but they represent the negative and critical view of the great man. Other dialogues may be grouped as political-cum-philosophical, viz. *The Republic, Politics*, and *The Laws*. *The Republic* occupies the central place among Plato's dialogues. It represents the summation and consummation of his vision and thought. It is his *magnnm opus*. No other dialogue of Plato shows an equal knowledge of the world and contains more universal thoughts, and no other dialogue makes the splendid synthesis between the life and philosophy. In it "the philosophy reaches the highest point to which ancient thinkers ever attained". Still other dialogues dealing with his mystical metaphysics are *The Timeus, The Parmenides* and *Phaedo*.

The Central Idea in Dialogues

The central idea, pervading all the works of Plato, lies in the stream of thought which in various ways stresses that while unhappiness is due to ignorance, the one way to deliverance or the attainment of happiness lies in the pursuit of knowledge culminating in the perception or the vision of the highest good. Knowledge as such is a profoundly practical affair. Its attainment produces elevation of human spirit from the physical to the spiritual plane. It brings about deliverance from the thraldoms of the flesh. Such knowledge is not possession but realisation, not information but enlightenment. It means awareness of being, truth, good, beauty. It expresses itself in ideas, feelings, actions and, in the whole of life's activities. Knowledge is virtue, and virtue is knowledge. There is an abiding tendency in each man to seek truth and good. But, accustomed as they are to living in the darkness of the cave they find it painful to come out and see the light of the day.

SUBJECTS OF PLATO'S DIALOGUES

1. Hippias Major. Unless we define our ideas, clarify our mind, and know precisely what virtues are, we cannot have right conduct and our life cannot be truly virtuous.

2. Hippias Minor. Those who fall to temptations are always inferior to those who do not, or do on purpose. No man does wrong out of knowledge or intention. All wrong doing is due to ignorance, and therefore, involuntary.

3. The Ion. The poet is not a conscious artist for he writes in moments of inspiration which take him out of himself. He is a mouthpiece of a power which he does not understand and cannot explain.

4. The Chardimdes. It stresses the importance of right conceptions and definitions. Unless we know accurately and define justice, truth, and temperance we cannot really be just and temperate. It discusses temperance which is contrast of folly lying in forgetting oneself in the moment of triumph and prosperity. It is the easy and natural self-restraint of a man. It is a sort of quietness and slowness as against undignified and ungraceful hurry.

5. The Laches. It deals with courage which it defines as certain persistence or endurance. It is wise resolution or persistence. Acts of courage involve the sacrifice of the lower pleasure for the higher. True courage ultimately consists in the knowledge of goodness. Only the philosophers therefore, can be truly good and courageous.

6. The Lysis. It describes friendship as a condition of attraction between two opposites. The highest friendship, however, can be possible only between those who are truly good, and engage in the common pursuit of the supreme good.

7. The Cratylus. It discusses the use and function of language.

8. The Euthedemus. It rejects the contention of the Sophists that goodness can be taught. The virtuous life depends only upon the knowledge of the supreme good. Knowledge of the good is no art, for while it involves the awareness of good and evil, it results only in virtuous activity and in no other.

9. The Gorgias. It deals with rhetoric but its real theme is the way the good life can be lived. The real power lies not in oratory but in goodness. A genuine statesmanship consists in the tending of the soul. To increase wealth or power is no service to the state. The truest service is to enable and inspire the citizens to develop their goodness. It works out the application of the conception of "the tendency of the soul to the whole complicated business of life".

10. The Meno. It contains the Platonic doctrine of knowledge through reminiscence. Learning is a recalling or remembrance of the past life which flashed to the mind when some object stirs in it an association of ideas. The object gives the cue and the soul responds to it. Truth is our recovery of what we have lost. The soul of itself advances towards the object of knowledge. Knowledge is not given or granted, or received or acquired. There is a need of an impersonal memory to account for the *a-priori* discovery of fresh mathematical truths. There is a distinction between higher and lower goodness between higher and lower knowledge.

11. The Euthyphro. It maintains that all virtue is knowledge of the good. Any one virtue if pursued in fulness will cover the whole of human conduct.

12. The Apology. It is an attempt to justify Socrates. It raises the problems whether obedience should be paid to the will of the state or to the sense of justice with which it conflicted, or should be the citizen conform by promising silence or speak out his voice of warning and denunciation? The answer of Socrates is a classic of human culture — "Acquit me or condemn me: I shall never alter my ways". But one should defy law only for the sake of conscience, not for that of life. If a law is bad, one must resist, but one must show loyalty to the state by courting punishment happily.

13. The Crito. It explains why Socrates refused to avail of the chances of escape which were provided to him by his friends. It emphasises the contribution of law to civilised living: "By law the citizen is legitimately born into his citizenship; by law he is educated into the capacity to use his citizenship. By the grace of the law, he is what he is; he owes obedience to it as he does to his parents. Further, every man who regards himself to be a member of the state has thereby subscribed to the obligations of membership."

14. The Phaedo. It considers the tendency of the soul as the highest pursuit of life, and describes soul as made up of a divine stuff. The divinity of the soul makes for its immortality. It renders death into "an entrance on better life". To a philosophic man, the body is a hindrance to the care of the soul and an obstacle to the comprehension of reality, or of truth, goodness, and beauty. One can comprehend absolute Good or reality only when one becomes free from the trammels of the flesh. The life of the philosopher must be a rehearsal of death

15. The Protagoras. It teaches that all virtues are one knowledge. It contrasts the Socratic from the Sophist morality.

16. The Republic. It represents the fulness of Plato's thought. It is an attempt at the complete philosophy of life. It concerns itself with the state and justice. Primarily, it is a philosophical treatise. It begins with the question as to what is happiness, and extends to the higher question of justice. Plato describes the ideal state so that philosophy has a home to live and deliver its goods; the philosophic man and philosophic state are two sides of the same coin.[2] The Good can be envisioned only by a striving and aspiring soul through a most intimate and incommunicable personal insight.[3] The purpose of Plato here is to assert the truth that the eternal laws of morality are in the system of the universe. That is why a psychology of man and a metaphysics of the world enter into the plan of the *Republic.*[4]

17. The Timeus. It maintains that in physical sciences, all our results are tentative, and that what we reach with our present light is likely to be modified or even superseded under further enquiry.

18. The Phaedrus. It examines the use of rhetoric which necessarily leads to the vital issues of virtuous conduct. It also discusses the method of dialectical reasoning which exhibits the alternative rhythm of intuition and intellect employed in the mathematical sciences to comprehend the premises and deduce the conclusions of demonstrative proof.

19. The Parmenides. It is a philosophical treatise dealing with the theory of ideas. There is a discussion of two classes of Ideas — Mathematical Ideas of unity and plurality and the Ideas of value such as justice, beauty, goodness and the like. The latter predominate in the earlier dialogues in which Plato has followed most faithfully in the footsteps of Socrates, and in the *Symposium* and the *Phaedrus.* The former come into prominence in the *Phaedo* and the *Republic.*[5] While parmenides makes a criticism of the theory of Ideas he admits that philosophy cannot do without them.

20. The Theatetus. It contends that there can be no knowledge without Ideas. The contention of Protagoras that is the measure of all things, and that right conception is knowledge, are also rejected. The dialogue, after refuting Protagoras, establishes the doctrine of Ideas.

21. The Sophist. It describes Sophists as jugglers and illusionists, and underlines the inadequacy of all absolutist theories.

22. The Politics (or the statesman). One of the last works of Plato it was intended to be a logical exercise in the art of definition by way of differentiation rather than a political treatise.

23. The Philebus. It stresses that the good is not what we know as pleasure

2. Paul Friedlander, *Plato : An Introduction*, p. 6.
3. A.E. Taylor, *Plato : The Man and His Works*, p. 273.
4. Ernest Barker, *op. cit.*, p. 171.
5. Sir David Ross, *Plato's Theory of Ideas*, pp. 84-85.

of delight but thought, intelligence, memory and true judgement. It means a condition of the soul in which man remains happy, unmoved by the setbacks and successes of life.

24. The Laws. It restores what the *Republic*, had dislodged, namely the supremacy or sovereignty of Law. From the *Republic* to the *Laws* the change is great. '... it cleaves Plato's political theory into two distinct halves: On the one side is the guardian of the Republic unfettered by law; on the other is the guardian of the law who is its servant, and even is described as its slave."[6] In the laws rulers have private property and family and communism has been abandoned. The ruled have a voice and a vote in the election of their rulers. Plato calls law and civilization the differential of humanity. Laws stands for a compromise between the ideals of kingship and democracy, and supports division of powers between the people and the ruler.[7]

SOCRATIC INFLUENCE ON PLATO

Sabine has rightly pointed out, "The outstanding fact of Plato's intellectual development was his association as a youngman with Socrates, and from Socrates, he derived what was always the controlling thought of his political philosophy, the idea that virtue is knowledge." It has been rightly maintained that the image of his teacher never faded from the mind of Plato. In fact Socrate's influence upon Plato is so penetrating that it is difficult to distinguish between the ideas of the two. It is more so since we know the ideas of Socrates generally through the dialogues of Plato. However Socratic influence upon Platonic thinking is more exclusive in the following spheres:

1. Virtue is Knowledge. Socrates considered virtue and knowledge as synonymous. Knowledge, according to him, was not for knowledge but for virtue. It was not merely a collection of information but a basis for character formation. A knowledge which has no impact upon conduct is meaningless. Knowledge gives birth to the virtues of courage, temperance and justice etc. It was on the basis of this idea of Socrates that Plato developed his concept of the philosopher king in *The Republic*. Thus both Plato and Socrates do not distinguish between ethics and politics.

2. Theory of Reality. According to Socrates, the virtue of a thing is not in its existence but in its fulfilment. It aims at virtue. It was on the basis of this that Plato maintained that the world of ideas is more real than the world of things.

3. Theory of Knowledge. Knowledge, according to Socrates, is of two types: casual, and the true knowledge. The latter knowledge is the self-knowledge. Knowledge is concerned with conduct and character. It influences the total personality. All the virtues depend upon knowledge.

4. Philosophical Method. Socrates invented the question answer method of philosophical discussion. Plato has followed this method in his dialogues. In

6 Ernest Barker, *op. cit.*, p. 341.

7 John Burnett, *op. cit.*, p. 1.

this method, the inquirer analyses the thoughts of various thinkers upon a problem and arrives at the truth by their constructive criticism.

5. Art of Government. Socrates has considered the ruler as a philosopher. His contemporary Athenians considered him as a Sophist as his criteria was also humanist and yet his thinking was different from that of the Sophists on the following counts:

(i) While according to Sophists the world is mechanical, Socrates considered it as purposive.

(ii) According to Sophists goodness is an art which can be achieved by specialised knowledge. According to Socrates, on the other hand, goodness is not an art but an innate power of man.

(iii) While, according to Sophists, man is the measure of all things, according to Socrates, the criteria of different things are established according to their different purposes.

(iv) The theory of knowledge presented by Socrates was very much different from that of the Sophists.

(v) According to Sophists the social rules are not based upon the Nature and the traditions but they are man-made. According to Socrates the traditional laws are above man. It is hence that he embraced death while following the law.

The above distinctions between the thought of Sophists and that of Socrates shows that they had real differences. While Socrates was a citizen of Athens, the Sophists were foreigners. While Socrates did not charge any thing as his fee for education, the Sophists used to make charges. Socrates, therefore, was not a Sophist. At the age of 70 he was charged and sentenced to death. His death shocked his disciple Plato. It influenced thinking men everywhere. It encouraged enquiry into freedom of thought. Socrates laid emphasis upon reflective thinking. He preached that man should himself decide about the true and the false and follow the path directed by his soul. Besides having individual decisions the individual should follow the laws of the state which are obligatory upon him. The greatest contribution of Socrates is his dialectical method which was later on utilised by his eminent disciple Plato.

THE REPUBLIC

"Plato is philosophy, and philosophy is Plato," says Emerson; and awards to the *Republic* the words of Omar about the *Koran* : "Burn the libraries, for their value is in this book."[8]

Concepts of Knowledge and Government

The fundamental idea of the *Republic* came to Plato in the form of his master's doctrine that virtue is knowledge. The good is objectively real. In other words, what men want depends upon how much they see of the good, but

8. Emerson, *Representative Men*, p. 41.

nothing is good merely because they want it. From this it follows that the philosopher ought to have decisive power in government, and that it is his knowledge alone which entitles him to this.

Plato started by dividing the citizens into three classes : the common people, the soldiers, and the guardians. The last, alone, are to have political power. There are to be much fewer of them than of the other two classes. In the first instance, it seems, they are to be selected by the legislator; after that, they will usually succeed by heredity, but in exceptional cases a promising child may be promoted from one of the inferior classes, while among the children of guardians a child or young man who is quite unsatisfactory may be degraded.

Plato believed that every form of government tends to perish by excess of its basic principle. Aristocracy ruins itself by limiting too narrowly the circle within which power is confined. Oligarchy ruins itself by the incautious scramble for immediate wealth. In either case the end is revolution. When revolution comes, it may seem to arise from little causes and petty whims: but though it may spring from slight occasions, it is the precipitate result of grave and accumulated wrongs; when a body is weakened by neglected ills, the merest exposure may bring serious disease.[9] "Then democracy comes; the poor overcome their opponents, slaughtering some and banishing the rest: and give to the people an equal share of freedom and power."[10] Even democracy ruins itself by excess — of democracy. Its basic principle is the equal right of all to hold office and determine public policy. This is at first glance a delightful arrangement; it becomes disastrous because the people are not properly equipped by education to select the best rulers and the wisest courses. "As to the people they have no understanding, and only repeat what their rulers are pleased to tell them;"[11] to get a doctrine accepted or rejected, it is only necessary to have it praised or ridiculed in a popular play. Mob-rule is a rough sea for the ship of state to ride: every wind of oratory stirs up the waters and deflects the course. The upshot of such a democracy is tyranny or autocracy; the crowd so loves flattery, it is so 'hungry for honey', that at last the wiliest and most unscrupulous flatterer, calling himself the 'protector of the people rises to supreme power."[12]

The Problem of Psychology

Behind the problem of political philosophy lies the problem of psychology. Plato writes in the *Republic* that "governments vary as the characters of men vary:... states are made out of the human natures which are in them."[13] The state is what it is because its citizens are what they are. Therefore, we need not expect to have better state until we have better men; till then all changes will leave every essential thing unchanged. "How charming people are! — always

9. *Republic,* p. 556.

10. *Ibid.,* p. 557.

11. *Protagoras,* p. 317.

12. *Republic,* p. 565.

13. *Ibid.,* p. 544

doctoring, increasing and complicating their disorders; fancying they will be cured by some nostrum which somebody advises them to try, never getting better, but always growing worse....Are they not as good as a play, trying their hand at legislation, and imagining that by reforms they will make an end to the dishonesties and rascalities of mankind — not knowing that in reality they are cutting away at the heads of a hydra?"[14]

Plan of Education

One cannot fail to be astonished at the amount of space which Plato has devoted to education in the *Republic.* Rousseau said that the book was hardly a political work at all, but was the greatest work on education ever written.

Two Parts of Education

Plato planned, for a state-controlled system of compulsory education. His educational scheme falls into two parts : the elementary education, which includes the training of young persons up to about the age of twenty, and culminates in the beginning of military service : and the higher education, intended for those selected persons of both sexes who are to be members of the two ruling classes and extending from the age of twenty to thirty-five.

1. Elementary Education. The plan of elementary education given in the *Republic* was rather a reform of existing practice than the invention of a wholly new system. The curriculum is divided into two sections, gymnastics for training the body and music for training the mind. For the first ten years of life, education shall be predominantly, physical; every school is to have a gymnasium and a playground; play and sport are to be the entire curriculum : and in this first decade such health will be stored up as will make all medicine unnecessary. But mere athletics and gymnastics, Plato thought, would make a man too one-sided. "How shall we find a gentle nature which has also great courage? — for they seem to be inconsistent with each other."[15] We do not want a nation of prize-fighters and weight-lifters. Perhaps music will solve our problem : through music the soul learns harmony and rhythm, and even a disposition to justice;" for "can he who is harmoniously constituted ever be unjust? Is not this, Glaucon, why musical training is so powerful, because rhythm and harmony find their way into the secret places of the soul, bearing grace in their movements and making the soul graceful?"[16] Music moulds character and, therefore, shares in determining social and political issues. It is valuable not only because it brings refinement of feeling and character, but also because it preserves and restores health. There are some diseases, Plato writes, which can be treated only through the mind[17] : so the Corybantic priest treated hysterical women with wild pipe music, which excited them to dance and dance till they fell to the ground exhausted, and went to sleep; when they awoke they were cured.

---

14. *Republic,* p. 425.
15. *Republic,* p. 375.
16. *Protagoras,* p. 326.
17. *Charmides,* p. 157.

It is easy to exaggerate the influence of Sparta, upon Plato's theory of elementary education. Its most genuinely Spartan feature was the dedication of education exclusively to civic training. But its content was typically Athenian, and its purpose was dominated by the end of moral and intellectual cultivation. In fact, Plato's plan of training represents an Athenian, not a Spartan conception of what constitutes an educated man. "Any other conclusion would have been unthinkable for a philosopher who believed that the only salvation for states lay in the exercise of trained intelligence."[18]

2. Higher Education. Higher education, which is regarded as the most original and most characteristic proposal in the *Republic*, was to be given to the members of both sexes after an elimination test and was meant for the members of the guardian classes. It extended from twenty to thirty-five. This period was divisible into two parts, i.e., twenty to thirty and thirty to thirty-five. In the first, young persons were to be helped to choose their true vocations in life and get trained in them. There was to be a systematic scientific course. Dialectical power must be developed. Military training must also be given. At the age of thirty, a second elimination test would follow. This test is far severer than the first. Those who fail will become the auxiliaries, or executive aides and military officers of the state. Those who pass this test will be the perfect guardians and will get a further five years' course of training in Mathematics, Astronomy and Logic.

Need of Education

"This conception of Plato was not an innovation," says Sabine. What all he did was that he transformed the existing system of education to fit for the realisation of his ideal state. The Athenians concentrated upon intellectual and cultural activities. They neglected self-discipline and stability of character. In contradiction to it, in Sparta, the emphasis was upon military training, the young men tended to grow up strong and hardy but rough and uncultured. Spartan education was highly disciplined, imparting courage into the pupils. Athenians were trained in many subjects, with the end of making them better men. In his theory of education, Plato combined all the worthy features of Athenian culture and Spartan discipline and organisation, and blended them together. His system of education drew inspiration mainly from Sparta rather than his own city-state, Athens. He maintained that, as in Sparta, the education should be strictly under the control of State.

Reasons for Criticism of Existing Systems

1. Democracy. Plato was prompted to go against the existing system because the Athenian Democracy was inefficient, uninstructed and unenlightened. Selfish and corrupt statesmen ruled the country.

2. Sophists. In those times there was every likelihood of people getting corrupted by the teachings of Sophists.

18. Sabine, *A History of Political Theory*, p. 65.

3. Mental Malady. It was a necessary element in the Platonic Philosophy, as the realisation of the ideal state and thereby justice could be achieved only by highly developed intellectuals. According to Prof. Barker, "It is an attempt to cure a mental malady by mental medicine."

THEORY OF EDUCATION

Aims and Ideals

1. Realisation of Good. The essence of Platonic theory of education was the realisation of the idea of good. It was intended for the enrichments of the soul and the broadening of the spirit. As Plato called it, it is the 'one great thing' which will turn the 'inward eye' towards the 'inner light."

2. Citizenship. Plato believed that a state-regulated education could create the spirit of devotion in a citizen. It could make him or her contribute his or her best to state in one's own particular station in life. If the citizens are well-educated, they will readily see through the difficulties and meet emergencies as they arise. Education was calculated to promote justice. It was to enable a man to fulfil his duty. Public education was, therefore, a direct corollary of Platonic justice. As Barker points out, "Plato considered education as a means of social righteousness and realisation of truth and not of social success."

3. All Round Useful. The real aim of education was to make a man and woman socially, economically, intellectually and politically all round useful and fit. Plato believed in the perfect ability and plasticity of human nature. Through education the ruler could mould the character of the individual and train the citizens in unselfish devotion to duty and thereby to produce a harmonious state. Plato's theory of education meant to turn the state of injustice and lack of discipline into a 'just' state. Therefore, he made education compulsory and State-controlled.

4. More than Information. For Plato, education meant a great deal more than merely imparting information. It did not mean the storing up of external knowledge but the bringing of the soul into proper environment for its development. It involved the re-direction of the whole personality, the turning of the eyes of soul towards the light which hitherto had been unperceived. Plato said, "There is a faculty residing in the soul of each person and an instrument enabling each of us to learn." The soul, being an imitative thing, is not passive but active. The function of education is not to put ideas or knowledge into it; it is rather to draw out the best talent in it. Objects are not presented to the soul, but it moves towards them because it feels attracted towards them. The re-direction of the soul must be achieved by turning it towards the right object.

5. Provision of Suitable Environment. The quality of the soul is to be imitative. Surround it with the right kind of environment and it will begin to assimilate itself. The main problem of education is to discover how to provide the individual with the most suitable kind of environment. The most important thing for the educator is to place the individual in the midst of those things in whose likeness one wants it to grow. The aim of education is to enable the soul to see the beautiful and good.

6. Vision of the Absolute. The earlier education was predominantly social in character; its aim was the preparation of the citizens for the proper discharge of their duties. At the highest stage the purpose of education will be to bring the soul to a knowledge of the good vision of the Absolute. In this state the education was to be general and vocational. Education must help the individual to discover his or her vocation in life.

Life Long Education

Since the soul reacts on its surroundings at all stages of its development, education was a matter of life-time. Because it is a living and developing entity, it is affected by different agencies and media at various stages of its growth.

1. Infancy and childhood. During infancy and childhood, the soul is more susceptible to fancy and imagination . The character is trained through emotions at this stage. Therefore the aim of education during this period will be to stimulate the love of the beautiful in all its varied appearances. Here cultivation of virtue was a certain type of attitude towards things and man was more important than imparting of knowledge.

2. Adolescence. During the stage of adolescence and maturity when the reasoning powers began to develop, the soul is reached through reason. Here the education means the development of the understanding through science and philosophy.

3. Youth. In youth, education would be both physical and intellectual. The object of education would be acquisition of truth.

4. Innovations in Education. Plato's theory of education is truly innovative. He improved upon the current Athenian practice. He was possibly the first feminist. He was for giving the same type of education to both boys and girls. He believed that there was no difference in kind between the native capacities of boys and girls. He felt that the state was being deprived of services of half of the population by denying the education and the rights of citizenship to women. He advocated women emancipation and equal education for them along with the men. The women were to be eligible to the same offices as men.

Stages of Education

Plato has given a detailed curriculum of his state controlled system of compulsory education for both sexes. It was divided into two stages, called the elementary and higher education. This distinction is based on age differences and on class differences. Elementary education is the training of the youth and of the military class. It is the training of the character through emotions. It is the cultivation of the virtues of courage, self-control and discipline. Higher education is the training of the middle age. It is the training of the ruling classes or guardians. It is the training of reason and understanding through science and philosophy.

1. Elementary Education. These are as follows:

(i) *First Stage*. Upto the age of six, the imparting of instruction is not so important as to learn the lessons of good manner and good taste. A child should learn simple religious truths. He should also learn to hate and love things. In childhood, first impressions occupy a privileged place. The elementary education begins with the training in music.

(ii) *Second Stage*. In the second stage of elementary education, from 6 to 18 years, it will be supplemented by music for the soul or mind and gymnastics for the body. This education should be both physical and intellectual. Music comprised of literature, poetry, singing and all finer arts and gymnastics included bodily exercise, diet and medicine. Temperateness, grace, rythm and harmony penetrate in the soul through music. Gymnastic hardens the body and music brings gentleness. Both should be harmoniously blended so that the child may be neither too rough nor too soft. Plato was against poetry initiation and dramatics. He asked for a severe state censorship for stories, poetry and music. He recommended a drastic reform in them, he stressed on cultivating memory and the study of natural science. Science, according to him, developed thinking power and led to the understanding of the good.

(iii) *Third Stage*. In the third stage of elementary education, i.e. from 13 to 20 years there was to be given an exclusive training in gymnastics and military service in order to prepare them for the defence of the country in the eventuality of any war, it is mainly for military class.

2. Higher Education for Guardians. This was as follows:

(i) *First Test*. At the age of 20 years an elimination test will take place and less talented will drop off while the more promising will undergo another course of education lasting for 10 years. This stage is mainly for the guardian class. It is predominantly scientific in character, comparable more or less to modern university education. Its aim is to make the selected few to become the guardians or rulers of the state. Just as the special qualification of the warrior class is courage, the special virtue of the ruling class is wisdom. The courses of study at this stage aim at making the recipients wise through the study of sciences like Mathematics, including Arithmetic, plane and solid Geometry, Astronomy and Logic. Mathematics trains a mind to think clearly and precisely. Through higher education development of individual personality takes place.

(ii) *Second Test*. At 30, a second selective test will be held. The less gifted will be made subordinate officers and the more gifted will undergo a further course of training for another five years, i.e. from 30 to 35 years of age. Now they will study Mathematics and develop their power of dialectics. Dialectics attempts to arrive at proper definitions. It is, therefore, the corner stone of human knowledge. It is the instrument by which knowledge of the pure ideas is attained which constitute the highest reality. The highest of these ideas is the idea of the Good. It is the cause of all living being and it results in the beautification of his soul. He becomes fit to be the philosopher-ruler of the state. In the words of Sabine, it constitutes "the most original as well as the most characteristic proposal in *The Republic*." Plato had put into practice such a course of study in his own Academy opened before the completion in *The Republic*.

(iii) *Practical Education after 35.* At 35 guardians occupy positions of authority in the state. They now get practical experience through dealing with the day today problems of administration for 15 years. Education does not come to a stop here. According to Plato it is a life-long process. So long as the individuals are receptive to knowledge they may continue education even after this period. They would pass most of their time in philosophical pursuit at the age of 50 but they would also devote themselves to the hard duties of public life, hold offices for their country's sake and exercise power in the best interests of the people in order to make them just and happy. After retirement from public service the guardians had to concentrate on the realisation of the Idea of Good.

According to Plato only a perfect type of education may create perfect state. The political authority should be blended with broadest knowledge and culture and the philosopher should be the embodiment of highest political virtue, spirit, swiftness and strength. He should represent the knowledge in action. The guardians must be given special training. The system of education outlined above was meant to produce such a selfless ruling class.

Curriculum of Education

Plato's education has its objective in the realization of truth, a truth which is comprehensive, not limited or narrow. Plato, therefore, believes that development of the mind, body and soul is essential. For this reason he divided the curriculum into three parts:

1. Bodily Development. Plato's philosophy believes bodily development to be of the utmost importance in education, but this bodily development is achieved not merely through exercise and gymnastic activity, but also through a regulated and controlled diet. The educator must guide and train the educand to attend to his food. He must be a kind of doctor who advises a particular kind of diet after acquainting himself with the weaknesses of the educand's body. This must be done in order to get out of these debilities and finally to lead to complete development of the body.

2. Educational Impressions. But it must be remembered that bodily development is only a means to mental development, because a healthy mind resides only in a healthy body. Although much importance is attached to bodily development, even greater importance is attached to mental development. Being under the influence of Pythagoras, Plato recommended the teaching of mathematics as of supreme importance. The first step in the teaching of mathematics is the teaching of arithmetic, geometry and algebra should then be taught. Plato believed that the teaching of mathematics can remove many mental defects. In addition to mathematics, Plato considered the teaching of astronomy as of great significance, as part of higher education.

3. Training in Music. In order to achieve balance in education, Plato stressed the value of musical training as a supplement to training in gymnastics. Exercise is the source of bodily development while music helps in the development of the soul. But music and literature taught to the student must be capable of building character. Plato suggested that the child's curriculum should be purged of all literature and musical epics which tended to generate such qualities as cowardice, weakness, selfishness, egoism, etc. He was critical of the epics of Homer and other contemporary poets on this ground. Plato considered balance in human life to be of the greatest importance, because in the absence of such a balance, man should neither fulfil his social obligations nor enjoy his own private life to the full.

Hence it can be concluded that Plato suggested a balanced curriculum for education.

Role of Educator

In Plato's plan of education, the educator is considered to have the greatest importance. He is like the torch bearer who leads a man, lying is a dark cave, out of the darkness into the bright light of the outside world. His task is to bring the educand out of the darkness of the cave into the light of the day. He is thus the guide.

In his methods of teaching Plato believes imitation to be of the greatest importance, for he realizes that the child learns a great deal through imitation. He will acquire the behaviour of the people among whom he is made to live. Hence, keeping in mind the status of the child, he should be made to live among people from whom he can learn good habits and avoid bad ones.

Education According to Classes

Plato's plan of education does not envisage uniform education for one and all. He accepted the concept of social stratification that since different individuals have to perform differently, and suggested in order to train each one in his own respective sphere. He believed that different individuals are made of different metals. Those made of gold should take up administration and government, while those made of silver were best suited for trade and defence. Others made of iron and the baser metals should become labourers and agriculturists. The state must make different arrangements for the education of these different kinds of people, although Plato implicitly agrees that education of governing classes is of the greatest importance. The education of the other classes in society does not concern him very much.

Faced with the problem of determining the class of each individual, Plato suggested various kinds of tests to be conducted at different age levels. In the first place, primary education will be given to all between the ages of seven and twenty, following which a test shall be administered to everyone. Those who failed the test are to be sent to labour in the various occupations and productive trades. The successful candidates will be sent to the armed forces where training will be imparted to them for the next ten years. This will again be followed by a test, the failures will be compelled to remain in the armed forces while the successful ones will be sent to join the government. Then this governing class will be subjected to further education in science. Later on, one from among the governing class will be elected as the philosopher administrator whose task will be to look after the government and education of the state. This individual will occupy the highest position in the land, his word will be the law of the land. Apart from this supreme individual, all other members of the governing class *will continue to receive education throughout their lives, most of this education* consisting of teachings in philosophy. It is thus evident that Plato granted the highest place to philosophy in his educational scheme.

EVALUATION

As has been pointed out earlier, Rousseau was correct when he commented that Plato's *Republic* is the finest textbook on education. But it must be admitted that Plato' s scheme of education suffers from certain defects and shortcomings, which have been enumerated below.

1. Little Education to the Productive Classes. In any society the labouring or productive class is invariably the largest in size. In Plato's scheme of education, this class is granted only primary education, which implies that higher education of all kinds is intended only for the soldiers and the governing classes, assuming that the labouring class has no need for such an education. Plato's dictum was that the productive class actually required no more than primary education.

2. Absence of Variety. Plato's educational plan pays no attention to the individual differences between one individual and another. He suggested the same kind of education should he given to an entire class of people according to a uniform curriculum. This will inevitably lead to the creation of only one kind of citizens, thus inevitably leading to deadening monotony and lack of variety, which kills all future progress.

3. Stress on Philosophy. Some people get the impression that Plato's insistence on philosophy is exaggerated, and that it could only lead to an increase in the numbers. But it must be remembered that Plato has stressed the importance of both bodily and mental development and in this respect, he has achieved a remarkable harmony of both.

4. Neglect of Literary Education. Plato's curriculum also neglects training in literature by stressing the importance of training in mathematics.

In spite of the above defects, Plato's concept of education has influenced educational philosophy in almost all ages. In particular, his influence can be seen in the idealist philosophy of education. And, many of the finest teachers still consider Plato as their only true guide.

COMMUNISM OF WIVES

Plato supports communism of wives among guardians. The children of guardians shall be taken from their mothers at birth and brought up in common: their particular parentage will be lost in the scuffle. All the guardian-mothers will care for all the guardians-children; the brotherhood of man, within these limits, will graduate from phrase to fact; every boy will be a brother to every other boy, every girl a sister, every man a father, and every woman a mother.

However, community of wives does not mean, according to Plato, indiscriminate mating; rather there is to be strict eugenic super-vision of all reproductive relations. The argument from the breeding of animals here starts its wandering career: if we get such good results in breeding cattle selectively for qualities desired, and from breeding only from the best in each generation, why should we not apply similar principles to the mating of mankind?[19] For it is not enough to educate the child properly; he must be properly born, of select and healthy ancestry; "education should begin before birth."[20]

Functional Specialisation

Plato argues in the *Republic* that the eugenic society must be protected not only from deterioration within, but also from enemies without. It must be ready to wage successful war. Our model community would, of course, be pacific, for it would restrict population within the means of subsistence; but neighbouring states not so managed might well look upon the orderly prosperity of our Utopia as an invitation to raid and rapine. Hence, while deploring the necessity, we shall have, in our intermediate class, a sufficient number of well-trained soldiers, living a hard and simple life like the guardians, on a stated modicum of goods supplied by their 'maintainers and forefathers', the people. At the same time, every precaution must be taken to avoid the occasions of war. In short, the perfect society would be that in which each class and each unit would be doing the work to which its nature and aptitude best adapted it: in which no class or individual would interfere with others, but all would co-operate in difference to produce an efficient and harmonious whole.[21] That would be a just state.

This completes the general outline of Plato's theory of the state. Starting from the conception that the good must be known by methodical study, the theory constructs society around this idea by showing that the principle is implicit in all society. The division of labour and the specialization of tasks are the conditions of social co-operation, and the problem of the philosopher-king is to arrange these matters in the most advantageous way. Because human nature is innately and inherently social, the maximum advantage to the state means also the maximum advantage to citizens. The goal is, therefore, a perfect adjustment of human beings to the possibilities of significant employment which the state affords. The remainder of Plato's argument might also be described as a corollary. The idea of the good, in fact, is the source of all truth, of knowledge, beauty and of moral goodness. It is the source of all knowledge as well as the highest object of knowledge. It illumines the intelligible world. Its apprehension by the soul is Knowledge, its indwelling in the soul is Virtue, its shining forth to the soul — through the medium of sense — is Beauty, and its manifestation in the state is Justice.

Plato in the *Republic* did not consider law as an essential element of the

19. *Republic*, p. 459.

20. *Laws*, p. 789.

21. *Republic*, pp. 433-34.

state. He did not wish to bind the hands or limit the powers of the philosopher-king with the rules of law as to force an expert physician to copy his prescription from the recipes in a medical text-book. He trusted the wiseness and sincerity of the philosopher-king. Hence the omission of law was not a matter of caprice but a logical consequence of the philosophy itself. But Plato soon became doubtful about the success of his own plan regarding the ideal state. It ran quite contrary to the deepest convictions of the Greeks about the moral value of freedom under the law and of participation by the citizens in the task of self-government. Hence, Plato became more practical in his outlook towards the state and gave the law its due place in his later works, the *Statesman* and the *Laws*. Plato sketched out a legal system to help, guide and restrain. Here, the imperfect governmental machinery.

Chapterwise Contents of Republic

The Republic is not so much a treatise on political science as a treatise on education and justice. It is been widely praised by ancient and modern scholars alike. According to Barker, "It is an attempt at complete philosophy of man." In the words of Sabine, "In it practically every side of Plato's philosophy is touched upon or developed and its range of subject matter is such that it may be said to deal with the whole of human life." In this work the books first and second are elementary and discuss the nature of justice and moral duty. The books second, third and fourth discuss the system of education and the different classes in society. The books fifth, sixth and seventh have presented the concept of communism and the philosophical bases of an ideal state. The books eight and ninth discuss the deformities of the state and the citizens. The Tenth book discusses Plato's Philosophy of art and his theory of soul. Thus it is clear that *The Republic* was an attempt at a complete philosophy of man. It discussed social ideals, moral ideals, educational system, the family, theory of property and the ideal state. It is a dramatised philosophy of human life. Among the most important problems discussed in *The Republic* are nature of justice, nature of virtue, system of education, ideal citizens, ideal government, ideal state and the means to realise all these. Plato was not satisfied with the contemporary system of government in Athens. This Government was in the hands of selfish and ignorant rulers. Keeping these defects in view Plato has drawn a picture of welfare state. Thus *The Republic* is a mixture of ethics and politics. Besides giving a view of the contemporary political system it presents the ideal state of Plato's imagination.

Critical Evaluation

The following arguments have been advanced against *The Republic* of Plato:

1. Utopian Ideal. The ideal state of *The Republic* is Utopian. It cannot be applied to existing state. In fact no ideal of a state can be equally valid in all times and climes. As the circumstances change so should change the idea of an ideal state.

2. Applicable to Small State. The optimum population of an ideal state according to Plato, is 5040. It goes without saying that this cannot be applied to any existing state. It was applicable only to a city state which were small and self-sufficient.

3. Negligence of law. By entrusting the ideal state to the Philosopher King Plato neglected the value of the law. The order of the Philosopher King was itself law. This cannot be accepted by the modern political scientists.

4. Absolute Power Corrupts Absolutely. By entrusting absolute power of the state in the hands of the Poilosopher King Plato provided a scope for a lot of corruption. He forgot the psychological dictum that absolute power corrupts absolutely.

5. Separation of Political and Economic Powers. In the modern state the political and the economic powers go together, as the state cannot achieve its aims without economic power. Plato in his *The Republic* kept the rulers free from economic powers. It is difficult to understand as to how could they effectively use their political power in the absence of economic power.

6. Negligence of Lower Class. Plato, in *The Republic*, did not give any political right to the servants. Deprivation of the lower class of all political advantages is against the theory of justice. No modern political scientist can agree to the deprivation of political rights to a government by the modern political scientists almost unanimously.

7. Impractical Communism. Plato's theory of the communism of women and property for the ruler class is absolutely unpsychological. It is unjust to women and completely immoral. Therefore, all discussions concerning communism is impractical.

In spite of the above criticisms of the political philosophy of Plato, as advanced in *The Republic*, it had wide influence in medieval and modern writings in political science. Plato's political ideas influenced not only the ancient Cicero but also the modern Thomas Moore, Rousseau and August Comte. He also influenced the German and British idealistic thinkers. Both the communist and the fascist thinkers have been widely influenced by Plato's thought.

THE LAWS

In the *Laws*, Plato suggests a number of useful checks on the vices of different forms of government. Every citizen is to be allowed to have his share in the government of his state according to his ability. The law is now, the surrogate for that reason which Plato had sought to make supreme in the ideal state and which he still regarded as the supreme force in nature. The chief virtue in the ideal state had accordingly been justice, the division of labour and the specialization of functions which puts every man in his proper place and 'gives him his due' in the sense that he is enabled to bring all his faculties to their highest development and allowed to put them to the fullest use. In the state of the *Laws* wisdom is crystallized in the law: no such flexible adjustment of the individual to the state is possible, but the regulations made by the law are assumed to be the best possible 'on the whole'. Consequently, the supreme virtue in such a state is temperance or self-control, which means a law-abiding disposition or a spirit of respect towards the institutions of the state and a readiness, to subordinate oneself to its lawful powers.

However, on the close examination of the *Laws* he finds that Plato never definitely decided that the theory developed in the *Republic* was erroneous and to be abandoned. He repeatedly stated that his purpose in the *Laws* was to describe a second-best state, and he sometimes put this assertion into conjunction with his strongest statements about the importance of law. Without laws men "differ not at all from the most savage beasts," and yet if a competent ruler should arise, they would have no need to be ruled by laws, "for no law or ordinance is mightier than knowledge."[22] In fact, the state ruled by law was always a concession to the frailty of human nature and never something which he was willing to accept as having a right to stand on a parity with the ideal. Still if the knowledge necessary to make the philosopher-king is unattainable, then Plato is clear that the common moral consciousness is right in believing that a government according to law is better than a government by men, rulers being what they are. The relation between the two theories is not at all satisfactory; "the ideal is logically irreproachable but not attainable in fact, while the second-best state is not impossible to attain but is shaky in respect to its credentials."

The State as an Organism

Plato could never appreciate a democratic state. He was the most formidable opponent that democracy has ever had. He attached little value to and took little interest in the majority of producers. He compared the state to the human body, stating that when a finger is hurt the whole body feels the pain, and that when a member of the state is hurt all will likewise suffer. The state is the best in which the unity is that of the natural man. The happiness of the whole was more important than that of the part. The happiness of the state came before that of any one of its three classes. The life of every individual had meaning only from the function he performed in the organism of the state. The supreme good was the unity of the whole. But it does not mean that Plato completely sacrificed the individual to the state. The state exists for the perfection of the individuals within it, and the development of the individuals within it perfects the state. In the *Republic* there is no difference between the laws of public and private morality. The state conforms to the ideal of the individual man, and leaves to a later age the assertion that what is morally wrong can be politically right. Plato's description of the unjust states hammers home the lesson that it is the falling away in personal conduct that leads to the lowering of tone in public life and to the passing of power into unfit hands for "constitutions are not born of oak and rock, but grow out of the characters in each city."[23] So

22 *Laws*, 874 c; 875 c.

23 *Wayper*, C.L., *Political Thought* (1958), p. 37

the "celestial city, like the Kingdom of God, is really within us, and in our daily actions it is up to us to try to fulfil its laws, so far as is possible to live like an immortal," as Plato says in the *Laws*. George Herbert's "Who sweeps a room, as for Thy laws, makes that and the action fine" is fully Platonic. "It is unimportant whether the perfect state exists anywhere or will exist in the future," Plato writes, "for the first man fulfils the law of that state and of no other." And, in view of the above consideration, it is wrong to say that Plato tried to sacrifice the individual to the state. In fact, he, to quote Wayper, "has founded human personality not on man-made law but on eternal standard."[24]

While writing his famous work *The Republic* Plato's life was full of painful experience of democracy. Therefore, he severely condemned republican form of Government. On the other hand, while writing *The Laws* he was older, more experienced and the memory of the death of his teacher Socrates was not so acute. Therefore, Plato's attitude towards democracy in this new book appears to be wider and more comprehensive. This book was written when Plato returned from Seracuse. In comparison to other dialogues this appears to be a more mature writing. In this writing Plato's experience of the role of a philosopher king in Seracuse was quite useful. After teaching for 30 years in his academy Plato realised that the ideal state must be based upon realities of Greek life. His failure in appointing a philosopher king in Seracuse led to his arrest and slavery which also very much shocked him. Barker has rightly pointed out, "The lessons which he professes to derive from history in the third book of *The Laws* are really derived from the history of his own life."

Comparison of the Republic and the Laws

The following distinctions between *The Republic* and *The Laws* make the above statement more clear.

1. Supremacy of the Law over the King. While in *The Republic* the king is the supreme, the law is supreme in *The Laws*, it was so, because now Plato realised that the ideal of a philosopher king is far for being practical.

2. Mixed Constitution. While *The Republic* considered rule of a philosopher as the best, *The Laws* presented a constitution which was a combination of democracy and monarchy.

3. Relation of Self-restraint and Justice. While in *The Republic* self-restraint is under justice, in *The Laws* justice is under the guidance of self-restraint. It is hence that now Plato maintained that philosophers should control the producers. He pointed out that the ideal state should be based upon self-restraint, only then can justice be established.

4. Distinctions in Systems of Education. There are important differences between the educational systems presented in the two books under comparison. In *The Republic* education aimed at the establishment of an ideal state under a philosopher king, while in *The Laws* the aim of education was to establish a system in which each citizen may himself follow the laws. While in *The*

24. *Ibid.*, p. 38.

Republic education was provided only to the guardian class, in *The Laws* it was available for all the citizens. While in *The Republic* education aimed at the good of the males, in *The Laws* equal arrangement was made for women's education. The two books again differ concerning syllabi of education. While *The Republic* prescribes syllabi for the guardians *The Laws* outlines syllabi for all the sections of people. Finally, while in *The Republic* the educational system was completely under the control of the state, in *The Laws* the public too could arrange for education. *The Laws*, however, prescribes nothing about higher education.

5. Distinctions Concerning Communism. Both these books supported the idea of communism and yet they differ in details concerning its application. In *The Laws* all the restrictions upon personal property and the family were abolished. It emphasises a plan for equal distribution of land. In place of communism of women it supports a scheme for provision of communal rule.

6. Distinction in Division of Labour. Both these books equally support division of labour and yet they differ about details in its application. In *The Laws* trade and craft was entrusted to the foreigners. The owners of land were citizens but the labourers were slaves. The only function of the citizens was to administer the state.

7. Distinctions Concerning Family and Marriage. The two books differ about the details of the social institutions of family and marriage. In *The Laws* women were given equal rights along with the men. According to Plato, marriage could always be solemnized between healthy male and female having opposite but complementary qualities with the sole function of producing children for the state.

8. Distinctions Concerning Administration. The two books differ in details concerning administration of the state. In *The Laws* Plato prescribed several restraints upon the rulers. The authority of the state was vested in a board consisting of 37 elected members whose age was between 50 and 70 years. Under them there was an administrative committee consisting of 360 persons of which some were elected and some appointed through a lottery system. Besides this committee, a committee of 10 members was appointed to see that the constitution functions properly. The job of justice was entrusted to a system of jury.

The above comparison between the prescriptions of *The Republic* and *The Laws* may lead us to the conclusion that in the latter Plato was more realistic than in the former. In other words, "Plato's Republic over shadows his Laws, yet the latter has a practical value deprived to the former." The most important contribution of *The Laws* is the establishment of a rule of law in place of minority. Man needs law due to two reasons, firstly, as every individual cannot understand them he does not act accordingly. Therefore, there should be a rule of law in society so that social welfare may be achieved and the capacities of the citizens may be fully utilized. While temperamentally man goes in the direction of passions, the law leads him in the direction of reason. Therefore, man should always follow the law. The deficiencies of the law can be fulfilled by the customs. Laws should be formulated by the legislators. The Law is supreme in the state and the Government should follow it. Only a state based upon the laws can achieve universal welfare. The guardians have a right to reform the laws. Therefore in spite of being supreme the laws should be flexible. Their fundamentals should be mentioned while enacting them. In order to apply the law, education and intellectual development should go side by side with the punishment and force. Law is another name for morality. Just as the moral conduct is based upon the nature and reason of the man similarly conduct according to law is based upon the human nature and reason along with the fear of the state.

Plato has advocated a mixed constitution in *The Laws*. He enumerates the merits and demerits of monarchy and democracy and finally arrives at a combination having the merits of both these systems. This mixed constitution was not idealistic in nature but aimed at providing better administration. It admits relative importance of both war and peace though it considers a peaceful king as a better king. According to it justice and self-restraint are related in a state.

THE IDEAL STATE

In arriving at his concept of an ideal state Plato has less used his experience and more his imagination. Right from the beginning he has made it clear that he did not aim at drawing a picture of state which is found anywhere but an outline of an ideal state. Therefore he was hardly concerned as to how far the ideal state was practically realisable. According to him society is based upon man's needs. Everyone needs food, clothes and house etc. These needs cannot be fulfilled alone. The multiplicity and variety of needs gives birth to the sense of cooperation among different individuals. They get united and organise economic associations. Some take to agriculture, some to weaving and others to building houses. Thus there are different types of craftsmen in a society. As the needs of the individuals grow, the number of these artisans multiplies and one finds the goldsmith, the ironsmith, the carpenter, the physician and scores of other specialised trades. Of these each individual selects only that concerning which he has maximum capacity, and no one interferes in other's activities. This leads to increase in efficiency and quantity and quality of production. On the basis of this division of labour Plato has classified citizens of an ideal state into three classes: The Guardians the Auxiliaries and finally the Farmers and the Artisans.

Basic Principles

His ideal state was based upon four fundamental principles:

1. Classification of citizens in three classes.
2. Establishment of justice.
3. State controlled systems of education.
4. Communist social system.

According to Plato, each should have three traits wisdom, spirit, and appetite. These are found in everyone and yet they differ in quantity from man to man. Thus, while in some persons wisdom is predominant, in others there supremacy of spirit or appetite. A man adopts a role in society according to supremacy of a quality in his soul. The state is a bigger form of the individual. Therefore, in the state as well Plato has admitted the above mentioned three traits and a corresponding three-fold stratification. The appetite encourages production which increases the capital and finally the state. The state takes care of the property sometimes even by means of war which is not possible without state. Therefore spirit is needed along with appetite. The rulers need wisdom in order to keep proper proportion of spirt and appetite in the state. In the words of Barker, "Appetite may have drawn men together by an economic nexus; spirit may have added a new military bond, it is reason that holds 'men together by teaching them to understand, and through their understanding, to love one another'." Thus in a perfect state all the above mentioned qualities of the soul are found in perfect unison. Ultimately the state is not an economic organisation for the fulfilment of physical needs of life, nor is it a military organisation for the defence of the country. It is a rational organization aiming at mutual knowledge and love of the citizens which is the basis of unity in a state. As Plato has rightly said, "States do not come out of an oak or a rock but from the characters of the men that dwell there in." It is hence that the soul of the state has been imagined on the pattern of the human soul. In the words of Barker, "It is parallel between the consciousness of man, whether acting as a whole or in its several functions and the consciousness of a state expressed in the whole life of the community and in that of its separate classes." Plato believed that if the individuals belonging to the three classes in a state perform their functions most efficiently and sincerely, a state will evolve in which there were no class struggle and the ideal of competition will have no place. The citizens will be non-selfish, and peace and prosperity will grow. Only then justice could be established in a state.

The Philosopher Ruler

Of the above mentioned three classes in the state Plato has considered the guardians as the supreme since they represent wisdom in a state. He entrusts the function of administration in the hands of this class. Wisdom, according to him, not only makes us understand others, but also to love them. In the words of Barker, "Reason in its alliance with spirit has caused the soldier to know and to like, and therefore to protect, the citizens, whom he guards; but reason in its purity causes the ruler to comprehend and out of his comprehension to love and serve, the state which he governs." The source of the unity of the state is neither passion nor spirit but the wisdom . Therefore, the guardian class is the most important and ablest class in the state. Plato has called them the philosophers. Therefore, he cherished the ideal of philosopher king. When philosophers are kings, all weaknesses of political life will come to an end and ideal state will be established. In the words of Plato, "Until philosophers who are kings of the kings, and princes of this world, have the spirit and power of philosophy....cities will never have rest in their evils.'' Thus it is clear that Plato was in favour of a higher form of democracy. He was fully conversant with the weaknesses of the socio-political life in the democratic state Athens. Therefore, he was opposed to democracy even more than monarchy. According to him, even if one ideal philosopher king is available in the state he should be entrusted with all the political power.

Comparison with the Varna System

Platonic classification of the state into three classes is very much similar to the Indian classification of society into the three varnas, the Brahmins, Kshatriyas and the Vaishyas. But, while according to Plato, those who do not fall in any of these classes are slaves, the Shudras of Indian varna system were not slaves. While Plato has named the tendencies of these classes as gold, silver and copper, the Indian varna system considers their qualities as Satvic, Rajasic and Tamasic. The function of the rulers according to Plato was to achieve good in society and to serve the people. Similarly, the functions of Brahmins in Indian social system was to serve the people through education and teaching. The Indian system, however, was better in entrusting the function of administration to the Kshatriyas, the warrior class in consultation with the Brahmins. This is more so, since in ancient days the ruler had often to wage war and therefore he should have been a warrior and not a philosopher. In Indian system the philosopher was not the king himself but a close adviser of the king in different affairs of the state. This system was more practical, more psychological and logical, since in it the power of mind and the power of arms were kept separate so that nobody may be corrupted.

The Concept of Justice

Platonic ideal state cannot be understood without understanding his concept of justice. Justice is the basis of the state. Ideal state is not possible without realisation of justice. While justice is the life, the ideal state is the body. According to justice every citizen performs the function of which he is the most capable and does not interfere in other's functions. Thus each class efficiently performs its role in the state. Therefore, the state naturally progresses towards peace and prosperity. The ideal state is thus founded upon justice.

Status of the Laws

In the ideal state of Plato the law does not have the higher status. According to Plato, as the establishment of justice itself may lead to peace and prosperity therefore, there is no need of imposition of laws upon the citizens. As the establishment of justice will eliminate all the conflicts, punishment will not be needed any more. If the people are good the law is not needed. The laws and punishments are required only in a society where the character and conduct of the people is not based upon justice.

Status of Civic Virtues

Just as the rulers of the state had specific qualities, the ruled should also imbibe specific virtues in an ideal state. These virtues, according to Plato, are : perfect intellectual development, physical beauty, capacity of discussion, aspiration for knowledge; pity, sympathy and love towards fellow citizens and finally hatred towards those polluting social life. Thus it is clear that the ideal state of Plato cannot be achieved without much efforts. It requires a particular type of environment which can be established by a communistic economic system and a specific type of education.

Communism

In his ideal state Plato has conceived two types of communism : the communism of property and the communism of family. Man' s attachment is based upon greed of personal property and the love of personal family. These are the two most important sources of corruption in a state. Therefore, in order to relieve the guardians and the warriors from the anxieties and attachments, Plato prescribed communism of property and women to these two classes. Politically it is necessary that the economic and political power should vest in the hands of people who are free from conflicts concerning personal property and the family attachments. Communism of family aimed at freeing the rulers from the worries of the family so that they could devote themselves completely to the administration of the state. Communism was applicable only to the rulers and the warriors, the producers were free to have personal property and personal family.

Finally, the ideal state was established by means of an ideal system of education. The education, according to Plato, aims at developing wise rulers and virtuous citizens. It provides highest knowledge to man since man has an instinctive urge of curiosity. The highest ideal is the idea of social good. The philosopher king should know this highest ideal and the ultimate truth. Knowledge is the quality of human soul. Education aims at enlightening this spiritual insight. Both intellectual and physical education are equally necessary. While man should know more, he should also be more healthy. Therefore, the syllabi of education prescribed by Plato, includes music, painting and gymnastics along with science and philosophy. In brief, Plato aimed at evolving ideal citizens and able rulers through a system of education.

Critical Evaluation of the Ideal State

The above concept of an ideal state advanced by Plato has been widely scrutinised and criticized. The following are the most important arguments in favour of the ideal state:

1. Though it is difficult to realise on this earth, the concept of Plato's ideal state is based upon eternal ideals found in every age. Therefore, in spite of being utopian it wielded wide influence upon people in different societies.

2. The concept of ideal state encouraged the contemporary city states to remove their defects and to progress on the path of evolution.
3. The concept of ideal state was not purely imaginary, it was based upon Plato's experience in city states. The political systems of both Athens and Sparta have provided material for it.

In comparison with arguments in favour, more arguments have been given against Plato's concept of an ideal state. Of these the most important objections are as follows:

1. Plato has not clearly established the relation between the politics and ethics. In his ideal state the city and the citizens become one.
2. The organic relationship of the individual and the state in this ideal has been extended to a limit where no distinction can be made between the two.
3. Plato's division of human nature into wisdom, spirit and appetite and his comparable classification of human society accordingly is neither logical nor scientific since the society is not an organism.
4. The man cannot be an integral person in the ideal state since his role was confined specifically to a particular field of action.
5. The producer class has not been given a proper place in the ideal state. Plato has not advanced any scheme for his education and evolution. He has not pointed out any way for this class to ascend to the governing class of the rulers.
6. The state of the women and the communism of property is against the fundamental values of any human society.
7. In the ideal state the guardians may enjoy bliss by being absolutely tree from the attachments of life and death. It is difficult to understand as to how such spiritual persons can run the day to day welfare of a mundane state. It was hence that the Indian varna system did not entrust the job of administration to the Brahmins but to the warriors. On the other hand, Plato prescribes absolute authority for the rulers which may ultimately lead to their absolute corruption.
8. Plato has absolutely neglected the slaves in his ideal society. Unless something is done to improve their status an ideal state cannot be realised. The principle that the life of the citizens should be completely controlled is not practical.
9. Plato has not thrown any light upon the appointment of the rulers, the method of punishment and the establishment of the law courts.

THE PHILOSOPHER KING

Need and Value

According to Plato, "....the human race will not see better days until either the stock of those who rightly and genuinely follow philosophy acquire political authority, or else the class who have political control be led by some dispensation of providence to become real philosophers.'' Thus Plato believed that unless the administration of the state is entrusted in the hands of the philosopher king, peace and prosperity cannot be achieved. Only the rule of a philosopher king can free the body politic from its defects.

Plato said ''Until philosophers are kings or the kings and princes of this world have the spirit and power of philosophy, and political greatness and wisdom meet in one, and those commoner natures who pursue either to the exclusion of the other are compelled to stand aside, cities will never rest from their evils.''

Therefore, Plato planned a system of education which may give birth to philosopher kings. This idea was very much influenced by politics of Athens. Plato was against the democratic system of Government in Athens as it was the cause of the death of his teacher Socrates. Therefore, he strongly maintained that the rulers should he selected not because of their popularity, but by their education and ability. A philosopher king is a repository of all human virtues. He is equally anxious to put them into practice to realise the social good.

Characteristics of Philosopher King

In brief, the philosopher king has the following characteristics:

1. Wise. Of the three classes in society the philosopher class represents wisdom. Therefore, it stands in need of a particular type of education.

2. Communist. Plato prescribed communism of family and personal property for the philosophers so that they may live as members of the joint family free from the attachments of personal families.

3. Altruist. The philosopher king was absolutely altruistic. For him the good of the state was the highest good. This altruism was encouraged by communism of personal property and women.

4. Well educated. An able administrator should be a scholar of philosophy and a good politician. Therefore, Plato devised a long system of education for the rulers which aimed at establishment of an oligarchy of philosophers. According to Zeller, ''The platonic state can only be an aristocracy of virtue and intellect exercised by one or few.''

5. Authoritarian. Plato entrusted absolute power in the hands of the philosopher king so much so that he can be termed as an authoritarian. And yet in order to curb authoritarianism he prescribed that the philosopher king should follow the following rules laid down in the constitution of the state:

(i) The rulers should extend the state only as much as necessary to keep it self-sufficient and unified, it should be neither bigger nor smaller.

(ii) The ruler should not encourage too much prosperity or poverty in the state because this will lead to evolution of two contrary classes who may conflict and increase instability in the state. Therefore, the ruler should not allow too much imbalances in the increase or decrease of wealth.

(iii) The ideal ruler should see that each citizen follows his duty and does not interfere in the performance of duties by the other people.

(iv) The ruler should make no changes in the system of education prescribed in the state.

Critical Evaluation

The following criticisms have been advanced against Plato's ideal of a philosopher king:

(i) *Impractical Ideal.* The ideal of a philosopher king is far from being practical. Firstly, it is difficult to find a person equally conversant in philosophy, mathematics and social life. Secondly, a philosopher king, in order to succeed, not only needs the knowledge of philosophy and mathematics as prescribed by Plato, but a sound knowledge of psychology, economics, law and political science.

(ii) *Sanction to Authoritarian Ruler.* Plato's sanction of total power to the ruler tends to make him authoritarian. It has been rightly said that power corrupts but absolute power corrupts absolutely. The restrictions prescribed by Plato to curb this authoritarianism were far from satisfactory.

(iii) *Lower Status of the People.* The provision of unlimited power to the ruler will inevitably lead to a lower status of the people who will be deprived even of the fundamental human rights.

(iv) *Distinction between Philosophy and Administration.* The personality traits born due to philosophy are hindrances rather than help in the function of administration. Therefore, we cannot hope that a philosopher will be a better administrator.

(v) *Absence of People's Contribution in Administration.* Plato did not make any provision for the role of public opinion in a state. It is doubtful as to how the state can be administered successfully without taking into consideration the public opinion and without active cooperation of the people to the rulers.

THE DEMOCRACY

Plato had a bitter experience of democracy in the form of death of his teacher Socrates. He therefore advanced the following objections against democracy:

1. Mobocracy. Democracy is mobocracy since a mob alone rules a democracy.

2. Anarchy. Democracy becomes anarchy since there is no principle of unity or discipline among the three elements of soul and society.

3. Disorder. The principles of liberty and equality, considered as the basis of democracy, lead to disorder, if followed unlimited. In a democracy the human beings, like animals, claim equality and liberty in every field of life.

4. Equal rights to unsuitable persons. Democracy does not distinguish between the able and the disable. Plato, on the other hand, supported rights according to abilities. He condemned prescription of equal rights to all the people without consideration of their abilities.

5. Unjust. Democracy fosters injustice. Plato based his ideal of justice upon division of labour and specialisation so that each person may be given a role according to his abilities. On the other hand, in democracy, every one is free to choose a role according to his own sweet-will and no principle can be prescribed for this purpose.

6. Absence of a philosopher king. In a democracy some selfish people collect votes from the public and become rulers. In such a situation the ideal of the philosopher king cannot be realised in the state.

In spite of the above criticisms Plato was not as much against democracy as he appears to be in his book *The Republic*. Gradually, his opposition was diluted and in his work *Politics*, he considers democracy as better than oligarchy, a precise inversion of his earlier stand concerning democracy. In his later work *The Laws*, he considers democracy based upon laws as second to the ideal state.

WAS PLATO A FASCIST?

It has been said that "One of the main causes of Plato's pervasive and persuasive influence is that he is the ablest exponent of the aristocratic theory of the state and the acutest critic of the democratic way of life." Thus, Plato has been considered the first fascist in history. The incident of the trial of Socrates and his consequent death in a democracy had shocked Plato and therefore he mentioned many defects in the system. This led some of the political scientists to brand him as the father of Fascism and a totalitarian.

Similarities with Fascism

Though, this remark is not absolutely correct and yet one can find the following similarities between Plato' s political thought and the system known as Fascism :

1. Rule of Minority. Like Fascism Plato also entrusts the rule of the ideal state to a minority.

2. Authoritarianism. Like Fascism Plato entrusts unlimited rights to the ruler. He was considered as above the laws, traditions and public opinion and nobody could control over him. Thus in his system the ruler becomes an authoritarian.

3. Opposition of Democracy. Condemning democracy in his book *The Republic*, Plato said, "The laws of democracy remain a dead letter, its freedom is anarchy, its equality the equality of unequals." Thus, he considered democracy as a corrupt rule.

4. All Powerful State. Like Fascism Plato made his state all powerful. He gave no fundamental rights to the individual against the state and considered him as a means in the hands of the state.

5. Negation of Equality. Like Fascism Plato rejected the principle of equality as applied to the citizens of the state. He classified the producers, the warriors and the rulers in separate classes and made special provisions for the ruler class. He considered the individuals belonging to the ruler class as superior to the other two classes.

6. State as the Ultimate End. According to the Philosophy of Fascism it is said that "All within the state, none without the state, none against the state." In other words, fascism does not accept any thing against the state or outside the state. Plato has given similar rights to the state.

7. Importance of the Laws. Like Fascism Plato considers the law as an end and the individual a mere means to it. The fascist Mussolini gave the laws the highest place in his state.

8. Emphasis on the Duties of Citizens. Like Fascism Plato nowhere mentioned the rights of the citizens but laid exclusive emphasis upon their duties only. In a fascist state the citizen should not criticise the government, have faith in the rulers, follow their commands and sacrifice even their lives for the fulfilment of the duties of the citizens. Plato has given similar instructions to the citizens.

9. Fascist Educational System. In fascism the state governs the educational system. Similar is the case in Plato's plan of education. Like fascism his aim of education was the creation of able rulers and warriors. The Syllabi of education was planned by the government and executed for the welfare of the state under direct state supervision.

10. Racism. Like Fascism Plato also admits the distinctions due to race. He considered some people as superior to others by birth and thought that they alone have a right to rule the others.

Distinction from Fascism

In spite of the above similarities between fascism and the political thought of Plato, the following differences should also be remembered:

1. Historical Gap. While the fascist thought was born after the first world war in 20th century, Plato presented his political thought four centuries before Christ. Thus there is a long gap between them.

2. Distinctions in Attitude. In spite of considering the state as all powerful, Plato never supported its extension while on the other hand, the fascist thinkers consider extension of the state as empire as a necessary step in its evolution.

3. Anti War. Plato was against war while according the fascism war is necessary for the progress of the state.

4. Support of Communism. Plato presented the principle of communism of property and women. Fascism, on the other hand, is against all communism.

5. Idealism. Plato was an idealist. He presented plan of an ideal state. Fascism, on the other hand, is absolutely realistic in approach.

6. Philosophical Distinctions. In Plato's thought political thinking is based upon philosophical principles. The fascist philosophy, on the other hand, is based upon political thinking.

7. Ethics and Polities. According to Plato politics is the handmaid of ethics, according to fascism, on the other hand, ethics follows polities and politics is the highest ethics.

8. Systematic Thought. Plato's thought is systematic and scientific. On the other hand, fascist political thought lacks system and sequence.

The above discussion of the similarities and distinctions between the political thought of Plato and that of fascism leads us to the conclusion that neither was Plato the originator of fascism nor was he the first fascist in history. Both Plato and fascism opposed democracy but, as is clear by the above mentioned discussion, they do so for different reasons. Plato opposed democracy because in its system his teacher Socrates was given poison. Gradually, as the memory of this shocking incident diminished in his mind, his criticism of democracy was diluted. Plato's political philosophy was a result of his critical evaluation of the contemporary political systems. Fascism was a result of very different conditions. Therefore, it is not proper to call Plato's political thought fascist purely on some external similarities. Plato has not presented completely indentical views in all his works. In *The Republic* he supported an authoritarian state, while in *The Laws*, he considered laws as the most important in the state. The political thinkers branding Plato as a fascist forget that his political philosophy was a result of gradual evolution. In his later writing *The Laws* he presented a more balanced political thought.

GREEK ELEMENTS IN PLATO'S POLITICAL THOUGHT

In spite of his criticism of almost all the contemporary political theories, one can find the following Greek elements in his political thought, particularly the influence of the political systems prevalent in Sparta and Athens:

1. Like Sparta Plato advised the rulers to have food in public restaurants.

2. Like Sparta his rulers could not keep silver and gold. The philosopher king could not have gold or silver.

3. Like the system of compulsory military education in Sparta; Plato also emphasised physical and military education in his system of education.

4. In Sparta even the women had to exercise physically. Plato also prescribed the same.

5. Trade was prohibited for the rulers in Sparta. Similarly Plato also prohibited trade and commerce for the rulers in his ideal state.

6. In Sparta male and female were considered as equal. In his ideal state, Plato also provided equality to male and female.

7. In Sparta the state was supreme. Plato also held the state as supreme and the citizens secondary.

8. Plato's plan of education was organised on the pattern of curriculum in Athens and planned according to the pattern of Sparta.

9. In contemporary Greek society pornography had evil influence. Therefore Plato prohibited all pornographic literature and art in his ideal state.

10. There were city states in Plato's time. Therefore, he also decided 5040 as the ideal population for an ideal state.

11. In contemporary Greek society the custom of slavery was prevalent. Plato has considered it as universal and necessary for the state.

12. Customs similar to communism of property and women could be observed in contemporary Sparta. It was on the basis of these customs that Plato provided communism of property and women in his state.

13. The ideal state envisaged by Plato in his book, *The Laws* was similar to the state in Athens.

UNIVERSAL ELEMENTS IN POLITICAL THOUGHT

The above mentioned Greek elements in the political thought of Plato should not lead us to the conclusion that it has no universal element. There are two aspects of his political thought — applied and ideal. While the applied aspect is no more relevant today, the ideal aspect can still lead the political thinkers of our time. In brief, the following universal elements can be seen in the political thought of Plato:

1. Rule of Reason. Taking reason as the highest element in man Plato laid down that the rule of the state be entrusted in the hands of rational individuals. His ideal of the philosopher king is still important.

2. Theory of Justice. Justice, according to Plato, means following ones duties and not interfering in other's functions. Even today this principle is laid emphasis upon in the definition of justice.

3. Division of Labour. Plato wanted to allot different functions to different classes of people according to their abilities and capacities. This principle of division of labour had universal significance.

4. Equality of Women. Plato gave equality to women along with men in the social system. This principle has universal significance even now.

5. Communism of Property. Plato advocated the principle of communism of property for his rulers. From the point of view of communist philosophy today this principle is the most important in a human society.

6. Rule of Law. Rule of law was the most important in Plato's political system. From the point of view of modern political science, the rule of Law is the most important trait of a modern state.

7. Value of Education. Plato laid down the principle that educational system should be correlated to the type of society that we cherished. In order to run the state properly provision should be made for the rulers. The education of the citizens should be the function of the state. This idea is relevant even now. Today in most of the states the education is controlled by the state. Every welfare state considers it its duty to arrange for different types of education for different sections of society. Education today is the responsibility of the state.

On the basis of the above mentioned universal elements in the political thought of Plato it can be concluded that though his political thinking was based upon contemporary city states, his political thought is equally valuable to the bigger states of our own time.

IS THE REPUBLIC A UTOPIA?

The following points prove that *The Republic* is not a utopia:

1. Comprehensive Masterpiece. '*The Republic*' of Plato is his masterpiece. It is a treatise on justice. It is a treatise on political science and jurisprudence. Rousseau called it a treatise on education. To quote Sabine, "Its range of subject matter is such that it may be said to deal with the whole of human life." It deals with many subjects interwoven into one whole. In this book, Plato discussed every possible thing on earth including justice, education, eugenics, abortion, nudism etc. Hence, Sabine has rightly said that "The Republic defies classification."

2. Definition of Ideal State. As a consequence of Socrate's death and the decay of Greek polity Plato was provided with a point of view to criticise the city-state and also with a method that let to the conception of an ideal state. '*The Republic*' presents Plato's Ideal State. Plato gave his own definition of Ideal State. He placed it high above the existing systems. State, according to him, was a perfection to serve as a model, to be the criterion by which the existing systems can be estimated and an ideal to be emulated. Dunning says, "Plato's 'Republic' is a mere romance." But on the other hand, Barker points out that "Republic is not a city of nowhere, it is based on actual conditions, it is meant to mould or at any rate to influence actual life." This is due to the reason that Plato never divorced himself from earthly realities. He may equally be called a realist as well as an idealist.

3. Based on Actual Conditions. '*The Republic*' was based on actual conditions of Greece. In Plato's view Greek States were diseased because in them the elements of reason (which creates ambition) and appetite (parent of greed and social cleavage) were overgrowth. Plato wanted to cure these diseased states by the rule of Reason. Training of reason by scientific and philosophic education and liberation of Reason from greed and appetite by a system of communism were the two remedies employed by Plato to eliminate defects in existing city state.

4. Deduction and Induction. This statement of cure like the statement of disease is based on actual fact. Training and the mode of education suggested by Plato was the same as was actually given in academy. The system of communication; though it goes beyond anything that existed in Greece, is the extension of elements that Greece had known. So the Republic was not only a deduction from first principles it was also an induction from facts of Greek life.

5. Influence on Actual Life. '*The Republic*' was meant to influence actual life. Political reform was the aim of the work. As Plato was a practical idealist, he was an actual politician in intention. He fell short of a perfect idealist just because he was so eager to realise his ideal. As he himself said about his '*The*

Republic', "It is not impossible, nor do we speak of things that are impossible, though by even ourselves they are admitted to be difficult in enactment." What Plato said about state and government was not a mere dream. It was possible only when kings become philosophers or philosophers kings. Granted the philosopher and the means, the ideal could be realised.

6. Practicability of the Idea. At the end of the IX book, Plato said, "Ideal city is founded on words because on earth it nowhere exists." Plato doubted whether the ideal could be realised as it is. But the ideal, in spirit as a force in all societies, may be certainly hoped to realise. Plato was not greatly concerned with practicability of his ideal. The enquiry was for the sake of an ideal and not for proving that such a thing could exist in fact. Fact, in its approximation to perfect truth, must fall short of the theory. Action must lag behind thought. Thoughts can think of actual conditions. Mind constructs a picture of the world, as it would be. If the true principle of human life had free play such a picture is not a dream. It is abstraction indeed, but everything depends upon the society in which one lives. If the society puts away these old conditions and adopts new, then the dream may become true. Even if this is impossible the dream has still its value. It tells us as to what is good and what should be our aim. Thus, it directs us to move in right direction. It directs us to distinguish between different elements of life. It gives us control over lives.

WAS REPUBLIC A MERE ROMANCE?

The following points may be noted in favour of the comments:

1. Abolition of Necessary Things. Plato wanted to abolish things which men still regarded as inevitable. Private property, family and democracy exist even now. No civilized society or no state can be turned into a single family. Human nature demands personality and life of family. It also demands voice in the direction of public control. Plato goes far from realities when he wanted to abolish these three things.

2. Neglect of Evolution of State. Plato regarded state as organic but did not recognise organic growth. He did not think that state can develop into an ideal by the passage of time. He thought too much in terms of creation. He believed in a permanent ideal and did not believe in evolution. Political theory must deal with ideal. It must consider what the state might be and not what it is. It must investigate what is the right state, and the right state must be an ideal State.

3. Testing Actual by the Ideal. In VIII and IX books of '*The Republic*' Plato sought to judge the actual states by the degree to which they are interior to ideal state. This judgement took the form of corruption, in successive stages, of that ideal state.

4. Not Historical but only Logical Order. Plato did not give historical but only logical picture of the course that corruption of ideal state would take. If the ideal state is a perfect product of perfect mind successively inferior types of states are the product of successively inferior types of mind. Stage by stage, state is made to depend upon worse elements of human soul : until in tyranny it depends only on worst element of appetite.

REPUBLIC WAS NOT A MERE ROMANCE?

The following points may be noted in criticism of Dunning's remarks:

1. General Rule of Change. Aristotle maintained that constitutions do not change in the sequence Plato suggests. Oligarchy does not always pass into democracy or democracy into tyranny. In actual life, democracy may pass into oligarchy as readily as into tyranny. But Plato's rule cannot be denounced *wholly since it embodies the general rule of constitutional change.*

2. Condemnation of Tyrant. Plato's purpose of giving the system of ideal state was the condemnation of tyrant.

3. Explanation of Corruption to Show Need of Education. *The Republic* gives explanation as to why is a state corrupted and how can it become ideal. Corruption of state implies corruption of its citizens. Ideal state is ideal because it represents a type of mind in which perfect adjustment of faculties has been realised. Hence one way of reforming a state is readjustment of faculties of its members. Such readjustment can only be affected by education. Hence, the *practical result of Plato's sketch of constitutional change and corruption is that* education is the one and only way of political reform.

4. Determination of Justice and Injustice. *In his The Republic* Plato wanted to determine what is justice and injustice and he wanted to determine that justice is happiness and injustice misery. To attain this object, Plato wanted to determine how much happiness and misery did a man attain in various degrees of unjust states.

5. Harmony of Reason, Spirit and Appetite. The ideal state was based on the harmonious union of three elements of Reason, Spirit and Appetite in which reason is dominant. In the next forms of state reason loses its due place and spirit obtains control. Three succeeding forms — oligarchy, democracy and tyranny are all based on the supremacy of appetite. Democracy represents not only the necessities but also luxuries etc. Tyranny rests only on wild appetite for luxuries.

6. Psychological and Economic Interpretation of History. Excessive increase of anything often causes a reaction in the opposite direction. Oligarchy pursues wealth till it perishes of it. Democracy pursues freedom till it is ruined by it. In oligarchy, with the increase of wealth, poverty automatically increases. Class consciousness develops resulting into class war and revolutions. Thus Plato's interpretation of history, though primarily psychological, was also economic in nature.

7. Basis in Contemporary History and Politics. Plato's account of the different forms of perverted states was based on his knowledge of contemporary history and his own experience of politics. Features of Timocratic state were found in Crete and Sparta. Athens was the sketch of his democracy.

REPUBLIC DEFIES CLASSIFICATION

1. Contradictory Estimation. Athens was the cradle of modern civilization. Plato was the greatest apostle of this great culture. This explains Barker's remark that an Englishman will feel more at home with the works of Plato in the 5th century B.C. than with the Memories of Frederick the Great, who lived in the eighteenth century. Almost all the thinkers till the beginning of the twentieth century, till Nietsche and other Nihilists destroyed its value, drank to the very rich foundation of knowledge and wisdom in the Republic. To quote Catlin, "The old man is dead since 22 centuries ago, but as human nature has not died, the abstract truth stated by him still holds good." At the beginning of the human civilization, Plato stood like a colossus. He has been subject to plaudits and at the same time poisonous invectives. His thought has been complicated by the zeal of the modern commentators, who have enuended, conjectured, transposed and inserted with energy and diversity that leaves the reader in a hopeless confusion. His philosophy is contradictorily estimated.

2. Scientific Genius and Political Insight. However, "*The Republic*", is an impressive embodiment of scientific genius and political insight. That is why the remark of Sabine that it defies classification. Rousseau called it a treatise on education. According to Barker Plato's conception of justice is the hinge of his thought and the text of his philosophy. Any estimate of Plato's 'Republic' is bound to miss the mark as it deals with almost all the subject under the sky. Most of the problems touched by Plato are still the issues for debate and discussion. The range of Plato' s thought is so extensive that one feels that he is always amidst us.

3. Secret of Comprehensiveness. The secret of all comprehensive nature of Plato's Republic lies in the fact that he was the first great systematic and scientific philosopher. His greatness rested on the fact that he was the first thinker to define an abstract thing. According to Dunning, this made Plato's *mind run riot* with the result that his philosophy proceeded with a poetic vagueness. Its understanding is more a matter of feeling rather than of cold reasoning.

4. Duality of Human Nature. Plato was the first philosopher who found the dualities in the human nature, viz, the ape and the angel together. This recurring note in his philosophy, as Sabine points out, made the fathers of Christianity regard him as a Christian.

5. Wide Scope. It is difficult to put any label to Plato's profound work, '*The Republic*.' In this book, by the dialectic of dialogue, Plato discussed every possible thing on earth, like the conception of good, the location of justice, the place of education, eugenics, abortion, nudism and what not. The scope of this treatise is so wide that it easily speaks how Plato was a versatile genius.

6. Despondency. Plato lived in an age when Athenians were still suffering under the weight of defeat in the Plopponesian war and the death of Socrates. The general dependency and the disillusionment of the Grecian civilization prompted Plato to portray an ideal state and give new interpretation to the institutions and ideas to suit a renovated state. Hence, the wide sweep of his philosophy defying categorisation.

7. Definition of Abstract Truth. Plato's central theory in '*The Republic*' is the definition of abstract truth from which all the interesting subjects were discussed. If one accepts the definition as given by Plato and the method by which he came to practical realities, one is bound to agree to all his conclusions.

8. Method of Argument. The importance of Plato's philosophy is due to the fact that he proceeded by argument not by intuition or sentiments.

9. Opinion of Dunning. Even among the professors of political science opinions diverge about Plato's importance. Dunning is of the opinion that the discovery of the general idea is the achievement of first rate magnitude in the history of human intellect. This alone made Plato to treat Political Science as only of incidental importance. Bowles considers '*The Republic*' to be primarily a philosophic discourse, into which the ideal state is brought incidentally. In the words of Dunning, the treatise was essentially a romance embellished with a series of brilliant but not carefully correlated essays on morals and metaphysics.

10. A Model State. Dunning argued that Plato's conception of Ideal State was only intended for the purpose of drawing a moral. Plato never lived in a realm of fancy and imagination. As Barker points out, it is not an ideal state in the clouds, but a state which is intended to serve as the practical political system for the Greek world. It was a perfection to serve as the model. It was the criterion by which the existing systems could be estimated or emulated.

11. Virtue is Knowledge. In his exposition of philosophy, Plato believed faithfully in the Socratic doctrine that 'virtue is knowledge.' He maintained that real virtue and real knowledge is only perception of this idea. Good in its true sense, may be known only when one has attained this absolute and abstract knowledge. An all-wise philosopher is the king or the philosopher ruler. He alone can materialise the ideal state.

12. The Human Nature. After having stated what is true and virtue and who is the person that can attain it, Plato discussed the earthly realities. According to him human nature is composed of three psychological characteristics: reason, spirit and appetite. Reason dominates in the guardians, spirit in the military men and appetite in the workers and the artisans. This statement shows how shrewd was Plato in concluding that all men are not equal in mental abilities. Accordingly, each person should specialise in his own field. This is known as the functional specialisation.

13. Role of Education. Then Plato look up the problem how best to develop the special and unique attributes of each class, he advocated a system of state education. Further, while discussing the philosopher rulers he found that often the rulers in the actual state are distracted by two institutions, called the family and the property. This logically led him to discourse on communism. Thus, from the first step of definition of what is real virtue, Plato derived all these important conclusions.

14. Impact of Contemporary Conditions. A close scrutiny of Plato's philosophy indicates that he took cue from the existing conditions in his discussions on many topics. For instance, Sabine says that his thought on education was only a running commentary on the existing institutions. His advocacy of the communism of property was a direct reaction to the corruption of the Athenian rulers. However, in his treatment of education and communism, Plato exhibited an extraordinary brilliance. To illustrate, the manner in which he dwelt on the mental growth of the individuals under the impact of education is typically modern. It is only after divining certain rhythmic course in the growth of the intellect, that he prescribed the period of education.

Critical Observations

The philosophy of Plato may be criticised from the following points of view:

1. Weak Link to Realities. The first is the weak link by which Plato came to practical realities. This is the Achille's heel in his philosophy. This is because if one accepts the three psychological characteristics of human nature and their location in three classes of society. What Plato said is true, but unfortunately human nature possesses traits like emotions, instincts, passions and morbidity as well.

2. Authoritarianism. Popper in his book *'Open Society and Enemies'* states that Plato's philosophy leads to a world of absolutism and the authoritarian views. This view cannot be accepted. Plato never meant rulers but only path finders. According to Collingwood, the philosopher was only to be a friend and guide. Elliot and MacDonald point out that in ancient empires of Egypt, Babylon, Assyria, Summeria, Persia and India, the priests were the advisers of the monarch controlling the state. Mandarian class in Chinese Empire and Oenero of Japan were like Platonic Guardians. So was the case with the party elite of Soviet Russia according to Marxian philosophy. The necessity for a healthy intelligentsia in any progressive and happy civilization is a biblical truth. Without such a group of people a civilization is threatened with imminent destruction.

3. Nietzsche's Criticism. Thus, the philosophy of Plato is so extensive in its ramification that it is next to impossible to give it a trade label. All the old problems discussed by him are eternal problems. *The Republic* has come round again in present time in eugenics, nudism, abortion, feminism, communism, class-war etc. In conclusion, one is reminded of the poignant criticism by Neitzsche that while emphasising on specialisation Plato heralded the age of degeneracy since specialisation and expert knowledge is always the curse of civilizations. It was only the happy versatility of the Greeks as symbolised in Euripides, Homer, Archimedes, Hipporitus and a host of others, that is responsible to call the Grecian civilization as the cradle of the modern civilization. A community is dynamic whenever versatile genius is abundant. A parallel instance is the Hindu civilization in the Gupta period with the illustrious Nagarjuna,

Aryabhatta, Charaka, Kalidas and a thousand others. This indicated that in spite of the supreme excellence of Plato, he missed the mark.

PLATO'S PRAISE OF PHILOSOPHY

Plato was the first great systematic and scientific philosopher of polities. He was the first man to define an abstract thing. This, says Dunning, made Plato's mind run riot with the result that his philosophy came to have a poetic vagueness whose understanding is more a matter of feeling rather than of cold reasoning. In the words of Catlin, "The old man is dead 22 centuries ago, but as human nature has not died, the abstract truth stated by him still holds good." Plato was the first philosopher who found the duality in human nature, *viz.* the lower man and the higher man. This recurring note in his philosophy, as Sabine points out, made the fathers of Christianity regard him as a Christian.

Republic : A Philosophical Discourse

Both Dunning and Bowle consider Plato's "*The Republic*" to be primarily a philosophical discourse into which the ideal city was brought incidentally. In the words of Dunning, "The treatise was essentially a romance embellished with a series of brilliant but not carefully co-related essays on morals and metaphysics."

Praise of the Philosopher

In his exposition of philosophy Plato believed faithfully in the Socratic doctrine that Virtue is Knowledge. In his times Socrates threw the challenge that if there is any valuable thinking, it must be defined. So Plato, his disciple, said, that real virtue was only the ultimate "Idea" of Good and the real knowledge was only the perception of this idea. Good in its true sense could be known by only one that had attained this absolute and abstract knowledge. An all-wise philosopher alone could attain to virtue. It was knowledge alone which entitled him to exercise decisive power in government. When this all-wise philosopher is the king or the philosopher ruler, then alone will come into existence his ideal state.

Rule by the Philosopher King

Thus, in Books V and VI of '*The Republic*', Plato depicted, how an ideal state is to be ruled by philosophers. Why did Plato say so? It was due to the bad political and social conditions of city-state of Greece of his time. Degeneration of Athenian democracy, Peloponesian war, factionalism, clashes of economic interests in the society were the causes responsible for Plato's conception of philosopher king. The execution of his master, Socrates, made him all the more disgusted with the then existing democracies. He was led to believe that human race will not see better days until those who rightly and genuinely follow philosophy acquire political authority. In Plato's words, "Until philosophers are kings or the kings and princes of this world have the spirit and power of philosophy and political greatness and wisdom meet on one, cities will never have rest from their evils."

Plato wanted to base his state on absolute wisdom, absolute truth, justice, reason and scientific laws. Hence according to Plato, the government must be directed and controlled by knowledge. The only true knowledge is philosophy. Hence the government must be controlled by the philosopher. The philosopher-ruler knows the good of a state as the physician knows health. It is knowledge alone which distinguishes the true statesman from the false as it is knowledge that distinguishes the physician from the quack. The philosopher ruler is as gentle and noble as a god. He loves knowledge. He can discriminate between good and bad. Hence, his rule will be the rule of universal reason and higher than any fixed laws. To Plato, discretion, if it is wise, is higher and better than the straight jacket of law. With a philosopher king the laws would be the dictates of reason and this discretion will surely be better than inflexible laws. The philosophy will be above laws and selfishness.

Virtues of the Philosopher

The philosopher must rule because then alone there could be an end to political selfishness and incompetence. He alone can think of his office not as an opportunity but as a sacred duty. He loves truth and can see the unity of all knowledge. He knows what is Justice, Beauty and Temperance. He uses his knowledge to mould the character of those over whom he rules. His knowledge is at once his right and duty to rule. "He has the noblest gifts of nature and makes highest use of them." He fosters the spirit of justice in an appropriate manner. He represents knowledge in action. He embodies in himself justice "the highest of all political virtues." He is just and gentle. He shows the due proportion in all things developed by the study of metaphysics, higher mathematics and from contemplation of the Good. "None of the graces of a beautiful soul are wanting in him." He is a passionate seeker of truth and wisdom.

The Ideocracy

The ideocracy on which Plato builds up his ideal state, led him to tolerate aristocracy of intellect but his best reference was for a philosopher king. He was a true statesman. His monarchy was the best form of Government. A philosopher king should be no more burdened with laws than a medical practitioner with medical rules. Plato favoured absolute monarchy of philosopher king. Justice was the corner stone of the Platonic state. Justice lies in rendering to a man his due which the philosopher king would do. He will pursue no other object than the welfare of the community. He will rule the state in accordance with his own free judgement and will be responsible to his own conscience alone.

Limitations on the Philosopher-King

Although the philosopher-king was to be absolute ruler untrammelled by written laws, Plato did not keep him free of all restraints. He must respect the fundamentals of the state. These fundamentals relate to :

(i) Regulation of wealth and property in the State,

(ii) The size of the state,

(iii) The rule of justice, and

(iv) The system of education.

Thus, even the philosopher king of Plato was subservient to the fundamental social order. The following charges have been made against Plato's attempt to place philosophy on the largest pedestal:

1. Aristocracy. Wisdom is never the monopoly of a few individuals, however well they are trained. To say that philosophers alone possess the great knowledge is to censor all new ideas and there by live in stagnation. Plato was so much impressed with the idea of philosopher-king or lover of philosophy that he totally neglected the idea of law or the influence of public opinion. There is a whole world of difference between knowledge and experience. Plato ignored the Greek conception of the state as being an association of equals, owing only to the sovereignty of law. He reduced the majority to the status of automata. It is very difficult to locate a true ruler to limit laws on the one hand and public opinion on the other. After all laws are also the product of practical thinking and experience of legislators.

2. Absolutism. Plato's grant of monopoly of political power to philosopher king or to aristocracy of intellect makes the ruler absolute and degenerates it into enlightened tyranny. Untrammelled by laws the king may identify his own intellect with public interests. A philosopher given to abstract thinking cannot be practical. He is likely to loose touch with reality of public life and introduce harmful changes in public institutions. He may not be fit to take decisive action in moments of crisis. His scheme of education is more likely to create men of ideas than of action. In the words of Jowett, "The philosopher-ruler is apt to be looking into the distant future or back into the remote past and unable to see actions and events of the present."

3. Reversal in the Laws. If Plato's scheme of the rule of philosopher were practicable, he would not have discarded it in the "Laws." '*The Laws*' was written in an attempt to restore law, which is indispensable to accomplish the results under existing circumstances. Plato himself modified his earlier doctrines of private property, education, training and family ties. He did not propose for his philosopher ruler any study of law or finance or military tactics. Abstract sciences like mathematics or dialects are no preparation for a man of action which a philosopher ruler has to be. The experience of history shows that such rulers have failed. They have brought more misery than good to those entrusted to their care. They introduced revolutionary changes without due preparation and experience.

4. Aristotle's Criticism. Plato's belief that the philosopher, by renouncing property and women, would become highly altruistic was questioned by his disciple Aristotle. According to Aristotle, a denial of these things would lead to recklessness, carelessness and such other traits. Aristotle maintained that even the wisest ruler cannot dispense with law, because the law has an impersonal quality, which no man, however good, can attain.

5. Closed World. In his book '*Open Society and Enemies*' Popper states that Plato's philosophy led to a closed world. The absolute authority given to the philosopher-rulers meant a totalitarian state. However, Plato never meant his philosopher rulers to be dictatorial. Collingwood in Hobhouse Lectures showed that it meant only path-finders i.e. their duty is that of a guide, a friend, a mentor and a philosopher. They are supposed to appreciate the signs of the time. Plato insists upon the necessity of knowledge for those who rule. Their training, even in abstract thinking is for civic action. Pursuit of the Idea of the Good must materialise in healthy social action. Philosophic education, civic training and rigorous communistic asceticism were calculated to create a type of guardians who were not dreamers but practical idealists.

6. No Utopia. In concluding this argument, one is tempted to say that Plato never lost himself in a world of ideas as is thought by Dunning. There is nothing dreamy and wishful about his philosophy. In a way, this philosopher-ruler can be found in the past, in the present and may be in the future. Elliot and McDonald said that self-appointed people trying to guide a society is a common theme in the political history of the world. They show how the Egyptian Polity, the Babylonian, Assyrian and Sumarian Empires were guided by a handful of men who can be called the philosopher guardians of the state. The early Indian history is also not an exception for the reason that it was the priestly class possessing the mastery and monopoly of the knowledge in Upanishads and Vedas, who guided both the rulers and the society. Again, it is interesting to note that till very late in the Japanese history the Genero, the elder statesmen of Japan were the masters of the nation. Coming to the present day, one can find the philosopher rulers in the Marxian Communism since only a handful of picked people, conscious of the Marxian philosophy, must guide the people through the final stage of the human society, namely the proletariat dictatorship. Thus a more liberal interpretation of Plato's philosophy shows that he is still in the midst of us.

SYSTEM OF GOVERNMENT IN 'THE LAWS'

In his book '*The Laws*' Plato asserted the fundamental principle of sovereignty of laws. He expressed the view that in the second best state law is sovereign and supreme and the government with all its organs is subordinate to it. No body of magistrates, no council or senate, no assembly, however broad, is above the law. But Plato does not maintain this thesis in the twelfth Book. The most important reason for the absence of any sovereign body in the government is that the constitution of the sub-ideal state must be of mixed type. It should be a reconciliation of monarchy with democracy, the principle of knowledge with the principle of liberty. A mixed constitution can hardly contain a single sovereign authority. To quote Prof. Barker, "It is impossible to say of the constitution of Sparta, whether it is a monarchy, or an aristocracy, and tyranny or democracy, it must be equally impossible to say of the state which Plato builds in the Laws that it is ruled by any one sovereign authority."

Platonic State of Laws

In the Platonic State of Laws, the electoral authority is a popular assembly. It elects the council and the various executive magistrates. This popular assembly is the whole body of 5,040 citizens, arranged in four classes on the basis of qualifications, and the differences in the amount of the property possessed by them. It is compulsory for the first two classes to attend the meetings but for the 3rd and 4th class attendance is optional. No citizen of any class may attend these meetings unless he bears arms and has gone through military service.

Function of the Assembly

The function of the assembly is to elect the guardians of the law and the council. It also elects a number of local officials and generals of the army. The 37 guardians of the law are to be elected by a Triple ballot. In the first ballot 300 are elected; in the second ballot 200 are eliminated and only 100 are elected. In the third and final ballot 37 are elected from the hundred candidates who remain.

Election of the Council

The election of the council is much more elaborate than that of the assembly and the election of 37 guardians. While in the election of the guardians of law the system of classes finds no place, it comes into operation in the election of the council. The Council is to consist of 360 members. These members are elected annually, 90 members are elected from each of the four classes. The first stage in the election is the selection of candidates. Candidates of different classes are to be selected in different ways. The first two classes are elected by the citizens compulsorily. For the fourth class, the first two classes must necessarily vote, the other two may vote or abstain. The second stage is the stage of voting. The third and final stage is the election by lot of 90 members from the 180 candidates. In this way the election to the 360 member-council is completed.

Barker's Comment

Commenting on this system, Barker says, "The effect of this system is that the first two classes will tend to exercise a preponderant voice in the selection of candidates. At the same time all the classes may join in the original selection of candidates in every class, all classes must join in the process of elimination; and the use of the lot is meant to secure equality in the final stage. The whole system is a carefully calculated combination of universal suffrage with class suffrage, and again of what Greeks regarded as the aristocratic method of election by voting with what they regarded as the democratic method of the lot." Plato defends the system as a mean between the monarchical principle of wisdom and the democratic principle of liberty.

Functions of the Popular Assembly

The popular assembly plays a double part as an electorate and as a judicature but it has no deliberative functions. The functions of the popular assembly may be described as follows:

(i) It elects the council;

(ii) It elects the local officials of the city and market;

(iii) It elects the generals of the army;

(iv) It has cognizance of public suits against those who have injured the state;

(v) Its consent is necessary it any law has to be changed;

(vi) It has the power of extending the stay of resident aliens beyond the appointed period of 20 years.

Sub-Divisions of Council

Plato proposed that the council should be divided into 12 parts. Each of these parts should act for a month as the main organ of the government and the presiding officers in the state. Each division, during its tenure of office, receives in audience, foreigners and citizens and resolves the meetings of the assembly, whether it be for election, for justice or for a change in the laws.

Executive Magistrates

Again, each division in its turn will act in conjunction with the executive magistrates, who are the guardians of the law. The magistrates are 37 in number. They are elected by the assembly for a period of 20 years. At the time of election the age of the magistrate should not be less than 50 years. He must not hold office on attaining the age of 70.

Grades of Courts

As regards judicial institutions of the state, Plato distinguishes between private and public suits. For private suits, there are to be three grades of courts:

1. Voluntary Court. This is composed of neighbours and friends who know the issue best. This court has 'Greatest Competence.'

2. Tribal Court. The judges of this court are to be chosen by lot. In such court, the principle of a popular judicature is recognised. As Prof. Barker points out, "That principle is one on which Plato lays emphasis; all should have a share in jurisdiction, for the man who does not share in the power of sitting with others in justice is apt to think himself utterly without any part in the state."

3. The Court of Selected Judges. The judges are annually chosen by all the magistrates of the state in conjunction. The sittings of these courts shall be public and decisions delivered in open court.

System of Government

The form of Local Government described by Plato is small. A state of 5,040 persons can need little beyond its central government. In the central city these are :

(i) *City Inspectors*. The city inspectors are concerned with the care of the city, its buildings, its roads, water supply etc.

(ii) *Inspectors of the Market Square*. The market inspectors superintend the market square and its buildings and are concerned with the care of the city, its buildings, its roads, water supply etc.

Both type of inspectors, however, have a petty jurisdiction.

Commenting on the 'system of Government in the Laws' Prof. Barker says, "There is popular assembly, an elected council and an executive of guardians of the law. There are military and local officials besides court of justice. The popular assembly is to be built upon a system of classes and a distinction is drawn between the classes which must and those which may, attend. Every citizen is a member and may vote in all its meetings. The council is elected on a system which combines regard for wealth with regard for universal suffrage. The guardians of the law will be freely elected by all the citizens, and from all the citizens. The military officials are partly recruited by popular election and partly nomination. The courts of law are largely based on the principle of a popular judicature. The local officials of the city and market are elected not indeed from all but at any rate on all.

PLATO'S "STATESMAN"

If *Republic* was a treatise on ethics and education, Plato's *Statesman* can be considered a treatise on politics. He did not abandon his idealism in the *Statesman*. Here his idealism has gave place to some kind of realism or practical idealism. Plato was more logical and exact in this book. He pointed out that what a man ought to be and do, if he is to rule. What is the part played by politics and political science in fostering education? Plato came to the conclusion that politics should aim at educating people in virtue and justice.

Change of Attitude

In *Statesman*, Plato changed his attitude towards law as reflected in his classification of states in this book. In his classification, he confined himself to actual states and preferred law abiding states than to lawless states. He also showed distinction between the theories of government and the theories of politician. He declared that an ideal ruler is not merely a politician or a more administrator. He must be an ideal philosopher. According to Plato the duty of such a ruler is not only to administer the state but to make men adopt the ideal standards of good and justice. The ruler and state is good or bad only if this is achieved or not achieved. If the ruler is learned and a philosopher, he should not be fettered by laws. But as such individuals are rare, law, which contains practical wisdom and experience of the past age, is essential. Thus Plato gave importance to laws in this book.

CLASSIFICATION OF GOVERNMENT

Plato mentioned six kinds of governments according to the number of rulers, *i.e.* ruled by one, few or many and whether these are law abiding or lawless. Classification of government according to the nature of the ruler is as follows :

Government directed by law		**Government not directed by law**	
1. **Rule of one**	: Monarchy	1. **Rule of one**	: Tyranny
2. **Rule of few**	: Aristocracy	2. **Rule of few**	: Oligarchy
3. **Rule of many**	: Moderate Democracy	3. **Rule of many**	: Extreme Democracy

In the above mentioned classification, Plato said that whenever the rule is of one, i.e. monarchy is the best form from the point of view of the good of the people in a law governed state. But monarchy may perverse in tyranny which is the worst form of government. The rule by a small number of ablest men who devote themselves to the service of the state is aristocracy while its perverted form is oligarchy in which the rulers rule for their own benefit. The rule of many, i.e. democracy is the worst form of a state directed by law because it reflects the rule of an average man who is incapable of political speculation. But democracy is the best form of government in a state which is not governed by law. Thus Plato came to the conclusion that Democracy is the worst of law abiding states but the best of lawless forms. As such democracy is higher than oligarchy. This reflects total abandonment of the attitude toward democracy adopted in *The Republic*. To quote Barker "Seeing the virtue of law, as the fruit of experience and invention of wisdom, Plato can now see the value of democracy which is based on the rule of law." Thus he supported democracy supported by Rule of Law.

The central theme of *The Republic* is that the world would not cease from evils unless philosophers are kings. Thus Plato gave the panacea for all the ills of the state in the union of wisdom and power in the same individual or group of individuals. But failure of this experiment in Sicley, forced him to give up his ideal. According to Barker he still believed that "It is not impossible nor do we speak of things that are impossible, even though by ourselves they are admitted to the difficult." However he drifted to sub-ideal state in *The Laws*.

Plato's approach is more realistic in '*The Laws*', than his approach in *The Republic*. In this book, he attempted to discover a legal system, to help, guide and restrain the imperfect governmental machinery. Experience forced him to be more realistic and modify his views about many things such as communism of property and wives. In *The Laws*, Plato admitted that private property and family are indispensable for human beings though even now he did not give them full support. He allowed both private property and marriages under strict control than the system proposed in '*The Republic*'. The only real restriction on marriage is with a view to prevent the perpetuation of really bad types of humanity. Similarly in case of women, Plato placed emphasis on domestic duties though he allowed them same education as to men and to take part in political affairs of the state. He was, however, in favour of establishing censorship over the intellectual and moral and artistic interest of the citizens. Thus he came to the conclusion that "Law is the expression of reason and since the reason is sovereign, law should take the form of a sovereign command"

Political Power and Wealth

Plato allowed wealth to share with intellect and philosophy, the monopoly of power in his book "*The Laws*". He preferred landed property than commercial wealth to share the monopoly of power. Thus, he showed preference to agriculture in his conception of city states but he tried to limit the landed property through the state. Thus, he preferred Chinese set-up giving preference to farmers than Russian set-up giving -preference to bureaucracy and workers. He divided population into four classes on the basis of wealth in land. At the lowest ladder, people were to be allotted a definite area of land, the produce of which may enable the owners to maintain bare necessities of life. The other three classes were allowed to have double, triple and four times respectively of the landed property assigned to the lowest class. But nobody was to be allowed property more than allotted to his class. Surplus land was to be confiscated by the state. Plato believed that vast differences in holdings may destroy the harmony of the state and give rise to conflict between the rich and the poor. It may result in the corruption and inefficiency of the state. In *The Republic*, Plato proposed complete abolition of property for the guardian class but in *The Laws* he makes a retreat and provides land with proper safeguards against concentrations of property.

Administrative Machinery with Proper Checks

In '*The Laws*', Plato suggested many useful checks on the abuses of different forms of governments. He allowed every citizen to have his share in the government of his state, according to his ability to do so. He outlined his scheme of machinery of government with necessary checks.

1. Board of 37. Supreme authority of the State was to be vested in the board of 37 whose members were to be between the ages of fifty and seventy. Plato gave preference to old age as it brings experience and stability with it. These members were to be chosen by elections and were to be guardians of law. This board was to function as supervisory body. There was to be an administrative council of 360, appointed to execute the orders of board of 37. These men were to be chosen by election and vote, based on possession of land. Plato liked jury system in which every citizen of either sex would take part.

2. Administrative Council. Finally, there was to be council of administrators.

3. Council of Ten. These were to ensure the proper and smooth working of the whole constitution to watch the correct execution of laws and to prevent unconstitutional laws being proposed.

4. Council of Twenty. The council of ten was to be assisted and advised by a council of twenty priests famous for virtue and by a council of twenty young men to counteract the conservatism of the older men. Thus, he favoured mixed and balanced form of government with proper checks.

In *The Laws* there is no insistence on exclusive right of reason to rule over appetite. Plato put emphasis on the free concord of appetite with reason. According to Sabine, this was brought about through the virtue of self-control of temperance which may be defined as a law abiding disposition or a spirit of respect towards the institutions of the state and a readiness to subordinate oneself to its lawful powers. Thus in the ideal state of '*The Laws*', Plato proceeded from harmony between the different individuals. According to Barker, "Its unity springs out of sympathy. Issuing as it does in sympathy, self-control brings in a different atmosphere from that of the Republican atmosphere less rare but human; less clear but also less cold." In his book '*The Laws*', Plato makes an attempt to trace "the development of human civilization, mark its stages, not the causes of progress and decay and by analysis of whole derive the laws of political stability, which the wise statesmen will observe in order to direct and control the changes that beset human society." In *The Laws* Plato did not provide for collective farming but insisted on private possession and common use.

Principles of Society

In his book "*The Republic*", Plato offered a sound analysis of the most general principle underlying human society. His most original idea was of the philosopher King ruling without any restriction of laws, which he developed on the basis of Socratic doctrine of the identity of virtue and knowledge which led him to reject the democratic ideal of citizenship which was the very essence of the city state. In '*The Laws*' Plato tried to make good his omission of law by returning law to its proper place. Such a task required complete change of his psychology of the human mind and of his theory of knowledge. In *The Laws* he suggested a really careful analysis of actual institutions and laws and the attachment of such studies of history. He also suggested the principle of balance of a mutual adjustment of claims and interests as the proper means for forming a constitutional state. It was from these beginnings in *The Laws* that Aristotle started, without abandoning the general principles stated in *The Republic* he adopted almost in every case the hints thrown out in *The Laws*, enriching them with more painstaking and more extensive examination of the empirical and historical knowledge.

Difference in Political Thought

Political thought of Plato is quite different as represented in '*The Republic*' and in *The Laws*. The fight of imagination which charms us in '*The Republic*' gives way to realistic approach in The Laws. It may be said that "*The Republic*" is based on ideal but "*The Laws*" is based on experience and imagination modified by realistic approach. In *The Republic* Plato started with the assumption that government is purely a matter of scientific knowledge and it leads to the conclusion that the philosopher King as the enlightened despot, is best and highest. This led Plato to ignore the necessity of consent, public and law because the ideal ruler did not stand in need of these things.

COMPARISON OF THE INFLUENCE OF THE REPUBLIC AND THE LAWS

1. Influence on Communism. Hegel's glorification of the state and monarchy and his fascist theory of the government and Roman Church with its emphasis on the infallibility of Pope, hierachical organization and theory of education to clergy, comes nearer to Plato's political thought. Though his thinking about communism did not exercise much influence but Prof. Maxey calls 'Plato Reddest of reds.' Prof. Jazzi compares modern communism with the conception of Plato's communism in *The Republic*. There are differences between modern communism and the communism of Plato, but perhaps '*The Republic*' is the book which gives clear conception of communism and in a way of fascism also. As such according to Prof. Maxey, "Virtually all socialistic and communistic thought has its roots in Plato, were he alive today he would be 'the reddest of reds'. He adds "It (Russian communism) departs from Plato in too many important aspects....Notwithstanding this, there is enough of Plato in Soviet system to evoke profound reflection on the deathless might of vital political ideas." Thus, there are germs of communistic and socialistic thought in the thinking of Plato and so it can be said that his political thought affected communistic and socialistic theories in a modified way and his views on human inequality, opposition to democracy, liberty and support to powerful ruler led to Fascist ideas.

2. Influence on Aristotle. But *The Republic* had little influence on the thought of Aristotle, who was very critical of the concept of the philosopher King who rules unfettered by laws. Aristotle criticised the communism of wives as well as communism of property most vehemently. "*The Laws*" exercised a far greater influence on Aristotle as well as on subsequent thinkers because it was more realistic and conformed to the Greek ideal of constitutional rule and participation by the citizens in the deliberative functions of the state. In '*The Laws*' Plato put emphasis on law and the conception of mixed constitution for securing the stability of the state.

The Laws exercised a profound influence on Aristotle and other thinkers. Aristotle placed emphasis on sovereignty of law and brought about the conception of rulers as guardians of law and its servants. By saying that a man outside lawful state can either be God or beast, Aristotle echoed the conception of Plato as expressed in '*The Laws*'. Aristotle was indebted to '*The Laws* ' for his theory of mixed constitutions. Ideal state as depicted by Aristotle resembled to sub-ideal state of Plato as stated in '*The Laws*'. On account of this, some scholars are of the opinion that Plato's second best is Aristotle's best state. Professor Barker has pointed out a large number of points in which there is similarity between '*The Laws*' of Plato and *Politics* of Aristotle.

EVALUATION OF PREVALENT THEORIES OF JUSTICE

In his interpretation and enquiry into the nature of justice, Plato has followed the dialectic method. As in his espistemology and ethics so here also before finally presenting his own idea of justice, Plato has evaluated the following four theories of justice prevalent in his time:

1. Traditionalism. According to Polymarchus, the son of Cephalus, justice consists in giving to each man what is proper to him. Thus it is speaking the truth and paying the debt. In other words, justice is an art which gives good to friends and evil to enemies. Criticising this theory of justice Plato has advanced the following arguments.

(i) If justice is an art or a capacity it can be equally used for good or for evil like the capacity of a physician or a soldier.

(ii) It is difficult to distinguish between friend and foe and therefore on the basis of this theory we cannot decide about our ideal conduct about them.

(iii) Good is good for both friend and foe. Evil even towards enemies cannot be called justice.

2. Radicalism. According to this theory, prevalent in Plato's time, justice is the interest of the stronger. This theory was supported by Sophists including Thracymachas. According to Thracymachas justice is the interest of the stronger. One should act according to his capacity and he should achieve whatever is possible for him. As the state is the strongest of all whatever the state does is just. In other words, justice is the will of a ruler who wills his own good. Criticising this theory of justice Plato had advanced the following arguments:

(i) If this theory is true about the ruler it may lead us to the conclusion that justice is the realisation of others' interest. In other words, that man is just who satisfies the ruler and one who satisfies himself is unjust.

(ii) On the basis of this theory we cannot explain the contradictions found in the activities of different rulers at different times and in different countries. If an action is right for one ruler it should be right for another as well.

(iii) Thus this theory leads us to the contradictory situation that opposite actions are equally good. It cannot however give us any universal standard of justice which may be followed by every one.

(iv) Therefore, it is not a rational principle, since a rational principle is always universal.

(v) It cannot be that guiding principle of a rational person who is more concerned with the achievement of justice in his own light.

3. Pragmatism. According to this theory, justice is the child of fear. Glaucon, the originator of this theory, presented a theory of social justice followed later by the social contract theory of Hobbes and Rousseau. Justice, according to it, is born out of traditions. It is thus not natural but artificial. In ancient times people used to heap injustice upon others who succumbed to it. These people were weak and therefore, could not oppose the strong. They, therefore, arrived at a sort of social contract that they will neither do injustice to others nor tolerate injustice. This social contract led to certain conventions in human society. These conventions resulted into social ethics. This social ethics lies between the two extremes of doing injustice and tolerating injustice. As against this explanation of justice on the basis of social customs and traditions, Plato has advanced the following arguments in criticism:

(i) There is no evidence of any age in the evolution of human civilization when men did arrive at some sort of real and overt social contract. If there was any contract between human beings, it was only tacit and implied.

(ii) There is a spontaneous tendency among human beings to recognize the rights of others. This innate tendency has resulted in the historical fact that people agreed not to do injustice nor to tolerate it.

(iii) People naturally believe that the ruler should rule with justice and the rulers also know that their rule depends upon this will of the ruler. It was on the basis of this natural tendency of a relationship between the ruler and the ruled that some scholars have arrived at the false theory that the state is the result of some real historical social contract between the ruler and the ruled.

(iv) Law is not artificial or merely conventional. It may be called artificial so far as it is a product of human mind. It is, however, a codified form of the general will, the will of the society, according to which we ought to do certain actions and ought not to do others. The sanction behind the law and its obligation is not simply due to the political pressure but depends upon the human preparedness to follow the law. Even if law is obligatory one accepts it only because it is not imposed by sheer brute force. Law is based upon right will which also leads us sometimes to oppose the law.

4. Rationalism. Justice, according to Socrates, is an art. Art aims at removal of the defects of things. For example, a physician removes the defects of the body and the teacher removes the defects of the mind. An ideal teacher is a person who develops the capacity of the mind of the student removing all the detects and incapacities. Similarly, a ruler is successful only if he removes the defects from the ruled. He is following the art of justice so far as he is absolutely unselfish and aims at the good of the ruled. Accepted that a person utilises his art for his living and even sometimes for the satisfaction of his selfish ends, but this is not the ideal condition. In the ideal condition, the artist is unselfish, totally devoted to the intrinsic aim of the art, without any selfish and narrow end to achieve and always acting for the improvement of his art. It is hence that Plato in his *The Republic* advocated the rule of a philosopher king for the achievement of ideal republic.

PLATO'S THEORY OF JUSTICE

The acme of the political philosophy of Plato is the theory of justice. This may be called the theory of social justice since, as has been pointed out, state was a means for the whole of the society. Therefore, political justice is a corollary of the theory of the social justice. The theory of justice has been elaborated in Plato's famous dialogue *The Republic*. In this work the books first and second discuss the theory of justice while political justice has been discussed in the books two, three and four. *The Republic* was concerned with the nature of justice, its characteristics and how it can be dispensed with in the society and state. This theory was developed on the basis of imagination of an ideal state, how a state ought to be. It was not based upon a survey of the actual facts in Greece or elsewhere. Therefore the discussion is mostly philosophical. Obviously, it has led to many grave errors from the point of view of practice. And sociologists and political scientists have amply criticised the social philosopher for his neglect of the facts. It has been pointed out that Plato started philosophical speculations concerning the concept of justice without any reference to social facts leading to ideas which only show that philosophical reflection in this branch of knowledge is useless. This, however, is too harsh a criticism of the philosopher. Plato's insight into the nature of social justice has been the torch bearer of thinkers in this field in ancient and modern times.

Quality of the Soul

In *The Republic* the nature of social justice has been discussed in the form of a dialogue between Socrates and some of his friends concerning the aim of human life, the structure of human personality and the parallelism between the individual and the society. The philosopher pointed out that just as in the individual different aspects must be given their due and no one aspect should be allowed to dominate all the rest for all the time, similarly in society the different classes must be given what is due to them and no single class should be allowed to dominate all the other classes without any restriction. Justice, according to Plato, is the quality of the soul. Therefore, it does not depend upon any external source of power. It is the voice of conscience of man. The human personality is guided by three tendencies: knowledge, physical tendency and the spiritual tendency. Of these tendencies the spirit should rule and the rest should be ruled. Similarly, in the society, persons who are primarily spiritual should be appointed the guardians of the state and the others should be ruled by them. Reason, courage, temperance and justice were the four ideal values to be equally followed by the individuals and groups. Of these justice was chiefly the function of the state. The ideal state dispensed ideal justice. Justice, again, resulted in happiness both in the individual and the society. Justice means harmony and rythm in the individual and the society.

Organic Theory of Society

Thus it is clear that justice, according to Plato, is primarily an ethical concept not a jural one. It insists upon following one's duties in the path of morality. It maintains the necessity of following the spiritual impulse. Plato has, however, committed a mistake in holding the organic theory of society in which different parts have all intrinsic and vital relationships with each other. As has been pointed out by modern sociologists and political scientists, society is not an organism. While organism has an internal relationship between different parts, some of the relationship in the social groups are external. Again, there is hardly any parallel between the human body and the human group. In the human body every cell is an integral part of the body, but it has no identity out of it. In the human group, on the other hand, the individual, in spite of having internal relationships, maintains his individuality. While in body no harm is done if a part is not given any freedom apart from the body, in the social group the freedom of the individual cannot be denied. Plato's conception of social justice, on the basis of organic theory of society, resulted in totalitarianism which tended to annihilate all the freedom of the individual. In his ideal republic the guardians were given all the powers of the rulers and the ruled were not given any freedom to criticise them. Whatever may be its reward in terms of political efficiency, it is definitely against the democratic emphasis upon liberty. Again, it could not lead to fraternity among the members of the society. Therefore, in spite of the fact that Plato sought to create an ideal society through his concept of social justice, it resulted into practices contrary to human good.

Integral Approach

The most important characteristic of Plato's theory of justice is its integral approach. It looks to all the sides of the individual personality and the body politic. It aims at giving justice to every part of the individual and each class of society. However, in maintaining a hierarchy like the varna system in India and adhering to it too rigidly, he arrived at a concept which was a negation of his essential purpose.

Characteristics of Justice

Plato's theory of justice exhibits the following characteristics:

1. Based upon Social Stratification. Corresponding to the three elements of a soul Plato has pointed out a three-fold social stratification involving the guardians, the soldiers and the general people such as the artisans, farmers etc. According to him, justice consists in the fulfilment of duties by all these three classes in a state.

2. Innate Tendency. Justice, according to Plato, is innate. It is the quality of the soul. It is the voice of conscience.

3. Functional Specialisation. Plato classified society into three classes according to the three human tendencies: the cognitive, the conative and the affective. While the guardians represent the first, soldiers the second, the third is represented by the general masses. Thus Plato arrived at a functional specialisation among citizens.

4. Philosopher King. Justice, according to Plato, is possible only in a state where the philosopher rules since the philosopher, according to Plato, is the wisest among human beings.

5. Communism. In order to keep the guardians free from personal worries and envies, Plato has advocated communism of property and women among guardians and soldiers.

6. Two Types of Justice. Plato has classified justice into two types : Social and Individual, both of which are intimately related.

7. Universal. Justice, according to Plato, is the same everywhere. It is the universal principle.

8. Moral Concept. Platonic concept of justice is not jural but moral. Fulfilment of justice does not so much require fulfilment of jural duties but the following of moral obligations.

9. Freedom for Women. The establishment of justice, according to Plato, requires freedom for women. Women should be given equal rights in the state to participate in all the activities alongside with men.

10. Education for Justice. In order to prepare the citizens for the realization of justice in the state, Plato has advanced a scheme of planned education.

The Individual Justice

Justice, according to Plato, is the spirit by which men are animated in the fulfilment of duty. In human mind there are three elements : reason, spirit and appetite. While wisdom is the virtue of reason, the courage of the spirit and the temperance of the appetite, justice is the virtue which maintains harmony in all these three. Thus, according to Plato, each part of human mind must get its due satisfaction and ultimately there must be a harmony between different parts of the individual. Only such harmonious individuals can create a harmonious society and a harmonious state. Social justice is not possible without individual justice. In fact, the social justice is based upon the individual justice. In other words, only in a society where individual justice is generally found, social justice can be achieved.

Social Justice

Just as in the individual, there are three elements, similarly in a society there are three types of men corresponding to it. These types of men are classified according to the predominance of some one part out of the three pointed out above in the individual source. Thus some people are predominantly rational. They are more adept in rational persuits. Some other people are strong in spirit and therefore more active. The majority of the people are neither strong in reason nor in spirit but only in passions. These are required to be controlled by the other two. On the basis of this classification of the individual types in society, Plato has established a three fold functional social stratification in which the philosophers are at the apex, the soldiers in the middle and the artisans, farmers etc. at the base. Each of these parts of the state should carry on its own activity. According to Plato the man should practice one thing only and that is the thing to which his nature was best adapted. Justice according to Plato, is of two types – justice concerning the individual and justice concerning the state. Both the types of justice have been conceived on parallel principles. Justice everywhere is the principle of harmony among the constituents. In the justice concerning the state all the citizens should do their duty. The ideal virtue of the ruler is to rule the state with wisdom and temperance. The main virtue of the ruler is wisdom. Justice, therefore, is the virtue of the wise. The ruler is among the wisest persons in the state. That is why Plato has recommended that philosophers should rule the society. In an ideal state justice is given to each individual, who in his turn fulfils his duties towards the state. For the citizens, therefore, justice means fulfilment of one's duties. In the ideal state each citizen fulfils the duties according to his status and role. Thus, justice is the basis of all the virtues. No ideal state is possible without justice. The situation contrary to justice means that some one part of the state is allowed to dominate the other parts. On the other hand, justice is the elimination of such a possibility. Plato's theory of justice hits at selfish individualism. Individual according to him is a complex whole and not a single unit. His aim is not personal pleasure or pleasure of any one part of it. He should realise satisfaction of all his parts resulting into harmony and happiness. Plato has accepted organic theory of state, according to which citizens are the constituents of the body politic, their pains and pleasures are the pains and pleasures of the state. It is desirable that this theory maintains an intimate relationship between the ruler and the ruled but by comparing human individuals with the parts of the body political, Plato finds place for totalitarianism. Later on fascist states were built up on Plato's social philosophy.

Criticism of the Theory of Justice

The following criticisms have been advanced against Plato's theory of justice explained above:

1. Concept of Moral Justice. Plato's theory of justice is the concept of moral Justice. He has therefore laid more emphasis upon the duties rather than the rights. Undeniably, emphasis on rights keeps the society united and in the state of solidarity, exclusive emphasis, however, leads to exploitation. Both rights and duties are important in an ideal society.

2. Centralization of Power. Plato provided wide powers to the philosopher king. He, however, forgot the psychological principle that absolute power corrupts absolutely. Even the wise person becomes corrupt if he is allowed absolute power.

3. Disadvantages of Functional Specialization. Though some sort of division of labour is necessary for the harmonious growth of every society, yet too much functional specialization leads to the hindrance in the all-round growth of individual personalities. By prescribing division of labour based upon inherent tendencies Plato prescribed a division of labour in society solely according to these functions. He forgot the principle that heredity alone is not responsible for the personality traits. Personality is governed both by heredity and environment. Laying exclusive emphasis upon heredity, Plato prescribed education suitable for different functions in society. He, therefore, in spite of his ideal of harmony and justice, laid the foundation of the system of society and the system of education which tended to develop one-sided personalities.

4. Fascism. As has been already pointed out, Plato's theory of justice lays a foundation for fascism. According to it each citizen is expected to show absolute loyalty towards the state, which in its turn, is also powerful. Modern thinkers are against entrusting all powers to the state which invariable results in curbing the freedom of the individual.

5. Guardian's Freedom from Law. While Socrates gave so much importance to law that he refused to escape from the prison, Plato considered the guardians of the state above law. In fact what he calls justice is the dictate of the indwelling spirit of the guardians. True justice, however, cannot he based upon personal conscience. Plato's theory of justice does not provide a sound basis for law. Law is different from loyalty. It is concerned with regulation of society and the state, while on the other hand, morality is concerned with the ought and the ideal. Neglecting this distinction between moral and legal obligation Plato has failed to provide sound basis for either.

6. Passive Concept. Plato's concept of justice is extremely passive. Being primarily individual and moral it cannot be the basis of jural regulation. He does not provide any solution in the conflict between desire and duty, duties and rights.

7. Emphasis on Unity than Diversity. In spite of maintaining some sort of relationship between the unity and diversity, Plato has laid too much emphasis upon the unity of the state. In his search for unity he arrived upon such absurd ideas as communism of women and abolition of marriage and family. He provided too much authority to the state, so much so that it reduced individual to a mere cell of the state organism.

In spite of the above criticism of Plato's theory of justice and our conclusion that the theory does not provide a sound basis for body politic, we must remember that Plato was first a philosopher and then a political thinker. As we have already pointed out, his political philosophy is in fact based upon his social philosophy. His theory of justice is not concerned with legality but with social morality. It is, therefore, neither a subject of law nor a subject of individual ethics or a confusion of the two. It is rather a harmony of the two. It studies the means by which goodness can he achieved in society. It seeks to arrive at the essence of morality, which according to it, is the fulfilment of one's duties in society. This society, again, is not legal and based upon the legal rights. It is a moral society based upon moral duties. Justice in fact is the inner spirit which guides men in the fulfilment of their duties. It is closely connected with self-control. It involves both harmony and symphony, the two bases of an ideal society.

COMMUNISM

Plato's ideal state represents a new social order in which the guardian class and warrior class live in a state of special regimentation. Representing the element of reason and spirit, they are made to renounce the appetite. For this purpose, Plato advocated system of communism of property and wives which was not wholly without local institutional and ideological Greek support. There was a minor touch of communism in Sparta as shown by the common messing out of private lands. Wives were lent by husbands to others for the purpose of the state. In 'Crete', there was public tilling of public lands. In 5th century B.C. in Athens, communistic theories appeared showing a distinct tendency to idealise the ancient people, who held things in common. In his 'Protestilaus' Euripides advocated communism of wives. Plato's communism of wives and property had psychological as well as practical basis. He brought out communism of wives in two waves, i.e. emancipation of women and reform of marriage.

Ideas that Lead Plato to Communism

Plato put state before the individual and divided the community on the basis of functional usefulness. Each man was to do the duty for which he is best fitted. He had to merge himself in the state and render the greatest possible service to the state. As Plato was a thorough collectivist, who ignored the individuality of the citizen, some writers consider him fascist and others as communist. Individual must not have other interest than those of state. He was not to be allowed to collect and keep property as owner. Plato feared that a desire to collect and own property, would lead to selfish personal ambitions and would bring about a clash between an individual's personal state and with those of the rulers of the state.

The Communist Social Ideal

Long before Karl Marx, the father of modern communism, presented his theory, Plato in Greece derived a social philosophy based upon communist ideals. This ideal was first presented in his dialogue *The Republic*, which was later on improved in another dialogue *The Laws*. The aim of Platonic communism was moral evolution. While through education he wanted to prepare a social environment conducive to his plan. Communism was the means for maintaining unity in the state. Plato wanted to reform the individual and society through spiritual means. His communist system aimed at creating an ideal environment for the moral growth of the guardians. The mind of man is the creator of the state and therefore if the state has to be reformed, men's mind must be reformed. Justice is not something external, but a tendency of the mind. It can be, therefore, achieved only in a right thinking mind. The nature of the mind, however, is very much governed by the social circumstances in which one has to work. The creation of justice in society depends upon the condition that should be created which lays emphasis upon fulfilment of duties. Fulfilment of duties, again, depends upon the condition that impediments to it are removed.

Platonic communism is not an original idea. Communist system was prevalent in Greece long before the advent of Plato. In Greece the ownership of land was generally collective. In Athens the state was considered the owner of all the forests and mines and the care-taker of the individual property. In Sparta the produce on individual lands was commonly distributed. The people considered it their right to take food in other's homes. They could use other's horses, dogs and slaves for their personal good. The dramatist Eurepides has referred to the communism of women. Thus Plato's ideas concerning the communism of property and women were very much borrowed from contemporary circumstances. It is a different matter that while we have forgotten about the circumstances of his time, his ideas have widely influenced different branches of knowledge.

Communism of Property

In the third book of his famous work *The Republic*, Plato has explained his theory of communism of property. In the first place the guardians may be allowed to keep only the minimum property with them. No guardian should be allowed to have a home or a treasure which is only his own. He should be provided materials to be used just as it is provided for others. He may be given only so much as is neither short of nor more than necessary. During the time of war the warriors should be provided food and other materials gathered at one place. So far as gold and silver are concerned, the guardians do not need them as they are pure gold in their spirits. Guardians are not allowed either to possess or even to touch silver and gold. They should not use ornaments of silver and gold nor should they use golden and silver utensils. Only in this way can they defend their states. If, on the other hand, they are allowed to possess and store gold and silver, land and animals, they will become ordinary household persons full of selfishness and egoism. They will thus fail to protect the state and involve in personal rivalries and conflicts.

Principles of Communism of Property

Plato's communism concerning property was based upon the following considerations:

1. The Individual is not a Separate Unit. In his book *The Republic* Plato has rejected the idea that the individual is an isolated unit and aims at fulfilment of his desires. He, on the other hand, maintained that the individual is a unit of society and he should see satisfaction in the fulfilment of his social duties. He should, therefore, share all his properties with everyone else. This is particularly true about the guardians who are responsible for the growth of the state.

2. The Ideal of Justice. Communism of property was a means for the realization of the ideal of justice. Justice is possible only when each member of society honestly fulfils his duties. In an ideal state the guardians should be selfless and without any strings of property etc. It is only then that they can show wisdom and courage and remain free from fashions, characteristic of the general people. In fact they should totally sacrifice the economic possessions so that they may become free from passions and their soul may achieve the virtues of wisdom and courage. In the absence of such sacrifice their reason will be either passive or weak and will surrender to the passions.

3. Realisation of Ideal State. An ideal state can be realised only if its guardians are kept free from personal property and the bonds of marriage and family. This is possible only through communistic provisions.

4. Pragmatic Argument. Plato has advanced a pragmatic argument in favour of his communism of property. He pointed out that if the guardians are allowed economic possessions, they will tight among themselves. Experience shows us that concentration of wealth in the hands of few people results into conflict and disharmony. For the psychological and pragmatic point of view, therefore, the guardians should be free from the bonds of personal property. In the ideal state of Plato only the general masses consisting of artisans, farmers and others had the right to personal property. But even this class is very much controlled by the state as too much poverty or too much prosperity is equally harmful for the maintenance of justice in the state.

5. Maintenance of the Unity of the State. Plato's communism aimed at maintaining the unity of the state. Abolition of private property will end selfishness and possessive tendencies. The guardians will therefore work more efficiently. They will also easily secure love and cooperation from other people. They will be particularly loved by the general masses who possess some sort of personal property. As they will have no personal property there will be no mutual envy and conflict resulting into the solidarity of the state.

Criticism of Plato's Communism of Property

The following arguments can be advanced against Plato's concept of communism of property:

1. Autocracy. In the communism of Plato the two upper classes, the guardians and the warriors, have to forego personal property in the interest of society in general. This is an extreme demand which may result in reaction in favour of autocratic tendencies. In this sense the economic communism leads to political autocracy. It may be said that his communism was developed with a political aim.

2. Reduction in National Income. When the two upper classes in the society will not have personal property, they may not work hard for the growth of national income. This may lead to its reduction.

3. Against Psychological Principles. The most common argument advanced by those thinkers to oppose the abolition of personal property, is psychological. According to these thinkers man has a natural tendency of possessiveness. If all personal property is abolished he will be left with no incentive in his life. Property is a means for the self-expression of the individual. In its absence the two higher classes in society will be deprived of the means of expression which may ultimately tell upon the harmonious development of their personalities.

4. Too Much Right to the State. Communism of property means state's possession over property. Thus, this theory is against the freedom of the individual and in favour of wide power to the state.

5. Communism for Guardian's Alone. It may be noted that Plato's communism of property was mainly for the guardians while the artisans, farmers and businessmen were allowed to retain personal property. This is against the law of justice, according to which, no section of society, superior or inferior should be used for the good of other parts of the society. The guardians should not be used as means for the good of other sections of society

Communism of Women and Children

Along with the abolition of private property, Plato has recommended communism of women and children for the guardians. He has, therefore, abolished marriage and family in the guardian class. Property and family are the two sources of attachment in man resulting in selfishness. Plato thought that if the guardians are freed from both the bondages they may easily become unselfish and follow their duties. Communism of women has been prescribed in two ways. Firstly, the women were set free from the bondage of the family. They were provided similar education along with men, thus securing equal opportunities for their development. Freedom from the family could give them sufficient leisure to help the guardians in their job of ruling the state. Secondly, the guardians were not permanently married to particular women. Thus Plato abolished the institution of permanent marriage. The right to progeny was given to wise and able persons. They should be mated with women having similar qualities thus resulting into birth of suitable progeny. Plato suggested marriage festivals in which ideal men were freely allowed to mate with ideal women. Children resulting from such festivals were to be brought up by the state and the parents had nothing to do with them. The age limit for participation in this process was maximum upto 50 years. After that the male and female were allowed to be absolutely promiscuous. If, however, this promiscuity resulted in birth of children, they should be silently disposed of. This communism of women and children was based upon the following principles and aimed at realizing the following aims:

1. Establishment of equality of male and female in the ideal state.
2. Birth of physically and mentally superior progeny in society.
3. Provision of opportunities for maximum development to females as well as males.
4. Nationalization of the family.

Criticism of Communism of Women

Plato's theory of the communism of women and children has been bitterly criticized. On the basis of this theory thinkers have commented that in the absence of social facts, the speculations of social philosophers arrive at absurd conclusions which are not worthy of serious attention. However, the following arguments may be considered against this theory:

1. Elimination of Family. While Aristotle, after Plato, maintained that the family like the state, is a natural institution, Plato abolished the family. The family was eliminated in the interest of the state. By elimination of the family Plato unwittingly sought to destroy the very foundation of morality which he so much wanted to establish in human society.

2. Elimination of Marriage. Plato's strictures concerning marriage are wrong both from psychological and social viewpoint. Psychologically human beings need marriage and therefore, some sort of marriage institutions have always been prevalent in human societies. Plato's idea of communism of women resulting into elimination of marriage is psychologically harmful both for male and female guardians. From the social point of view, it will result into promiscuity leading to moral degeneration. The provision of marriage for the layman and negation of it for the two higher classes may lead to inequality between these two sections.

3. Immoral System. It is really strange that Plato, primarily a moral thinker, could suggest abolition of family and marriage, the two social institutions which form the basis of all social virtues. The virtues including that of temperance and wisdom cannot be developed without a permanent institution of marriage. Communism of women will lead to incest and all sort of illicit and immoral relationship. The idea of the search for ideal pairs by the state is hardly practicable. The idea of mating able male and female could be a good idea in animal husbandry but it is hardly suitable for human society.

4. Against the Good of Women. Nor does the theory of communism of women fulfil the interest of the women themselves. Male and female are in fact complementary to each other. They do not require identical status in both. Equality of women only means provision of opportunities for their development. It does not mean converting them into males. Plato has himself accepted that the functions of male and female are different. It is hence difficult to understand how his system of communism of women will be useful for women themselves. The women are not suitable for the job of the warriors. Temperamentally they are more suited for upbringing of the family. Plato's provision of comradeship to them in the two higher classes can be hardly considered as an ideal opportunity for them.

5. Neglect of Children. The institution of family provides the ideal situation for the growth of children. The idea of communism of women hitting at the institution of family will result into neglect of children. The arrangement that all the males and females mating during a particular festival of marriage should be considered parents of all the children born as a result of this festival, is hardly suitable from the psychological point of view. The psychology of parenthood is purely personal. No one loves other's children as much as he loves his own. Plato's provision of general parentage will only result in the general neglect of children.

The above evaluation of Plato's theory of communism of property, women and children amply demonstrates that he had much bias in favour of the good of the state as resulted in provisions which may lead to a barbarous primitive society full of inequalities and short of all soft virtues. A social philosophy, not finding suitable place for soft virtues, may however, result in the creation of a society which will not be suitable for growth of human values.

THE DEMCROCY

Origin of Democracy

About the origin of democracy Plato said, "So democracy, I suppose, comes into being when the poor conquer, and kill some of the other party and banish others, and share out the citizenship and government equally with the rest; and the offices in it are generally settled by lot."

Variety and Richness in Democracy

According to Plato, democracy produces variety and riches. As he says "First of all, then, they are free men; the city is full of freedom and liberty of speech, and men in it may do what they like."

"Where there is liberty of action, it is clear that each man would arrange his own private life in it just as it pleases him."[25]

"Consequently, I suppose, all varieties of men would be produced under this system more than anywhere else."

"In fact, this is the most beautiful of constitutions. It is decked out with all sources and conditions of manners, as a robe of many colours is embroidered with all the flowers of the field, and what could be more beautiful."

"Because of this liberty: All sorts of constitutions are there; and if anyone wants to fit up a city, as we have been doing, it is only necessary for him to go to a city governed by a democracy, and choose whatever fashion of constitution pleases him, as if he had come to a bazaar of constitutions; then, having picked out his pattern, he can make his city accordingly."[26]

"These things, then, and other such like them are in democracy; a delightful constitution it would be, as it seems; no governor and plenty of colour; equality of a sort, distributed to equal and unequal alike."[27]

The Democratic Man

Describing the democratic man, Plato said, "A young man brought up as we described, in parsimony and ignorance, gets a taste of the drones, honey, and finds himself among wild beasts fiery and dangerous, who are able to provide pleasures of every variety and complexity and condition: there you must see the beginning of his inward change from the oligarchic to the democratic."

"As the city then was changed by the alliance coming from without to assist one party within, like to assist like, so the young man changes by a crowd of desires from without coming to assist one of the parts within him, a crowd akin and alike."

"And if another alliance comes from somewhere to assist the oligarchies part in the man from the father, perhaps, or others of the family, who warn and

25. Warmington, E.H. and Philip G., Rouse (Ed.), *Great Dialogues of Plato*, Trans. by W.H.D. Rouse, Mentor, New York, 1950, p. 355.

26. *Ibid.*, p. 356.

27. *Ibid.*, p. 357.

reproach him — then there is faction and anti-faction and a battle ensures within him against himself."[28]

"And sometimes, I suppose, the democratic part retreats before the oligarchic, some of the desires are destroyed, and some are banished; a little shame comes up in the young man's soul, and it is brought into order again."

"Then they draw him back to the same associations, and they spawn secretly and breed multitudinous brood."

"So in the end, I think, they storm the fortress of the young man's soul, and they find it empty of learning and beautiful practices and without words of truth, which are indeed the best sentinels and guardians in the minds of men whom the gods love."

"No liars and impostors, I suppose, false words and opinions, charge up and occupy the place of the others in such a man."

"So then the young man comes back among these lotus-eaters and makes his home there openly; if any support comes from his family for the thrifty part of his soul, those bragging words bar up the gates of the royal castle in him and will not let in even these allies, nor even receive any embassy of words from his older friends in private life, a battle follows, and they win; shame they dub silliness and cast it forth, a dishonoured outlaw; temperance they dub cowardice, trample it underfoot and banish it; they persuade the man that *moderation and decent spending* are clownishness and vulgarity, and drive them out beyond the border by the help of gang of unprofitable desires.

"And so having purged and swept clean of such things the soul of this man, who is now in their power and being initiated into their grand mysteries, they proceed at once to bring home again violence and anarchy and licentiousness and immodesty with a long train of attendants, resplendent with garlands about their heads; and they glorify them and call them by softnames — violence is now good breeding, anarchy is liberty, licentiousness is magnificence, immodesty is courage. There, you see more or less how the young man who was being trained among necessary desires is led into the emancipation and release of unnecessary and unprofitable pleasures."[29]

"And so he lives, I think, after this, spending money and pains and study upon unnecessary pleasure no less than the necessary. But if he is fortunate and not too dissolute, if as he grows older the great riot abates a bit, he receives back again parts of the exiles, and does not yield himself wholly to the intruders; he carries on his pleasures, maintaining if you please a sort of the equality among them, he gives over the rule of himself to any pleasure that comes along, as if it had gained that by lot, until he has had a ought, then to another again, without disrespect for any, but cherishing all equally."

"And not a word of truth does he receive into the fortress of his soul, he will not even let it into the guardhouse. If anyone tells him that some pleasures

28. *Ibid.*, p. 358.

29. *Ibid.*, p. 359.

belong to beautiful and good desires, others to those which are vile; some he should practice and respect, others he should chasten and enslave at all such warnings, he nods his head up and says, "Not at all, they are all equal, and to be respected equally."[30]

"And so, he spends his life, every day indulging the desire that comes along; now he drinks deep and tootles on the pipes, then again he drinks water and goes in for slimming; at times it is bodily exercise, at times idleness and complete carelessness, sometimes he makes a show of studying philosophy. Often he appears in politics, and jumps up to say and do whatever comes into his head. Perhaps the fame of a military man makes him envious, and he tries that; or a lord of finance — there he is again. There is no discipline or necessity in his life; but he calls it delightful and tree and full of blessings, and follows in his days."

"So you see, I think is a variegated man, full of all sorts of conditions and manners, this is the beautiful, many-coloured man exactly like that city, one whose life many a men and many a women would envy, having in himself patterns of innumerable of constitutions and characters."

"Very well, let such a man be ranked besides our democracy as the democratic man rightly so called."

"So the oligarchy was destroyed by the insatiate desire of riches, and disregard of everything else for the sake of money-making."

LIBERTY

Describing liberty in democracy, Plato said, "Liberty, that, I suppose, you would always hear described as most beautiful in the democratic city, and therefore this is the only city where a man of free nature thinks life worth living."

Dangers of too much Liberty

Warning against too much liberty, Plato said, "When a democratic city atheist for liberty gets worthless butlers presiding over its wine, and has drunk too deep of liberty heady draught, then, I think if the rulers are not very obliging and won't provide plenty of liberty, it calls them blackguards and oligarches and chastises them."[31] The following are the results of too much liberty:

1. Familial Disorganisation. The father gets into the habit of behaving like the son and fears his own children, the son behaves like a father and does not honour or fear his parents, 'must have liberty' he says. Settler is equal to citizen and citizen to settler, the foreigners are the same.

2. Educational Disintegration. "Teacher fears pupil in such a state of things, and plays the toady; pupils despise their teachers and tutors, and in

---

30. *Ibid.*, p. 360.

31. *Ibid.*, p. 361.

general, the young initiate their elders and stand up to them in word and deed. Old men give way to the young; they are all complaisance and wriggling, and behave like young men themselves so as not to be thought disagreeable or dictatorial."

3. Urban Disorganisation. "Mob liberty can go no further in such a city, when slaves bought with money, both men and women, are no less free than the buyers. Ah, I almost forgot to tell how great equality and liberty there is between women and men, between men and women."

"The domestic animals how much more free and easy they are in a city like this than is others, no one would believe who had not seen it. There's really nothing to choose between missus and bitch, as the proverb goes. Horses and asses, if you please, adopt the habit of marching along with the greatest freedom and haughtiness, bumping into everyone they meet who will not get out of the way; and all the other animals like wise are filled full of liberty."

4. Social Disorganisation. "To sum up, observe what comes of all these things together; how touchy it makes the people. They fret at the least hit of servitude, and won't have it; for at last, you know, they care nothing for the laws written or unwritten, that no one may be their master in anything.

According to Plato too much liberty in democracy makes it tyranny, as he said, "This then, my friend is the beginning from which tyranny grows, much a beautiful, bright beginning."

"The same as in the oligarchy, the same disease which destroyed that gets in here, stronger and more violent from this liberty, and enslaves democracy. And in fact that is what generally happens in the world. To do anything too much tends to take you the opposite extreme, in weather and in plants and in living bodies," and so also in constitutions most of all.

"For too great liberty seems to change into nothing else than too great slavery, both in man and in city."

"Then it is likely that democracy is precisely the constitution out of which tyranny comes; from extreme liberty, it seems, comes a slavery most complete and most cruel."

Three Classes in Democracy

According to Plato there are the following three classes in a democracy :

1. The Rulers. "One, a class such as we have described, grows here because of democratic licence, no less than in the oligarchic city. There they get no training and gather no strength, because they are excluded from the government as being held in no honour, but in democracy this is the dominant class, all but a few. The fiercest part of them talk and act while the others swarm round the platform and buzz; they never tolerate anyone who speaks on the other side, so that all business of state is managed by this class, with a few exceptions."[32]

---

32. *Ibid.*, p. 363.

2. The Aristocrats. "Another class, besides, is always being separated from the mass."

"When all are busy in making money, the most orderly by nature, I suppose, generally become richest."

3. The People. "People will be the name of the third class, all who are handiworkers and outside politics, without much property of their own. This is the largest and most sovereign class in democracy when it combines."[33]

Protectors in Democracy

According to Plato, "When the Protector of the people finds a very obedient mob; when he will not abstain from shedding tribal blood; when he drags someone into court by the usual unjust accusations, and incurs bloodguilt by destroying the life of man when, with unholy mouth and tongue, he tastes a kinsman's gore; when he banishes and executes, when he hints at abolition of debts and partition of estates — surely for such a one the necessity is ordained that he must either perish at the hands of his enemies, or become a tyrant, and be a wolf instead of man?"[34]

"Meanwhile your protector himself does not lie low, grand in his grandeur, at all; no, knocks down crowds of others and stands towering in the coach of state, Protector no longer by Tyrant finished and complete."

"Well, then at first, in the early days, he greets everyone he meets with a broad smile; says he is no tyrant, and promises all sorts of things in private and in public, frees them from their debts and parcels out the land to the people and to those about him, pretends to be gracious and friendly to all the world."

"As to outside enemies, when he has made terms with some and destroyed others, I take it, and when all is quiet from that source, he is for ever stirring up some war in order that the people may want a leader."

"And moreover, in order that they may become poor by having to pay taxes, and stick to their daily round, and be less likely to plot against him."

"And if he suspects that any harbour a free spirit and will not endure his rule, he wants an excuse to destroy them by exposing them to the enemy. For all these reasons the tyrant must always be stirring up war."[35]

REASONS FOR HOLDING OFFICE IN THE REPUBLIC

"For this reason then," Plato said, "good men are not willing to rule either for money or for honour. They do not wish to exact pay openly for their rule, and to be called hirelings, and they do not wish to take it themselves from their rule secretly, and be called thieves; nor again for honour, for they are not place-hunters. Therefore constraint must be put upon them and a penalty if they are to become willing to rule, and that is really why it has come to be thought

33. *Ibid.*, p. 364.

34. *Ibid.*, p. 365.

35. *Ibid.*, p. 366.

an ugly thing to present yourself willingly for office and not to wait for construing. But the greatest penalty is to be ruled by a worse man, if one it not oneself willing to rule. This I think distinguished men fear when they do accept office; and then they enter upon their office, not as coming into something good, or expecting to enjoy it, but as a grim necessity, being unable to entrust it to men better than themselves, or as good. For in fact if a city of good men could be, they would fight to avoid ruling, just as they fight now to rule; and then it would become quite manifest that indeed a true ruler's nature is to look for the subject's advantage, not his own. So every man who knows what is what would choose rather to have benefit from another than to benefit another and have no end of trouble."

SECOND BEST STATE

Plato made everything subordinate to the ideal of the philosopher king who also knew; what is good for men in the state *'The Republic'*. He excluded law altogether from the Ideal State. In the estimate of his political philosophy, the reemergence of law in his later writings is a matter of great importance. This implies drastic changes in all the underlying principles of government. Government in '*The Republic*' is by the specially chosen and specially trained men. In '*The Laws*' is a government in which law is supreme. The state governed by law as given in *'The Statesman'* and the laws is different from the conception of Ideal State. It formulates the second Best State. However, while sketching his second alternative, Plato was always haunted by the Ideal State as given in his 'Republic'.

Causes of Second Best State

1. Experience. The second state of Plato's is described as a half way house between the ideal and actual state. It is because of the fact that Plato modified his original ideal state, he considered it to be too good for human nature. Experience forced him to modify his views. Some scholars think that this was due to the disappointment of Plato on his failure to establish an ideal state in Syracuse. This cannot be true because even while Plato was writing his '*The Republic*' he said in a letter to his friend, Dion, "Let not Sicily nor any city any where be subjected to human masters — such as my doctrine — but to laws subjection is bad both for masters and for subjects." That is why Sabine says that it is safe to conclude that Plato never made any sudden changes in his convictions and that he was aware over a long period of years, that the omission of law from the ideal state was a cardinal difficulty.

2. Realist Approach. Plato repeatedly said in the book called '*The Laws*' that this purpose is to define a second best state. He was convinced that his Ideal State is always good but it is not possible to attain it due to frailty of human nature. It was perhaps the sobriety and wisdom that came to him in his old age which made Plato realise this.

3. Compromise. Another reason why he made the law to occupy a prominent place in his state is that Plato totally went against the Grecian thought. The

Greeks of those times believed that to suffer injustice is better than to do injustice. Therefore in his second best State, Plato tried to compromise the principles of his state to the popular feeling. Plato, in his early works, drew inspirations from Sparta. In later years he tried to amalgamate the best both in Sparta and Athens. In *The Laws* he borrowed more from Athenian constitution than from that of Sparta.

4. Philosopher Guardians are Difficult to be Acquired. By the experience that the philosopher-guardians are difficult to be acquired, Plato made law supreme in his state. He said that the rulers of this state must be the slaves and servants of law. They are not high above it for the reason that they are not totally dominated by reason which will enable them to understand true justice. Hence Plato remarks that 'without laws men differ not at all from the most savage beasts'.

5. Statesmen. In this sub-ideal State, Plato described psychology of human nature to be that of self-interest and temperance. His ripe wisdom taught him that it is not possible to get the philosopher-guardians, but it is possible to produce statesmen who can be bound by the sovereignty of law. Law has no limited functions. Plato called his second best state as the golden ground of the law. The supreme virtue in the state is temperance or self-control. It means a law abiding disposition or a spirit of respect towards the institutions of this state. It is readiness to subordinate oneself to its lawful powers. Admission of law in Plato's alternative scheme implies that the available human knowledge is not enough to secure a philosopher.

6. Rule of Law. Plato accepted this compromise with bitterness. He now appreciated a mixed state, where we find the combination of monarchical principle of wisdom with the democratic principle of freedom. His purpose was to achieve harmony by balancing forces. In the Republic there was no scope for freedom and conflict between the interests of the individual and the state.

7. Constitutional Subjection. In *The Republic* subjection is ethical but in *The Laws* subjection becomes constitutional.

Deduction from First Principles

'*The Republic*' of Plato was a deduction from the first principle, he used the existing practices only to illustrate his propositions. In '*The Laws*' he tried to trace the growth of human civilisation from herdsmen to statesmen and from families to city states, and, thereby principles of political stability useful for the statesmen. It was found a great contribution to the philosophy of state. '*The Republic*' shows extremism for realising the ideal state, '*The Laws*' depicts modernisation. Plato tried to show that the arbitrary power of monarchy, tyranny and democracy ruins itself by excess of things. According to him, power of monarchy needs moderation by wisdom and liberty of democracy by order. Besides, in '*The Republic*' Plato admits the claims of only one class, but in *The Laws,* he allows those of other classes also in order to achieve the most law abiding state.

The Republic dealt with the whole philosophy of man but in '*The Laws*' Plato primarily deals with politics, and explains at length political institutions and physical, economic and social assets of state.

Characteristics of Second Best State

Following are the characteristics of Plato's second best state :

1. Model State. Plato considered the community of race, language, law and religion as desirable factors for his sub-ideal state. *The Laws* is a pragmatic approach with an object to serve as a model for scientific students of jurisprudence and politics who may be called upon to act as advisers to the practical statesman engaged in founding a new community or remodelling an old one.

2. Change in Classification of States. The conception of the second best state made Plato change the classification of the states. He calls tyranny as the corruption of monarchy; the rule of a few as the aristocracy and its corruption as oligarchy. And finally, there are two types of democracy, the one is moderate and the other is the extreme form. Monarchy is best from the point of view of the good of the people in a law governed state. Democracy is the best form of government. The degenerations or corruptions of his ideal state Plato has given as timocracy (military state), oligarchy (government by the rich), and tyranny.

3. Prominence to Law. Plato grudgingly gave prominence to law. He said that if a competent ruler (a philosopher-king) is available there is no necessity for the supremacy of law, because nothing can be greater than knowledge. But he readmits law simply because individuals are not competent to always find out what is best in social life. Law makes them realise that common good is prior to individual good. This law is guided by reason. It is evolved by the education and appeal to the mind. It represented a return to the general Greek idea of the role of a fundamental law.

4. No Communism of Women. In his second best State, Plato gave up the communism of property and wives, which he advocated in his '*The Republic*'. He simply put certain restrictions on the property and the family life. He did not advocate radical changes. Permanent monogamous unions with public supervision were accepted as the lawful forms of marriage. Women were to give birth to children only between the age of twenty and forty. Every couple was required to produce a certificate of good health before mating.

5. No Communism of Property. As regards property, an individual was given right to private property under strict state supervision. Plato fixed the number of citizens at 5,040. Wealth was to come from land since commerce was still taboo. The land was to be equally divided among the citizens. It was to be inherited but not divided or alienated. The produce of the land was to be consumed in common at a public mess. The cultivation of land was to be done by slaves or serfs. Personal property was permitted but its amount was limited. Plato prohibited to any citizen a personal property exceeding four times of the lot of land. The purpose was to exclude large differences between the rich and the poor. Plato did not permit his citizens to engage themselves in business, trade or industry. He prohibited the taking of interest for loans and the possession of gold and silver. Thus, instead of a complete abnegation of property as advocated in *'The Republic'* Plato gave a new and modified communism with division of land accompanied by safeguards against concentration of wealth. He gave a new division of labour. Agriculture was the function of slaves, trade and industry that of resident aliens and political functions were the privilege of the citizens.

6. Religion. Plato had forceful opinion about the religion of the city states. He said that the individual must offer his rituals and ceremonies under the auspices of the state and not according to his own free will. He thought that private religion withdraws men from their allegiance to the state. He was even in favour of a new creed of religion for his state that proposed to penalise disbelievers by law. He proposed imprisonment and even death to atheists.

7. Education. There is not much difference in the scheme of the education as given in *The Laws*. Compulsory and similar education for all men and women, distrust of poets, censorship of art and literature, training in gymnastics and music all remained unchanged. In school the education was to be imparted in public regulated schools by paid teachers, under the directions of a magistrate, who was the chief of all the magistrates.

8. Share in Government. Every citizen, in Plato's second best state was to have his share in the Government according to his ability. The supreme authority was to be vested in a board of 37, who were to be old men between 50 and 70 with mature judgement and experience. They were to be guardians of laws, and chosen by three-fold election. The functions of this board of chief magistrates were supervisory. The citizens are divided into four classes. The first of them to have land, the produce from which would just enable them to maintain life. The three higher classes were to hold double, triple and the four times respectively of the landed property assigned to the lowest class. There was to be an administrative council of 360 appointed to execute the orders of the board of 37 magistrates. Plato assigned to each of the four classes one-fourth of the members of the council. There was penalty for rich citizens, if they fail to cast their votes. In the case of council the number of persons elected was double the number of seats to be filled and the final choice was made by lot. "This concession to democracy", says Sabine, "was certainly very slight and grudgingly made on account of the discontent of the masses."

9. Nocturnal Council. There was another Nocturnal Council, a body of the ten eldest of the 37 guardians. Its members were supposed to have the knowledge needed for the salvation of the state. They were to ensure the proper and smooth working of the whole constitution. They were to watch the proper execution of laws and to prevent unconstitutional laws being proposed. This council was to he aided and advised by (i) a council of 20 priests known for their virtue, and (ii) a council of 20 young men to contract the senile conservatism of the older men. In the words of Sabine, "It is evident that this Nocturnal council stands in the place of the philosopher king of *'The Republic'* and that its inclusion in *'The Laws'* is a flagrant violation of loyalty to the Second Best State''. It was nothing but oligarchy and democracy, leaning rather to oligarchy.

Concluding Remarks

Thus, Plato's concept of a Second Best State was not due to the repudiation of his ideal state. He was a philosopher but also played the role of a law giver. Secondly, while estimating his later works, one must complement him for his quick realisation about the baseness of human nature and the impossibility of realising his ideal state. As a result he did not doggedly cling to his ideal state thereby forgetting all the realities of life. He modified his fundamental principles in *The Laws*. He suggested the principle of balance of a mutual adjustment of claims and interests as the proper means for forming a constitutional state. However, Plato still had a nostalgia for his ideal state. To quote Maxey, ''Disillusion coupled with advancing years may have chilled his poetic enthusiasm and venomed the barbs of his irony, but they did not impair the clarity of his vision or shake his loyalty to the ideal. He still seeks the city of light hoping if not believing, that philosophers may be kings and kings philosophers.''

The political philosophy of Plato was not an abstraction. It had an intimate relation with local Hellenic ideas and institutions. Every philosopher formulates his theories on the basis of the ideas of his precursors and also the material conditions prevalent in his time. We find in Plato both the Hellenic and also the universal elements.

HELLENIC ELEMENTS IN PLATO'S THEORY

The defeate of Athens by Sparta in the Peloponesian war made the Athenians ponder over the causes of their defeat and downfall of their civilisation and culture. Socrates inspired his disciple Plato in these speculations. Plato was himself disillusioned by the democracy which put his master Socrates to death. Plato lived during the decline of Hellenic civilisation and culture. This period and not one preceding it left an indelible impression on his mind.

Influence of Sparta

Plato may have laid the foundations of *The Republic* on abstract thought and dialectics. The ideal state constructed over it however, had many similarities with Lycurgean institutions. Sparta played an important role to influence the thoughts of Plato.

1. Most of the elements of Plato's ideal state portrayed in *'The Republic'*, were Spartan. These are common meals for rulers, community of property, military training of the youth, gymnastic exercise for women, the subordination of the individual completely to the state, the equality of sexes, state controlled education for both men and women, the hatred of the poets and the ban on entry of ruling class into trade.

2. In Sparta, the governing class confined itself only to state duties and the system ensured a rigid uniformity among citizens.

3. The Spartans ruthlessly sacrificed every individual or family interest to the state.

4. Women shared the training of men and were lent out by their husbands to procreate for the state.

5. Gold and silver by certain classes and written laws were in disfavour.

6. The weak and deformed babies were 'exposed' on eugenic grounds.

Synthesis of Sparta and Athens

All these traits of Sparta, besides her successful military career and political efficiency, impressed all thinking Greeks including Plato. Plato did not fail to see the intellectual backwardness of Sparta. Hence he did not borrow wholesale from Sparta in his *'The Republic'*. He tried to strike a balance between physical fitness of Sparta and intellectual keenness of Athens. *The Republic* was written when Athens was passing through the most demoralised state. Therefore the contents of *The Republic* are more Spartan than Athenian.

Athenian Model in the Laws

By the time *The Laws* was written by Plato, Athens had recovered her lost position to a great extent. *The Laws* depicts Athenian classification of the population according to wealth, the organisation and functions of the administrative council, recognition of law as the golden cord of the state, the prohibition of interest on loans, the mode of choosing magistrates by election etc.

Hellenic Elements

1. Slavery and Trade. Plato did not denounce slavery nor did he condemn trade or disallow enslavement of the Greeks. He thought and wrote in terms of the city states of ancient Hellas. The guardians of the laws and the Nocturnal council strongly suggest the Senate of the Areopagus. Plato fused the individualism of Athens with specialisation and absolutism of Sparta.

2. Institutions. Plato's Ideal State depicts the Spartan institutions. There is also resemblance between Plato's Ideal state and Pythagorean League, an aristocracy by virtue. The literary and philosophic touch in Plato's scheme of education for the guardians was Athenian in origin from which Hellenism of Plato is clearly borne out.

3. Training. The idea of training came to be accepted during the time of Plato, when a professional soldier, Iphicrats had astonished the world by showing what a body of light armed, professionally trained troops could do even against the heavy infantry of Sparta.

4. Negative Influence. In a negative way also the Hellas influenced Platonic thought. The civic unrest in Athens was primarily because of great diversities of wealth which are inconsistent with good government. The factions between the rich and the poor drove Plato to advocate the abolition of property. In the words of Sabine, "The abolition of marriage was probably an implied criticism of the position of women in Athens, where her activities were summed up in keeping the house and rearing her children." In his communism of property and wives Plato was not only influenced by Spartan system and also from other Hellenic practices as well as theory, Greek hunters could, by common custom take out of other people's stores. In Greek, public lands were tilled by public serfs, and the income was used for common meals and general expenses of government. Pythagoras remarked that friends should have all things in common. Herodotus recorded that the Agathyrsians held their women in common. Euripedes advocated the community of wives.

5. Educational Tradition. (i) Plato was in agreement with general Greek tradition that the chief function of education was to train a citizen in the true spirit of the constitution of the state. It was to enable him to play his due part in the state.

(ii) People of his time chose education for the children as their fancies prompted or as the custom of the day provided.

(iii) Plato's educational system combined the curriculum of Athens with the administrative organisation of Sparta. That is why Sabine remarked that it was a running commentary on the existing institutions.

(iv) Plato's aversion to poetry resulted out of experience. Poets told the stories of Koruous eating his sons and daughters, talked loudly of adulteries of Aphrodite and the escapades of Leuns in the form of a swan, bull etc. Taking these into consideration, Plato put a virtual ban on poetry; that poets make states too unstable. It is evident from the above facts that there was positive Hellenic influence on Plato's thought.

UNIVERSAL ELEMENTS IN PLATO'S THOUGHT

Plato' s writings do not have only topical interest, they contain a good deal of what is of universal value useful to mankind for all times and climes. He was one of those greatest philosophers who have contributed a great deal of original matter to human thought. *The Republic* was the greatest of Utopias and the whole tribe of Utopian philosophers followed it. The Ideal State portrayed in *'The Republic'* was laid in heaven and could never be realised. However, the Ideal State was meant to be a model to be emulated. Plato was trying to show in principle and in theory what the state ought to be. He did not worry about its practicability. This was something of permanent value for political science. Plato was the first philosopher who dealt with political problems which even now remain the same. His treatment is an important legacy of his political thought.

Plato's emphasis on such issues as justice, emancipation of women and their equality with men, the rule of intellect, functional specialisation and his principles of eugenics are of permanent importance in his political philosophy.

1. The Guardians. It is a universal truth laid down by Plato that only very few people have the capacity to rule and the general mass is incapable of dealing with political problems. It is a fact that many modern writers and thinkers are very much disappointed with democracy. The clergy of Europe in medieval history almost resembled the philosopher guardians of Plato. They ruled for about a thousand years and their eminence rested on their mastery of religious books, and their disposition to a life of meditation and simplicity. In the later half of the period they were also free from family cares. According to Will Durant, "The communist rulers of Russia after 1917 reminded us of *The Republic*. Essentially he (Plato) is right is he not? What this world needs is to be ruled by its wisest men. It is our business to adopt his thought to our own times and limitations."

2. Factors of Decline and Growth of the State. According to Wayper, Plato portrayed the unjust state in order to bring home the lesson that the fall of ethical conduct is the cause of lowering the moral standard of public life. In the words of Maxey, "His ardent analysis of the fatal tendencies of free enterprise in an acquisitive society has been echoed again and again in the history of Western civilisation." Again, "Plato's analysis of the factors in the growth and decline of states and their cycles of change reveals a genuine appreciation of the materialistic forces of history causation. Like Marx and Lenin, he proposed to work with history and not against it."

3. Social Idealism. Plato is the precursor of all great lovers of social idealism. Milton, Locke, Rousseau, Goethe etc., drank deep from his philosophy.

4. Role of Unconscious and Subconscious. Modern psychology is indebted to Plato's *Republic* in showing the importance of the unconscious and subconscious in education and significance of dreams in bringing out the lower nature of man.

5. Ideals of Education. Plato's ideal of education continuing throughout life and extending to both sexes and the ideal of unity and correlation of knowledge will be always emulated by men.

6. Philosophy of Law. The modern statesman and legislator has much to learn from Plato's system of jurisprudence, his distinction between civil and criminal laws and his insistence that laws should be reformatory rather than punitive and, therefore, must have explanatory preambles.

7. Fascism. Modern Fascism bears a close resemblance to Platonism although there are some essential points of difference as well. Both have democracy, human equality and liberty. Both advocate dictatorship of an all-wise man and regimentation of civil life. Both believe in definition of state.

8. Registration and Standardisation. Plato's suggestions regarding an official survey and registry of all titles to real estates and regarding official standardisation of weights and measures are universal in practice.

Concluding Remarks

Plato has profoundly influenced Rousseau, Auguste Comte, Sir Thomas More and also the German and English schools of Idealists. Thus Plato's thought has tremendous universal importance. Modern world has followed him a great deal in all spheres of life. Plato was like a philosopher of his own description. The profound nature of his philosophy, his grasp of the fundamentals of life and his political radicalism made Plato a helpful guide for all times and places. The ideas propounded by him still loom large on the present age. Barker remarked that an Englishman feels more at home with the works of Plato in the 15th century B.C. rather than with the members of Frederich the Great who lived in the 18th century. To quote Prof. Smith, "We are the Greeks." In the words of Catlin, "The old problems (of Plato) have all come round again. The old answers are still true. Eugenics, nudism, abortion, feminism, communism, proletarian democracy, division of labour, class-war, scientific expertise — all the problems are here."

BOTH INDUCTION AND DEDUCTION

Both Induction and Deduction are means to arrive at universal truth. In induction, we arrive at universal from particulars. On the other hand, the deductive method means to take on universal truth and then to come to the particulars. Plato used deductive method in his writings. At the same time, he used inductive method also. Deductive method had a firm hold on Plato. He, however, tried to give a colouring or embellishment to deductive method by the help of inductive facts. He was deductive in his arguments but he used inductive facts to prove that human nature is weak and frail. Hence one cannot say that either deductive or inductive method was the basis of his philosophy.

1. Virtue or Knowledge. In his exposition of philosophy, Plato believed faithfully in the Socratic doctrine that virtue is knowledge. In his times, Socrates, threw the challenge that if there is any valuable thinking, it must be defined. So, naturally, Plato his disciple, said that real virtue was only the ultimate idea of 'Good'. Virtue is knowledge and it can be acquired by the philosopher guardians of the ideal state. When this all wise philosopher is the ruler, then alone will come into existence his ideal state.

2. Functional Specialisation. After having stated what is true virtue and who is the person that can attain it Plato came down to earthly realities. He did not merely live in his fancied world of abstract thinking. He maintained that human nature is composed of the psychological characteristics. Reason will dominate in the philosopher-ruler or king, the spirit will dominate in the military guardians, and appetite will dominate in the workers and artisans.

From this psychological proposition Plato argued by deduction that as men are endowed with different capacities, they must try to develop that quality alone. That is to say that each person, according to his ability, must specialise in his own field. This is called the functional specialisation.

3. Education. The next question was how to develop this ability. In order to make men perfect in their own respective fields Plato advocated a system of state education. With the help of education, the individual will be able to perceive the ideal of 'Good'. It will result in the beautification of soul which means the inward eye of the individual will totally perceive the inner light.

4. Communism. While discussing about the philosopher rulers, Plato found by induction that often the rulers in the actual state were distracted by two institutions called family and property. By deduction he pleaded to destroy both of them.

5. Inductive Method to Modify Deduction. Plato has used inductive method to modify his deductive conclusion. He borrowed certain things from the ancient thought. 'The first thing he borrowed from Sparta was discipline. In Sparta men used to dine at common table and they were most disciplined people. Plato tried to develop a sense of discipline among the Athenians also, as stated in his Ideal State. Dunning says, 'Plato Spartanised his Athenians'. However, Plato modified his deduction on the basis of induction arrived at by his actual experience in the Greek world around him during his time. He suggested that the education should be imparted by the state as was done in Sparta. Education leads to the realisation of the 'Good'. He shaped the existing education to his own purpose. Plato had before him the example of Sparta where boys were taken from the parents at the age of 7, and brought up and educated by the state. The weak and deformed babies were exposed to death. Wives were lent to procreate for state purposes. In Sparta, people, especially the ruling class, used to take their meals on one table and discuss their problems. The system of dining together at one place was one minor detail of communism that was borrowed by Plato from Sparta. In Crete there was public tilling of public estates.

The classification of states as detailed by Plato in his writings was based on the different degenerated states in Hellenic world. The guardians of the laws and the nocturnal Council strongly suggest such an influence. The constitution of Plato's second best state contains many Athenian institutions such as the four-fold classification of the population according to wealth, the organisation and functions of the administrative council, the prohibition of interest on loans, the mode of appointment of magistrates by election and drawing of lot. Plato thought and wrote in terms of the city states of ancient Hellas. He fused the individualism of Athens with specialisation and absolutism of Sparta. The censorship of art and literature and hatred of poets were borrowed from Sparta. There is also resemblance between Plato's ideal state and the Pythagorean League, an aristocracy of virtue.

ARISTOTLE'S CRITICISMS OF PLATO

The circumstances make the man and social environment influence the thought. No one can think in vacuum. As the temperament and surroundings of Plato and Aristotle differed, so their political thought was bound to differ. Aristotle gained his substance of political thought from Plato but due to different temperaments and back ground they differed because thoughts reflect the image of a man. Plato and Aristotle differed widely due to their temperamental and other differences. Aristotle vehemently criticized many conceptions of Plato.

1. Ideal and Method. Plato believed ultimate good is to be found in the ideal, i.e philosophy in universal forms. Aristotle based his thought on contrary assumption that reality is not to be found in Idealistic or perfect ideas. He laid emphasis on experience and observance which is called philosophy of individual experience. While Plato followed inductive Aristotle followed deductive method, based on observation, comparison and conclusion etc.

2. Approach. Plato was imaginative, Aristotle was reactionary. Plato was eloquent and Aristotle was exact. From general concepts Plato drew logical conclusions. Aristotle slowly worked from various facts. Plato painted a picture of ideal commonwealth. Aristotle provided the material requisites out of which a model state can be constructed.

3. Status of the Individual. Plato wanted total assimilation of individual in the state but Aristotle allowed private rights to individual.

4. Outlook. Plato's outlook was literary, Aristotle's outlook was scientific. Prof. Maxey has labelled 'Aristotle as a first scientist.'

5. Maths V/s Biology. Plato was a lover of Mathematics. He wrote "Let no one devoid of interest in Mathematics enter here." As mathematics deals with number and figures which are straight and fixed, so Plato thought of real world as consisting of eternal, immutable and fixed archetypal essence of things. Aristotle was a lover of biology which deals with the facts of growth or development. As such Plato's universe is Static but Aristotle's dynamic.

6. Style of Writing. Plato was a master artist in the use of words. Aristotle was careless on style but placed emphasis on meaning. Plato is poetical, Aristotle is philosophical.

7. Assumptions V/s Testing. According to Prof. Borule, "Where Plato is set on constructing a planned state in the light of assumed principles and will often brush aside practical objections, Aristotle is constructing and testing his hypothesis by the facts."

It is said that a thinking man is either a Platonist or Aristotian. It means that the two philosophers are quite opposite to one another. Aristotle criticised Plato very harshly and devoted Book II of the politics to criticise, Plato's *'The Republic'* and *'The Laws'*.

8. Realism. Aristotle complained that the ideas of Plato are brilliant but too radical and imaginary to be realised in the realistic words. To quote Aristotle, "Let us remember that we should not disregard the experience of ages; in the multitude of years, these things, if they were good, would certainly not have been unknown; for almost everything has been found out although sometimes they are put together; in other cases men do not use knowledge which they have." Prof. Sabine remarks "Aristotle is the soberer, if less original genius." He was imaginative and synthetic in his philosophy.

Plato based his philosophy on ideas and ignored historical facts. He imagined schemes of Government without much reference to actualities. Aristotle put emphasis on facts, their collection and examination. He possessed thorough knowledge of political institutions of past and present and attached great importance to them. As Aristotle liked definite and scientific knowledge, so he favoured Plato's sub-ideal state of *The Laws.* His biologist view can be traced back to his descent from a family of medicos and scientific interest to his early life at Sagira, where the scientific culture of Macedon prevailed.

9. The Philosopher King. Aristotle clearly distinguished between the theoretical and practical exercise of reason which was not known to Plato. Due to this reason, he rejected the most profoundly original doctrine of Plato that the states should be ruled by philosopher King. Aristotle divided sciences into theoretical, practical and productive classes. He considered Mathematics, Physics and Chemistry in theoretical science which comprehend the world of nature, Ethics and Politics in practical sciences, which study the working of mind and building, sculpture and painting in productive sciences. As per Aristotle "the prime qualification of a Statesman is not knowledge but practical wisdom which is acquired by long experience with the work handling men and their affairs" and not by the study of Mathematics or Dialectics as supposed by Plato. Politics or state craft not theoretical knowledge will enable a statesman to govern in a proper way. As such Foster remarks, "Aristotle's own treatise on Politics is a work of just such practical reason. It is a handbook for statesman containing the wisdom as distilled as it were from the collective political experience of the Greek states."

10. Unity of the State. Aristotle argued that the unity of state as emphasized by Plato would destroy that differentiation of function which is the law of Nature. He maintained that such a unified state would destroy the self-sufficiency of the state as "the nature of state is to be plurality, and leading to greater unity, from being a state it becomes a family, from being a family an individual." As such attainment of greater unity would be the destruction of the state, Aristotle said a unity based on the removal of all destruction in individual is fatal to the state just as identity in musical tones is fatal to musical harmony. Aristotle believed in the maxim that unity lies in diversity. He believed that Plato's system of state would create perpetual disunity and discord; because of the two diverse and antagonistic elements of educated guardians and uncultivated masses.

Aristotle's criticism of uniformity applies only to upper classes of Plato and not to the majority class for which Plato allowed diverse functions and interests. He is not fair in criticism of Plato. Plato never sought to reduce the state to the unity of an individual. He provided three clearly distinguished classes and recognized the diversity of functions. As such Plato's state is as diverse as that of Aristotle.

11. Communism. Aristotle harshly criticised Plato's conception of communism. In order to achieve unity of the state Plato desired to abolish family and private property. Aristotle desired to create unity in the state by educating the people in the spirit of the constitution. He laid emphasis on moderation, individual liberty and private property which are essential for development of individual's personality and for the benefit of the people.

(i) *Communism of Properties.* Aristotle believed that common ownership of property leads to common neglect as everybody's business is nobody's business. People pay most attention to their own property. In a system of common property those who work hard and get little will have a grievance against those who work little and get much. There will be no incentive to hard work because it is love of private property which arises due to wickedness of men, but in communism these may arise also due to its very nature. As those who travel together and have a common purse come to quarrel, same may happen in case of common property.

Aristotle believed that sense of private property is a source of great pleasure as it is a form of self-love. Private property can be used for charity, benevolence and for the benefit of humanity etc. It gives a man a sense of independence. If men are deprived of property, they will have no attachment to the people and hence will lose all interest. Property is essential to enable to perform their duties well. According to Aristotle personal attachment alone can develop sociable character. He advocated that property should be owned privately but must be shared in common. In this way, he secured the advantages of individualism and communism. Communism will upset the natural inequality of capacity and industry of individuals. Moreover, human selfishness cannot be eradicated in this way because it is inherent in the nature of man. It can be minimised only by properly educating the people to common use of their private possession. Denial of certain minimum of property will check the fullest development of individuality. It will result in the impoverishment of the whole state. Private ownership brings economic and moral advantage, common use following from private spirit produces that unanimity which is desired most. But Aristotle is against the accumulation of wealth beyond the need of good life. He wanted to improve the institution of private property by proper custom and registration etc.

(ii) *Communism of Children.* To Aristotle, Plato's communism of the children is unnatural and foolish. Plato believed that the unity of state is best achieved when all the citizens say 'mine'' and 'thine' for the same things, i.e. when all of them regard all children as their own and none of them has a separate private home. In this way, a man will feel an equally high affection for all the children in the state. But Aristotle is of the opinion that this communism will not result in greater love for all common children but no love to any, because the sense of personal possession and exclusive relationship is the only basis of affection. If it is extended, it may be reduced to merely friendship. The children will be neglected because every body's business is nobody's business. It is far better to be a real cousin than a Platonic son. In Platonic plan each man will have a thousand sons and every child a thousand fathers. Public creche can be a poor substitute for the home and mother.

(iii) *Communism of Wives.* Community of wives means that every man's wife will be the wife of every other man. Practically, this may bring discord and may give rise to jealousy. All the guardians cannot be in actual possession of one wife. Unknown relationship may result in unholy acts between blood relatives and may create suspicion among them.

It may be noted here that perhaps Aristotle misunderstood Plato because Plato never contemplated nationalisation or socialisation of women of guardian class so that wife of every man may be the wife of every other man. His aim was abolition of permanent marriage and provision for temporary mating between properly selected pairs. However, human nature is more akin to Aristotle's permanent marriages than Plato's temporary marriages. Even modern communism did not believe in communism of wives.

Plato thought family and property as source of evil and therefore sought to abolish them. But Aristotle found them deeply rooted in human instinct and saw much good in them. He abhorred the idea of throwing the baby along with the bath. He clinged to the experience of ages and thought that Plato was too radical and speculative in his political philosophy to be a good guide in practical life. To Aristotle, the home and family is the great school of wisdom. The lessons learnt by the affection of parents in the family later extend to wider life of the society. Family is the natural unit of human life. Private property a necessary part of social economy. This realism made Aristotle the philosopher of medieval world.

12. The Ideal State. Aristotle vehemently criticized the Plato's ideal state. Experience is a better guide than expert knowledge. While Plato believed in wisdom of few, Aristotle believed in collective wisdom. He would like to give equal share to all citizens. Plato favoured the philosopher King, i.e. the enlightened ruler but Aristotle favoured constitutional rule because philosopher guardians can never be always altruistic as was supported by Plato.

Aristotle also criticised Plato for the neglect of overwhelming population of non-guardian class for which Plato did not provide education. Aristotle feared, it may result in class conflict and mutual jealousy. However, it may be noted here that in his ideal state Aristotle himself did not grant rights of citizenship to lower class stating, "From the hour of their birth some are marked out for subjection, others for rule."

13. Criticism of the Laws. Aristotle criticised *'The Laws'* of Plato on the following grounds:

(i) He opposed the increase of warriors from 1000 to 5000 as it will make sub-ideal state too large.

(ii) Plato should have defined the limit of population and the amount of property. Aristotle objected that if other property can be four fold why did it not apply to land also.

(iii) Aristotle was of the opinion that Plato's system of double election will transfer the power of election into the hands of a clique. Plato mixed oligarchy and democracy, he did not mix tyranny and democracy which are worst institutions. Plato grudgingly accepted law to be supreme in his second best state as a concession to human frailty, but Aristotle believed that law is the product of human progress by stating that "the law is reason unaffected by desire".

EVALUATION OF ARISTOTLE'S CRITICISM

(i) In his criticism of the Plato's ideal state Aristotle is neither fair nor always accurate. It is unfair because it was ideal and not to be followed in practice. Ideal state is to serve as a measuring rod to judge their nature.

(ii) Plato did not destroy differentiation as Aristotle thought but clearly emphasized three classes in the ideal state.

(iii) Plato's communism was meant for only guardian classes.

Impact of Plato on Aristotle

What Aristotle criticised he adopted later on. One impact of Plato on Aristotle, when he said that great majority of men are natural dunces and sluggards, infanticide is to be replaced by abortion, offices should be reserved for the best equipped and so on. According to Sabine, "In his construction of the ideal state almost every subject discussed is suggested by the laws and there are many parallelism (even verbal) in small points." To quote J.P. Suda, "There is no doubt that Aristotle never misses an opportunity to criticise his master, and is more conscious of his difference than of points of agreement with him. These differences should not be allowed to minimise or conceal the great extent of what is common to them." It is true that the keen intellect of Aristotle did not allow him to be blind follower of Plato and accept all his teachings. But he made Plato's teachings the main basis of his own thinking and developed them along the lives determined by his earlier biological studies and scientific temperament. As per Will Durant, Aristotle says, "Dear is Plato, but still dearer is truth." To quote Foster, "Aristotle is the greatest of all Platonist, that he is permeated by Platonism to a degree in which perhaps no great philosopher besides him has been permeated by the thought of other."

According to Wayper, "In spite of Aristotle's criticism, usually niggling though occasionally trenchent of Plato, the difference between them is more formal than real." C.E.M. Joad holds the same view, and he says that Aristotle has a habit of starting and starting avowedly from positions which are antithesis of those of Plato and ending in conclusions which are scarcely if at all distinguishable from these of his predecessor." Dunning states, "He (Aristotle) differs from his master Plato, much more in the form and method than in the substance of his thought."

Similar Points

Aristotle remained Plato's disciple for 20 years in his Academy. According to Sabine, "Every page of his (Aristotle's) later philosophical writings bears witness of this connection."

1. Greek Legacy. Both Plato and Aristotle were product of Hellenic civilization. Both commonly inherited the legacies of Homer to Socrates. As per Foster "Both of them looked with alarm on the instability of Greek political life and on the moral anarchy which they believed to be its cause and both accordingly believed that the remedy lay in education for a better living. Both believed that good life could only be lived in a city state of moderate size. It could not be attained by all men but those who have sufficient schooling to do so. Both therefore wished to limit citizenship so as to make this possible and both thought it right that manual labourers should be slaves or non-citizens.

2. Aims of the State. Ideas of Plato and Aristotle were identical in setting up an ethical purpose as the chief end of the state. Both believed that the real aim of the state should be moral improvement of its citizens. The state ought to be an association of men living together to achieve the best possible life. The state alone is self-sufficing in the sense that it alone provides all the conditions with in which the highest type of moral development can take place. Both believed that man is a social animal and the state is necessary. Both regard state as a moral and spiritual entity as they believe that "Good" is the ultimate end of the state although in case of Plato it is absolute and in case of Aristotle it is relative.

3. Conservation. Both are conservative and confine their ideal to the state as the basis of their political thought. Both are influenced by Athenian and Spartian outlook and champion the cause of oligarchy. Both oppose Democracy. Plato hated lower class and Aristotle defended slavery. Both place emphasis on check of population by birth control and destruction of unhealthy children. Both are metaphysical in so far as they say that nature has made some men of gold, silver and copper.

4. Ethics and Politics. Both are of the opinion that Ethics and Politics constitute a single and indivisible science and their thought possesses ethical character. Both believe that the life which is worthy of man is a life of virtue and that it is possible for an individual in and through membership of the state.

5. Support of State. Aristotle and Plato both oppose sophism and hold that states come into being for the sake of life and continues for the sake of good life. Both aim at the unity of the state but their methods differ. They equate state and society and give no right to individual against the state. Both plead against trade and industry and usury. Both possessed encyclopaedic knowledge and were giant philosophers.

6. Importance to Women. According to Barker, Aristotle gives equal importance to women as Plato did. He attacks Plato's ideal state but not his sub-ideal state. This is the reason that Aristotle's ideal state is considered as Plato's second best state.

7. Importance to Education. Plato and Aristotle, both gave equal importance to education. In reality, "Aristotle was a genuine Platonist in so far as he believed that the greatest need of the times was the proper education of the rulers." As per Plato, education is the instrument through which the ideal of state can be realised. According to Aristotle, though it is not the medium but still it occupies a prominent place in his best average state. Aristotle discussed the place and importance of education is the best practicable state.

8. Importance of Law. In constructing his ideal state, Plato stated that when men are without laws, they did not differ at all from the most savage beast. Aristotle said, "Man when perfected is the best of animals but when separated from law and justice, he is worst of all.'' Plato came to the conclusion that it is not possible to procure philosopher guardian, so he supported law in the state. Aristotle borrowed the origin of state from Plato as stated in *The Laws* that first, there were isolated families then villages and then came the state. The requirements of his ideal state such as the specifications regarding population in character, size, nature and situation are derived from *The Laws.* Aristotle's best is, Plato's second best. His remarks while introducing the best state are inspired by Plato's discussion on the physical, economic and social factors which govern the nature of state. Influenced by *The Laws* of Plato and Aristotle stated that in any good state, law and not any person whatsoever must be made sovereign.

9. Support of Middle Path. Plato condemned excess as dangerous. Aristotle was an exponent of the golden mean. Both stated that man is a political animal and can only develop himself in the state. Aristotle's classification of the state is similar to that of Plato because the names of the classified states are the same even though the methods are different. For both individual and the state are complementary and not contradictory.

10. Best State. Both possess aristocratic temper. Plato supported philosopher guardians and Aristotle limited citizenship. Both believed that among persons some are marked out for subjection and others for rule. Both opposed democracy.

According to G. Grote, ''The organisation of government proposed by Aristotle in the last two books of his politics, as representing his own ideas of something like perfection were incidently propounded upon the Republic of Plato from whom he differs in the important circumstances of not admitting either community of property or community of wives and children. Each of these philosophers recognized one separate class of inhabitants relieved form all private toil and all money, getting employment and constituting exclusively the citizens of the commonwealth; the remaining inhabitants are not a part of commonwealth, they are only appendages to it, indispensable indeed but still appendanges in the same manner as slaves are kept.'' Grote feels that Aristotle's best state where he deviates from *The Republic* largely copies Plato's *The Laws.*

Aristotle's best state is a compromise between three things: a romantic Platonic aristocracy; a sound balanced feudalism; and some democratic ideas but feudalism was the best of it. Aristotle requires that all citizens should have the right to participate in the government. Aristotle maintained that not only slaves but all members of producing class are excluded from participation in state affairs and citizenship. Thus, he supported Plato that the working classes must not rule and the ruling class must not produce. As such he repeats his contention that ''the first principle of all action is leisure.''

11. Slavery. Somewhat grudgingly Aristotle followed Plato, his teacher, as closely as his temperament permitted. As such he endorsed and systematised Plato's rationalistic theory of slaves, though in some minor points, he slightly mitigates Plato's theory of slavery and duly censors his teacher, Plato for being too harsh.

Concluding Remarks

As per Zeller Aristotle "can inspire us in the same way as Plato does." His work is direct and more professional than Plato's work. It may be said that "in fundamentals of his political philosophy, Aristotle was a faithful disciple of Plato." To sum up in the language of C.E.M. Joad, "In the end he (Aristotle) is found to have done little more than to dot the 'i's and cross the 't's of the proposition, already reached by Plato." Lastly we agree with Sabine that "Aristotle's theory of political ideals stands upon the ground which he had clearly occupied because of his association with Plato.

QUESTIONS FOR EXERCISE

1. "The image of his (Plato's) teacher never faded from his mind," Explain.
2. "Plato represented the greatest legacy bequeathed by Socrates to Mankind." Discuss.
3. "The Republic did not spring at once to life, self begotten in Plato's brain it had its prelude and preparations in previous thought." Explain and discuss.
4. "The James...like character of the Republic presents two forms one a Hellenic State, the other a kingdom of philosophers." Explain and discuss.
5. "The Republic and The Laws are the communist dictates. Plato is the first communist or fascist thinker." Catlin "The Republic did not spring at once to life, self together in Plato's brain, it had its prelude and its preparation in previous thought." Barker.
6. "Republic is the crowning achievement of Plato's Art and Philosophy". The Republic is not only deduction from first principles, it is also an induction from the fascist statements of Greeek life, illustrate.
7. "Plato's Republic is an exposition and an evolution of Socratic principles." Discuss.
8. Examine the view that the Platonic Republic ... must be considered as a brilliant exercise of philosophical imagination.
9. "The Republic is not a work upon Politics but the finest treatise on education that ever was written." Rousseau. Explain
10. 'The theory of the state in Republic culminates in the conception of justice.' Discuss Plato's theory of states. How does this theory of state culminate in his conception of justice?
11. "So striking is the part played in Plato's ideal state by education that some have considered this to be the chief topic of the Republic". (H.G. Sabine). Explain.
12. "Plato's Republic overshadows his Laws, yet the latter has a practical value denied to the former." Discuss and compare The Republic with The Laws.

13. "The State ruled by law is a concession to the frailty of human nature" (Sabine). On what grounds does Plato justify the statement?
14. "The Platonic state can only be an aristocracy, a government of virtue and intelligence exercised by one or a few." Edward Zeller. Elucidate this remark keeping in view Plato's dislike for democracy.
15. "Plato seeks superman, who will create a state as good as ought to be. Aristotle seeks a super science which will create a state as good as can be." Elucidate and discuss.
16. "Not one of them is a state, but many of them, for any state, however small is in fact divided into two, one state of the poor, the other that of the rich and these are at war with one another." (Republic). Discuss.
17. "The state is the individual wit large." — Plato. Comment.
18. "The truth is that the state in which the rulers are most reluctant to govern, is always the best and most quietly governed than the state in which they are most eager." — Plato. Comment.
19. "In a democracy even the horses and asses have a way of marching along with all the rights and dignities of free man ... all things are just ready to burst with liberty." — Plato. Comment.
20. "What Aristotle calls the ideal state is always Plato's second best state." — Sabine. Explain.
21. "Until the philosophers are kings or kings and princes of the world have the power of philosophy cities will never have rest from the evils." Comment.
22. What were Plato's objections against democracy?
23. "One of the main causes of Plato's pervasive and persuasive influence is that he is the ablest exponent of the aristocratic theory of the state and the acutest critic of the democratic way of life."

    Do you agree? Is it correct to say that one could trace the germs of totalitarianism in Plato's political thought?
24. Describe the Hellenic and Universal elements in Plato's works.
25. "Plato's Republic is a mere romance."(Dunning). Explain.
26. "It is easy to interpret the Republic as a Utopia, a city in the clouds, a sunset fabric seen for an hour in the evening and then fading into the night....But the Republic is not a city of nowhere. It is based on actual conditions; it is meant to mould or at any rate to influence actual life."(Barker) Discuss.
27. "The Republic" of Plato defies classification. (Sabine) Comment.
28. "The Republic" aimed at the representation of human life in as State perfected by justice and governed according to the idea of good. (Staulham) Discuss.
29. "Until philosophers are Kings, or the Kings and princes of this world have the spirit and power of philosophy and political greatness and

wisdom meet in one....cities will never have rest from their evils....(Plato). Examine Plato's contribution to political thought in the light of this remark.

30. "If political power and scientific knowledge (Philosophy) are not united in one person, then there is no end of evil for the state and also for mankind in general." Discuss.
31. "Plato's philosophy is the most savage and most profound attack on liberal ideas which history can show."(Crossman) Discuss.
32. Analyse the system of Government as portrayed by Plato in the 'Laws.'
33. "The 'Republic' and the 'Laws' are communist tracts. Plato is the first communist." Catlin. Do you agree, If so, how would you reconcile the other view equally strongly propounded that Plato is first among fascist?
34. "Republic" said Rousseau "is really the first treatise on education that was, ever written." Amplify this statement.
35. "So striking is the part played by Plato's ideal education that some have considered this to be the chief topic of the Republic." (G.H. Sabine). Elucidate.

    Discuss Plato's concept of Education and function of Education in his ideal state.
36. "Justice is the order of the state and the state is the visible embodiment of justice under the conditions of human society."
37. "The Republic aimed at the representation of human life in a State perfected by justice and governed according to the idea of good." (Staulham).
38. "The fundamental issue of Republic is the discovery of nature and habitation of justice." Discuss this statement and examine Plato's conception of justice.
39. "Justice is the hinge of his (Plato's) thought and the text of his discourse." (Barker) Discuss.
40. "Plato's communism is a heroic remedy for a desperate evil the union of political power and economic temptation in the same hands." Explain.
41. "Both the community of property and the community of families, as I am saying tend to make them more truly guardians." (Plato) Discuss.

    OR

    Give a critical evaluation of Plato's communism of wives and property.

    OR

    Is it correct to describe Plato as totalitarian? Give reasons in support of your answer.
42. "Other regulations concerning their properties and families tend to make them more freely guardians. They will not tear the city to pieces by differing about "mine", "not mine", each man dragging any aquisition he had made into a separate house of his own, where he has a separate

wife and children and private pleasures of his own.'' Discuss with reference to the peculiar character of Plato's communism.

43. ''In respect to wives and children, Plato is definitely propounding a system of 'communism' in the sense of common ownership. But it is to a very small extent that Plato recommends common ownership of property.'' — M.B. Foster. Discuss.
44. ''Any city, however, samll, is in fact divided into two, one the city of poor, the other of the rich.'' — Plato. Explain.
45. ''Plato's Republic is not only a deduction from the first principles, it is also an induction from the facts of Greek life''. Elucidate.
46. ''The comments of Aristotle on Plato's Republic and Laws are full of inaccuracies and inconsistencies.'' — (Jowett). Explain this statement.
47. Aristotle's theory of political ideals stands upon ground which he had clearly occupied because of his association with Plato. — (Sabine). Discuss.
48. ''Indeed it is generally true that it is difficult for men to live together and to be partners in any form of human activity but it is specially difficult to do so when property is involved' — Aristotle. Explain.

7

Aristotle (384 B.C. — 322 B.C.)

Among the pioneers of human knowledge Aristotle was undoubtedly, the greatest. To quote Frank Thilly, "In its scope, Aristotle's philosophy is perhaps the most comprehensive synthesis of knowledge ever achieved by the mind of man. No other thinker, ancient, medieval, or modern — with the possible exception of the German philosopher Hegel — has incorporated into his system so great a bulk of knowledge."[1] Aristotle's philosophy included almost all the sciences and humanities such as logic, mathematics, physics, biology and psychology, metaphysics and ethics, politics and aesthetics. His range was encyclopaedic, original as well as creative. He was not merely an eclectic. Far from it, he was the original genius behind the original growth of not only so many social sciences but also the physical sciences. From the criteria of breadth, originality and influence Aristotle was undoubtedly, "master of those who know".[2]

BIOGRAPHICAL SKETCH

Born in 384 B.C., in Stagira, a city of Greece, Aristotle had a silver spoon in his mouth right from his childhood. His father, Nicomachus, was the court physician of Philip of Macedon. Aristotle entered the famous Academy of the Great philosopher Plato at the early age of 17 years. He stayed there for almost 20 years as a student and a teacher. In 347 B.C. after the death of his master Plato, Aristotle left the academy and started travelling. He went to Assos in Mysia and from there to Mitylene. He was called by the king Philip to look after the education of his son Alexander the great, in 342 B.C. For seven years he was the tutor of Alexander after which he returned to Athens to establish the school known as *Gymnasium.* It was also known as Peripatetic school because of the habit of Aristotle of walking while lecturing. His method of teaching was not only through lectures but also through dialogues. After the death of Alexander the great he was accused of sacrilege. He left Athens for Euboea where he died in 322 B.C.

Aristotle was a master of dialectic. He was a great observer, a voracious reader and a specialist both in natural sciences as well as in philosophy. Among

1. Frank Thilly, *History of Philosophy,* p. 118.

2. Gomperz, *Greek Thinkers*, pp. 18-19.

his writings one finds not only on metaphysics and logic but also on human sciences like psychology and ethics and politics as well as upon natural sciences.

WORKS OF ARISTOTLE

It has been said that Aristotle wrote as many as 400 books.[3] Each book, however, means a chapter of a book as we generally understand by the term 'book' today.

Aristotle's works have been classified into those of logic, metaphysics, ethics, politics, rhetoric, psychology and natural sciences. In these fields his important works are as follows:

1. Logic. Aristotle's views concerning logic are available in his work *Organon.* This work includes categories, rules of interpretations, analytic and fallacies etc. This great work is divided into different books on these different topics.

2. Metaphysics. On *Metaphysics* includes as many as 14 books of Aristotle.

3. Ethics. Aristotle's famous works *Nicomachean ethics* consists of 10 books on different topics concerning ethics. Another important work on ethics is *Eudemian ethics.*

4. Politics. Aristotle's famous book *Politics* consists of 8 books. Besides this important work he also wrote another book entitled *On the Constitution of Athens.*

5. Psychology. Aristotle's famous work *On the soul* consists of 8 books on different topics concerning human psychology. Besides, he also wrote small independent treatises on memory, dream etc.

6. Natural sciences. Aristotle has a wide influence on almost all the natural sciences due to his pioneer work in different fields. Of these the most important are: *Physics* (eight books of which Book VII is an interpolation); *Astronomy* (four books); *Origin and Decay* (two books); *Meteorology* (four books); *Cosmology* (spurious); *Botany* (spurious); *History of Animals* (ten books, Book X spurious);

PLATO AND ARISTOTLE CONTRASTED

Political philosophy of Aristotle is empirical and descriptive in comparison with radical and abstract nature of Plato's philosophy. The central theme of his politics is moderation, golden means or balance. According to Catlin, "After Confucious, Aristotle is the apostle of common sense and golden mean." Moreover, the digressions or confusions of Aristotle led to the opening of new chapters in political science. He tried to reconcile ideals with actualities. In doing so he travelled far away from his master, denied the scope of political science and dealt with most of the modern problems.

Theories of Aristotle are based on historical knowledge. He condemned Plato for paying insufficient attention to history and for imagining schemes of

---

3. Zeller, *Outlines of the History of Greek Philosophy*, p. 158.

Government without due references either to the nature of human animal of the actual forms of Government.

First Political Scientist

According to Sabine, "The true romance of the Republic is the romance of free intelligence, unbound by custom and untrammelled by facts." But Aristotle gave due importance to fact as his biological training and scientific studies made him a careful and systematic observer. Politics became empirical and inductive in his hands. As such he may be considered the father of study of comparative government. He pioneered the new method of first knowing the constitutional history and then arriving at general conclusion. According to Sabine, "Aristotle is the founder of historical method which has been on the whole sound; and the most faithful that the study of politics has evolved." To quote Karl Fredrick "He (Aristotle) was the first man in the world's literature who applied a deeply inductive (experimental) or comparative method to the diverse phenomenon of the state." Similarly Maxey also calls him as first scientist.

Realist in Approach

Aristotle not only collected facts but also stressed the problem of value and importance of ethical judgements. He judged the importance of the facts in terms of the end or purpose of the state because politics was to him the culmination of ethics. Unlike his idealist teacher Plato, he was the first realist in political thought. While Plato argued in the imaginary world of dreams or of idealism, Aristotle dealt with reforming of actuals. Aristotle has been honoured with the title of father of political science. Hence his love of facts checked him from being too radical. He remained confined to reformation as he believed that the ideal must conform to actual facts. He followed middle path and separated ethics from Politics.

Cautious and Moderate

An Aristotle was descriptive and empirical he did not have the bold sweep and courage of Plato to destroy all that stood in his way. He was more cautious and moderate. He was reformer and not a revolutionary. His ideal state which he proposed in book III was never realised because his ideals were sunk in the mid-stream of realities. Hence Prof. H.G. Sabine remarked "What all he wrote was a book not on ideal state, but on the ideals of state." However, he brought Plato's ideal down on earth and adopted it to the practical politics of the city state. This new line brought him rich dividend. This revolt against Plato opened new vistas in political science and made it an independent subject.

DIFFERENCE BETWEEN PLATO AND ARISTOTLE

While pointing out difference between Plato and Aristotle Maxey says "As Plato is father to the idealists, romanticists, revolutionists and utopians of political philosophy, so Aristotle is father to the realists, scientists, pragmatists and utilitarians." All who believe in new worlds for old are disciples of Plato, all who believe old world made new by the tedious and toilsome use of science are disciples of Aristotle. He adds "Where Plato lets the imagination take flight. Aristotle is factual and dull; where Plato is eloquent, Aristotle is exact; where Plato leaps from general concepts to logical conclusions, Aristotle slowly works from multitude of facts; where Plato gives us an ideal commonwealth that is the best which his mind can conceive; Aristotle gives us the material requisite out of which by adopting them to the circumstance, a model state can be constructed."

1. Rule of Law. A great drawback of Plato's philosophy is that it is cut up in two halves. In *The Republic,* he supports the absolute rule of philosopher King unchecked by law or public opinion, but in *'The Laws'* he realised the necessity of laws and public consent grudgingly. Aristotle not only restored law to its proper place but also established sovereignty of the law in the state. He took hint from Plato and said emphasis on law by saying "Man, when perfected is the best of animals but when separated from law and justice, he is worst of all. He believed that the collective wisdom is superior to that of even wisest rule in making of law. He supported law not as a necessary evil but as a mark of good state. Sabine says, "Even the wisest ruler cannot dispense with law because the law has an impersonal quality which no man, however good can attain." The Law is reason unaffected by desire or objective truth.

2. Constitutional Rule. Unlike Plato who believed in the rule of autocratic philosopher King, Aristotle believed in constitutional rule, the constitutional ruler, who rules over willing subjects because he rules through law and constitutional rules and regulations and not by whim or caprice of ruler or rulers. As against a personal or fictional interest it is a rule in the public interest. Thus Aristotle supported constitutional rule. He was correct as historically the rule of despot has been replaced by constitutional rule in the world.

3. Scope of Political Science. Plato confined political science to the narrow limit of ideal state but Aristotle widened the scope of political science by including study of actual states. He held that political science should teach the art of governing and organizing all types of states, good as well as bad. He even discussed how the tyranny may be preserved. He used inductive method in his writings. He defined and described the features of various forms of government. He analysed the cause of their decay and suggested the best way to preserve them. He divorced ethics from politics. According to Aristotle "The complete art of statesman must take government as they are and do the best it can by the means it has. It might even divorce itself from moral considerations altogether and tell the tyrant how to succeed in tyranny." Thus the widening of the definition and scope of political science is Aristotle's profound contribution to the subject. He was the first political scientist to give independent status to political philosophy.

4. Importance of Law. Aristotle puts emphasis on constitutionalism, making law sovereign and governments the servants of law. These conceptions gave inspiration to St. Thomas, Richard Hooker and Burke etc. He coined the main problem of politics as the reconciliation of individual liberty and state authority. Unlike Plato, he laid stress on the value of public opinion. He believed that masses not the experts are better judge, and therefore masses should be the final judge, and not the expert judges or expert bureaucracy. Thus he gave sovereign power to people to whom officers are accountable. He held that the aggregate value and ability of the masses are greater than the wisdom of a handful experts of law or experienced bureaucrats. He favoured a vague sort of democracy. He believed that permanent exclusion of the multitude from all offices is dangerous because it produces widespread discontent. Thus in comparison to Plato, Aristotle gave more rights to common people.

5. Value of Democracy. Aristotle hated democracy though he possessed keen insight even about democratic set-up. If he opposed democracy, he was a greater democrat than the modern democrats, who pay lip service to democracy and wield powers of cruelty, despotism and utter neglect of general public in the name of democracy. According to Aristotle, democracy is that form of government in which the poor who constitute the majority are supreme. It may be also defined as the policy based on the principles of civil equality and freedom. Aristotle supported elections to be conducted on the basis of adult suffrage or by lot or rotation without any proper qualification. The tenure of office remains of short duration in democracy so that all may get opportunity to share them. Thus while Plato believed in philosopher king, Aristotle gave final power to citizens.

6. Division of Power. According to Aristotle deliberative assembly, judicial hierarchy and magistracy are the organs of the government which lead to similar conceptions of executive, legislative and judicial organs. Montesquieu is indebted to Aristotle for his theory of separation of powers. Aristotle conceived the conflict of exploiter and exploited, haves and have nots which was developed later on by Karl Marx. His classification of governments and the discrimination between the various forms of oligarchy and democracy rests on economic background. He maintained that prosperity and stability are secured easily in a state where extreme wealth on one side and appalling poverty on the other side did not exist while a strong middle class exists which avoids extreme paths and follow the path of golden mean.

Practical Wisdom of Aristotle

Aristotle's conception of forms of government is sound and even applicable today. His conception of revolution shows his clear insight and minute observation. He was in a sense the forerunner of Marx in conceiving that conflicts are produced due to economic causes. He pleaded that the main cause of revolution is inequality and perverted ideas of justice. He tells us in detail about the causes of revolution and also suggests remedies, by which these may be prevented. Thus he was probably a forerunner of Machiavell. His thought exerted a profound influence on medieval political thought. According to Dunning, "The capital significance of Aristotle in the history of political theories, lies in the fact that he gave to politics the character of independent science, which he achieved by separating politics from ethics which were blended in Plato's thought." Foster says, "There is probably no parallel in the history of mankind either to the vastness of his intellectual achievement or to the extent of subsequent influence."

ARISTOTLE'S DEBT TO PLATO

Aristotle never missed an opportunity to criticise his master. He was more conscious of his differences than of the points of agreement with him. These differences, however, should not blind any one to discern the indebtedness of Aristotle to Plato. Understandably his keen intellect did not allow him to be a blind follower of Plato and to accept what the master taught him. However, he made the master's teachings the basis of his own thinking. He developed them along the lines determined by his earlier biological studies and scientific temperament. As Will Durant puts it, to Aristotle, 'dear is Plato but dearer still is truth.' Foster pointed out that Aristotle was the greatest of all Platonists, that he was, 'permeated by Platonism to a degree in which perhaps no great philosopher besides him has been permeated by the thought of another." To quote Wayfer, "In spite of Aristotle's criticism, usually niggling though occasionally trenchant, of Plato, the difference between them is more formal than real." In the words of C.E.M. Joad, "Aristotle has a habit of starting avowedly from positions which are anti-thesis of those of Plato, yet ending in conclusions which are scarcely if at all distinguishable from that of his predecessor." Dunning says about Aristotle's relation with Plato, "He differs from his master Plato, much more in the form and method than in the substance of his thought. Most of the ideas which seem characteristically Aristotelian are to be found in Plato. But Platonic expression of them is generally in the form of a suggestion or allusion or illustration; while in Aristotle they appear as definite, clear-cut dogmas, bearing an unmistakable relation to the general system of scientific doctrine. This contrast is rooted in the respective intellectual peculiarities of the two philosophers."

Similarities in Plato and Aristotle

Aristotle had similarity with Plato. He remained the chief disciple of Plato for 20 years at the Plato's Academy. He was to head the Academy after Plato's death but Spensippus became its director and Aristotle could not succeed. According to Sabine, "Every page of his (Aristotle) later philosophical writings bears witness to this connection." The following similarities may be seen in Plato and Aristotle.

1. Inheritance of the Legacies. Both Plato and Aristotle commonly inherited the legacies of Homer to Socrates. In the words of Foster, "Both of them looked with alarm on the instability of Greek political life and on the moral anarchy which they believed to be its cause; and both accordingly believed that the antidote lay in education for a better way of living. Both believed that the good life could only be lived in a city state of moderate size, could not be attained by all men, but only by those who have sufficient means and schooling to do so. Both therefore wished to limit citizenship so as to make this possible, and both thought it right that manual labour should be done by slaves or by non-citizens.''

2. Political Ideal. Aristotle's political ideal was quite at one with Plato's ideal. It was setting up an ethical purpose as the chief end of the state. The real purpose of state was the moral improvement of its citizens, because the state was an association of men living together to achieve the best possible life. This was the meaning of a state. The state alone was self-sufficing in the sense that it alone provided all the conditions within which the highest type of moral development would take place.

3. Conservatism. Aristotle, like Plato, was conservative. He also confined his ideal to the city state as the basis of his political thought.

4. Athenians. Both were Athenians but under the influence of Sparta they protected oligarchical character of society.

5. Early Education. Both were of the view that education should begin when a child is conceived.

6. Control of Population. Both laid stress on check of population by birth control and destruction of unhealthy children.

7. Metaphysical. Both were metaphysical in so far as they said that nature has made some men of gold, others of silver and copper.

8. State as Moral and Spiritual Entity. Both regarded the state as a moral and spiritual entity as they believed that 'Good' is the ultimate end of the state. In the case of Plato, it is absolute and in the case of Aristotle, it is relative.

9. Ethics and Politics. Both hold that Ethics and Politics constitute a single and indivisible science. Their political thoughts were ethical in character. Both believed that the only life which is worthy of man was a life of virtue. It is made possible for an individual in and through membership of the state. Aristotle agreed with Plato against the Sophists that the state comes into being for the sake of life and continues for the sake of good life.

10. Unity. Both aimed at unity, but their methods differed.

11. State and Society. Both equated state and society and gave no right to man against the state.

12. Against Trade, Industry and Usury. Both were against trade and industry and usury.

13. Political Ideals. Plato was firm to his ideal to the end. Aristotle borrowed ideals from Plato but as modified and tested according to practical experience. That is why Plato is known as idealist and Aristotle as realist. All the same, according to Barker, Aristotle borrowed many points to the extent of verbal copying. He gave equal importance to women as Plato did. He attacked Plato's ideal state and not his sub-ideal state. Aristotle's Ideal state is considered Plato's second best state.

14. Place and Importance of Education in the Ideal State. Aristotle was a genuine Platonist in so far as he believed that the greatest need of the times was the proper education of the rulers. To Plato education was the instrument through which the ideal state could be realised. To Aristotle even though education is not the medium, it occupies a prominent place in his best average state. He discussed at length about the place and importance of education in his best practicable state. Unfortunately, it was not carried to its logical conclusion, due to his death.

15. The Laws. In constructing his ideal state Aristotle considerably depended on *The Laws* of Plato. In his '*The Laws*' Plato stated that when men are without laws they differ not at all from the most savage beast. To quote Aristotle, "Man, when perfected is the best of animals, but when separated from law and justice he is worst of all." This is almost verbal copying. Plato said that as it was not possible to procure philosopher guardians, law must be made sovereign. Aristotle also made the law sovereign in his state. Again, Aristotle borrowed the origin of state from Plato who stated in *The Laws* that first there were isolated families, then villages, and then came the state. The requirements of Aristotle's ideal state, like the specifications regarding population, its character, size, situation and nature were derived from *The Laws.* Though, his Ideal state differs greatly from the Ideal State of *The Republic* but it resembles as good ideal the sub-ideal state of *The Laws.* In other words, Aristotle's best is Plato's second best. While introducing the best state Aristotle's remarks were inspired by Plato's discussion on the physical, economic and social factors which govern the nature of state. Grote recognises that Aristotle's best state, where it deviates from that of *The Republic,* largely copies Plato's *The Laws.*

16. Golden Mean. Plato argued that excess is dangerous. Aristotle was considered one of the greatest exponents of the golden mean in politics.

17. Nature of State. For both, Plato and Aristotle, man is a political animal and can only fulfil himself in the state. The classification of the state by Aristotle is almost similar to that of Plato. The name of the classified states are the same even though the methods are different. For both the state and the individual are complementary but not contradictory.

18. Aristocratic Temper. In both, Plato and Aristotle, there is a kind of aristocratic temper. Plato with his philosopher guardians and Aristotle with his limited citizenship exhibited aristocratic temper.

19. Debt to Republic. In the words of G. Grote, "The organisations of government posed by Aristotle in the two last Books of his Politics, as representing his own ideas of something like perfection, is evidently founded upon *The Republic* of Plato, from whom he differs in the important circumstances of not admitting either community of property or community of wives and children. Each of the philosophers recognises one separate class of inhabitants, relieved from all private toil and all money getting employment, and constituting exclusively the citizens of the commonwealth. This small class in fact the city, the commonwealth, the remaining inhabitants, are not a part of common wealth, they are only appendages to it, indispensable indeed, but still appendages in the same manner as always are kept."

20. Theory of Slavery. Aristotle grudgingly followed his great teacher as closely as his temperament would permit. He endorsed and systematised Plato's rationalistic theory of slaves. He slightly mitigated Plato's theory of slavery in some minor points and duly censored his teacher for being too harsh.

21. Best State. Aristotle's best state was a compromise between three things: a romantic Platonic aristocracy; a sound and balanced feudalism; and some democratic ideas but feudalism was the best of it. With the democratic ideal Aristotle pleaded that all citizens should have the right to participate in the government. But, this of course, was not meant to be as radical as it sounds. He explained that not only slaves but all members of the producing classes may be excluded from citizenship. Thus, with Plato, Aristotle maintained that the working class must not rule and the ruling class must not produce. It is in the same vein that he repeatedly insisted that "the first principle of all action is leisure."

It is said that Aristotle made a profession of Platonic philosophy. He only systematised Platonism. Zeller said that Aristotle "can inspire us in the same way as Plato does. His work is direct, more professional than Plato's has been." It is true to say that "in fundamentals of his political philosophy, Aristotle was a faithful disciple of Plato." To conclude in the words of C.E.M. Joad, "In the end he (Aristotle) is found to have done little more than dot the i's and cross the t's of the propositions already reached by Plato."

FATHER OF POLITICAL SCIENCE

In comparison with the radical and abstract nature of Plato's philosophy the political philosophy of Aristotle is empirical and descriptive. In spite of many repetitions and certain inconsistencies the central theme of Aristotle's *Politics* is balance or moderation. Catlin remarked that, "After Confucious, Aristotle is the supreme apostle of common sense and the Golden mean." The confusions on digressions of Aristotle were responsible for opening new chapters in political science. Aristotle aimed at the reconciliation of ideals and actualities. In doing so he dealt with most of modern problems. He deviated a long way from Plato, but for this very reason he widened the scope of political science.

1. Father of the Study of Comparative Government. Aristotle's theories were based on a detailed knowledge of the past history and on a reliance on the teachings of experience in history. He condoned Plato for paying insufficient attention to history and creating schemes of Government without due preference either to the nature of human, animal or actual form of government. According to Sabine, the true romance of the Republic is the romance of a free intelligence, unbound by custom and untrammelled by facts. But Aristotle had a great love for facts because of his biological training and scientific studies, which made him a careful and systematic observer. He had an extraordinary knowledge of the political institutions before he wrote his *'Politics.'* Political studies thus became empirical or inductive in his hands. He may, therefore, legitimately be called the father of the study of comparative government. His great achievement was his new method of first knowing the constitutional history and then arriving at general conclusions. To Sabine Aristotle is the founder of the "historical method which has been on the whole the soundest and the most fruitful that the study of politics has evolved." In the words of Karl Frederick, "He (Aristotle) was the first man in the world's literature who applied a deeply inductive (experimental or comparative) method to the diverse phenomenon of the state."

2. Return to Actuals : Ethics and Politics. Besides attaching great importance to collection of facts, Aristotle stressed the problem of values and importance of ethical judgements. He judged the significance of the facts in terms of the end or purpose of the state. Politics was to him, the culmination of ethics. He was the first realist as against idealism of Plato. While Plato raved in the imaginary world of idealism, Aristotle dealt with the reforming of actuals. That is why Plato could not be honoured with the title of "Father of Political Science." It has been bestowed upon Aristotle, "It was his great regard for facts which prevented Aristotle from being radical; he could not be anything more than a reformist. A person who attaches great importance to the accumulated wisdom of past cannot become a revolutionary. The whole bent and bias of his mind led Aristotle to believe that in order to be effective an ideal must not go against the actual state of affairs."

3. Empirical and Descriptive. Aristotle never completed his ideal state for which he gave introduction in his Book III. It is because of the reasons that these ideals were sunk in the mid stream of realities. According to Sabine, "What all he wrote was a book not on an Ideal state, but on the ideals of state." This is due to the reason that he was more empirical and descriptive. He did not have the bold sweep and courage of Plato to destroy all that stood in his way. He was more cautious and moderate. He was more of a reformatory than revolutionary. What he did was to bring the ideal of Plato down to earth. Accepting Plato's general view of proportion and harmony, Aristotle adopted it to the practical politics of the city state. This new line, this revolt on Plato was fruitful in the sense that it opened new world in political science.

4. Plato v/s Aristotle. Pointing out the difference between Plato and Aristotle, Maxey said, "As Plato is father to idealists, romanticists, revolutionists and utopians of political philosophy, so Aristotle is father to the realists, scientists, pragmatists and utilitarians. All who believe in new worlds for old are disciples of Plato, all who believe in old worlds made new by the tedious and toilsome use of science are disciples of Aristotle." Again, "Where Plato lets his imagination take flight, Aristotle is factual and full; where Plato is eloquent, Aristotle is exact; where Plato leaps from general concepts to logical conclusions, Aristotle slowly works from multitude of facts; where Plato gives us an ideal commonwealth that is the best his mind can conceive, Aristotle gives us the material requisites out of which, by adopting them to the circumstances, a modern state can be constructed."

5. Value of Laws. The chief defect of Plato's political philosophy was that it was cut up into two incompatible halves. His ideal state of *'The Republic'* had absolute rule of the philosopher-king, untrammelled by law or consent of the people. But his second best state of *"The Laws"* gave importance to laws and public consent. This he did grudgingly. Therefore, he was not able to restore law properly. It required complete revision of the psychology and the theory of knowledge underlying *'The Republic'* Aristotle took up the hint and the direction suggested by Plato. He restored law to its proper place. He established sovereignty of law in the state. *The Laws* made him regard law not as make shift but as an indispensable condition of a moral and civilised life. An introductory passage in Aristotle's *Politics* was written with one of Plato's remarkable utterances in his mind: "Man, when perfected, is the best of animals but when separated from law and justice, he is the worst of all." Aristotle believed that in the making of law, the collective wisdom of people is superior to that of even the wisest ruler. He regarded supremacy of law as a mark of good state and not merely as an unfortunate necessity. In the words of Sabine, "Even the wise ruler cannot dispense with law because the law has an impersonal quality which no man, however good, can attain." The law is "reason unaffected by desire."

6. Constitutional Rule. Due to his regard for law, Aristotle laid emphasis on constitutional rule. It was to him, consistent with the dignity of the subject, whereas a personal or despotic rule was not. According to Aristotle, the constitutional ruler rules over willing subjects. He rules by consent. Constitutional rule is the rule in the public interest as against a fictional or personal interest. It is a lawful rule in the sense that the government is carried on by general regulations and not by arbitrary decrees.

7. Study of Actual States. Aristotle did not like to confine the scope of political science to the construction of the ideal state as it was for Plato. Aristotle wanted that political science should be widened to include a study of the actual states also. Political Science should teach the art of governing and organising all types of states, good as well as bad. Aristotle discussed how even tyrannies may be preserved. He did not use the deductive method of Plato but used descriptive or inductive method while dealing with the actual states. He defined and described the features of various forms of government. He gave the cause of their decay and the best ways to preserve them.

8. Ethics and Politics. Aristotle divorced politics from ethics and thereby seemed to be most modern. The middle portion of his *'Politics'* is entirely empirical and moral considerations are put aside. At places his treatment is almost Machiavellian. However, he did not reject the ethical purpose of the state. He retained the basic ideal derived from Plato. He went farther than his master, and in so doing he introduced fundamental modifications. Besides the moral end of the state, he included in his new and more general science of politics, an empirical study of elements of state, both political and social, of actual constitutions, their combination, and the consequences which are bound to follow from these combinations. In the words of Sabine, according to Aristotle,

"The complete art of the statesman must take governments as they are and to the best it can with the means it has. It might even divorce itself from moral considerations altogether and tell the tyrant how to succeed in tyranny." This widening of the definition and conception of political science is Aristotle's profound contribution to the subject.

9. Definition of Political Constitution. Aristotle defined a constitution as an arrangement of citizens. It is the expression of the kind of life which the state is designed to foster. A change in the form of government would signify a change in the constitution or the underlying kind of life that the citizens are trying to realise. Aristotle was shrewd enough to observe that a political constitution is one thing and the way it works is a different thing. A given form of government would work in a very different way if a new social class acquires ascendency. Aristotle did not fail to notice that the political structure of a state depends upon the social and economic structure of society. He recognised the importance of economic influences as well as of geographical conditions on political organisation and activity. The character of a constitution and its actual working depends upon the way in which the three elements of the state deliberative, judicial organs and magistracy are constituted.

10. Profound Political Generalisations. Aristotle's works contain many profound generalisations which may be applied to political life in all times and climes. For instance, 'Man is a political man' and 'state came into being for the sake of life, it continues for the sake of good life.' The themes underlying the thought of Plato, Aristotle gave them their classical expression. To him, the purpose of the state was not to extend its dominion or enrich its people, but to widen knowledge, promote virtue and ability of the mass. This led him to favour a vague sort of democracy. He gave ultimate sovereign power to the mass of citizens though the actual reigns of government would be in the hands of the best citizens only. He warned that permanent exclusion of the multitude from all offices is dangerous because it produces widespread discontent.

11. Definition of Democracy. Aristotle did not agree with the current definition of democracy as the form of government in which the masses are supreme. According to him, democracy is that form of government in which the poor, who constitute the majority, are supreme. It may be defined as the polity based on the principles of civic equality and freedom. To be equal the citizens must all have an equal right to share in the work of government. All the citizens must all have an equal right to share in the work of government. All the citizens are rulers as well as the ruled. Elections to various offices should be based on universal suffrage and should be conducted by lot or rotation. Elections should have no property qualification or only nominal one. The tenure of offices should be short in order that all may be able to share them.

12. Three Organs of Government. Aristotle guided the modern political science in analysing the governmental power into three organs — executive, legislative and judicial. However, his three demands of government deliberative, magistracy and judicial organ cannot be completely identified with them. In his theory of separation of powers, Montesquieu drew a lot of inspiration from Aristotle.

13. Inter-relation of Politics and Economics. Aristotle's remarkable political insight is also shown by his realisation of the inter-relation between politics and economics. He clearly explained the conflict between haves and have-nots. His classifications of government and the distinctions between the various types of oligarchy and democracy ultimately relied on economic issues. He went on to show that stability and prosperity are secured easily in a state where there are no extremes of wealth and poverty and a strong middle class exists.

14. Foundation of Political Science. Aristotle's forms of government are sound. These are applicable even today. He was fully aware of the importance of economic element in producing conflicts. Perverted ideas of justice and inequality also cause revolutions. He gave a number of causes of revolution and also suggested remedies as to how the revolutions may be prevented. He influenced *'The Prince'* of Machiavelli. His *Politics* exerted a profound influence on the thought of the Middle Ages and that of Christendom. Dante called him the 'master of them that know.' In the words of Dunning, "The capital significance of Aristotle, in the history of political theories, lies in the fact that he gave to politics the character of independent science." It was accomplished by him by the disentanglement of political from ethical conceptions, whereas the two were completely blended in Plato's Thought. His doctrine of the golden means was precursor of the modern notion of political checks and balances. His good common sense and golden means led him to refute Platonic communism. His political philosophy was more individualistic than that of Plato. As such he may be said to be the father of modern Individualism as well as the modern theory of popular sovereignty. According to Karl Frederick, "Aristotle is the founder of Logic, of Political Science and of system of scholastic." He has been of service to conservatives and aristocrats of egalitarian democracy, to the historical and later to the sociological school. While Plato soared in the heights of the ideal, Aristotle's objective was not the ideally best but the best attainable. Aristotle laid the foundations of real political science by his keen and practical political insight and systematic treatment of the subject.

STATE AS NATURAL

Aristotle said, "Man is a political animal, destined by nature for political life." This implies that "The state is a creation of nature and man is by nature a political man. And he who by nature and not by mere accident is without a state, is either above humanity, or below it." The solitary man is either a beast or a god, state is a natural institution and not a conventional institution as the sophists supposed or as enunciated by the social contract theory. Surprisingly enough, contractualists like Hobbes, Locke and Rousseau, totally forgot Aristotle's natural origin of state while dealing with the controversy about its origin.

1. Origin in Gregariousness. Aristotle traced the origin of state to the gregarious instinct of man. Man cannot live alone. That is why when one is to be given punishment he is made to live all alone. Being a social animal, it is man's nature to associate himself with his fellow men and form associations. The state is one of such associations. It is as natural to man as the family or clan. It is as natural as water to a fish. It is the medium without which human faculties can never come to their full compass.

2. For the Sake of Life. The naturalness of state is clear from the fact that it came into being for the bare needs of life and it continues for the sake of good life. According to Aristotle man cannot realise the destiny of his life without the state. The state to him, is an association of unlike persons who, by nature, associate together to satisfy their common social and economic needs, desires and racial instinct by mutual exchange of goods and services.

3. Logical Development of Family. The association of male and female for the perpetuation of the race, and of master and slave for the production of subsistence, give rise to family or household, which has its social or moral use. This stands as long as men are not satisfied with a bare existence and the satisfaction of their elementary wants. Urged by their nature to seek a fuller life, households are compelled to combine together into a village for the better satisfaction of their wants and then into a city or polish or state, of such size and nature as to be self-sufficing. Thus, the state stands at the top of the pyramid which springs from families and villages. It is a logical development of family. The institution of family is the first foundation of the state. It is not a deliberate human creation. It fosters human growth. It is hereby that man begins to learn the virtues of civil life, thus the sources of social and political life are found in family. It is in the family that the three elements essential to the building of a state spring up, viz., fellowship, political organization and justice. As the state is the logical end or development of the family, it is equally natural. It should foster the development of the individual which starts in the family but is achieved partially in it. If this full development of man were possible in family or a village, the process of forming associations would not have proceeded further.

4. Perfect form of Association. According to Aristotle, self-sufficiency can be attained only in the state. It is the culmination of widening circles of human association based on human wants. It is not merely an economic association but also a moral community. It is the perfect form of association. Man is naturally a political animal. He can attain the true end for which he is made.

5. Moral Self-Sufficiency. According to Plato and Aristotle, self-sufficiency reached in city-state, does not mean economic self-sufficiency. It cannot be achieved even by a big state of the present day. The state provided all the conditions and the environment necessary for the moral development of the individual. To quote Foster, "The lower forms of society, the village, or example, prove inadequate not only because they do not supply the needs of man's animal nature, but also because they do not adequately supply the needs of his rational nature. These latter can be supplied only in a political, as distinct, for example, from a purely economic society."

6. Natural Destination. Thus, man is a political animal because his natural destination is the state. Man would be a brute without social life. Most animals are gregarious, but man alone is political. What makes him political or rational being, distinguished from the lower form of animal life, is his faculty of speech and organised association with his fellows. It enables him to distinguish between good and bad, between the just and the unjust and associate himself with his fellows in the pursuit of good life. This human faculty of speech also suggests the naturalness of the state.

Aristotle said, "The state is a natural association for it develops organically from the most primitive but natural associations, i.e. the household and the village. It is the end of them and is, therefore, a creation of nature. It is necessary for man who is by nature a social or political animal. Man fully develops his personality only in the state, of which he is a natural, integral and organic part. The individual is to the state as a part is to the whole." Membership of the state is the end or destiny of human life. Man finds true meaning and significance of his life only in and through relation to the state, without which he would decay and die.

7. Association of Associations. To Aristotle, the state is not an association of isolated individuals, but an association of individuals already united as members of smaller groups. It is an association of associations. Unlike Plato, Aristotle preserved the family and village in the state. He described the state as a union of families and villages for a happy and self-sufficing life. State is the supreme association as it is the highest of all and embraces all the other associations. State is the highest form of association, because it aims at the highest good which is the good life of the citizens. Thus for Aristotle the state is the final, perfect and natural association originating in the bare needs of life. It continues to exist for the sake of complete life. Complete life does not mean fulfilling merely earthly purposes. It continues to exist for the sake of complete life. Complete life does not mean fulfilling merely earthly purposes. It also aims at ethical and intellectual objective. Therefore, the final goal of human life is the spiritual enrichment. For this the state provides much greater field than the family and the village.

8. Community of Good Life. An association, therefore the state implies not merely being together but living together for something higher than mere existence. It is not an insurance against mere insecurity of life and property. It is a community of good life. It is biologically a superior association embracing all other lower forms of associations. It is the whole, of which associations and individuals are parts. The whole is prior to the parts. It is the whole which lends significance to the parts. While in the order of time the state is preceded by the family or household and village, in the order of thought, it is prior to both. It thus precedes the individual. Only in the state can the human being rise above the brute and become a man. When isolated man is not self-sufficient, independent or perfect. It is the state alone that man finds the perfection of life. This is so because the state alone can secure social peace and order and provide diversity of interests necessary for complete and good life. The state is natural in the sense that it is an institution for that moral perfection of man to which his whole nature of imminent impulse drives through various forms of society.

9. Abiding Place in Scheme of Things. The state is natural, not because it is independent of human volition but because it has its abiding place in the scheme of things. All the other associations attain their full perfection only in the state. They are incapable of separate and self-contained existence. To quote Aristotle, "Men live social and political life, not by choice but because of their inherent natures, their needs and desires and weakness and strength make them to do so. Unequal and non-uniform natural endowments, intellectual, moral and physical, compel associates, and therefore, a social and political life. Societies and state were necessary for the well being of men and were therefore, as much a product of Nature as man himself."

10. Organic Theory of State. The state is an organism, according to Aristotle. Like an organism it is composed of diverse parts interdependent on each other. They share in full the life of the organism and live because of the relation to the whole. Aristotle drew a close analogy between human organism and the state. It is not possible to understand the rights and duties of man apart from his relation to the state. However, Aristotle's organic conception of the state does not regard the state as a super-being, distinct from and above the citizens as enunciated by Hegel. Aristotle did not believe in absolutism, although state and society were the same thing for him. To him, the state was prior to man. He said, "The state has no end other than the promotion of the happy or virtuous life of the citizens....It is necessary for the development of human personality but has no independent purpose of its own."

11. Aims at Highest Good. Every association aims at some good. The state, the highest of all associations, however, aims at the highest good. The functions of the state are implied in Aristotle's definition of the state as the union of families and villages in a perfect and self-sufficing life, by which we mean a happy and honourable life." They can also be deducted from Aristotle's oft quoted statement that "the state came into being for the sake of life, but continued for the sake of good life." Aristotle did not limit the scope of state activity to mere exchange of services. The state is there to ensure a complete and virtuous life.

12. Functions of the State. The purpose of the state is not only to extend its dominion or enrich its people, but to widen knowledge, promote virtue and to secure justice to all. It has a positive function of promoting good life and not merely restraining or curbing the vicious tendencies of its members. Thus Aristotle went beyond the modem writer Green, who described the function of state simply to remove hindrances to good life, but not to make men good.

13. Identity of Individual and State. Life Plato, Aristotle found a close identity between the individual and the state. Like an individual, the state must show the virtues of courage, self-control and justice. The virtues of the state and the individual are the same. Both try to attain positive good and happiness, internal and external, which can be done, among other things, by conforming to moral law.

14. Difference between the Family and the State. Since the state originated historically from the household, Aristotle examined the nature of difference between the two natural institutions. As against Plato, who said that a small state and a large household are identical, Aristotle opined that the two institutions do not differ in degree but in kind. He abolished private family and property in order to make the state a large family. According to Aristotle, "There is only one kind of relationship, that of the ruler and the ruled; but in the household there are three different relations, viz. those of husband and wife, parents and children, and master and slave. The relations of the ruler of a state to each of the citizens is the same. But the head of the family stands in the three different relations to the wife, the children and the slaves." While the household fulfils their physical needs, the state fulfils the intellectual and moral needs of citizens.

ARISTOLE'S MAGNUM OPUS 'THE POLITICS'

Aristotle was a versatile genius. His knowledge was encyclopaedic. He wrote on ethics and metaphysics, art and poetry, economics and politics, physics and mechanics, physiology and medicine, astronomy and logic. He has been called "philosopher" of the ages. He is the father of realism. His most famous work, '*The Politics*' is a classical statement of Greek political thought. It is a justification of existing institutions like the state, slavery and family. It is meant to suggest remedies for the ill of the body politics of the city-state. Aristotle's political thought is ground mainly in this book.

Aims and Objectives

Plato was imaginative and poetic. He reasoned deductively from abstract philosophical conceptions of justice and virtue. On the other hand, as Gettle has pointed out, Aristotle was practical, logical and systematic. He reasoned inductively from a comparative and scientific study of the governmental systems that were actually in existence. His discussions, based on history and observations, are clear and precise with relatively little poetic or allegorical 'embellishment.' Aristotle's *'Ethics'* discussed the nature of individual happiness. In '*The Politics*', which is intimately connected with his *'Ethics'* Aristotle treated of the state as one of the chief means through which an individual attains the happiness. Thus, the object of Aristotle's *'The Politics', is* both practical and speculative, i.e. to explain the nature of the best state in which the end of happiness may be best realised.

Work of Master Intellect

In the words of John Bowle, "Aristotle, besides being a shrewd judge of character and situations is the greatest of early scientists. "*The Politics* was only a small part of this writings. Scientific interests overshadowed his ethical and political thought. Aristotle immensely powerful, classifying, assimilative mind broke away from the clear cut geometrical pattern of '*The Republic*' and *'The Laws'. The Politics is* a different book. It is a quarry of arguments and profound definitions, the thought behind them becoming apparent as the argument proceeds. The philosophical premises of *The Politics* were similar to that of Plato. Aristotle, however, did not argue about them. Plato was set on constructing a planned state in the light of assumed principles and often aside practical objections. Aristotle constantly tested his hypothesis by the tacts. *'The Politics'*, was the work of a mind of immense power, with enormous reserves. Aristotle, however, had little consideration for the reader. He followed his own thought for his own satisfaction without much regard for his audience. In *'The Politics'* sometimes there seems a staggering callousness and lack of imagination; at others a penetrating insight; and there is ironical humour and biting understatement. "The book is the work of a master intellect, not over touched with pity, drawing on great erudition."

Contradictory Opinions

To John Bowle, *'The Politics' is* an incomplete work. It is a heap of arguments and theories, sometimes repeated or left unfinished. Scholars have expressed almost contradictory opinions about its worth. Dr. Zeller euologizes *'The Politics'* as the richest treasure that has come down to us from antiquity, the greatest contribution to political philosophy that we possess. On the other hand, Dr. Taylor holds that no work of Aristotle is quite so commonplace in its handling of so vast a subject.

Unfinished Work

These contradictory remarks about *'The Politics'* are because of the fact that it is an unfinished work. It contains frequent repetitions, omissions contradictions, obscurities, inaccuracies and inconsistencies. If at one place reference is made to a topic as it has been discussed earlier without its having been touched at all, at other places references are made to what is discussed at later stages. Sometimes there are abrupt changes in the discussion of topics in the book as a whole. The only explanation for these defects is that *'The Politics'* as it is, is an incomplete book. It appears to be the result of either notes taken down by Aristotle's pupils or rough notes prepared by Aristotle himself for lectures delivered at different times and put together in the form of a book at a later date. It is because of the reason probably that Aristotle did not find time to give finishing touches to his book. One does not get the polish, form and beauty of Plato's classic, *'The Republic'*. However, in spite of the rugged nature of this book its central theme is balance or moderation. Hence the remark of Catlin that "After Confucius, Aristotle is the supreme apostle of common sense and the Golden Mean". Moreover, the confusion of Aristotle is responsible for opening new chapters in political science and giving to politics the character of an independent science. The main theme of Aristotle is to reconcile ideals and actualities. Naturally, this attempt gives us a hazy picture.

Treatise on the Art of Government

Aristotle's *'The Politics'* is of great help to constitution makers and legislators. It provides rules to construct best possible politics for securing happiness or a life of complete virtue. It is not a systematic study of political philosophy. It is rather a treatise on the art of government. In it, Aristotle analysed the evils that were prevalent in the Greek cities and the defects in their political systems. He gave practical suggestions as to the best way to avoid the threatening dangers. The general nature of his political thought may be inferred from the point of view of the work as a whole and from the rational principles underlying his political advice. The subject of Aristotle was not so much the ideal state but the ideals of the state.

Subject Matter of the Politics

What was the original arrangement of the book, *'The Politics'* is not known. Traditionally, the eight books can be roughly divided into three groups. According to Barker, these differ from each other in matter as well as treatment.

(i) *Common Foundations.* The First group consisting of Books, I, II and III can be taken to be the common foundation from two different constructions independent of each other.

(ii) *Principles of Best State.* The Second group containing Books VII and VIII deals with the principles underlying the best state, which may be supposed to be the first construction. Aristotle's treatment of the subject here is idealistic like Plato. His Ideal state described therein resemble the sub-ideal state of Plato as portrayed in *'The Laws'.*

(iii) *Analysis of Constitution.* The Third group of Books IV, V and VI constitutes the second construction. Here Aristotle explained the nature of constitutions, their distinctions and the changes required. In this section, he left aside ideals and dealt with the actual. His approach was quite empirical. He criticised Plato here.

Two Main Divisions

Some critics like Jaegar would divide *'The Politics'* into two main divisions instead of three. According to them, *'The Politics'* was written in two stages, according to the development of Aristotle's political thought.

(i) *Theories of Ideal state.* The first stage, consisting of Books II, III, VII and VIII, covers the works dealing with the Ideal state and with previous theories of it together with criticism of Plato. It seems to have been written long after Aristotle's departure from Athens after Plato's death.

(ii) *Study of Actual States.* The second stage, covered by Books I, IV, V and VI, relates to the work dealing with a study of actual states, mainly democracies and oligarchies. It discusses causes of their decay and finds out means of their stability. This portion seems to have been inserted in the middle of the original draft in order to give it the shape of general treatise on political science. According to this arrangement, Book I, was written last. It constitutes a general introduction to the treatise as a whole. The first stage of Aristotle's thought, as given above indicates the influence of Plato's idealism. Here he constructs the Ideal state, on the lines of Plato's *'The Laws'.* In the second stage, Aristotle seems to have emancipated himself from composition of *'The*

Politics' extended over about 15 years. From being originally an ethical treatise, it became a detailed and scientific appreciation of the political facts. For want of revision by Aristotle, the result is confusion produced by the desire to unite together into one whole two independent parts differing from each other in their subject matter, tone and purpose, dealing with ethics and politics.

CONTENTS OF 'THE POLITICS'

1. Book I. The general introduction in *The Book I* opens with an inquiry into the nature of the state. To quote Aristotle, "Since men aim at the good, the state, which is the highest form of community, aims at the highest good." Biologically and economically, Aristotle traced the origin of the politics and gave his profound definition that man is a political animal. The solitary man is either a beast or a god. By the gift of speech and sense of moral values man is distinguished from the other animals. The state is natural to man. In the words of Aristotle, 'For man when perfected, is the best of animals; but when separated from law and justice he is the worst of all, since armed injustice is the most dangerous; and is equipped at birth with the arms of intelligence and wit, moral qualities which he may use for the worst ends." "The principle of order", continues Aristotle, "in political society is justice, the bond of men is state." By justice, Aristotle meant a far reaching principle of harmonious balance. He also examined the structure of the household, the question of property and the natural position of a slave, whom he defined as one "by nature not his own, but another's human being, also a possession". Being the child of his times, Aristotle took slavery for granted. In dealing with the subjects of household and their management, he raised the question of the relations between husbands, wifes and children. He touched on the importance of education. He discussed at length the subject of property and money making, legitimate and otherwise. He strongly objected to usury as unnatural.

2. Book II : Discussion of the Ideal State. *Book II* begins with Aristotle's discussion of the Ideal state. It is mainly concerned with a criticism of Plato's *'The Republic'*. The two challenging Platonic ideals of community of property and of women are discussed and refuted here. To quote Aristotle, "The principle of reciprocity is the salvation of state". He admonished that not suppression but reform of private property is necessary. He advised that not only property but also passions should be regulated. This is still valid in all our modern disputes. Property is essential so that men should perform their duties well. Aristotle pointed many difficulties in the community of wifes and children. He said that by this affection would become watery and morale low. In his view, family is to be esteemed for its development of that natural affection from which wider devotion might stem. Aristotle maintained that the guardians in Plato's Ideal state would probably quarrel. "And if the guardians are not happy, who are?" Aristotle maintained that personal attachment alone will make men develop a sociable character. Property should be limited according to the number of children. Aristotle also discussed the subject of crime. He said, "The greatest crimes are caused by excess, not by necessity.'' He also deals with the judicial questions and law courts.

3. Book III: Forms of Government. The third book describes the main forms of constitutions normal as well as perverted. It deals fairly exhaustively with monarchy. Aristotle defined the state and citizenship. He said, ''A state is a body of citizens sufficing for the purpose of life.'' The citizens are those adults and heads of household, who by reason of birth, have a right to take part in the government and the administration of justice. The state is necessary for the achievement of good life. Men are intimately bound up with states. If a state is bad, the man who is a good citizen in it must be a bad man. Not all persons are capable of achieving this end. As women and children have limited and imperfect reasons and the slaves almost entirely lack it, they are incapable of citizenship. Men must be judged on merits and not by birth. According to Aristotle, there are three groups of citizens: slaves by nature, freemen capable of development but deprived of the opportunities thereto; and citizens proper.

Aristotle's classification of states is similar to that of Plato. The governments which aim at the good of the community as a whole are relatively normal. There are: royalty, aristocracy and constitutional governments. Those governments which aim only at the good rulers are perversions. These are: tyranny, oligarchy and democracy. The merits and demerits of these forms of government have been exhaustively discussed by Aristotle. He particularly abhorred democracy as it fails to recognise the importance of human differences. A mob follows demagogues in terms of passion. It lacks statesmanship. Aristotle remarks that for men of pre-eminent virtue there is no law; they are themselves a law. He decided that the best law is preferable due to its being passionless. He said, ''He who bids the law rule may be deemed to bid God and reason alone rule, but he who bids men rule adds the element of the beast, for desire is a wild beast, and passion perverts the minds of rulers, even if they are the best of men.'' This principle is obviously of great importance. It points out the way to a wider conception of law.

4. Book IV : Analysis of Constitutions. Now comes the more concrete analysis of particular constitutions and states. It forms the middle section of *'The Politics'* . It is inserted between the more general discussions contained in the chapters which make up the beginning and ending of the work. Here Aristotle abandoned the discussion of general study of institutions. In Book IVth he remarked, ''Political writers, though they often have excellent idea, are often impractical. We are concerned with what form of government are most tolerable in different conditions and the causes of the ruin and preservation of states.'' Aristotle reviewed forms of government other than monarchy. He dealt not only with main types but also with sub-species and varieties. There are various kinds of democracies and nature of demagogues; aristocracies and politics or constitutional governments which are a fusion between democracy and aristocracy. Aristotle regarded tyranny as the worst form of government. It is the arbitrary rule of an individual who is responsible to no one and governs all alike with a view to his own advantage and not of his subjects, and therefore against their will. In Aristotle' s view, the best kind of constitution should show a preponderance of the middle class interest, "for those who are of the middle condition pass through life safely and are most amenable to reason ." Friendship will be most likely among equals. Large states are more stable than small ones since they contain a larger middling elements.

5. Book V : Causes and Preventions of Revolution. The Fifth book in *'The Politics'* ideals with the causes of revolutions and their preventions. According to Aristotle, inferiors revolt in order that they may be equal, and equals revolt in order that they may be superior. He was fully aware of the importance of economic element in producing conflict. However, he perverted ideas of justice. Inequality causes revolution. Concentration of power creates arrogance in the one group and resentment in others. Election intrigues, disloyal and dishonest officers and an attempt to combine dissimilar elements in a state are the causes of dissentions. The failure to attach due importance to small changes is also dangerous. Oppression of the people and rivalries between demagogues or oligarchies etc. create revolts. According to Aristotle, "The best way to avoid revolution is to preserve a friendly atmosphere and never wrong the ambitions in a matter of honour or the common people in a matter of money." Spirit of reverence for law, both on the part of the rulers and the ruled, and the wisdom of the rulers, who keep on good terms with their subjects are the two methods to avoid revolts. Excuse of external danger will overcome internal dissension. Sound defence against foreign aggressor and unity amongst the ruling group are stability of the government. Polity prevents any one from becoming too strong. There is to be a mean between democracy and oligarchy. The citizens must be educated in the spirit of the constitution. Aristotle also described the time honoured methods of tyrants and how they are overthrown.

6. Book VI : Organisation of Democracies and Oligarchies. The Book VI deals with the Organisation of democracies and oligarchies. According to Aristotle, the best kind of democracy is agriculture, for few farmers want to bear nuisance of office. Mob democracy is the worst but finds many supporters since "most persons would rather live in a disorderly than in a sober manner." Demagogues maintain their power by bribing the electorate. Aristotle discussed the right distribution of offices and the need to audit public accounts.

7. Book VII : Construction and General Principles of the Best State. Book VII is return to the construction and general principles of the best state. It should have been put after Book III. "True happiness is", said Aristotle, "more often found with those who are most highly cultivated in mind and character." The subordination of politics to ethical purpose is apparent here. This book "is one of the wisest achievements of the Greek mind." Laws, aiming at maintenance of power and "warlike pursuits, though generally to be deemed honourable, are not the supreme end of all things, but only a means, and the good law giver should inquire how states may participate in the good life." Aristotle insisted on the small size of the state, for experience showed to him that very large states cannot be very well governed. The state must be self-sufficing; situated near the sea, but not on it and within closed walls. Aristotle advocated common meals in the well ordered city. True happiness depends on right type of education. Education should foster reason and control appetite. Marriage should take place at the age when parents are most likely to have five children. It should be 18 for women and 37 for men. Aristotle advocated birth control by abortion to avoid overpopulation. He said, "Let there be a law that no deformed child shall live."

8. Book VIII: Education. Aristotle prescribed the methods of bringing up of children and proper diet. The Book VIII is mainly concerned with the function of education. After a further enquiry into the principles of education, Aristotle insisted that children should be kept away from any vulgar influence. All paid employments absorb and degrade the mind. Things must be done for their own sake, not to benefit others. Leisure is of the utmost importance. The good man must clearly be an amateur and never a technician. To Aristotle, "To be always seeking after the useful does not become exalted soul." This shows a touch of romanticism and idealising of an aristocratic way of life.

To Aristotle in education habit must come before reason. Therefore, physical training is most important. Children must not be brutalised; that is the Spartan mistake. Courage is found in brave men and not in barbarians or animals. Music plays an important role in building character. Modes and melodies should be employed which are ethical. 'It is evident that our youth should be taught the Dorian music' maintained Aristotle. The VIII chapter ends with the profound observation that education should be based on three principles: "the mean, the possible, the becoming, these three." The 'mean' implies a first balance of faculties, mental and physical, the whole disciplined by a habit of calm and self-control. The 'possible' means two things: (1) no man can achieve what is beyond humanity to win, (2) a man's education and ambition should fit his ability. Finally, the 'becoming' is the result of the achievement of the 'mean' and the 'possible'. "The development of a man's full faculties in the way appropriate to his talent and surroundings, which gives him style and assurance, is the true mark of a right adaptation."

Such, in brief, is the subject matter of Aristotle's *'The Politics'*. Its analysis is profound, the purpose noble, and the setting foreign. All the essential problems have been raised in it. It stated the truth than man is, and must be, a political animal, that the community and the individual are bound together. To conclude, "Where Plato attempts to impose a pattern of events, Aristotle, with an equally strong ethical purpose, wrestles with facts and deduces his principles from them; combines a scientist's respect for the facts with the shrewed judgement of a man of the world; further he has a clear vision of the moral purpose of society, which is to secure the good life."

THEORY OF REVOLUTION

The kaleidoscopic changes in the government of the Greek city-states due to dependence on political life gave food for thought to Aristotle. He was led to devote considerable attention to the subject of revolution. He delved deep into the causes of revolution. He searched for political stability. This made him formulate his views on the remedies to revolutions. In Book V (in some editions Book VII and VIII) of *'The Politics'* Aristotle made a masterly analysis of contemporary political evils. He showed ripe political wisdom and suggested preventives for revolution. His analyses of the causes of revolution were unsurpassed by any subsequent thinker. These are applicable even today to some extent. He may be considered a 'founder of the realistic school of politics.' He was a precursor of trend from monarchy through oligarchy and tyranny to democracy as the result of social and economic changes. He found the main source of fictional contents in the discrepancy between the political ability of the different classes of citizens and the actual authority that they possess.

Empirical and Objective Treatment

Aristotle's treatment of the subject of revolution is the most empirical and full of objectivity. He suggested ways and means as to how the oligarches, democrats and even tyrants may maintain themselves in power and safeguard their empires against revolutionary changes. Here Aristotle comes closer to Machiavelli. Here politics is separated from ethics. This book on revolution can be divided into two parts; Part I deals with advice to oligarches, democrats, aristocrats, monarchs and tyrants on how to keep themselves in power. Part II gives the philosophical basis of good and stable government.

What is Revolution?

What is a revolution according to Aristotle? As different from revolution of the kind of French Revolution or Russian Revolution it is as follows:

1. Change in the Constitution. Revolution to him, means a change in the constitution of the state, whether great or small.

2. Change in Given Group. The constitution may remain unchanged but the political power may change hands.

3. Change in Form of Government. A revolution may make an oligarchy more or less oligarchic or a democracy more or less democratic. As such, the overthrow of oligarchic rule by the democrats or of democratic rule by an oligarchic action is also regarded revolution.

4. Change in Institution or Set of Persons. It has the following characteristics. A revolution could also be directed against any particular institution or set of persons in the state without any change in the form of government.

Thus, for the Greeks every constitutional change was a social and political evolution. According to Sabine the part of *'The Politics'* dealing with the subject of revolution reveals Aristotle's political penetration and mastery of Greek Government.

Causes of Revolution

1. Dis-satisfaction with the Existing State of Affairs. Dis-satisfaction with the existing state of affairs widespread or confined to a small group is the general cause of revolution, according to Aristotle. It is apt to be expressed in violence. It may be suppressed, or it may succeed in overthrowing the existing regime.

2. Source of Revolution. Aristotle is of the opinion that while diagnosing the cause of revolution one must consider (i) the temper of those who make it, (ii) the motive of the revolution, and (iii) the causes and occasions of a revolution. The source of revolution may generally be found in one-sided or perverted notions of justice that men entertain.

3. Inequality. Every form of government has its corresponding idea of justice and public morality. But inequality is the most general cause of revolution. In the words of Aristotle, 'Everywhere inequality is the cause of revolution but an inequality in which there is no proportion, for instance, a perpetual monarchy among equal; and always it is the desire of equality which rises in rebellion.'' Since men crave equality, a feeling of injustice arises among those who see others possessing privileges which they do not share. The proper apportioning of political power is, therefore, fundamental to the security of the state.

4. Types of Equality. The democrats believe that because by nature men are equally free, the masses of citizens should be given absolute equality. The oligarchs hold that because men are unequal in wealth, ability and birth, they should have proportionate equality. This represents the state of mind of the authors of revolutions. In short, all revolutions are ultimately due to the innate desire in the average citizens to have honour, gain, equality of opportunities and rights. Thus the stability of a state is directly proportional to the satisfaction of this craving for equality. Disturbance in the proportionate equality causes revolt. When the balance between oligarchic and democratic elements is tilted it results in revolt. Therefore, to conclude, a mixed form of government is the best containing both oligarchic and democratic elements.

5. Disproportion. Aristotle remarks, "Inferiors revolt in order that they may be equal, and equals that they may be superior.'' Revolutions spring from a disproportionate increase in any part of the state. They are often occasioned by trifles; some are gradual and imperceptible, others sudden. The failure to attach due importance to small changes is also a danger.

6. Concentration of Power. Concentration of power creates arrogance in one group and resentment on the part of others. An attempt to combine dissimilar elements or races in a state is bound to produce instability and perpetual dissention.

7. Carelessness in Public Appointments. Carelessness in admitting disloyal and dishonest persons to offices in the state, who start oppression of people also creates dissatisfaction.

8. Psychological Causes. (i) Love of gain and honour, (ii) Insolence, (iii) Fear, (iv) Contempt, (v) Undue importance of individuals are some of the particular causes of revolutions as distinguished from occasions of revolutions.

9. Election Intrigues. Election intrigues pervert the purity of government and bring about a change in its form.

10. Political Faction. Sometimes political differences, friendship or dynastic and family feuds lead to formation of factions which upset the constitution.

11. Terrorisation. Terrorisation on the part of rulers to maintain their power is a sure cause of revolt.

12. Immigrant. Universal passion for privileges and difference in interpretation of justice, equality and liberty, especially in case of immigrant foreign race leads to revolutionary changes. Every class interprets them to its own advantage.

13. Different Conceptions of Justice. In the words of Sinclair, "Since justice and friendship are the moral bases of the state, injustice and ill-will are the most potent causes of discontent and instability. The absence of proportionate equality, of a fair deal, leads to a lack of justice and splits the city into actions. There can be no fellow-feeling when one section of the community is convinced that its rights are being denied to it and that justice is not being done." The democrats create oligarchic rule because they think that in spite of being the equals of those who have the advantage, they are being denied of their share. The oligarchs feel that they are not getting their due in a democracy when they deserve political power on ground of superiority in wealth etc. These differences in conceptions of justice tend to produce revolutionary temper.

14. Specific Causes of Revolutions. Aristotle also examined the specific causes of revolutions in various forms of government:

(i) *Democracy.* Democracies are usually overthrown by the excess of demagogues, who widen the gulf between the poor and the rich by attaching the latter individually and collectively, which leads the rich oligarchs to combine against the popular government. They appeal to passions and instincts of the demagogues.

(ii) *Oligarchy.* Oligarchies are overthrown by either revolts due to their oppressive rule or by rivalry between the oligarchs which leads them to play the demagogue.

(iii) *Aristocracy.* Revolutions arise in Aristocracies because of the jealousy created by narrowly restricting power and honours of state to a small circle and because of imbalance in various elements, i.e. oligarchic and democratic, also due to foreign influences.

15. Undignified Rule. Lastly, monarchies are overthrown because of the undignified rule or contemptuous behaviour of the king. Fears, terror and court dissentions lead to conspiracies against the throne. Tyrannies are peculiarly liable to be overthrown by the influence of neighbouring state of an opposite character.

Preventives for Revolutions

Aristotle has made a number of practical suggestions concerning the methods by which various forms of government may be successfully maintained and revolution prevented. Suggestions as to how to avoid revolutions are equally illuminating as their causes. These are as follows:

1. Balance. According to Aristotle, the best way to prevent them is to preserve a friendly atmosphere, to counteract discontents, to act moderately, to avoid extremes, and "never wrong the ambitions in a matter of honour or the common people in a matter of money."

2. Wisdom. Aristocracies and oligarchies may continue despite very imperfect constitutions simply through the wisdom of the rulers, who keep on good terms with their subjects.

3. Reverence for Law. Another most essential thing is to inculcate the spirit of fairness and of reverence of law, both on the part of the rulers and ruled. Lack of government and growth of arbitrariness change the good into bad forms. It is unwise for the ruler to rely on his capacity to deceive the people.

4. Close watch. The ruler must be on the watch to defeat the small changes in the constitution or the beginnings of a revolt and they should be nipped in the bud.

5. No-monopoly. Offices must not be monopolised by a few families or a class of citizens. Political power should not be allowed to concentrate in one or a few hands, offices and honours should be awarded on considerations of distributive justice. Various classes in the state should be treated with consideration and equally associated with the government. No man or class or citizens should feel that they cannot hold political power. It should be open to merit.

6. Offices without salaries. The surest way to satisfy classes and masses is to throw the office open to all but without salaries.

7. Smaller offices long tenure, Big Offices short tenure. Smaller offices should have long tenure and higher have a short tenure. In the words of Aristotle, "The ruler should give moderate honour for a long time rather than great honour for a short time, for men are easily split, not everyone can bear prosperity."

8. No Office to Aliens. Strangers and aliens should be kept away from the important political offices.

9. No Bribery. The state should be so administered and so regulated by law that its magistrates or holders of offices cannot possibly get a chance to make money bribery or illegal gratification etc.

10. Gradual Access to Power. No one must be allowed suddenly to rise in power, i.e. access to power should be gradual and slow.

11. Offices by Loyalty, Capacity and Integrity. The highest offices in the state should be given only on considerations of loyalty to the constitution, administrative capacity and integrity of character, but each citizen must have his due.

12. Public Scrutiny. For the sake of gaining popularity and political stability the financial and the administrative machinery, particularly the former, should be open to public scrutiny.

13. Feeling of Emergency of Foreign Attack. The ruler or government should keep before the public the danger of foreign attack in case of internal revolt. Excuse of external danger will overcome internal dissention. According to Aristotle, the ruler should invent terrors and keep distant dangers near so as to maintain loyalty. A feeling of emergency must be maintained. This is in close resemblance with Machiavelli.

14. No Factionism. The ruling group must remember their common interest and not give way to faction.

15. Watch on Distribution of Wealth. A close eye should be kept on changes in the distributions of wealth, since these have important political effects.

16. Sound Defence. Sound defence against foreign aggression makes a ruler popular.

17. Patriotism. Patriotism of the people must be kept on the feverish pitch.

18. Regulation of Marriages and Friendships. For the sake of security of the state Aristotle permits interference in the private life of the individual also. He says if marriages and friendship lead to revolt, they should be regulated by the state.

19. Observation of Political Mean. Oligarchies and aristocracies should not relax their constitutions to be converted into democracies. The oligarchic and democratic spirit should not be pushed too far. The mean must be sought. Polity or a mixed form of government containing both oligarchic and democratic elements is the most natural and enduring. It is the Aristotle's panacea against revolutions, as it is based on popular will. Stability of a state depends upon the satisfaction of the craving for equality. Equipoise and balance can he maintained only with this form of government. Only by proportionate equality and by giving to each his due, stability can be maintained.

20. Respect to Property and Dignity. In democracies the property of the rich and in oligarchies the rights and dignity of the poor should be respected.

21. Diplomacy in Public Relations. The tyrant must chop off the inconvenient tall poppies. He must employ spies, especially female spies, foment quarrels, and keep people busy and poor. He must show zeal for religion but with dignity and reserve. He must show favours personally but punish through others.

22. Education. The citizens should be educated in the spirit of the constitution. The best guarantee of stability is education, adopted to the form of government of the state.

Distributive Justice

Aristotle touches the subject of distributive justice while dealing with revolution. It plays an important role in the stability of state. To Aristotle complete and absolute justice means virtue in action or excellence of character. It lies in conforming to law. But justice in narrower sense is particular justice. It is nothing but observing the rules of equality. To be just is to assign a man his due, i.e. to share offices and honour in proportionate equality with others. This particular justice has two aspects: corrective and distributive justice.

(i) *Corrective Justice.* The corrective justice is mainly concerned with voluntary commercial transactions like sale, hire, furnishing of security, etc. and other things like aggression on property, life, honour and freedom.

(ii) *Distributive Justice.* Distributive justice, on the other hand, means giving to all what is their due and according to their contributions to the society in the form of wealth or virtue. It is mainly concerned with political rights. Every form of government has its own standard of distributive justice. For instance, as Aristotle points out, "In a democracy, the standard is descent while in true aristocracy it is virtue." According to Aristotle, a virtuous state discards both the democratic and oligarchic criteria. It assigns honour, offices and power to virtue. A virtuous citizen has moral wisdom, military strength and property and efficiency in some particular direction. Distributive justice is nothing but proportionate equality. By countering inequality of the equals or the equality of the unequals, it lessens frictions and confusions. It gives offices, honours and other regard according to the social performance and contribution to the society. At the same time it prevents encroachment by one member upon the sphere of another.

According to Aristotle office and honours should not be restricted only to the virtuous few. It should be open to all the citizens. Collectively, people make an important contribution to the state. They must be proportionately rewarded. In electing and judging the magistrate there is collective wisdom of the people. Every class has something to contribute and thereby entitles itself to some share in political power. To be stable, a state needs more supporters than enemies. Aristotle wanted to reconcile principle of democracy with his philosophy of justice and thereby evolve a liberal constitution of today. However, Aristotle's concept of distributive justice cannot apply to modern big states but only to city state of his times. Modern notion of distributive justice is based on duties rather than rights. It is particularly the duty of the citizens to pay proportionate taxes to the state. The offices and honours must go to meritorious persons.

On Tyrants

While discussing on revolution Aristotle was led to deal with tyrants. He tells what methods do the tyrants use to maintain their power, how are they usually overthrown and what preventives they can use to preserve their regimes. Here Aristotle keeps aside his ethical considerations. He separates politics from ethics, and thereby seems to be modern.

In Aristotle's days a tyrant was an enlightened despot. According to Aristotle, by an efficient system of espionage especially through women spies, a tyrant maintains himself in power on the basis of a vigilant watch over the unruly element. He always diverts the attention of his subjects from internal maladministration and injustice through successfully waged foreign wars and to glories to victories won. He keeps patriotism of the people on the higher pitch. He sows quarrels among the various classes of his subjects. He impoverishes them as to require the support of his guards. The people are prevented from conspiring if kept at hardwork. The tyrant lops off those who are too high. He takes measures to prevent people from knowing one another well. He prohibits intelligent discussion. He tries to destroy the intellectual life of the citizens. He attempts totally to render them incapable of political speculation which is dangerous for a tyrant.

A tyrant is surrounded by bad men. He dislikes anyone who wants independence. Women and slaves support him. Under him all these have a good time. While destroying the intellectual life of his subjects, the tyrant should try to improve their material well-being. He should dispense justice to rich and poor alike. He should show favour himself but punish through others. The tyrant should remain austere and wide awake. He should appear to do everything for the public good. He should show sympathy and concern for the people and thereby gain the goodwill of the people. He should refrain from taking material gain for himself through his power and position. He should be earnest in the service of the Good and in promotion of fine arts. He should cloak his feelings and actions and show self-confidence in the interests of state. In Aristotle's own words, "Let his disposition be virtuous, or at least half virtuous and if he must be wicked, let him be half wicked only." Here the whole picture presented by Aristotle is a masterly performance outclassing Machiavelli on this ground and valid in any age.

THE IDEAL STATE

Distinction from Plato

Aristotle sketches his best state in tradition of Greek writers to paint the picture of the best state. In latter writings, however, he deviated to a large extent from his Ideal state. In Book III of his *'The Politics'* he admitted his failure to complete the account of the Ideal state. Fortunately it led him to more fertile fields. Strictly speaking, there was no total abandonment of the Ideal state. It was described as what is known as his best practicable state. Aristotle's best state is different from that of his Master Plato. Plato's was an Ideal state, which could not be achieved anywhere else than in the world of imagination. Ideal state of Aristotle can be attained everywhere and under every set of circumstances.

Life of Virtue is the Objective

Both for individuals and states the best and happy life is the life of virtue. It includes external good sufficient for the performance of good actions. To quote Aristotle "True happiness is more often found with those who are most highly cultivated in mind and character and have only a moderate share of external goods, than among those who possess external goods to a useless extent but are deficient in higher qualities." Here as elsewhere in *'The Politics'* the subordination of politics to ethical purpose is too clear. After defining his objective or true end of the state, Aristotle built up a picture of the kind of city the state is likely to realise and of the education on which it must be founded. For this purpose he drew considerably on *The Laws* of Plato.

Criticism of Power as Good

Aristotle dismissed the widely held view that power is good in itself although it was on this assumption that most politics were conducted. He said, "Although in most cities, law may be said generally to be in a chaotic state, still if they aim at anything they aim at the maintenance of power." Again, "Warlike pursuits, though generally to be deemed honourable, are not supreme end of all things, but only a means, and the good law giver should inquire how states may participate in the good life." Further he added, "A peaceful career devoted to self-perfection through the harmonious and increasing activity of all the elements of political and social organisation is the true ideal and that which involves complete happiness for both state and people."

Which Government is the Best?

In deciding which form of government is the best, Aristotle maintained that political institutions must correspond to the character and needs of the people concerned. Therefore, an ideal state is possible only in ideal conditions. So he discussed what is the best attainable in actual practice or under given conditions. The ideal or absolute state should be ruled by the ideal virtue. According to Aristotle the best must rule. If one man is pre-eminent in virtue, the form of government is royalty, otherwise it is pure aristocracy. In other words, if men of pre-eminent excellence could be obtained, Aristotle believed that monarchy and aristocracy are the best forms of government. Taking human nature as it is, he was inclined to favour a moderate democracy.

Three Kinds of State

Aristotle had studied over 150 constitutions and it is upon the study of these that he pictures his state. This vast knowledge made him all the more idealist. He concluded that the same type of the state cannot be the best everywhere and at all times. Because of this reason he did not give any categorical answer to the question as to what form of state is the best absolutely. He laid down before his readers three kinds of states, i.e. (1) which is the best absolutely; (2) which can be attained and attained by actual men; and (3) which is the best under a particular set of circumstances.

Principle of Golden Mean

Setting aside the consideration of the first type of state, Aristotle enters in the discussion of the second type, i.e. the state which can be actually attained. The criterion of goodness that Aristotle applied here is that of golden mean beside Plato's theory of virtue. In human society, extremes of wealth make people haughty, arrogant and unsubmissive. The extremes of poverty, on the other hand, make them, wretched and submissive. Thus a class which cannot obey can be only ruled despotically. There can be no real state where a population is divided into two classes of very rich and very poor. It is no rule that there can be no real friendship between the classes, and friendship is the essential principle of all association. Thus, to avoid the political extremes Aristotle advocated the principle of golden mean. That policy is the best where the middle class is stronger, either or both of the extremes.

The Stability Criterion

The middle class people do not plot against others, they are not themselves plotted against. They pass through life peacefully. A large middle class brings stability to the state. Stability is the criterion. That constitution is the best which lasts the longest under the circumstances. In this sense, democracy is the best, where the poor greatly exceed the rich in number. Oligarchy is best where the superiority of the rich in resources and power compensates for their inferiority in members. That polity is best where the middle class ruler is clearly superior to all the best. In such a state the citizens have a moderate and sufficient property. Aristotle wanted maximum number of people to participate in the public life. He expected all the citizens to have civic virtues, political knowledge and high moral and intellectual qualifications as against Plato's small number of guardians. This was Aristotle's best constitution on the average. It was the best attainable.

Order of Preference of State

Aristotle's order or preference of states is as follows: 1. Ideal Royalty, 2. Pure Aristocracy, 3. Mixed Aristocracy, 4. Polity, 5. Most moderate democracy, 6. Most moderate oligarchy, 7. The two intermediate varieties of Democracy and Oligarchy and 8. Tyranny. Polity stands fourth in the above list of Aristotle's preference. However, he calls it is as the best practicable state. A mixed constitution embodies the best elements of each of the other forms and has stability and harmony. It brings about a happy balance of oligarchic and democratic elements or of quality and quantity. The oligarchic elements in the polity bring in the prestige of birth, wealth, status, education and experience. The democratic element strengthens it with the prestige of members. Aristotle wanted to maintain a balance of power to the middle group with some property. It is imbued with more wisdom than the mob. However, it has danger of being turned from general welfare through the prejudice of vested interests. Aristotle desires something like the Platonic arrangement, yet all possessing some power and each performing the functions best suited like Plato, he believed that rights and duties should be proportionate to qualification. Unlike Plato, be believed that all classes have some qualification for some participation in government. He preferred a practical balance to check extremes, his 'Polity' was a means to escape from the cycle of political changes. According to him, the cycle goes on with an unchanging radius and endless succession.

DESIRABLE FEATURES OF THE STATE

Aristotle proceeded on to discuss the most desirable features of the city state, big population, size, topography, character of the people and so on, after determining the forms of the state which are best under different conditions and circumstances. In the determination of these, Aristotle applied his old formula of the golden mean.

1. Population. Aristotle did not give any definite size of population. However, he said that the state should be of a manageable size. His views on the size of population cannot apply to modern states. According to him, the citizens must know each other in order to judge and elect officers according to merit for good government.

(i) *Optimum Theory*. The population should not be so small as not to become even self-sufficing. Nor should it be too large as to become unmanageable. Obviously, what Aristotle approved of was the population of a city state, not of a nation-state. His optimum theory of population visualized that the citizen body should be large enough to ensure its military and economic independence. But it should not be so large that it cannot be seen at one view.

(ii) *Quantitative Limitation*. A very populous state cannot be well governed. Aristotle, therefore, wanted that population growth must be checked. His eugenics, was less severe than that of Plato. It was nevertheless concerned with improving quality and limiting quantity. To quote Aristotle, "Let there be a law that no deformed child shall live, but where there are too many and the state of feelings is averse to the exposure of offspring, let abortion be provoked before sense and life have begun."

(iii) *Marriage*. According to Aristotle, marriage should take place at the age when the parents are most likely to have five children. This age is 18 for women and 37 for men. Marriage should take place in the winter at the season of the north wind. Procreation should cease when fathers reach 50 or 55. Those who are over-athletic will not be the best parents. The temperament of an athlete is not suited to the life of a citizen, to health or to the procreation of children.

(iv) *Adultery*. About adultery, Aristotle said, "Let it be held disgraceful if during the time of bearing children anything of the sort occurs. Let the guilty persons be punished by a loss of their privileges in proportion to the offence."

2. Territory. Following are the criteria of territory:

(i) *Self-Sufficient*. Experience shows that very large cities cannot be very well governed. Hence the size of the city should be moderate. A large territory means the natural beauty of state. It must be economically self-sufficing. It should be in such size and extent as may enable the inhabitants to live temperately and liberally in the enjoyment of leisure.

(ii) *Hard of Access by Enemy and Easy for Citizens*. The state should be hard of access to the enemy but easy of access to its own inhabitants. It should be situated near the sea to procure what is necessary from abroad. But it should not be too near to sea to be attacked by others. It should stimulate commerce and sea faring class. It should not be unduly small enough to be taken in at a single view, and be such that it is just self-sufficient.

(iii) *The City*. Thus, the city should be fed, beautified and protected. Its economy should be planned and sensibly directed. It should face east, as east winds brings health. There should be an abundance of springs and fountains. The water should be pure, strong walls are necessary. The public and religious buildings should be built on the highest spots. They should be spacious to accommodate priests and magistrates. Slaves should live separate from citizens. There should be two market places, which are also places of assembly, one for free citizens and the other for traders. The market for citizens should be near the public. Aristotle has given detailed features of water supply and defence buildings.

(iv) *Common Meals.* Aristotle greatly admired Spartans. As in the city of Sparta, he wanted that there should be one common meal table, by taking meals together the citizens come to know each other. It promotes stability and unity of the state.

(v) *Arrangement of Property.* The best arrangement of property is, according to Aristotle, as follows: "The land must be divided into two parts one public and the other private....half the public land, being appropriated to the service of the gods, the other used to defray the cost of the common meal; the private land should, of course, be fairly distributed among citizens, each citizen getting his share of land cultivating it with the help of slaves."

3. Character and Classes of the People in the State. According to Aristotle, the state should have a climate which produces high spirited and intelligent people like the Hellens. In character and ability the citizens should combine the spirit and courage of the northern races with the intellectual keenness of the Asiatics. All elements which are essential to make the state self-sufficing should be present to such agriculturists, artisans, warriors, well-to-do persons, priests and administrators. All except the first two classes should be given the privilege of citizenship. The citizens must own the land individually except for the common land. They will perform different functions during different periods of their lives. When young and strong they will be warriors; when old and wise they will be administrators, while priesthood shall be constituted of those who are too old for the service of the state. This arrangement will complete their civic training. It will teach the citizens their duty of ruling and being ruled.

4. Education. Following are characteristics of education:

(i) *Aims and Objectives.* According to Aristotle, virtue and goodness in state is not a matter of chance. It is the result of knowledge and purpose. Animals are creators of habit. Man alone has reason. Education should foster reason that it may control appetite. The perfection of the community depends upon the perfection of its constituent members. The perfection of the citizens can be achieved only through the cultivation of moral and intellectual excellence.

(ii) *Compulsory Public Education.* A system of uniform compulsory public education, without any regard for birth or occupation, is the first essential of the best state, according to Aristotle. The administration of such a system is the most important function of government.

(iii) *Educational Legislation like Plato.* Aristotle's project of educational legislation was of the same general character as that of Plato. It aimed at mental culture rather than practical utility. It laid due stress upon the physical side of the training. It attached a moral significance and a character making influence to music. Education was same to all. The educational system was calculated to make good citizens, soldiers and administrators.

(iv) *Early Childhood.* Aristotle like Plato, started with the unborn baby although education actually starts from the age of seven. He gave rigid regulations for time and conditions of marriage and procreation and care of infants. From birth till the end of the 7th year, children should to be properly fed and given muscular exercises. They should be trained to withstand the rigours of climate. They should be given plenty of milk, which is the best food for human beings. Upto the age of 5, children should only play. The games should be miniature representations of the later life. Children should be kept away from bad company and indecency of speech. They must not go to the theatre until they are of an age 'to sit at the public table and drink strong wine.' They must be allowed exercise and amusement, so long as it is not vulgar. To Aristotle, Plato was wrong in attempting to check the loud crying and screaming of children, for those contribute towards their growth and in a manner exercise their bodies.

(v) *Late Childhood.* In the next period, they should be made to learn by doing things instead of reading about them. In late childhood, stress should be placed on gymnastics for beauty, grace and symmetry of body. Music should be taught, which is not only amusement but a moral discipline and rational form of enjoyment. Children should hear those mode of music that promote ethical behaviour. Music reinforces the physical development made by gymnastics. It produces a sound mind in a sound body.

(vi) *Early Manhood.* In early manhood the citizens should be educated for the service of the state. Citizens should be taught to obey when young and rule when old. On first becoming citizens they should study philosophy in a practical way.

(vii) *Late Manhood.* With growth of age the citizens should be assigned posts of less activity and more thought, till they devote themselves exclusively to speculative philosophy, which, according to Aristotle, is the highest of human developments. The very old, who approach nearest to the gods, become priests and live in communion with them.

(viii) *Cycle of 7 Years.* According to Aristotle, education should begin with the body first, then with appetite and lastly with reason. His educational system runs in cycles of seven years. In the first 7 years of infancy education is at home. In the next two periods of 7 years each, the state takes charge of the pupil. To quote Aristotle, "From seven to puberty the emphasis is on a proper development of the body, while from puberty to the age of 21 cultivation of mind receives special attention."

(ix) *State Control.* Like Plato, Aristotle insisted that education should be controlled by state, which will bring uniformity in it and which will instruct the citizens in the spirit of its constitution. His system of education was confined to the citizens only. Aristotle is guilty of creating a chasm between the citizens and non-citizens in the state. Aristotle's system of education proposed to introduce education in the best state in order to make a citizen socially, morally and politically high.

Concluding Remarks

To sum up, Aristotle's best state is "neither too rich nor too poor, secure from attack and devoid of the desire for great or wide expansion of trade or territory, homogeneous, virtuous and cultured, a defensible unambiguous community, self-sufficient but not aggressive, great, but not large; a tight tittle independent city over which the supreme power will rest in a true aristocracy." Aristotle firmly refuted the assertion that laws and morals are matters of convention in this best practicable state. Here once again he was one with Plato in considering laws to be a thing higher than the common custom and usage.

Criticism

1. Typical Greek State. Aristotle's best state, as conceived above, seems to be a typical Greek state of his time. In spite of his vast knowledge and long stay in the capital of the Macedonian empire, he could not suggest a bigger state, nor could be put forward the idea of a federation or a confederation. Despite the fact that they had the best of the brains the world has ever produced Greek politic could not last long. It soon fell prey to other states.

2. Support to Slavery. Aristotle expected the institution of slavery to exist. He has reasons to support and justify its existence.

3. Unfinished Scheme. The subject of education was left unfinished.

4. No mention of Actual Government. Aristotle makes no mention of the actual governmental machinery of his ideal states. It may be due to a part of *The Politics* having been lost to us.

Despite all these defects, the world is indebted to Aristotle for the idea of democracy that he initiated. He has also been regarded as the founder of the three departments of the state: Executive, Legislative and Judiciary. No doubt his best state is defective in certain respects but at the same, it forms a precedent upon which rests the modern system of government to a great extent.

ARISTOTLE'S IDEAL STATE AND PLATO'S SECOND BEST STATE

According to Barker, in the later writings the consuming fire of Plato's early enthusiasm gave way to sober realities. Grudgingly and half-heartedly he stated here a second type of best state. He believed that human nature is too low to realise his ideal state. Aristotle's approach was more empirical and descriptive. The whole science of politics, according to him, included the knowledge of both political good and also of political mechanics. Sabine calls this enlargement of the definition of political philosophy as Aristotle's most characteristic contribution. The widening of the scope of politics in the writings of Aristotle made him to compromise the ideals of Platonic state with those of practical realities. For Plato the second best state was a forced constitution due to frailty of human nature. In the case of Aristotle, it was a full-fledged conviction. It has been rightly said that the ghost of Plato made Aristotle fully captive. The following are the similarities in the ideal state of Aristotle and Plato's second Best state:

1. Law as Necessary Condition. The first striking similarity between the ideal state of Aristotle and the second best state of Plato is with regard to law. Law is not a make shift but a necessary condition for moralised and civilised life. Plato made law supreme in his state. He regarded it as the wisdom of the ages. He applied it from marriage to the burial of the dead. In this, there is a striking parallel to Aristotle's ideal state. Aristotle maintained that when perfected, man is the best of animals, but when separated from law and justice, he is the worst of all. In making a law, the collective wisdom of the people is superior to that of even the wisest law-giver. However, Aristotle, like a true Greek, places the sovereignty of law above the sovereignty of the people. The supremacy of law is accepted by him as a mark of good state and not merely as an unfortunate necessity or as a concession to human frailty. In the words of Sabine, "Even the wisest ruler cannot dispense with law, because the law has an impersonal quality which no man, however good can attain." The law is "reason unaffected by desire."

2. Diluted Communism. Aristotle attacked tooth and nail the Platonic conception of communism as stated in '*The Republic.*' 'However, he is one with communism as diluted in *The Statesman* and *The Laws* of Plato. In his later works, Plato spoke of common ownership of land, but he also recognised ownership of private property. This thing was totally given up by Aristotle in his Ideal state. However, like Plato, Aristotle would like that there should be one common meal table, because taking of meals together would promote stability and unity of the state. He would divide the land into two parts, one public and the other private....half the public land being appropriated to the service of the good, the other used to defray the cost of common meals. Although Aristotle disliked the community of wives as given in Plato's Republic but he was one with Plato in allowing women to have education and in being similar in intelligence with men with slight difference. One thing about which Aristotle was not clear is whether women should be allowed an equal opportunity to take up public offices or not.

3. Higher Place to Ethics. Both Plato and Aristotle gave a higher place to ethics in their ideal state. Aristotle's political ideal was one with Plato's in setting up an ethical purpose as the chief end of the state. The real purpose of a state ought to be to help the moral improvement of its citizens. The state ought to be an association of men living together to achieve the best possible life. This was the 'idea' or meaning of a state for Aristotle. The state alone is "self-sufficing" in the sense that it alone provides all the conditions within which the highest type of moral development can take place. The only difference between treatment by Plato and Aristotle is that the former described his true state as law abiding and the latter described it as working for the general good.

This is only a minor difference as both of them believed that morality should cover the activities of the state.

4. Eminent Role to Education. Both Plato and Aristotle provide an eminent role to education. The chief function of the state according to them should be to provide a scientific course of education designed to cultivate moral, intellectual and physical excellence in its citizens for the due performance of their civic functions. The first necessity of an ideal state is the system of uniform, compulsory and public education. Aristotle's educational scheme generally resembles that of Plato. It was meant for leisured citizens. It aimed at moral and mental culture rather than at practical or professional utility. It laid emphasis on gymnastics and music; the former helping in bringing beauty, grace and symmetry in the body and the latter in producing a sound mind.

Plato gave a good deal of attention to describing education at length. In the case of Aristotle, the details are lacking. According to Sabine, it may be due to the reason that Aristotle was not able to furnish the necessary details due to his early death. It may be safely said that the discussion of Aristotle on liberal education and his contempt for the useful is a little higher than as given by Plato. Aristotle agreed that children have to be taught some useful things but to be always seeking after the useful does not become exalted. There is an apparent touch of romanticism and idealising of an aristocratic way of life in Aristotle's scheme of education.

5. Similarity in Details. There is an all round similarity in the details given by Plato for his second best state and those given in the case of the ideal state of Aristotle. Plato told why that his second best state cannot be located on the sea-shore. The Ideal state must be agricultural. It should have all the machinery of a democracy like the Assembly, the Council of Peers and Magistrates etc. While accepting all these things, Aristotle did not fall in line with the first detail, viz. that the state should be only inland.

6. Democracy. In his '*Statesman*' and '*The Laws*' Plato cherished a mixed state based upon the principles of monarchy and democracy. He preserved the spirit of the philosopher king as absolute and made it function through a democratic apparatus. In the case of Aristotle, the belief in democracy is much great, because the state exists for the good of the citizens. The political relationship must be of such a kind that the subject does not wholly resign his judgement and responsibility. Constitutional rule is consistent. By constitutional rule Aristotle means that it should be in the public or general interest. It should be carried out by general regulations and not by arbitrary decrees as it is the government of willing subjects. The constitutional ruler rules by consent. He is quite different from a dictator. This was a great advance on Platonic thought. But unfortunately, it was not examined systematically and thoroughly.

7. Classification of States. The division of states into six categories by Plato was totally accepted by Aristotle; the only difference being that while Plato described his true state as law-abiding, Aristotle called it as existing for the general good.

8. Principle of Separation of Powers. The principle of separation of powers was accepted both by Płato and Aristotle. Proper organisation and duties of executive, legislative and judicial reigns were examined. Since men crave for equality a feeling of injustice arises among those who see others possessing privileges which they do not share. The proper apportionment of political power is, therefore, fundamental to the security of the state.

9. Acceptance of Slavery. Both Plato and Aristotle could not conceive of state without being based on the system of slavery. Their states could not function without leisured citizens who used to get leisure only by employing slaves for their household and other duties regarding their livelihood.

Concluding Remarks

The essence of Aristotle's ideal state was the uniting of empirical investigations with the more speculative consideration of political ideals. For Aristotle moral ideals were always the ends for which the state ought to exist, what he discovered was that these ideals were infinitely complicated in the heavens but as forces working in and through agencies by no means ideal. In short, Aristotle's ideal state was Plato's Second Best state annotated, underlined and confirmed.

Definition of Constitution

Aristotle defined constitution as the arrangement of the offices of state determining which of its members shall hold different offices, especially the highest. It is a plan or scheme in accordance to which government is carried. The constitution determines the state and the nature of the ruling class determines the nature of constitution. Constitution is not merely a legal basis of state structure but it expresses the whole of the national life. It is a way of life of its citizens. It is the ideal for the realization of which citizens are united in the forming of a state. Aristotle attached utmost importance to constitution.

Distinction Between State and Government

Aristotle was first to point out distinction between state and government. State was the assemblage of body of citizens. The government consists of those citizens who held the supreme political power of the state and they execute and perform the political or ruling functions. Government may change with the change of those who hold highest offices but state changes only with the change in constitution.

Nature of Sovereignty

Aristotle was of the opinion that sovereign belongs to elective government. He is one with Dicey, who says that in England parliament is sovereign because it can change anything without the concurrence of any other authority. Aristotle believed that sovereignty should go to most virtuous. Location of supreme power in the state was a very important consideration, to Aristotle. It may be possible that the majority of the citizens may not be able to give judgement on the technical details of administration, still they have enough commonsense of deciding to whom they should delegate political power and authority to make laws. They possess enough commonsense to choose their rulers and bring to book those who misbehave. Thus Aristotle was vaguely in favour of giving ultimate sovereignty to citizens though actual work may be carried out by the best administrators. Thus he favours sovereignty of people and gives ultimate power neither to parliament nor to Supreme Court but to people.

Sovereignty of Law

In order to prevent the abuses of sovereignty of people, Aristotle placed sovereignty of laws above it. He favoured laws because he held that law represents the body of rules which have been determined beyond the passions of a man. If law represents the rule of reason based on traditional wisdom, it gives stability to the state. Representing the practical wisdom and experience of ages law is essential for proper conduct of a man and for the proper working of governmental machinery. Law, according to Aristotle, is not the 'will' of the sovereign or rules promulgated by ruling elite class to perpetuate its rule but practical experience and wisdom of ages and rule of reason. He discarded the conception of Plato who prefered rule of philosopher King and supported law as necessary. Aristotle gave preference to law as such. He was the first man to defend constitutionalism. Thus he was the forerunner of St. Thomas Acquinas, Hobbes, Locke and Montesquieu, Catlin, Marshall, Dicey etc.

Usefulness and Importance of Law

Aristotle believed that men not only require proper training at an early age but the watchfulness of perpetual discipline throughout life, in order to be kept within the bounds of morality and virtue. No amount of moral exhortation will suffice to enable a common man swayed by passion and self-interest to restrain and control himself, to curb a man's selfishness and passion. A coercive legal authority is necessary for this. The brute in a human being cannot be prevented and kept under control merely by pious and moral teachings. It can only be controlled by fear of punishment. The fear of law is the beginning of wisdom. Man only listens advice or reason in the shape of law because it is supported by force. A judge or king or ruler is more easily corruptible because he is liable to be swayed by prejudice, greed, passion and lust for power or sex. Law cannot be corrupted because it is passionless. The passionless authority of law gives to magistrate authority, a moral quality which it could not otherwise have.

Plato said that man acting legally is best of all animals, while when separated from law and justice, he is worst of all. Subjection of law leads to perfection of man as such, Aristotle stated that life in subjection need to constitution not to be regarded as slavery hut as the highest welfare.

Classification of Government

The government in a state could be constituted on the basis of 1. birth, 2. wealth, 3. number. A monarchic government based on birth suffers from the defect that one ruler may be most wise and efficient and benevolent but his son or successor may not inherit these qualities. A government based on wealth may not be good as wealth is no criterion of a man's moral or intellectual talent and efficiency. The basis of number is better than the two because wisdom lies in multitude and it is easier for a single man to err than for numerous persons to make a mistake. However, Aristotle classified government on the basis of number to hold sovereign power on the basis of the ends or ideals in view, whether it is for general welfare and good or for selfish and corrupt motive of rulers.

FORMS OF GOVERNMENT

Efficient or moral form	*Corrupt form*
1. **Monarchy** — with supreme virtue as its guiding principle.	1. **Tyranny** — representing force, descent and selfishness.
2. **Aristocracy** — representing a mixture of virtue and wealth.	2. **Oligarchy** — representing the greed of wealth and selfish motives.
3. **Polity** — representing martial and virile virtues, power resting with the middle class people.	3. **Democracy** — representing the principles of equality with power in hands of the poor.

Aristotle's monarchy, representing the rule of one man is based on hereditary succession for common good; and tyranny is its perverted form. An ideal person who may create rule of philosopher king is not easily available. Even if such a man may be available it may not be true for his successor. Aristotle recognised five kinds of monarchy, i.e. Spartan type, oriental, hereditary, disposition old heroic, guardian. Aristocracy is difficult to be realized as in man selfish motives gain supremacy over motives of common welfare and as such aristocracy degenerates into oligarchy. Polity is the government of all, for the good of all, but as poor persons are always more numerous than the rich, so polity gets perverted into democracy. Aristotle considers polity having a mixed form of Government and supremacy of middle class as the best rule. By democracy Aristotle meant direct democracy, as such his ideas do not apply to modern representative democracy. Aristotle held wealth as the deciding factor if a rule is by more than one man. Aristocracy always degenerates into oligarchy, in which rich persons rule for their own benefit and polity degnerates into democracy in which poor persons rule. Aristotle believes that four elements always struggle for power in a state i.e., 1. Birth, 2. Virtue, 3. Wealth and 4. Liberty. It depends on efficiency of the group in which only determined and efficient persons succeed. Thus, Aristotle lays emphasis on economic factors and efficiency and capacity and will power of the ruling elite class.

Cycle of Change

Aristotle believes in famous cyclic order according to which Governments are not static but dynamic. Every form of Government changes but changes do not follow any set rule, any fixed manner as history is a very complex phenomenon. The conception of Aristotle that change is inevitable law of nature is correct but his conception that monarchy changes into tyranny, tyranny into aristocracy and aristocracy into oligarchy, oligarchy into polity and polity into democracy is not correct. Complex changes take place in historical process. Various forms of Government such as Parliamentary, Presidential, Federal or Unitary or Imperialistic rule or Communist rule etc. were not known to Aristotle, so his idea about fixed change of circle cannot be accepted.

Criticism

1. Aristotle did not regard democracy as a good form of Government but now it is regarded as the best form of Government.

2. Many forms of Government such as Constitutional monarchy, Dictatorship, Totalitarian Government or one party Government such as of Fascists and Nazies were unknown to Aristotle, so his classification is unsuitable to modern age.

3. It is wrong to say that Democracy is the Government of poor people. In U.S.A. and in capitalist democracy bourgeous and in communist democracy workers rule so Aristotle's conception does not apply either to capitalist or to communist democracies of modern age.

MIXED CONSTITUTION

It was a Hellenic tradition to express the ideas about the best state. Following that tradition, Aristotle also painted the picture of the best state. Unlike his teacher Plato, Aristotle was a realist, so he painted the picture of best practicable state which can be attained anywhere under every set of circumstances.

Life of Virtue and Happiness

Aristotle holds that true happiness is more often found with those who are most highly cultivated in mind and character and have only a moderate share of external goods. Among those who possess external good to a useless extent most are deficient in higher qualities. Thus Aristotle believes that the best and happy life for the state and the individual is having enough external goods for performing good action. He subordinates politics to ethical purpose, and refuted the view that power is good in itself on which politics is conducted. He states that war like pursuits, though generally deemed to be honourable are not the supreme end of all things but only a means. The good lawgiver should enquire how states may participate in the good life. Peace has her victories no less glorious than war and the true ideal of people and state is to gain life of virtue and complete happiness.

The Best Government

While discussing about the best form of government, Aristotle concluded that a political institution must correspond to the character and needs of the people concerned. As such ideal state can be possible only in ideal conditions the best state should be ruled absolutely by virtue. If one man is of pre-eminent virtue, form of state may be royalty. If few, it may be aristocracy which are the best form of Government. But it is difficult to find a man of pre-eminent virtue or a few selfless men of pre-eminent virtue, so taking into account the fraility of human nature as it is, Aristotle favoured a form of moderate democracy.

After studying about 200 constitutions Aristotle came to the conclusion that the same type of state cannot be best everywhere at all times. Leaving aside the first type of ideal state, he discussed about the state which can be actually attained according to circumstances and conditions prevailing at that time. Aristotle assumed golden mean as a criterion of goodness besides Plato's theory of virtue. In human beings excess of wealth make people haughty, arrogant and unsubmissive while extreme poverty makes people slavish; degrading and submissive and unable to oppose tyranny. The arrogant rich knows only how to crush the masses and submissive poor people know how to work slavishly. In a state where there is extreme poverty and richness, there can be no real state. As there cannot be friendship between the two which is the essential principle of all associations, so Aristotle suggested the principle of golden mean to avoid extremes. The middle class people neither plot against others, nor are they plotted against, and they pass their tenure of life peacefully and give stability to the state. Thus Aristotle favoured the middle class.

Aristotle believed that the stability is the touchstone of the best state. Democracy in which poor dominate is tolerable, is better due to superiority of talent or power but polity is the best and superior to all the rest where the middle class rules. In such a polity the citizens have a sufficient property and moderate ways of living. Aristotle desired that the maximum number of people should participate in public life as he wished that all the citizens of state should have civic virtues. Such a constitution was his average or best attainable constitution.

Classification of States

Aristotle prefered states in the following order: 1. Ideal monarchy, 2. Pure Aristocracy, 3. Mixed Aristocracy, 4. Polity, 5. Most moderate democracy, 6. Most moderate Oligarchy, 7. Middle or medium varieties of democracy or Oligarchy, and 8. Tyranny.

Though polity comes fourth in Aristotle's preference but he called it best practicable state. This shows that unlike Plato he was aware of human weaknesses and selfishness. He did not long for the philosopher king but made a realistic approach. He believed that mixed constitution brings stability and harmony, a happy balance of oligarchic and democratic elements of quality and quantity. The oligarchic elements in polity bring prestige of birth, wealth status, education and experience while the democratic elements strengthen it with numbers. Aristotle desired to give balance of power to middle class, who may be more intelligent than masses and may not work for the vested interests but keep in view the welfare of masses. He wished something like Platonic arrangement, yet, he desired to give some power and functions to all for which they may be best. Like Plato, he believed that rights and duties should be proportionate to qualifications yet he favoured to give chance to all classes in participation of Government to keep practical balance to check extreme. He desired to check the cycle of political changes in his polity which according to him goes on with endless chain of succession. Thus he favoured mixed Government with checks and balances in which middle class gains upper hands.

Constituents of State

After discussing about forms of the best states under different circumstances, Aristotle discussed about population, territory, topography character of the people of city states and so on. In this discussion he also followed is formula of golden mean; in his ideas he was greatly influenced by the set up of Greek city states.

1. Population. Aristotle held that there must be a certain minimum of population to make the state self-sufficing but he did not lay down maximum or minimum limits. He said that the population should be such so that the citizens may know each other and may elect right persons. This conception points out to Aristotle's inclination towards city states.

2. Territory or Size. Aristotle stated that the size of the state should be neither too large nor too small. It should be small enough to permit the holding of periodic assemblies for deliberative purpose which may be known at a glance. For the best state personal knowledge and personal intercourse with one another is necessary, so that unity of purpose and interest may be maintained. The territory of state should be difficult of access to foreign invaders but easy to check an enemy. It should be on the bank of sea to encourage import but not too near so as to encourage adventures. To Greek mind big empires were foreign to their conception. Hence Aristotle confined his thoughts only to city states though Alexander whom he taught, created first world empire in western countries.

3. Character of People. Aristotle takes Greek virtues as model for characters known to history. He stated that in character and ability the state should resemble Greeks who combine the spirit and heroism of northern races and intelligence of orientals.

4. Classes in the State. According to Aristotle to make it self-sufficing, the necessary classes in the state are agriculturists, artisans, warriors, wealthy people, priests and administrators. He was not in favour of granting rights of citizenship to agriculturists and artisans but to all other classes. Land should be in the possession of citizens who should perform different functions in different periods of the time according to laws. They should fight in army in their young age and work as administrators in old age and as priests in very old age. Thus Aristotle gave importance to age and experience like other thinkers of ancient times.

5. Education. Like Plato, Aristotle believed that virtue is teachable. He placed emphasis on education. He believed that the tone of society and character of people depends upon education to a considerable extent which cultivates intellectual, moral and physical excellence and enables the citizens to do their duties efficiently. Aristotle prescribed a system of uniform, compulsory and public education more cultural than practical.

6. Other Requirements. Among other requirements of his best state Aristotle mentioned best means of defence against foreign attack, water supply, topography, fortifications and arrangement of streets and communications etc. He believed that there should be a popular assembly for deliberative work composed of all. There should be a system of magistracy, i.e. executive body and a system of judiciary. Thus Aristotle was the forerunner of three organs of Government, which was developed by Montesquieu and followed in U.S.A. and many other countries.

Aristotle believed that extreme democracy m which all the offices are open to all citizens endangers the stability of state. To minimize this danger, that polity is the best in which minimum property qualification may be prescribed. It will bring the rule of middle class and stability. Aristotle desired reasonable equality of property rights between the citizens. He disfavoured all aggressive wars because the ideal of state should be virtue and not power. The state should possess the capacity to achieve and infuse virtue in citizens.

Thus Aristotle's best state was secure from attack. It followed golden mean, the middle class was devoid of desire for territorial or trade expansion, homogeneous, virtuous and cultured, unambitious community, self-sufficient but not aggressive, independent and medium sized ruled by a true aristocracy. Aristotle placed emphasis on law in his ideal state. He rufuted that laws and morals are matters of convention. The features of his ideal state tally with the ideal of best state as depicted by Plato in '*The Laws*.'

Criticism

1. Guided by the ideal of Greek city states Aristotle's conception does not conform to modern great states like U.S.A., U.S.S.R., China or India etc.

2. Aristotle did not mention about actual governmental machinery in his ideal state.

3. He left subject of education unfinished.

4. His ideal of states failed to save Greek city states from ruin.

5. His ideal of small states cannot be accepted now.

6. As his book remained unfinished, his conception about ideal state is incomplete.

In spite of these defects, Aristotle gave us ideal of democracy and of mixed constitution based on rule of law and on checks and balances. He was the founder of the three departments of state, i.e. Legislative, executive and judiciary. He formed a precedent upon which rests modern system of Government of U.S.A. He to a large extent emphasized middle class rule, based on rule of law. He thought that the law is reason unaffected by desire. Thus he was the founder of many ideas which are still followed in a modified way.

ARISTOTLE A CONSERVATIVE

Aristotle tested the political ideal of Plato with actual practice. He was an empirical philosopher, who widened the scope of politics and thereby enriched it throughout the Middle Ages. He was called 'The Philosopher'. He was known to have been called by Dante as the master of them that who knew. It was he who inspired and attracted most of the thinkers during the medieval period. The extensive knowledge exhibited by Aristotle proved a fertile field for many new ideas. Conservatism, democracy and socialism are the ideals found in his philosophy in a raw material form. He was never a conservative, democrat or socialist in the modern sense. Extensive discourses enable us to find the seeds of the three doctrines in his writings.

1. Support to Rituals, Traditions, Customs and Usages. Aristotle can be called conservative due to the reason that he said that character depends upon the way a man is brought up. This meant that the rituals, traditions, customs and usages do shape the character of man. Naturally, Aristotle showed great regard for these things in Greece of those times. He nationalised existing institutions. He ruled out traders and artisans from citizenship. Any person who holds the existing order to be respected is conservative. Hence Aristotle has been rightly called conservative.

2. Support to Slavery. The way in which Aristotle regarded the slave system of those times shows him to be a conservative. He maintained that just as subjection is good for beast, so also is the slave system for some people. The brawn must serve the brain. However, one cannot accuse Aristotle of cruelty or harshness towards slaves. He himself married a give from an ex-slave family. He also took a concubine from slave class. Finally, in his will, he provided for the freedom of the slaves in his household. In short, he neither bettered nor worsened the situation. He tried to explain the slave system by the reason of heredity. He canonised it.

3. Limited to Polis. Aristotle's whole philosophy and outlook was conceived in the Polis. His vision never widened beyond the limits of the city states. He considered slavery to be central and congenial to the attainment of good life which is the end of the state.

4. Trust in Law. Aristotle trusted the law more than any other previous thinker. The law is sovereign in the state. In the Grecian life, law is regarded with great sacredness and respect. By making law to be the sovereign of the state, Aristotle once again placed the existing belief on a high alter.

5. Distrust of Amateur and Adventurer. Catlin maintains that Aristotle's distrust of amateur and adventurer is a conservative outlook. A mere expertise in the art of statesmanship and statecraft is no guarantee of success in the modern world. Catlin says, "the successful ruler must be a pressman assisted by Goebbles."

ARISTOTLE AS A DEMOCRAT

1. Central Theme. Aristotle may be called a democrat for the reason that the central theme of his philosophy as stated by him in his metaphysics is, "no universals exist apart from the individual." This means that things must proceed from individual human beings but not from abstract principles. This is equal to the democratic principles which put value on each individual. Aristotle was in favour of individual liberty for development.

2. Limited Sense. It may be doubted as to how can he be called a champion of democracy when he totally disregarded a part of the population as not-being fit for citizenship. Still he was a democrat in the limited sense of the term due to the reason that all citizens are on equal level. His master Plato on the other hand, considered the majority of the citizens to be the meek and dumb herd.

3. Participation of Citizens. According to Aristotle, each citizen should have a share in the state activities. It is only those who participate in the administrative and judicial organisation of the state, that are to be called the citizens, according to him. Modern democracy means equal participation of all the citizens in the activities of the state. This also is the opinion of Aristotle.

4. Faith in Collective Wisdom. Aristotle had faith in collective wisdom. He had a distrust in the superiority and correctness of a few individuals. He often repeated that when a large number of people are gathered together and when different points of view are expressed, there is scope for greater wisdom. Here it may be mentioned that Aristotle did not believe in the full participation of women in the political field. This cannot be a point against his democratic tendency for the reason that it was only in the twentieth century that most of the democratic states placed women on a footing of equality. A democratic state like Switzerland had not given political rights to women even till late twentieth century.

5. Liberal Democrat. Aristotle was not a proletarian democrat. He did not believe in mob democracy. He was the liberal democrat opposed to all forms of dictatorship even that of the philosophers. He did not believe in the class-rule of Plato or Marx. He realised the soundness of the political judgement of the common man. He believed that, "It is possible that the many of which each individual is not a man of talent, are still collectively superior to the few best persons."

ARISTOTLE A SOCIALIST

1. Equitable Distribution. Aristotle can be called a socialist for the reason that he thought that there should be an equitable distribution of wealth but not equal distribution. Though he condemned the type of economy advocated by Plato but he too was for a regulated type of economy. He said that there should be a private ownership of property but it should be shared in common.

2. Emphasis on Middle Class. In Aristotle's best practicable state, the middle class formed the backbone. It is they who are neither too rich nor too poor. Modern socialism also banks mostly on the middle class who are neither capitalists nor communists.

3. Against Interest on Lending. Aristotle was also against 'interest on lending,' which he thought would lead to the concentration of wealth in a few hands. The growth of modern capitalism is the direct result of banking and credit organisations. When Aristotle was against lending on interest, he may be safely called a socialist in ideas.

4. Against Speculation. Aristotle insisted that strong measures should be taken against speculation. It is one of the method which often disturbs the economic equilibrium. While thinking that it must be suppressed, Aristotle reviewed the state like a socialist which wants the state to be an umpire between the conflicting economic interests of the citizens.

5. Against Extremes of Wealth and Poverty. Aristotle believed that extremes of wealth and poverty are the main source of evil in human society. There can be no peace in the state where population is divided into two classes of too rich and too poor. These will be hostile to each other. This will lead to class war. There can be no real friendship between these classes, and friendship is the essential principle of all associations.

To conclude, Aristotle is somewhat a conservative, a democrat, and a socialist rolled in one. He was not an advocate and a pioneer of these doctrines. They existed only in embryo form in his political philosophy. Scholars have even found him to be a fascist though this is rather far-fetched. He was a Biologist, Mathematician, Metaphysician and even a Humorist who said that a beautiful lady needs no introductory letter.

PLATO'S SUPERMAN V/S ARISTOTLE'S SUPER SCIENCE

In the universe of political philosophy Plato and Aristotle are the two greatest stars. The former is known as the first poetic philosopher in the history of political thought. His disciple and successor, Aristotle was the father of political science. According to Dunning, both were the greatest apostles of the Greek culture. Almost all the thinkers till the beginning of 20th century drank deep from the rich fountain of knowledge and wisdom provided by Plato and Aristotle. Plato stands like a collossus at the beginning of the human civilisation. His fame greatly rests upon his masterpiece '*The Republic*'. It is an impressive embodiment of scientific genius and political insight. Dunning calls this work essentially a romance consisting of a series of brilliant metaphysical essays wherein politics has been incidently discussed. Plato believed that the ideal is the real. The Ideal state presented in his '*The Republic*' was meant to be a model for all times and climes. It was to be the criterion by which the existing systems can be estimated and an ideal to be emulated. Plato wanted to show what in principle the state ought to be rather than what it can be. He wanted to give the 'Ideal' of the state. He did not worry about the practicability of the 'Ideal'.

On the other hand, Aristotle was soberer, if less original genius. He dealt with a vast range of subjects in his works. His political philosophy was empirical and descriptive in comparison with the radical and abstract nature of Plato's philosophy. He had a pragmatic approach. He was concerned. . . with what can be in political science. His central theme was balance and moderation and the reconciliation between ideals and actualities. In the words of Catlin "After Confucius, Aristotle is the supreme apostle of common sense and the Golden Mean." Drawing out a beautiful distinction between the two philosophers, Prof. Maxey said, "Plato can bring out conceptual commonwealth to conform with the absolute perfection of his dreams, because he sees human nature as plastic only within the orbit of its inborn potency and perfectable only to the extent of its ability to build on things as they are."

Plato's Deduction

Plato's was deductive philosophy. He used inductive facts only when he accepted the human nature to be weak and frail. He started with a certain assumption and then deduced conclusions logically from it, brushing aside whatever came in the way of his arguments. His first point was that what we see is simply a shadow of the idea which is the final goal of mankind. Man should try to achieve that object as far as possible. That ideal can be reached by rational man. Now the question is as to how to develop this ability. For this purpose Plato advocated a system of state education. With the help of education, the individual will be able to perceive the Idea of Good. It will result in the beautification of soul. It means that the inward eye of the individual will totally understand the inner light.

Plato's Induction

After having stated that virtue is knowledge and how to train individuals in order to attain that, Plato came down to earthly realities. He pointed out that all men are not equally competent to receive education because of natural division of aptitude and ability found in them. According to Plato, human nature is made of three psychological characteristics called reason, spirit and appetite. He assumed that in the philosopher guardians, reason will dominate while in the military guardians the spirit will dominate. Those of third class will be dominated by appetite. They will look after the production of material goods essential for the sustenance of man. In this classification of human beings, man was primarily concerned with what ought to be. He did not bother about the birth or sex of the guardians. Those who are incompetent even if they are the children of guardians should not be appointed to those posts, and if they are fit for the highest duties of the state, then no matter if they are women or slaves they should be assigned those jobs.

While discussing about the philosopher guardians, Plato found that often the rulers in the actual states are distracted by two institutions called family and property. Hence in order to realise philosopher-guardians he did not hesitate to sweep clean of both of them. In their place, he advocated for common meals, state regulated mating, infanticide etc.

During his later writings, *'The Statesman'* and *'The Laws'* Plato realised the impracticability of his ideal state as portrayed in *'The Republic'*. He grudgingly recognised the sovereignty of law due to fraility of human nature. He postulated his second best state in *'The Laws'*. However, he stated at many places that there was no need of this state if the philosopher guardians could be made available. The institution called the Nocturnal Council was nothing more than a device to usher the philosopher guardian through the back door. Throughout his writings, Plato's main problem remains to be the search of a philosopher guardian or the philosopher-king or super-man who will guide the state.

Realism of Aristotle

Aristotle's approach was entirely different from that of Plato as given above. Although he also started with the construction of his ideal state like other Greek philosophers he abandoned his attempt later when he started discussing the political actualities. He came to certain conclusions after the analysis of many constitutions. In his best attainable state, Aristotle showed that he was a realist dealing with common men and not with super-men or philosopher rulers of Plato. He placed the sovereignty in such a state in the hands of the middle class which ensured great stability. But this sovereign class was not to have unfettered authority. It was subject to laws. Unlike the philosopher king of Plato who was above the laws in Aristotle's state there was the sovereignty of law. He did not share Plato's idealism and his hatred for existing laws, practices and institutions. His sense of reality and compromise did not allow him to portray an Ideal state and made the state colourless. To quote Wayper, "He began by the method of observation and of deducting general conclusions from actual practice which as it were, anchored political thought to earth. His interest in the politics, his concern with the best good in existing circumstances, his conviction that we must take states as they are and do the best we can with them, his belief that political thought must combine a knowledge of political good and a political mechanics, his insistence on the value of the rule of law or disembodied wisdom, his realisation that some constitutions would not grow in certain soils, all played a great part in the development of political thought."

Dealing with Actual States

Before Plato, Aristotle stated that the ultimate aim of the state is the realisation of good life. But he dealt with actual states. He pointed out various methods to maintain them including tyranny. His methods of averting revolutions were not based on ethical or idealist principles. They were based on pure and simple expediency as for example, to create imaginary fears to maintain security. In the words of Sabine, "Both democracy and oligarchy tend to degenerate into tyranny which is bad in itself and also unlikely to be successful. The almost cynical freedom with which Aristotle advises the tyrant precedes Machiavelli. The traditional tactics are to degrade and humiliate all who might be dangerous, to keep subjects powerless and to create divisions and mistrust among them."

Moderation Principle

According to Aristotle, *moderation* was the true key to success. He always endeavoured to maintain a balance among the conflicting forces. There is nothing like what ought to be but only what can be. He emphasised climate, geography, social character, customs etc. as the determining factors of a state. He maintained that one must make the best out of a given situation but should not aspire for an ideal. In the words of Maxey, "Plato's state is a fabric of abstract ideas to be translated into reality by a philosopher king who will sweep away all existing institutions and employ genetics and education to create a new and better race of men in a perfect social order; Aristotle's is a fabric of material already for use by any intelligent statesman who dares to try his skill at weaving them into patterns approximating the ideal. Yet both thinkers display the same ethical ferver, the same passion for order, the same love for moderation, the same faith in humanity, and the same concern for the realisation of good life."

Some critics like Dr. Popper accuse Aristotle of vulgarising political science because of his practical approach. He had to earn his living by drafting constitutions for innumerable city states, that came up like mushrooms during his times. Sabine compared the two philosophers in these words, "In originality and boldness of speculative construction he was by no means the equal of Plato and the underlying principles of his philosophy were all derived from his master. In the power of intellectual organisation especially in the ability to grasp a pattern, or a tendency in vast and complicated mass of details he was not only superior to Plato but the equal of any thinker in the later history of science." To conclude with the remarks of Maxey, "As Plato is father to the idealists, romanticists, revolutionists and utopians of political philosophy, so Aristotle is father to the realists, scientists, pragmatists and utilitarians. All who believe in new worlds for old are disciples of Plato: all who believe in old world made new by the tedious and toilsome use of science are disciples of Aristotle."

IDEALS AND ACTUALS

Aristotle never completed his ideal state for which he gave introduction in his Book III of *'The Politics'*. This was because of the reason that the ideals were sunk in the mid-stream of realities. Hence Sabine said "What he wrote was a book not on an Ideal state but on the Ideals of the state." As compared to Plato Aristotle was more empirical and descriptive. He did not have the bold sweep and courage of Plato to destroy all that stood in his way. He was more cautious and moderate. He was more a reformer than a revolutionary. This new line he took up did lead to significant results. His revolt on Plato was fruitful. He opened new world in political science, political future became much wider in extent and scope.

1. The Law. The conflict between the ideal and the actual was first found with regard to law. With Plato, Aristotle agreed that law is not a make shift but the wisdom of the ages. It meant that law must be supreme and cannot be changed. However, according to Aristotle, law was relative to the constitution. A bad state will have bad laws.

2. Virtue and Wisdom. Aristotle agreed with Plato that wisdom and virtue may have an absolute claim, but while dealing with the actuals, he said that virtue and wisdom may be changed according to social and economic status of a state. This means that there was conflict between the wisdom which Aristotle believed as an ideal in Book III and wisdom that he found in Book VII and VIII, of his *'The Politics'*.

3. Varieties of State. Aristotle took wholesale the six-fold classification of states given by Plato, but when he came to speak of actual states, he told us of more varieties. He thought that Monarchy and Aristocracy alone can be regarded a ideal state. But when he turned to the examination of existing monarchies, he dropped the idea of the ideal state. Now he spoke about the kingship of Sparta, Persia and Oriental Monarchy.

This collision between the ideal state of Book III and actuals that Aristotle came across was due to the reason that he was a disciple of Plato. The ideal state of Plato took such a firm hold in his mind that he could free himself from it only at a later stage. His greatness consists in the fact that his idea was softened and moderated by the hard facts of realities. In the words of Sabine "He is more soberer than Plato though not an original genius."

4. Constitution and Government. This compromise of the ideals with the actuals resulted in profound discoveries. In the beginning, Aristotle spoke of the constitution as a kind of life and government as the expression of the kind of life it is to develop. But when he met realities, he said that constitution is a body of rules and regulations by which a state is to be managed.

5. Divorce of Politics from Ethics. Aristotle divorced politics from ethics or morals, thereby destroying the work of Socrates and Plato both. He said that politics must enable the state to make statesmen perfect in the art of government. He went to the ridiculous extent of even giving advice to the tyrant as to how he can regulate and maintain his tyranny.

6. Popper's View. The important role played by actuals in the philosophy of Aristotle was described by Popper in a funny manner. In his interesting analysis of Aristotle in his second volume of *'Open Society and its Enemies'* Popper feels that Aristotle's interpretations of the good society were coloured by his necessity for making a living as a popular teacher and by drafting and selling constitutions for various city states of his times. This is because of the fact that he was poor whereas it was never a necessity with Plato who was aristocratic.

In spite of becoming incompatible with the actualities Aristotle's Ideal state brought a rich harvest to political science. His new conceptions like the constitution, divorcing of politics from ethics, the influence played by social and economic factors and his recognition of the fact that ideal is an ideal, had far-reaching consequences to the political science. These came to be developed as various manifestations of political science. In short, the incompatibility of his ideal and his actuals did not drag. Aristotle's contribution into a quagmire led to finding of new paths.

CONCEPT OF CITIZENSHIP

As Aristotle spent most of the time in analysing the actuals of constitution, he was made to define the meaning and status of citizens and slaves. The slave was a man in subjection. The citizens of the state went in subjection to their rulers. What justifies this subjection ? In trying to give answer to this, Aristotle landed himself in difficulties. As Doyle puts it "repeatedly Aristotle strove to find an appropriate answer to this, but he was defeated repeatedly."

Who are not Citizens?

Before giving us the true definition of a citizen, Aristotle points out that all those who live in a particular territory are not citizens. There are certain classes which are to be excluded from the citizenship. Citizenship is the special privilege of a few members in any state. This is not equivalent to the modern conception which calls a person a citizen provided he is a resident of the state for a specific number of years.

Special Characteristics of a Citizen

Accordingly, Aristotle pointed out special characteristics of a citizen. These are not residence, descent or legal privilege, but civic functions not for a limited time but indefinitely. He who participates in the administrative, deliberative and the judicial organisation of any state is a citizen. Thus, citizenship signified the enjoyment of political rights and duties. The state was coincident with the group of persons exercising these rights and duties. The Greeks regarded citizenship not as something guaranteeing rights but affording opportunities of service to the city state. The state is made up of citizens, which are those adults and heads of households, who by reason of birth, have a right to take part in the government and the administration of justice, which is its highest function.

Definition of State

From this, Aristotle arrived at a definition of the state. A state is a body of citizens sufficing for a purpose of life. Life in a Grecian sense was both political and social. The state is necessary for the achievement of good life. All persons, who are necessary for the existence of a state, are not capable of achieving this end. According to Aristotle, women and children have limited and imperfect reasons and the slaves almost entirely lack it. All those are incapable of citizenship. Children who may participate in the political activities of the state in future, cannot be called full-fledged citizens. Aristotle calls them citizens only in a qualified sense. Slaves are excluded from citizenship by definition. They are those people whose toil is a necessity. Those who are manual labourers are unfit for citizenship. Citizenship is confined only to those fortunate few who happen to carry out the political functions of the state.

Comparison with Plato

Aristotle's concept of citizenship is less democratic and more exalted than that of Plato. To Plato, the citizen body included the entire passive, uneducated and non-political demagogues of the city state. According to Aristotle a citizen is that who has the capacity to rule and be ruled in turn. Aristotle has excluded a majority of population besides slaves and foreigners including traders, workers, artisans, women and children from citizenship. Thus his concept was less democratic than that of Plato. Plato gave the right of citizenship to a wider population. However, according to Plato, all citizens do not take part in the functions of the state. Only the guardians class is concerned with the state duties. The non-guardian classes have simply to obey and do nothing else. Aristotle's concept is more exalted than that of Plato.

Economic Qualifications of Citizenship

According to Aristotle, a citizen must be rich enough to have leisure. He should have no economic worries so that he may be able to participate in the functions of the state actively. But most of the population is poor. This means that they will be deprived of this political right. Only the rich will participate in the functions of the state. Hence they will identify their wealthy interests with the public interests. To Aristotle, property was necessary for citizenship. It afforded leisure for speculatation and public works. It created an interest and faith in the safety of the state. Aristotle discarded the Platonic view that the capacity to rule is the exclusive monopoly of a few individuals such as guardians. Yet he was more reactionary than Plato. Whereas Plato made the producing class an organic part of the state, Aristotle made them instruments and not members of the state. Plato assigned obedience to his labourer citizens and no higher political functions. Aristotle cut the society into two rigid parts, one of which the working classes, merely existed as a means for the welfare of the other, the leisured citizens.

Citizenship and Goodness

A good citizen is not always a good man. A person performing political activities in a bad state can be called a good citizen but not a good man. A good citizen and a good man may be found only in an ideal state. The virtues and excellence of all citizens are not the same. They have to perform different functions in the state. Each polity exercised different moulding influence on civic virtue and citizenship. Good citizenship depends on different things in different polities. For example, the virtues of a citizen in a democracy are different from those in an oligarchy.

Functions of Property

According to Aristotle, an essential qualification of a citizen is to have property. This was to ensure leisure, i.e. freedom from cares and worries from the necessities of life. It is indispensable for the proper performance of the political duties. The working classes, though necessary for the state, cannot be granted citizenship because they have neither the ability nor the leisure for performing political duties properly.

Limitations of Aristotle's Theory

Aristotle assigned to his citizen the functions of a jury and legislator because of direct democracy in his days. His concept of citizenship, therefore, is not applicable to a modern state, particularly one with representative government, where every citizen cannot be legislator and there may be jury system. In modern state a citizen does not rule, but chooses his rulers. Aristotle failed to foresee the possibilities of representative government. He excluded a major portion of population from citizenship to arrive at a lofty concept of citizenship. But in so doing he deprived them from the educative and ennobling effect of the functions of citizenship. Every voice in the choice of government has its own civic and ethical value. A large indifferent and unenfranchised class is bound to tone down the civic excellence of the state. In this respect, Aristotelean idea of citizenship is very conservative. One should not forget that every philosopher is the child of his time and so was Aristotle in advocating citizenship to leisured persons.

VIEWS ABOUT SLAVERY

Definition of a Slave

According to Aristotle the state is made up of households. The parts of the household are those individuals who compose it. A complete household consists of slaves and freemen. Aristotle considered slaves the parts of household management. This management necessitates the possession of the different kinds of the instruments. Some of them are living while others are lifeless. Property is a part of the household because a man cannot live happily unless he be provided with property. A slave is a living possession. He wholly belongs to his master. To quote Aristotle, "The master is only the master of the slave, he does not belong to him, whereas the slave is not only the slave of his master but wholly belongs to him. Hence we see what is the nature and office of the slave he who is by nature not his own but another's and yet a man is by nature a slave, and he may be said to belong to another, who being a human being is also a possession. And a possession may be defined as an instrument of action, separate from the possessor."

Slavery a Natural Institution

Slavery, according to Aristotle is not a man-made institution. It is a natural one. It must, therefore, be retained and maintained. In support of this plea Aristotle advanced a number of tacts. He believed in the natural inequality of mankind. Men are, by nature or heredity, roughly divided into two groups. The first are those in whose soul nature has implanted the governing principle. The second are those in whom the submitting principle ruled is a thing, not only necessary but expedient; from the hour of their birth some are marked out for subjection, others for rule. It is not only true in mankind, but everywhere in nature. This phenomenon of subordination of the inferior to the superior is common with all things. It is just as well as natural and advantageous to both.

It originates in the constitution of the universe. Man has since ages dominated over woman, animal and children even in man, soul rules the body."

Characteristics of a Slave

1. Instrument. Economy necessitated the possession of instruments, some living and some non-living. A slave is a living possession. He is an instrument of action. He wholly belongs to his master whereas the master does not belong to the slave. Aristotle defined a slave as one 'who can be and, therefore, is another's and he who participates in reason enough to apprehend, but not to have reason.' A slave is, thus, a human being who differs from his master in not possessing reason, he differs from lower animals in being able to comprehend it. He cannot do any thing on his own accord. He requires some one to direct and guide him. Like wealth, he is an instrument of the household. He is one who performs action rather than carries on production.

2. No Rational Characteristics. Reason distinguishes a master from a slave. Its presence enables the master to command, its absence in the above makes him obey order. Master represents mental and the slave physical strength. The combination of the two is necessary for household purposes. Therefore, slavery is natural. This explanation of slavery however, landed Aristotle into a confusion. It is due to the fact that among the slaves he found men who came from noble families and who by accident became slaves. In order to reconcile this phenomenon he admitted that some part of slavery was legal and conventional. But he never gave up his general assumption that wholesale slavery was the result of natural differences in man.

3. Useful to Both Master and Slave. Aristotle justified slavery on the ground that not only is it useful for the master, it is equally useful for the slave himself. It secured the best conditions for him. A slave's association with his master brings him derivative excellence. By providing leisure to the master, a slave enables him to attain virtue. He is thereby like an instrument to produce much. As the slave is incapable of attaining virtue in himself, he does so by sharing his master's life. This relationship is of mutual benefit for both.

4. Necessary for Welfare and Security of Family, Society and State. According to Aristotle, slavery is good for the welfare and safety of the society. In society, its rational element should rule over the physical. Each natural household requires slaves for its proper management. Therefore slavery is an essential part of natural arrangement. Nothing can be done without instruments. A carpenter needs his tools for his work. A student cannot write without a pen. Similarly, the slaves are necessary for the maintenance of a family. Slavery is an essential part of the family unit. Efficient management of state depends upon the leisure of its citizens. This can be provided only by the slaves who look after the needs of household. Therefore, slavery is necessary for the state as well. Without slaves the progress and prosperity of the state will suffer.

Slave by Nature or by Law

Aristotle distinguished between a slave by nature and slave by law. He generally disapproved slavery by law, i.e. slavery by force such as in the case of prisoners of war. His concept of slavery and citizenship was very arrogant. He went even to an extent that all the barbarians (therefore meaning non-Greeks) furnish the natural order of slaves. He introduced a racial theory of politics, which according to Elliot and MacDonald, reached its climax in the hands of Nazi philosophers. Aristotle considered slaves merely chattels of citizens. Even Plato did not drive them to this position, Plato allowed slaves to possess some private property. Even though Aristotle believed in collective wisdom, a large part of the population from citizenship. He was not a humanitarian. He stood only for the elite of the people but not for the whole population.

Qualified Approval to Slavery

Aristotle qualified his approval of slavery to some extent. According to him, a child of a natural slave is not necessarily a natural slave. He observed that a Greek should not enslave a Greek except only causally. Only persons of other races which are inferior to the Hellenes should be slaves. It was inconceivable that a barbarian should have a Greek slave. The slaves must be treated kindly though in the interest of the master, a slave is, as it were, unanimated part of his master's body. He should be given the hope and chance of emancipation as a reward for good conduct. Prisoners of war should be enslaved only if they are intellectually inferior to their victors. Being the believer of golden mean Aristotle would neither allow slave hunting nor moralise over the abolition of the institution of slavery like the Sophists. He proposed to emancipate a slave who has developed his reason and capacity for self-direction. The position of slaves was comfortable in Athens.

Confined to Greek City States

Aristotle's conception of slavery and citizenship did not go beyond the horizons of the Greek city states. Even during his life time the signs were found that the Greek city state is not the only cultural spot of the world. This blindness of Aristotle to the new cultural forces and his attachment to the Greek view of life, made him unprogressive in his political philosophy. He never laid down a fixed criterion for the determination of who is and who is not a natural slave. He advocated merciful treatment of the slave, but his definition of a slave gave the latter the status of a beast or an instrument of action. According to his definition a modern worker is no more than a slave. It may be said to his credit that though he allowed slavery as a social necessity he insisted on its reformation. In his will he laid down about the emancipation of his own slaves.

Postulates of Slavery

Aristotle's theory of slavery rests upon the following postulates:

(a) By nature men are unequal and divided with respect to their capacities for virtue.

(b) It is possible to determine who is virtuous and who is non-virtuous.

Slavery secures the best conditions for the slave. A slave shares his master's life and therefore, in a way his excellence. Slavery is justifiable as it leads to the attainment of virtue by the master through the leisure it affords him. In Aristotle's time slavery was a necessary part of natural economy and stability. Emancipation of slaves would not only upset the balance of power in the city-state. It might have brought down whole social fabric under the weight of a huge mass of emancipated slaves.

Arguments for Justification

Aristotle justifies the institution of slavery on the following grounds:

1. Natural Inequality of Mankind. Men are by nature inequal with respect to their capacities for virtue. Nature has no endowed men with similar quantities. Nature desires that men should not be mentally and physically equal. There are persons who possess high sense of reason and who are fit to command. There are others whose intellectual standard is low and who are fit to obey only. Nature wills that the former type of people be masters and the latter slaves. Thus, slavery is in accordance with nature.

2. Superiors Rule Over Inferiors. Aristotle said, "For that some should rule and others be ruled is a thing, not only necessary, but expedient. From the hour of their birth, some are marked out for subjection, others for rule....for a being endowed by nature with mind capable of reflection and foresight is by nature the superior and governor whereas he whose excellence is merely corporal is formed to be a slave."

3. Subordination of Inferior to Superior. Slavery is just one more manifestation of the general rule of the nature of the subordination of the inferior to the superior. In the words of Mulwain, "Slavery in short; is only one more manifestation of the general rule of nature. But wherever several parts combine to form a whole, there invariably appears a subordination of some of these parts to others, a relation of rule and subject of some kind, as of man over man, as of man over the beasts, the soul over the body....and if this suggestion is natural, it is just."

4. Secures Best Conditions for Slaves. Slavery secures the best conditions for the slave. Therefore it was justified by Aristotle.

5. Master Needs Slaves. According to Aristotle, in order to lead good life a master needs slaves.

Limitations of Slavery

Sophists like Antiphone and Alicdamas were of the opinion that slavery is an subversion of nature. They deemed the institution of slavery unjust because it existed by convention and not by nature. They held that all men are equal. Contrary to this, Aristotle seeks to justify slavery but with limitations. These limitations were the following:

1. Slave by Nature or by Law. A distinction should be made between a slave by nature and a slave by law.

2. No Legal Sanction. Aristotle does not approve of slavery by law.

3. Friendly Behaviour. While dealing with the slave, the master must not misuse his authority. He should behave like a friend with his slave.

4. Emancipation. The slaves should be given the hope and also the opportunity of emancipation.

Aristotle goes to the extent of saying that a master cannot lead good life without slaves.

Criticism of Aristotle's View

1. Classification Unjustified. Aristotle holds that human beings are dividable into two classes superior and inferior. Superiors were those who are endowed with the capacity for virtue. Inferiors were those lacking this quality. But human beings cannot be divided into two such classes. It cannot be said that any person or a group of persons lacks the capacity for virtue entirely.

2. No Criterion for Classification. Aristotle said that human beings are dividable into two classes but he did not fix any criterion for this purpose. In such a case, how is it to be determined whether a person belongs to the superior class or to the inferior class.

3. Racial Prejudice. Aristotle held that all non-Greeks are barbarious. He is of the opinion that war prisoners, if they are not Greeks, may be justifiably made slaves. This view cannot be justified by any cannon. It seems that Aristotle's views on slavery were evolved due to his racial prejudice.

4. Contradiction. On the one hand Aristotle recommended a humane treatment of slaves by the master on the other hand he treated slaves as animate instruments of action who cannot apply reason. These two views are contradictory to each other.

5. Wrong Emphasis on Heredity. Aristotle's emphasis on heredity does not stand to reason. His opinion is not convincing that some persons are by nature slaves. It would be totally wrong to say that a slave has no reason. A slave also possesses some reason and if proper facilities and environment are provided, reason can certainly be developed in slaves.

6. Vast Majority Slaves. Aristotle held that some people are born to command and others to obey. If this view is deemed right, then a vast majority of the people today would be slaves.

7. Against Freedom and Equality. Freedom and equality is the slogan of the present day. Aristotle's justification of the institution of slavery being the very negation of this slogan, is therefore, unjustified.

8. Countless Classes. Aristotle said, 'Nature ordains that the superiors should command and interiors should obey'. But in such a case there will not only be two classes in the society but countless classes, because every person in some way or the other is superior to some one and inferior to others.

THEORY OF PROPERTY

Plato was of the opinion that a small state and a great household are essentially the same and 'the government of both is but one science.' But Aristotle disagrees with this view. It was Aristotle who, first of all, worked out the fundamental principle that the character and distribution of wealth is the determining factor in fixing the form of government. He held that every citizen requires private property and the discipline of family life. He regards these institutions as belonging to all by the order of the nature. "Like Plato, Aristotle was obliged by practical considerations to fall back upon property as a surrogate for virtue. Neither thinker believed that property is a sign of goodness, but both reached the conclusion that for political purposes it offers the best practicable approximation to it."[4]

Definition and Type of Property

Property, according to Aristotle, "in the sense of a bare livelihood seems to be given by nature herself to all, when they are grown up. Property is of two kinds: Inanimate or Animate, private or local. Private property must be protected by the state otherwise somebody else will take possession of it. It is necessary for the existence and proper functioning of the household. In the words of Maxey, "The things which are necessary for life such as food, clothing and shelter constitute property. The instinct of acquiring property in man is natural. But the amount of property required by the family is limited by its needs, to have in excess is bad as to have less than what is required." As Foster has said: "A hammer must be heavy in order to serve its purpose; but the object of the hammer maker will not be to make it as heavy as possible. The same function of the hammer maker will observe this limit. The essence of Aristotle's saying is that all true wealth must be limited."

Justification of Private Property

To justify private property, the following arguments have been advanced by Aristotle:

1. Necessary Part of Social Economy. Private property is a necessary part of social economy. In the words of Aristotle, "When every one has a distinct interest, men will make more progress because every one will be attending to his own business." Ebenstein is of the view that Aristotle links the idea of self-interest with that of social progress. Where self-interest is involved, the individual concerned will do his best and his best efforts will in turn benefit the society.

2. Gift of Nature. The instinct of acquiring property is the nature's gift to man.

3. Necessary for Household. Natural property is necessary for the existence and proper functioning of the household. In the words of Maxey, "It is nature's own way of assuring man the wherewithal to live."

---

4. Sabine, G.H., *A History of Political Theory*, G.G. Harrap & Co. Ltd., London, 1948, p. 108.

4. Essential for Good Life. The instrument of private property is essential for leading good life.

5. Development of Personality. Property is necessary for the development of individual personality.

6. Source of Pleasure. The ownership of property is a source of pleasure. Aristotle said, "Almost all men love money." Thus on psychological ground Aristotle defends private property.

7. Sense of Civic Responsibility. The ownership of private property creates a sense of civic responsibility in the owner.

8. Training in State Management. Private property makes a man know the art of managing it. The experience thus gained will also be useful in the management of state affairs.

Modes of Holding and using Property

According to Aristotle, the following are the three modes of holding and using property:

1. Private ownership but common use of property.
2. Common ownership but private use of property.
3. Common ownership and common use of property.

Of the above Aristotle preferred the first mode. He said, "It is clearly better that property should be private but the use of it common."

VIEWS ON FAMILY

Plato's communism of wives did not appeal to Aristotle. He called Plato's theory unnatural and fanciful. To him, family was a natural association of which man becomes a member from the time of his birth. It is as natural as the state. Marriage is a holy institution and family is the basis of the state. Household constitutes the historical origin of the state. Aristotle does not agree with Plato's view that a small state and a big household are essentially the same and the government of both is also the same. The state and the family are not the same. Family satisfies the elementary needs of the man. It exist for satisfying the physical needs while the state satisfies the moral and intellectual needs. State is an association of associations. It is the highest of all associations.

INFLUENCE OF THE POLITICS

Aristotle has been called the father of political science. He struck a new ground in political science. Herein lies his importance in the history of political thought. In the annals of political philosophy, his place is enviable. He opened new avenues to political science. He was a pragmatist thinker. He based his conclusions on the data collected from observations. In his *'History of Classical Scholarship'* Sandays observes, 'No single thinker, not even Plato has had as much impact as, was of Aristotle's on intellectual and institutional history of later centuries."

Practical political philosophy began with Aristotle in the west. With his systematic treatment of the science of politics, he laid the foundation of political science. Max Learner says, "The religious systems were philosophically uncreated and needed a logic and critical framework and these Aristotle made available." Barker remarks, "It is perhaps in Marsiglio of Padua that Aristotle's influence is most remarkable. The Prince of Machiavelli was influenced by the commentary on the last chapter of Aristotle's book dealing with revolution."

To understand the influence of Aristotle's *The Politics* one will have to make a systematic study of the Hellenic and the universal philosophy of the late thinkers.

(a) The Hellenic in Aristotle

In the words of Prof. Dunning, "The foregoing sketch of Aristotle's work should at least suggest the importance of the purely Hellenic elements in his political philosophy. His historical research went far beyond the confines of Hellas but the system which he framed was determined in its most essential characteristics by the conditions that prevailed within those continued." The following show the Hellenci elements in Aristotle's political philosophy:

1. Superiority of Greeks. Superiority of Greeks over other races.

2. The City State. The city-state as representing the best form of political organisation.

3. Slavery. The inherent necessity and justice of slavery as the basis of social organisation

4. Leisure. The incompatibility of bread winning pursuits with the moral and intellectual attributes of good citizenship.

5. Education. The supreme importance of state directed and controlled education and training in the maintenance of political virtue.

6. Authority of Law. The subordination of all personal motives and conduct to the 'dictates of law' conceived either as of formulated wisdom of some individual of almost super human sagacity.

Dunning adds, "In the course of ages most of these ideas either have passed entirely out of consideration or have been so modified as to lose the significance which Aristotle attaches of them."

(b) The Universal in Aristotle

Dunning says "....When we look further into his philosophy, beneath the general outlines determined by these Hellenic dogmas, we find a long series of principle which are as ultimate as human nature itself, and which, in almost the exact shape in which Aristotle formulated them are features of political science at the present day. " Following are the universal elements in *'The Politics'*.

1. Liberty and Authority. In the words of Dunnings, Aristotle puts forward, "The distinct and unequivocal conception of the ultimate people of politics, i.e. the reconciliation of liberty and authority." Aristotle held that the law is supreme and all must be subordinated to it. He meant by liberty "subjection to unselfish and constitutional authority and obedience to right and proper law." He denounced complete liberty and perfect equality. In his *The Politics,* he observed the tendencies of extreme democracy, "Equality is held to signify the rule of the majority and liberty and equality to mean that each may do as he will. Hence, in democracies each follows his own inclination. But this is evil. For life in subjection to the constitution is not to be regarded as slavery, but as the highest welfare."

2. Constitutionalism. Aristotle's emphasis on constitutionalism reveals his universality. He held the law as the sovereign and the government as its servant. In the words of Ebenstein, "The concept of the rule of law of the constitutional state is perhaps the most-important legacy, Aristotle has bequeathed to posterity". Dunning also points out that "the ultimate idea of sovereignty Aristotle discerns, rather than adopts the theories of modern times. He realises the significance of a determinate human superior, whose undoubted will is final, but he recurs again to the thought of a law controlling even this sovereignty. He prefers that the ultimate human superior should be the whole people, but he qualifies the solution firstly, by limiting it to a society in which the quarrel level of virtue, i.e. of moral and intellectual attainment is high, and, secondly, by limiting the field of sovereign legislative activity to the region not previously occupied by law.

3. Aims of the State. Aristotle held that the state came into being for the sake of life and it continues for the state of good life. The aim of modern state is the maximum welfare of the people.

4. Importance of Public Opinion. Aristotle was of the opinion that the work of officials is best judged by the masses or not by the experts. This attaches great importance to public opinion and has a great appeal to the modern political thinkers.

5. Ownership of Private Property. Aristotle defends the ownership of private property and his plea holds good even today.

6. Theory of Separation of Powers. The modem theory of separation of power owes its origin to Aristotle.

7. Theory of Golden Mean. Theory of the golden mean is a forerunner to the present concept of political checks and balances. In the words of Catlin, "After Confucius, Aristotle is the Supreme apostle of commonsense and of the Golden Means. The practical nature of his philosophy is not virtue but it is necessity to virtue. Man cannot live on poetry alone, but they need satiating, their gastric desires too."

8. Inter-relationship of Politics and Economics. Aristotle's narration of inter-relationship between politics and economics has universal element in it. He held that economic influence upon political organisation is very important. To quote Dunning, 'The permanent and universal side of his philosophy is peculiarly illustrated by the importance which he attaches to economic influence in the political organisation and activity. From the theoretical view point the validity of private property is maintained, and from the practical point of view the eternal friction between those who have and those who have not is made to explain many of the most conspicuous phenomena of government. On this turn his classification of forms, his adjustment of administration machinery and to a great extent, his explanation of revolution. And from this is derived that doctrine which has been so impressively confirmed by later history, that stability and prosperity are most to be found where extremes of wealth and poverty are unknown and middle class is the strongest."

9. Father of Modern Individualism. Aristotle holds that 'individual is prior to the state' which shows that he is in fact an individualist. He is therefore, regarded as the father of modern individualism.

10. Philosopher of the Ages. Aristotle has been regarded as the 'philosopher of the ages. His influence on later thought was immense. According to Sandys, "No single thinker, not even Plato has had as much impact as Aristotle on intellectual and institutional history of later centuries. There were four centuries when Aristotle's shadow was only visible." Rome and Spain kept the study of Aristotle alive. In Paris University in the whole Europe, Aristotle's study was revived. It formed the base of all Christian philosophy. During the medieval times, St. Thomas Acquinas incorporated logical conclusions of Aristotle. To quote Max Learner, "The religious systems were philosophically uncreated and needed a logic and critical framework and these Aristotle made available. To St. Thomas as well as to his teacher Albert the great law was identical with reason. Both of them regarded that the best forms of government were those which organised on the basis of virtue. Both regarded the mixed constitution as the best." Prof. Barker remarks "Aristotle taught St. Thomas, he taught Richard Hooker who drew from the origin the theory of law and government. The judicious Hooker was in turn one of the masters of Locke....Theory of Locke descended in turn to Burke....There is not only an analogy...between the climate of Aristotle's Politics and the climate of English political thought in the seventeenth and eighteenth centuries. There is also some measure of affiliation." Aristotle's influence over Marsiglio of Padua can be seen in his *'Defensor Pacis'* which was more or less an adaptation of *Politics'*. According to Barker "It is perhaps in Marsiglio of Padua that Aristotle's influence is most remarkable."

In his *'De Monarchia'* Dante refers to *'The Politics'* again and again, Machiavelli was greatly influenced by Aristotle. No less was his influence over the utilitarians of the first century and the idealists of the nineteenth century. Rousseau, Hegel, Kant, Bradley, Bosanquet: T.H. Green and Laski, all were indebted to him.

To sum up *The Politics* of Aristotle is one of the greatest classic on political science. It is said that *'The Politics'* is an unfinished treatise and often obscure but the half-understood words of Aristotle have become laws to thought to other ages. To quote Zeller, "*The Politics* of Aristotle is the richest treasure that has come down to us from antiquity. It is the greatest contribution to the field of political science that we possess."

QUESTIONS FOR EXERCISE

1. "The capital significance of Aristotle in the history of Political theories, lies in the fact that he gave to politics the character of independent science." — Dunning. Elucidate.
2. "In the fundamentals of his political philosophy, Aristotle was a faithful disciple of Plato." Discuss.
3. "In the fundamentals of his political philosophy Aristotle was faithful disciple of Plato." Explain.
4. "Aristotle's theory of political ideas stands upon the ground which he had already occupied because of his association with Plato." Explain and examine this statement.
5. "State is natural. It came into existence for the sake of life and continued for the sake of good life." (Aristotle) Discuss this statement critically.
6. "The State is prior to the individual." (Politics) Discuss.
7. "Man is a political animal, destined by nature for political life." (Aristotle). Discuss.
8. "State exists for the sake of good life, and not for the sake of life only." (Aristotle). Elucidate.
9. "No Aristotlean work is quite so common place in its handling of a vast subject as The Politics." (Taylor) Discuss.
10. "The Politics of Aristotle is the greatest contribution in the field of political science that we possess." (Zeller). "No Aristotlean work is so common place in the domain of a vast subject as the Politics." (Taylor).
11. "The cause of sedition is always to be found in inequality." Aristotle. Explain.
12. "It is inequality, as we have seen that is everywhere the cause of revolution." Explain this with reference to Aristotle's principle of distributive justice.
13. How did Aristotle come to the conclusion that "the best political association is the one which is controlled by the middle calss.?"
14. "What Aristotle calls the Ideal State is always Plato's Second Best State." (Sabine). Discuss.
15. "Life in subjection to constitution is not to be regarded slavery but as the highest welfare." Aristotle. Explain this clearly bringing out Aristotle's conception about constitution and sovereignty.
16. "The more perfect the admixure of the political elements, the more lasting will be the constitution." (Aristotle). Explain.
17. "Plato seeks a superman, who will create a state as good as ought to be, Aristotle seeks a super-science, which will create a state as good as can be." (Maxey). Discuss.

8

Epicurean and Stoic Political Thought

POST-ARISTOTLEAN ERA

Limitations of City-States

In the writings of Plato and Aristotle, the Greek Political thought reached its zenith. These were based on the city state which was considered the best and the highest form of political and social organisation. To them, the city-state was essential for good life. Good life was identified with political life. Political life was necessary not merely for satisfaction of material needs, but also for the spiritual realisation. Both Plato and Aristotle failed to note the inadequacies of city-state as a political unit. Both of them were totally unaware of the part played by foreign affairs even in the internal economy of the city-state. Self-sufficiency could not be attained by it. Policy of isolation was bound to result in stagnation in that very culture and civilisation which Aristotle regarded as city-state's crown of glory. Later political necessity drove the city state to seek alliances with other cities. These federal alliances impaired the independence of their members. They failed to make permanent and stable states.

Epicureans, Stoics and Cynics

Though there was magnificence in the philosophy of Plato and mighty mastery of constitution in the philosophy of Aristotle, they failed to influence the centuries in the immediate future. Sabine has described it as a magnificent failures. During this gap came the philosophy of the Epicureans and the Stoics and Cynics, Contrary to earlier philosophers they were defeatists in their approach.

Military Empire

The free life of Greece were brought to an end even before the death of Aristotle. The empire of Alexander, the Greater and later, on the empire of Rome dealt a death blow to free life in Greece. Now the military empire became typical form of political organisation. The Greek political institutions survived merely as phases of local government in the Roman Empire. Greek thought was so intimately connected with Greek institutions that the decline of one necessarily meant the decline of the other.

Negative Attitude to City State

The post-Aristotlean philosophers adopted a negative attitude towards the city state. They did not identify good life with political life. On the contrary, they felt that keeping away from the membership of a state was necessary for good life. Both Epicureans and Stoics maintained that a wise man should reduce to the minimum, his participation in the life of the community. The Greek political philosophy became more individualistic than before. A tendency to distinguish the individual from the state emerged as against the merging of the individuality of a man in the state in the philosophy of Plato and Aristotle. Self-sufficiency, which Plato and Aristotle regarded as an attribute of the state, became an attribute of and individual human being. The happiness of the individual became the subject of serious thought.

FACTORS OF CHANGE

Following factors contributed to this radical change of attitude. After the swamping of city states of old Greece by Philip of Macedon and his son Alexander the great, the city states seemed altogether out of date. In the words of Sinclair, "They were powerless and useless in its traditional functions as an arbiter of morals and social habits." Now, larger and more compact political units were needed. City states were too small to be self-sufficient and to defend themselves against powerful neighbours. The notion of an empire or world-wide order with something like an impersonal government and universal law was quite alien to old Greek thought and culture. It was totally new to the European mind. They failed to anticipate the shape of things to come. All they said about them was a friendly criticism. They firmly believed in the inborn greatness of the city state's civilisation.

1. Elimination of City Patriotism. The establishment of the Macedonian and later on the Roman Empire made Greek political philosophy more universal or cosmopolitan. The ideal of the citizenship of a city state was replaced by the ideal of the citizenship of the world. In the words of Gettell, "Universalism and individualism replaced city patriotism."

2. Individual Higher than State. Participation in civic functions was considered to be more important than personal rights and duties in the city states. No individual could separate himself from common life and set up his personal happiness as an end to be sought for itself. Now, the city state no longer remained as the playing point to Greek enthusiasm. The offices of the state did not possess the same attraction for men of ability. Their observance of civic religion failed to give the people social and emotional satisfaction. The loss of political freedom weakened the patriotism of the people. It led to the separation between the state and the individual. They began to think of the individual rather than of the state. They began to find a sphere of private and personal life. Ethics and philosophy came to be sought after more than ever before. Greek thinkers ceased to think on the city-state and concentrated attention on religion and ethics. It resulted in the growth of two schools of thought, e.g.

Epicureanism and Stoicism. In place of devotion of the city state, they laid stress on the ideals of personal character and private happiness.

3. Revolt of Downtrodden. The treatment given to the slaves foreigners and even artisans class in city states was far poorer than what they said about the higher classes. So when the objects of worship of the earlier philosophers, viz., the city states, began to decline they had their revenge. The germs of this negative attitude towards city state and its values were hidden in the very pages of the *The Republic* and *The Politics.* Plato allowed active citizenship to two upper classes and ignored the third and the largest. Aristotle gave the right of citizenship only to the leisured classes. It was but natural that the vast bulk of the downtrodden ones must develop an attitude of indifference towards the city state.

4. Ideal of Stoicism. Aristotle considered Greeks to be superior to the barbarians. He justified slavery. Alexander mixed the two and upset the whole concept. The Greeks lost freedom and were now under foreign domain along with barbarians. Now, they found it easier and more natural to develop the idea of common citizenship of the world and denounce slavery. Idea of equality of men under a universal law was held by Stoicism correctly.

5. Epicureanism and Cynicism. The failure of the philosophies of Plato and Aristotle created a void. This was filled by the two schools of Epicureanism and Cynicism. The keynote of these was escapism or withdrawal from the vigourous political life as advocated by the earlier writers. Both of these divorced ethics from politics. They did not care very much for the laws of morality. For Epicureans and the Cynics the ideal was the securing of the happiness of the individual. Both found the substance of life in the internal and not in the external life of an individual. Though they differed in regard to the summum bonum or the highest good of life, they agreed on minimum participation in the life of the community and in individual self-sufficiency. They said that cultivation of personal character is the best guarantee of private happiness. They claimed to have derived their inspiration for Socrates. This period was one of the empire building and the welding of civilisation. It was devoid of any great political philosopher.

EPICUREANS AND STOICS

1. Similarities. In Greece, the two schools of thought developed after Plato and Aristotle were Epicureanism and Stoicism. They were philosophical in nature. Their outlook on life was more individualistic and more cosmopolitan as compared with that of Plato and Aristotle. They wanted individual self-sufficiency independent of society. Individual had to learn living in new form of social union larger than city-state. Both the schools agreed in making individual happiness the aim of life.

2. Differences. However, they defined happiness and the method by which it might be secured. The Epicureans advocated the temperate satisfaction of every desire, sensual and intellectual. The Stoics taught the suppression of the emotion and the subordination of immoral desires to the demands of reason.

VIEWS OF EPICUREANS

Epicurus (306 B.C.) founded Epicureanism. It was also expanded by the Roman poet Lucretius. It was developed over by Cyrenaicism, established by Aristippus who claimed to have derived his ideas directly from Socrates. According to it, the greatest aim of life was the greatest happiness. This was nothing but absence of pain or worry. Epicureans, however, identified happiness with virtue. A wise man would reduce his desires to minimum. He lived on bread and water only. Maximum happiness could be achieved by making oneself independent of state and by withdrawing from cares of public life, because active membership of the civil society creates desires and ambitions in a man. Even family life should be avoided as much as possible, as it adds to the worries and pain. Being free from these worries one could devote one's energy to self-improvement internally or to the pleasure of the soul rather than of the body.

Deterioration in Political Thought

Epicurean principle that happiness is the aim of life brought deterioration in Greek political thought. The high principles of right, virtue and justice gave place to the low notions of happiness or utility. Epicureanism was the basis of utilitarianism. The Epicureans based the state upon individual self-interest. They believed that men were essentially selfish. The authority alone may curb individual selfishness. As common superior authority, law is an agreement of utility and expediency. Law is required by the individuals in order that they might be secured against violence and injustice. The social contract theory of the state was now foreshadowed. To Epicureans and Cynics political life was burdensome. They maintained that a wise man will not take part in politics unless his interest absolutely demands it. The Epicureans urged submission to any government that maintained peace and order and ensured easy social intercourse. Efficient despotism to them was as good as democracy. They were in line with Hobbes in ascribing origin of the state to the need of security. They taught submission to any efficient *de facto* government, a doctrine that suited to the situation. After the conquest of Greece by Alexander this was founded by Zeno about 300 B.C. Zeno was the pupil of Creates who was the leader of the Cynic School. Stoicism influenced first Greece and then the Roman thinkers like Cicero, Seneca, Emperor Mercus Aurelius etc.

PHILOSOPHY OF STOICISM

Stoicism was more important than Epicureanism as it exercised greater influence on the development of political theory and Roman jurisprudence in its formative stage. It formulated the concept of the Law of Nature based on reason and cosmopolitanism or world-citizenship. These became part and parcel of western civilization and culture.

The Aim of Life

As for the Epicureans so for Stoics also the aim of life was to achieve human happiness. But while the Epicureans allowed a moderate indulgence in both physical and intellectual desires, the Stoics were against physical satisfaction. They advised pursuit of intellectual pleasure based on reason and not on feelings. They agreed with the basic ideas of Cynicism such as perfect self-control, independence from circumstances, self-sufficiency and life according to Nature. But the nihilistic doctrines of cynicism were constructive and positive. Stoicism gave shape to the political thought from Cicero till 18th Century.

Concept of City of God

For Stoics, true happiness lay in virtue. Virtue in its turn was nothing but following the law of nature, which was definite, unchangeable and based on reason. Thus, life according to law of nature was to live according to reason. However, an individual was not to follow one's individual reason, but the reason as shown by universal approval or judgement. As the source of natural law human reason did not mean the independent judgement of the individual but the common judgement of mankind. Men, by natural law have equal rights. A cosmopolitan political theory was created upon this doctrine. All men, whether Greek, slaves or barbarian, are naturally brother fellow citizens in a world republic. This city of God is an abstract conception like Plato's ideal city found in *The Republic*. Subjection to one law by all individuals is the doctrine of natural equality of man. This was alien to natural inequality and fraternity which have been borrowed from Stoicism. Brotherhood of man depends on the observance of Natural Law, which unites all men into one great community. Universal natural law and individual citizenship were Stoic ideals. The significance of these conceptions in a society accepting slavery is evident.

Concept of Natural Law

The Stoics conceived of nature as the embodiment of universal law. As the creative source of law, it was the revelation of nature. The law of nature was therefore fixed and immutable. It was the reflection of the process of nature, in harmony with human reason, the divine element in the universe. In this form the idea of natural law was handed down through Roman law and through medieval political thought.

Concept of Nature

The Stoics rejected the crude naturalism of Cynics, instead they substituted the idealistic view of life. According to them, Nature was not a jumble of events or chaos. It is a rational system or order filled by divine reason. They recommended resignation to the course of things. They supported an indifference to the events of fortune and values of social life. For them the life according to Nature meant life according to law. Nature was the manifestation of the single and homogeneous spirit of the world based on reason. The law of Nature is that common universal divine and good rule of reason, which governs creatures combined in a natural association. Natural law is objective reason. Civil law must be based on Natural law which is the sovereign universal standard of right or wrong.

Status of State

According to Stoics individual is a unit by himself, self-sufficient and distinct from the society. The stoic philosophy was the negation of Platonic and Aristotlean philosophy. According to Plato and Aristotle good life could be lived only within the state. To the Stoics, the good man was different from the good citizen. Ethics and not politics was the controlling or guiding force. Private life was more important than public life. Participation in politics was condemned. But according to Stoics, in spite of his individualism a wise individual would recognise society, even though as a necessary evil. He would do all he can to help it. Stoics believed in the general depravity of mankind. They justified the existence of the institution of government. This belief overshadows the cardinal Christian doctrine of original sin.

Wide Influence of Stoicism

For the Stoics justice represented a form of universal reason. It was based on the sense of equality among human beings. They did not advocate the abolition of slavery. They pleaded for mercy to be shown to the slaves as freedom of spirit was the true freedom and its lack true slavery. Thus they gave to the world the notion of equality based on universality of naturally law. After the death of Aristotle till the advent of Christianity they played a tremendous part in moulding human thought. The Stoic philosophy greatly influenced the writings of Cicero and the doctrine of original sin of Christianity. It became the characteristic philosophy of the Roman rulers.

The Stoics developed their ideals of brotherhood of man and of world state. It represented an ideal Universal Empire of Reason, from a philosophic and humanitarian point of view. The conditions of the time soon became favourable to their political application. Empire of Alexander broke down the barriers between Greeks and barbarians. Diverse people became members of one political system. Universal law and universal citizenship was realised under the Roman Empire. The Roman jurists adopted the idea of law of nature and principles of common justice to all men. Christianity adopted the conception of human brotherhood. It expanded it all over the civilised world.

QUESTIONS FOR EXERCISE

1. What are the characteristics of Post-Aristotlean political thought in Greece. Give a brief account of the Epicurean and Stoic thoughts.
2. "After Aristotle the character of political thought in Greek underwent a radical change." Explain the statement with reference to the Stoics in Epicureans.

9

Roman Political Thought

According to Will Durant, "Law was the most characteristic and lasting expression of the Roman spirit. As Greece stands in history for freedom, so Rome stands for order, and as Greece bequeathed democracy and philosophy as the foundation of individual liberty, so Rome has left us its laws and its traditions of administration as the basis of social order."[1]

The impact of Plato and Aristotle on the Roman political outlook was so much so negligible that it has been called a magnificent failure.[2] With the rise of empires the polis passed into oblivion as the centre of intense political activity, and men were rendered into spiritual exiles. They found themselves lonely in a vast world where they could be either individuals withdrawn unto themselves or broadminded citizens of the world. As the individuals left *deracine* as a result of the eclipse of the polis they began to make souls for themselves.[3] They began to think of themselves as distinct items of humanity. The death of Aristotle, marks the close of one era and the commencement of another, a legitimate turning-point in the history of political theory.

According to W.W. Tarn, Man as a political animal, a fraction of the polis or self-governing city-state, had ended with Aristotle; with Alexander begins man as an individual. This individual needed to consider both the regulation of his own life and also his relations with other individuals who with him composed the inhabitable world: to meet the former need there arose the philosophers of conduct, to meet the latter certain new ideas of human brotherhood. These originated on the day .... when, at a banquet at Opis, Alexander prayed for a union of hearts (hymonoia) and a joint commonwealth of Macedonians and Persians.[4]

C.F. Angus puts it, "Metaphysics sank into the background and ethics, now individual, became of the first importance. Philosophy is no longer the pillar of fire going before a few intrepid seekers after truth; it is rather an

1. Will Durant, *The Story of Civilization III : Caesar and Christ*, p. 391.
2. G.H. Sabine, *op. cit.*, p. 123.
3. C.F. Angus, *The Cambridge Ancient History*, Vol. VII, p. 210.
4. W.W. Tarn, *Hellenisitic Civilization*, p. 69.

ambulance following in the wake of struggle for existence and picking up the weak and the wounded.[5]

Stoicism was the doctrine most characteristic of the post-Aristotelian or Hellenistic period. It accorded little importance to metaphysics. It valued virtue. It considered God as the soul of the world and every human being as a spark of the Divine fire. It upheld belief in the law of nature. It held that there was virtue in life to the extent that it conformed to nature. It had a cosmopolitan outlook. Marcus Aurelius supported belief in the *daemon* as the only guide to man and his outlook was cosmopolitan:

"My city and country, so far as I am Antoninus, is Rome, but so far as I am a man, it is the world. Love mankind, follow God ... and it is enough to remember that law rules all."[6] Stoicism stood for the whole world as one community in which gods and men lived together, the former as lords and the latter as subjects. It saw men united in a fellowship through their partaking in reason. It provided a spiritual basis for the growth of a humanistic system of laws, particularly of the laws of nature.

POLITICAL CAREER OF ROME

Roman mind was consolidative, i.e. legal and not speculative. As the Polybious and Cicero were poor comparison to Plato and Aristotle, Romans did not contribute much to political philosophy. But the political institutions and the legal system of Rome moulded Western political thought and substantial parts of the laws of France, Germany, Poland and of South American states are based on Roman law. When Christianity became the state religion, church of the Roman Empire became centre of Roman Catholic religion.

Rome started her political career as a monarchic city state. She achieved greatness as a Republic and declined as an imperial and despotic power. Monarchic form of Government was replaced due to conflict of patricians and the plebians. It started her aggressive career and founded one of the greatest and most stable and longest empire which world has ever seen. It evolved a political system and universal legal system. Roman empire lasted about 2000 years and influenced the whole of Europe.

Roman Political Institutions

In Rome Plebians, i.e. common people succeeded in a *Comitia centuriats*. A Republic was set up about 500 B.C. to consult replaced kings. There were assisted by Proctors, and consors and latter on by the Tribune, the peoples representative. Romans conquered many other states which were governed by Prefects. Later on military dictatorship was established and popular assembly lost its power. The ideals of democracy, liberty and autonomy were replaced but the ideals of unity, order, universal law and cosmopolitan outlook gained ground. They evolved a common official language and a universal legal system

---

5. C.F. Angus, *op. cit.*, p. 231.
6. Quoted by Ernest Barker, *The Legacy of Rome*, p. 32.

and common citizenship, which were followed by British, French and Russian empires to some extent.

Impact of Greece on Rome

The development of Roman law was influenced by intellectual impact of Greece upon Rome. According to Molluruain, the arrangement of Roman law in the form of twelve tables was largely due to the influence of Greeks. The tables were based on the laws obtained from Greek city states. The Greek influence on Rome increased vastly when Romans conquered Greece. It became a fashion in Rome either to send his ward for study to Greece or to keep a Greek tutor. Greek political thought gave ethical and humanistic basis to legal system.

DEVELOPMENT OF ROMAN LAW

1. Jus Gentium. As foreigners flocked in Rome a special magistrate was appointed to decide the cases of conflicting nature. He decided the cases on the basis of common practices, supplementing them with rational and ethical considerations. At the end of his term, he collected his decisions and published them. New proctor took into consideration the edicts of his predecessor and added his own. Thus a new law of *Jus Gentium* came into existence.

2. Juscivile. The Roman law, called *juscivile*, applied to Romans only. While *Jus Gentium* was common to whole Rome *Jus civile* was applied to Romans only. In the formative stage the doctrines of political relations were held and taught by Greek thinkers of those days. There were combined with principles drawn from Italian customs, to be handed on to the new people of Europe as the basis of their law and politics. This combination and transmission together constituted the chief role of Rome in the growth of western political thought. In practical importance it was a role second to none.

3. Jus Naturale. Later on principles considered to be inherently reasonable irrespective of their being found in law gave rise to *Jus Naturale*. *Jus Naturale* began to be regarded higher than *Jus Gentium* which was based on generally recognized principles. According to Sir Fredrich Pollock it became an ultimate principle of fitness with reference to the nature of man as a rational and social being which is, or ought to be the justification of every form of positive law. *Jus Naturale* thus became a touch stone of ethical criticism of positive law.

While *Jus civile*, based on twelve tables was applicable to Romans, *Jus Gentium* was applicable to foreigners and the people of Roman empire. The *Jus Naturale* belonged to philosophers and influenced the work of Jurists and Proctors. Under the Roman empire these systems were mixed into one universal law applicable to all the subjects of the empire. The Roman outlook became wider, humane and less narrow when ideal of justice borrowed from stoicism was added. According to Sabine "Belief in justice is the crowning glory of Roman jurisprudence." They believed that justice must be done though heavens may fall.

Roman Concept of Law

To Greeks, Law was the expression of passionless reason. Its sanction was ethical or religious. In the beginning Roman law was also a mixture of religious regulations and customary rules. However, in a vast empire containing people of diverse faiths, it was not possible to keep the law and religion and so law became secularised, positive and secular to a great extent. However the Roman law was not a product of legislation in the modern sense of the term. Roman jurists and philosophers conformed to the higher law of nature. They were deeply influenced by humanistic doctrines of Stoicism. In the words of Sabine, "Roman law preserved the spirit of civic phrase, that we are servants of the law in order that we may be free."

Social Contract and Theory of Natural Rights

Romans believed that the king is the source of law. During the close of middle ages they drifted to the theory that king is the agent of people, this theory used to explain the sovereignty of the national king. Stoicism thought that all men are born free and are equal in natural rights. This was used by the opponents of royal power in constructing the theory of social contract and natural rights which served as the basis for revolution and democracy. The conceptions of *Jes Jentium* and *Jus Naturale* were worked out by Grotious in international law. Thus in Roman juristic conception one finds the germs of social contract of natural law and of international law.

The idea of contract played a great part in Roman legal theory. Even the creation of law followed the social contract. The laws were made by magistrates in cooperation with popular assemblies. As Gettle put it, "Law was not a command imposed by sovereign upon his subjects, but a contract arranged among the constituent organs of the state offer negotiations." The private law of Romans was based on the idea of contractual obligation between the individuals. Romans thought that people worship God in bargain for certain benefits from him.

POPULAR SOVEREIGNTY

Romans thought that the state is a legal sovereign though the political sovereignty resides in the people as a whole. According to Gettle, "The early kings, the republican magistrates, and in theory at least, emperors, received their authority from the citizens and acted as their agents, and were responsible to them for exercise of their duties. The will of the emperor had that force of law because in theory people have delegated to him their entire authority." This delegation is irrevocable and therefore revolutions are unjustified. Later on with the development of power of the king, this conception gave place to divine authority of emperor, who delegated his authority to state officials.

IMPERIUM AND REX

Though Roman empire began under monarchy, they never believed that any individual had a particular and absolute title to rule over them, because of any hereditary claim or divine antecedents. Any Roman could fill the office of the ruler but once chosen, the king held office for life. He could not be deposed constitutionally. The subjects owed absolute allegiance to him. He possessed the absolute power of the state. He was the high priest and held imperium for peace and war. Power was given to him though this gift was absolute and irrevocable. At his death, however, the imperium returned to the burgesses or the representatives, the procters. An inter Rex was appointed for a temporary period through whom power came to next Rex or King chosen by people. This idea was interrelated to their conception of popular sovereignty. Both were complementary to one another.

ROMAN CONTRIBUTION TO POLITICAL THOUGHT

1. Conception of Universal Brotherhood. With the expansion of Roman Empire, Romans developed wider outlook, ideals of human brotherhood and of equality of men before law. The cosmopolitan outlook of Rome and astoic-Christian conception of the brotherhood of man laid the foundation for the modern point of view of universal brotherhood and modern ideas of U.N.O.

2. The Principle of Colonial Rule and Local Self-Government or Municipal Administration. Limited local self-government was permitted to the provinces. As people realised the value of Roman order, the ghost of Rome haunted during the middle ages. Roman law and language spread all over the world. Roman law is taught to Indian students in Indian universities even upto now. The Christian Church organised itself on the model of Roman empire. Caesar, Imperium and theory of world unity influenced the course of political philosophy. Roman law and its legal system influenced whole mankind.

3. Concept of Secular Law. It has its sanction in the will of the ruler. It is the main contribution of Romans to the theory of law and jurisprudence. It brings us to the idea that the state is distinct from society. It is more of a legal structure than an ethical association.

4. Legal Personality of the State. Romans also propounded the idea of legal personality of the state.

5. Mixed Constitutions. Romans also believed that mixed constitution in the best.

6. Contractual Theory of Law. Romans propounded the contractual theory of law which meant that laws are contract arranged among the constituent organs of the state after negotiations.

7. Imperium. It means lawful but not necessarily actual authority. The Roman idea meant that the authority is trust on the public will. Thus, the greatest contribution of Romans is in the field of law and jurisprudence.

8. Stable Empire. Romans contributed to building of a stable empire. They compelled subject people for submission. They developed conception of integrity of empire and commerce. These replaced liberty by the notion of peace, order and protection of Government established by law.

9. Sense of Security. By uniform political and legal system and common official language, they developed a sense of security in the Roman Empire.

10. Centralised Administration. Centralised despotism with local self-government in colonies and provinces was key to Roman administration.

11. Cosmopolitan. Cosmopolitan outlook and international law were developed by Romans.

POLYBIUS (204 TO 102 B.C.)

Polybius was the first political philosopher, who wrote on Roman government and its constitution. Born in 204 B.C. and died on 102 B.C. he was a Greek hostage upto the time Romans conquered Greeks. Polybius wrote his *History of Rome* in which he admired Roman polity which enabled Rome to become a great political power. Polybius began his history by dealing with the cause of the origin of the state. He narrated the various types of government monarchy, aristocracy and democracy in Aristotlean manner. He declared that the differences between the three types were external rather than internal or ideal. He displayed that the pure forms of these are unstable because of the rivalry shown by the elements in the states representing other two types. He recognised a natural cycle of change in the form of government in the state. According to him, change took place in them in following cycle; monarchy, tyranny, aristocracy, oligarchy and democracy and mobocracy and, then the new cycle again. The constitution of Rome was of a mixed form and therefore better than a constitution of pure types because it embodied a system of checks and balances among the different organs. These ideas effected makers of American Constitution which is based on checks and balances.

Polybius possessed the practical political wisdom, which Aristotle had considered an indispensable qualification of a successful ruler. This is the reason why "whatever the Romans did by the advice of Polybius turned out well" but whenever they did not listen to his instructions they went wrong.[7] Most states belonging to the Achean League obtained the leave of Rome that Polybius should frame constitutions and draw up laws for them. Polybius was Ivor Jennings of Rome, an accomplished constitutionalist, a seasoned expert on the affairs and intricacies of politics.

Polybius was a bridge between the two cultures of Rome and Greece. He interpreted both to each other and acted as an intellectual bridge between the two. He performed this role well as he was Greek in race and training and Roman in outlook and sympathy. The practical bent of his outlook was due to the circumstances of his life and compulsions of the times. He had grown up as son of a statesman and at a relatively early age been initiated into the politics of the Achean League and Rome where the highest ideals of Hellas had flowered into a new and vigorous life. The watchwords of equality, free speech and democracy were his knowledge from his boyhood as he had watched the ideals in their application to the practical affairs.

7. Pausanius quoted T.R. Glover, *The Cambridge Ancient History*, Vol. VIII, Chap. 1, p. 1.

Polybius was also something of a historian. For him, history rather than philosophy was the proper subject of study for the ruler, and in his insistence on it he appears to be a precursor of Machiavelli long before him. As he had played a great part in the Achean League, he was able to write history from the standpoint of, and with sympathy for those who had been engaged in making its events and moulding its course. Though an inhabitant of Megalopolis in Arcadia, a leading city in the Achean League he was forced by circumstances to spend mature years in Rome. What happened was that after the victories of B.C. 168 the Romans imprisoned and took away one thousand of the leading men of Greece to Rome and kept them there for seventeen years. Polybius was one of these very prisoners of war. Since he was an intelligent and learned man, the Roman King felt drawn toward him and called him at his court. There he developed intimacy with younger Scipio, the son of Acmilius Paullus and the conquerer of Perseus. Polybius was at Scipio's side at the critical moment of his life; watched the burning of Carthage and confided to his friend his strange foreboding that another great city would suffer a similar fate. Polybius was thus, a man who had known the best of the two worlds. In his early years he had watched the movements of Greek politics, republican and monarchical; in the older years he stood in the inner circle of the Roman government.

In history Polybius chose the element of chance as his theme: The meteoric rise of Rome to the pinnacle of glory and power, in particular, constituted the mystery he wanted to unravel in his historical studies. On the stage of history Rome had made her *debut* as an empire in just fifty years: in this men might have naturally read the hand of Fourtune (Tyche).

To quote Polybius, "The very element of unexpectedness in the events I have chosen as my theme is enough to challenge and incite every man, old or young to the study of my treatise. For who among men is so worthless or spiritless as not to wish to know by what means and under what kind of polity the Romans in less than fifty years have succeeded in subjecting nearly the whole inhabited world to their sole government — a thing unexampled in history."[8]

Polybius was not a fatalist. He did not believe in fortune as a determinant of history. He refers to fortune only in order to underline the necessity of exploring the underlying causes behind the movement of history. He said it was improper and vulgar to explain things and events in terms of fortune. He himself explained the rise of Rome to the heights of power and glory not in terms of fortune but in those of the character of her citizens, soundness of her institutions, and above all, of the happy blending of the different governmental principles in her constitution. Rome's rise was something to be explained in terms of reason and performance.

RULE OF DECLINE

In his *Histories* Polybius enunciated a theory of the law of decline to explain events and achievements in history. He found an immanent tendency

8. Quoted *Ibid.*, p. 15.

of growth and decline at work in nature. Aristotle had also believed in a law of growth but had stopped there; Polybius held that the process of growth is, of necessity, followed by a reverse process of decline. "There is in every body or polity or business a natural stage of growth, zenith and decay; ... and everything in them is at its best at the zenith," thus wrote he. The reason why Rome was ultimately triumphant over Carthage in the Hannibalic War is to be found in the fact that the political fortune of Carthage gas waning and of Rome waxing.

THEORY OF CONSTITUTIONAL CHANGE

In pursuance of his belief in the historical law of growth and decline Polybius advocated a cyclical theory of constitution change. He considered mixture of governmental principles as a cause of the strength, unity and stability of the Roman constitution. He derived his concept of mixed constitution from the examples of Sparta, Carthage and Rome. The Spartan constitution contained four organs of government all of which worked in a team-spirit, viz. the Council (Gerusia), the Assembly (Appela), the Kings and the ephors. Likewise Rome there were three organs in government, viz. the Consuls, the Senate and the popular assemblies. The Consuls were at the head of all public affairs with magistracies working as their subordinates. They consulted the Senate on urgent matters and promulgated *Senatus Consulta.* They summoned the Assembly, presented bills and carried out the decisions of the majority. They controlled the operations of war and spent as much public funds as necessary. The Senate administered the public treasury and controlled all revenue and expenditure. It decided the manner in which the embassies should be received and answered. The Assembly conferred honours, adopted or rejected laws, deliberated on war and peace, and ratified alliances and treaties.

The three organs in the Roman government exercised intra-governmental checks upon one another. In the operations of war the Consuls could not do without the people and the Senate. Without the co-operation and help of the latter they could bring no military operations to a successful conclusion. They needed the people as well for the ratification of treaties and terms of negotiations. When the Consuls laid down their office, they had to give their account to the Assembly. The Senate had to consult the people and take its opinion into account on matters of public importance. In public and private affairs the people, had to depend upon the Senate. In this sort of constitutional mixture Polybius found his theory of mixed constitution at its best working.

The mixture of political principles had been there in Plato's Laws and Aristotle's Politics, but there the mixture was more of social classes than of governmental principles. To them, the mixture characterised the whole state; but to Polybius it characterized the government only. The difference, thus, is fundamental.[9] Whereas in Aristotle we find a fusion of political principles, in Polybius we find a system of checks and balances within the highest governmental organs of the state.

9. C.H. McIlwain, *op. cit.*, p. 100.

The mixture had been there in the constitutions of Carthage and Sparta as well, but the amount of mixture was greatest in the Roman constitution. Just as there is tendency of inevitable decline and growth in nature, so there is also in constitutions. But the tendency of decline works most with the constitutions which are unmixed. History reveals a cyclical development: The cycle runs from despotism to monarchy, then to aristocracy followed by oligarchy to democracy. Democracy is followed by mobocracy, and mobocracy is followed by despotism.

However, constitutional breakdown takes place, only when the people concerned become involved in it. They become so involved owing either to their hostility to the over great or because they are courted by the demagogues and falsely made to feel that power lies in their hands. Polybius explained constitutional change in some such way: Political life begins with the rule of the stronger. It evolves slowly into monarcy based on law and cônsent. When monarchy comes justice and other virtues strike roots in the life of the state. When, however, the king insists that his word is law, the elite of society rises against him and establishes aristocracy. But when the aristocrat begin to seek power and glory for themselves, people rise in reaction against them and the result is democracy. No constitution can escape the law of decline. Democracy too is superseded by oligarchy when the economically privileged class attains to superiority in the state. When the people use bribery and corrupt the rulers, democracy gives way to mobocracy under which, led by some demagogues, the rich are slain and exiled and their properties *looted* and appropriated. Despotism appears again, and the process repeats itself endlessly.

MIXED CONSTITUTION

The tendency of decline can be checked, by the adoption of the mixed constitution. Polybius advocated mixture of the principles of three good forms of government, viz. monarchy, aristocracy and democracy. As the three principles were fused in a happy synthesis in the constitution of Rome it attained strength and stability. The government in Rome developed within itself a system of checks and balances. The Consuls represented the principle of monarchy, the Senate of aristocracy and the popular assemblies of democracy. It was in time of crisis, however, that the mixed constitution, was particularly of great importance, for then every organ of government vied with another in performing its role best and defending the state. It ensured the vigour of the constitutional machine and strengthened the stability of the constitution. In peace time also it made for wisdom and moderation of the conduct of affairs. "Since the three organs can thus hamper and support one another, their working mixes the best results in all circumstances, and it is impossible to find a more perfect form of governmental than this. When common danger threatens the Romans from abroad, compelling them to think and act in complete unity, the strength of the constitution becomes so great that no necessary measure is neglected, for all determined to deal with the situation and decisions which are taken carried out.

without delay, since all combine, collectively and individually to accomplish the object which they have undertaken.''[10]

According to Polybius, mixed constitution imparted invincibility to Rome and made for her successes in everything undertaken by her. It liberated her from all fear from without. It enabled them to enjoy the prosperity and wealth earned by their victories. In its constitution each organ kept its own place either because the other opposed its efforts or because it was too much afraid of their interventions to make the attempt at all.

INSTITUTIONAL METHOD

Polybius applied institutional method to the study of politics. He tried to relate the international status of a country to its home politics and institutions. He perceived a correlation between the internal and environmental settings. Rome's rise to the world's supremacy was the work of not a few heroic individuals and military leaders but of high political standards and practices and sound administrative institutions and working. While the Greeks had studied political institutions in relation to the good life of the polis, Polybius studied the same in terms their structural and functional role. He considered the institutional fabric of the state as the chief determinant in the formation of its overall strength.

CRITICAL EVALUATION

However Polybius over-emphasised the role and importance of the principle of mixed constitution behind the strength, greatness and stability of Rome as a state and as a power. In addition to this principles, a number of factors must have been at work and contributed to what greatness and capacity to survive Rome possessed, such as the morale of the citizens, the military strength and capability, economic capacity, sound leadership, traditions of civility, homogeneity of the people, the geopolitical situation and others. The soundness of institutions is indeed a major factor making for the strength of a state but behind that soundness lie a variety of other social and psychological factors and complexes. Polybius admitted that the greatness of Rome was due to the character of her citizens and the soundness of leadership. But he considered the mixed constitution as the most potent factor responsible for the miracle that Rome was in history. Rome's internal strength, depended on a tenacious principle of unity expressed in the form of citizenship. This principle had a remarkable elasticity. It adapted itself for a time to the alien conditions of a growing empire.[11]

Over-emphasis on the merits of the mixed constitution has been objected to by critics like Mommsen and Hegel. Mommsen writes "There is hardly a more foolish political speculation than that which derives the excellent constitution of Rome from a judicious mixture of monarchical, aristocratic and democratic elements, and deduces the successes of Rome from the excellence

10. Quoted Leon Homo, *op. cit.*, p. 117.

11. R.M. MacIver, *op. cit.*, pp. 113-14.

of her constitution."[12] Hegel also observed, "How blind are they who can imagine that institutions, constitutions and laws can persist after they have ceased to be in accord with the morals, the needs and purposes of mankind and after the meaning has gone out of them."[13]

Mixed Type Most Stable and Best

Polybius believed that the best safeguard against political revolutions was the incorporation of the best elements of all the three pure forms of Government in the constitution. It was achieved by the Roman Republic wisely and advantageously. In the Roman constitution, the Consuls represented the monarchic principle, the senate represented aristocratic element and the popular assemblies represented democratic element. Polybius checked, watched and controlled other two elements. He based his ideas on Aristotlean conception. His democracy is identical with Aristotle's polity and Ocholocracy with his extreme democracy.

Subsequent historical facts proved that the conception of Polybius was correct to a great extent. British constitution was considered best due to its mixed character. Polybius idea of checks and balances was upheld in U.S.A. Dictatorical and communist states did not accept this conception due to different social set up. But the decline of dictator's power has again proved the utility of mixed constitutions. Polybius was the first political theorist to bring out the importance and advantage of mixed type of Government. It was grasped by Motesquieu and incorporated in many constitutions in modified form.

POLITICAL THOUGHT OF SENECA

Seneca divided human history into several periods. The most ancient period, according to him, was the golden period as the society was free from all defects and perversions. Gradually, the human society analysed the causes of the corruption and degeneration. According to him, the most corrupting cause of the golden period was economic. He considered the concept of property as the most defective and harmful for society. He pointed out that in the golden period there was no idea of property. During that period the property belonged to the whole society. All the persons had equal social status without any distinction of high or low. There was no problem in this society based on equality. Gradually, the concept of property dawned in human society. With it grew the distinctions of high and low, small and great, rich and poor. This led to the degeneration of the entire society. Conflicts about property started growing. Political power was needed to settle the conflicts concerning property. Laws and constitutions were developed. Behind all these was the evil nature of man. This evil nature, however, is natural to man. This interpretation of human nature by Seneca was borrowed by Christian thinkers and led of the concept of guilt in Christianity.

---

12. Mommsen, *History of Rome*, Vol. IV, p. 247.

13. G.H., Sabine, *op. cit.*, p. 531.

CICERO (106 TO 53 B.C.)

Cicero was born in 106 B.C., when the political constitution of Republic was failing. His purpose of writing was to commend the national virtue of public service and to recast them with the old method of government. He wrote about a century after Polybius. He was the greatest Roman representative of the Stoic school of Political philosophy. His was the age of military dictators like Morius, Sulla, Pompey and of Julius Caesar etc. But he was an ardent supporter of republicanism. He wrote to increase the power of senate and magistrates. Like Polybius, he believed that the mixed constitution is the best. His *De Republica* written on Plato's model and *De Legibus* represent an appeal for the revival of old spirit by restoring old constitution with its healthy system of checks and balances.

Importance of Cicero's Writings

Importance of Cicero's writing does not lie in his originality of thought but in the manner of their expression. Characteristically, he was not a political philosopher but a lawyer and statesman, whose works and reflection were on politics rather than on political science. Sabine holds that Cicero lacked the originality to strike out a new theory for himself with Roman experience and in defiance with Greek sources. According to Foster, "much that he writes, is directly inspired by Plato and Aristotle." He himself stated that his works were compilation. According to Sabine, an idea once embeded in his writings was preserved for all time to the reading public and became immortal.

Cicero championed the cause of moderation, concord and constitutionalism. He took these ideas from Polybius but amended them in the light of his own understanding of Roman history. He brought *Jus Naturale* of Stoics and supported Natural law and human equality to be realised in Roman Empire. His ideas are the treasure of mankind.

Following the footsteps of Plato in his *De-Republica*, Cicero painted the picture of his ideal state. He copied Plato in supporting justice as the main theme. But unlike Plato his ideal is co-related to reality. While Plato was an idealistic thinker of city state, Cicero has the practical sense. Cicero was influenced by Stoic philosophy. According to Dunning, Cicero confined himself to the consideration of Roman state and its history as illustrating and embodying the ideal of political science.

Like Greeks, Cicero believes that the state is the natural outcome of the social instinct of man. He supported stoic conception of the state as a rational and desirable institution. But he differed with Stoics and considered the state as a political institution distinct from the society in general. He separated state and government and placed the ultimate authority in people, the government acting as their agent. He held commonwealth as moral community and regarded as people's affairs, in which a group of persons possess the power of the state and its law.

Difference with Plato

Plato confined political authority in guardian class, but Cicero believed in *Rex Populi* in which people are involved. When legally and rightly exercised political authority is the corporate power of the people, the magistrate are merely creatures of law. The motto of the state is to supply its members with the advantage of mutual and just government. Cicero regarded state and its laws subject to natural law or law of God. Force is an incident. It is justified only because it is required to give effect to the principles of justice and right. Authority proceeds from the people. It should be exercised according to law and moral grounds. Cicero's ideas achieved universal acceptance and profoundly influenced the western political thought.

Difference from Aristotle

According to Dr. Carlyle, no change is so startling as a change from Aristotle to Cicero.

1. Equality. Aristotle stated that some should rule and others should be ruled. He restricted his rights of citizenship to a narrow circle though his circle is greater than that of Plato. But Cicero believed in the equality of man. Slave is not a living instrument as Aristotle said but a wage earner hired for life. Some measure of dignity and respect is due to every man. A man should to be treated as an end and not as means.

2. Democracy. Cicero gave preference to democratic mixed Government but Plato and Aristotle condemned democracy and preferred Monarchy and Aristocracy.

3. Democratic Outlook. Plato's outlook was fascistic, Aristotle's conservative but Cicero's outlook is democratic.

4. Practical. Plato paints idealistic picture of his state but Cicero's approach is practical.

5. Universal Brotherhood. Aristotle and Plato dealt with city states but Cicero dealt with great Roman empire and so his outlook is broad based on universal brotherhood.

6. Natural Law. Greeks were ignorant of natural law. Cicero gave a concept of natural law applicable to whole mankind and said that state laws are subject to natural law of God.

7. Rule of Law. Plato gave prominence to philosophy, Aristotle supported law but Cicero supported rule of law as right reason, conformable to nature, universal and eternal "a state is nothing but partnership in law."

8. Right. Greeks thought rights is source and content its antecedent to and independent of law. But Cicero differed and reversed the process.

9. Liberty. Cicero believed in liberty unlike Aristotle who believed in slavery. He stated that liberty has no dwelling place in any state except that in which the people's power is greatest and surely nothing can be sweeter than liberty; but if it is not the same for all, it does not deserve the name of liberty.

10. Popular Sovereignty. Plato believed in the rule of philosopher king, Aristotle in the rule of limited class of citizens but Cicero's state is based on popular sovereignty where office holders act merely as the agents of public, who delegates authority to them for discharge of their duties only.

11. King. Cicero, unlike Plato and Aristotle, believed that the state is not prior to individual and the King is representative of law.

12. Roman Law. Cicero identified Roman law, based on the principle of equality and justice, with the Stoic law of nature.

13. Authority. According of Cicero, Authority proceeds from the people and should be exercised through laws on moral grounds. Thus we may conclude in the words of Gettle, "His ideas of natural law and justice sank deeply into Roman legal thought and influenced the later imperial jurists and imperial writers. And his idea of world unity and of universal law and authority remained central principle of political thought through out medieval age and to some extent in modified form even now."

POLITICAL THOUGHT OF CICERO

Saving Republican Constitution

Cicro was the Roman political writer who exercised an enduring influence throughout the ages. He was responsible for the introduction of the Stoic philosophy in Rome. These were the last years of the Roman Republic. Cicero saw the republican constitution crumbling before his eyes due to the civil war between two powerful factions in Rome. He wrote against the background of the political failure of the republican constitution. It is necessary to distinguish between the immediate purpose for which he wrote and the long time influence that he exerted. Though his influence was very great what he attempted was a total failure, aimed at restoration of Republican constitution. He wanted to commend to his fellow countrymen the traditional Roman virtues of public service. Due to the extension of its dominion economic changes divided the Romans into two hostile classes, the wealthy nobles, who composed the senate, and the poor commons or the proletariate represented in the assemblies. The recurring deadlocks between the two organs broke into civil war. Cicero wanted to save the constitution falling to ruins. His two works *'De Republica'* and *'De Legilius'* aimed at recalling the Romans to the old method of forming their government. These works, however, had no effect during his life.

Importance of Style

The importance of Cicero's writings lies in the originality of their expression of his ideals. He was not a professional political philosopher or a leader of school. He was a lawyer and statesman. His works are reflections on politics rather than on political theory. To Sabine, Cicero lacked the originality to strike out a new theory for himself in tune with Roman experience and in defiance with his Greek sources. Cicero's ideas were derived from earlier philosophers and from the notions generally current during his time. His works indicate the development that had taken place in the political theory since the classical philosophy of Greece. To quote Foster, 'Much that he writes, is directly inspired by Plato and Aristotle themselves'. As Cicero himself admitted, his work were compilations. However, an idea once embedded in his writings was preserved for all time to the reading public and became immortal.

Constitutionalism

Cicero fervently believed in moderation, concord and constitutionalism. He attached much importance to the excellence of mixed constitution and the theory of historical cycle of the constitutions. He derived both of these ideas from Polybius. He however tried to modify them in the light of his own understanding of Roman history. He brought *Jus Naturale* of Stoics from the heaven to earth. Natural law and human equality both were realised in the Roman Empire and consequently, it became a permanent treasure of mankind due to Cicero.

Practical Purpose of Cicero's Writings

The practical purpose of Cicero's writing, *De Republica,* fashioned on the model of Plato's Republic was to set forth the concept of an ideal state as Plato had done in his *'Republic'*. The main theme of both the books is the nature of justice. But unlike Plato, Cicero's ideal state is in close relation to reality. In the words of Dunning, 'He confines himself to the consideration of state and its history as illustrating and embodying the ideas of political science. He was a conservative. He believed in constitutional government. Plato was a philosopher of City-state. Cicero had the sense of the world nurtured by Stoic philosophy.

Origin and the Nature of State

Cicero agreed with the fundamental Greek theory about the origin and nature of the state. He believed that the state was the natural result of the social instinct of man. He followed, in general, the Stoic idea of the state as a rational and desirable institution. He did not accept the Epicurean idea of the state as an artificial creation, resulting from individual self-interest. However, unlike Stoics, he viewed the state as a political institution distinct from society in general. He further separated state and government. He placed the ultimate authority in the people as a whole with the government acting as their agent. He regarded the state as a 'Commonwealth', a moral community. He called it a group of persons who, in common possess the state and its law. He regarded the commonwealth as the people's affair.

Different from Plato

Cicero agreed with Greeks on the origin and nature of the state but he differed from Plato. His state is not a hierarchy like that of Plato in which the few exercise political authority and the rest belong to it and are not of it. It is a Rex Populi. The whole people are concerned with it. When rightly and legally exercised political authority is the corporate power of the people, the magistrate, who exercised it is the creature of law. The state supplied its members with the advantages of mutual aid and just government. The state supplied its members with the advantages of mutual aid and just government. The state and its law is the common property of the people. Its authority arises from the collective power of the people. The state itself and its laws are always subject to the law of God or the Natural law. 'Force is an incident and is justified only because it is required to give effect to the principles of justice and rights'. Thus, according to Cicero, the general principles of government were (a) authority proceeds from the people, (b) it should be exercised only by warrant of law, and (c) it is justified only on moral gounds. These general principles achieved universal acceptance after Cicero. Standing prominently in his political philosophy, these principle later formed a part of intellectual equipment of Western political thought.

Classification of Government

In his classification of government into Royalty, Aristocracy and Democracy, Cicero closely followed Polybius. Each of these possessed certain advantages, each was subject to decay that resulted in a corrupt form and led to a cycle of revolutions. Of the simple forms, Cicero considered monarchy best, aristocracy next and republic least desirable. To contract the revolutionary cycle he preferred a mixed form of government, combining the excellences of each simple form but avoiding their weakness. This was the idea of Polybius, who illustrated it by an elaborate exposition of the constitutional development of Rome. In this way, the Republican system of Rome was a perfect example of the checks and balances for stability and good government. He showed that monarchy was discarded because the king became the tyrant. The Patrician aristocracy, over bearing in its monopoly power, was forced to yield to the restraint of Polybius. Cicero's idea of checks and balances was less mechanical than that of Polybius.

Idea of Natural Law

What gave importance of Cicero in the development of European political thought was his most valuable work on the idea of Natural Law. In the border region, where ethics, jurisprudence and politics meet, Cicero presented ideas which give him an important place in the history of political theory. These ideas were the development and practical application of the concept of natural law. Here he followed the doctrine of Plato that the principles of right and justice are eternal and immutable. Cicero followed the idea of the Stoics that a supreme universal law existed in nature. As Dunning puts it, "In Greek philosophy the distinction between 'right' and 'law' had been recognised but right had been regarded as in source and content antecedent and largely independent of law...Cicero reversed the earlier Greek conception of the relation between Law and Rights and proceeded to make right in every sense subordinate to and dependent upon Law."

Law of God

Cicero's ideas on Natural law were in no sense original, they were only a restatement of the Stoic doctrine. However, he was mainly responsible for spreading them through Western Europe from his own days down to the 19th century. He believed that there is a single universal law of nature governing the whole world. It has arisen equally from the fact of God's provisional government of the world and from the rational and social nature of man which makes them akin to God. As Sabine puts it, "It is same every were and is unchangeably binding upon all men and all nations. No legislation that contravenes it is entitled to the name of law, for no ruler and no people can make right wrong." In Cicero's own work, (in De Republica) a true law is "right reason consonant with nature, diffused among all men, constant and eternal; which summons to duty by its command and hinders from fraud by its prohibition....To invalidate this law by human legislation in never morally right". Again, "God is the author of this law, its interpreter and its sponsor. The man who will not obey it will abandon his better self". Thus it may better be termed as the Law of God.

Synthesis of Ethics and Politics

According to Cicero, Law of Nature is self-imposed. It may be of the nature of a moral law. Law of Nature is the single system of law governing the entire universe to which all natural things have an obligation to conform. Inanimate things are bound to pay obedience to it by natural necessity. Animals have instincts by which they conform blindly. Man is obliged to obey by his reason. Man's reason is capable of discovering this law to him, and of directing his conduct in conformity with it. Plato assigned this part only to the philosopher king. The allegiance which a citizen owed to the laws of his state is conditional and not absolute. If these laws do not conform to the Law of Nature, they do not deserve to be called laws. On the other hand, submission to the Law of Nature is unconditional and absolute. In the words of Gettell, Cicero believed that "moral principles are as applicable to political matter as they are in private matters, and that true law is right reason, conformable to nature, universal and eternal."

Doctrine of Natural Equality of Men

In Cicero the doctrine of Law of Nature is combine with the doctrine of natural equality of men. This doctrine is the profoundest contribution of Stoicism to political thought. He said that men are equal in possession of reason. It raises them above the level of beasts. It makes them equal in the eyes of God. Inequality is a vice. It is man made and not natural. This belief brings Cicero and Stoics nearer to us than to Plato and Aristotle. To Cicero equality was a moral requirement and not a fact, it had no democratic implications. According to Dr. Carlyle, it is the dividing line between ancient and the modern political theory.

Citizenship of the World

As subject to the same law and sharing in a common justice all men constitute members of a society co-extensive with humanity and transcending the difference of race and language. The whole universe must be conceived as one common wealth of which all men, good as well as bad, are members. This is the restatement of Stoic conception of citizenship of world.

Modern Elements

Cicero's concepts of equality of man, supremacy of law, universal brotherhood and natural law are indicative of modernity of his thought. Natural law and equality of men are the two principles on which modern democracy is based. Christianity incorporating most of the Hellenic Philosophy and Roman Law, from which most of the legal systems of the west have been derived, have been the two channels through which these ideas have come to us.

Difference from Greek Thought

According to Carlyle, no change in political theory is so startling in its completeness as a change from Aristotle to Cicero. Cicero differed from the Greek thought in the following respects:

1. Closer to Kant than Aristotle. For Aristotle, relation of free citizenship can only exist between equals, but because men are not equal, Aristotle inferred that citizenship must be restricted to a small carefully selected group. Cicero, on the contrary, infers that because all men are subject to one law and so are fellow citizens, they must be in some sense equal. Some measures of dignity and respects is due to every man. Slave is not, as Aristotle said a living tool but a wage earner hired for life. Kant said that man must be treated as an end and not a means. Astonishing fact is that Cicero is closer to Kant than he is to Aristotle.

2. Mixed Democratic Government. While Aristotle and Plato perferred Monarchy and Aristocracy, Cicero advocated mixed government, preferably democratic.

3. Particular State. Cicero gave a particular state, not an ideal state of Plato's Republic.

4. Universal Brotherhood. Greeks dealt with city states. Cicero conceived a universal brotherhood. He had a sense of the world brotherhood. Both Plato and Aristotle had no place for mankind in their political theories. For them all the non-Greek world was barbarian, and so could be enslaved without any question of injustice. Cicero had a more universal outlook.

5. Concept of Natural Law. Cicero gave a new concept of natural law which was unknown to the Greeks.

6. Law based on rights. Greeks thought that right is in source and content antecedent to and independent of law, Cicero reversed this process.

7. Rule of Law. Cicero's state depended more upon law than that of Plato and Aristotle. Philosophy and not law is the main theme of Plato's Republic and Aristotle's Politics. To Cicero, the rule of law is more important.

8. Liberty based on Popular Consent. Cicero went farther than Aristotle in his stress on popular consent as the foundation of the legitimate government and liberty. He said "Liberty has no dwelling place in any state except that in which the people's power is the greatest and surely nothing can be sweeter than liberty; but it is not the same for all, it does not deserve the name of liberty."

To sum up, in the words of Gettle, Cicero's ideas of justice and natural law sank deep into Roman legal thought and profoundly influenced the later imperial jurists and the early Christian writers. And his idea of world unity and of universal law and authority remained the central principle of political thought throughout the whole medieval period.

DEVELOPMENT OF ROMAN LAW

The greatest contribution of Roman political thought is in the juristic field. It is still taught to the students of law in Western and in Indian Universities and all over the world in majority of countries.

Roman law grew slowly, in the beginning it grew with religious precepts, customs and rules of equity. With the passage of time distinction began between divine functions and rational customs of men. About 450 B.C. the customary rules of Romans were codified into the twelve tables. It brought symmetrical classification and clearness into the laws. Codification hitted hard the clarity of the laws and the powers of nobles, who were the sole interpreter of laws in their own interest. Cicero stated that laws govern the magistrate."

Common men called Plebians now knew their laws. The future laws passed in their favour were recorded and became part of codified law. It gave inspiration to legal thought in Rome and yielded place to secular authority and, man made laws. The Twelve Tables were supposed to contain all laws which were filled by adding new body of laws passed by legislative bodies with the consent of the people. This gave rise to Roman diction that Roman laws represent the will of the state. In the beginning these were passed and modified by plebiscite but later on by constitutions of the emperors. Lawyers were jurists and not philosophers. Twelve Tables was broken down by the edicts issued by proctors, responses drafted by Juris consults and the constitutions proclaimed by emperors. Law was not only expanded but also rationalised. Proctors and juris consults laid down new judicial principles of general application and the important notion of *Jus Naturale* were recognised.

With the expansion of trade and commerce in Roman Empire foreigners flocked to Rome. A special magistrate was appointed to decide their fate as these had to deal with foreign merchants of different countries. In it proctor Perogrinus embodied principles of natural equity and customs and laws common to nations subject of Rome. Principles of equity representing abstract principles of justice, dictates of reason of universal application, brought into existence conception of *Jus Naturale*. *Jus Gentium* meant laws common to all nations. As slavery was prevalent during those days among all nations so it was acceptable to *Jus Gentium*. But as nature has created all men equal so slavery could not be accepted or supported under *Jus Naturale*.

Nettleship holds that the *Jus Gentium* meant the usage of world of all mankind. It was intended to express common usage and customs, picked up in war commerce or travel. Sabine, on the other hand, holds that *Jus Gentium* was and never was anything else, but a portion of the positive Roman law with commercial usuage and other sources of law, more specially the procterian edict, clothed in a concerted form. The *jus gentium* was that part of the private law of Rome which was essentially in accordance with the private law of other nations, more especially that of Greeks.

Fusion of *Jus Gentium* and *Jus Naturale* made Roman legal system comprehensive and more liberal. Legal appeals from all part of Roman empire were sent to professional juris-consults and their opinions were considered as good as law. The Jurists had to lay down general principles of universal application and were responsible for the creation of a scientific system of jurisprudence like code of Justinian. As the Jurists were Stocis notions of brotherhood of man and the universality of law prevailed in their rules. They believed that law is an impersonal reason.

Corpus Juris or Code of Justinian

Next to Bible and Christian teachings, code of Justinian made profound influence on the western world. This code contains the following :

1. The Institutes 533 A.D. It contains legal notions given in the ideas of Marcian and Florentins. The legal jurists collected their opinion on expressed opinions of the best legal minds.

2. The Digest. Published in 533 A.D., it contained select passages from the legal pronouncements of collected lawyers.

3. Novel. A collection of collected lawyers.

4. Collection of Laws. A collection of imperial laws and decrees relating to public and private laws from the beginning of the empire.

(i) *The Laws of Nature*. Gins divided laws as *jus Gentium,* i.e. *Gentium*, i.e. law of notions, *Jus civile,* i.e. law of nature embodying abstract principles of right. According to *Gins Jus Naturale* law presents ideal law. It is a law which nature has taught to all mankind. Ulpain says that the law of nature was ideal law, while *Jus Gentium* and *Jus Civile* are supporters of it.

(ii) *Slavery*. Aristotle defended slavery but Gins holds slavery as unnatural and artificial. Ulpain regarded slavery as wickedness of mankind. Cicero and Seneca pleaded for the humane and kind treatment to slaves.

(iii) *Property*. Roman Jurists believed that during primitive golden age there was no property. They believed that property came in existence due to greed of man. They supported its retention because in every known stage of human history property always existed and is necessary for human existence.

(iv) *The Civil Law*. Law has been defined by great jurist, Salmend, as "sovereign body as interpreted by judges." It is not necessary that it should be related to morality or justice. But Roman conception of law was based on ethical principles of morality. Gins stated that the law is right reason embodied in state. Ulpain said that the law stood as a criterion to judge what was just or unjust and enabled man to do good and just. As per Justinians justice represented a constant and perpetual disposition of the will which renders to each one what was his due. Thus Romans believed that object of law was to make man good. Justice is to give every man his right.

(v) *Imperium*. Romans sought source of political authority in imperium which meant that people delegate authority to rulers. Gins said that authority were people,who delegated their authority to ruler. *Rex Legius* possesses the force of law because it was finally based on the will of the people. The people gave all authority, i.e. Imperium and its powers to the ruler. Thus lawyers gave us new theory of delegation of authority or Imperium by the people to the ruler. As authority once delegated cannot be taken back, so the authority of King became supreme and he became not only the fountain of law but above law. Thus on the one side, Emperor got authority as delegation from people and on the practical side he became supreme. But people remained the ultimate source of authority.

Importance of Roman Law

Romans made everlasting contribution in the field of jurisprudence and law. Roman law served as the basis of common law of the church. It influenced the legal world. In Western Europe and in America all the countries have been influenced by it. It is still taught all over the world. According to Rudolf Stammler: "Belief in justice is the crowning glory of Roman jurisprudence." In the words of Sabine, "A conception of Natural law and belief in justice and equality of man etc., are important contribution of Roman Political thought."

INFLUENCE OF ROMAN INSTITUTIONS

Rome did not contribute much to the political philosophy. Her political institutions and legal system, however, exerted a tremendous influence on political evolution. For many centuries after her the idea of the state was based on the institutions that Rome had established.

(i) *Law*. The whole of Western European law is based on the Roman law.

(ii) *Jurisprudence*. The importance of the Roman system of jurisprudence lies in the fact that it is a universal and comprehensive law. It represents the crystallised experience of multitude of people living in the vast Romans world, as expressed by trained Roman jurists. It is comprehensive and refined. It represents a people who had a genius for law. Those who wanted to be called civilised adopted it. It represented the superior civilisation of a world empire. Its civilising influence cannot be over emphasised.

(iii) *Canon Law*. The Roman law became the basis of canon law, when Christianity became the state church of the Roman Empire. It is the outcome of the patience of many centuries and is the symbol of the greatness of the Roman Empire.

DEPARTURE FROM TRADITIONAL GREEK VIEW

Roman concept of law shows a radical departure from the traditional Greek law. The Greeks did not separate law from religion.

1. Concept of Law. Romans did not consider a human superior to be the source of law : its source and sanction was religious or ethical. Law was the expression of passionless reason. In Rome the final result of the legal development was the secularisation of law. If forms the basis of the civil law of many countries in the world. Modern conception of law as the command of a definite human superior rests on it. Romans taught mankind that the popular will is the source of all law. They distinguished between law and morality.

2. Codification of Roman Law. Roman laws in the beginning were a mixture of religious regulations and customary rules. The Romans did not know that the state could create law. The violation of a customary law was sin against the God. It was not an offence against the state. In about 450 B.C. Roman laws were codified in the form of twelve tables. The law came to be considered as the will of the state. It formulated and sanctioned it. The religious element was pushed in the background. In a world empire consisting of diverse people the law could not remain attached to religion. The practical necessity divorced law from religion and ethics. It made law secular. However, the Roman law was not the product of legislation in the modern sense of the term. Roman jurists and lawyers always thought that the positive law enacted by the state must conform to the higher law of nature which sets up certain norms. They were deeply influenced by the humanistic doctrines of stoicism. As Sabine puts it, Roman law preserved the spirit of Cicero's phrase, "We are servants of the law in order that we may be free."

3. Stoic Doctrines of Jurists. Towards the close of the Middle Ages when the study of Roman law was revised, the Roman dictum that the will of the prince is the source of law, was separated from the Roman idea that the prince is the agent of the people. It was used as the basis for the theory of the sovereignty of the national king. The Stoic doctrines of the jurists were that by natural law all men are born free and that all men are equal in natural rights. These were revived by the opponents of royal authority. They built on it the theory of social contract and actual rights. It served as the basis for revolution and democracy. The concepts of *Jus gentium* and *Jus naturale* played an important part in the creation of the theory of international law. It was finally worked out by Grotius.

4. State as Legal Person. Greeks, especially Plato, had merged the individual in the state completely. The Romans, on the other hand, separated the individual from the state. Both state and individual were allotted definite rights and duties. The state was not considered non-essential. The Epicureans considered it natural and necessary. Individual rather than the state, was made the centre of legal thought. To protect the rights of the individual as a legal person, was the essence of all functions of the state. The state was viewed as a legal person, exercising its authority within difinite limits. This was the basis of Roman private law. The idea of legal personality of the state influenced the medieval thinkers distinct from society, as it was based on the abstract idea of the state.

5. Delegation of Authority. The state was the legal sovereign. The political sovereignty, however, was made to reside in the people as a whole. As Gettell put it, "The early kings, the republican magistrates, and in theory at least, even the emperors, received their authority from the citizens, acted as their agents, and were responsible to them for the exercise of their duties. The will of the emperor had the force of law because, in theory, the people had delegated to him their entire authority." This delegation of authority was by a governmental contract, and not by a social contract. The delegation was irrevocable. It could not be withdrawn. There was no redress against the abuse of delegated authority by the officials. Revolutions were unjustified. The Roman lawyers based despotic rule on the basis of the consent of the people. All citizens had equal political rights. In the citizens as a body was considered a divine gift. The emperor ruled by virtue of the Divine will and delegated his political authority to the state officials.

6. Idea of Contract. The idea of contract played a large part in Roman legal theory. The creation of the law took the form of a contract. In agreement with the popular assemblies the laws were made by the magistrates. The magistrates proposed and the assemblies ratified the new laws. In the words of Gettell, "Law was not a command imposed by a sovereign upon his subjects, but a contract arranged among the constituent organs of the state after negotiation." Roman contract was involved even in religious thought, the worshipper used to worship in bargain for certain benefits from gods. The private law of the Romans was based on the idea of contractual obligation between the individuals.

7. Concept of Imperialism. Before the Christian Era had begun, Rome had developed into a world state. For the spread of commerce and expansion of the empire a vast network of roads had been constructed. The Roman laws kept order in the empire. It promoted not only expansion of empire but also the development of commerce. The Romans preferred order to the Greek notion of liberty. Individual liberty was crushed for the maintenance of order. In contrast to the Greek ideas of liberty and democracy, Romans placed chief emphasis on the ideas of law, order and unity. The weakness of the Greeks was in their failure to unite. Faction fight cost them political independence. On the other hand, Rome subjugated the whole western world. It united her population. It resulted in the establishment of similar political institutions and legal system. This similarity of conditions created a sense of unity in different people.

8. Foundation of Modern Democracy. In order to realise unification and establishment of peace and order, Rome was compelled to destroy the Greek conception of freedom and democracy. It made the state highly centralised and all powerful. The vastness of the empire made centralised despotism a political necessity. Democracy and freedom became impossible. The Roman despotism, however, made modern democracy possible. It levelled down local jealousies and class distinctions. It put into political practice the ideals of human brotherhood and of equality of men before the law. The foundation of the modern point of view of law was laid by the cosmopolitan power of Rome and the Stoic-Christian conception of the brotherhood of man.

9. Principles of Colonial and Municipal Administration. Romans laid down the principles of colonial and municipal administration. Self-government was permitted to the provinces. The subject peoples realised the value of Roman order. They felt a loss of something valuable when the Roman empire fell to pieces. They did not establish the conception of civilised life. The provinces continued to flourish long after the capital itself broke down. Rome regained a name of much power when the actual city was ruined. Her language and law spread over the world. The church built up its organisation and its authority on the model of Roman empire. Caesar et Imperium, Theory of world-unity etc. these Roman words were long powerful in political thought.

10. Idea of Sovereignty. Almost unaided by Greek thought the Romans developed one more important idea called Imperium or sovereignty. They believed that each community has its inherent power of issuing commands to its individuals and of exacting obedience from them. This authority of issuing commands and compelling obedience to them was called by them Imperium. This is sovereignty as we call it now. Its possession was the characteristic of every community. Romans did not develop this idea systematically. They however, built up a magnificent system of laws upon it : Imperium or sovereignty. The people had no share in its exercise. On the death of one king it passed on to his successor.

11. Social Control Theory. In the Republican year, the Imperium was divided among the public officials. These were accountable to the people for its exercise. This shows that imperium resided in the people organised in their assemblies. No individual had a particular and absolute title to rule by virtue of any hereditary claims of divine antecedents. Thus arose the social contract theory. According to it the people possess the ultimate authority in the state. They could not exercise it themselves. So they delegated it to or vested it by their will in one or more persons. Having once delegated it, they could not withdraw it. They had to respect and obey them. The rule that the people are the sole repositories of state power and that the emperor is their agent did not die out, even during the imperial era. As a matter of fact the emperor was responsible to none. He alone had the right to command and exact obedience.

12. Popular Sovereignty. The idea of imperium as a trust prevented its wielder from becoming a tyrant. It prevented acting against the welfare of the people. During the monarchy it was a reality. It was only a theory during the empire. The exercise of imperium was believed to rest on the consent of the people. The Romans believed in the theory of popular sovereignty.

QUESTIONS FOR EXERCISE

1. "In the general development of political thought, the importance of Rome is very great but this importance results from neither striking originality, nor from any considerable new contribution to the world's

stock of political ideas, it was owing wholly to the Greek political part that Rome played in laying the legal and political foundation of the Western world." Elucidiate the above and bring out the chief contribution of Rome to the development of western civilization.

2. "Belief in justice is the crowning glory of Roman jurisprudence" (Sabine). Elucidiate.
3. Polybius was the first political theorist to bring out the importance and advantages of mixed type of Government. Discuss and Explain.
4. Explain the political thought of Seneca.
5. "Time is right reason" Cicero. Comment.
6. How far is it correct to say that Cicero's thought is a synthesis of Platonic and Stoic ideas in the context of Roman states?
7. Explain the principle of Cicero regarding the natural law and discuss its importance in the history of political philosophy.
8. What was the influence of Roman political thought on the development of the European political thought?

10
Christian Political Thought

Jesus had no interest in political thought. Christianity in its earlier stages was only a religious movement. It had nothing to do with political doctrines. The early Christians were bound together by spiritualities. They had not temporal or political bonds. They emphasized the principle of Golden Rule. The morality of the individual was instruction. The authority of Government was minimum. Jesus distinguished the spiritual kingdom from the kingdoms of this world. The ideas of the early Christians on political topics were mostly Stoic in character. They believed that an individual must render obedience to duly constituted Government. They had faith in the equality of men in the eyes of God. They believed in the divine government of the world. St. Paul called natural law as written in men's hearts and revealed by reason. It was distinct from the law of the state.

By being connected with the Christian conception of the fatherhood of God and brotherhood of man these Stoic ideas received a deeper meaning. The democratic idea of human equality found stronger support in the idea of brotherhood of men. This was common participation in Divinity. The Stoic conception of cosmopolitanism acquired a fuller and deeper significance through the Christian conception if the kingdom of ends.

DIVINE RIGHT OF KINGSHIP

Jesus Christ said, "Render unto Caesar the things that are Caesar's and unto God the things that are God's". St. Paul expressed it in his own characteristic way, "Let every soul be subject unto higher powers. For there in no power but of God: the powers that be are ordained of God. Whosoever therefore resisteth the power, resisteth the ordinance of God; and they that resist shall receive unto themselves damnation." What is implied by the above quotation of St. Paul is that civil Government or state is a Divine institution deriving its authority from God and not from the people as believed by Romans. Thus the obedience to secular authority became a fundamental principle of Christian thought. According to the Christian doctrine, obedience to the civil authorities is a religious obligation. To disobey the ruler is to disobey God. The state is to be obeyed because of religious duty. It was also a political necessity. The state exists to maintain justice. It therefore has a sacred character. Its ruler is God's servant, the obedience is essential. This reverence is, however, to the office of the ruler rather than to his person. What Christianity upheld was that divine right of kingship and not of kings.

STATE AS NECESSARY INSTITUTION

The Apostles stated these ideas for properly adjusting the relations of the early church to the Roman Government. It was also because of the desire to contract the anarchical tendencies in the early Christian societies. In theory, the church fathers held that all men are equal. There ought to be no Government whatsoever. Anarchy was a legitimate state of affairs. Gradually, they recognised that the state was essentially based upon Stoic philosophy, that man is naturally social and that government is necessary for people, it is essential to obey the law of the state. In the words of Gettle, "The Christian Writers, in adopting the Stoic rather than the Epicurean attitude towards the state and in adding the Christian conception of the divine order in human society, laid the foundation for the political thought of the following thousand years."

KINGSHIP AS TRUST

As a consequence of the fall of man from original innocence to the depraved condition, political authority was instituted by God. Thus civil Government of coercive authority is the result of human sin. This does not mean that it is itself sinful. God himself established state for the maintenance of justice. To drive out the original sin or disobedience of God by Adam in eating the forbidden fruit and the consequent depravity of human nature, the Government is a necessary controlling and correcting agency. It is a necessary evil. Its importance increased the remedies for man's constituted, civil authority. This is due to its sacred character, its head is the vicar of agent of God. According to St. Paul, however, the king was not the lord of the people. He was their first servant in order to minister their needs. In his own words, "whosoever will be the chiefest shall be the servant of all." Kingship was regarded as a trust throughout the Middle Ages.

CAUSES OF DIVINE SANCTION TO THE STATE

The attempt at giving a divine sanction to the representing secular power was due to following reasons:

1. Counteracting Anarchism. There was the desire to counteract the evils of anarchism taught by some early thinkers.

2. Imperial Adoption and Endowment. The empire had adopted and endowed the church. The church showed its gratitude by exalting the position of the empire.

3. Jewish Theory of Divine Kingship. The Christian fathers inherited this theory. The church doctrine that the ruler derived his power from God was the chief difference between the church fathers and the Roman legal writers, the latter traced all authority to its ultimate source in the people. Later, medieval political thought gave considerable attention to the contrast between these principals. This delegation of political authority to the state amounts to a repudiation of the contractual basis of political obligation.

TWO FOLD HUMAN DUTY

Deverting to the quotation of Christ: "Render unto Caesar the things that are Caesar's and unto God the things that are God's." This Christian teaching implies a sphere of life beyond political one. Some things belong to Caesar. There are other things which belong to God and which must be rendered upto him. It means that man has a two fold duty: one to civic authorities and the other to God. In case of clash between the two, one should obey God rather than the political authority. In other words, passive obedience to the powers that he was enjoined, Government was conceived as means of carrying out of God's will on earth, and meekness and humility was insisted upon. But when the state interfered with the teachings of the church obedience was permitted. The injunctions to obey God rather than man led to the passive resistance of the martyrs.

TWO TYPES OF WORLD

The Christain doctrine stressed on theoretical duty of obedience to civic authorities. However, its ultimate loyalty to God or church made it incompatible with the Roman concept of unlimited and undivided devotion to the state. Therefore, the Christians were persecuted by Roman emperor Marcus Aurelious. Moreover, this aspect may be contrasted with the state. The Christian doctrine separated the spiritual from temporal sphere of the state, the idea to realise all the values of life through membership of the state. The Christian doctrine separates the spiritual from temporal sphere or takes the ultimate values of life totally out of the political sphere. In the words of Bowle, "It pulls the individual out of the organic community of the city or temple and sets him into a world beyond them. It undermines the whole structure of the more primitive, less individualised community and the psychological solidarity which had kept earlier societies strong and stable, if insensitive. Although St. Paul preached for obedience to civic authorities, yet held that Christians should seek settlement of their disputes not in pagan courts but in Christian courts according to Christian law. It amounted to setting up a state within a state."

DUAL HUMAN NATURE

Rendering unto Caesar things that are Caesar's and unto God things that are God's implies that man has a dual nature and is subject to two authorities. As body belongs to the civil society, his material or temporal interests are bound up with his membership of the secular state. Therefore obedience to it becomes a mundane necessity. As spirit man has different interests and a different destiny. He becomes a member of the kingdom of ends which is within him. His spiritual interests are in keeping of the church and not the concern of the civic society. The spiritual interests are more important than physical interests. In case of conflict between loyalty to the state and loyalty to God the latter should always take precedence over the former. Stoics also thought of the membership of two states — the state of birth and the world at large. The Stoic idea of citizenship of the world is, however, different from the Christian notion of membership of the city of God which is based on the cleavage between body and soul.

THEORY OF TWO SWORDS

Primitive Christianity was politically indifferent, unfavourable for political speculation and mainly concerned with the problem of salvation of the soul. As the conditions changed, Christianity became the official religion of the Empire and the church its adjunct. Both came to have close relationship. It was admitted that they should help each other. The church was to preach the duty of civic obedience. The state was to protect and help the church. As the church came to be organised on its own doctrines and acquired large property, it began to claim autonomy in spiritual matters. Thus arose the problem of proper relation between them until the later part of the 11th century. This principle has been termed as the theory of two swords.

STATE AND CHURCH

A man has to subject himself to the rule of the secular state for his physical and economic well-being and for the enjoyment of worldly peace and prosperity. On other hand, he has to submit to the discipline imposed by the church authorities for promoting his spiritual welfare and for attaining salvation. A sword symbolises rulership. According to early church fathers, "God gave one sword to the emperor and the other to the Pope. It was the main function of the civil authority to maintain peace and order and dispense justice, while the business of the clergyman was to minister to the spiritual welfare of the citizens and help them to attain eternal salvation." Two authorities were now bound within each other's way to prevail. Jesus's saying implies that these should subsist between the two orders. "The Christian ruler would seek guidance from the church authorities in spiritual matters and the bishops would assist the civic authorities in dealing with secular matters and make use of imperial laws for the course of temporal affairs only."

Statement of Pope Gelasus I

In a letter to the Roman Emperor Anastasius, Pope Gelasus I gave an authoritative statement to the doctrine of Two Swords. He wrote, "Auguste Emperor, this world is governed by two powers — by bishops and by kings; of these the responsibility of the priests is the weightier since they have to render an account to God even for kings themselves...You devoutly bow your head to the bishops who are charged with the administration of holy things; you address yourself to them to be conducted in the ways of salvation; and in all that regards the reception and administration of the sacraments, you acknowledge that far from having any power to command, you are bound to obey them...in all such concerns you depend upon their judgement, and that you have no right to subject them to your will...The ministers of religion obey your laws in all that belongs to the temporal order, because they know you have received your powers from above."

Controversy Between Pope and Emperor

If line could be drawn to divide secular from spiritual elements, there would have been no difficulties in the application of this doctrine. But the feudal order was so complex that the jurisdictions of the two parallel and autonomous Government overlapped. Each began to fell that the other was interfering in his sphere. In the 11th century, a great controversy started between the relations of the pope and the emperor. It lasted several hundred years with many ups and downs.

The conception of natural law, as worked out by Cicero and suggested by St. Paul, was adopted by the early church fathers. They taught that men are by nature free and equal. They recognised slavery as lawful. They considered it a punishment as well as a remedy for sin, due to the fall of man from the state of the nature where all men were equal. They declared that all men are free whatever the physical disabilities imposed upon them. Spirit of slavery is discipline by God for the good of the soul of the slave. As a punishment for human sin slavery must be accepted as such submission to God's will. However, the masters must treat their slaves with mercy and consideration. Though it was contrary to the teachings of Christianity, the Christian Church tolerated slavery for centuries.

POLITICAL THOUGHT OF ST. AUGUSTINE (354 — 403 A.D.)

Contemporary Circumstances

St. Augustine was one of the greatest church fathers. He greatly influenced political thought. He was the son of a pagan father and Christian mother. He was educated at Madaura. He was the Bishop concerted to Christianity by St. Ambrose of Milan. He was the Bishop of Hippo in North Africa. He was the most important figure in the history of the Christian Church after St. Paul. He lived in the early part of the 5th century. It is often called the formative period of Christian thought. It was a period of transition from the ancient to the medieval age. The medievalism began with St. Augustine. Europe had gained religious unity after the spread of Christianity in the Roman Empire. The Church and the state were not hostile to each other. This period was critical for Christianity. The barbarian attacks brought ruin to the empire of Rome. It had been the most stabilising factor for about eight centuries for the civilised world. The fate of civilization and Catholicism alike hung in the balance. Finally, Rome was sacked and plundered by King Alaric and the Goths in 410 A.D.

Influence of the Fall of Rome

Rome was the symbol of all that was potent and enduring. Its fall caused great disturbance and confusion in the minds of pagans and Christians alike.

Pagans were the enemies of the church. They attributed the fall of Rome to Christianity. They pointed out that so long as the Romans worshipped the old gods of city-state like Jupiter, Naptune, Iris etc., success followed in their footsteps. Rome grew from a city-state to great world empire. When Romans abandoned the old gods and adopted Christianity, Rome met its fall. The Christians refuted this contention of the pagans. They were themselves terror stricken that their faith and religion could not save Rome from this disaster. Not only the fate of the Empire was the cause of concern to the thinking people but the state of affairs in the church was also no less source of the concern of thinking people but schisms appeared within it. Its well known solidarity disappeared. Heresy was rampant. News sprang up, especially in North Africa.

Augustine's Defence of Christianity

St. Augustine took up the defence of Christianity by explaining the cause of the fall of Rome. He shared the suppression of heresy and the combat of paganism. He used his philosophical genius to strengthen the church and for the depiction of its ideals. He wrote voluminously.

Political Principles in Christian Thought

St. Augustine was the first Christian intellectual who found a place in history. His work a mine of ideas in which both Protestant and Catholic writers of later times have dug. In his "*Essays on Government*" Barker says, his writings were a mine of ideas which expressed an abounding gift of self-expression. He adds that St. Augustine possessed a remarkable style of Latin which was atonce marvelous, subtle and sinuous. To quote Bowl, "St. Augustine's is a highly trained claim that his spiritual experience supersedes the best classical thought. The classical outlook, it is argued, was over-intellectualised. The Greek and Roman philosophers were attempting to live by reason alone and never tapped the spiritual energy of the whole man. He found tne final symbol of the complete harmony of the whole — by surrender to a power beyond the self, personality regains its full integrity and a harmony of intelligence, will and energy is secured." Bowle described the writings of St. Augustine as "the record of an ultra-sensitive mind dealing with the demands of an exacting life, and of a powerful intellect which finally found peace by an act of faith."

The City of God

Political philosophy of St. Augustine is contained in his book *'De Civitate Dei'* popular by known as 'The City of God'. It is divided into 22 books. The first ten book are the defence of Christianity from pagan attacks. The remaining 12 books are concerned with the construction of the city of God. This works contains two of Augustine's most important ideas, namely, the conception of Christian commonwealth and the culmination of spiritual development of mankind. St. Augustine thus described the immediate cause of the writing of this book "Rome, having been stormed and sacked by the Goths, under Alaric, their king, the pagans made an attempt to attribute the calamity to the Christian religion...It was this which kindled my zeal for the name of God and prompted me to undertake the defence of the city of God against its assailants."

Religious Interpretation of History

St. Augustine ridiculed the idea that Rome fell because of Christian religion and because of disfavour of pagan gods. He traced history to show that Rome had earlier also met such a fate when those old gods could not save it either. He interpreted the course of human history in terms of the Eternal Will of God. The things are moving in such a way that finally the kingdom of god will be established on earth. Thus the sack of Rome was a blessing in disguise as it led towards that goal. The story of mankind depends not upon a chance but upon the eternal purpose of the creator. Behind everything there is divine will.

Philosophy of History

Like Hegel and Marx, St. Augustine saw the world process as a vast drama unfolding itself in time. The human history was seen as a continuous conflict between the powers of darkness and powers of light in which the later will finally win. Augustine believed in predestination. To him, the worst evil had some good in it. The evil of fall of Rome would be attended with the good of the founding of the city of God. Christianity would be the religion of the rulers and the ruled. It would save the state from any catastrophe.

Man as a Citizen of Two Cities

According to Augustine man is a citizen of two cities, namely the city of his birth and the city of God. This is because man's nature is two-fold. He is both spirit and body. The earthly city is founded due to the impulses of lower human nature. This is the kingdom of satan, 'Civitas Terrona'. It is embodied in the empires of Asyria, Babylonia and Rome. Hence they fell. The city of God is founded in the hope of heavenly peace and spiritual salvation. As body man is a member of the earthly state, as spirit he belongs to the city of God, its membership is indispensable for the salvation of his soul. Since the inception of Christianity in the world, human history has been the dramatic struggle between these two states or cities. Those earthly states that accept Christianity came nearer to the city of God which will finally emerge victorious.

Contrast of the Two States

Augustine further compared both these states. The earthly state was by its very nature impermanent and perishable. The city of God was permanent and enduring. In Sabine's words, "All earthly kingdoms must pass away, for earthly power is naturally mutable and unstable; it is built on those aspects of human nature which necessarily issue in war and the greed of domination." Thus St. Augustine mixed together the conception of state of Plato and Cicero in the conception of city of God. He presented them in a setting of Christian theology. The city of God is universal in time and space. It is founded on love of God. The earthly state is based on self love. The city of God is an abstract conception. Describing the relation between the church and the city of God, Foster wrote,

"The church is both one section of the city, comprising these members who are all (or almost all) whome members of the city must have passed." Thus the membership of the city of the God is wider. It includes angels and such elects of God. One can become member of city of God only after accepting the membership of the church. The city of God is nothing but a Christianity church state. Non-believers were excluded from it. Both Roman Catholic Church and the city of God were closely connected though they were not identical.

Stoic City of God

Augustine's city of God resembled Stoic city of God. Though it is like Cicero's universal society it is not open to all human beings by virtue of their humanity due to the fall of man. Men can become its member only by the grace of God. Grace is given only to those who repose their faith in Jesus Christ. Grace is not for race, state or class. It is the real qualification for membership of the city of God. This city does not include the whole humanity. It is open only to the members of the Christain church. These members were bound into a unity by their common love and worship of God, without any distinction of class, race or state. This conception of the Christian church as the visible manifestation of the city of God prepared the ground for the idea of the universal Christian society living under one principle of life. This idea dominated throughout the Middle ages. The conception of the Holy Roman Empire was built upon the city of God. Hence St. Augustine is sometimes described as the man at the turning point of an age. He has been called the perfector of the old and the percursor of a new mode of thought.

Secular V/S Christian State

As Christian church is the visible embodiment of the Civitas Dei, so is Roman Empire closely connected with the earthly state of Civitas Terrona which is also an abstract idea like that of the earthly state of God. The association between the two led Augustine to depreciate the authority of the secular state in comparison to the church. Later medieval writers took up this idea in order to claim supremacy of the church. To Augustine all human history is the majestic unfolding of the plan of decisive salvation in which the appearance of the church marks the decisive moment. This idea was dominant in the thought of the Middle ages.

QUESTIONS FOR EXERCISE

1. "Render upto Caesar the things that are Caesar's and upto God the things that are God's." (Jesus Christ). Explain.
2. Explain the theory of Two Swords and bring out its bearing on Medieval Political Thought.
3. "The most important political ideas of St. Angustine are those which centre round the doctorinc of "two cities" the earthly city and city of

God. The city of God realizes in eminent degree two values justice and peace.'' (Foster). Explain.

4. 'Medieval thinkers' says Prof. Hearnshaw ''seems like student writing essays on political theory from text books three in number, the Bible, the Roman law and the Politics of Aristotle.'' Show the extent to which Augustine drew upon the three sources.

PART II — MEDIEVAL POLITICAL THOUGHT

11

Political Thought of Middle Ages

Middle Ages have been usually characterised as non-political. These times, on the whole, were barren of all political activities. However, there was political activity though it was not subordinated to theology. Middle Ages are known for giving ideas about monarchy. Monarchy was considered as the best form of government. Rather than the person of the monarch, stress was laid on the office or institution of concept of law. It was considered as belonging to the common folk. Law was the supreme authority behind the king for governing the masses. Universalism was preached. It was believed that spiritual and temporal authorities were of mutual help to each other. The authority of church and papacy grew. It was also supported by the feudal lords who wanted to see weak monarchs on the throne. Christian scholars studied Christian civilisation. Theology was given more importance. A movement known as scholasticism spread. It continued to influence the Middle Ages. Theory of Corporation was accepted as the principle of governing the people. Ultimate authority was not vested in the individual but in the organisation, assembly or council. Composite character of the state was stressed. The state was believed to be the result of a convention. This idea held ground for considerably long period. The sovereign was not absolute. She was bound by the rules of community and law of nature. This authority was challenged by the feudal lords and church fathers. The system of representation was quite common. The representative was considered a trustee and not an agent of the people. Medieval period was dominated by a struggle for supremacy between the church and the king. Both tried to establish their power and authority. The institution of feudalism meant a contract as well as personal loyalty. Both these things existed side by side. The whole system was complex and complicated.

Dark Ages

It is very doubtful to lay down a demarcating line between ancient and medieval period. Medievalism is not absolute. It is relative with reference to each country. Usually, Machiavelli (1469-1527) has been considered as the first modern thinker, with whom ends medievalism. The medieval period lasted for over 100 years. Usually, without any political speculation medieval age is called 'Dark Ages'. There was no origination of new ideas in political field. There was lack of intelligence among the rulers. Education was neglected. Differing from this usual idea Barker has said, "There was abundant political thought in the Middle Ages, just because they were ages of formation and formulation, in which the Christian Heaven, the great new thing in the world, was steadily permeating society and the fresh Germanic influx into the ancient world was finding its place and level." The idea of corporation and self-government was mooted. This was a step forward in support of monarchy.

CHARACTERISTIC FEATURES OF MIDDLE AGES

The Germans were not very intelligent. They believed in the supremacy of law, they gave birth to the idea of nationalism. The period was not dead absolutely. It had life in so far as political philosophy of breaking of new ideas was concerned. Following were the prominent features of the middle ages:

1. Monarchy
2. The Law
3. Universalism
4. Papacy
5. Scholasticism
6. Corporations
7. The State
8. Sovereignty
9. Representationism
10. Secular Spiritual Supremacy
11. Feudalism

1. Monarchy. Medieval political philosophy believed in the theory of divine origin of kingship. God was overlord of all kings. Earthly lordship flowed from the Divine Lordship. Monarchy was considered the best form of government and political organisation. However, Barker has said, "The popular business and popular right of critics of monarchy are cardinal tenets of medieval theory." Though the king was representative of God yet the community had a right to control him. Reconciliation between the two, though paradoxical, was realised throughout the Middle Ages. Due to the amalgamation of Germanic and Christian idea, the monarchy and not the monarch was exalted. The office and not the person was infallible. The subjects had to obey not the individual but the office. Unjust monarch could be disobeyed and resisted. In the exercise of his authority the ruler was not absolute. He was bound by certain limitations such as those of the law of nature and of the community etc. Monarch had to promote peace and justice. He had certain obligations towards community which he could not defy. He had to have regard for customs which were considered to be the product of wisdom of men. He was not supposed to make laws but only promulgate them. The laws made the king. In the words of Bracton, "The king himself ought to be under no man, but under God and under the law, because law makes the king." In the words of Sabine, "The king was not the head of the estate as he became in the era of absolute monarchy at the opening of modern period." The king protected the subjects. The kingship was a service rendered to the people. It was an obligation rather than a right. The monarch could either be hereditary or elected. He could be nominated by the Grace of God.

2. The Law. Throughout Middle Ages, the law was tribal and personal. It was never national or territorial. It belonged to the folk. It was a common possession of the people. Its source was unknown. The customs, Law of Nature and God's laws were the basis of folk laws. These were considered permanent and eternal. As the customs were the basis of laws, these were usually unwritten. Law was the custom of community. Its obedience was a habit. Real authority behind the laws was the will of the people. According to Sabine, "Law seems regularly to have been issued in the name of the whole people definitely with the sense that their consent is an important factor in its validity."

The law was the supreme authority in the state. Even the king was required to obey it. None was competent to revoke laws. Law alone authorised the king to rule. Government or the king was subordinate to law. The law was not subordinate to the government.

3. Universalism. Middle Ages believed in the idea of a universal or cosmopolitan society. This was borrowed from Roman idea of world civilization. The church and the state were two different aspects of same indivisible society. These were headed by the Pope and the Emperor respectively. But both were the members of the same society. Though both were different from each other in their jurisdiction yet they were of mutual help to each other. All believed that spiritual salvation is the sole aim of human beings. All human activities should be directed with this end in view. This goal was the be-all and end-all of all human efforts. Even political activities were directed to achieve this supreme end.

4. Growth of Papacy. The organisation of church into a mighty organisation was characteristic of the Middle Ages. It was a generation's conviction that church was essential for Heaven's blessings. The Pope ruled as the deputy of God on earth. He demanded that all Christians should obey him. The monarchs invited pope on their coronation ceremonies to seek his blessings. Gradually, the Pope began to interfere in the temporal affairs as well. Church organisation was gradually strengthened. The state became only its department. Gradually, due to the destruction of Holy Roman Empire and the rise of feudalism, the temporal authority was weakened. It gave the church an opportunity to exert itself. In the latter case it strengthened the hands of Pope against the Emperors. The feudal lords usually classed with the Emperors. It was against the interests of the feudal lords to have a centralised authority. They wanted to see a weak king on the throne. This could only be done through a powerful church.

5. Scholasticism. Middle ages are also known for scholasticism. It was represented by persons like Thomas Acquinas and Albortus Magnus. They realised the need and necessity of studying pre-Christian civilisation. They were not conservatives. According to Foster it was a representative civilisation and product of 'Union of Christianity with the ancient culture of the Graeco-Roman world'. They believed that philosophy had no conflict with theology. They assigned foremost importance to theology. To quote Dunning, "Scholasticism was a system of thought in which philosophy in the purely rational sense was subordinated to the established theological doctrines". Hearnshaw says, "Scholasticism of the 13th century is a master key to the understanding of medievalism". Foster said, "Scholasticism was the representative characteristic of the civilization of Middle Ages which arose from the union of Christianity with the ancient culture of Graeco-Roman world."

6. Theory of Corporations. The theory of corporation was another trait of the Middle Ages. Even the church and state were believed to be corporations. All human groups were considered as corporate. This theory was due to Dr. Gierke and Dr. Figgis Mitlad. It was widely used during the conciliar movement. The church was considered as the body corporate of the believers. By virtue of this theory, attempt was made to decentralise authority throughout the Middle Ages rather than allow concentration of power in the hands of a person. The Pope was like a presiding officer of the Church Council. The same principle was applied to the king in respect of his court councillors.

The theory of corporations also considered collective wisdom to be superior to the individual. As such the individual interests should be sacrificed before collective interests. It also promoted the idea that in spite of its non-composite character organically the state had composite character. Ultimate sovereignty resided in the people. The monarch was representative of the masses. Thus for of all purposes the theory contributed towards pluralist theory of sovereignty. Effort was made to distinguish between the state and the Government. Modern Fascists and the Syndicalists draw their inspiration from this theory.

7. The Origin of the State. Barring Acquinas all medieval thinkers believed that the state was the result of a convention. This was against the philosophy of Plato and Aristotle which preached that the state was the product of nature. With Romans and church fathers they believed that the state was the result of an agreement between the king and the subjects due to the sins of man. The theory held ground for a considerably long time. It was appreciated by modern thinkers till it was criticised by Montesquieu and Rousseau.

8. Sovereignty. In the Middle Ages there was no specific theory about sovereignty. Sovereign was not supreme over external and internal affairs. As Carlyle has said, "There is nothing more characteristic of middle ages than the absence of any theory of sovereignty." Divine reason and moral order prevailed over political authority. State was not considered absolute. Church authority also imposed limitation on the king. The Law of Nature also was limitation on the authority of the king. The law was considered supreme and unchangeable. The community had a control over the king. It could dispose him of, if he was tyrant or despotic. The sovereign authority was also challenged by feudal lords. They were always interested to see the king weak. The middle Ages did not like the idea of absolute sovereignty, they stood for limited or constitutional sovereignty.

9. Representationism. The Medieval Ages are known for the system of representation. The representative was, however, considered a trustee or agent of the people whom he represented. He was elected with the object of promoting the welfare of the people. Modern representative system is indebted to this age for this philosophy. The fundamentals of this system still remain unchanged.

10. Controversy over Secular V/s Spiritual Supremacy. It was believed throughout Middle Ages that the state and church were two different organisations. The church had autonomy and was free from temporal control. It had an independent character of its own. The temporal authority, however, did not wish to part with its traditional power. The king rejected the idea of absolute spiritual autonomy. This resulted in the theory of two worlds. It implied that spiritual and temporal aspects of a man should be separated from each other. Pope should be obeyed in religious matters. The king should be obeyed in secular affairs. However, the pope was superior to the king because he derived this authority from God. He could check the king by interdiction or ex-communication. On the other hand, the secularists pleaded that the king was representative of God on earth. It used to exercise both spiritual as well as secular powers before the establishment of the church. The church was a usurper. However, religion and not politics dominated the Middle Ages. Hence Dunning remarked that Middle Ages were unpolitical. No political investigation was carried out. This age was shorn of any new political philosophy.

11. Feudalism. Feudalism was an important institution of the Middle Age. It influenced economic, social and political life of the people. To quote Sabine, "Feudal institutions dominated the middle ages as completely as the city state dominated antiquity." Carlyle said, "It affected the life of the every class in the medieval community from the king or the emperor". Feudalism was the product of Roman and Teutonic institutions. It came to the fore front as the result of disruption of Roman Empire and subsequent anarchy. Barons got land from the monarchs and in turn gave it to the tenants who tilled the land. They were obliged to owe allegiance to the baron or feudal lord. In the words of Carlyle, "Feudalism is a system of relations, of judicial order and of political order". It was almost obligatory on the part of a tenant to work on the terms and conditions of a bond executed with the baron. It was expected to be honoured by the baron but was usually dishonoured by the baron. It was virtually withdrawn as the tenant withdrew his personal loyalty from the lord. *Prima facie* it might appear difficult to reconcile the ideas of contractual system with that of personal loyalty. However, it is a historical fact that the tenants worked on contract system. They owned personal loyalty to the immediate superior, they did not know about the king to whom their superior owed allegiance.

The feudal system continued throughout the Middle Ages. It was passed on to modern times in one form or the other as one of the legacies. However, its foundations were shaken in modern times, more especially by the socialistic countries and democratic institutions. Discussing the significance of Middle Ages Gierke said, "Through all the works of medieval publicists there runs a remarkably active drift towards monarchy and here we see a straight contrast between antique and medieval thinking." To quote Prof. Adam, "The work of the Middle Ages was not primarily progress, it was to form the organically united and homogeneous world out of heterogeneous and often hostile elements."

CONTRIBUTION BY GERMAN FOLK

According to Adams, the German people brought with them fresh vigour, youthful outlook, a new set of ideas and institutions which combined with the old and gave birth to new civilization. The Greeks and the Romans laid emphasis on the state but Germans had a very high idea of personal independence, of the value and importance of the individual man compared with the state. A Teuton was very jealous of personal independence as is depicted by the proud spirit of personal or individual war. They considered revenge as the duty of injured person. The unit was individual man, civil liberty was regarded as one of the most pernicious right to be jealously guarded by a Teuton. The private rights were considered inviolable and limited the sphere of the state.

Representative Government

Teutonic races introduced the representative institutions and spirit of local autonomy which had a profound effect on the growth of medieval and subsequent growth of political institutions and ideas. The primitive tribal organization was incompatible with the highly centralized and despotic government of the Roman Empire. Teutonic attack divided Roman empire into a number of loose knit kingdoms whose organisation was tribal. A sense of local institutions and feudal organisation saved the empire from complete anarchy.

German Characteristics

In Germany there was National Assembly consisting of all the freemen of the tribe. Its main function was to elect a chief and to decide necessary matters referred to it. Sometimes it used to assemble and to decide cases which might be placed before it. In addition to it, there were local representative assemblies in the hundreds in the cantons which decided matters of local importance and acted as judicial bodies. It survived till the revival of Roman law at the end of the middle ages. In England they provided the basis for the rise of House of Commons and establishment of local self-bodies like city councils and Borough councils etc. The germs of our modern legislature and local Assemblies lie in the Teutonic ideas of representation in middle ages. Their system of government represented a device that combined central control with local self-government and possible control over vast areas.

Constitutional Monarchy

For the early Teutons, freçmen had the right to choose their own Chief or King. Later on, it gave place to hereditary Kingship in other countries but in Germany it was preserved for centuries. In England monarchy became hereditary but the parliament claimed the right to choose successor in case of disputed succession and even to depose unpopular Kings or tyrants. Generally the law of succession of eldest son was in vogue but it was not so strong, as to rule out the principle of election by people. With the development of Christianity, was also added idea of rule of King due to grace of God. As such the King inherited his throne, owed his office to popular election and ruled by the Grace of God. They broke the principle of state absolutism. The King was subject to law, this was the corollary of his ruling by grace of God. Principle of election was used in the choice of emperors, so long as Holy Roman Empire remained into existence.

Legal System

Teutons developed conception of legal rights in their capacity as private persons. It had the right to be tried according to his own law. It was promulgated by assemblies acting as courts. Feudal customs were declared to have the force of law, and case law, based on common notions of justice, which helped in the development of unwritten law. In England this common law is still retained though in Europe, it has been replaced by Roman law.

Representative local self-government, elective or constitutional monarchy and a system of common law and ideals of individual liberty are the greatest boons which Teutons gave to the humankind and which had a profound influence on the development or representative and constitutional governments. In the words of Sabine, Teutonic people can be given credit of the idea that "the people was corporate body which expressed its corporate mind through magistrates and natural leaders. "In short nations of individual liberty or rights, representative Government" common law and of constitutional governments are their main contributions.

FEUDALISM

Disruption of Roman Empire gave rise to various petty local kingdoms. It brought into existence numerous feudal lords. According to Prof. Sabine, "feudal institutions dominated the middle ages as completely as the city states dominated antiquity." Thus Feudalism prevailed in middle period. Political feudalism means decentralization of the governmental authority. In this system the maintenance of peace and order and of deciding cases and of keeping armed forces rested with feudal lords. At the top were Popes and Emperors, next was the King who dealt with feudal lords and feudal lords dealt with subordinate lords and subordinate lords dealt with the individual or agriculturist who was called serf. Serf was at the lowest ladder. He had to pay tax and owe allegiance to his immediate lord. His condition was pitiable. Serf used to hold his fief from his immediate superior called his suzerain. Serf was called vassal and his immediate superior called his Suzerian. The relation between them was personal and natural. Suzerian had to take an oath of loyalty to his serf and to respect his rights and immunities. Vassal had to pay certain dues, attend his court, and to do military service whenever required. According to Sabine this feudal organisation maintained "an aspect of mutuality, of voluntary performance, and of implied contract which has vanished from modern relationship."

Suzerian of serf owed his duties to feudal chief. He was vassal and feudal lord was his Suzerain in the same way as he was of Serf. Feudal lords owed allegiances to their Kings. These feudal lords possessed power maintaining peace, order and justice in their territories. Army, court and state revenues were with the feudal lords. King was unable to interfere in their internal affairs. It depended on the ability of King as to what extent he was able to keep feudal barons under his control. The strong Kings were able to keep feudal lords under their thumb but if King was weak and feudal lord was strong, they used to care a fig for the King and sometimes feudal lords of the same King fought with one another and even with their own King. Thus though the King was theoretically supreme, he was sometimes unable to do what he desired.

On the economic side feudalism was a system of land tenures in which those who tilled the soil possessed only right of life interest. In theory land belonged to King who gave it to feudal lords as he was unable to till the land himself, feudal lord gave it to his subordinate and subordinate lord to tiller, i.e., on certain terms. Serf was bound to feudal lord and feudal lord to King. Thus there was a hierarchy who owed duties and obligations to one another. As the church was also owner of land so its bishops became spiritual as well as secular feudal lords. Thus feudalism prevailed not only in Europe but in Japan and in India also. Emergence of national states, rise of trading class and sacrifice weapons gave a death blow to feudalism and modern nation states came into existence.

Invention of gunpowder, renaissance, emergence of national states of England and France etc. under strong kings such as Henry VII and Louis XI, geographical discoveries, commerce and reformation gave death blow to feudalism in 15th century. New national states emerged with new political ideas of patriotism and democracy which brought medieval political thought to an end.

POLITICAL THOUGHT IN MIDDLE AGES

Precursor of Modern Age

"The middle ages, writes Ernest Barker, are the pit from which we were digged and the rock from which we were hewer. They are the beginning and the origin of the things that exist today."[1] Modernity in political theory has been a steady growth on the foundations laid in the middle ages. Most modern ideas can be traced in their origins to the medieval tradition. These include sovereignty, sovereign people, political representation, social contract, natural rights, natural law, positive law, limited government and consent as the basis of government, etc.

However, it would be a mistake to find the medieval ideas as precursors of the modern. The absolute authority of the medieval ruler is not a precursor of the Hobbesian sovereignty. M.J.Wilks and other who read sovereignty into the doctrine of Augustinus Triumphus commit this mistake. The concept of absolute authority there was also subject to a number of ethical and religious limitations. The factors which rendered sovereignty impossible were precisely the forces that facilitated the supersession of the medieval doctrine by the modern. These were:

(1) The existence of a multiple, trifaceted society,

(2) The notion that the power of the ruler was derived from the people,

(3) The conception of the state as an affair of the people,

(4) Revival of the Aristotelean doctrine that the government exists for the well being of the people,

(5) The Germanic notion that law was superior to both government and society,

(6) The existence of two powers papal and political, each limiting the other,

1. Quoted by Allen, *Medieval contributions to Modern Civilization*, p.168.

(7) Feudalism with its notion of contractual relationship between the king and his vassals,

(8) Christian emphasis on the sanctity of the life of the individual who in essence was divine,

(9) Superiority of the Church and its law to the state and its commands,

(10) The emphasis of the Church on the Stoic notion of man as a rational being endowed with equality, moral freedom and sense of responsibility,

(11) Natural law with reason as the sole criterion of the validity of law, and its associate idea of contingent obligation and private property as an inalienable and inviolable individual right.

RISE OF DEMOCRATIC TRADITION

Through their emphasis on these ideas the middle ages prepared the ground for the rise of the democratic tradition of thought and practice. The medieval political doctrine stood for the truth that the ultimate significance of human institutions consists in their capacity to help man realise his potentialities of growth and perfection. "We may eliminate the Church altogether but we cannot without incurring spiritual bankruptcy and undermining the foundations of our civilization, eliminate from our lives what the Church stands for. We need to consider what we the state and all our institutions are at, and why we are at it."[2]

The Christian ethics repudiated all distinction between high and low, bound and free, it taught that all men are equal in the eyes of God. It gave a new sanction and wider circulation to the Stoic doctrine of equality and brotherhood of man. Men are all brothers, because they are all children of God. Thus, every man became an end unto himself a spirit which mattered more than rank, wealth and power. The concept of the inner worth of personality received a great reinforcement at the hands of Christianity. But the concept of equality had only spiritual significance as it received its practical realization only in the Church.

Political Liberalism

In the later middle ages the diversity of religious faiths rendered conflict so recurrent and violent that men were forced to come round to the principle that difference of belief constitutes no bar to common citizenship—a principle which came, in the long run, to constitute the corner-stone of the political liberalism of the modern West.[3] The rise of the Church ruled out from the control of government, the creative sphere of cultural expression. The

2. R. M. Macre, *The Web of Government*, p.183.

3. Betrand Russell, *A History of Western Philosophy*, p.15.

undying fervour of oppressed religious convictions, secured for Western peoples the triumphant right of opinion. The existence of the Church contributed towards preservation of liberty and prevention of the rise of the omnipotent state. In its form society found an institution which could stand up against the state.

Political Obligation

St. Paul's declaration, "Render unto Caesar the things that are Caesar's and unto God the things that are God's" was a turning-point in the history of western political tradition. To the Greeks the state had been the highest institution which enjoyed exclusive loyalty of the citizens. In the Roman period, with the eclipse of the *polis* and rise of the empire, the citizen felt politically withdrawn. With the advent of Christianity man stood faced with two institutions claiming his loyalty, the state and the Church. The rise of Christianity posed a problem of two-fold obligation corresponding to the two fold destiny of man. It was never questioned that the state deserved loyalty. But it was asserted that the higher loyalty must go to the Church. Man was loyal to the state in respect of his temporal needs and nature. But with regard to his spiritual nature and needs he had to be loyal to the Church. The novelty of the Christian position lay in its assumption of a dual nature of man, and of a dual control over life and society corresponding to its two-fold destiny.

Religious Orientation

The most distinctive mark of the medieval political tradition was its deeply religious orientation. For the Greeks the highest duties of morality and religion met in the state. But for the Christian's the duties of religion were a paramount obligation that man owed directly to God. The Christian could never reconcile himself with the interference of state in his sacred and intimate relationship with the Lord. An institution which claimed tendance of the soul and its relationship with God as its primary concern was bound to assert its independence of the state.

SUPERIORITY OF THE CHURCH

The superiority of the Church was established by the last quarter of the eleventh century A.D. when Henry IV knelt in penitence before Gregory VII at Canossa.Until the onset of the ninth century it was believed that the western provinces of the Roman Empire were subject to the Emperor at Constantinople who was the sole source of authority. Charlemagne challenged this position and led to the foundation of the Holy Roman Empire by declaring that he derived his claim to legitimacy from the Pope of Rome. Since that declaration no one could be emperor unless crowned by the people.

Gelasian Theory

It was the Gelasian theory that had prevailed until the supremacy of the Church was established over the state. According to this theory, there were two governments with separate powers over the temporal and the spiritual realms. The burden of the Pope was viewed to be heavier because he had the duty to answer even for the kings at the day of judgement. By founding the Holy Roman Empire with his coronation in 800 Charlemagne effected the eclipse of the Gelasian theory with its concept of two parallel governments. As Church came out victorious against the state for three reasons : First, it had monopoly over education; second, the kings were perpetually at war with each other; third, rulers and people alike profoundly believed that the Church possessed the power of the key as it could decide whether a king should spend eternity in heaven or in hell.[4]

The Church was victorious also because, with the eclipse of the *polis*, a spiritual void had occurred in the life of man and church filled that void. "Something essential had gone from his life and for all great show of activity," writes Will Durant, "too often he felt that his existence was empty... The vacuum could be filled only by a religion which appealed both to the heart and mind, giving meaning to the aimless life of the new cosmopolitan and rootless Greeks".[5] The Church promised to work as a lever of imperial unity at a time when the Empire, stood on tottering foundations. As Will Durant observes: "It was because Rome was already dying that Christianity grew so rapidly. Men lost faith in the state not because Christianity held them aloof but because the state defended wealth against poverty, fought to capture slaves, taxed trade to support luxury, and failed to protect its people from famine, pestilence, invasion and destitution: forgivably they turned from Caesar preaching war to Christ preaching peace, from incredible brutality to unprecedented charity, from a life without hope or dignity to a faith that consoled their poverty and honoured their humanity."[6]

Universal Community

According to Gierke, "Therefore in all centuries of the Middle Age Christendom, whose destiny is identical with Mankind, is set before us as a single, universal community, founded and governed by God Himself Mankind is one mystical body; it is one single and internally connected "people" or fold; it is an all-embracing corporation (*Universitas*) which constitutes the Universal Realm, spiritual and temporal which may be called the Universal Church (*ecclesia universalis*) or ... the Commonwealth of the Human Race

4. Will Durant, *Christ and Caesar*, p. 93.
5. *Ibid*, p. 663.
6. *Ibid*

(*respublica generis humani*). Therefore that it may attain its one purpose, it needs one Law and one Government (*unicus princicatus*).[7]

Political theory of the Middle Ages is neither concerned with the state nor with the Church but with a universal Christian Society. In this *respublica Christiana* these two institutions are just two wings existing under the same Christian umbrella. The duality of the king and the bishop was crossed towards unity. By the subjection of the king to the Bishop in spiritual matters, and of the Bishop to the king in the temporal. Thus, the Middle Ages give a theory of the Christian Commonwealth in which the Church and the state exist and work side by side. Ernest Barker calls it a Community-State-Church having two governments — a secular government in things temporal and an ecclesiastical government in things spiritual.[8]

BIRTH OF STATE

In the Middle Ages the concept of state had a protracted and painful birth and its outlines were only indistinctly drawn. Emergence of the ecclesiastical and secular governments took long time fructify. Ecclesiastical government developed only when power was concentrated in the Pope and administrative, judicial and diplomatic machinery grew to sustain and consolidate his power. Acquisition of territories by the kingdoms and growth of governmental institutions resulted in a distinct secular organization when the two governments came into their own conflicts of jurisdiction arose. Revival of legal study helped emergence of the two governments. In the words of Barker, "Under the stern influence ... of legal formulation functions hardened into rights, superiority became authority, subordination turned into delegation. In general, the influence of legal thinking strengthened all tendencies toward the centralization of authority in the church as in the secular state.[9]"

Civil jurisprudence provided numerous precedents for imperial control of papal affairs and for the interpretation of papal powers. Imperial authority was ultimately based on the consent of the people. The canonists developed their own conception of imperial sovereignty or power over the empire. Systematization of canon law provided sufficient precedent for that sovereignty.

GROWTH OF NATURAL LAW

The idea of natural law received great elaboration in the Middle Ages. It was viewed as superior to all laws and beyond the touch of all earthly powers. Its principles were eternal and binding. It provided the criterion of the validity

7. Ibid, Otto Von Gierke, *Political Theory in the Middle Ages*, p.7.
8. Earnest Barker, *Principles of Social and Political Theory*, p.7.
9. Earnest Barker, *Essays on Government*, pp. 287-88.

of man-made law. It was the basis for statute law, a limitation on authority and a purpose for government. The medieval adherence to natural law precluded espousal of the concept of sovereignty at a political plane. It constituted the most serious limitation upon all authority. It prevented the growth of law as an expression of will. MacIver writes, "Whatever contradicted natural law contradicted, that which reflects the declared will of God. With such an idea suffusing the whole of medieval life, it is only with difficulty that we pass to a power in the prince to interpret natural law, and thence to law which is binding upon all because it is his will."[10] Natural law has been rated as the most characteristic and significant medieval conception. The state was viewed to be based on natural law first and last. As H.J. Laski said, "There is a sense, in fact, in which the basic idea of natural law is a necessary part or any political philosophy which seeks to be more than a doctrine or immediate expediency. It is glory of the medieval thinkers not only to have grasped that truth but so to have stated it as to make it an integral part of the heritage of mankind."[11]

Growth of Teutonic Law

In the development of the concept of law the Teutonic idea of law played a leading part. During fifth to tenth century three phases may be noticed in the growth of the Teutonic concept of law.

1. Law was primarily tribal as the custom of the tribe was exclusive in its scope, and the law was little affected by fresh conditions.

2. The emphasis was laid on the personality of law. It was conceived as belonging to the folk or the tribe. As McIlwain puts it, "Each member lived within the people's peace, and the law provided especially the regulations necessary to prevent that peace from being broken. The law in every case the law of the Tribe or folk which it ruled.[12] This phase was of crucial importance as it enabled Roman law to persist as local custom. Had it not so persisted the Renaissance of Roman law might never have come, and the entire development of political theory would have taken a different course. To quote McIlwain, " But for the effects of the personality of law there might well have been no Irnerius, no Bartolus, no Cujas, no Bodin".[13]

3. The conception of law as a personal attribute of the tribe was replaced by the conception of law as territorial. As kingship came into vogue, the law acquired uniformity. It come to bear the stamp of the territory in which it operated. But due to the diversity of law the king could not easily extend the jurisdiction of his courts to the entire length and breadth of his kingdom.

---

10. R. M. MacIver, *The Web of Government*, p. 183.
11. Quoted in R. G. Gettell, *A History of Political Thought*, p. 91.
12. McIlwain, G. H. *op. cit*, p. 178-9.
13. *Ibid*, p. 170.

Law as Custom

Throughout these phases the idea persisted that the law belongs to the "people" or the "folk". Under the Teutonic or Germanic conception, the folk was conceived to be made by the law than law made by folk. "Natural law was as good as people's custom. The custom which was rooted in the folkways was in no sense set off from natural law but rather was felt to be a twig of the great tree of the law which grew from earth to heaven and in whose shade all human life was lived."[14] It was by custom that the law of different Teutonic tribes was held to be binding. Its writing and formal promulgation were incidental, not essential. Law was not 'made', but 'proved' or 'found' as many jurists of the Middle Ages believed. Thus, the supremacy of the British Parliament over the Courts a medieval legacy. The king was considered as much bound by law as his subjects. He could not ride roughshed over the rights of his subject guaranteed by custom or law of the land. Every man was to respect the law according to his rank and order. No king could transcend certain limits without doing violence to the idea of law and morals. Thus, the Germans contributed towards the growth of an impersonal system of law which was another version of natural law, and which was different from the law of Rome. They habitually thought of as the immemorial custom of the tribe rather than as the legislative enactment of any supreme authority in the state.[15]

The wisdom underlying the medieval notion of law persists to day as law is supposed to embody the subjective principle of the will of the government or of the people. The distinction that is made between the constitutional law and the ordinary law is an assertion of some objective principle of validity. Even if constitutions are "made" today it is in correspondence of some rational standard, prevailing customs and traditions. While the medieval law represented the custom of the people, modern law represents the wisdom garnered by a people from which customs themselves derive. Medieval jurisprudence, however, assumed a 'continuous co-operation between the king and his subjects, both being, so to speak, the organs of the realm to which the law belongs'. In medieval times even the conception of delegated power was crossed by the notion that authority was inherent in persons who, were agents of the king. Even in the seventeenth century Sir Edward Coke could think of the crown, the Parliament and the courts of common law as enjoying inherent powers under the law of the realm.[16]

Thus, throughout the Middle Ages, following matters were universally taken for granted the validity of natural law and its binding authority over rulers and subjects, the obligation of kings to govern justly and in accordance

---

14. Sabine, M H. *op. cit*, pp. 180-1.
15. McIlwain, G.H., *op. cit*, p. 17.
16. Sabine, G.H. *op. cit*, p.186

with laws, sanctity of constituted authority both in Church and state and the unity of Christendom under the parallel powers of *imperium* and *sacerdotium*.

PROBLEMS OF SOVEREIGNTY IN THE MIDDLE AGES

In medieval political theory the notion of sovereignty emanated from the conception of the world as an organic entity governed by one God. The king was called a sovereign because as the *viceregent* of God he was above and beyond the community. One of the supporters of the Pope Wilks vigorously backed the idea of the omnicompetent sovereign.[17] He saw in this theory the origin of the modern idea of the totalitarian state.[18]

The Pope must have absolute power because he represents "the point at which heaven and earth meet, because he is the soul which provides the connection between the body politic and the Godhead. Once the divine infallibility of the Pope is accepted there could be no real limitation of papal power without at the same time infringing the omnipotence of God.

But the doctrine of absolutism was crossed by many other rival doctrines. As the theory of natural law went against a true conception of monarchy, the only real alternative, as Augustinus Triumphus revealed, was to make "rightness" dependent upon the will of the ruler himself.[19]

LIMITED V/S CONSTITUTIONAL MONARCHY

The medieval tradition made a sharp distinction between 'limited monarchy' and 'constitutional monarchy', and upheld the former. The former is limited by extra-constitutional whereas the latter is limited by constitutional factors. The king in modern times is viewed limited not only by laws defining his sphere of authority but also by a competing authority such as the House of Commons in England. In the middle ages, as McIlwain points out, government was limited, in modern times it is limited in a much more positive way by the actual inclusion of a popular element among the organs of government themselves.

In the medieval times the king could be an autocrat but never a despot. His will was law only if expressed in a particular way and subject to particular principles. As John of Paris put it, neither Pope nor king could take a subject's goods without his consent.

CRITICAL EVALUATION

1. Unreal Theory. However the medieval tradition limited the king to his proper sphere of action, in practice, it always left him in office alone,

.17. Wilks, M.J. *op.cit*, p. 151.

18 .*Ibid*. p. 158.

19. *Ibid*, pp. 153-54.

supreme and irresponsible. Political theory in the middle ages, writes H. J. Laski, was not based upon an actual observation of the conditions of politics and social life. The concept of the king under law was a theoretical fiction rather than a political fact. Even, under feudal system any lord could, in theory, be compelled to respect the rights of his vassals, but no coercive remedy was available if he encroached upon a vassal's rights. While there was no such doctrine that the king can do no wrong, there was no effective check when he was inclined to do one.

2. Lacking Historical Perspective. Medieval political theory, lacked historical perspective as there was no immediate impact of events on doctrines which mark the religious wars of the sixteenth century in France, the great rebellion in England or the synchronization of socialism with the industrial revolution. In so far as political theory came to be written by men like Wycliffe in terms of feudal institutions it remains even more remote from the facts thereabout than the classical idea.

3. Abstract Theory. The revival of Aristotelianism and Roman law tradition made for the medieval political theory abstract. While the medieval ruler continued to appear as a vicar of God, Thomas Acquinas and John of Salisbury tended to think less in terms of an over-righteous ruler than in terms of abstract ideals like natural law.

QUESTIONS FOR EXERCISE

1. "Universalism was the keynote of medieval political thought." Explain.
2. Examine the view that Middle Ages were essentially unpolitical.
3. What are the chief characteristics of the political thought of the Middle Ages.
4. Write brief essay on the characteristics and problems of medieval political theory.
5. "The Middle Ages were essentially unpolitical." Comment on this statement with reference to the method and content of medieval thought.
6. "The note of all medieval thought is universalism." Write a critical estimate of medieval political thought.
7. "The ghost of Rome haunted middle ages." Explain.

12

Power Controversy Between State and Church

Before the establishment of Church, the king was considered as the most powerful authority in the state. He was the supreme overlord in the land. His authority was unquestionable and undisputed. He combined in one both temporal and spiritual authorities. The controversy between church and state, however, grew and the church began to assume more and more powers. The pope assumed the power of ex-communication. He directed the subjects to defy the orders of a defiant prince. The church made definite and pointed effort to exert and assert its authority against the state. However, when the Roman empire was enjoying glory and was at the height of its power no attempt was made to decide whether the emperor derived its authority from God or the masses. There was also no division of powers between the church and the emperor. Both could not reconcile themselves to the ideas that they had co-eval powers. However, it was usually believed that the church and the state were two departments of the same social organisation, their clash became acute in 11th century. Emperor Henry VI and Pope Gregory got each other ex-communicated to open a sharp controversy, which lasted for more than two centuries. Till the 18th century the position of the church was sound. In the 18th century, due to decentralisation and disintegration of the Roman Empire, the situation changed when secular authority of the king began to establish supremacy over papal authority. The weakness of the feudal system and the establishment of nation states highly elevated the position of monarchy. The conflict was primarily over the jurisdiction between the two officials of the same state. According to Maxey, "At first the church distinctly had the better of it. No temporal lord was strong enough to prevail against her. Her enormous wealth, her universal and smoothly functioning organisation, her highly centralised political system, her hold upon the superstitions of classes and masses enabled her to rout all oppositions. Upto the 13th century, it was known as the age of enthroned papacy and the church triumphant. The position changed for the better for the monarchies in the 14th century. In the following conflict and controversy both the rival parties had their own claims."

Arguments for Papal Supremacy

The church tried to claim its jurisdiction even over temporal affairs after 9th century. The Pope Gregory who had a dynamic personality and high character was successful in introducing many changes in the church organisation. He could also solve many problems and remove many difficulties which had weakened the church. This enhanced the prestige of the church. Hence some of the thinkers accepted that the church had jurisdiction over the princes. The weak Roman empire which was facing and fighting the strong feudalism practically accepted unquestioned supremacy of the Pope and the church. It could not face the strong and militant organisation of the church. The following arguments were given for Papal supremacy.

1. Oneness of Mankind. According to the church father, mankind was one. This oneness could be achieved only when God governed the people and the state, through his representative. The Pope was their priest and their king, their spiritual and temporal monarch, their law giver and judge in all cases supreme. The church claimed that for the sake of oneness and unity of mankind the Pope alone should be made superman. The king could not touch spiritual aspect of mankind. In the words of Grieke, "The head of all this embracing state is Christ. But as the unity of mankind is to be realised already ,in this world, His celestial Kingship must have a territorial presentment....The Pope is the wielder of what is in principle an emperor over the community of mortals. He is their priest and their king, their spiritual and temporal monarch, their law giver and judge in all cases supreme."

2. Idea of Supremacy of Soul. The church argued that as soul was superior to the body similarly the church was supreme over the state. While the state represents body the church represents soul. Pope was superior to the king. Spiritual development was the concern of the church. The development of body was the concern of the state. The emperor was the highest vassal of the pope. The pope was the guardian of kingship. It was his duty to protect and enhance the prestige of secular authority. The pope was the competent authority to hear complaints about the king. He had definite and clear superiority over the king.

Arguments for Secular Supremacy

To face strong arguments of Papacy the monarchs or the kings could advance equally weighty arguments. They exercised uncontrolled sway over the secular affairs. However, usually the monarchs adopted defensive attitude and were not on the offensive. They effectively repulsed the onslaught and did not take offensive attitude. They agreed that the church and the state were two distinct organisations. They agreed that the state should content itself by claiming rights and supremacy over the secular and not over temporal affairs. Thus the secularists were moderates and never extremists. According to Sabine, "The position taken by the imperialist parties to the investiture controversy was on the whole more defensive than that of the Papalists." The claim for church supremacy over secular affairs was challenged on the following grounds for secular supremacy:

1. Theory of Divine Origin. The secularists claimed that the state was of Divine Origin and it was not a mere delegation of authority by the church. As the king was deputy of God on earth he was exclusively responsible to God for all his actions. The state had as much Divine blessings and sanctions as the church and thus was at par with church. Therefore, the question of subordination of one over the other does not at all arise. "Fear God and Honour the king," was a commonly acceptable idea.

2. Moral Basis of the State. The secularists agreed with Greek thinkers that the state was based on morality and that it was one of its foremost duties to promote morality and justice. Therefore, they felt that it was not the duty of only the church to promote morality. The state had a share in it. The state was as much responsible for enforcing morality as the church itself.

3. Gelasian Argument. The theory of two swords gave a specific and clear idea that the state and the church were two separate departments. Hence the secularists claimed that the two departments were equally independent. They pleaded that according to this theory, the state was independent of the church.

4. The Theory of Harmony. The church and the state were believed to be two essential social organisations. Social harmony could develop only when both worked in close cooperation with each other. The harmony could be achieved only if Pope claimed supremacy over religious affairs and left the state with exclusive control in temporal affairs.

5. Biblical Arguments. The secularists quoted from the old as well as New Testament, which said that, "the powers that be are ordained by God. Whosoever, therefore, resisteth the powers resisteth the ordinance of God". They claimed that the state was responsible to God alone and to none else.

6. The Theory of Two Swords. This theory propounded that the church and the state were two distinct and different organisations. According to Carlyle, it was believed by the exponents of this theory that, "Of these the greater weight is with the priest in so far as they will answer to the Lord even for the kings in the last judgement." This theory is also known as Gelasian argument.

7. Divine Sanctions of the State. The Church Fathers believed that the state has divine sanction only through the authority of Church. It has no Divine origin. The state originated due to the sin of the man. It is governed by human laws whereas church is governed by Divine Laws. Human laws are inferior to divine laws. As such, secular officers are subordinate to spiritual officers.

8. Church Obligation. To Church Fathers it was their foremost duty to do spiritual doctoring for the state. They claimed that they can discharge these duties and obligations only if they have a right to interfere in state affairs. If this right is denied the church shall not be in a position to discharge this obligation properly. The church must interfere in state affairs.

9. Arguments from Bible. The Church Fathers supported their arguments from Bible also. According to them, old Testament is the testimony by way of preaching that jews were governed by the priests from the time of Moses. The first king was coordinated by the priest. They also supported their argument from The New Testament by quoting the famous argument 'Feed my sheep.' It implied that Pope was the guardian of the flock of Christ and thus the protector of all including the king.

10. Coordinating Power of Church. To Church Fathers the church was the coordinator of all authority. After the fall of Roman empire church was the only agency which coordinated all activities. While all other agencies were unstable, church was the only stable agency. It was through church alone that all social, political and economic ferments could be checked. Therefore, this coordinating agency must be strong, powerful and influential.

11. Historical Argument. The supporters of church pointed out that it was a historical fact that monarchs sought the blessings of the Pope. They quoted historical example of coronation of Emperor Charlemagne by Pope Leo III where the Pope conferred authority on the monarch to rule. It was argued that if the Pope could bless a monarch he could also ex-communicate the inefficient secular ruler.

12. Moral Argument. Morally, the state is inferior to church. Therefore, there is no justification for the officers of the church to obey the officers of the state. On the other hand, there is every justification for the officer of state to obey the officers of the church.

13. Will of God. Church Fathers claimed that it was the will of God that church should govern the Christians. The church could ex-communicate and punish all those who did not obey it, as the disobedience of the church was the disobedience of God. The church could punish those who refused to carry out the will of God.

14. Legal Argument. During 11th century, one of the important Roman Jurist Bortolus, clearly stated that legally sovereignty was inalienable and to dispute it was sacrilege. The other jurists agreed that the power of the Emperor was unshaken. The will of monarch was the command and thus unquestionable. Holy Roman Emperors were the rightful successors of the empire of Rome. As the emperors enjoyed unquestioned authority, their successors should also enjoy that authority undisputed and unquestioned by the church. According to hereditary law of Roman Empire, the state was the private property of the monarch and thus unquestionable. Inspite of the above arguments of the secularists the Popes enjoyed a superior power over the king. Hence, it has been said, "The Papacy was the ghost of the Roman Empire, sitting crowned on its grave." The Popes took full advantage of the downfall of the Roman Empire, they established and stablised their supremacy.

QUESTIONS FOR EXERCISE

1. In the eleventh and twelvth centuries political writing was in the main controversial, centering about the contest between the Popes and the Emperors over the boundaries of the secular and ecclesiastical authorities." (Sabine). Explain and examine the arguments given for papal supremacy and secular supremacy.
2. "The starting point of all medieval rising in the politics was the dogma of two powers the sacred authority of the priests and the royal power. (Dunning). Explain.
3. Summarise briefly the chief arguments of Sacredotal pre-eminence put forward by the church during the Middle Ages.
4. Give some account of the work of the more prominent defenders of the independence to the secular authority during the Middle-Ages.
5. What were the principal arguments used by the protagonists of the Church in the Church—State controversy during the Middle Ages.
6. Write note on 'The Investiture Controversy'.
7. State and examine the ecclesiastical argument for the supremacy of the church over state in the Middle Ages.

13

Papalist Thinkers of Medieval Age

The Papalists

The Papalists believed in the supremacy of church. They had full faith that in Church— State controversy church had prior and pride place. Since soul has positive and definite supremacy over the body, so the church which represents soul has supremacy over state which represented body. The relation of church with God was direct whereas that of state with Him was indirect. Of the Papalists Gregory VII and John of Salisbury were extremists. St.Thomas Acquinas was a liberal Papalist.

GREGORY VII (1013-1080)

Gregory VII was one of the staunchest supporters of church. He strongly pleaded that the church should be absolutely free from the control of secular authorities. He said that Pope and the Bishops were absolutely free and under the Divine Law. He was a great practical reformer. As a Pope he introduced many changes in the institution and organisation of church itself. He was responsible for 'Monastic Revival' movement which enhanced the prestige of Papacy. He established the image of a sovereign Pope who was arbitrator in all disputes and supreme mediator in questions of war and peace.

1. Supremacy of Church. Gregory VII was in favour of strengthening the institution of Papacy. He pleaded that the Pope should not only be supreme in spiritual but also in temporal matters. According to him the humblest church officer occupied more exalted place as compared with even a responsible secular officer. As soul is always superior than body, those who are associated with the soul must enjoy supremacy over those connected with body. The state is a product of sin. It aimed at punishing the people for their sins. The church stood to promote justice and aimed at maintaining that. However, it was in their mutual interest that both should work in close harmony with each other. Both authorities are appointed by God to rule over the world. The church has full authority to declare the laws of Emperor as unconstitutional, but a monarch could not declare papal command as illegal.

In the words of Maxey, "None may nullify a decree of the Pope or pass judgement on his acts, but the Pope as vicar of God may nullify the decrees of all other earthly powers."

2. Theory of Justice. Gregory's theory of Justice aimed at the supremacy of church. Justice is possible in a society where Pope had undivided, undisputed and unquestionable authority over church. The clergy should have no desire for marriage nor attracted by economic gains. The Pope had ultimate authority to admonish or banish even a king if he violated the principle of divine laws. The Pope is the final authority to decide about the extent of violation of a particular Divine Law.

3. Theory of Subordination of State. The supremacy of church means it is absolutely and completely subordinate to the church. Gregory most logically developed the theory of subordination of state. According to him, since the king was himself Christian, therefore, in spiritual matters he is always subordinate to church. Political rule is more or less a large scale highway legal robbery.

4. Institution of Kingship. According to Gregory VII the institution of kingship began due to the ignorance of the people and because of "greed and intolerable presumptions to make themselves as masters of their equals." The state originated because of the sins of the people, there is not much role of the institution of kingship as such. Church should exercise control over the monarchs because of their being Christian. Kings should be disciplined Christians. Pope should have control over the spiritual and moral affairs. Secular rulers are small men, secular authorities should fear papal authority.

5. Dignity of Church. According to Gregory, Divine Government is superior to all secular governments. Gregory was much indebted to St. Augustine for his political philosophy as well as method of writing and expression. Gregory banned the investitures of the officers of church by lay secular princes. He pleaded that those princes who disobeyed Divine Laws had no right to demand allegiance from their subordinates. All such subordinates were absolved from the oath of allegiance which they had taken in respect of such a prince. The king had absolutely no control over the clergy in any respect. The Pope had every right to admonish a king who transgressed divine law. Righteousness could only be spread by exalting the authority of the church by all means. It was an institution for the purification of mankind. Hence it is most essential for man's welfare.

JOHN OF SALISBURY (1120-1180)

About the book *Policraticus* (1159) Ebenstein has said that "There is perhaps no single doctrine that he can claim to have discovered first; yet his book is one of the most influential medieval political statements because of the originality with which he combines existing isolated ideas into a new pattern."

John's second treatise '*Metalogicum*' has also drawn much from the writings and philosophy of Aristotle. He was highly indebted to Aristotle for his philosophy and ideas. His writings were ethical rather than legal or constitutional. There is however nothing very original in his writings. Being a close follower of Gregory VII he repeated his basic ideas. He established supremacy of the church by extensively quoting from the Bible and other religious classics. However, he was bold enough to point out the evils of church including the sale of justice and the greed of the clergy etc.

He was a man of letters and he had modern outlook and liberal views about many problems which faced his times. About his '*Policraticus*' it has been said that it was a turning point of medieval history. His ideas can be discussed under the following headings:

1. Organic Theory of the State. John of Salisbury agreed with Cicero that the state is a commonwealth and an organic entity. There is close resemblance between human body and body politic. The state is ruled and governed by certain moderating reasons. Prince in a state is like the head, senate like heart, judges like eyes, ears and tongues, soldiers like arms and artisans like the feet of the man. As the soul rules the body from within it, the church also rules the state. As soul is superior to body so church is superior to the state.

2. Theory of Tyrannicide. Tyrannicide is an integral and inseparable part of political philosophy. As soon as a king ceases to rule in accordance with the established laws of the land he ceases to be a king and becomes a tyrant. No king should ever try to transgress the limits of laws. He should have great respect for them. No ruler has a right against the people. A tyrant might even be slain without any offence to religion. Poison should be avoided as a method of slaying an unrighteous Emperor. As far as possible the subjects should pray for getting rid of such a monarch. John has been much criticised for his support of tyrannicide.

3. The Ideal State. John tried to portray an ideal state. It is based on the fundamental and basic principle that religious authority is superior to secular authority or that religion is superior to worldly affairs. Church is superior to the state. In an ideal state, there should be perfect adjustment. The king should love justice and have Sagacious mind. His just will is a good law. A king, however, deputises for the church, whose authority over him is unquestionable. The king is not above laws. Every secular law must be in accordance with the Divine Law. Each secular law is dependent on spiritual law. It is subject to the interpretation given by spiritual authority, the Pope. Perfect adjustment of things is possible only when there is obedience to Divine Laws.

4. Subordination of State to Church. According to John though the church and the state had different functions to perform yet broadly speaking the church represented both and a king draws his authority from the church. The king was the agent of church. It is the duty of the church to exercise control over secular affairs. It should see that secular laws were is accordance with Divine Laws. The Pope should not actively interfere in the affairs of the state. King's authority is passed on to the king through the agency of the church. Relation of church with God is direct while that of state is indirect. It is the duty of the state to serve the church because it has superiority over the state. To quote Maxey, John believed that, "The power which the prince has, is therefore, from God, for the power of God is never lost, nor severed from him, but he merely exercises it through a subordinate hand, making all things teach his mercy and justice. The state stood for maintaining peace, law and order and giving a secure and safe life to the citizens. These aims could be achieved by close cooperation between the church and the state." John used to say, "The prince therefore, is in a sense the minister of priestly office, and one who performs that part of the sacred functions which seems unworthy of the hands of priesthood."

5. Theory of Two Swords. John believed in the theory of two swords. As a strict follower of the theory he believed that it was intentional that the church parted with secular and retained spiritual authority. Had church so desired it would have retained both. According to John, "This sword (Coercive jurisdiction in temporal matters), then the prince received from the hand of the church although she herself in no sense holds the sword of blood. She nevertheless possesses this sword, but she uses it by the hand of the prince of whom she confers the coercive power over the body, reserving the authority over spiritual things for herself in the pontiffs."

6. Theory of State. According to Salisbury, monarchy is the only ideal form of government. Other forms of government deserve no attention. A monarch has certain duties to perform towards his subjects as well as the priests. God is the source of life of state, which he passes on to the king through church. Various parts of state are bound together by law and justice. A good state is one which is governed by reason and which promotes security and welfare of the subjects.

7. Ideas About the King. John discussed in considerable details about the duties and qualities of a king. The king is bound by Divine and Natural Laws. He must do justice at all costs. He should remember that there is always a punishment for an unjust ruler in store. He should strive to promote the welfare and interests of common man. He should always realise that he is only the minister of common interest. He should be like a good doctor prepared to use bitter medicines for the welfare of the patients. Hanging a person is just like cutting one's own limbs. A king should try to do justice. A good king should combine godliness as well as justice. The king can be good and ideal only if he is loyal to the church and devoted to spiritual pursuits.

8. Role of Law in the State. John is remembered for assigning a definite role to law in the state. A prince is a servant of law. A king should act as the minister or servant of the people. The people should be ruled by law alone as it was God sent. Law is not merely a code. It aims at eternal justice and equity. Monarchs must be subjected to the authority of eternal law. Monarchy is not a private office but a public utility service. It is in the interest of the monarch himself and for better performance of service that restriction of law is imposed and considered essential. Law is the only point which distinguished a monarch from a tyrant. It has definite and superior place in the state. It regulates the conduct of even the monarchs. In the words of Maxey, "Law, says John is but the interpreter of God's equity and justice and the prince is merely the minister for common interest and the bond servant of equality."

Contribution of John of Salisbury

John of Salisbury is known as a liberal thinker. His works are termed as turning point of medieval ages. His importance lies in the following ideas:

1. Prince Subordinate to Law. John gave the idea that law has a definite and specific place in the state and that a prince is subordinate to laws. A king must respect the law. He should not only obey them but should act in accordance with them. The real distinction between a monarch and a tyrant is that the ruler who ruled in the spirit of law is a monarch otherwise he is a tyrant.

2. Moral Support to Kill the Tyrant. John was the first important political thinker of middle ages who gave moral support to the idea that tyrant should be slain and that the subjects are absolved from the oath of allegiance which they had taken in respect of such a ruler.

3. Systematisation of Political Philosophy. Though John was not an original thinker, yet his importance lies in systematising and synthesising the existing ideas. He has given systematic treatment to the political philosophy of his times.

4. **Theory of Two Swords.** John was the first original thinker who gave the idea that the church had two swords. It was of his own accord that the church delegated its temporal authority to the state as it did not wish to use coercive and bloody temporal authority.

5. Church Directly Related to God. John also developed the idea that church had direct relation with God and relationship of God with state was indirect.

6. State as Commonwealth. John developed Cicero's idea that the state is a commonwealth. He influenced Nicolas of Cusa in developing his theory of Medicine. Thomas Acquinas borrowed from him the idea that church is the soul of state.

7. Sovereignty Flowed from the King. John expounded the philosophy that the people have a right to disobey a king who has tyrant. He gave the idea that sovereignty of the king flowed from the people. This idea occupied the mind of every important thinker who followed him. Indirectly it refuted the theory that Middle ages were barren of all political activities.

8. Organic Theory of State. John gave the idea of organic theory of the state which was subsequently developed by Herbert Spencer.

QUESTIONS FOR EXERCISE

1. Discuss briefly political idea of Hildebrand (Gregory VII).
2. 'Gregory's theory of Government in the church was monarchical, not in the sense of the feudal monarchy but more nearly in the sense of the imperial Roman traditions.' (Sabine). Discuss.
3. Discuss the political ideas of John of Salisbury and estimate his importance as a political thinker.
4. Show the importance of the work of John of Salisbury in the development of theory of state.
5. Explain the contribution of John of Salisbury to the political thought and estimate his importance.
6. Trace the growth of medieval political thought in Europe through the writings of John of Salisbury (1120-1180).
7. Discuss the views of John of Salisbury on the relationship between Church and State.

14

Thomas Aquinas (1227-1274 A.D.)

St. Thomas Aquinas is generally acclaimed as one of the greatest political thinker. He was born in 1227 and died at the age of 47 in 1274. According to Foster "he was one of the greatest systematic philosopher of the world." He holds that the distinctive thing about Aquinas was that he assimilated into the unity of a single system the different trends of thought which has previously been apart. He represents, perhaps as no other medieval thinker does, the totality of medieval thought.

Contemporary Circumstances

Thomas Aquinas lived at a time when the organisation of church was fairly developed. Roman church had become a gigantic spiritual organisation. Feudalism has considerably declined. Nationalism was striking at its roots. Aristotle was again being seriously studied. All this was weakening papal authority, church supremacy was being refuted. The church was in need of an exponent who could expound church philosophy in the most systematic way and bring Christianity in harmony with diplomacy. This task was admirable accomplished by St. Thomas and so much by the originality of his ideas or brilliancy of his ideas as by his extraordinary gift of combining and unifying very different elements of thought in an apparently logical and convincing system. He struggled to establish the supremacy of church over the state.

St. Aquinas was a follower of Christian religion. He made Aristotle the cornerstone of his philosophy. He also freely borrowed from the writing of Stoics, Cicero and other Roman lawyers. In subordinating state to church, he followed St. Augustine. From John of Salisbury, he borrowed the idea of supremacy of law and also that of executing a monarch who was tyrant. He was influenced by scholasticism which aimed at synthesising all branches of knowledge and attempted to reconcile faith and reason. His works were synthetic. He followed Aristotle's philosophy that the state is natural to man. The general theory of law, as expounded by Aristotle, is visible in his philosophy. He died at the premature age of 47 yet he left much behind him.

INDEBTEDNESS TO ARISTOTLE

In Aquinas, Aristotelean philosophy was revived. Aquinas is Aristotle renamed. In the words of Dunning, "Doctrine of Aquinas presents the reconciliation of St. Augustine and Aristotle." Aquinas borrowed rather too much from Aristotle. He tried to represent Aristotle's philosophy by adjusting Christian doctrine and harmonising the both. But he was not a blind follower of Aristotle. He differed from him when his doctrines clashed with those of Christianity. Foster says, "The greatest of the task of reconciliation which Aquinas has to perform was to reconcile the philosophy of Aristotle with the truth of Christian revelation." Aquinas followed Aristotle because he felt that his ideas were based on reason and proved sound logically. Aristotle's philosophy so much appealed to him that he has been characterised as Christianized Aristotle. He borrowed from Aristotle in these respects:

1. Aristotle's Method. Aquinas' method of approach was both scientific and Aristotelean. He posed a question and pointed out various arguments and difficulties which might come. One by one he dealt with them and put his idea as a solution. Such a solution was based on Christian philosophy. He dealt with all the objections to the Christian philosophy connected with that problem and ultimately he gave his own ideas and solution to the problem posed by him. This method of study was very much Aristotelean.

2. Purpose of the State. Aquinas borrowed from Aristotle the idea that the state made a man moral. It has a specific mission and certain educative functions to perform. The purpose of the state is not only to make people moral but also virtuous and induce them to lead a happy life. He did not agree with church fathers that the state existed only for the purpose of maintaining law and order. To him the state is not a necessary evil. He agreed with Aristotle that the state is the only social organisation covering all aspects of human life. However, to Aquinas the church was superior to state.

3. Nature of Society. Aquinas agreed with Aristotle that society is mutual exchange of services for the sake of good life alone. Society promoted good and happy life. But whereas Aristotle's conception was narrow that of Aquinas was comparatively broader. Aristotle took into consideration only secular aspect of society. For Aquinas, a perfect society is one in which secular and religious organisations existed side by side and where religion has priority over the secular organisation.

4. Nature of Man. Aquinas agreed with Aristotle that man is a social animal and that without society he can not exist. He also believed that the state is natural to man. Thus he repudiated the idea of the traditional Christian that the state is the result of the fall of man and that it is a sort of punishment to human beings.

5. Ethics. In the sphere of ethics Aquinas also borrowed from Aristotle. For him it was a source of happiness and a method for pleasure giving. But whereas for Aristotle it was worldly pleasure, for Aquinas it is spiritual salvation without which earthly happiness has no meaning and is thus incomplete.

6. Teleology. Aquinas borrowed from the concept of teleology. Everything in this universe is moving towards a particular object and under subordination to an end. Even human life has an end. But for Aristotle this was a rational contemplation while Aquinas believed that not reason but soul is the loftiest and that salvation can only be possible through deep faith and by the Grace of God. The highest goal for everything in the world should be deep faith supplemented with reason.

7. Nature. Both Aristotle and Aquinas agreed that nature is an axiom but whereas for Aristotle this earthly nature was everything and there was nothing beyond that, for Aquinas this is only superficial and there is another nature beyond the worldly nature which is most important.

8. Justice. Aquinas agreed with Aristotle on the concept of justice based on equality. It is perpetual. It gives everyone its own right. It lies in the laws of the state. While for Aristotle human law is everything Aquinas subordinates human law to natural law. For Aristotle there is no subordination of human law to any superior law but for Aquinas, human law is bound to be subordinated to natural laws. Foster has rightly summed up his ideas in this regard by saying that, "His system depends upon the assumption that this superstructure can be raised upon the Aristotelean foundation without the need of essential modification of the Aristotelean doctrine itself. In fact this society must loose the character which Aristotle attributed to it."

IS AQUINAS A MERE MEDIEVAL ARISTOTLE?

Aquinas has been called a medieval Aristotle. A.P.D. Entreves maintains that his political theory was but one aspect of a great enterprise of reconciling Aristoteleanism and Christianity, or of grafting on to the teaching of the Church the old and yet newly discovered wisdom of Greece.[1] His theory has also been called a Christian coping upon an essentially Greek substructure.[2] But an adequate survey of Aquinas' ideas drives one to reject the views and agree with G.H. Sabine's opinion that Thomas valued Aristoteleanism only as a better philosophical support for well-founded (Christian) beliefs.[3]

Aquinas was the best interpreter of the spirit of his times, and of their deepest aspirations. His philosophy represents the *Zeitgeist*. It is a grand

1. A.P.D. Entreves, *op. cit.*, p. xxxvi.
2. W.J. Jones (Ed.), *Masters of Political Thought*, Vol. 2.
3. Sabine, G.H., *op. cit.*, p. 216.

synthesis of diverse ways of thought and outlook. As the thirteenth century was one of a clash of the philosophy of Aristotle and theology of Christianity, Aquinas resolved this clash by effecting a synthesis between the two, but in this synthesis he did not surrender his basic Christian ground. He gave reason its due, and accommodated, it within his great Christian system. Despite Aristotelean influence, his *weltanschauang* remains Christian.

Aristoteleanism is merely an adjunct of Thomism. Aquinas uses Aristoteleanism to support his profound faith in the truth of Christianity. Critics of Christianity has viewed faith to be opposed to reason. Aquinas asserted that faith was only a fulfilment of reason, rather than its antithesis. He used Aristotle to buttress the position he had already taken against the onslaughts of the iconoclass; used it to support the convictions he had reached without reference to it. As Bertrand Russell observes, "There is little of philosophic spirit in Aquinas. He does not engage himself in an enquiry the result of which it is impossible to know in advance. Before he begins to philosophize, he already knows the truth; it is declared in the Catholic faith. If he can find apparently rational arguments for some parts of the faith, so much the better; if he cannot, he need only fall back on revelation."[4]

Differences from Aristotle

Prof. Foster points out that Aquinas sets, in every department of philosophy, a Christian coping upon a Greek substructure. This is wrong as the differences between him and Aristotle are far-reaching and profound.

1. Aristotle believes in the *polis* as the only setting where a true political life can be lived. While Aquinas believes in the empire or the Christian Commonwealth of which the state and the Church constitute just two wings.

2. While to Aristotle, the *polis* is a self-sufficient moral community which is also natural and organic. Aquinas does not consider state to be self-sufficient. He views man to be a spiritual creature in his essence whose highest goal lies in the liberation of the soul from the bondages of the flesh. Man can attain this liberation only by means of grace and revelation.

Man is a moral being. Hence needs the state. But as a spiritual being he can be satisfied with nothing short of the Church. In the eyes of Thomas only the *Respublica Christiana* can be considered self-sufficient or the institution of the highest self-fulfilment. Life under state is a mere stepping-stone to the one under the Church. Morality is subservient to spirituality; so is state to the Church.

3. The organic state of Aquinas, too, differs from the organic polis of Aristotle. Aquinas derives his concept of organism as a feature of state from his

4. Bertrand Russell, *op. cit.*, p. 474.

larger conception of Republica Christiana, as already noted.

4. Unlike Aristotle's state the state of Aquinas does not entirely absorb the life of man. To Aristotle, a citizen is higher than man: To Aquinas man is higher than the citizen. The state of Aquinas touches only the externals of personality; the inner spiritual being remains beyond the hand of the state. The state stops at the gate of life; the Church reaches of sacred sanctuary of spirit.

5. Contrary to Aristotle, Aquinas upholds the ideal of spiritual blessedness of which Aristotle is all unaware.

6. To Aristotle, the best practicable system of rule is polity; but to Aquinas, both in theory and practice, it is monarchy that is the best.

7. In the special function that Aquinas assigns to aristocracy we find an echo of Aristotle's idea of a mixed constitution; but his stress on consent as the basis of government or on election of the king more shows a preference for the Roman practice which merely recognizes that the king derives authority from the people.

8. Aristotle nowhere advocates overthrow of any government bad or tyrannical; Aquinas does.

9. Aristotle rather writes from the standpoint of the powers that be. But being a Christian Aquinas advocates loyalty to higher principles and higher institutions than the state and its laws.

10. Aquinas does accept the Aristotelean definition of law as expression of pure reason. To him, there are higher laws than the positive law or even natural law. To him all laws are lower or higher manifestations of a cosmic reality. And in virtue of his theory of natural law he improves upon Aristotle's notion of state as a natural institution. Unlike Aristotle he stress that no life can be truly natural unless it is perfectly just.

Aquinas, thus, is not a medieval Aristotle. His originality, in fact, consists in his adaptation of Aristotle to Christian dogma with a minimum of alteration. As G.H. Sabine observes. "Thomas at least had no desire to depart from the great body of political and social tradition that had descended to the thirteenth century from the Fathers of the Church; so far as his inheritance was concerned, as in the case of the whole body of Christian belief, he valued Aristoteleanism less as a means of making innovations than as a better philosophical support for well-founded beliefs."[5]

The above study of the ideas of Aquinas leads us to conclude with J.W. Allen that "The schoolmen seem to have got little from Aristotle, for all their talk of him. They Platonised him and they Christianized him but they never

5. Sabine, G.H., *op. cit.*, p. 216.

understood him. Aquinas, in some respects, is a Stoic, in some, neo-Platonist, never an Aristotelean."

Aquinas was a great system-builder and synthetizer in philosophy. His philosophy is capable of constructing a rational scheme of God, Nature, and Man within which society and civil authority find their due place. Beyond building a system, he gave to Christian civilization a systematic and rational philosophy of a kind it had not known before.[6] His thought was purely impersonal because it was most universal—a thought that weds mind and mystery in the heart of being.[7] "The universal inheritance taken up in its entirety and in its entirety reconstructed, born again, in the intellect, is quite the opposite of eclecticism and a mosaic of opinions. A immaterial word infinitely complex in structure and perfectly one in essence, was vitally begotten in the womb of the mind."[8]

Influenced by Aristotle Aquinas stands for the idea of a fundamental harmony between human and religious values, between reason and faith. Human values and truths are not obliterated by the revelation of the higher ones; however modest and low they deserve to be considered as possible tools for the great task of building up Christian civilization. Whereas the Aristotelian view of the state as a natural institution was, for others a challenge of the Christian idea of the existence of higher and ultimate values, for Aquinas it offered a condition and means for the existence of a higher order as natural law is but a part of the eternal law of God. Aquinas considers the action and value of the state, as part of the natural order, entirely subservient to divine direction. He thus makes a thorough going reconstruction of the medieval political thought. Despite this reconstruction Aquinas remains true to the Christian view of man as ultimately a spiritual being who can never be completely absorbed by the state. 'Man is not formed for political fellowship in his entirety'.

SUMMA THEOLOGICA

St. Thomas discussed his views regarding Nature and God in his book *Summa Theologica,* but he could not complete it. As a great master of synthesis and codification he was content to leave his finest work unfinished, because he was conscious of the idea, that no single book and no single man could attempt to embrace all the mysteries of Nature and God. As he confessed to those friends who questioned him on this point, "all that he had written so far appeared to him as nothing in comparison with the wonderful things that God had been pleased to reveal to him recently."

---

6. Maurice Granston (Ed.), *Western Political Thinkers,* p. 29.
7. Maritain, *Political Thought in Perspectives,* pp. 126-27.
8. *Ibid.*

SUMMA CONTRA GENTILES

Another important book of St. Aquinas is the *Summa Contra Gentiles*. It was written during the years 1259-1264. It was mostly concerned with establishing the truth of the Christian religion by arguments addressed to a reader supposed to be not already a Christian; one gathers that the imaginary reader is usually thought of as a man versed in the philosophy of the Arabs. It tried to establish that what is demonstrable is, so far as it goes, in accordance with the Christian faith, and nothing in revelation is *contrary* to reason. But it is important to separate the parts of the faith which can be proved by reason from those which can't. Accordingly, of the four books, into which the *Summa* is divided, the first three make no appeal to revelation, except to show that it is in accordance with conclusions reached by reason; only in the fourth book were matters treated which cannot be known apart from revelation.

1. The First Book. It is concerned with the existence of God. The existence of God is proved, as in Aristotle, by the argument of the unmoved mover.[9] There are things which are only moved, and other things which both moved and are moved. Whatever is moved is moved by something and, since an endless regress is impossible, we must arrive somewhere at something which moves other things without being moved. This unmoved mover is God.

2. The Second Book. It is mainly occupied with the soul in man. All intellectual substances are immaterial and incorruptible; angels have no bodies, but in men the soul is united to a body. It is the form of the body, as in Aristotle. There are not three souls in man, but only one. The whole soul is present entire in every part of the body. The souls of animals, unlike those of men, are not immortal. The intellect is part of each man's soul; there is not, as Averroes maintained, only one intellect, in which various men participate. The soul is not transmitted with these men, but is created afresh with each man. There is, it is true, a difficulty; when a man is born out of wedlock, this seems to make God an accomplice in Adultery. This objection, however is only specious.

3. The Third Book. It is largely connected with ethical questions. Evil is unintentional not an essence, and has an accidental cause which is good. All things tend to be like God who is the end of all things. Human happiness does not consist in carnal pleasures, honour, glory, wealth, worldly power, or goods of the body, and is not seated in the senses. Man's ultimate happiness does not consist in acts of moral virtues, because these are means; it consists in the contemplation of God. But the knowledge of God possessed by the majority does not suffice; nor the knowledge of Him obtained by demonstration; nor even the knowledge obtained by faith. In this life, we can't see God in His

9. In Aristotle the argument leads to 47 or 55 Gods.

essence, or have ultimate happiness; but hereafter we shall see Him face to face. This will happen, not by our natural power, but by the divine light; and even then, we shall not see all of Him. By this vision we become partakers of eternal life.

In this book, St. Thomas also discussed sexual ethics and pleads for strict monogamy. Ploygamy is unfair to women, and polyandry makes paternity uncertain. He then passes on to sin, predestination, and election, on which his view is broadly that of Augustine. He seems to hold, with St. Augustine, that no reason can be given why some are elected and go to heaven, while others are left reprobate and go to hell. He also holds in this book that no man can enter heaven unless he has been baptized.

4. The Forth Book. It is concerned with the Trinity, the Incarnation, the supremacy of the Pope, the sacraments, and the resurrection of the body. In the main, it is addressed to theologians rather than philosophers.

The conclusion that St. Thomas draws in this book is that though revelation is above reason, it is in no way contrary to reason. Theology completes the system of which science and philosophy form the beginning, but never destroys its continuity. Faith is the fulfilment of reason. Together they build the temple of knowledge but nowhere do they conflict or work at cross purposes.

CONCEPT OF NATURE

The most important part of Thomas's philosophy is the picture which he draws of Nature. The universe forms a hierarchy reaching from God at its summit down to the lowest being. Every being acts under the internal urge of its own nature, seeking the good or form of perfection natural to its kind, and finding its place in the ascending order according to its degree of perfection. In all cases the higher rules over and makes use of the lower, as God rules over the world or the soul over the body. No matter how lovely it may be, no being is wholly lacking in value for it has its station, its duties and its rights, through which it contributes to the perfection of the whole. The essence of the scheme is purpose, subordination to an end. In such a structure human nature has a unique place among created beings, since man possesses not only a bodily nature but also a rational and spiritual soul by virtue of which he is akin to God. He alone of all beings is at once body and soul, and on this fundamental fact rest the institutions and the laws by which his life is directed.

CONCEPT OF SOCIETY

The entire social and political conception of Thomas, which can be gleaned from his two books, *Summa Contra Gentiles* and *De Regimine Principum,* particularly from the latter book, falls directly into his larger plan of Nature as a whole. Like Nature, society is also a system of ends and purposes in which the lower serves the higher and the higher directs and guides the lower. Following Aristotle, Thomas described "society as a mutual exchange of services for the sake of a good life to which many callings contribute, the farmer and artisan by supplying material goods, the priest by prayer and religious observance, and each class by doing its own proper work. The common good requires that such a system shall have a ruling part, just as the soul rules the body or any higher nature rules the lower."[10] Thomas compared the founding and ruling of states, the planning of cities, the building of castles, the establishments of markets, and the fostering of education to providence whereby God creates and rules the world.

CONCEPT OF THE STATE

Aquinas was of the opinion that man was a social and political animal and that the state was essential not only because it checked human evil, as it was held by the early medieval Christian thinkers but also because an individual could not realize himself fully in its absence. Also, Aquinas attempted to support his earlier contention that the higher always rules over the lower by holding that as one man was superior to others in knowledge and justice, it was good that he should rule over others for their benefit. In Thomas's view rulerships was trust for the whole community. He justified the authority of the ruler because he thought that whatever the ruler did, he (the ruler) did for the common good. The moral purpose of the Government, according to Thomas, is paramount. Broadly speaking, it is the duty of the ruler so to direct the action of every class in the state that men may live a happy and virtuous life, which is the true end of man in society. Ultimately, of course, this must lead to a good beyond earthly society to a heavenly life, but this is beyond human power and is in the keeping of priests rather than of rulers. But it is characteristic of Thomas that he should regard an orderly political life as a contributing cause even to this ultimate end. More specifically, "it is the function of the earthly ruler to lay the foundations of human happiness by maintaining peace and order, to preserve it by seeing that all the needful services of public administration, of judicature, and of defence, are performed, and to improve it by correcting abuses wherever they occur and by removing all possible hindrances to the good life."

The moral purpose for which political rule exist implies that authority ought to be limited and checked by the law. Thomas's dislike of tyranny was as great as that displayed by John of Salisbury though he explicitly disavowed the latter's defence of tyrannicide. Justifiable resistance is a public act of a whole people, and the right is safeguarded by the moral condition that those who resist are responsible for seeing that their action is less injurious to the general good than the abuse which they are trying to remove. Thomas's

10. Sabine, G.H., *A History of Political Theory* (London, 1948) p. 219.

interest was essentially in the moral limitations laid upon rulers, and the legal or constitutional phases of the subject seem not to have concerned him. He was explicit on the point that a king's power should be 'limited' (*temperature*) though he never explained exactly what this meant. As a moralist, he broadly held that the end of the state, as also of the individual, was the realization of good in a virtuous life. To him, the source of all political authority is God who is the Supreme Governor of all things. From God the legitimate authority to govern passes to the whole community. The people under God are sovereign and they may delegate their authority to a monarchical, aristocratic or republican form of government.

CONCEPT OF GOVERNMENT

St. Thomas was conscious of the purpose of the government. He held that all governments were good or bad according as they worked. The main aim of a man was to lead a virtuous life and that of government was to promote virtue among men to enable them to achieve eternal salvation. The character of a government should be determined according to the fulfilment of this object. Like Aristotle, Aquinas divided the governments into monarchy, aristocracy, polity, tyranny, oligarchy and democracy. He preferred monarchy to a democracy. His preference for monarchy was in line with his earlier argument that one God rules the universe, and one soul rules the body. According to him, the monarchical form of government is the best, because it gives to the state important advantages of unity, regularity, experience and an analogy with Divine Rule. Tyranny he considered the worst type of government. The degeneration of a monarchy into a tyranny, could be possibly prevented if the monarchy were a limited one. The best form of government is an elective monarchy in which a monarch should be made to take an oath to observe the constitution of the state so that if he breaks the oath he can be justifiably deposed. "The king must work for the sake of the kingdom and not *vice versa.*"

SUPREMACY OF CHURCH

Aquinas regarded the rule of God as superior to that of man. He held that a secular ruler could properly perform his functions only in co-operation with and under the guidance of the Church. Salvation was to be achieved not through reason but through faith. On all questions of faith the church was the final authority. The Pope must be obeyed by everyone, including the temporal rulers, in everything whether relating to temporal or ecclesiastical affairs. A king might be the image of God, but if he disregarded the Church he could be excommunicated. In assigning superiority to the Church over the most exalted of secular rulers, including the Holy Roman Emperor, Aquinas was only theorizing over a *fait accompli.* Besides, like all good medievalists, Aquinas believed in the fundamental importance of unity amidst universal disorder and anarchy, and believed that this unity could only be achieved by the supremacy of the Papacy over all persons and all classes, spiritual or temporal.

REPRESENTATIVE OF MIDDLE AGES

St. Thomas Aquinas has been frequently called as the representative of the middle ages. This implies that he combined in himself all the medieval doctrines :

1. Theory of Two Swords. The middle ages were known for the theory of two swords. Aquinas, like a true Papal supporter, believed that in the case of a conflict between the church and the state, the church has supremacy over the state.

2. Monarch. As a true medieval he supported the idea of monarchy as the best form of government because if promoted stability in administration. His monarch, however, was not absolute but bound by laws, more particularly by divine law.

3. Law. Like all other medieval thinkers Aquinas has given a preference to law everything else in the state. According to Sabine, "His reverence for law was such that he assumed its authority to be inherent and not dependent on any human origin."

4. Universalism. Like all other thinkers of middle ages Aquinas believed that there is a universal society with a papal monarch as the supreme head. Thus he believed in universal scholasticism. This was one of the prevailing movements of the middle ages admitted by Aquinas.

5. Aristoteleanism. There was a trend in the middle ages to revive the philosophy of Aristotle. Aquinas beautifully and faithfully accomplished this. He followed Aristotle, as long as he did not go against church.

Thus it may be said that Aquinas was the true representative of the middle ages. He combined in one all the characteristics and qualities of his age.

POLITICAL PHILOSOPHY OF AQUINAS

1. Origin of the State. Church Fathers believed that the state was the result of fall and sins of men and the government came into being to punish the people for their sins. Aquinas did not agree with this general belief. He believed that man was a social animal by nature and necessity and that state was natural to man. The people accepted the state for their fullest development and also for attaining perfection. State is natural because none can be self-sufficient. The aid and advice of others is always necessary for meeting our social requirements. The society is exchange of services and hence essential for human nature. The state has positive role to play and it has great educative value as well which is likely to be seriously jeopardised without state. The

Christians should have citizenship rights. The state should aim at making the citizen virtuous and moral. It should aim at providing knowledge.

2. Monarchy. Monarchy is the best form of government. State and no other institution can promote unity. It is the inevitable law of nature that the superior should rule over the inferior. As such, a monarch, who is definitely superior, should rule over the subjects. It is also in the interest of inferiors that they should be ruled by the superiors. For Aristotle slavery was justified on the grounds of inequalities whereas for Aquinas it was divine expedient. In the words of Maxey, "Whereas Aristotle has justified slavery on the grounds of inequalities of ability, the saint at Dominican saw it as a divine expedient for the punishment of sin, a righteous and holy institution which followers of Nazareth could conscientiously defend." In addition to this, monarch is like the heart of a state which should not be diversified but unified, it should present a united view.

3. Functions of a Monarch. According to Aquinas, rulerships is only a truth of office and a place of service. A ruler is required to contribute to the good and welfare of the masses. He should aim and act at promoting happy and virtuous life. He should maintain peace and order and provide all useful service needed for public administration. He should make adequate arrangements for giving justice to the people. He should remove hindrance and correct abuses. In democracy there are discussions which a monarch should avoid. A monarch should see that he acts in accordance with the laws not that he does not become a tyrant. Tyrannicide would lead to anarchy. There should be limitation on the authority of the king so that he does not feel tempted to become absolute.

4. Reason and Faith. Before Aquinas a controversy had been going on whether human behaviour should be guided by faith or reason. St. Augustine had stood for faith. But Aquinas tried to end this controversy by saying that both the faith and reason had common source, namely God. In the words of J.E. Greene, "Thus St. Thomas provided the synthesis between Christian dogma and the philosophy of the ancient not by a dualistic recognition of each but by unifying them as the emanation of Divine Being. This was his great achievement."

5. Slavery. St. Thomas Aquinas favoured the institution of slavery. Slavery is divine remedy for the punishment of all sins. It is also essential for stimulating bravery among the soldiers. It gives a warning to them that they should not get themselves vanquished. Aquinas agreed with Aristotle that some were born to rule while others to be ruled.

6. Classification of Government. Aquinas classified Government broadly on two principles, namely whether the supremacy is the product of sins of man, which to him culminated into slavery or whether that was the result of social instincts. It was this latter category which, to him, was the basis of civil government. Hence he attached importance to the civil governments which were of four types (i) Sacred, (ii) Royal, (iii) Political and (iv) Economic. No form of government is either absolutely good or bad. It depends on the functions which it performed and that how much virtuous it makes the citizens. Aquinas followed Aristotle in giving his classification of governments. He classified them into normal and preverted forms. In the former fall monarchy, aristocracy and polity (which is modern democracy). Their corresponding perverted forms are tyranny, oligarchy and democracy (which in the modern sense can correspond to Mobocracy). Aquinas, however, had definite preference for limited monarchy which he felt is a check on tyranny.

7. Functions of Government. A good government is only one which performs good functions. There was no other standard for measuring quality of a form of government. It should pave way for pleasure, happiness and a virtuous life. It should give better administration, justice and civic facilities. It should ensure defence of citizens. It should have a good system of coinage. It should maintain population. It should look after the needy. According to Sabine, "A ruler is justified in all that he does solely because he contributes to the common good. His power, because it is derived from God for the happy ordering of human life is a ministry or service owned to the community of which he is the head." Paramount function of the state is to promote moral life of the masses. The functions of the state are: (i) to look after the poor; (ii) to promote unity; (iii) to look after common, instead of individual, good and welfare; (iv) to introduce sound system of weights, measures and coinage; (v) to remove hindrances from the path of citizens for right living and virtuous life; (vi) to keep roads safe and free; (vii) to maintain peace and happiness and also protect property of the subjects; (viii) to avoid undue taxation and provide economic relief to the subjects; and (ix) to reward the worthy.

8. Welfare State. From the above mentioned functions of the state, it is clear that like a traditional Christian Aquinas did not favour the idea of assigning any negative functions to the state. On the other hand, he believed that the state was positively good. He thus mooted the idea of welfare state in modern sense of the term. In the words of Maxey, "The purpose of Government, he asserts is to elevate man to his true end, which is the life of highest virtue. Human wisdom and virtue are not sufficient for this, and consequent by pure royal authority must be reinforced by priestly authority under the law of Christ."

9. Sovereignty. Aquinas has given his ideas about sovereignty only indirectly. He maintained that sovereignty is derived from the people from political view point and from God from theological viewpoint. The sovereignty is indivisible. It is the only source of positive law, the end of which is temporal tranquillity of the state. A positive law, therefore, must derive from natural law and aim as common good. It must provide directives for human acts of justice. A bad law given by the sovereign leads to lawlessness and is thus *ultra vires.* Laws of tyrant sovereign need not be obeyed because obedience to the commands of such sovereign is a contempt of conscience. A sovereign drew his authority from the people. A monarch is a public person ruling for common goods. He is duty bound to institute good life among his people and also to preserve and promote that the source of authority of a king is nothing else, but popular will.

10. Supremacy of Church. According to Aquinas, a secular state should always work under the guidance of church. Without that it shall neither be in a position to give salvation to the people nor shall it promote virtuous life, for which it stood. Since the church is the guiding and controlling authority, therefore it is superior as compared with the secular authority, exactly in the same way as spirit has superiority over the matter. The church has authority to ex-communicate a ruler. Pope should be obeyed both in secular and religious affairs. Church is the only agency which promotes unity out of universal disorder and anarchy. It is supreme over all persons and classes. It is not to be disputed and is a *fait accompli.* For harmonious working it is essential that both the church and the state should work in close cooperation with each other. Church cannot keep feudal vassal, as it is the privilege of the king. The authority of the church over the state is indirect rather being direct. As such the interference of church in the state affairs should be minimum. Interference cannot be warranted without valid or serious causes. According to Dunning, "The initial assumption of his whole philosophy was that certain truths and those of the highest importance to man were not demonstrable by reason but must enter human cognition through faith and immediate divine relevation." According to him, "It was the duty of the political rulers to administer secular affairs in such a way as to further God's will and to this extent the official of the state must be subject to the priests and to the Divine Law of the church." In the words of Maxey, "The Pope as the head of the Christ's church, has authority covering all matters of sin, and this places him on a plane above all kings and civil rules. He is the royal head of system of government which transcends all temporal affairs and includes within its jurisdictions, all Christian people and their sovereigns. Temporal authorities are to be obeyed in so far as their limited power is sufficient for the realisation of the Christian state but beyond that point papal supremacy is not to be denied."

11. Private Property. Thomas Aquinas favoured the institution of private property. He was of the view that private property is needed for three following reasons:

(i) *Incentive.* Every person is more careful to produce and procure that which belonged to himself alone. In the absence of sense of possession no body will be willing to put labour and will make every effort to avoid that.

(ii) ***Responsibility.*** Private property provides a sense of responsibility which is always more conductive for the conduct of human affairs.

(iii) ***Peace.*** When each one is satisfied with what is his own a peaceful state is likely to be ensured.

Aquinas was firm that private property is not opposed to natural laws. In his own words, "The right to private property is not opposed to natural law, but in addition to it, is devised by human reason."

PHILOSOPHY OF LAW

1. Definition of Law. One of the most important and lasting contribution of St. Aquinas to the political philosophy is his idea about law and justice. According to Sabine, "Human law is for him part and parcel of the whole system of divine government whereby everything both in heaven and earth is ruled." To him law was the rule and the standard of human action. Its end is to promote happiness and common good. It should be created by multitude and for the multitude. It should be brought to be notice of all concerned for their implementation. To be law an action must be promulgated by a competent authority. It should not be opposed to the general wishes of the people. A law is a degree as well as reason. Since there was nothing absolute in the universe, law cannot be exception to this rule. Law is interlinked with reason and must be in conformity with that. It is of practical reasoning and universal and natural. Everything else is under law which can not easily be changed. Law should never be against human nature. It should always express reason. It should have the approval of the masses in order to become effective for implementation. It is connected with justice. According to Dunning, "Thomas's theory of law is the channel through which the doctrines of Aristotle, the Stoics, Cicero, the Roman imperial jurists and St. Augustine blended into a rounded whole were transmitted to modern times." According to Sabine, "An unlawful ruler was not primarily a violator of human rights and institutions though he was that but a rebel against the whole divine system by which God rules the world."

2. Nature of Law. According to Aquinas, the will of the sovereign has the force of law, otherwise the sovereign will be saviour of lawlessness rather than that of law. He said that "Law is in all those things that is inclined to something by reason of some law." He added, "Just as nothing stands firm with regard to the speculative reason except that which is traced back to the first in demonstrable principles so nothing stands firm with regard to practical reason, unless it be directed to the last end which is the common good and whatever stands to reason in this sense, has the nature of law." He said that law is not in person but each one is a law to himself. He was of the view that laws ought to be changed; not in view of any improvement, but for the sake of a great benefit or in the case of a great urgency.

3. Structure of Law. Aquinas built up a structure of law in which the most important position was given to Eternal Law. Briefly speaking, structure of law as defined and given by Aquinas is as follows:

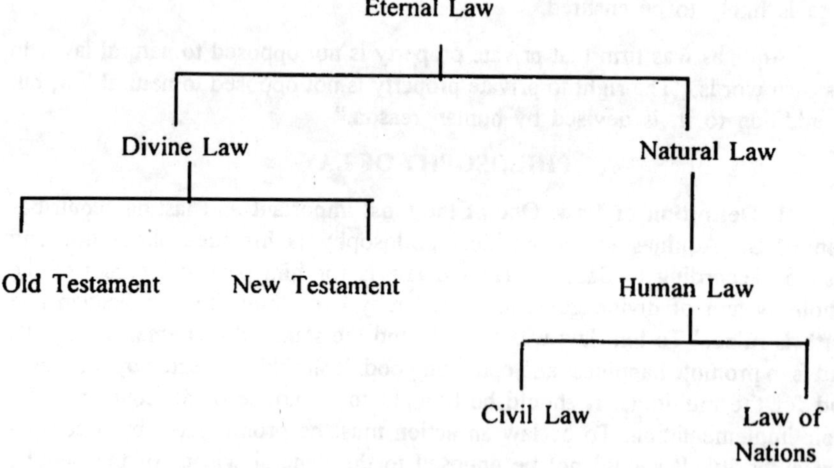

4. Classification of Laws. Aquinas has given four fold classification of Laws namely (i) Eternal Law, (ii) Natural law, (iii) Divine Law and (iv) Human Law.

(i) *Eternal Law.* It governs both animate and inanimate kingdoms. It governs the whole universe. It functions in different ways both in the rational and irrational worlds. It is identical with reason and is truth in itself. It is the type of law through which God governs the whole of universe. It is cosmic in character. According to Sabine, "It is the eternal plan of Divine wisdom by which the whole creation is ordered. In itself this law is above the physical nature of man and in its entity beyond human comprehensions, thought it is not for this reason foreign or contrary to human reasons."

(ii) *Natural Law.* It is the type of law which influences people to dictate the reason of eternal law. It is a type of law which is written in the heart of the people. It is a reflection of divine reason in human beings. It helps in distinguishing between good and evil and also in seeking good and avoiding evil. It helps the people in developing the idea that men should live in society. Salient features of this type of law thus are the following:

(i) It distinguishes between good and evil.

(ii) It helps in seeking good and avoiding evil.

(iii) It develops the idea that man is bound to live in society.

(iv) It gives the idea of self-preservation.

(v) It helps in educating the people.

(vi) It creates desire for seeking truth and developing intelligence.

(vii) It is unchangeable.

(viii) It is positive law both in nature and character.

According to Sabine, "It is manifest in the inclination which nature puts in all beings, to seek good and avoid evil, to preserve themselves; and to live as perfectly as possible the kind of life suitable to their natural endowments....Natural law enjoins all that is implied to give these human inclinations their widest scope."

(iii) *Divine Law.* It is the outcome of commands of God through revelation. It is not the result of natural reason but gift of God. It varies from community to community and changes from time to time. According to Sabine, "By Divine Law he meant substantially revelation. An example would be the special code of laws which God gave to the Jews as the chosen people or the special rules of Christian morals or legislation, given through scripture or the church."

(iv) *Human Law.* It is the outcome of human customs and conventions. It has its origin in human wisdom. It is positive in nature. It is promulgated by the princes. It is not supposed to be against human reason. It should aim at common rather than individual welfare. These laws should only touch temporal and not spiritual affairs. It is derived from natural law and is subordinate to it. According to Foster, "Human law is the system of rule for the regulation of man's conduct worked out for human reason from the principles of Natural laws."

5. Law and Justice. According to Aquinas justice is the basis of law. It is expressed only through law. It is something eternal and gives everyone its due. It is proportionate equality. Aquinas, however, distinguished between corrective and distributive justice. If the laws are unsound, justice naturally cannot be sound. There is close bearing if laws on justice. Both are interlinked and interconnected.

Implication of Theory of Law

Aquinas's theory of law has many far-reaching implications. He worked out relationship between eternal law, natural law and human law. He combined the concepts of laws of the Greeks, Romans and Christian church fathers. He made uncompromising appeal to reason. Even under special circumstances unreasonable law should be obeyed to avoid social disturbances. Aquinas gave due importance to moral elements in law and so also to the common good of the community. He made political obligation a voluntary affair. Perhaps for the first time Aquinas declared that the source of law was multitude itself.

Significance of the Theory

While discussing significance of Aquinas's discussion of law Sabine says, "It was significance of his point of view that he was thus able to find a conception of law which he conceived to be applicable to a range of phenomenon so well and to modern thought so diverse." To conclude with Dunning, "St. Thomas's theory of law and justice is the channel through which the doctrines of Aristotle, Stoics, Cicero, the Roman Imperial jurists and St. Augustine blended into a rounded whole were transmitted to modern time."

CONTRIBUTION OF AQUINAS

St. Thomas Aquinas was one of the most outstanding personalities of the middle ages. He was an intellectual and liberal thinker. He attempted to revive Aristotelean philosophy in so far as it did not come in conflict with the church philosophy. He was the best scholastic. He was an influential writer and a systematic philosopher. He represented middle ages. His contribution to the political philosophy is as follows:

1. Welfare State. In his philosophy Aquinas mooted the idea of welfare state. By pleading that the state should upkeep the population, look after the poor, promote justice and make roads safe and living peaceful he safely planned the idea of welfare state which is being adhered even today.

2. Constitutional Government. Aquinas favoured the idea of monarchy as the ideal form of government. But to him that was not absolute but limited one. According to him, monarch should be bound by the laws of the state because their violation would make him a tyrant. By imposing limitations on the authority of monarchs he put forth the idea of the constitutional government which is today considered as the ideal form of government.

3. Classification of Laws. Another contribution of Aquinas is the method with which he has classified laws based on reason. He did not make law the command of the superior but only a product of reasonable thinking. No law should be obeyed for being merely a command of the superior. Dictates of law should be honoured because of their being based on sound reasoning alone. In addition to this, he has tried to link laws with justice. To quote Carlyle, "His treatment represents a very important aspect of the significance of the rational element in law."

4. Revival of Aristotle's Philosophy. Aquinas borrowed heavily from Aristotle in many ways. He was so much indebted to him that he has been called as 'Christianized Aristotle.' He is mainly responsible for the revival of Aristotle's philosophy in the West. He agreed with his philosophy so long as it did not clash with church ideals. He made an effort to merge the doctrines of Aristotle with traditional doctrines. In the words of Sabine, "Aristotle was not merely revived but made the corner store of Roman Catholic philosophy."

Grahman says, "None before no one after 15th century had studied Aristotle as thoroughly as Thomas had done."

5. Basis of State. Aquinas was the first political thinker in the middle ages who declared that the state is not the result of fall of man or due to his sins. It is a moral institution and stands to promote the welfare of its subject. It has no contractual origin. It is an outcome of social instinct of man. The state is not only required to perform negative function of punishing the guilty but positive functions of promoting virtue and good life. It is a moral institution. It has great educative value. This Aquinas was the first thinker in middle ages who attached natural and moral basis to the state and these are appreciated even today.

6. Personal Authority. Dunning has characterised Aquinas' most important contribution that authority was personal rather than impersonal. According to him, impersonal concepts like nature and reason had no importance but only personal God had force and value.

7. Systematic Knowledge. Aquinas maintained that philosophy should best be studied in a systematic way and the diametrically opposite ideas can be studied by way of synthesis. His system was so perfect that Foster has described him as one of the greatest systematic philosophers of the world. He assimilated various fragments of knowledge and combined them together into a solid philosophy. He systematised reason with faith. He tried to reconcile the two. He was a compiler and systematiser of ideas. He was an exponent of new philosophers. According to Foster, "Aquinas is one of the great systematic philosophers of the world."

8. Secular State. It was due to the efforts of Aquinas that the old idea that the religions acting through the machinery of the state should dominate science and philosophy, was substituted by national sentiment for religious authority as the dominating force behind Government. In this way he contributed to the idea of nation state.

9. Natural Law. Aquinas gave the concept of natural law in a very systematic manner. He subordinated human law to natural law. His ideas about natural law influence the thinkers of Glorious Revolution, including Locke. In the words of Sabine, "The underlying moral relations between Natural Law and Human Law were still for Locke substantially what they were for Thomas." Maxey has said, "In reviving the Roman doctrine of Natural law and in stressing the rational elements in human law St. Thomas made a far reaching contribution to political thought."

10. Reconciliation of Church and State. Aquinas was a staunch supporter of church. He would not tolerate any secular interference in church affairs. But he made a sincere effort to reconcile church and state authorities. He felt that the conflict arose because both tried to do the same job, namely moral uplifting of the people. If moral uplift was left to the church and political one to the state, there would be no clash between the two. It was not dignified and honourable for the priest to interfere in state affairs without solid reasons.

11. Welfare of the People. Another contribution of Aquinas is that he did not ignore the masses and cared for their welfare. He said that the ruler should look after the poor masses, he should make roads secure for them and so on. He believed that the masses should care to see that the laws of the state were not violated by the ruler and that he did not turn himself to be a tyrant in any way. He pleaded for imposing checks on the authority of monarchs, though he did not suggest any effective measures.

Summing up Aquinas place in history Sabine says, "The conception of a Christian society, as it has been transmitted in the Christian tradition, Thomas took to be eternal. Controversies might come and go, but they could not make essential changes here. His philosophy sought to find the reason for it as it was believed to be; to construct a rational scheme of God, nature and man within which society and civil authority find their due place. In this sense Thomas's philosophy expresses most naturally the convictions, moral and religious, upon which medieval civilisation was founded." One of his outstanding twentieth century follower Anton Pagis says, "He stood on a giant past and though he himself was as giant he always looked upon his intellectual structure with genuine humility." To quote Dr. J.E. Greene, "Aquinas was the greatest synthesizer of theology and philosophy."

QUESTIONS FOR EXERCISE

1. Consider St. Thomas Aquinas as the highest expression of Medieval Political Thought.
2. 'A Christianised Aristotle,' bring out the aptness of this description of St. Thomas Aquinas.
3. Analyse the political thought of St. Thomas Aquinas. How far does it mark a turning to that of Aristotle.
4. "Thus in every department of philosophy, Aquinas sets; as it were, a Christian calling upon a Greek substructure," (Foster). Elucidate the above and show how St. Thomas Aquinas attempted the medieval synthesis between the church and Aristotle.
5. "It is necessary that the will concerning the things commanded be a will controlled by some reason it is to bear to the character of laws." (St. Thomas Aquinas). State and elucidate St. Thomas's theory of law.
6. "It is not, therefore the final end of a society to live according to virtue,

but by means of a virtuous life to attain to the enjoyment of God." (Aquinas), Comment.

7 "Since law is the rule and standard of human action, it is necessarily related to reason." (Aquinas). Comment.

8. "St. Thomas Aquinas represents as no medieval writer does the totality of medieval thought." Explain.

9. "By his laws and commands he (the king) must keep his subjects from wickedness and lead them into works of variety." (St. Thomas Aquinas). Discuss.

10. "Scarcely was Thomas's system complete before the seams of his great structure began to open." (Sabine). Discuss the difficulties inherent in the political and philosophical system of Thomas Aquinas.

11. It is necessary that the will concerning the things commanded be a will controlled by some reason it is to bear the character of law. (St. Thomas Aquinas). Comment and elucidate St. Thomas's theory of law.

12. "Law is nothing but an ordinance of reason for the common good promulgated by him who has the care of the community." (Aquinas), Comment.

13. "The greatest mind of the 13th Century a saint Aristotle." Discuss this statement with reference to St. Thomas Aquinas in the realm of political thought and law.

14. "In the court of conscience, there is no obligation to obey an unjust law." (St. Thomas Aquinas). Comment.

15. "Since law is a rule and standard of human action, it is necessarily related to reason." (St. Thomas). Comment.

15

Sacerdotal Thinkers of Middle Ages

JOHN OF PARIS

Early Life

John of Paris (1269-1306) represented the spirit of his age. He said that the faith is necessary for the slavation everywhere and spiritual interests are similar in whole Chiristendom. Hence a universal church and unity in religion is desirable. But in secular matter language, customs and manners differ from province to province and country to country. The political requirements of England are different from French and those of Germany from Italy. Therefore on secular side natural units are kingdoms or national states. There can be as many kingdoms as the diversities of political interest may demand. There is no need of unifying power or centralized state administration.

Views About States

John refuted the theory that the state is rooted in human sin. He propounded Aristotelean theory that the state is necessary for good life and without it independence, social and personal virtues, cannot develop. In this way he used the naturalness of the state to support its independence from the control of the Pope or the church.

He opposed Aristotle that the higher controls the lower or lower is subordinate to higher. He agreed that the spiritual authority of the church is superior in dignity to the secular power of the prince but held that it does not mean that the former is superior to the latter in each and every respect. Superior dignity does not mean superior power. A teacher or preacher possesses greater dignity but less temporal power. Similarly though secular power is lower in dignity it is superior in temporal power. Both derive their authority from God. It is wrong to say that the secular power derives authority from the church. Aristotle's theory that the higher controls the lower does not bring us to the conclusion that the spiritual power should control the secular power.

John attacked the legal validity of donation of Constantine. He stated that the Emperor had no right to alienate any part of the Empire. If he possesses such a right it does not apply to France as France was never under the control of the Empire Moreover, when France became free, the Pope had no right to exercise any control over the independent western kingdom of France through his henchman Emperor.

Defence of Property

John stated that every individual has full right of ownership and use over his property and these rights belong to him who acquires property by dint of his labour and industry. The only right that the ruler possesses is to regulate the use of property in public interest and tax it. So far as church property is concerned it belongs to church as an organization and the Pope is only steward or manager of that property to administer it for public good. The prince does not possess power to the ownership of property or to administer it, but he possesses the power of regulating its use for public good. The Pope possesses the right to administer the church property and to use the layman's property for the protection of common faith.

Limited Authority of Church

John stated that the right of the church is limited to the duty of preaching, teaching and administering the church property. Communication amounts to protest and not to deposition. The right of deposition if at all valid belongs to electors and not to the Pope. The Pope possesses power over spiritual matter and does not possess any control over secular matters. According to Sabine, "coming from a church man....limiting of church's authority is very strange."

About the ecclesiastical powers of church, John stated that he is the administrative head of church organisation and not the supreme authority. The final authority resides in the general council of the church which can depose a Pope for corrupt practices. John of Paris justified resistance to Pope who abuses his authority. Thus he supported secular state and popular sovereignty against the Pope.

Contribution

According to Sabine, "Without presenting a systematic political theory, the work of John of Paris was highly magnificent both for its own time and for the future. As Frenchman as well as clergy, he made a strong case on both his historic and legal grounds for the independence of the French monarchy." He adds "Substantially his argument is a protest against the invasion of religion by law and against investing the Pope with a sovereign power medelled on the legal position of the Emperor." John supported conception of national states against the universal state of Dante. His ideas have more rational application of Aristotelean theory of self-sufficiency community than of Thomas or Dante, as such his theory is known Anerroist Aristotelism.

DANTE (1265-1321)

Dante was a very great poet and a political thinker who supported the cause of empire. He was more logical in his exposition of imperial theory than Marsiglio of Padua. He was born in Florentine in 1265 and died as an exile in 1321 at Anerona. He was a great literary genius perhaps the greatest poet of medieval age. He was drawn into the conflict against the Papacy because he thought that the wars among the secular rulers are created due to papal interference. He became aggressive when Papacy was transferred to Aninguonn. He felt that disputes of the states can be wiped out under an all embracing authority of the Emperor and by excluding Pope from any secular authority. He possessed the experience of Italian politics and was a party man and believer in Roman supremacy to rule a vast empire.

De Monarchia

Dante's great work *De Monarchia,* is a sincere an strong plea for the restoration of a world empire as the pre-requisite of lasting peace and of depriving the Pope from the secular power. According to Dunning "De Monarchia contains the most complete and perfect system that we have of imperialistic philosophy.

1. Central Theme. The central theme of *De Monarchia,* is monarchy. By monarchy he means the universal dominion over all things. Temporal state is the state in which all the petty states and pincipalities would be united as semi-autonomous members. In this ideal empire whole Europe was to be organized. Dante holds that peace is necessary for realization of rational life and only universal empire can maintain peace. His arguments may be summarised in the words of Doyle, that all men have the same end which is the realization of potentialities of human reason. This end can be realised only through a cooperative social process, no individual or small group of individuals could achieve it themselves. The whole of mankind must move forward in harmonious effect of sustained co-operation towards the complete realization of the whole potentiality of the human intellect. Defection in honour of few of the members prevented the fulfilment of the ideal. He believed that only a universal emperor can have power and strength to keep under control and check the forces of disruption. Dante supported the common and universal law as a bond of cohesion and unity among the mankind. He desired for an universal monarch to enforce universal law. His ideal for universal empire was based on the Roman Empire which maintained peace in Europe for many centuries. He believed in an universal empire to maintain peace all over the world.

2. Realisation of Potentiality. Civilization would press on to complete realization of whole potentiality of human intellect.

3. Empire Based on Service and Law. Dante desired world empire for the welfare of mankind and not for the sake of ruler. To Dante, the Empire was "Law personified, law throned and crowned and invested with majority and honour." Dante thought of a supreme law rather than of a super state. Supreme law may be called justice administered by emperor, not swayed by passion. According to Pollock, Dante's monarch is not a universal despot, but governor of higher order, set over the princes and rulers of particular states and keeping peace between them. He is to have the jurisdiction, in modern language of an international tribunal. In the second book he tried to prove the claim of Romans for world empire. Thus he defended superiority of Roman ruling class.

4. Church and the Empire. In the third book Dante tried to prove that secular authority is derived, not from the Pope but from God directly. Man according to Dante is worldly and possesses spiritual leanings, so he needs both spiritual and secular authorities to guide him. The Pope represents spiritual and the emperor temporal authorities and both derive their power from God directly. The two have their different sphere of work and must not encroach upon each other's jurisdiction. Christ said, "my kingdom is not of this world," so the Pope most not interfere in secular affairs. The two powers Imperium and Sacredatium are combined only in God and none else. The spiritual power dealt with the eternal matter which he called the celestial paradise and earthly paradise has no place for it. Only the universal monarch should preside there with no rival claimant to supremacy exercising a subversive influence. Dante made an effective breach in the theology of the schoolmen by denying their basic assumption that man had one end in life.

5. Defence of Empire. In this way Dante proved the complete independence of the empire and repudiated the claim of the church to exercise central control over secular authority. He first proved that the office of monarch was necessary for maintaining peace and well being of the world and then stated that he derives power from God and not from ecclesiastical authority. As such Church or the Pope have no place in a secular state and cannot control it because its sphere is heavenly life and celestial paradise.

Comparison with Acquina and Salisbury

1. Inspite of the fact that Dante is ranged against Thomas Acquina and John of Salisbury in the controversy between the papacy and the empire, he was at one with them in his fundamental convictions. Firstly like them he believed in a single universal society containing all mankind and governed by the divinely ordained authorities the emperor for secular things and the Pope for spiritual things. In the days of Dante, Christendom was divided into fragments of various kingdom but Dante overlooked this fact of contemporary life and looked back to Roman Empire as his ideal preached for the world empire on its basis. As such the saying that the ghost of Roman Empire haunted

the middle age is fully applicable to Dante's ideas as he dreamt of the world empire on the basis of Roman Empire quite contrary to the realities of contemporary world because he was poet.

2. Secondly, Dante accepted the dual nature of man and accepted the medieval tradition of the dual government in the single universal society because man possessing both spirit and body is of dual nature. He further held that no one should interfere in the sphere of the other. Thus he desired to raise the theory of two swords and the maxim that give unto Caesar the things that are Caesar's and unto God the things that are God's. He differed very much in general background of his thought from other supporters of secular cause like John of Paris, William Occam and Marsiglio of Padua. His ideas belong to 13th century rather than to 14th century.

3. Both St. Thomas Acquina and Dante were influenced by the ideas of Aristotle Dante attempted to prove his conclusion syllogistically, starting from generally accepted principles to such saying of Aristotle that nature makes nothing in vain and deducting conclusions from them. Thus he tried to prove the universal desirability of peace and that it could be realized only in a universal empire of universal monarch. Thus in fundamental assumptions Dante resembles St. Thomas Acquina who also built assumptions on the basis of Aristotelean philosophy and unified power and the ideas Roman Empire. Sabine said that they are one in their fundamental convictions but St. Thomas Aquina supported the cause of the Church and Dante of a universal Empire through philosophy and herein lies their difference inspite of their similar fundamental convictions. He was a minor thinker but a great poet.

WILLIAM OF OCCAM

The last medieval thinker to support the cause of secular independence against papal claim was William of Occam or Ockham. He was born near about 1290 and died near about 1349. He was an English Francis can and a colleague of Marsiglio of Padua in the University of Paris. He was ex-communicated along with Marsiglio of Padua by Pope John XXII for his attack on papal authorities. Like Marsiglio he took refuse in the court of Emperor Lewis and championed his cause against the Pope. He was scholastic theologian on Aristotelean philosophy and had a great influence. He was more conservative and moderate than Marsiglio in his attack against papacy. Following true scholastic fashion, he always presented both sides of the case and made his own suggestions instead of making dogmatic statements. Unlike Marsiglio, he did not oppose reason and faith. Contrary to Marsiglio he wielded a great influence over his own generation which declined later on.

Political Ideas

His political ideas resemble the ideas of Marsiglio. He was a dialectician rather than a philosopher. He held that church and state are useful institutions in their respective spheres. State to him was like a body and church like a soul. Thus he gave church a little higher position. Main theme of his thought is that every kind of authority whether it is secular or spiritual must be limited to the purpose for which it has been created and should act for common welfare based on reason. If anyone who wields the authority crosses its limits he should be deposed. Marsiglio placed authority of deposition in the hands of citizens in case of the Emperor and to general council in the case of general body of Christian in the church. Ockham knew that neither the general people had the ability to control the Emperor nor general body of Christians to control the Pope. As such he suggested that the Emperor and the Pope should be bound by law of nature. He was of the opinion that a universal empire in spiritual and temporal side was an impossibility.

Arguments Against Supremacy of Pope

Being annoyed by undue interference of Pope John XXII in secular matters he declared that the Pope had no right to interfere in temporal matters as his authority was limited to spiritual matters only. He stated that the pope could have only those powers which would be safely and prudently committed to one man, for the sake of common utility in regard to all things, morals and the spiritual needs of believers. He refuted that the Pope is infallible and did not give any power to the Pope or priests. He deemed it unreasonable to give universal supremacy to Pope. He believed that the whole body of Christians is superior to Pope and as such he could not exceed to what was necessary for the common welfare of citizens. He disbelieved that Peter gave absolute powers to the people both the spiritual and temporal matters. Christ himself did not give the powers to Pope. He did not authorise the Pope to deprive Princes of means of their property, rights and liberties. Moreover, the Pope could not go against Gospel and his resistance is justifiable, if he exceeds his limits.

He did not allow Pope the right to interpret gospel which was to be exercised by the wisest persons famous for their piety and integrity in the service of the church. He gave to the Pope the position of the head of the church whose function was to secure eternal salvation of soul. He stated that the papal jurisdiction is of service and not of powers. He desired to vest whole power in the general council organized on the federal basis. He proposed that all Christians should choose their representatives of both the clergy and laity and even the women. He held that body to be the true representative of Christians. This body would have the power of interpreting scripture, settling matters of disputes and of excommunication and of desposing the Pope. The Pope should neither possess the power of convening the council nor of presiding over it.

William hated the clerical love for wealth and property and believed that possession of wealth made it secular minded. He desired that the church property should be treated on equal terms with that of other property and should not be exempted from taxation or appropriation. He supported the punishment of clergy by secular power for violation of laws. He desired that both church and state should respect the rights of one another.

Conclusion

William did not give despostic powers either to the emperor or the Pope. The Emperor should make his rule just and useful to the people and confirm to the will of God, natural reasons and equity and to international law. Emperor's authority is to be exercised within the framework of law. He desired checks on the despotic powers of both the emperor and the Pope and supported ultimate powers of the public like Marsiglio.

Later on the controversy between the Pope and the Emperor ended and the problem of constitutional or despotic rule came on forefront. The concilliar movement was an attempt to solve the problem but if failed on sharp rocks of realities.

QUESTIONS FOR EXERCISE

1. What role John of Paris played in building up medieval secularism?
2. Briefly analyse the political thought of John of Paris. What is his contribution to the growth of medieval political thought?
3. Write a short essay on Dante's De Monarchia.
4. Dante's De Monarchia has been described as the most complete exposition of imperial philosophy. Show how this is so.
5. Examine Dante's argument for a universal secular empire in his De Monarchia.
6. Estimate the contribution of Dante to political thought. Are his method and basic ideas different from those of St. Thomas Acquina.
7. Write a short essay on William of Occam.

16

Marsiglio of Padua (1270-1340 A.D.)

Marsiglio of Padua, was one of the strongest champions of secular cause. His philosophy was original in nature and character. He has been characterised as one of the greatest political thinkers in Europe after Aristotle. He practised medicine and was also devoted to church to the extent that he even became Archbishop of Milan. It was only subsequently that he changed his ideas and joined the Court of Emperor Louis IV of Bavaria. Gradually, he developed hatred for Papacy, which he felt had degenerated itself and was not performing functions worthy of religious organisation. This degenerated character of church turned his ideas from religion to politics and made him a strong secularist.

The idea of Marsiglio of Padua are embodied in his work entitled *''Defensor Pacis''* completed in 1324 Sabine wrote about it, "The Papal condemnation of *'Defensor Pacis'* named John of Padua, a professor at Paris and the author of several commentaries on Aristotle from the Averoist point of view, as co-author with Marsiglio. There have been numerous efforts to distinguish parts written by John, but both the recent editors are emphatic in asserting unity of authorship, both on the stylish grounds and because of the well knit structure of the book." The book was addressed to Lewis the Bavarian. It was based on the theory of city-states. It dealt with the problems connected with them. It pleaded that Papacy was the cause of disunion in Italy. It developed the theory of Canon Law. It sought to fix limitations as the book was devoted to classification of states and their underlying principles. The second part attacked church organisation and discussed mutual relations of the two. Third part of his book summarised the first two parts. The author borrowed much from Aristotle and tried to plead that religion should be regulated by society and must fall within the control of human community. He sought to root out the ideal or Papal supremacy and to explode the myth of Divine appointment of Pope. He tried to bring forth evils of church organisation. This eventually made him a secularist. He criticised church by saying that it was cumbersome and unnecessary.

INDEBTEDNESS TO ARISTOTLE

Marsiglio was so much indebted to Aristotle that it has been said that his '*Defensor Pacis*' completed the work left undone by Aristotle. He did not rule out religion. He wanted to follow it in quite a different and logical method. Following points show his indebtedness to Aristotle:

1. Idea of Self-Sufficiency. Marsiglio was influenced by Aristotle in the idea that the state is self-sufficient. The state is essential for the development of the subjects. Whereas the concept of self-sufficiency was theoretical in Aristotle, it had practical bias in Marsiglio.

2. Classification of State. Marsiglio borrowed from Aristotle the idea that the states are both normal and perverted and the standard of judging the form of Government is whether the ruler ruled the subjects for self or for collective interests.

3. Source of Law. Marsiglio borrowed from Aristotle the idea that the community and not any individual is the source of law. Only few can make laws for their own selfish interests. Universities are the mainspring and source of law.

4. Natural and Living Character of State. With Aristotle Marsiglio believed that the state is natural to man. It can be compared to a living organism. Various organs of the state should work in close co-operation with each other for its smooth working.

5. Wisdom of Multitude. Another idea borrowed from Aristotle was that the multitude has better wisdom than the few. Wisdom of multitude is dependable in all actions rather than wisdom of a single individual.

6. Origin of State. With Aristotle Marsiglio believed that the origin of the state is in the social instinct of human beings and that it is an expansion and growth. It exists for the needs of the people.

7. Supremacy of Legislature. Marsiglio was indebted to Aristotle for the idea that the legislature is superior to the executive. The executive is only the agent of legislature. A good executive is required to perform the functions assigned to it by the legislature.

8. Preference for City State. Both Aristotle and Marsiglio had definite preference for city state over the nation state. They felt that it in only in the city state that the people can expect development, perfection and happiness.

9. Rationalism in Philosophy. Like Aristotle Marsiglio was a rationalist who believed in rational methods and investigations in the studies. He gave preference to reason over faith in politics. Due to this rationalism he wanted to separate religion form politics. He developed complete disregard for degenerated church.

10. End of the State. Marsiglio borrowed from Aristotle the idea that the fullest development of the citizens is the end of the state. Only by promoting welfare of its citizens and subjects the state should justify its existence.

11. Nature of State. Marsiglio was indebted to Aristotle for his idea about state. The nature of state is a living being. It should perform necessary functions for the development of human life. No organ of state should interfere in the affairs of other parts. Such an interference usually leads to disorganisation. The city is perfect community. City states are better than empire states. Reason is essential for maintaining civil government, peace and order. The state should follow rationalism. The state is just like organs of human beings and various parts of the state had corresponding organs in the human body. States are normal as well as perverted. The basis of distinction between the two is whether the rulers ruled for common or self welfare. The state is a natural whole representing all classes in a society. It is a symbol of self-sufficiency. It aims at general welfare. It should be outside the control of all external forces. It should be independent. It should promote good life. In a healthy state the ultimate sovereignty is vested in the people. People are the masters of the state. The state should respect the people.

MEDIEVAL POLITICAL THINKER

Marsiglio of Padua has been called the most brilliant thinker of the entire middle ages. Marsiglio's theory, writes George Sabine, is one of the most remarkable creations of medieval political thought and showed for the first time the subversive consequences to which a completely naturalistic interpretation of Aristotle might logically lead. The theory reached a high level of logical consistency and it included many elements which attained their full importance only much later. Its purpose was to define and limit the pretensions of the spiritual authority to control, either directly or indirectly, the action of secular governments, and to this end he went farther than any other medieval thinker in placing the church under the power of the state.[1]

Marsiglio remained a typical medieval thinker. He represented the transitional phase of the later middle ages. The centuries from the eleventh to the fourteenth constitute the transition from the early to the later middle ages. The transition is marked by the reinstatement of the Roman law in its completeness for the first time since the break-up of the Empire of the West. In the thirteenth century Europe had its first direct contact with the ethical and political writings of Aristotle. By the eleventh century the counterclaims of Empire and Papacy had become distinct enough to bring about the first of the great contests between them, that of Pope Gregory VII and the Emperor Henry IV. The period is

1. Sabine, G.H., *op.cit.*, 3rd Ed. p. 252.

also marked by the formation of the*Corpus Juris Canonici,* the growth of a system of common law in England and its beginnings in France, and by the development of medieval estates and of representative institutions and ideas almost everywhere in Europe. It was marked by an unprecedented outburst of polemical writings which accompanied the struggles of the Popes and the Emperors. During 1052 to 1112 as many as fifty writings appeared on the imperial side and sixty - five on the papal. The ecclesiastical literature was written not solely for the monasteries or the schools but aimed to make its appeal to people. The controversial literature, though centering round the Investiture Question touched on the most fundamental problems of the origin, the nature, extent and sanction of all forms of authority both spiritual and secular, and in some cases, it anticipated "theories of the state that we are prone to think of only as modern."[2] The basic question underlying the entire controversy was whether the King could freely choose and control his own feudal vassals without clerical interference, and whether the same time the Church could exclude from its sacred offices those whom it considered unworthy.

State v/s Church

In the matter of investiture the clerical party was not disposed to deny some right of royal interposition for which there were long-standing precedents. Nor could the adherents of the King ignore the fact that the election of bishops rightfully belonged to the clergy and the people, not to the prince. The contest for supremacy was not between two rival institutions, a State and a Church, it was between two sides of human life, two elements in the constitution of main, two powers that claimed his obedience, the *regnum* and the *sacerdotium.* 'Theocracy or imperialism the contrary solutions, came back to the same single idea, unity.' In the entire middle ages Christendom constituted an all-embracing corporation (universitas) or the Universal Realm, spiritual and temporal which may be called the Universal Church *(eclesia universalis)* or the Commonwealth of the Human Race *(respublica generis humani).* It was only the growth of the nation-state that weakened the medieval insistence on unity.

The Pope claimed to represent or symbolise the unity of the Christian commonwealth: Thus Gregory VII demanded the right to establish new provisions for the needs of the time, but not any legislative authority. He did not act contrary to the medieval distinction between *leges* as mere administrative provisions and fundamental principles founded on the Scripture and the traditions of the Church on which Gregory based his whole claim to superiority over bishops and kings. St. Aquinas had taken the position that the Pope had an indirect rather than a direct authority in temporal matters. The contrary

2. McIlwain, C.H., *op. cit.,* p. 203.

theory that papal power should directly control all temporal administration was a mainly a logical development of the institutional conception of the Church rooted in Roman jurisprudence, and one strengthened and elaborated by the canonists rather than by theologians.[3]

Throughout the middle ages, the conflict between the Church and the State, or rather the Pope and the King remained a live issue. Augustine was so deeply engrossed in the theological defence of Christianity against paganism and heresy that he could scarcely define the boundaries between political and ecclesiastical power.

The View of Gelasius

At the close of the fifth century Gelasius defined the relations between the two swords or authorities. According to him, Christ divided the two offices assigning to ecclesiastical authority the spiritual and religious, welfare of men, and to political authority the care and administration of political matters. Both derived their authority from God. Both were supreme in their own respective sphere. The Church was to recognise the authority of the state in temporal matters. The state was to bow to the supremacy of the Church in spiritual matters. But Gelasius did not raise or answer the question as to who was to decide whether a particular question belonged to the spiritual sphere or the temporal. He only assumed that they would co-operate with each other. He did not visualise any possibility of strife between the two wings of the *respublica Christiana.* He also weighed his doctrine in favour of the Church by mentioning that its burden was heavier than that of the state because the priest was answerable for the souls of all-subjects, lords and kings.

View of the Papalists

From the ninth century onward the doctrine of heavier burden became, a positive claim for more dignity and authority in the church even in relation to temporal matters. As the conflict between the church and the empire grew, particularly from the tenth to the twelfth centuries the papalists claimed supreme authority for the church, insisting that all authority ecclesiastical and secular was originally given to the church. The church received its authority directly from God whereas the state received it from the church as the intermediary between God and society. The papalists, did not demand that the pope should actually rule and administer the Empire. He should rather control emperor's action from the standpoint of Christian values. He should protect the subjects when the rulers had deviated from the path of righteousness so that he could censure and admonish the emperor and excommunicate and depose him if necessary. The imperialists, however, claimed that both the state and the church had received authority directly from God. They did not go

3. *Ibid.*

beyond restating the Gelasian doctrine of equality and equilibrium between secular and spiritual authorities.

Role of Roman Church

The Roman Catholic Church represented itself as the guardian of all Christendom. The Roman Popes continued struggle with expanding German power. The papacy also collides with French and English kings. Its principal adversary was German Monarchy which threatened Italy and the Roman Churches most directly. Being feudal holders of land, the Bishops too were vassals of the king, and the loyalty of the vassal to the king was expected to be very intimate. As the clergy in the middle ages enjoyed for long a monopoly over learning, they were entrusted with important administrative positions in the courts and chancelleries of Europe.

First Great Conflict

The first great conflict occurred in the eleventh century when in 1076 Emperor Henry IV deposed Pope Gregory VII. Shortly thereafter the Pope not only deposed the emperor but also excommunicated him and relieved the subjects from their oath of allegiance. Until the end of the thirteenth century the conflict dominated the theory and practice of politics.

Pope Boniface VIII

Pope Boniface VIII (1294-1303) was the last Pope to make claims of world rule and the first to descend from the summit of glory to humiliation. In defeating the German emperors the Popes has learned to rely heavily on the French Monarchs; yet France was most destined to explode the papal claim to world hegemony. The church needed more and more money as it grew into an ambitious power. Its financial needs clashed with the needs of the new national monarchies, particularly France and England. In 1296 Boniface declared in a bull (order or proclamation) that laymen have no jurisdiction over the clergy, over both the persons and goods of the ecclesiastics without prior papal permission, and that no temporal ruler was permitted to levy taxes on church property, and nor was the clergy permitted to pay them. Both England and France refused to recognise a financial state within state. They emphasised their sovereignty. As the church property was vast they could not afford to exempt it from taxation. In England King Edward I threatened that the king's peace could not be had for nothing. In France King Philip IV firmly rejected Boniface's interference in French finances, and the Pope was powerless to enforce his bull. In 1302 Boniface issued the bull *Unam Sanctum,* which stated that neither salvation nor remission of sins outside the holy catholic and apostolic church was possible, and that the temporal authority should be subject to the spiritual. Philip IV took up the gauntlet thrown down by the Pope Boniface and planned to bring him before a General Council of the Church to be held in France and to have him deposed for heresy, murder, sexual immorality and other crimes.

Role of Marsiglio of Padua

Marsiglio of Padua came at a time when the Pope had to yield before the French Monarch. Boniface was succeeded by Pope Benedict XI who established a concord between the Holy Sea and the kingdom of France by annulling all excommunications, bulls and decrees of his predecessor against Philip and his counsellors. Benedict was succeeded by Clement V who followed the policy of his predecessor. Clement praised Philip for defending the faith against Pope Boniface. Clement did not go to Rome but set up his court in Avignon in southern France where he and his six successors, all French, resided in what has been called the 'Bobylonian captivity'. The French era of the Avignon papacy was followed by the great Schism (1378-1417) during which there were two Popes, one at Avignon and another at Rome. There was also a rivalry between Rome and Constantinople. After the Great Schism, the Protestant Reformation drastically diminished the jurisdiction of papal authority by reducing the Roman Catholic Church to one among many.

Biographical Antecedents

Marsiglio represented the principal revolutionary changes in the later middle ages, namely, the growing vehemence of the anti-clerical felling, and the decisive defeat of the papacy, the secularization of life, the rise of the bourgeoisie, the growth of the cities and the formation of national states. He was a student of philosophy, law and theology and an inhabitant of the Italian city of Padua which was known for its study spirit of liberty. Marsiglio was of middle class origin and his mode of thought, skeptical, realistic and empirical was characteristic of the city with strong secular and republican traditions. His practice of medicine imparted a more critical and scientific cast to his outlook. Like Aristotle he used commonsense and empirical verification rather than abstract speculation and authoritative dogma. He had spent his youth as a student and teacher in the University of Paris of which he was Rector for a short period in 1312. Paris at that time was a great centre of scholarship and secularism in Europe. It was here that Marsiglio deeply imbibed the spirit or secularism of rather anti-clericalism and developed friendship with John of Jandun who is also said to have collaborated with him in his *Defensor Pacis*. He developed a full-fledged doctrine from current isolated arguments and discerned in contemporary events the shape of a future world. He is considered the most original thinker because he broke the fetters of his age to a great measure and rejected outright any clerical control of thought or government.

The Defensor Pacis

According to McIlwain the *Defensor Pacis* was constructed by Marsiglio by combining two separate treatises, one an interpretation by John of Jandun on Aristotelean principles, of political institutions in general, somewhat after the manner of the *De Regimine principum* of Egidio Colonna; and the other was a discussion of the question of church and state written by Marsiglio himself. The first contained the *Dictio Prima*, or the first three books of the Pacis. The second furnished the material of *Dictio Secunda,* or Book II of the Defensor . The basic question of the Defensor, however, has been raised by Marsiglio himself by saying that 'Church and state constitute a problem which Aristotle never considered'. Moreover a recent investigation of John of Jandun, the Averroist philosopher's own undisputed works by professor. A Gewirth shows that John held views on Government which emphasised its ethical function in the usual scholastic manner, and that these views are quite remote from those expressed in the *Defensor.*[4]

Marsiglio and John of Jandun were fugitives to the court of Louis of Bavaria (1314-1346), now claiming the imperial title in the teeth of Pope John XXII who still attempted to vindicate the outdated papal ambition to supervise and confirm imperial elections. Marsiglio wrote his *Defensor Pacis* as an address to Lewis the Bavarian. As for his secularism he derived it from three sources: (i) from the republicanism of the city to which he belonged; (ii) from the anticerical feeling prevalent in his time particularly in France; and (iii) from the philosophy of Aristotle which reached him through the Averroists like John of Jandun. Previte Orton states a partial truth when he says that Marsiglio's theory of secular government was based directly upon the practice and conceptions of the Italian city states. It may be admitted that as a patriotic Italian his enmity for the papacy needed no more stimulus from Germany than Dante's. As a citizen of the Padua he needed to feel no more friendship for the empire than the interests of his city demanded. He wrote not to defend the empire but to destroy the whole system of papal imperialism that had developed in the practice of Innocent III and the theory of the canon law. His object was "to define and limit in most drastic manner the pretensions of the spiritual authority to control, either directly or indirectly, the action of secular governments, and to this end he went farther than any other medieval writer in placing the church under the power of the state. "He has rightly been called the first Erastian."[5]

Marsiglio considered his *Defensor* as a supplement to Aristotle's Politics, particularly to that part of it which discusses the causes of instability and suggests remedies for stability. There was one respect in which, because of historical development of the western society, the Aristotelean analysis of the causes of change stood incomplete— that is, it did not, as it could not, consider church or religion as a cause of change and as a problems that called for solution. Aristotle did not know that civil discord could take place as a result of the claims of the Pope to supreme power, particularly those of the recent

4. John B. Morrall, *Political Thought in Medieval Times,* p. 104.
5. Sabine, G.H., *op. cit.*, p. 293.

Popes that filled all Europe particularly Italy with strife. Marsiglio sought the remedy for this, the religious cause of civic discord. He found it in the Aristotelean principle of a self-sufficing community capable of supplying both its physical and moral needs.

ARISTOTELEANISM AND CHRISTIANITY

As a medieval thinker Marsiglio, following the Averroists, accepted the truth of Christian revelation. Unlike Thomas Aquinas, he held that the rational conclusions of reason or philosophy might be quite contrary to the truth of faith. Aquinas attempted a reconciliation between Aristoteleanism and Christianity. Marsiglio rejected this reconciliation. He also accepted the Averroist contention that theology contributes nothing to rational knowledge, and that happiness is attained in this life without the aid of God or religion, and that moral living according to the teachings of Aristotle's Ethics suffices for salvation. From a rational point of view Marsiglio, like the Averroists, takes human societies to be self-sufficing in the fullest sense. Religion has social consequences apart from its truth and may therefore be regulated by society. Whatever effects it may have in the life to come may be left to the future and the church. Spiritual interests are identical with the other worldly interests and are logically irrelevant. On the other hand, moral or religious concerns that do affect the present life all without exception fall with in the control of the human community.

IMPACT OF ARISTOTLE

1. It is difficult, however, to accept the contention of Morrall[6] that Marsiglio's Aristotle was the empirical scientist rather than the metaphysician, and that he leaves out of account the Aristotelean concept of the good life as the final cause of politics, and instead his discussion turns on the efficient cause, the actual technique whereby government may function in the smoothest possible way. The state cannot be self-sufficing for man unless it is a full-fledged moral community which can provide an alternative to the church for the kind of moral guidance man needs for the elevation of his personality.

2. Marsiglio may be described as "the first political sociologist of the Middle Ages"[7] inasmuch as the *Defensor* sketches the development of human society, closely following Aristotle's scheme of evolution from family via village to *polis*. Marsiglio traced in this development from the family to the *polis* a growing specialization and differentiation of activities, all paving the way to attainment of a common end, the acquisition of those things necessary for life and even the good life.

---

6. John B. Morrall, *op.cit.*, p. 105.

7. *Ibid.*, p. 107.

3. Marsiglio accepted the Aristotelean concept of the state as a perfect community which has attained the limit of self-sufficiency, which suffices not only for living but also for living well: Now, since we have determined, writes Marsiglio, that the state exists for the sake of life and the good life as its end, we must next discuss that life and its modes.[8] Following Aristotle he defines "state" as a kind of "living being" composed of parts which perform the functions vital to its existence. The excellence of state consists in the orderly working of each of its parts. Strife arises when one part does its work badly or interferes with another part. Again, following the Greek master he derives the state from the family and considers the city to be a perfect community.

4. As a typical medieval thinker Marsiglio admits that "good life" has both moral and spiritual connotations in the sense that it means good in this life as well as in the life to come: Knowledge of the good in this life is the proper subject of philosophy while that of the good for the life to come is the concern of theology. The first is based on reason, the second on faith or revelation. Reason shows the need for civil government as a means of peace and order for this life. Religion is useful to this life as well as to life after death.

5. Marsiglio follows Aristotle also in the enumeration of the classes or parts which make up society. These are three, viz.,

(i) farmers and artisans who supply material goods and the revenue for government;

(ii) the soldiers, officials and priests who make up the state in strict sense of the term; and

(iii) the clergy who fulfil the purpose of religion and also its other-worldly purpose which cannot be comprehended by reason.

Role of Clergy

The function of the clergy, according to Marsiglio is to know and teach those things which, according to Scripture, it is necessary to believe, to do or to avoid in order to obtain eternal salvation and escape woe. He admits that there should be a special class devoted to worship. He considers religion important. But he makes politics autonomous and does not allow religion to interfere with it. Rather he allows politics to interfere with religion in sc far as the same functions as a social phenomenon and produces social results. But in so far as religion is other-worldly, it should be beyond the touch of the state. Marsiglio thus has "walled off Christianity as in its essence, supernatural and beyond rational discussion."[9] Whatever reverence faith may deserve as

---

8. Ewart Levis, *Medieval Political Ideas,* Vol. I, p. 185.

9. Sabine, G.H., *op. cit.,* p. 255.

a means of eternal salvation, it has become simply irrelevant from a secular point of view. Being irrational or superrational it cannot be brought into a consideration of rational means and ends which means that secular questions have to be decided on their own rational merits without reference to faith.

In all secular relations, the clergy, according to Marsiglio, is merely one class in society along with other classes. From a rational point of view the Christian clergy are like any other priesthood since the truth of what it teaches it beyond reason and applies to a life beyond life. It follows that in all temporal concerns the control of the clergy by the state is in principle exactly like the control of agriculture or trade. In other words, religion is a social phenomenon in as much as it uses material agencies and produces social consequences. In these respects it is subject to social regulation at need like other human interests. As regards its truth that is something about which reasonable men cannot dispute or discuss: "As he says, ...And whatever that second kind of living, namely the eternal, may be, a university of philosophers could not prove by logic, nor was it a self-evident matter, and therefore, they were not concerned to teach in regard to those things that exist for its sake."[10] Such a separation of reason and faith produces religious scepticism and even anti-religious secularism. It is true that it makes spiritual interests too sacred for reason to touch but practically there is little difference between too sacred and too trivial. The church becomes part of the secular state in every respect in which it affects temporal matters.

FORMS OF STATES

Marsiglio accepts the Aristotelean classification of constitutions. He considers monarchy, aristocracy and constitutional system as the good types and tyranny, oligarchy and mobocracy as bad types. He also accepts the criterion of the distinction applied by Aristotle, namely whether the government governs for the good of the people or for its own good. But he improves upon Aristotle by accepting the further criterion that in the good forms of government the ruler governs for the general good *in accordance with the will of the people.* Likewise, the bad or the perverted constitutions are those that are for the benefit of the rulers *without* the *consent of the governed.* Ebenstein calls it a fundamental revision and transformation introduced in Aristotle by Marsiglio.[11]

Marsiglio departs from Aristotle even more drastically when he abandons the criterion of the object of government (the common good) and replaces it with *that of the method of government* according to which political rule is "over either voluntary or involuntary subjects." Modern liberal democratic theory emphasises that democracy in government is primarily a question of

10. Lwart Levis, *op. cit.*, Vol. I, p. 135.

11. Wm. Ebenstein, *op. cit.*, p. 262.

method the consequences of which can be good or bad. Marsiglio anticipated the modern assumption that the proper method of government, that is consent, is more likely to produce good ends than are undemocratic methods though employed for the ends of society as a whole. "The consciousness of dynamic relations between means and ends" says Ebenstein, "is one of the main contributions of modern philosophy, and Marsiglio points in this direction by stressing the problem of government is one of means as much as of ends."[12]

THEORY OF LAW

Marsiglio achieved his complete break form Aristotle in his conception of law as a manifestation of political authority. He displayed vigorous independence and originality of outlook. Right from the days of Aristotle down to Thomas Aquinas, the writers had taken for granted that law was anexpression of reason, and therefore, something objective, impersonal and universal. Will or volition was not considered as of any significance in making the law. Aquinas defined law as the *ordinance of reason* for the common good. He divided law into four categories, namely, eternal, divine, natural and human. Which were four forms of reason. But Marsiglio made only two divisions, divine law and human law. He replaced reason by will. Whereas for Aquinas law was an expression of a rational principle, for Marsiglio, it was a command of the superior. *Divine law*, accordingly, was a command of God directly, without human deliberation, about voluntary acts of human beings to be done or avoided in this world but for the sake of attaining the best end, or some condition desirable for man, in the world to come. He defines *Human law* as "a command of the whole body of citizens, or of its *prevailing part*," arising directly from the deliberation of those empowered to make law about voluntary acts of human beings to be done or avoided in this world, for the sake of attaining the best end, or some condition desirable for man this world. By human law he means "a command the transgression of which is enforced in this world by a penalty or punishment imposed on the transgressor."

The two kinds of law are distinguished by the kinds of punishment attached to each for its violation. Divine law, is sanctioned by rewards or punishments to be meted out by God in a future life. There is no earthly penalty for its violation but only a penalty in the life to come. Human law therefore is not derived from divine law but is contrasted with it. Any rule that involves an earthly penalty belongs to human law and has its authority from human enactment. The spiritual teachings of priests do not properly constitute a power or authority as these lack coercive force in this life. But the case is different when a human legislature delegates such a power to priests.

---

12. *Ibid.*

Marsiglio's theory of law is important also because of the emphasis it placed upon the element of command as its essential principle, and rendered important or rather decisive the will of the legislator and his power to impose the will. It admitted that law means a rule of reason or of intrinsic justice but it clearly regards law, at least in its juristic sense, as characterised by its emanating from a constituted authority and carrying a penalty for its violation. Whereas Aquinas presented divine and human law as well as eternal and natural law as all of a piece, the emphasis of Marsiglio was on the sharp distinction between the two forms of law.

To Marsiglio, law is a coercive command of the legislator enforceable in the courts. While he expects human law to be ordinarily consistent with divine or natural law, he concedes the possibility of false conceptions of the just and beneficial becoming laws when there is given a command to observe them. Because of his refusal to identify human law with divine authority or reason, Marsiglio was driven to find the source of validating law in the human society itself. Thus he held that 'the source of law was the people or the prevailing part of the same'.

The legislator, or first and proper efficient cause of law, is the people or whole body of citizens, or a *prevailing part of it*, commanding and deciding *by its own choice or will* in a general assembly and in set terms that something among the civil acts of human beings be done or omitted on pain of penalty or temporal punishment.

Human law, thus, arises by the corporate action of a people setting up rules to govern the acts of its members, and from it follows that conversely a state is a body of men who owe obedience to a given body of laws. As Sabine observes, the result is the same whether the law is used to define the state or the state to define law, since either implies a corporate body competent to control the behaviour of its members. The source of legal authority is always the people or its prevailing part even though in a particular case it may delegate its authority to a commission to play that part, or even to an emperor in case of an empire. While Marsiglio was thinking of a people in a city state, the definition applies to any state whatsoever.

THE LEGISLATOR

Marsiglio has used the term "legislator" in the traditional Roman sense and not in the modern positive or democratic sense, though in a city state he might have done even that. He probably used the concept in the sense of a political sovereign when he applies it to the 'people' whom he views as the constituent power of the state which alone has the authority to make the constitution. He also admitted that the people may entrust the task to some person or body of persons who can be legislator only in a relative sense and for a particular time and in accordance with the authority of the primary legislator. By legislator he meant only that the whole people makes its law in the sense that all authority is to be conceived as the act of the people and is to be exercised in their name. He expressly provided for the case in which a commission acts with derivative authority. The conception was prevalent in ancient Greece where the Athenian jury was addressed simply as 'Athenians'. And also in Rome where the members of the Senate were addressed as 'Romans'. It was also not much different from the medieval fiction by which the whole realm was supposed to be consulted in a parliament. In fact, Marsiglio considered a people's legislation as including custom as well which he calls part of law.[13]

REORGANISATION OF CHURCH

Marsiglio condemned church which had degenerated itself. Church is part of social community, like physicians the clergy should advise about the performance of religious rites. The church fathers should not own any property. As donation given by the community church property is subject to taxation. State represents the will of community. Every church officer can be deposed of by the community. Church should be distinguish organisation being spiritual. There should be a church council which should manage all church affairs. It should also interpret religious books. Collectively, the Council is superior to Pope. Pope should be elected and made responsible to this Council. The Council should have the power to depose a pope for his misbehaviour. The Pope has only human and no divine rights. The clergy has no coercive authority. According to Sabine, "The clergy, being themselves merely a class set apart to perform religious service, are subject to regulation like any other class and like laymen are amenable to the civil courts for violation of human law." There is no spiritual offence. Every offence is *ipso facto* offence against human law. Excommunication belongs wholly to the civil power. The church is primarily responsible for creating disunity among the nations. The only remedy to church evils was that it should be deprived of all coercive powers and authority. To quote Maxey, "By a series of usurptions, it is argued, the Pope has gained a fictitious power which he uses with disastrous consequences to the peace of nations. To correct this, all clergy, including even the Pontiff himself, should be deprived of all corrective authority and all power to impose the observance of divine law."

RELATIONSHIP OF CHURCH AND STATE

Marsiglio of Padua was one of the strongest of the secularists. He did not directly write in support of the empire, yet criticised church organsation. The people should enjoy civil happiness. There is definite contradiction between spiritual and secular interests as the two are incompatible. A true clergy

13. *Ibid.*, p. 258.

should have no love for wealth and property. They should feel pleasure in poverty. Church property is subject to taxation. The church should not claim any share in secular authority. The church should only perform religious rites and promote love for Faith. They should teach truth. Like any other citizen, they should obey secular law. They should help people in getting eternal salvation and escaping from woes and miseries. They should also help people in knowing religion. According to Dunning, "Not even the purely ecclesiastical penalties of interdiction and ex-communication can be employed save by the authority of the legislator for their application by irresponsible persons with the peace and quite of the faithful, which it is the function of the secular ruler to defend." The church should preserve its past tradition of helping the state by way of controlling the people in the fear of going to hell. The church is therefore to assist the state in checking crimes. The clergy has no right to forgive the sins of any person. The church should be under the state for the sake of unity and peace. There should be no discord between the two authorities which claim equality among themselves. Pope has no special powers. Papal sovereignty was not supported either historically or by any other way. The Pope does not enjoy any pre-eminent powers over the bishops. Ranks in church organisation have no Divine sanction but are of human origin and even these are mostly unnecessary. In temporal matters church should be part of the state. It should not exercise any coercive powers. These should be left to the care of the state only. In temporal affairs, like every other citizen, clergy and the pope should be under the coercive authority of the state. This temporal authority is superior to religious authority.

TYPES OF LAW

According to Marsiglio the laws are of two types, namely 'Divine Law' and 'Human Law'. Law should be to the advantage of community as a whole. He said, "It is an imperative expression of the common need, formulated by reason, promulgated by recognised authority sanctioned by force." According to him, Divine Law is animated from the authority of God. Human Law is the command of community as a whole. It is the outcome of specific human deliberation whose violation is an offence punishable by temporal authority. Thus Divine Law is concerned with future life. Human law is concerned with the present life. In Human Law there is a specific authority to promulgate and enforce law. In Defensor Minor Marsiglio defines the two kinds of law by saying: "Divine Law is a command of God directly without human deliberation, about voluntary acts of human beings to be done or avoided in this world but for the sake of attaining the best end, or some condition desirable for men, in the world to come." Again, "Human Law is a command of whole body of citizens, of its prevailing part, arising directly from the deliberation of those empowered to make law, about voluntary acts of human beings to be done or avoided in this world, for the sake of attaining the best end, some condition desirable for man, in this world. I mean a command the transgression of which is enforced in this world by a penalty or punishment imposed on the transgressor."

AUTHORITY OF LAW

One of the essential ingredients of law is that it should be promulgated by the competent authority. Breach of law should be a punishable offence. Those held responsible for execution of law should have punitive powers. Marsiglio said, "It is an imperative expression of common need, formulated by reason, promulgated by recognised author, sanctioned by force."

SOURCE OF LAW

The source of law according to Marsiglio is the legislator. He expresses his will either directly or through Assembly of citizens. The people are sovereign in a state. The law and authority should be enacted and enforced in the name of the people. A legislature is supreme in the state. It should elect executive and judiciary. The executive is primarily responsible for good government of the people. In the event of failure it can also be removed by the legislature. For good and smooth running of the government it is essential that all organs must work smoothly and in close cooperation with each other. As Marsiglio put it, "The legislature, the first and proper efficient cause of law, is the people of whole body of citizens or a prevailing part of it, commanding and deciding by its own choice or a general assembly and in set terms that something among the civil acts of human being be done or omitted on pain of a penalty or temporal punishment."

SOVEREIGNTY OF THE PEOPLE

According to Marsiglio, the people should be sovereign in a state. This is in the collective interest of the community as a whole, combined wisdom is always better than individual wisdom. The people could collectively find defects in the laws. The people were the best judge to enact a law. Collective virtue could better be promoted by the community as a whole. Laws enacted by the community have no chance of being enacted in the interest of a single class. These will also be readily obeyed. Elected monarchy is the best form of government. Monarch should be responsible to the community as a whole. He should only perform administrative functions. He should not go beyond them. The people have a right to remove a king from authority who abuses his powers or exceeds his legitimate rights. In order to make the rule of the people effective it is essential that the people should be educated. The state should arrange for the education of the people. It should see that there is not much of disparity in wealth between various classes in a society. The state should regulate economic life of the people. A monarch should be elected by the people. Monarchy brings unity in executive because authority is vested in the hands of one person. In the words of Maxey, "The head of the Government should be elected or appointed by the people, and should be circumscribed in such a way that he cannot put himself above law," To quote McIlwain, "It is clear from all this that the king is servant as well as the creature of the people. But he is a servant entrusted with enormous powers, and while the great limitations often affect the tenure of his power or a wrongful use of it, they put scarcely any limits to its legitimate extent."

CONTRIBUTION OF MARSIGLIO

Marsiglio has been considered as one of the most important secularists of his age. His theory was one of the most remarkable creations of medieval political thought. Unlike many other political thinkers of middle ages he had original thoughts. His important contribution to political thought is the following:

1. **Forerunner of Renaissance.** He brought to the front the idea that the church has degenerated itself. It is not delivering spiritual goods. Thus he was the forerunner of renaissance movement.

2. **Absolute Authority.** Marsiglio gave Austin the idea about absolute sovereignty. The sovereignty has coercive authority without which sovereign could not exercise his powers.

3. **Separation of Ethics and Politics.** Marsiglio separated ethics from politics. He gave definite and superior place to state. He paved the way for the philosophy of Machieavelli.

4. **Democracy.** Marsiglio gave a definite and superior place to the people. He helped the cause of democracy.

5. **State.** Marsiglio did not put state at par with the church. He gave a superior position to the state. This brought modernism in his ideas.

6. **Separation of Powers.** Marsiglio distinguished functions of all the three organs of government. He was the forerunner of the theory of separation of powers as expounded by Montesquieu.

7. **Limited Monarchy.** Marsiglio was the first medieval thinker who gave the idea of limited or constitutional monarchy. In the words of McIlwain, "He seems to be the first writer who has clearly in mind a perfectly normal feature of monarchy, a preference for something like a modern limited monarchy with another government organ independent of prince clothed with authority to judge him."

SUPREMACY OF STATE OVER CHURCH

Purpose of Marsiglio

Marsiglio was a supporter of secularism. He thought that many of our present day problems could be solved if the church did not interfere in the affairs of the state. He said that the Pope is the chief disturber of peace in Europe. He sought to destroy the whole system of Papal imperialism. To quote Sabine, "His object was to defend and limit in the most drastic manner the pretensions of spiritual authority to control either directly or indirectly, the actions of secular Governments." Doyle has said, "The purpose of the author was to destroy the whole system of papal absolutism by proving that the Divine appointment of the Papacy on which the entire authority of its claim rested was myth and that the church was an unnecessary encumbrance to the state." As McIlwain has quoted, "The chief disturber of the peace of Christendom is the Plentitude Potestatis of the Bishop of Rome called Pope." In his book *Defensor Pacis* Marsiglio said that in addition to old causes which were disturbing the peace of the state, are "desire and undertaking whereby the Roman Bishop and his clerical coterie in particular are aiming to seize secular rulerships and to possess excessive temporal wealth." This is another cause for disturbing peace of the state. Main arguments advanced by Marsiglio for supremacy of the state are as under:

1. **Importance of Present Life.** The church very strongly argued that the people should be more careful for the next life and for making next life happier, church alone could help. The church fathers argued that the church was in this way superior to state. Worldly pleasures were also considered inferior to spiritual salvations. The present life should be considered only means to an end, the end being the next life. The present life was in no way an end itself. Marsiglio strongly refuted this theory. The present life is as important as the next life. In fact, it is much more important. It is wrong to say that it is only means to an end. On the other hand, it is an end itself.

2. **Church Itself Preferred Temporal Life.** In those days the clergy were amassing wealth. The church had a lot of property under its possession and control. This made the church an strong and powerful enemy of the state. According to Marsiglio, a true clergy should not possess wealth or property. The clergy and the Pope should lead a life of poverty. The very fact that the Pope was living a luxurious life was in itself an indication that the church itself preferred temporal rather than spiritual life.

3. **Church Fathers Should be Spiritual.** Marsiglio maintained that if the church fathers wanted to be spiritual, it is most essential that they should not be secular. Wealth, property and power should have no meaning with them. Church property is a kind of donation made by the community to the priest for worship.

4. **Church, A Department of the State.** Another argument advanced by Marsiglio was that the clergy is one of the class, along with other classes in the society. As such they have no right to seek exemption from taxation. They should obey secular laws, in the same manner, as these are obeyed by others. Church is a department of the state.

5. No Right to Interfere in Secular Matters. The function of the church is to promote faith, so that the people can obtain salvation. As such it has no right whatsoever to interfere in secular affairs.

6. State as Penal Authority. Marsiglio said that the nature of Divine Law is such that it needed no coercive authority. There was no penalty for violation of Divine law. No authority on earth has any justification to inflict any penalty for breach of Divine Law. The power of ex-communication is vested wholly in the civil power. According to Dunning, "Not even the ecclesiastical penalties of indirect and ex-communication can be employed save by the authority of the legislator; for their application by irresponsible persons interferes with the peace and quiet of the faithful, which it is the function of the secular ruler to defend."

7. Sovereignty of Executive-Pope is Not Sovereign. Even within the church the Pope is not sovereign. Sovereignty resides in the General Council and not in the Pope. The people have exclusive power to appoint executive of the priests. As the Christians spread among all the sections of the society, therefore they have a right to appoint executive for the priests.

8. Pope is Not Superior. It has been argued that Pope is superior to all Bishops, clergy and laymen and supreme in secular and religious affairs. Pope is like a Bishop and all the Bishops are equal. Pope of Rome is in no say superior over all other bishops.

Different views have been expressed about Marsiglio's view concerning secular supremacy. Alan Gewrith said, "There is then an important ambiguity in Marsiglio's doctrine whereby priesthood is a part of the state dedicated to the sufficient life in both worlds participating in the coercive authority required for the state's functioning, and at the same time is prohibited from such participation and inculcates values contrary to this worldly sufficient life." Sabine said, "Few theorists in any age, and none in the middle ages, care to go as far as Marsiglio in whittling down the spiritual freedom which formed the permanently important claim fostered by Christianity." Dunning said, "It goes without saying that *Defensor Pacis* embodies the more radical antagonism to the Pastime Dogma in all its bearings."

QUESTIONS FOR EXERCISE

1. "Marsiglio wrote to defend the empire but to destroy whole system of Papal-imperialism" Sabine. Discuss.
2. Explain the debt of Marsiglio of Padua to Aristotle and bring out the element of modernity in his ideas.
3. What part Marsiglio of Padua play in building up the medieval secularism.

4. It in not the priest that forgives sin, God alone judges in these matters. Explain.
5. "The legislator or the first the proper efficient cause of law is the people of the whole body of the citizens or prevailing part of it." (Marsiglio of Padua). Comment.
6. "Essentially Marsiglio's political philosophy was a recurrence of the theory of the City State, competent to regulate every branch of its civilisation." Explain.
7. "Human law is a command of the whole body of the citizens, or its prevailing part." Comment.
8. "Marsiglio of Padua is the most original thinker of middle ages." Discuss.
9. "In some respects Marsiglio is prophet of the Reformation and even of Rousseau; but on the whole he expounds his own age." (Barker). Examine this statement.
10. 'Marsiglio's theory is one of the most remarkable creation of medieval political thought." (Sabine). Comment.

17

End of Medieval Period : Conciliar Movement

With the publication of *Defensor Pacis* the controversy between the church and the Empire subsided and after it Churchmen and political philosophers began to discuss the proper form of the Church government as the cause of the independence of secular powers settled in the favour of secular rulers.

The attempt to settle the form of Church government was made at the councils of Constance (1414-1418) and Basle (1431-1449). It is known as the conciliar movement in history. It is itself insignificant in the history of political thought but the offshoots and repercussions that came out of it are important. From 11th upto 14th century medieval thinkers debated about the controversy between the Empire and the church but in first half of 15th century emerged conciliar movement which represents the last important phase of modern period.

Environment

In general, during this period, the church organization was corrupt from top to bottom. It was bitterly attacked by John of Paris, Marsiglio of Padua, William Occam, Wycliff John Huss etc. during the 14th century. Despotic and absolute papal rule meant much more than the rigid control of the Pope. The Pope heard appeals relating to religious matters from the different parts of the continent. Large sums of money used to go to the papal authority. Thus the problem of papacy was the concern of the Christian people of the whole Europe. The creation of two rival popes using all theological powers and political chicanery made papal authority notorious and the popes lost prestige and splendour in the eyes of the public. Great schism of (1378-1417) made matters worst.

The Babylonish captivity under which the Popes lived at Avignon from 1309-1376 under the influence of the French monarchy made matters worse because all Christians believed Rome as the headquarters of the Pope. In 1377

Pope Gregory XI returned to Rome and Babylonish captivity came to end. However, due to the creation of the Popes, at the Avignon and the other at Rome, each claiming themselves as rightful Pope made great schism. Italy, Germany and England favoured the Pope at Rome while France, Scotland, Castile and Naples followed the Pope of Augnon. The schism showed the degeneration of the Pope. Hence a general demand of purification of the Church through the general council instead of the old despotic Papacy came to forefront. This movement is known as conciliar movement.

Two Stages

There were two stages in the growth of this movement :

1. In the first stage John of Paris, Marsiglio of Padua and William of Occam in 14th century put forth the demand of the general council of the church as the final authority and as the sole repository of power.

2. In the second stage the dream materialized and three councils were held to deal with the problem. Nicholas of Cusa, Gerson, Preire P. Ally were the prominent leaders who took part in the movement in its second phase. The protests of Marsiglio of Padua, John of Paris and Occam against the absolute authority of the Pope coupled with the scandalism of schism, gave birth to the Conciliar movement. It turned it into a popular demand and tried to bring change.

Purpose of the Movement

According to McIlwain, "The essential point in contention of the reformers was the assertion of the competence of universal council of the church to adjudicate a disputed claim to papal authority with so important corollary that the jurisdiction of this council is higher than that of the Pope." The proper system of the accounts of the church was to be maintained in order to ensure legitimate expenditure of money for the Church purpose and to curtail the luxury and extravagance of the papal court. The schism was to be healed by the appointment of one Pope instead of two rival claimants to prevent discord and to achieve harmony. Wycliff of England and Huss of Bohemia desired restraints on absolutism of Pope through popular discussion. The reform of the head of the church, moral reform of the clergymen and suppression of heresay were the objects of conciliar movement.

Attempts to End Defects

In order to reform the church and to remove above-mentioned defects, many meetings of the general church council took place. The meetings were held as the council of Pisa 1409, the council of Padua 1423 and the council of Constance (1414-1448). Of these the council of Constance and Basle was very important. The council of Constance and Gerson demanded another council. It won the support of calling the meeting of the council at Constance, which was the most representative council. But since no resoluteness was shown in reforming the church in head and members, so no success was achieved. The views of Huss and Wycliff were condemned as heretic. Huss was burnt alive though he had been invited under the guarantee of protection. John Gerson who was the chancellor of Paris University was the leading theorist of the council. Through his efforts the schism was healed. It was agreed that the plenitude of power belonged not to the Pope but to the General Council as representative of all Christians. Discussions ended in the famous decree of 1415, which has been described by Dr. Figgi's as "probably the most revolutionary official document in the history of the world. According to Jesus Christ "Where two or three are gathered together in my name, then I am in the midst of them." These words were taken to imply the superiority of Council over the Pope. The Pope as the executive head of the church was only an authorised agent of the community. Christ thus opposed infallibility of Pope.

According to Sabine "The church, being a complete and self-sufficing society, must possess all the powers needed to ensure its continuance, its orderly government and the removal of the abuses as they occur. Consequently, the spiritual powers with which it is endowed is vested in the church itself in the whole body of the faithful as a cooperate body, and clergy including the Pope are merely the ministers or agents by which society acts."

In 1417, another decree was passed by the general council by which after every ten years meeting of church council was proposed and its independence was guaranteed from the control of the Pope. These decrees were ratified in 1439. After the healing of schism and with the appointment of one Pope, the zeal of reforms took wings. But nothing material was achieved for the reformation of the church, the Pope continued his work as in the past and abuses remained unchecked as before.

As the council of Basil failed to achieve the constitutional rule in the church or anything substantial, so the movement failed. According to Sabine "A council which itself was a prey to every form of national jealousy was ill qualified to attack the stupendous mass of vested interests that made up ecclesiastical patronage."

Arguments for General Council

The sovereign power lies in the general council and not in Pope. Mixed form of Government consisting of the Pope cardinals and prelates is better than the supremacy of the Pope. Pope is simply an administrator and not maker of law so not above the law. The Church as a whole makes law and the Pope is responsible to the General Council of the Church which is the true representative of the Christians. The community has inherent power to make their own laws, set up its own ruler. The difference between lawful government and tyranny is that the former rests on the will of the people inherent in the community and does not depena on the whims of the rulers. Papal decrees should depend on the popular acceptance. Notions of natural rights should be in conformity with the basic functions of the Pope.

The council represents the people and only its consent gives the binding force. The church is a perfect society so it can reform itself and can even depose the Pope. Nicholas of Cusa stated, "Since by nature all men are free, any authority by which subjects are perfected from evil and their freedom is restricted to doing good through fear of penalties comes from harmony and from the consent of the subjects, whether the authority resides in written law or the living law, which is in the ruler. Kings are therefore to be regulated by the general part of the society."

This paragraph of Nicholas of Cusa shows verbal similarity with the later revolutionary thoughts. The main point of the Conciliar theory is that the whole body of the church is the source of law and the Popes with its hierarchy are merely its administrators. According to Nicholas, Government is a co-operative enterprise, concordantia or harmony and not delegation of power from supreme head.

Failure of Conciliar Movement

The Conciliar movement was a failure, first, because it lacked competent leaders and intellectuals, who could have driven home its ideals to contemporaries, secondly, because, it sought to effect in the Church a constitutionalism that was fast getting out of date in secular society from where it arose, and thirdly, because centralization of power which it opposed was the tendency of the time.[1] Even so, it represented the emergence of the conception of the national kingdom as a political power not bound by the traditions of the Holy Roman Empire. It forced the Pope to sign *concordat* with each state in which he allowed the king to remedy some clerical abuses and guarantee some regalian rights within his dominion. These concordats were a tacit 'acknowledgement of the sovereignty of national states'. They marked the virtual end of the medieval theory that Christendom in its secular aspect is one great state as in its spiritual it is a single Church. Inference was soon to be drawn that the Church was in every nation, instead of embracing all nations. It meant that its functions were primarily spiritual and that its participation in secular matters was never justifiable except for a spiritual end. It stood for the important ideal that 'lawful authority is a moral force while despotism is not, and that society itself embodies a force of moral criticism to which even legally constituted power is rightly subject.[2] The movement worked in an atmosphere which was medieval, it represented a spirit that was modern, and in fact, it

1. Sabine, G.H., *op. cit.* p. 282.
2. *Ibid.*, p. 283.

paved the way for the dawn of modernity in political theory. It supported the idea that the powers of state were not the private rights of a group of individuals but the public rights of a constitutionally established authority or assembly. The king, according to this idea wielded authority as bearer of a permanent dignity and not in his individual capacity. He was not above the state but part of it.

Causes of Failure

1. The conciliar movement represented the spirit of Constitution against the absolute power of the Pope. But the movement failed because there were mutual suspicion, jealousies, little harmony in Europe and little zeal for constitutionalism and reform.

Thus it failed to draw up federal constitution for the whole Europe. Consequently, autocratic forms of government came into existence both in ecclesiastical and secular fields.

2. The growing national sentiment gave a death blow to the ideas of conciliar movement. With the growth of national states, all persons became interested in their own national interests and problems and showed little zeal for the reformation of the Church.

3. It lacked popular support of the masses. It was too academic and remained confined to universities.

4. There was no strong leader whose influence may be helpful in setting aside the differences for the general cause. Leaders like Luther and Calvin could have overcome national jealousies but there were no such leaders.

5. According to Cook the caution and moderate approach was also responsible for its failure. It led them to conservatism.

6. The old tradition of papal authority proved too strong as soon as conservatism took its hold upon the general council.

7. The Pope was able to play one faction against the other and thereby not only saved his position but made it strong.

8. The organization and the bureaucracy was more clever than its leaders who were merely academicians.

9. The leaders of the movement failed to show originality and borrowed ideas from Marsiglio and Occam failed to get popular application.

10. Finally national Kings disfavoured the centralization and dreaded the rival of the power of the Pope which always kept them in check, so they tried for its failure by hook or crook.

11. Moreover time was not yet ripe for constitutionalism as autocratic governments existed everywhere in Europe.

Significance of the Conciliar Movement

Inspite of the fact that the movement failed in its objective of the establishment of the supremacy of the church council, it accomplished following things :

1. It stated that the church was superior to the Pope and that general council possesses the final authority.

2. It demanded a representative government for the Church.

3. It was careful not to exercise authority against the safety of the church.

4. Failure was a blessing in disguise as protestanism emerged through Luther and Calvin etc. which reformed Christianity.

5. The Church became better organized and efficient.

6. The Papacy was re-organized and re-established on the national basis.

7. It resulted in the establishment of national church which recognised the rights of layman.

8. It was democratic, federal and national in tendencies and these tendencies later on affected church as well as the states.

9. It sponsored the idea that power was the trust and it must not be misused. The current of the governed is the essence of the government and the representatives should be consulted in important matters.

10. It put emphasis on the constitution in preference to the absolute or despotic rule.

11. It recognized the growing spirit of nationality.

12. The germs of the revolution of 1688 and 1789 are traceable to it.

13. It gave notions of liberty, equality and fraternity.

14. It stated that the ultimate power belongs to masses.

15. It made democratic notions popular even in the church which was believed to be of divine origin.

16. It propounded the idea of national rights.

JOHN GERSON

John Gerson was the Chancellor of the Paris University. Influenced by the writings of Marsiglio of Padua, he developed the idea of communal sovereignty. He pleaded for the mixed form of government, having monarchic, aristocratic and democratic elements both for the church and the state. He was opposed both to absolutism of the Pope as well as extreme democracy of whole body of believers. He was in favour of giving supreme authority to general council in the church. According to him the pope was merely administrative head of the Church whole authority may be defied in the interest of the Church. He even favoured the authority of King to depose ecclesiastical head if he acts contrary to natural or divine laws. According to Gettell, Gerson aimed to preserve the right of Pope and King, within definite limits and at the some time secure the liberties of the people. Gerson held that a church body was superior to the Pope. It could depose him, if he abused his office. He framed his principle so skilfully that while giving supremacy to the general council to the church, he did little violence to the traditional theory of Pope. Gerson frequently suggested that the assertion of conciliar supremacy is mainly to be justified by the scandal of the schism and the mortal peril of the Church. He was one of the greatest leaders of conciliar movement.

NICHOLAS OF CUSA

Nicholas of Cusa was a cardinal born in 1400 and died on 1446. He took more democratic view than Gerson. His book *The De Concordantia Catholica* gives the best exposition of the conciliar movement. It has been described by Dr. G.N. Figgis as almost the last book which treats Christiandom as a single organic system in which a complete theory of politics in whole and parts is set forth. It gives philosophic expression to the constitutionalism. It embodied the main principles which underline theory of constitutional government and educated them with a university that increased their significance. It is original and profound and deals with the deepest movements of the age.

Thought

Nicholas believed that peace and unity in the church is the crying need of the day. He reconciled divine with human authority and united secular to the spiritual. He stated that power ultimately comes from God but immediately from people. As quoted by Sabine he said, "Since by nature all men are free, any authority by which subjects are prevented from evil and their freedom is restrained doing good through fear of penalties, come solely from harmony and from the consent of subjects ... power could be set up only by the choice and consent of other just as law also is set up by consent." Briefly it means that by nature all men are free and equal so authority and superior power emerges from the consent of the governed. The law is found in the consent of the people neither the Pope nor the ruler derived power from God. Sovereignty resides neither in Pope nor in the General Council but in the people of whole Christiandom. There should be representative Government in every form of society, secular or spiritual. Thus Nicholas was a great champion of democracy, liberty, equality and sovereignty of the people. In his idea there were the germs of cry of liberty, equality, fraternity and sovereignty of the people for future revolution.

CHARACTERISTICS OF MEDIEVAL THOUGHT

The middle ages did not produce giants like Plato or Aristotle. There was little originality in political thought. As Prof. Hearnshaw remarks, Medieval thinkers seem like the students writing essays on political theory from text books, mainly three in number the Bible, the Roman Law and the Politics of Aristotle. Their main themes were universalism, supremacy of church, the monarchical government in the church and state. But their ideas of popular sovereignty, representative government and of kingship and natural law corporations need a little clarification.

1. Medieval Idea of Kingship. The king was representative of God on earth. The King was under the God and the law. Kings were believed to be made for the people and not people for the kings. It was his bounden duty to further and maintain peace and justice. The king inherited his throne elected by the people and ruled by the grace of God.

2. The Law. According to Teutons the law was the common possession by which the group was held together. While the modern democrat is prepared to respect law in so far as he can regard himself as its author, medieval obedience was founded on the opposite sentiment that laws were respectable so far as they were not made by man. As such, divine law was respected more than human or man made law.

3. Idea of Representation. In modern age representatives are elected but in medieval age, office holders were considered as trustee of the people and were charged with the mission of their people. Representative ideas reached to perfection during conciliar movement through the ideas of Gerson and Nicholas of Cusa which gave us notions of popular sovereignty, liberty, equality and justice etc. These later on brought revolutions of 1688 of England and 1789 of France and in 1776 in U.S.A.

4. Natural Law. Conception of Natural law began with the Stoics. Cicero stated that the law of nature springs from God. It is the basis of all morality. It ought to prescribe the provisions of positive law. Romans believed that the law common to all nations is the law of nature. This concept became highly influential in the growth of Roman legal system and jurisprudence. It was supposed as the ultimate source of law. It as a touch stone limited the validity of positive laws themselves. This gave rise to the theory of Natural law.

5. Corporations. During conciliar movement, the concepts of Roman law about universe were pressed into service to define the character and significance of corporate entities like the church, the church council, the state, the universities, free cities and communes. These are partial wholes having an aim and an end of their own and therefore a will and personality of their own. The church was conceived of as a corporation consisting of all believers and endowed with ultimate and residuary powers. The general council of the church was conceived as the corporate representative of the church of which the Pope was presiding officer. Later on these rights were conceded to the representative assemblies or groups by recognising them as a great corporate and juristic person which passed the way for popular sovereignty and modern ideas of pluralism.

6. Popular Sovereignty. Leaders of conciliar movement supported popular sovereignty, liberty, equality and fraternity and representative guides both in church and the state. These ideas developed into modern representative democracies which are main gifts of modern age. Thus conciliar movement supported democratic ideals against the supremacy of Pope and rulers. It favoured ideas of popular sovereignty. So it proved useful for further progress and brought medieval controversy and ideas to an End. Democratic ideas and the attempt of reconcilement between spiritualism, secularism and democratic ideals possess philosophical value. These can help in solving conflict between secularism and newly emerging religious ideals and democratic ideas with necessary changes and modification to suit modern environment and set up.

ORGANIC STATE AND LIMITED GOVERNMENT

The growth of the concept of the organic state led to the idea of kingship as an office rather than a personal attribute. Baldus formulated the concept of state personality but he never attributed will or substantive personality to the state as for example Maitland or Rousseau subsequently did. He rather held that the jurisdiction delegated by the prince ceased at the death of the delegator. It was John of Salisbury who in his *Policraticus* propounded the first organic theory of the medieval times. A state, he said, is a certain body endowed with life by God. And, if state is a whole, then all its parts have equal value and role. The king belongs to this whole as much as do the people, and both are under the laws that sustain the state.

Emphasis on organic state in medieval theory was derived partly from Aristotle as in Marsiglio, and partly from the Christian conception of the world as an organic mystical body with Christ as its head, priesthood as its soul and the faithful members as its body. The papal and political orders did not represent any negation of this organic conception, for they were but two sides of the same great organism and functioned in a harmonious concord.[3]

The concept of organic body politic led to the emergence of many important ideas in political theory. It gave rise to the notion of membership to answer to the positions filled by individual men in various institutions. It gave rise to the idea of differences in rank, profession and estate so that individuals stood as socially grouped and differentiated.

3. Gierke, *op. cit.* p. 24.

FEUDALISM

Feudalism was fundamentally a personal, private, and non-political system. In this system, it was not the claim of the state but of a Lord, not the welfare of a whole but the right of a master which inspired and maintained the obligations of men to one another. The king himself ruled or reigned as of personal right with the result that the people were "his people" and the country his country. The powers of the feudal lord were definitely limited and his relations with the vassals were defined by contract.

The theory developed that everything had moved from some one, had at some time been granted by some one, and it continued to be held of them. His interest in the thing granted did not cease with the grant. If he had granted land as lord to a vassal, his rights over the land remained except for the particular interest he had parted with.[4] Tenure also affected the personal status of the grantee as it made him a peer of his co-vassals of the same fief so that he was entitled to a judgement of these peers before he could be lawfully punished for a wrong or deprived of a right. The grantor was now his lord with definite rights over him and definite obligations to him of a continuing character, and he, as a vassal, had a reciprocal duties and rights in relation to the lord.

The basic tendency of feudalism was individualistic. It promoted the ideas of loyalty and contract. It compelled lord and vassal to obey and maintain the law which prescribed their mutual rights and obligations. It was a system of contract under which man could say to his lord, "I will be to you faithful and true on the condition that you keep as I am willing to deserve, and all that fulfil our agreement was when I to you submitted and chose your will.[5]

DEMOCRATIC INSTITUTION

As a result of the Teutonic influence, there developed a device of government that combined central control with local initiative and made possible popular control over large cities and area. Under this influence England embarked upon a great experiment conducted for seven centuries and produced in the long run a remarkable system of democratic institutions. The Great Charter which constitutes the foundation of modern parliamentary democracy was produced at the outset of this experiment. There were also other experiments in representation specially in the Church Councils and local councils, in the conduct of business of the guilds and in trials by jury. There were other parliaments than that of England. The Parliament of France, and specially of Paris were executive judicial councils. The most momentous innovation was,

---

4. McIlwain, C.H., *op. cit.*, p. 181.

5. Ernest Barker, *Essays on Government*, p. 88.

of course, the summoning of the burgesses in England. It was, as MacIver writes, a step toward nationalism in its true political sense and the beginning of the longest of all marches toward democracy.[6]

It was significant for the growth of the democratic tradition that the Teutonic possessed the right of electing their king, though there was a general tendency towards the principle of heredity. Under the influence of this idea the German Emperor seldom possessed any real governing power. The English king owed his authority to the people. Thus the Teutonic principle of elective monarchy, contributed towards the growth of the modern democratic and constitutional government.

To sum up, the medieval mind, created great systems of civil and canon, law maritime and mercantile codes, charters and municipal freedom the jury system and the habeas corpus, and the Magna Carta of the, aristocracy, courts and curias prepared for States and Churches modes an mechanisms of administration employed to this day. Representative government appeared in the Spanish Cortes, the Icelandic Althing, the French Estates General, the English Parliament.[7]

It is hard to imagine, writes G.H. Sabine, that liberty could have played the part it did in European political thought if ethical and religious institutions had not been conceived to be broadly independent of and superior in importance to the state and legal enforcement. Particularly, the belief in spiritual autonomy and the right of the spiritual freedom left a residuum without which modern ideas of individual privacy and liberty would be scarcely intelligible.[8]

It was the great merit of the medieval tradition to have stressed the supremacy of law and natural law, subordination of government to public opinion and customs of the people and moral restraints on power if not the responsibility of the rulers to the ruled. As D'Entreves observes, "The idea that authority, whatever its origin, its forms, or its aspects, has in itself some element that never is and never can be merely human: that, therefore, duties, and obedience is due less to men than to principles; that it is the subservience to the divine order of justice which alone can legitimate political rule and give it a divine character; such principles, which medieval thinkers continued to develop from the original source of Christian experience, have become outstanding landmarks of Christian political thought and must remain such unless Christianity abdicates all hopes of constructive action and takes refuge in a passive acceptance of the powers that be."[9]

6. MacIver, R.M., *The Web of Government*, p. 185
7. Will Durant, *The Story of Civilization : The Ages of Faith*, p. 1083.
8. G.H. Sabine, *op. cit.*, p. 166.
9. D'Entreves, *The Medieval Contribution to Political Thought*, p. 10

QUESTIONS FOR EXERCISE

1. What were the aims and objects of conciliar movement ? Why did this movement fail to achieve any reform in the government of the Church ?
2. Write a short note no conciliar movement and determine its contribution to political thought.
3. Write a short note on Gerson and Nicholas of Cusa.
4. What were the characteristics of Medieval Political thought. How do they differ from ancient thought and what influence did they exert on early modern thought.
5. "The middle ages were essentially unpolitical" comment.

PART III – MODERN POLITICAL THOUGHT

18
Niccolo Machiavelli (1469-1527 A.D.)

The central political problem of the transitional periods F.J.C. Hearnshaw writes, "was the position of the new national state and its secularised government in respect of the old cosmopolitan authorities, and in relation to the Christian principles which had so long dominated Western affairs. The central social problem was how to restrain and limit the dangerous liberty of the emancipated individual, and how to turn to the advantage of the community the experience of his egoistic activity."[1]

Between the death Marsiglio of Padua in 1323 and the birth of Niccolo Machiavelli in 1469 a period of 'strange interlude' took place. It constituted one of the most momentous epochs of change in the history of Western civilisation. It marked a time of momentous beginnings and of equally momentous endings of much that had been counted fundamental since the end of classical civilisation. Remarkable developments in the art of printing, the discovery of America by Columbus, the opening of unknown continents, the rise of unforeseen possibilities of commerce heralded a new era.

PROBLEMS OF MODERN POLITICAL THOUGHT

1. Modern State as a Means Not End. Plato and Aristotle thought that the state is a natural association in the sense of being a natural growth resulting from the deeply rooted social nature of man. To Aristotle, "It came into existence for the sake of life and continues for the sake of good life." He goes a step further and says that it is contrary to human nature to lead a solitary life and one who leads a solitary life must either be a beast or God. Thus according to Plato and Aristotle men reach the highest development possible for them in and through the membership of the state.

1. Hearnshaw , *The Social and Political Ideas of Some Great Thinkers of the Sixteenth and Seventeenth Centuries*, p. 10.

The Sophists, the immediate successors of Plato and Aristotle, refuted their theories and held that state is an artificial continuance designed by man to achieve some ends. State is contrary to natural order of things. The more radical of them thought that the right of life according to nature was to live through domination over others so far as one's power permitted. One should obey its laws when one must and ignore them when one can. Roman thinkers gave prominence to law and Christian thinkers both to God and state. Modern age began with Machiavelli who gave prominence to power.

Hegel calls state as the march of God on earth but Communists consider it as an organisation by which the economically stronger groups exploit the weaker sections. The individualist consider state as a necessary evil. Anarchists are of the opinion that human nature reaches its highest development in a stateless society. Even Karl Marx and Lenin said that there can be no freedom so long as the state remains into existence. M.K. Gándhi abhored the omnipotent power of the state. He said that man has a soul but state is a soulless machine.

2. Nature of Government. Political organization is the essence of the state in which a few govern and many obey. But who has the right to rule over his fellowmen and why? There are conflicting views about this question.

3. Functions of the State. Some support the rule of wise, some of military while some give prominence to wealth or noble birth etc. Interesting questions and conflicting opinions arise about the organisation and forms of government. There are conflicting views about the end or purpose of the state. Individualists say that its purpose is to maintain peace and order. That Government is the best which governs the least. The socialists desire to increase the functions of the state and consider it as an instrument of promoting good life to citizens. On the other hand, anarchists recommend its total abolition. At present socialists views have gained prominence.

4. Law, Rights and Duties. Connected with the government is the problem of law and that of rights and duties of citizenship and how to reconcile man with society.

These are some of the main problems of political science. The task of historian of political thought is to present the views of great thinkers in a detached way and present a balanced and objective view for the convenience of a reader or student which may enhance their knowledge and may help in creating useful citizen with enlightened outlook.

BIOGRAPHY OF MACHIAVELLI

The Spirit of Renaissance

The Renaissance in Europe produced one man of supreme eminence in political philosophy: Niccolo Machiavelli. His political philosophy was scientific and empirical, and was based upon his own experience of affairs concerned to set forth the means to assigned ends, regardless of the question whether the ends are to be considered good or bad. When, on the occasion, he allowed himself to mention the ends that he desired, they were such as we can all applaud. Much of the conventional obloquy that attaches to his name is due to the indignation of hypocrites who hate the frank avowal of evil-doing. There remains, a good deal that genuinely deserves criticism, but in this he is an expression of his age. Such intellectual honesty about political dishonesty would have been hardly possible at any other time or in any other country, except perhaps in Greece among men who owed their theoretical education to the sophists and their practical training to the wars of petty states which were the political accompaniment of individual genius in classical Greece as in Renaissance Italy.

Three great writers were produced by Italy in the sixteenth century Machiavelli, Ariosto and Tasso. He was the son of a Florentine lawyer, who was neither rich nor poor, and who held a minor post in the government. When he was in his twenties Savonarola dominated Florence and made a great impression on Machiavelli, for he remarked that "all armed prophets have conquered and unarmed ones failed," proceeding to give Savonarola as an instance of the latter class. On the other hand, he mentioned Moses, Cyrus, Theseus and Romulus. It is typical of Renaissance that Christ is not mentioned.

His Interest in Politics

Right from his boyhood, Machiavelli had an absorbing interest in politics, the technique of influence, the chess of power. Immediately after Savonarola's execution in 1498, when he was twenty-nine years of age, he was appointed secretary to the *Dieci Della Guerra* a Council of Ten for War. He held that post for fourteen years. He was of the view that a national militia should be formed with good equipment and training. It should serve as the last firm line of the republic's defence. After long hesitation, the government accepted his plan and empowered Machiavelli to execute it. In 1512, Julius II, furious against Florence, for having refused to join in expelling the French from Italy, ordered the armies of the Holy League to suppress Florence. Florence was taken and Machiavelli lost both his reputation and government post. Unfortunately at this time he was supposed to be involved in a plot to re-establish the Republic. He was exiled from Florence. He retired to a farm in the country, where he devoted himself to rustic employments and to literature, and his most important works were produced in this period of his life.

For want of other occupation, Machiavelli became an author. His most famous work *The Prince,* was written in 1513. It was dedicated to Lorenzo the Second, since he hoped to win the favour of the Medici. Its tone is perhaps partly due to this practical purpose. His longer work, *the Discourses,* which he was writing at the same time, is markedly more republican and more liberal. At the beginning of *The Prince,* he said he will not speak of republics in this book, since he had dealt with them elsewhere. Those who do not read also the *Discourses* are likely to get a very one-sided view of his doctrine.

Writing in the age of Alexander VI and Julius II, Caesar Borgia and Medici, Machiavelli realized that contemporary polities was not based on good Christian ethics but on self-interest. The Italian society of the 16th century, though intellectually brilliant and artistically creative, was a prey to the worst political corruption and moral degeneration. Injustice, cruelty and murder were the ways of government. Faith and truthfulness had little place in the conduct of people. Force and craft had become the master-keys to success and selfishness, profligacy and debauchery were running rampant. It was a society which illustrated Aristotle's saying that "man, when separated from law and justice, is the worst of all animals."[2]

The beginning of the 16th century witnessed a revolution which sought to transfer "the allegiance of the human spirit from clerical to civil authority."[3] Medieval institutions had to give place to new institutions in conformity with the spirit of the time. The *Sacerdotum* vanished as a power and the Church was reduced to the position of a voluntary association or a partner of national government. During this period there gradually emerged the institution of absolute monarchy as the prevailing form of government in Western Europe. In contrast to this, the Italy of Machiavelli presented a picture of disunity and disrupted monarchy. The states of Venice, Florence, Naples, Milan and the papal states were pitted against one another in internecine wars and conflicts, and no power appeared strong enough to unite the whole country. To Machiavelli who was deeply influenced by these conditions, therefore, it was supremely important that Italy should be consolidated as a strong power under an absolute monarch.

Machiavelli's writings do not belong to the domain of political theory. He writes mainly about the mechanics of government, about the means by which the states may be made strong, about the policies by which they can expand their power and about the errors that lead to their decay or destruction. It is, a Prof. Laski says, "a grammar of power of the use of the sixteenth century Italy." Building upon his observation and experience he explained with realism and incisiveness the way in which alone, as he knew contemporary Italy, the state could be made strong and enduring. He did not inquire whether it was right to attain position in that way; nor did he bother that other and better ways did or did not exist. He sought two essential things: first, the rules to

2. Sabine, G.H., *A History of Political Theory* (London, 1948), p. 338.

3. Figgis in *Cambridge Modern History,* Vol. III.

enable a person to realize his will in a world where such realization was the highest ambition without regard to its moral character, and second, how, in a world of fraud, force and passion to maintain what one has obtained. Political and military measures were his sole concern and he divorced these from all moral, religious and social considerations except for the purposes of political expediency. The prince must "know well how to use both the beast and the man." "Right and wrong have nothing to do with government." Success justifies all means, for success brings power, unity and stability. Beyond this criterion of success Machiavelli refused to go. He put his position lucidly in these words: "A prince, therefore, who desires to maintain himself must learn to be not always good, but to be so or not as necessity may arise. For, all things considered, it will be found that some things that seem like virtue will lead you to ruin if you follow them; whilst others that apparently are vices, result in your safety and well-being."[4] And again be said, "Many have pictured republics and principalities which in fact have never been known or seen, for how one lives is far distant from how one ought to live, that he who neglects what is done for what ought to be done, sooner effects his ruin than his preservation....hence it is necessary for a prince who wishes to hold his own to know to do wrong and to make use of it according to necessity."[5] The prince Leviathan of Machiavelli is not to concern himself with standards of rightness or religion in realizing his aim. He has to be very shrewd and diplomatic, to be good or bad as occasion demands and to use force without the consideration of its moral validity. The test by which he judges the actions of rulers is their ultimate success in obtaining, preserving and increasing their power. Thus, politics becomes an end in itself and means are sacrificed for attaining it.

CONTEMPORARY ENVIRONMENT

A man of very sensitive nature and penetrative observation, Machiavelli very much influenced by the political and intellectual tendencies of his age. Up to 16th century the conciliar movement favouring constitutional government in the church and the state had disappeared beneath the wave of a monarchist reaction. In spiritual sphere the Pope succeeded in establishing supremacy over church council. In secular sphere national monarchs crushed feudal aristoc-racies and feudal assemblies. In Italy no strong man appeared on the scene. It was divided in many states such as Venice, Florence, Naples, Milan and the papal states etc. It thus became the battleground of intriguing and ambitious potenties local as well as foreign. In such an atmosphere, public morality became extremely low and leaders were guided by selfish motives. This situation pained Machiavelli and restoring prosperity to Italy became a master passion with him. He propounded the idea of national state and secular thought.

4. *The Prince,* XV.

5. *Ibid.*

Machiavelli was very much influenced by the environments and growing spirit of renaissance. He gave a new outlook by exploding the shells of scholastic dogma and domination of religion and morality over politics. He was the creature of the Renaissance and a child of his times and environment. In the middle ages church or religious dogma dominated the political thought but the renaissance impelled men to examine ideas free from religious domination. How it was possible to formulate political theories on a purely secular basis. Machiavelli stood on a borderline between the middle and the modern ages. He gave birth to a new era in the modern age by freeing politics of the vassaldom of religion.

During, the middle ages, political thought laid emphasis on the salvation of soul and God in the light of Christian theology. With the Renaissance, man instead of God, earthly enjoyment instead of salvation of soul, gained prominence. A new tendency developed to concentrate on this world, on the enrichment of personality and beauty in all forms. Rationalism brought into existence a new outlook based on reason. Individualism laid stress on the dignity of man. Nationalism replaced the universalism of the middle ages. The new ideal put emphasis on individual success in this life and in this world. It demanded self-assertion, ruthlessness and disregard of conventional morality. Idealistic approach gave place to realistic approach. Power became an end in itself. With the decline of religion the motto of life became end justifies the means. Machiavelli was as true representative of his times as is depicted by the subject matter of his study, his arms and ideals, his empiricism, his rationalism, his realism, his pragmatism his individualism, his nationalism and his hednotic morality. Machiavelli gave prominence to secular thought.

Influence on Machiavelli

Machiavelli was profoundly influenced by Aristotle. He believed that human nature and human problems are almost the same at all times and places. Therefore he interpreted the present with the help of past. He studied contemporary problems and politics, analysed these formed conclusions and then summoned history to substantiate them. In this way his method was historical.

Importance of Machiavelli

Machiavelli believed that there is but one criterion in the realm of state craft and in the affairs of government by which to judge the character of an action and the results. To quote Maxey, Niccolo Machiavelli is perhaps the most universally reprobated figure in the history of political literature, the man whose percepts are universally, disavowed in principle but actually followed in practice.

FIRST MODERN THINKER

No political thinker can think in a vacuum but in no system of political philosophy, the influence of environment is more manifest than in that of Machiavelli. According to Dunning, "The brilliant Florentine was in the fullest sense the child of his time." He discarded religious thinking and said, "end justifies the means.''

Historical Background

The end of middle ages and the beginning of modern period started with two movements known as Renaissance and Reformation. Renaissance came forth in Italy by the revival of ancient thought and learning which had been buried deep by Christianity in medieval age. Roman thought and Greek philosophy had been really burdened with the medieval thought. In the medieval ages people pondered about the spirit, salvation and God Renaissance made the study of man instead of God as the centre of political thought. It inspired scholars to study the things from rational rather than clerical point of view. It revolutionized the attitude of man towards religion and morality. It was something mere than more revival or recovery of ancient learning. It was rebirth of emotions and of faculties which have remained dormant for long. It awakened in man a new consciousness and new values of life. Secular study now dominated the academic sphere instead of religion. This world came to have more importance than the next world. It set aside conventional morality. Development of personality and the spirit of individualism emphasized the dignity of man. Machiavelli was the creature of this renaissance which dominated Italy in general and Florence in particular. He stood on the border line between the middle and the modern ages. He freed the political thought from shackles of religions. With the renaissance, came new conditions and new individual success in this life and in this world. The success demanded self assertion, ruthlessness and disregard of conventional morality. Power became the new deity, good in itself and end in itself. Machiavelli was the true representative of his times who preached that the end justifies the means and power of is good in itself.

The age of Machiavelli has been called the age of bastards and adventurers. It was a society intellectually brilliant and artistically creative. But it was a victim to worst political corruption and degeneration. Cruelty and murder were normal methods of government. Force and craft were keys to success. Society was leaderless. According so Sabine "Machiavelli's was a thought of the masterless man. In Italy there was internecine war and disorder. Due to wars and Italy became a Cockpit of Europe. Church according to Machiavelli has kept and still keeps our country (Italy) divided.''

In such an atmosphere, Machiavelli lived and wrote books. This degenerating and depressing state of Italy could not leave uninfluenced and unmoved a sensitive patriot and keen observer like Machiavelli. The challenge of the day was the solution for this chaos of depravity by strongman. Dunning remarked, "The era was of the strong man and Machiavelli's writings give copious evidence that he realised this fact''. Unity, prosperity and independence of Italy became a master passion with him. His works *"The Prince''* and *"The Discourse''* show that he was fully conscious of the fact that the contemporary politics was based on violence and fraud and not on good Christian ethics. These books reveal him as a practical statesman concerned about the mechanism of government and how it can be made strong.

Spiritual Ancestry

Machiavelli was largely influenced by Aristotle. He brushed aside the teaching of scriptures and of the church father. He did not pay attention to the controversy of church and the state. He separated politics from the church. He believed that human nature and human problems, were almost the same at all times and places. He thought of enlightening the present with the help of past. He studied contemporary politics, analysed it, formed conclusion and took help of history to support his conclusions. He chose selected examples from ancient history to substantiate his conclusion and to propagate his ideas.

Historical Method

Machiavelli claimed to have followed historical method though strictly his method was not historical because he did not take pains to draw conclusions from historical facts, but utilized carefully selected instances of history to support his presumptive arguments. He was primarily a student of practical and not of speculative politics. As a realist in politics, he cared little for political philosophy. His writings tell us about the art of government rather than the theory of the state. He was more concerned with the actual working of the government machinery than with the abstract principles of constitution. His main theme was preservation and continuation of the state. He believed that public morality was different from private morality. Man's virtue is measurable by his power and fame and lies in a combination of force and intellect. For such a "virtue there is little place for any restraints imposed by general principles which natural law implies."

NATIONALIST AND PATRIOT

In 16th century in Italy, where Machiavelli lived and wrote his famous political works, the medieval order had collapsed. The feudal lords had vanished but, unlike other European lands such as U.K. Spain and France, no strong central authority unified the country. In Italy, there were many small states who used to fight. Political life was chaotic, laden with treachery and intrigue. Morals had decayed. Men tended to live by their units, serving their own selfish interests without consideration of others, or of society as a whole. The pope, nominally superman spiritual authority in Christiandom, had become a prince among the many, who divided the country between themselves. Machiavelli noticed the game for power. He concerned himself with political state craft, but not with political science. He was more a mariner's compass or the whether cock than a pioneer for new philosophy. He preached opportunist philosophy. However he broke totally from ancient moorings, when he gave an insignificant place to morals, ethics and religion in politics. According to Dunning, he was more unreligious than irreligious and more unmoral than immoral. He was critical of Pope because he was responsible for the division of Italy into a number of princely states and was not strong enough to unite Italy under himself or to permit anyone else to unite it. He was critical of religion because Christian principles seemed to him to make men feeble and more disposed to endure injuries than to avenge them. He desired to make religion as hand maid of politics to be served as a device to use it to make it easier to rule over a body of people. In ethical sphere he did not ask whether power was good or evil but he wanted to know has to preserve and also to increase it. He stated that the state knows no morals and the end justifies the means. Public morality is quite different from private morality. Thus Machiavelli discarded the medieval conceptions of religion, morality and ethics. He used historical method to support his contentions though in a defective manner. His belief in free thinking, advocacy of a national army, the criterion of state as extension, his idealization of Prince point out his new thinking.

The National State

Machiavelli's greatest contribution is the nationalistic outlook. He popularised the name 'state' in the way in which it is used today, something having a definite territory, population, government and sovereignty. He made politics a common subject to be discussed by common men. These made him a modern thinker.

While the keynote of medievalism was universalism, Machiavelli was the herald of the modern nation state. He supported national monarchical states. He said "the only way to establish any kind of order is to establish a monarchical government to curb the excessive ambitions of feudal lords and corruption of powerful individuals."

Patriotism

Machiavelli was a patriot. He wrote for the glorification of Italy without any mental reservation of being either a confirmed monarchist or republican. He subordinated all considerations to his motherland. He himself stated that after putting all other considerations aside, the only question should be what cause will save the life and liberty of country. He passionately desired to find some means by which Italy could be united. He made strong plans to maintain internal peace, resist aggression by foreign states and expel the foreigners from her soil. His books tell the methods by which the state can be made strong, the policy by which it can expand its power and the errors which it must avoid if it is to prosper and flourish. He came to the conclusion that the main purpose of politics is to preserve and increase political power; that is the criterion by which he measured the success or failure of Government.

Nationalism

Machiavelli also gives us glimpses of democratic principles. His statement that property and women should not be confiscated and fraud must be used in war shows him as a person interested in the welfare of his countrymen.

He was one of the founder father of nationalism. During his life time he was much impressed by the French and Swiss national army so he condemned the keeping of mercenary troops. Though he does not use the term nationality in the modern sense but he was aware of the forces which make a state united against other state, i.e. a common tradition, a common language, a common history and a common system of law. Thus understood these factors produce the sentiment of nationalism in modern age. His advocacy of the expansion of the state upto the limits of ethical homogeneity clearly pointed out to the fact that he was the forerunner of the theory of national states and of wise and strong ruler.

He advocated for strong and wise ruler to keep order and promote the interest of the state. In this sphere he was the first political psychologist. He proposed a strong absolute monarchy, again anticipating later political developments and theory of sovereignty. As such he is considered as first original modern thinker. He must be given his due for having stumbled on those principles which spelled into mighty streams in later centuries. His particular emphasis on the part played by the state is of great significance as it was through this instrument that the national, states came into existence. He was a herald of nationalism. All these make him an important initiator of contemporary political philosophy. He united political theory with political practice, separated religion from politics and preached for strong national states and patriotism. Thus, he was the first modern thinker.

THE HUMAN NATURE

Machiavelli discussed at some length about human nature. He gave a very dark picture of Human Nature. He equated it with animal nature. Human beings are ungrateful and selfish. As put forth is his books his views about human nature are as follows :

1. Self-centred. Man is self-centred, he thinks about his own interest rather than the interest of any body else. He always cares for himself. He is a greedy and sensual creature.

2. Aggressive. Human beings are aggressive. Every one is interested to acquire more and not interested in leaving what has been once acquired. Men are always fighting with each other, thereby creating conditions of anarchy.

3. Wicked. Human beings are always prepared to work against collective interests provided their own interests clash with them. All men are wicked in nature.

4. Timid. Man is always timid. Being timid he follows the line of least resistance. He wants to follow only well established customs so that he is not opposed by the society.

5. Acquisitive. Machiavelli was of the view that by nature men love private property more than their kiths and kins. Men can forget and forgive murder than patrimony.

6. Discontented. Every human being always remains unsatisfied and dissatisfied. No human being is content with his position. He is always after more and more power.

7. Stupid. Most people are stupid and irrational. They are always attracted by elusive good desire. Ultimately these result is ruin.

8. Love for Change. Human beings have love for novelty and change.

9. Ambitious. By nature men are ambitious. They desire many things which they cannot get with the result that they remain dissatisfied and discontented. Enemities and wars are the outcome of this desire.

Criticisms

Machiavelli has been criticised for his views about human nature.

1. Extreme picture. Human nature is not as bad as he has tried to portray. Human beings are of course not completely good but at the same time they are not completely bad as well.

2. Cause of Evil. Machiavelli has nowhere stated as to why the human beings are bad and selfish. He has given no rational explanation for that.

3. Will, Not Force, the Basis of State. Machiavelli's views about human nature also leads one to the conclusion that people came in the state due to fear. Today it is fully established that will not force is the basis of the state. In this regard his theory falls on the ground.

4. Not Incorrigible. Machiavelli is of the view that human beings are incorrigible. But this is not correct. With the help of education and making the people realise about anti-social activities, all human beings can easily be reformed to a great extent.

IMPLICATIONS OF MACHIAVELLI'S VIEWS ABOUT HUMAN NATURE

1. State Control. One serious implication of Machiavelli's views is that it leads to the conclusion that the state is to check the wicked nature of human beings who are selfish. The state should use maximum force. Social instinct had nothing to do with it.

2. Absolute Power. Prince is given absolute power. He is not to care for his wicked and selfish people but govern them with rod without caring for morality which too is not correct or desirable.

3. Politics a dirty game. The game of politics cannot be played with fair hands. It is a dirty game, which is not very healthy.

THE PRINCE

1. Purpose.

The Prince was written by Machiavelli with some definite purpose, and its tone is entirely different from that of the *Discourses,* which he had written at the same time. He regarded Italy of his time as an example of a corrupt society. Hence he stated that when the necessary virtues had decayed, there was no possibility either of restoring them or of carrying on orderly government without them, except by despotic power. He had in mind the necessity of the existence of a strong and unified Italy, which during his lifetime, as for many centuries longer, had remained divided politically. As a student of practical politics, he sought to determine the workings of a real, not of an ideal, political life.*The Prince* is concerned to discover, from history and from contemporary events, how principalities are won, how they are held, and how they are lost. Fifteenth century Italy afforded a multitude of examples, both great and small. Few rulers were legitimate even the Popes, in many cases, secured election by corrupt means. The rules for achieving success were not quite the same as they became when times grew more settled, for no one was shocked by cruelties and treacheries which would have disqualified a man in the eighteenth or nineteenth century. Perhaps our age, again, can better appreciate Machiavelli, for some of the most notable successes of our time have achieved by methods as base as any employed in Renaissance Italy.

2. Subject Matter

The Prince is the masterpiece of Machiavelli. It is generally taken as the source of his political philosophy. The treatise consists of 26 chapters. It deals with the rules for the guidance of a prince who has come to power rather unconstitutionally. It has now become a treatise on the art of government rather than a book of political science. It is a handbook of a politician rather than of the political philosopher.

3. Basic Principle

(i) ***State as Supreme.*** The basic philosophy of *The Prince* is that the state is the highest association. The subjects must completely merge themselves in the state. A successful state is one which is founded by a single man. The laws which he creates, reflect national character of the state.

(ii) ***Economic Success as Criterion.*** The scale for measuring the success or failure of a state is the material prosperity which it has achieved or is enjoying. A successful Prince might not be very much moral but he must adopt all those means by which he could remain in power. He must combine in himself the law and bruteness. He should use both as the time required. He must know how to play fox and lion. He must keep himself on guard from his neighbouring states. These were his likely enemies. He should command the confidence of the people not by giving powers to his subjects, but by spreading network of his intelligence and deception when necessary. He must catch and severely punish conspirators. This should be through execution rather than by way of confiscation of their property. The people can forget the execution of their ancestors but not the loss of their ancestral property. He must promote economic prosperity of his subjects. It is by this way alone that he can command respect of the people. A layman will judge the worth of the prince only through economic prosperity.

4. Dead to Sentiments

A good prince should be dead to all sentiments except those of love for his state. His personal glory is the glory of state. His personal honours and dishonours are deeply associated with those of his state. He must be ready to sin boldly for maintaining the integrity of the state and for glorifying it. He must also be ready to oppose every evil both from inside as well as outside the state. The evil must be replied with evil and that too with equal and if possible with more vigour and strength.

5. Above All Laws.

Machiavelli believed that the Prince is above all laws. The state security knows no laws. There are always two codes of conduct in a state one for the individual and the other for the stage. Both need not be combined at any stage. The individual has a different code than that of the state. It will be the end of the state if an attempt was made to combine the both. As the law giver the Prince is above all rules. The state knows no ethics. The ends justify the means. The prince must not bother to see the morality or immorality of the means. He could steer through both to achieve the ends. In the words of Maxey, "The Prince is advised, therefore, to be generous or niggardly according to state of public opinion as to lavishness or economy; to be cruel or kind as expediency dictates, to keep faith only when disadvantage will result from so doing, to strive ceaselessly and by all manner of means, to win glory and renown; and above all to avoid being despised and hated."

Criticisms

1. Not Original. Machiavelli's *The Prince* is neither the outcome of his original political philosophy nor it is something unexpected of him particularly in his time sand circumstances. As Villari says, "Anyone acquainted with the 'Discourse' and knowing the author's special purpose could have forecast nearly everything in '*The Prince*'. To quote Sabine "*The Prince* was a selection of the author's view for a special purpose and was occasioned, it is true, by a desire to obtain employment under the Medici..." Machiavelli was bound to give an idealist picture of the tyrant. In his philosophy Machiavelli has tried to combine despotism with individualism. The despotism of Prince and individualism of an individual were made to go together. He tried to combine the theories of revolution and stability together, this made his philosophy look like a patchwork of both. It is self-contradictory and at many places even results in the failure of his philosophy.

2. Despotic Violence. Machiavelli has given an absolute power to his prince. He forgot that absolutism is a position. This absolutism is made still more dangerous when it is supported by an absolute power saddled with violence. Absolutism combined with violence is a naked weapon which could be used most dangerously. He has given powers but proposed no checks to see that there was no misuse of these naked powers. Despotic violence is a powerful political medicine, needed in corrupt states and for special contingencies in all states, but still a position which must be used with greatest caution.

3. Debt of Aristotle. Machiavelli is indebted to Aristotle in the basic principles enunciated by him in his '*The Prince*'. Aristotle advocated that the state is the highest form of association and that the man can find his development only through the agency of the state. Aristotle laid equal stress on material prosperity of the subjects as a source for the stability of the state. Thus, Machiavelli was not original in his thinking even in this regard.

4. Path to Revolution. While giving powers of absolutism and despotic violence Machiavelli forgot that man is by nature conservative and preferred old over the new, loved traditions and had certain likes and dislikes. He suggested his prince to sacrifice the individual at the alter of the state. To play with individual code of morality and to differentiate it from that of state code is something dangerous. It can possibly lead to revolution as well. The state is individual writ large. In a healthy society both the individual and the state codes must go hand in hand. They should be complementary to each other. Character of a state is reflected by those of its citizens. It will therefore be wrong to put both at the opposite ends. Basic harmony is the most essential feature of national and individual code of conduct. Machiavelli thus paved the path for revolution if his philosophy is followed to its logical conclusions.

5. Uncivilised Society. Machiavelli is of the view that a successful prince must be cunning. He should not care for morality. Now, who can deny that the subjects usually follow ideals and precedents set by their rulers. An immoral prince could not expect to have moral subjects. A society consisting of immoral persons cannot be considered a civilised society. In his attempt and passion for giving powers to his prince Machiavelli had forgotten problems which were bound to arise out of his theory.

6. Narrow Nationalism. Machiavelli is known as a modern political thinker. This cannot be justified when he advises his Prince not to trust his neighbouring states. Machiavelli thus stands for narrow nationalism and not for internationalism. No doubt the conditions of Italy of his time warranted nationalism but as a modern political philosopher he should not have confined his political philosophy to a particular state. It would have given him more importance and made him more realistic had he given international outlook to his ideas.

7. State of Fear. Machiavelli does not advise the ruler to pay heed towards moral progress. Development of morality and moral character in itself ends many problems which a state is ordinarily supposed to face. The problem of a state which has subjects with high moral character are quite different from a state which has immoral subjects. "The greatest fault of Machiavelli lies in the fact that he builds his theory of state or rational presentation of state in an environment of fear or prohibition, a thing which is bound to react rather unfavourably on the moral progress of the state without which neither preservation nor expansion is easy of accomplishment."

8. Wrong Estimate of Human Nature. Machiavelli has tried to underestimate the character and intelligence of the common man when he says that men do not care for the politics which the state follows but that they are concerned only with the outward labels. He is basically wrong when he says that the man in the street will never and can never be an effective political participant and that he only follows a policy made for him and not by him. His philosophy boils down to the idea that the subjects are dumb creatures rather than intelligent human beings.

9. Contradictions. Thus '*The prince*' is full of contradictions. Machiavelli would have done more justice with this treatise had he not written it with a particular motive of finding a job under the Medicis. Since the treatise had an individual motive, it could not be objective.

ETHICS AND POLITICS

Machiavelli like Hobbes, believed that human being is essentially selfish and the only uniting factor in these selfish human beings is the desire for security. States could only develop and serve if they exploited this weakness of the human beings. The subjects join the state because they find themselves insecure without the effective protection of the state. Man has a tendency to acquire and to protect what has already been acquired by him. The desire is bound to result in anarchy, if it is not checked by the authority of a strong government. The people in general are bad, and the wise ruler shall formulate his policies on this assumption. While awarding punishments, the state must prefer patrimony to murder.

Ethics and Religion

Medieval political philosophers believed that the religion was the basis of the state. They felt that development of state could only be judged by the religious progress which is made. It was felt that the state was only a department of the church. Hence church fathers and papists assumed definite supremacy over state affairs. They pleaded that as soul has supremacy over the body so the church enjoys supreme position as compared with the state. Aristotle tried to differentiate between the state and church functions but his work was undone in middle ages by Conciliar Movement. Machiavelli divorced religion from politics and separated them completely from each other. He tried to subordinate religion to the state. At the same time he agreed that morality had its own limited place in society which must be preserved and exploited. Since he did not bother about the morality of means for achieving the ends, he can be called the founder of utilitarian ethics. He differentiated between public and private morality and assigned the former a preferential place and position over the later. Patriotism is the only end of a good citizen.

Normal and Perverted Government

Like Aristotle, Machiavelli classified the governments into normal and perverted forms. In the normal form the government is monarchy, aristocracy and limited democracy or constitutional democracy. Machiavelli, however, agreed with Polybius and Cicero that only a mixed form of government is the best or the ideal that is attainable one. As a realist he felt that in a state there should be close relationship between economic development and political stability. The stability of government depended on the economic development of its subjects. To quote Sabine, "Thus Machiavelli insisted upon the needs for legal remedies for official abuses in order to prevent illegal violence and pointed out the political dangers of lawlessness in rulers and the folly of vexations and harassing policies." Machiavelli liked rule of many on elected basis rather than rule of one on hereditary basis. He had definite preference for elected government over hereditary system. He argued that the people no doubt are unable to understand intricate and complicated policy matters but their sharing of government in ordinary affairs is bound to bring stability to state. He believed in the suppression of nobility as their interests were against the monarchy and middle class. Training and equipping of a citizens army is the primary need of a nation. For a successful ruler it was most essential to know the art of war. He pleaded for compulsory military training for all able bodied persons.

"Machiavelli hoped that somewhere among the tyrants of Italy, perhaps in the house of Medici; there might arise a Prince with a vision broad enough to see a united Italy and bold enough to make the vision real." In addition to this, he stood for republic form of government as one which was for him conducive to efficiency and also responsible for promoting individual liberty. It is, however, not clear as to why he has pleaded for liberty for those to whom he has characterised as selfish and hasty to be controlled with strong hands of a strong ruler. According to Sabine, "Thus it happens that the concluding chapter of The Prince, though doubtless sincere, is the exception rather than the rule in his usually sordid advice to princes."

Support to Aggrandisement

Machiavelli strongly believed in the dictum that the state should either expand or expire. He held the view that the state must go on expanding itself both in absolute monarchy or republic. From expansion he understood not blending of organisation but annexation of states to be dominated and governed by one Prince. He preached the use of arms for the purpose of achieving successful expansionist policy. He pleaded that a Prince should not depend on the policy of taxation, because that was not a dependable source of income. Prince should believe in royal plundering. A successful Prince ought to believe in outward shows for catching the imagination of his subjects as well as the subjects of other states. This outward shows will certainly influence all other subjects and create appreciation and respect for his state in minds of others.

Machiavelli's propagation of expansionist policy was based on local environments. It was possible in Italy of his days to follow this policy of expansion and annexation, as the state was disunited at that stage.

Selfish Human Nature

Behind nearly everything that Machiavelli said was his assumption that human nature is selfish, and that the effective motives on which a statesman must rely are egoistic, such as the desire for security in the masses and the desire for power in rulers. Government is founded upon the weakness and insufficiency of the individual, who is unable to protect himself against the aggression of other individuals unless supported by the power of the state. Men are always in a condition of strife and competition which threatens open anarchy unless restrained by the force behind the law. He frequently remarked that "men are in general bad, and that the wiser ruler will construct his policies on this assumption." Thus governments and politics are only the reflection of human nature. Human nature being what it is, politics would remain the same as Machiavelli described it. Some social scientists and psychologists have come to the conclusion that there are certain instincts, urges and passions in man which are ineradicable. Human nature, they say, has not changed for the last two thousand years. To Machiavelli also, human nature is unchanging. Wise men say, "he writes, not without reason that whoever wishes to foresee the future must consult the past."[6]

Machiavelli regarded Church as necessary for the health and prosperity of a state. He knew that a state could not flourish if the citizens were induced to serve it solely by fear of such punishment as the ruler could inflict. As such, he accepted religion in general but was against the evil effects of Christianity. "The observance of religious institutions," he said, "is the cause of the greatness of the republics; disregard of these institutions produces the ruin of the state."[7] He had respect for religious institutions, but he disliked Christianity as it was practised in his time. He condemned it as having failed to make good citizens. It diverted too much attention to heaven and enfeebled men by preaching the feminine virtues. The rebellion of Voltaire, Diderot, Paine, Darwin, Spencer and Renan against Christianity was quite different from that of Machiavelli. They rejected the theology of Christianity, but admired the Christian moral code. On the contrary, Machiavelli accepted its theology but rejected its ethics, its conception of goodness as gentleness, humility, non-resistance; its love of peace and its denunciation of war. For his part, he preferred the Roman ethic based upon the principle that the safety of the people or state is the supreme law.[8]

"Where it is an absolute question of the welfare of our country we must admit of no considerations of justice or injustice, of mercy or cruelty, of praise or ignominy; but putting all else aside we must adopt whatever course will save the nation's existence and liberty."[9] Alexander VI never did, nor thought of, anything but cheating, and yet he was eminently popular and successful. Romulus was equally justified in killing his brother for the sake of unity in the government. Frauds, cruelties and crimes committed in order to preserve one's country are "honourable frauds", "glorious crimes". There is no eternal or natural law, no right universally agreed upon and hence, thought Machiavelli, politics in the sense of statesmanship must be held completely independent of morality. Morality and religion are, at best, instruments of politics. This is what a modern politician or a statesman thinks of morality and religion. If a modern politician is justified in either separating morality and religion from politics or in subordinating them to it, Machiavelli was equally right in holding politics above morality and religion for the purpose of the unity of the government or of the nation. Only a staunch moralist or a redeemed religious man will not accept such a view of the superiority of politics, because he interprets life in a metaphysical sense and, as such, he is never attracted by

6. *Discourses,* III, 43.
7. *Discourses,* I, 11-12.
8. Durrant, Will: *The Story of Civilization* (Vol. V), *Renaissance,* p. 558.
9. *Discourses,* III, 41-42.

earthly virtue of power, fame, glory or national unity, etc. But Machiavelli was not a saint. He was an ordinary human being, who was moved by the force of the circumstances of his time and who was much more interested in the rebuilding of his country, Italy, which had lost its glory and strength and had become politically divided. He never attempted to idealize the state, but, on the contrary, he was concerned with the actual state of affairs, and did his best for the greatness of Italy in the face of peculiar circumstances of his time. Further, Machiavelli did not neglect the importance of religion in the life of a nation. He was conscious of the role which it plays in harmonizing the social and political life of the people.

Philosophy of State

Machiavelli's philosophy of the state, as it was, cannot be considered fully inimical to the civilizing forces of man as Laski thought, although there are chances of misunderstanding the former's doctrine. If the state has a moral basis[10] and it essentially stands for a moral purpose, and if moral of the state means the social welfare or the widest possible fulfilment of the material and cultural needs and desires of the people, then Machiavelli's *Discourses* gives a sufficient proof of his consciousness towards this ideal of the state. His preference for a princedom is purely conditional. Where virtue is lacking and people are corrupt and they have no respect for laws, it becomes necessary, according to Machiavelli, to establish some superior power which, with a royal hand, with full and absolute powers, may put a curb upon the excessive ambition and corruption of the powerful. Otherwise, a free state, as described above, is definitely far superior to an unfree state. A strong prince, with a coercive authority, is needed only under peculiar circumstances. This appears to be quite sound and convincing. To quote Russell, "The world has become more like that of Machiavelli than it was and modern man who hopes to refute his philosophy must think deeply than seemed necessary in the nineteenth century."[11]

Steps for Staying in Power

Machiavelli suggested following steps to the Prince for staying in power without care of ethics:

---

10. "The state is based on a common conviction about a *right order* of human relations and the obligatory nature of the order."
(E. Barker: *Principles of Social and Political Theory,* p. 199)
"It possesses power because it has duties. It exists to enable men, at least potentially, to realize the best that is in themselves....The state accordingly is subject to a moral test of adequacy."
(H. J.. Laski: *A Grammar of Politics*, pp. 27-28).
11. Russell, B., *A History of Western Philosophy* (George Allen & Unwin Ltd., London II impression 1947), p. 532.

1. Ruthlessness. The Prince should not hesitate to use power ruthlessly against those who tried to challenge his authority. If need be he should also become cruel as well. He should ruthlessly crush all opposition and not mind execution and bloodshed. He should not brook any opposition.

2. Fox and Lion. A good Prince should know how to be both a fox and a lion. He should not avoid using force. At the same time he should not exclusively depend on that. He should try to persuade the people of his politics and programmes.

3. Peace. The Prince should also try to see that there is peace and calmness in the country. He should see that the people can live a comfortable life.

4. Exploitation of Moral Virtues. A good prince should most usefully exploit moral feelings of the people such as humbleness and submission. If necessary he should also try to involve divine authority as well.

5. Firm in Decision. A Prince should take final and decisive action, no matter whether be commits mistakes. He should not even hesitate to declare a war but be firm in that as well. He should be in a position to take quick and timely decision.

6. Strong Army. A Prince should realise that no nation can survive without having a strong and powerful army. He should have strong, well equipped army consisting of patriots.

7. Good Soldier and Commander. Of a good Prince it is expected that he himself should be a good soldier and commander on the field. He should be well aware of war techniques and latest war equipments.

8. Exploitation of Patriotism and Sense of Duty. A Prince would deceive himself if he feels that he could create a strong army only with the help of money. Real strength of army did not lay in money but in the feelings of patriotism and devotion to duty which a Prince could create with his personal qualities.

9. Violation of Promises. Machiavelli was of the view that it was not at all essential for a prince to keep his promises. A prince should be most willing to violate all promises, if the interests and safety of the state so demanded. In his own words, "Where there is the equation of safety of motherland, there is to be no consideration of just and unjust, pityful or cruel, honourable and dishonourable; only that course is to be taken which will preserve the life and maintain the liberty."

10. Popular. As far as possible the Prince should try to win sympathy and cooperation of his people, then he should try to become popular. That will make his position solid and even the opposition of the few rich and noble will not then effect or influence his position.

11. Use of Fear. It is always better for a prince to create an atmosphere where his people fear from him. It is better to be feared than to be loved. He should only be feared but not hated. The love could change as soon as the ruler withdrew benefits and concessions.

12. Dishonesty and Fraud. According to Machiavelli, it was not always essential for a prince to be honest. Fraud was no dishonesty in politics. To preserve his position as well as that of the state he should be dishonest where necessary.

13. Abstinence from Wealth and Women. A successful prince must always abstain from property and women of his subject. He should very sincerely avoid both. He must realise that the people are usually touchy on both these things. He is sure to be hated if he touched any one of them.

14. Secrecy. It is in the interest of the Prince himself to see that he is in a position to maintain utmost secrecy. If he ensures that his plans do not leak out he is bound to be a success in running his administration.

15. No Friends or Foes. A Prince must realise that for the state there are no permanent friends or enemies. Accordingly, he should be on the look out of an opportunity to his advantage and should not miss it under any circumstances.

16. Selfish use of Education and Propaganda. By education and propaganda. The Prince should create an atmosphere by which the subjects should begin to feel that their interests are identical with those of the Prince and that the Prince can only deliver the goods to them.

17. Avoid Sychophants. The greatest weakness of a Prince can be his habit of listening to his own praise. Flattery is aimed to let down a Prince and result in his fall. Machiavelli has therefore, suggested that a Prince must keep the sychophants at a safe distance so that they do not influence this decisions.

18. Destruction of Vanquished. When a Prince conquers new territories where the people are in the habit of enjoying freedom, he must completely destroy that because freedom loving people cannot adjust to new circumstances easily.

19. False Show. A Prince may not be essentially good, but he should try to show that he is always good, sincere, humane and sympathetic. Thus, according to Machiavelli, the Prince should always pose to be good and doing everything for the welfare of his subjects.

20. Selective. As far as possible the Prince should not listen to every body because that is likely to lower his position. He should select few wise and intelligent counsels and listen to them patiently. IIc should not give everbody the liberty of coming nearer and closer to him.

21. Achievement of Prince. The Prince should know the opinion of the subjects as to whether they wish him to be miser or to lavishly spend from the public exchequer, accordingly, so that he can get their praise and cooperation.

22. Proper Estimate of Enemy. The prince should try to destroy the enemy in the initial stages so that he should not become a powerful person to challenge his authority. He should never under estimate or over-estimate the strength of the enemy but try to have proper intelligence about his real strength.

23. No Friends in Politics. The prince should make his friends realise that he was extending them every cooperation and in fact he should do that, but fully well realising that in politics there were no permanent friends. A friend of today can become a foe of tomorrow as well.

24. Expansion. Machiavelli said that either a Prince must expand or stagnate. There was no other way out. It was therefore, both in the interest of the Prince and the people that he must expand.

Thus Machiavelli has given unethical tips to his Prince to remain in power. Though outwardly he is condemned by many for his ideas, yet in real practice his ideas are very much preached by many politicians of even the modern world.

CONTRIBUTION TO POLITICAL THOUGHT

Machiavelli has been considered as the first political thinker in modern sense of the term. With him the political philosophy of the middle ages, with characteristic religious domination, began to be challenged. A plea was made for the subordination of the church to that of the state. His contribution to political thought is as follow:

1. Divorce of Religion and Politics. Credit goes to Machiavelli for boldly and clearly divorcing religion from politics. The religion should have no place in state activities. The Prince should not act according to the wishes of the Pope.

2. Distinction in Public and Private Morality. Machiavelli's another contribution to the political thought was that for the first time he distinguished between public and private morality, which he felt must be separated from each other.

3. Refutation of Natural and Eternal Law. Machiavelli was the first political thinker of this times to abandon the idea of natural law. In its place he gave the idea that the law was a positive rule created by the sovereign in the state. He did not believe that there were certain eternal laws. Thus he refuted the idea of natural or eternal law.

4. Rejection of Divine Law. Machiavelli also did not contribute to the idea of Divine Law. Man has no super natural ends and as such it is wrong to believe that Divine Law has any purpose to perform. In the words of Foster. "Machiavelli values religion only as an instrument to the ends of the state."

5. State as an End. As a modern thinker, Machiavelli made a valuable contribution by saying that the state was an end itself. He did not care for the morality of means. He believed that end always justified the means. For the first time he put forth the idea that individual conscience should be sacrificed over the state. Like a realist he believed that the history was an illustration of the strength and nothing else. Therefore he worshipped power as the only deity to be worshipped. Without power there was nothing a prince could rely upon.

6. Nationalism. Machiavelli was a symbol of nationalism. He pleaded that there is nothing above or beside it and that it is an end in itself. It may not sound us of much importance today, but it was his greatest contribution to the era in which he was living. In the words of Sabine, "Machiavelli more than any other political thinker created the modern political age. Even the word itself, as the name of the sovereign political body, appears to have been made current in the modern times largely by his writing."

7. Secularism. Machiavelli was again the first political thinker who believed in secularism. Living in the days of theocracy he stood for secularism which can in no way be underestimated.

8. Naturalistic Theory of State. Another contribution of Machiavelli to the modern political thought is that for the first time he pleaded that man had no super natural ends and was not governed by the divine law. He thus made the conception of naturalistic theory of the state a logical one.

9. Psychological Treatment. Machiavelli was the first political thinker who said that a ruler should try to psychologically deal with his subjects and should consider that before acting.

10. Farewell to Medieval Philosophy. Another contribution of Machiavelli was to the philosophy of middle ages. His conception of autonomous authorities, with which he replaced central authority is both original and novel in so far as his age was concerned. In an age of feudalism he shook its very basis and thus invited the wrath of the feudalists and forced that.

11. Elected Authority. Machiavelli was modern in suggesting that the republican form of government is the best one. He stood for elected rather than a hereditary head of the state. His conception of elected head of state fully materialised in the theory of general will as expounded by Rousseau.

12. Logical Concept of Sovereignty. Credit also again goes to Machiavelli for attempting to give logical conception of Sovereignty by defining it as independent and supreme authority both internally as well as externally. Even today this definition is considered as the most logical one. It was put on scientific basis by Austin.

13. Theory of Statecraft. Machiavelli contributed to the theory of state- craft when he shook the foundations of the age long Greek philosophy of 'city states' and in its place pleaded for national states. The conception of city states had outlived its utility. The world needed another conception which Machiavelli rightly pleaded. His conception of national state is being followed even today.

CRITICISMS

1. Nothing About Major Political Issues. Machiavelli's writings are full of contradictions and in many cases he cannot be called as a farsighted thinker. He discussed and talked about nothing else except the art of war and politics. He did not discuss and solve special, economic and political problems which are equally important and in some cases rather more important. Sabine says, "He writes about nothing and thinks about nothing except politics, statecraft, and the art of war. For deeper lying social question economic or religious he had no interest except as they bore upon politics."

2. State as One Man Show. Machiavelli was not farsighted when he made the state as one man show. The absolutism of Prince is not realistic, and may be counter-productive ultimately.

3. Divorce of Ethics From Politics. Machiavelli's belief that a cunning prince can produce or change social and economic and religious values to his own ends is not correct. All these values are correlated with politics and have a close bearing on each other. To think of divorcing one from the other or of making the one the handmaid of others is not proper and mostly not possible.

4. Mis-representation of Religion. Machiavelli mis-represented the religious thought of his age and tried to mould religion according to his political wishes. He thus earned the criticism of many. He was narrow in his thoughts and philosophy. He did not take a universal view of the religion. Had he written sometime after reformation he must have treated religion on quite different footings.

5. Too Much Stress on Force. Machiavelli laid too much and undue stress on the role of force in keeping the people closer to each other. By overestimating the use of force, he underestimated the part being played by willing cooperation of the people in coming nearer and closer to each other.

6. Diplomatic Literature. It has been said about Machiavelli that his writing are more an opportunistic literature rather than having any philosophical approach to the problem.

7. Only Political Institutions. Machiavelli only thought about political institutions and has not given due place and respect to other social and religious institutions.

8. Ends do Not Justify Means. Machiavelli is not correct in his ideas that the ends justify means. If his philosophy is taken to its logical conclusions then a class of politically corrupt people is bound to come to power, with all determination to hold all power and position at all costs.

9. Wrong Presumption of Human Nature. Machiavelli's whole philosophy is based on the presumption that human beings are wicked by nature. It is because of this wicked nature that the state came into being. Machiavelli committed a blunder by generalising human nature on what he had seen in Italy. Philosophy, he has failed to discuss as to why human nature is bad. He has failed to advance any reasons for that.

10. Over Stress on Law Givers. Another criticism advanced against Machiavelli is that he has over stressed the role of law givers and legislators in moulding religious and social institutions.

IMPORTANCE OF MACHIAVELLI

Following comments by many foremost scholars show the importance of Machiavelli in the history of Political Thought:

(i) L.A. Burd. In his Cambridge Modern History Vol. I, Burd has rightly assessed the position and importance of Machiavelli when he says, "Living at a time when the old political order in Europe was collapsing and new problems both in state and in society, were arising with dazzling rapidity, he endeavoured to interpret the logical meaning of events, to forecast the inevitable issues, and to elicit and formulate the rules which destined henceforth to dominate political actions where then taking shape among fresh forming conditions of national life."

(ii) Jones. "Machiavelli's insight that the state can be understood only in terms of human lusts and appetities and his supplementary recognition that the successful ruler must learn to control these forces, make an epoch in political thinking and constitute the basis for the whole modern development.

(iii) Maxey. "His passion for the practical as against the theoretical undoubtedly did much to rescue political thought from the scholastic obscurantism of the middle ages, and entitles him to recognition as the first, if not the noblest of the great pragmatists."

(iv) K.F. Geiser and O. Jazzi. "By the passionate and enthusiastic glorification of political crime he must bear the responsibility of having made from the diffused crimes of isolated princely criminals, a compact of philosophical doctrine which corrupted public opinion in many parts of the world and which envenomed still more an unscrupulous political practice."

(v) Alien. "Machiavelli detached the state from the church making it an organisation of force for the attainment of merely earthly ends."

(vi) Prof. Jones. "Neville Chamberlain, for instance, would have learnt a great deal about Hitler (hence how to deal with him) by studying Machiavelli, and if President Wilson had pondered cover 'The Prince', the disaster of Versaille might have never occurred."

(vii) Dr. J. P. Greene. "His realism and statism can be found in an accentuated form in Germany under Bismark. And finally, in our country, the dictators like Hitler and Mussolini serve as examples of what Machiavelli has described in 'The Prince'."

QUESTIONS FOR EXERCISE

1. 'Machiavelli is in political theory the representative of Renaissance.
2. Show how Machiavelli was a nationalist and also a patriot.
3. Briefly discuss Machiavelli's views about Human Nature as depicted in 'The Prince.'
4. "Men living according to their own will and fearing according to that of Prince, wise Prince establishes himself on that which is in his own control and not in that of others." (Machiavelli). Comment.
5. "A prince ... who desires to maintain himself must learn to be not always good, but to be so as necessity may require." (Machiavelli). Comment.
6. "It is not essential that the prince should have all the good qualities but it is essential that he should seem to have them." (Machiavelli). Comment.
7. "Seeing therefore, that it is of much importance to a prince to take upon him the nature and disposition of a beast of all the whole flock he ought to imitate the lion and the fox." (Machiavelli). Comment.
8. "A prince, therefore, who is wise and prudent cannot or ought not to keep his word when the keeping of it is to his prejudice, and the cause for which he promised removed." (Machiavelli). Comment.
9. "A prince is 'esteemed' when he is a true friend or a true enemy, when that is he declares himself without reserve in favour of some one or against another. This policy is always more useful than remaining neutral." (Machiavelli). Is this an acceptable thesis for the present day ? Give reasons for your answer.
10. "All states, all powers, that have held and hold to rule over men have been and are either republics or principalities" (Machiavelli). Comment.

11. "It is essential, therefore, for a Prince who would maintain his position to have learned how to be other than good and to use and not to use his goodness as necessity requires." (Machiavelli). Explain. Do you agree that the basis of state morality should be different than that of individual morality?
12. "Therefore a wise Lord cannot, nor ought he to keep faith when the reasons which caused him to pledge it exist no longer." (The Prince). Comment.
13. "Where if a Prince succeeds in establishing his authority the means will always be adjudged honourable..." (The Prince). Comment.
14. "The divorce between the principles of religion and those of politics in the writings of Machiavelli is more apparent than real." Comment.
15. "In the action of men, and especially of prince... the ends justify the means." (Machiavelli). Comment.
16. "Let the Prince then look to the maintenance of the state the means will always be deemed honourable and will receive general appreciation." (Machiavelli in Discourses). State and examine Machiavelli's political ideas.
17. "Machiavelli is perhaps the most universally reprobated figure in the history of political literature: the man whose precepts are universally disavowed in principle, but regularly followed in practice." Maxey. Explain and discuss.
18. "Machiavelli, more than any other political thinker, created the meaning that has been attached to the state in modern political usage." Discuss this statement.
19. "Machiavelli's philosophy was both narrowly local and narrowly outdated." Comment.
20. "Machiavelli was not a philosopher in the strict sense of the word. He was rather a man of affairs who found time to write down his impressions of the world and of man but who lacked the inclination or the ability to organise impressions into a systematic account." (W.T. Jones) Explain and Discuss.
21. "Machiavelli's thoughts, his mode of thinking, his whole outlook were far more un-medieval than was the thought of 16th century as a whole." Comment.
22. "No political philosophy can step out of the relationship in which it stands to the problems, the valuation of habits or even prejudices of its own times." Sabine. Explain.
23. "The whole of Renaissance is in Machiavelli." Explain.

19

Reformation Movement and its Thinkers

The great intellectual upheaval popularly called Renaissance, of which Machiavelli was the forerunner brought the middle ages to an end in all spheres of life. In the beginning of 16th century new forces were working in the economic, political and intellectual fields and new methods were initiated but Roman church remained uninfluenced by it. According to Adam's "In Government, in doctrine, and in life, it still placed the greatest emphasis upon those traditions which the peculiar conditions of the middle ages had built upon the foundations of the primitive Christianity, and it was determined to remain unchanged." The reformation brought about the change in church. It indirectly destroyed the conception that the church was the ultimate master of human affairs. It created the concept of national state and brought modern Europe into existence. If reformation marks the beginning of new phase in the history of European political thought, it represented of Teutonic people from the religious domination of races, who chose the era of supremacy of Papacy which regulated the relations between the rulers and the ruled. Politically, it represents the inspiration of young nations with national interests and ideals of their own against their universal domination of papacy. These national states brought about the national temporal policies of their own. Economically, the princes and the people wanted to take possession of the enormous riches and landed estates of the church.

INFLUENCE OF REFORMATION

In the 16th century political theory was very much influenced by the reformation movement. Though primarily clerical, the movement could not fail to have ethical and political significance. The opposition of reformers to sole indulgences signified a reunion of morality and theology. In their opposition to papal authority, the reformers found princes anxious to save their subjects from papal exploitation. The reformers helped the princes in seizing property under the jurisdiction of the church which increased the power of the rulers. In this way, they helped these rulers against the catholic church and papacy. They also helped them against the disorderly elements within the state by preaching the doctrine of passive obedience. They helped them in crushing feudal elements in king's war and common people in peasant's war. These brought absolute monarchy into existence. The union between religion and politics heralded by Machiavelli was restored by the reformation movement. It also marked the reunion of religion and ethics.

The reformation movement of 16th century replaced the religious prescription of the church by the notion of justification by faith. It denied the right of Pope to grant pardons. It weakened the church by Lutherian doctrine of justification of faith, it supported national states.

The fundamental doctrine of justification of faith lead to the growth of a marked individualism. After temporary culmination of rulers power it ultimately lead to the growth of individual liberty and democratic government as also the establishment of a strong united national state. According to J.M. Figis, "To the form of Government it was a reversion to the ideas of earlier middle ages which were largely disappearing under the combined influence of Aristotle and the Renaissance."

Martin Luther was the prominent figure in the initial stage of reformation between 1517-30. It gave rise to absolute states territorial and national in character, with power to demand the allegiance of all of its citizens lay and ecclesiastical.

During second stage of 1530-1564, Calvin's theories became predominent which demanded a rigorous organisation and disciplining of human nature. During the period of 1564-1618 democratic nations and ideas of rights of man began to take its shape.

General Political Influence

The political teachings of the great reformers did much to counteract the rationalising, non-moral and non-religious spirit of Machiavelli. Reformation rejected the idea of universal empire and universal church. It allied itself with the idea of nationalism and strong rulers. According to Dunning, "In monarchic lands the tendency of the reform was to enhance the hold of monarchical principle and in aristocratic government to confirm the principle of aristocracy. In both, the effect was to strengthen absolutism in the political sovereign." Luther preached the doctrine of passive obedience and Calvin supported Secular right of rulers and strengthened the power of rulers of national states.

MARTIN LUTHER (1483-1546 A.D.)

Biography

The originator or reformation movement Martin was born at Thuringia in 1483 and died in 1546. He joined an Augustinian monastery and became professor or theology. His visit to Rome made him anti-Pope. It convinced him about the need of the reformation of the church. He cannot be regarded as the child of renaissance. To quote Adam's, "He was not by nature the heir of its spirit, nor all its tendencies. He accepted its principles and its methods because they were necessary to him."

Ideas of Martin Luther

Martin Luther opposed the indulgences for the forgiveness of sins which meant that the sins of an individual can be forgiven and entry into heaven can be assured on payment of certain sums of money to the church. Due to the opposition, Luther was ex-communicated by the church. This act forced him to break with the church and to take help of the princes against the church and the emperor who supported the church. Princes helped him because they saw that they could increase the wealth of the state by taking over possession of the church property themselves or vesting it in an eccelesiastical body under their control and subject to its authority.

Luther created a distinction between spiritual and secular authority. He exalted the national state against the universal notion of church. He preached the Christian duty of passive obedience to the established social and political order. He preached that the secular authority is divine in origin of the church and the ruler is responsible only to God. It thus led to royal absolutism. Luther was not a systematic thinker on any subject as he did possess the requisite degree of coolness and patience. On the contrary, he was hot and impatient. According to Sabine, "Luther left more than he considered and on the whole knew better what he did not believe than what he believed. All his books are....items in an excited controversy. He brought Protestant religion."

He started as the champion of the right of individual judgement and freedom of conscience. He supported the princes in killing peasant mercilessly during peasant's war. He declared that he would suffer a prince doing wrong than a people doing right. He preached to peasants the doctrine of passive obedience and sided with the prince because he depended on the support of princes. He preached that the clergymen are ordinary citizens and therefore the subject of laws and courts of state. In this way he strengthened the monarchy. The Calvinist John Knox had to preach the duty of obedience to the state authority and resistance to the authority of the state in the interest of religion.

Luther did not believe in the essential equality of men. He stood for civil inequality. His doctrine of personal conscience freed the individual from the domination of the church. The doctrine of passive obedience enhanced the power of the state. These were gained at the expense of the church as also of Holy Roman Empire. According to J.M. Figis, "The unity and universality and essential rightness of the sovereign territorial state, and the denial of every extraterritorial or independent communal form of life are Luther's lasting contribution of politics." Luther and Calvin brought Protestant Religion.

JOHN CALVIN

Biography

John Calvin was a French. He was the first reformer who created a detailed system of doctrine for the reformed church. According to Dunning, "While Luther was the theologian, Malevetrethon the philosopher, and Zuingli the politician, Calvin was distinctly the law giver of reformations." In his *Institutes of the Christian Religion,* he tried to give a guidance as to what was necessary to do in order to live a good Christian life according to the injunctions of the Bible.

Ideas of Calvin

Calvin thought that the church must have a system of Government and discipline suited to itself and distinct from the secular one. It must have a body of elders to lay down the rules of proper conduct with power to punish the unbeliever and to exclude the state from clerical affairs and to exclude secular affair from its organization.

Calvin based his conception of state on sovereignty of God and the Fall of Man. According to Dunning, "He believed that the authority of Magistrate is the most sacred and honourable of all things pertaining to mere moral life." He believed that the state should maintain peace and order and protect life, liberty and property. It should guard truth and exclude idolatry and blasphemy from society. Every Christian had a moral duty to help the state in these functions. He preached obedience to establish authority but showed preference to aristocracy. His ideas were theocratic in principle and aristocratic in operation. He supported the right of resistance to ruler, if the ruler contravened the orders of God. He believed in the natural rights of law, liberty and freedom of worship. Those doctrines helped resistance in Holland, Scotland and France. According to Bowle, "Calvin's doctrine is hostile to Empire and Papacy." Calvin and Luther ushered a new era of reason and brought Protestant religion. Indirectly, they helped national states with strong monarchs.

QUESTIONS FOR EXERCISE

1. What do you understand by reformation? How did it contribute to the growth of modern political thought.
2. Write a short essay on Reformation and its influence.
3. Briefly analyse the importance of Martin Luther.
4. Briefly narrate the life of Martin Luther and discuss his political ideas.
5. While Luther tended to subordinate church to state Calvin drew a clear boundary line between church and state and would not surrender the peculiar function of church to civil authority. (Gettle). Discuss.

20

Jean Bodin (1530-1596 A.D.)

Born in a middle class family, Jean Bodin studied law at Toulouse a university outstanding in jurisprudence. A Protestant, Bodin represented the Third Estate in the Estates General in 1576. He was closely attached to the brother of King Henry III. He served in the legal branch of the royal administration.

CONTEMPORARY CIRCUMSTANCES

During his time the unity of France was seriously threatened by religious conflict. Calvinist Protestantism made incessant progress in France during the sixteenth century. The attempt to eradicate it by force was met by resistance. The War of Religion continued for a generation. Opposition to royal absolutism failed in France because it was allied with a medieval particularism incompatible with centralized national government. Differences of religion were inextricably interwoven with political and economic issues. By the middle of the sixteenth century the centralized system of French monarchy had proved to be subject to serious abuses so that they threatened to cost the crown the support of the higher middle classes upon which its power really depended. Abuses of taxation, the delay and withholding of justice and the venality of royal executives led to a reaction. It was the great weakness of the Huguenots that they were in general on the side of local privilege and against the King. In the long run, however, the crown defeated both reaction and revolution. Effective centralization became possible towards the close of the sixteenth century under a prevailing theory of royal absolutism. It meant the triumph of national Catholicism against the pretensions of the papacy defended by Jesuits and the forces of particularism represented by Calvinists. In the massacre of St Bartholomew (Aug. 24, 1572) religious conflict showed its ghastly phase and the spirit of intransigence grew on both sides.

THE POLITIQUES

The religious divisions engendered by the Reformation were interwined with deep-seated social and economic issues which rendered reconciliation difficult. France needed moderation and compromise rather than fanaticism and radicalism. From the sixties on a group of administrators, lawyers and publicists calls *politiques* organised themselves against the forces of fanaticism. The politiques were first charged with putting practical politics above pure principles. The charge was not baseless. The Politiques were Catholic but unwilling to sacrifice the interests of the French state and nation to those of the Roman Catholic Church. Their attitude of toleration was born of expediency rather than philosophy. Michel de l'Hopital, Chancellor of France and an outstanding leader of politiques had urged as early as 1560 to get rid of "these devilish word, these names of party, faction and sedition—Lutheran, Huguenot, Papist, and had asserted that a man does not cease to be a citizen for being excommunicated. If possible, the Politiques preferred religious unity as a stepping stone to building national or political unity. They were convinced that the unity of France was endangered by violence and civil war. They were the first organised and conscious expression of a 'Third force' in the face of rival factions. They may be defined as a group of Catholics who advocated toleration of the heretics for the sake of peace and national unity.[1] They appealed to the Huguenots to co-operate in the States-General for the salvation of France. The state could flourish even if it recognised two religions. The state, if not independent of religion, was independent of any one religion. The unity of which men spoke of did never exist in fact. They questioned the claims of the Churches to an exclusive possession of saving truth. They doubted the validity of any attempted to fashion the state after the Scripture or bring it into real union with any particular Church. Such endeavours led only to confusion and misery. They saw in toleration the only means to putting an end to civil war and preventing the break-up of France.

The Politiques, however, were not agreed themselves on the form of constitution that suited most to the interest and unity of Frances. Their views about monarchy too diverged widely: Most of the Politiques clung to the tradition of a monarchy limited by custom or some theory of a constitutional monarchy resting on the Estates of the realm. While they rejected absolutism of the King, they saw no justification for rebellion against him. "No violence, no cruelty, no tyranny, no circumstance whatever, wrote a Huguenot, justifies a subject in rebellion." Such an attitude was called for in the conditions that existed.[2]

The actual basis of monarchy in France and of the belief in the theory of divine right of kings remained, however, utilitarian. A theory of sovereignty in which law and right became one and in which no right exists except that of the sovereign's creation was held by no one in the sixteenth century. Such a view was wholly incompatible with the theory of divine right

1. Allen, J.W., *A History, of Political Thought in the Sixteenth Century,* Metheun, p. 170.
2. *Ibid.,* p. 377.

of kings. Those who lost faith in the divinity of right and of kings believed in the absolute right of the political sovereign.[3]

WORK BY BODIN

Jean Bodin was the best-known theorist of the *Politiques.* He was "the most powerful of the French and perhaps of all political thinkers of the century."[4] His *Six Books on the State* express the desire for strong government that makes contented and secure citizenship possible. Bodin produced a number of books which reveal sparks of brilliance in his thought. His first work, the *Methodus,* published in 1566 presented the view that the method of studying history was a method for the study of all questions concerning the State or any state. "He had in his mind", says Allen, "a plan of the synthetic philosophy of the universe to be built up stage by stage in logical sequences, and the execution of the plan proved a life-long engagement." Bodin brought out the study of the fundamentally important economic conditions of France and in his *Reponse* in 1568. With this remarkable book Bodin is said to have founded political economy. Allen also considers it as "the most original of all his contributions to the study of society."[5] In this book he analysed the causes of the rise of prices that was afflicting Western Europe. He stated the disastrous consequences of depreciation of coinage, advocated freedom of trade and suggested that the relations of states were determined largely by economic factors. No one before him had seen so clearly the nature and importance of economic processes for the life of states or had dealt with them so definitely as a whole. But the *Methodus* and the *Reponse* were works propaedeutic to his *magnum opus,* the *Six Books of the Republic* which summed up and stated all the results of his studies and meditations. His personal connection with politics and the parties of the day became close only after he had completed his ideal construction of the State. While Bodin was a member of the Politique Party, he had not written his Republic, says Allen, to serve the interests of any mere group. But the Politiques were not factionalist but nationalist in their outlook. All parties found in the book something to accept as well as something to reject. Bodin earnestly desired to help regeneration of his country and his mind was full of practical reforms. If he was more of a jurist than of philosopher, he was far more a philosopher than a party politician.

As a member of the Estates, General Bodin opposed the proposal to start a war against the Huguenots. He upheld what he regarded as ancient rules of procedure involving the right of the Third Estate to refuse to be dictated to by the other Orders. He asserted against the King the inalienability of domain

3. *Ibid.*, p. 393.
4. *Ibid.*, p. 394.
5. *Ibid.*, p. 395.

property. His whole attitude was highly detached and honourable, but the success of his opposition lost him the favour of the King. In the *Methodus* Bodin had laid down that the knowledge of God without which no real knowledge is possible, is best attained through the study first of man and of human society. In 1580 he produced that strange and repulsive book, the *Demonomanie de Sorciers* to establish the fact of sorcery and witchcraft against the sceptics and to provide a practical manual of legal procedure for the use of magistrates. Bodin was convinced that man lives constantly under the influence of good and evil spiritual beings. Sorcery was a danger arising incidentally from man's constant relation to a world of spirits. It was only in the last year of his life that Bodin gave to the world his final conclusions about the universe in a work called the *Universae naturae Theatrum.* Bodin had thus written his Republic with a profound awareness about the mysterious character of human life. He has been called a mystic though he desired to explain everything. As for has vast erudition the following remarks of Allen may be noted: "His reading must have been prodigious. He knew Hebrew and Greek and was in some degree acquainted with German and Italian. He knew the Talmud and the orations of Demosthenes and Plutarch. He knew the Roman historian and had drunk deeply of Cicero. He had some knowledge of the medieval Scholastics, though he knew the jurists better. He knew something of the law and constitution of all European states."[6]

RELIGIOUS OUTLOOK

Jean Bodin had a deeply religious outlook though he was not sectarian. But it is difficult to say what his religion was before he wrote the *Heptaplomeres.* It is significant that he was described as a Jew in religion, as a Calvinist and as an atheist. In this book Bodin appeared neither a Catholic nor a Calvinist nor a Christian of any sort at all, and his religion was not that of the Jews. He secrutinised Catholicism and Calvinism and the central doctrines of Christianity and Judaism. He stressed that every man must seek God, for atheism makes nonsense of the universe. He emphasise intense religiousness of man. He studies state and law in manner of acquiring the knowledge of God which unifies all knowledge. He saw the State as one manifestation of God's will. But he wrote the Republic not only to expound the nature of political society and the laws that govern it but also to lay down general rules of policy and to advocate a number of definite and circumstantial reforms in France. His determination to be practical led him to confuse right with power. He wrote as though force could create what he called sovereignty. In the long run, however, power lay with reason and virtue and it ultimately expressed the will of God. "The natural, that is the inevitable, is always the just because the inevitable necessarily expresses that will."[7]

---

6. *Ibid.*, p. 399.
7. *Ibid.*, p. 402.

INFLUENCES ON BODIN

Bodin claimed to be original in his approach to the state: He was influenced by the Old Testament and Italian Platonism. But no thinker before *him,* he hold, saw the state rightly. "Aristotle had based his work altogether too narrowly; he had groped in darkness and found little. Plato and More had constructed ideal states without reference to history or circumstance. Machiavelli had committed the fundamental mistake of supposing that the state could exist without a moral basis and without religion. He thus claimed to be an explorer and a discoverer in country almost unknown."[8] In one respect Bodin was indebted to Machiavelli. He drew upon the Florentine in writing of war. What Machiavelli says about the weakness of foreign mercenaries, the uselessness of fortresses, the illusion the money is the sinews of war appears to have been taken *in toto* by Bodin. He embodied Machiavelli's views on the subject wholesale in the Republic.

HISTORICAL METHOD

In the *Methodus* Bodin advocated historical method for the study of politics and state. It is part of a larger study of truth about the world and God. History, according to him, should be studied in three aspects : divine, natural and human. While God is the alpha and omega of truth, the things divine, natural and human can be rightly understood only in a reverse order. Knowledge of God is attained most surely through the study of man and nature. But these studies cannot be entirely separated. Divine history connects through religion with human history. The understanding of human history must commence with and be based upon a knowledge of ourselves. All historic change reveals itself ultimately in the psychological change. From the knowledge of the elements of human nature one may proceed to the study of the family, the primary and natural form of human association. Thence one must proceed to grapple with the history of civil and political society. The primary use of the study of history is to pave the ground for that of politics. It is to help our understanding of the nature, structure and functions of the state. It also helps us to explain the revolutions, the profound and radical changes through which human societies pass. The perspective derived from the study of history enables us to determine the best form of government and law under specific conditions.

The study of history must be made primarily in terms of the systems of law that prevail in society. The nature and ethos of a people, its character and manners, the nature of society and the modes of co-operation that cooperate in it, the forms of government and the changes these undergo, all are found in the systems of law. What is needed is a comparative study of all the legal systems, with constant reference to that natural law which is fixed by a law eternal.

---

8. *Ibid.*

Bodin begins his study not with the factors that derive from man's will but with those that derive from nature and are permanent. These include geographic and climatic conditions that have played a great part in determining the character of peoples, their laws and institutions. But the study of these factors alone is not sufficient. Study of the origin of man and his society is also necessary. Moreover, there exists, a mysterious correlation of human history with planetary movements and positions and with numerical and proportional relations. These things still need much study. But the knowledge of history is the only sure thread to guide us in the labyrinth of politics. Bodin sees in history the fact of progress and cause for hope. He writes, we are more moral than Rome and we have more knowledge. He cites the compass and America and the printing press. The art of printing alone is a greater discovery than any made by the peoples of antiquity. With these convictions fortified by the study of economics Bodin embarked upon the examination of politics. He saw France as Machiavelli had seen Italy a country disorganised by factions, increasingly disordered. On all sides irreconcilable views were being expressed of the nature of French monarchy, of the nature of state authority and the duty of subjects. In his Republic Bodin tried to give reasoned answers to all the questions that were hotly debated in France. He believed that for the solution to the problems to be reached what was most needed was an agreement on the fundamentals. The foundation of the ordered state must be dug deep. Formulae had to be found of general application by which all vexed questions of duty could be decided. Bodin tried to show that the nature and extent of political authority was involved in the history, the structure and the end of political association. He strove to find some principle of order and unity that could reconcile liberty with authority, define political obligation and satisfy conscience and reason. A well-ordered state could be built up only on the recognition of such a principle Bodin found this principle in his doctrine of sovereignty.

NATURE OF THE STATE

Importance of Family

Bodin's treatment of state resembles that of Aristotle. He analyses state in terms of the units that make it. The units are the households or the families. The family, is natural because it arises out of necessity from the nature of man. It is the primary and the inevitable form of human association. Man cannot be conceived of outside its pale. In order to maintain itself in existence family includes property. Man is the master of the family due to superior moral ability. It is woman's moral and intellectual inferiority that makes of her the natural subject of man. While woman represents appetite, man represents reason. Emancipation of woman is fraught with dangerous consequences for herself and for society as a whole. The rightly constituted family involves a *droit gouvenment.* It constitutes the first and natural form of the state. The authority of the head of the family is the only natural form of authority.

Constituents of State

But the family is not state. The state is an association of families recognizing *'puissance souveraine'* (sovereign power). Civil society precedes the state. State came into existence when the families fell into natural groupings. It formed a union for common purposes, such as worship, war, trade etc. War and conquest played an important part in the formation of the state. The state in its full-fledged form comes into being when *'puissance souveraine'* is recognised and the families constitute the infrastructure of the same. In the obsence of sovereignty states cannot be deemed fully developed. Sovereignty is a necessary mark of a true or well-ordered state.

End of the State

The end of the state is not mere happiness. Due to the absurd conception of unity as the end of the state men have advocated communism which is inconsistent with a well-ordered state. Equality of goods and services is contrary to human nature. The state rests upon the recognition of natural inequality and private property. The end of the state is the realization of total good for the body and the mind. The state must be equipped with the means of subsistence, otherwise it cannot take care of its proper ends, viz. moral and intellectual values. In a well-ordered state, government must concerns itself with justice, defence and economics. Realization of virtues and values is the final end of the state. Thus like the Greeks Bodin too stressed the moral nature of the state as truer than economic or utilitarian. His view of the state as essentially a moral adoring was if inconsistent with his notion of sovereignty as the chief mark of a well-ordered stated. He denied that a state is created by force but he considered *puissance souveraine* as an indispensable feature of a state. He failed to maintain the distinction between the state and the republic, the latter being a well-ordered system. The Republic must be sovereign, a state as such may not be. A fully developed state or the Republic is marked not only be the possession of sovereignty but also by its dedication to the highest moral goals of life. In the words of Bodin, "The fully developed state is one that satisfies all the needs of man."[9] A well-ordered state must possess sovereignty but it must possess more. Sovereignty is necessary to it but it alone does not make it complete or well-ordered.

CONTRIBUTION TO POLITICAL THOUGHT

Jean Bodin was one of the most learned scholars of his age. His political philosophy embraced all the important aspects of political philosophy. He followed historical and analytical methods of study. He believed in synthesis of all human knowledge. He was more modern then even Machiavelli. In his outlook he said that private property should be respected under all circum-

9. *Ibid.*, p. 412.

stances. According to him, social instinct is the basis of the origin of the state. Only heads of the family should be citizens of state. Morality controls law, human conduct and behaviour.

1. Origin of State. About the origin of the state Bodin tried to adjust Aristotelean and social contract philosophies. Nature has given liberty to all individuals. It regulates the conduct of the people, society and the state. The state is not individualistic. It is a product of social instinct of the people. It brought man out of family life and gave birth to statehood. This instinct is also responsible for promotion of social institutions and the birth of political institutions. The state owed much to force not only in growth but in existence and development. Bodin agreed with Aristotle that the state is an organic association including the family. The state is superior to all associations. The sovereignty is vested in it and not in the associations. By virtue of its sovereignty the state has a right to keep all associations in their respective fields of activity and areas of operation. The state is an aggregate of all small social institutions. As such it is their supreme authority. The state has a soul as well as a body. The subjects have an inherent right to hold private property as a right which they enjoy even in the state of nature.

Criticisms

(i) *No Idea of Pre-Political Society.* Bodin has failed to give any clear ideas about the conditions of the people in pre-political society. Without this, his ideas about the origin of the state can neither properly be followed nor appreciated.

(ii) *Purpose of State.* Bodin is not clear about the ends and purposes of the state. He is rather indefinite about this. In the words of Sabine, "The state has a soul as well as a body, and the soul is higher thought the needs of the body are more immediately pressing. In reality Bodin never gave a clear account of these ends of the State."

(iii) *Right in Property.* Though Bodin has given some place to force in his ideas, he felt that the right to hold property is inherent. The people enjoyed that in the state of nature. This is very close to Locke's philosophy. "But to combine an inalienable right in the family with an absolute power in the state is an insuperable logical difficulty."

(iv) *Property in Family.* Bodin's concept of property can become a check on the sovereign authority of the state. It is therefore not clear form his theory as to why this inalienable right in the family with an absolute power in the state is an insuperable logical difficulty.

(v) *Origin of State.* Bodin has been criticised for his failure to define as to what natural needs gave rise to state over and above those supplied by the family and other groups.

2. Citizenship. Since family is the basic unit in a state, therefore heads of the families and not individuals ought to be the citizens. Both the citizens and the slaves, who lived in a state, ought to be under the control of the sovereign. The nobles should have more rights in the society than ordinary citizens. Nobility has a particular position both socially and politically. Bodin is personally against communism. The best citizens are those who obey the sovereign without any hesitation, grudge on grumble. Bodin differed from Aristotle when he said that citizen is not a participant but a subject of the sovereign. He did not favour the idea of extension of citizenship rights to women and retail traders. These categories of persons usually do not share their responsibility in the state affairs. It is the foremost duty of the citizens to obey the commands of their sovereign. His privileges are in his obedience. His rights are hidden in the proper performance of his duty. Maxey says, "But the duty of obedience is always implicit in the fact of citizenship, and is never obligated or decreased."

3. Law of Nature. Law of nature distinguished between the right and the wrong. Morality controls law and regulates human conduct and behaviour. But law of nature controls affairs of the nation. As such even a sovereign need not venture to violate the law of nature. The law of nature alone differentiates state from other societies. It raises the state to superior status. Bodin differs from Machiavelli when he says that the state should upkeep the morality of the subjects through a code based on law of nature.

4. Forms of Government. Bodin was the first political thinker of the 16th century who made an attempt to distinguish between on state and the government. The supreme power which concerned the nation is the deciding factor about the form of government. The division of sovereignty or its functions is another name of anarchy. The forms of government are monarchy, aristocracy and democracy. The government is different from a state. Thus there can be democratic government even though the head of state might be a monarch.

Bodin classified monarchy into royal monarchy, despotic monarchy and tyranny. If a monarch respects the laws made by him and acts according to law of nature then royal monarchy is the best form of government. The form of government is bound to protect the property and rights of subjects. Tyranny is the worst of all forms of government. Bodin, however, does not suggest the subjects to disobey a tyrant who has rightfully come on the throne. Democracy is another name of inefficiency and fickleness. Monarchy is most suited in times of difficulty, national emergency and for the territorial expansion of the state.

Criticism

The forms of government as given by Bodin were not elaborate and suited to modern conditions. It is too much to expect from a thinker of 16th century to classify Governments suited to 20th century. Credit goes to him that he attempted to distinguish between the state and the government at an early state of development of political philosophy. No doubt today monarchy cannot be considered as the best form of government but keeping in view the conditions of his times it was the only solution to many of the problems of his age and he was but to support monarchy. Some of the modern eminent political thinkers have gone to the extent of suggesting that his attempt at classifying the government is more important than even his enunciation or theory about sovereignty. Maxey has said, "He was one of the first to appreciate the distinctions between the states and he sharply criticised Aristotle for not having perceived and made the distinction more clearly."

5. Revolutions. Bodin was very clear that the society is always undergoing constant changes. A revolution could take place either slowly or violently. But in all circumstances it was bound to change not only laws and religion etc., but also location of the sovereignty. There is no revolution in technical sense, if the sovereignty remains unchanged. If the sovereignty has changed its location, there is real revolution. The revolution can come by human, natural or divine reasons. The human reasons for promoting revolution are unlimited freedom of expression, non-censorship of news and injudicious right to wear arms. Physical environments have great influence on the retardation or acceleration of revolutions. The social problems, more particularly of confiscation of property and religious intoleration are the general cause of revolution. The government should attempt at preservation of property and religious toleration. Unlike Plato Bodin believed in the equality of wealth and its distribution to the extent possible. Hereditary and typographic factors are also responsible for bringing revolution nearer and nearer.

Criticism

Though Bodin's concept of revolution is realist but it is not conceivable to say that change in the location of sovereignty is the only deciding factor whether a revolution had occurred or not. The laws are the very basis of nation. If they change violently and drastically then there is revolution, no matter the sovereignty has changed its location or not. A sovereign might concede the request of his powerful senate. He may respond to the will of the people by either amending the laws or drastically changing them, thus he brings no change in the location of sovereignty but only in the character of the laws. By introducing the idea that change in laws is immaterial in revolution, Bodin underestimated the value and importance of laws and their role in regulating human conduct and behaviour.

6. Practical Administration. Bodin was the first political thinker who discussed real problems in practical administration facing a government. Every sovereign must have a senate or counsel general or the magistrates as his adviser. Without their sovereign these advisers have no status. The advisers may be those entrusted with the issuing of commands or those responsible for their execution. The state shall protect the population as that was real wealth of a state. Bodin favoured the idea of economic equality. Strength of a state depends on its financial resources. As such a sound state must build up its finances. If properly exploited trade and land could be the best source of national income.

The states should conclude international treaties as these promoted proper understanding and goodwill. The government must always remain alive to the social and economic conditions of its subject.

In so far as his ideas about practical administration were concerned Bodin did not agree with Machiavelli. Here he advised the state to conclude treaties with his neighbouring states. With Machiavelli, he did not advise the sovereign to think that the neighbouring states were his would be enemies and he should remain on guard against them. He stressed the importance of treaties as a regulating force.

7. Religious Tolerance. According to Bodin religion includes a spirit of obedience and respect for laws. As such it should be treated with respect. There should be no religious intolerance. The sovereign should not use force for conversion of religion. Religious intolerance is bound to be followed by bloodshed. Therefore, there should not be religious intolerance. Religious factions are more successful in bringing about the changes than political factions. Respect for religion is an essential feature of sovereignty.

CONCEPT OF SOVEREIGNTY

The concept of sovereignty is Bodin's real contribution to political philosophy. He for the first time tries to give systematic and tangible idea of what sovereignty is and under what limitations it should work. He was of the view that sovereignty originally vested in the people who have an authority to exercise that but it has become customary for the people to delegate their authority to a single person, called sovereign who also exercises that.

Bodin defined sovereignty as "supreme power over citizens and subjects, unrestrained by law". He called it a perpetual power as distinguished from any power that is limited to a specific period of time. It is an unlimited power of the state for making law for itself. The sovereign must exercise the right to make peace and war, to appoint magistrates, to decide all causes in the last resort and to grant pardons. Bodin does not quite separate the conception of sovereignty from the idea of a group of legal prerogatives. Mere customary law can derive authority only from the sanction of the Sovereign. It is unrestrained by law because the sovereign is the source of law. The sovereign cannot bind himself or his successors. He cannot be made legally accountable to his subjects. The law of the land is simply the sovereign's command. Accordingly any limitation on the sovereign's power to command can be only extra-legal. The power to give laws to citizens collectively and severally, without the consent of a superior, an equal, or an inferior is the primary attribute of sovereignty. The other attributes such as the power to declare war and treat for peace, to commission magistrate, to act as a court of last resort, to coin money and to tax—are consequences of the sovereign's position as legal head of the state. Enactment can change custom, not custom enactment.

Different Forms of Sovereignty

Different forms of government can vary only in the location of the power. In a monarchy sovereignty resides in the King and the function of the Estates is advisory only. If the King is bound by the advice tendered by the assembly or by the act of the Estates, then government is an aristocracy and sovereignty resides in the assembly. And, if the final power of decision rests with some sort of popular body, then government is democratic. Bodin's treatment of sovereignty postulates a clear-cut distinction between state and government. The state consists in the possession of sovereign power while the government consists of the apparatus through which such power is exercised. A monarchy may delegate his power widely and govern popularly while a democracy may govern despotically.

Function of Sovereignty

Sovereignty has its mark upon the entire body of the state including its subordinate organs: The function of Parliament is advisory in a monarchy. The power exercised by the magistrates is one delegated by the sovereign. All the corporate bodies which exist in the state owe their powers and privileges to the Sovereign. The powers of the corporations are constructively derived from the state even if they rest upon ancient usage and not upon charter or statute. Bodin wanted to represent the King of France as the head of the entire body-politic, and to make a foot-hold for the rights of the monarchy against all the survivors of the feudal age. He treated the estates as merely one of the corporations which the sovereign permit along with trading companies and eccelesiastical bodies.

Nature of Sovereignty

Sovereignty is a recognised and unlimited authority to make law. However it may have arisen, it is an indivisible power. There is no room for mixed government or separation of power. Often sovereignty is a mere legal fact. The mere existence of law implied the existence of a sovereign. Law must be conceived as command and command is an act of will. Expression of will must be single or there is no command. Once a sovereign will is recognised, its action cannot be limited by law. At the same time, the absolute law-making power which belongs to the community and is actualized in some legal sovereign cannot be a mere legal fact. It is mere legal fiction; for whatever law may say, no ruler can actually do whatever he pleases. The question with Bodin is never really one of legal fact but essentially a question of the obligation to obey.[10]

10. *Ibid.*, p. 414.

Bodin seems to asserts the existence of an unlimited authority in all republics to which all owe obedience as a duty. But he gives no answer as a whence this authority is derived and on what it is based. He viewed sovereignty to vest in recognition. He never suggested that he conceived of sovereignty as capable of existing unrecognized. He thought of this recognition now as creating the state, now simply as highly desirable and now connected with the conception of the true end of the state or even as necessary in view of that end. But he did not make it clear how this recognition originated or even why it is desirable.

Bodin also speaks of sovereignty as being established or appropriated by force; but sovereignty that is either inherent or necessary is not created by force in any sense, even though an actual sovereign may be. He also speaks of sovereignty as being conferred. But this is a mere transference of legal sovereignty from one hand to another. The people that confers it must, at least, have possessed it.

Bodin seems to hold that legal sovereignty must be the formal expression of a sovereignty inherent in the nature of a human association and determined by its ends. If the end is the realization of all possible good, if therefore, the government should have power to control all relations, the recognition of a sovereignty unlimited in law is a necessity. It is the symbol of the legality of the state. It is above other laws except those which it which it imposes upon itself of its own. Bodin defines sovereignty as the "Supreme power over citizens and subjects unrestrained by the law." Maxey says, "Living in a period of political chaos, and conceding that the religious and other disturbances of the time were attributable in the last analysis to the incompetence of political authority, Bodin naturally arrived at a view of the state which exalts unity and power."

Characteristics of Sovereignty

1. Perpetual. According to Bodin sovereignty has certain characteristics. It is perpetual and not meant for any specific period.

2. Inalienable. The sovereign cannot delegate this authority or power to an authority either without or within the state.

3. Unrestrained. The sovereign is the source of law and as such sovereignty is unrestrained by law. The laws of the land are under command of sovereign. As such to think of any legal bindings on this account is simply extra legal. By virtue of his legal authority the sovereign is competent to impose and collect taxes. The sovereign is not bound by his advisers. Advise rendered by them is simply a request. It is purely at the discretion of the sovereign either to accept that or not.

4. Supreme Authority. The sovereign is the head of the state and as such the head of all corporate associations because these corporate bodies exist only at the will of the state. By declaring that sovereign was supreme authority in the state, Bodin gave a rude shock to the claim of papacy for being a partner in supremacy. Sovereignty is the highest will that can exist in the human society. Maxey says, "It is the unity which stands above all diversity in human society, the centripetal force which exceeds any countervailing centrifugal forces."

5. Limitations of the Sovereignty. Bodin did not plead that the sovereign authority was unlimited and unrestricted. Under the following restrictions it was limited :

(i) *Laws of God and Nature.* The sovereign, though being the head of the state and foundation of law was not above all kinds of laws. He must obey the laws of God and Nature, which are above all other laws and product of right reasons of mankind and hence unquestionable and above everything else Sabine says, "For him as for all his contemporaries, the law of nature stands above human law, and sets certain unchangeable standards of right; it is the observance of this law that distinguished the true state from mere effective violence."

(ii) *No penalty for violation by Sovereign.* Bodin, however, has not suggested any penalty for a sovereign who violated the laws of nature, because he felt that for such violations he was accountable only to God alone and did to his subjects.

(iii) *Honour the Commitments.* The Sovereign is supposed to make certain promises at the time of his coronation. It is not legally challengeable in the court of law, yet morally he is bound to honour those commitments.

(iv) *Respect for property.* The sovereign must respect the institution of private property. He must not confiscate it without very valid reasons. The property is a social institution. Sovereignty is political rather than social. Both should not be intermingled.

(v) *Constitution.* The state is bound by certain laws called the constitution of the state. These are the basis for the every existence of the state. Once the sovereign has agreed and has given royal assent to the constitution he is bound to respect the constitution. Hence a sovereign should not defy constitution.

6. Rights of the Sovereignty

(i) *Dictation.* According to Bodin the for most right of the sovereign is to dictate and to expect obedience from the subjects.

(ii) *Imposition of Taxes.* The sovereign has a right to impose taxes individually as well as collectively and to make arrangements for their collection.

(iii) *Coining Currency.* The sovereign has a right to coin money for proper regulation of state transactions.

(iv) *Appointments.* The state has the right of making appointments. A sovereign must appoint all categories of officers in the state both for his own interest and in the interest of the state and the individuals.

CONFUSIONS IN THE THEORY OF SOVEREIGNTY

1. Sovereignty or Recognised Power. According to Bodin there must be recognised legal sovereign with unlimited powers in every state. It is not an adequate solution to the problems of the discovers of the state to say that sovereignty must be or is a recognized power. Bodin seems to think that the conception of legally complete sovereignty at once explains and justifies political society. It ensures order and unity, defines the duty of citizens and answers all questions. It has existed for long both in law and in fact. But Bodin is more concerned to argue that *it must exist,* because it is implied in the very notion of man-made law and because it alone explains political society. The long continuance of political society proves to Bodin that its existence accords with the will of God. As it is the will of God than man should realise good in political society, the sovereign prince may even be called God's vicar. But the reference to God seems to be a formality of the time in which he lived. His Prince is not like Barclay's who is sovereign by virtue of a special divine commission. Sovereignty is for him always a human creation. It arises from the nature of man and from human needs and aspirations.

2. Limited Sovereignty. "You can eliminate from Bodin's Republic all his references to God and to Prince as a lieutenant of God and yet the whole structure remains intact. But if you eliminate God from the system of Barclay his whole structure collapses."[11]

Bodin does not appear to conceive of sovereignty as necessarily involving a strictly unlimited power, even in law. His sovereign is limited in various ways: He is limited by natural law by which he is bound. He is also restrained by the fundamental laws of the realm, that is, by the *leges imperii.* He is bound to respect the sanctity of property and the family which together from the foundations of the state.

3. Restrictions Over the Sovereign. Bodin defines sovereignty as unlimited power to make law or to command, but the exercise of sovereign power in his state is by no means unlimited, for he allows a number of restrictions over the sovereign as he actually governs the state. Thus he never doubts that the sovereign is bound by the law of God and the law of nature. While he defines law as a sheer act of the sovereign's will, he never supposes that the sovereign could make law by mere fiat. The law of nature stands above human law and creates certain unchangeable standards of right. It is the observance of this right that distinguishes the true state from mere effective violence. There

---

11. *Ibid.*, pp. 415-16.

is, no doubt, no way to make the sovereign legally liable for violating the law of nature. Even so, natural law does impose some real disabilities on him. It requires the keeping of agreements and respect for private property. The sovereign's agreements may involve political obligations towards his subjects or towards other sovereign, and in such cases he is bound in fact if not in law It is difficult for him to keep these obligations of the sovereign exclusively on a moral plane and so apart from legal and political obligations. Bodin thus has no doubt what the magistrate will do when the sovereign commands something contrary to law. In cases of flagrant violations of natural law by the sovereign he will be or ought to be disobeyed. "Law is at once the with of the sovereign and the expression of eternal justice, and the two may be in conflict.[12]

4. Fidelity to Constitutional Law. Another confusion in Bodin's theory of sovereignty arises from his fidelity to the constitutional law of France. All his natural inclinations both as a lawyer and a moralist, were on the side of constitutional government and respect for ancient usages and practices of the realm. There were certain things which the King of France could not lawfully do. He could not change or modify the law of succession called the Salic Law and could not alienate any part of the public domain. At the same time, Bodin views the French King to be sovereign in full sense of the term. In fact king was, the example par excellence of a sovereign. Bodin admits the existence of a peculiar set of laws which are necessarily connected with the exercise of sovereignty itself and which even the sovereign cannot tough or change, namely the *leges imperii,* implying apparently that sovereignty itself would vanish with their violation. Thus, the sovereign is at once the source of law and the subject of certain fundamental constitutional laws which he has not made and cannot change.

5. Confused Attitude. Confusions in Bodin's theory of sovereignty arise from his confused attitude towards the realities of the French political system and towards sovereignty itself. He is not clear whether sovereignty is only legal or also factual. In fact, he was seeking to increase and consolidate the powers of the crown which was necessary under the circumstances. But as a convinced constitutionalist he was bent upon saving and perpetuating the ancient institutions of the realm. The idea behind the *leges imperii* was that except as an element of the realm the crown would have neither existence nor power. The idea behind the definition of sovereignty was that the crown is the chief executive, *pars principans,* of the realm. Bodin, is not clear who or what is more important the sovereign or the state: Sabine rightly observes, "For, if sovereignty means essentially the supremacy of the prince, then the political community has no existence except by virtue of the relation between the prince and his subjects, and it is impossible that the realm should have laws of its own

12. Sabine, G.H., *op.cit.,* p. 348.

which the prince cannot change. . . On the other hand, if the state is a political community having laws and a constitution of its own, it is impossible that the sovereign should be identified with the prince."[13]

6. Need of a Powerful King. In fact Bodin wanted a powerful king who could command the allegiance of the nation and keep it united and strong. Only a visible king, seen as a Vicar of God could hold the French nation together and make it strong. But a visible, really sovereign the king is not easy to insert into a system of juristic concepts.

7. Defective Method. The confusion is also due to the method of study aimed at building a synthetic, all comprehensive philosophy: It was a method that sought to combine history with philosophy, factual evolution with logical analysis. In the perspective of history, the realm of France, the political community must be taken as a single social organism, continuous and self-identical through an indefinitely long series of gradual changes. But from the point of view of analysis it would be equally necessary to make a cross-section through the historical stream and consider the formal relation between the part of the legal constitution. No analysis, Sabine remarks, would fit all stages of the story history, and for this reason the history would violate the canons of any formal analysis.

8. Views About Private Property. Another confusion in Bodin's theory of sovereignty arises from his view about private property: He considered private property an inviolable right even if it is based only upon a law of nature. He made it so sacred that the sovereign cannot touch it without the owner's consent. Taxation for him required the assent of the estates though he called it only advisory in capacity.

9. View of State. The confusion springs equally from his view of state and the definition he attempts of it. The right of property is an indefeasible attribute, a necessary concomitant, of the family, or its very basis, and the family is the unit existing independently and naturally out of which the state has arisen. Property is to the family what family is to the state: The institutions are inextricable interwoven. A well orders stated, however, requires a sovereign whose legal power is absolute. Bodin fails to combine the indefeasible rights of the family with the unlimited legislative power of the sovereign. The family is essential to the state as property is essential to the family; but the power to tax is the power to destroy. The state cannot process the power to destroy its own members. Bodin's thought thus breaks in two at the point where the theory of the family ought to be joined to the theory of the state.[14]

---

13. *Ibid.*, p. 346.
14. *Ibid.*, p. 380.

SOVEREIGNTY AND REVOLUTION

Meaning of Revolution

In his Republic Bodin also examined the causes and prevention of revolutions. He defined revolution as a displacement of sovereignty. A revolution does not occur so long as sovereignty resides in it place. Bodin discussed various causes of revolution, of various degrees of importance. His analysis of the means of prevention of revolution led him to cover every branch of administration and to display high political acumen and wisdom. The king, he held, should not ally himself with any faction but should follow a policy of conciliation, using repression cautiously and only where there is sure chance of success. He also made a firm defence of religious toleration which he treated rather as a policy than principle.

Theory of climate

The examination of revolutions lead Bodin to the more general subject of the relation of the physical environment to national characteristics. Here comes his theory of climate in which he anticipated Montesquieu. The peoples of the north, he said are large and physically vigorous but slow of movement and of mind. Southerners are slight of build, vivacious in manner and surpass in acumen and ingenuity. For political purposes, the middle region is superior where the two sets of qualities are mingled. This is shown by the fact that the great states as well as the science of politics have originated there.

Obligation of the Sovereign

Bodin also considered the obligation of the sovereign to keep faith in treaties and alliances. Here he deplored the growing belief that princes are not bound by promises to their own disadvantage--an implied criticism of Machiavelli. He revealed a growing sense of the need for restraining absolute sovereigns in their international dealings, a need which half a century later was stressed by Grotius in his attempt to formulate international law. Bodin also considered the finances of the state, its sources of revenue and desirability of the various forms of taxation. He also advocated revival of the Roman censorship both as a means of obtaining exact information about the resources of the kingdom and as one of moral purification. However, in the heart of this work, Bodin showed the superiority of kingship to other forms of government. He regarded a state governed by a sovereign king as the only well-ordered state. He also showed that heredity and even the Salic Law are founded not only in custom but in reason. Despite his admission that sovereignty may he vested in an aristocracy or in the people, he was convinced that in practice that leads to anarchy and to the ruin of subjects as well as rulers. The only well-ordered state is one in which sovereignty is undivided because it resides in a single person. But Bodin is never quite clear whether sovereignty is a quality which it is desirable for the state to possess but which actual states sometimes lack, or whether it is a quality which every state must of necessity possess. He seemed to defend the theory as if it were a universal logical necessity. At the same time he also believed that many or perhaps most states do not rise to the level of a well-ordered monarchy in which alone true sovereignty is possible. He, thus failed to separate the necessary from the desirable. Sabine comments, "Bodin states what was really a programme of reform under the guise of a pronouncement of eternal truth."[15]

Taxation and Sovereignty

It has been maintained that in giving the Estates power to freely grant or refuse taxation. Bodin took away the sovereignty he has given and handed it over to the Estates. It has been argued by A. Franck that his system really places sovereignty with a "people" and that he must have conceived the monarchy of France as a constitutional monarchy. Bodin's sovereignty really belongs, to the community itself. It is individual, perpetual and unconditioned, and the actual legal sovereign is a delegate who does not possess absolute sovereignty, even though no one may either command or punish him. But this view hardly expresses the truth of the matter: No doubt, Bodin held that sovereignty might be conferred by the people and that it originally belonged to them. But once conferred it is conferred for ever. Allen rightly says, "Sovereignty may be conceived, as the power of the state but Bodin thought of it always as power actualized in a legal Sovereign."[16] Essentially it is a power of making law. Such power according to Bodin, cannot be logically conceived as divided or as legally limited or conditioned. Nowhere in his Republic he indicated that he thought of the King of France as not in any way possessing sovereignty or of the Estates as having share in the same. Even so, the Prince has no arbitrary power to levy taxation because such power will be inconsistent with the purposes for which sovereignty exists or with the existence of the state itself. A family is the foundation of the state and property that of the family, to say that the Sovereign is not bound to respect property amounts to saying that he is not bound to respect the state itself. As Allen has remarked. "The necessity, for the Prince, of obtaining a grant before levying direct taxes on property is not derived from any sort of sovereignty of the people but simply from the fact that to allow the Sovereign the power to destroy the state is inconsistent with the ends for which sovereignty exists. Sovereignty must be conceived as absolute and legally unlimited in relation to the ends for which the State exists: It cannot rationally be so conceived except in reference to those ends".[17] But Bodin is no advocate of absolute sovereignty. He

15. *Ibid.*, p. 352.

16. Allen, J.W., *op. cit.*, p. 421.

17. *Ibid.*

thought of it as legally limited only by such *leges imperii* as were logically involved in the position assigned to an actual Sovereign. The Sovereign exist only to subserve the ends for which the state exists, and only in relation to those ends can it be conceived as existing at all. He is limited by the law of nature which expresses itself in the common consciousness of right and wrong. Right is something clearly known to all men. The Sovereign does not create it, and cannot. A Sovereign creating right would be an atheistic blasphemy to Bodin. He holds it right to obey the Sovereign in view of the ends for which sovereignty exists, but wrong to obey him if he commands injustice. Bodin's originality in the theory of sovereignty thus consists in the fact that he did not connect it specifically and directly with the will of God, and that it was a creation of man in the only sense in which man can create. It came into existence because the ends and the nature of human association logically implied its existence.

Two Notions of Sovereignty

But Bodin's mind seems to waver between the notion of legal sovereignty as complete and indivisible and the conception of sovereignty as necessarily limited by the nature and purposes of the state. No state can be well-ordered in which the Sovereign does not recognise limits to his right.

Bodin's Real Contribution

Bodin's theory of sovereignty must be viewed in the wider context formed by influences coming from different directions and springs including customary usage, natural law, law of God, institutions of private property and the family, climate and the basic laws of the realm called *leges imperii*. Allen has rightly said that Bodin's claim to special honour rests primarily on the fact that he, almost alone among the sixteenth century thinkers, made an honest effort to construct a comprehensive theory of political society. His originality, as Plamenatz points out, consists in a new way of looking at what men were already familiar with; the great monarchies of the West.[18] To explain these monarchies he put forward new ideas and enabled his contemporaries to see familiar things with fresh eyes. "He was less narrow, more elaborate and more moderate, more imaginative and more adequate in his views than anyone else moved to write about politics by the spectacle of a France in the throes of civil war." Further, as Sabine points out, Bodin conceived his political philosophy more broadly and executed it more impressively than any other thinker of the sixteenth century.[19]

A Janus-faced thinker Bodin looks in two directions, back into the past and forward into the future, laying the foundation, on the one hand for empirical social study with his theory of climate and on the other asking

18. Plamenatz, J., *Man and Society*, Vol. I, p. 115

19. G.H. Sabine, *op. cit.*, p. 352.

rulers to study astrology and medieval lore. He pointed ahead to the completely lay notion of sovereignty as a centre of force for administering the state and back to the conception of the ruler as God's Vicar, commissioned to carry out divine law on the earth.[20] Again, Bodin saw two things very clearly: one that the state is a natural instrument, and second, that there is a rational order in the universe superior to any man's will to which therefore he will ought to correspond.

Bodin, however, failed to connect his theory of sovereignty with his conception of the ends of the state and to adjust both to his theory of climate. He failed to account for the existence of sovereignty and to show how groups of families coalesce into a state by the recognition of it. He did not show in what sense sovereignty is the power of the state as distinguished from the power of a legal sovereign. He did not draw his constitutionalism and centralized power together. He accepted natural law which is the basis of the state structure as a tradition but did not analyse it. The ends of a well-ordered state, the nature of the subjects' obligation to obey and the relation between the state and its constituent families have not been fully analysed and explained. Bodin could not develop his theory of sovereignty in terms of power logically and systematically— a task which was later accomplished by Hobbes. He also could not effect the modernization and secularization of the ancient theory of natural law as an ethical foundation of political power, which was subsequently done by Grotius and Locke. Thus Sabine has rightly said, "The theory of sovereignty, though Bodin's statement of it was the clearest given in the sixteenth century, floats in the air, a feat of definition rather than explanation.[21] As for the state, Bodin's theory of it has been called "a grand edifice in the very latest Gothic, built up on disjointed and rotten foundations."[22]

Jean Bodin, however, paved the way for the empirical and sociological study of politics two centuries later. He prepared the ground for the coming not only of Hobbes and Locke but of Monstesquieu. He enunciated his concept of sovereignty and state in the sociological context of France. If Machiavelli suggested the need for a strong and centralised state, Bodin articulated it in his theory of sovereignty. And whereas Machiavelli made power an end *per se*, Bodin also looked at the ends which power ought to serve.

BODIN AND MACHIAVELLI

1. Limited Sovereignty. Bodin's greatest contribution to the history of political thought was his concept of sovereignty. Prior to him Machiavelli too

---

20. W.T. Jones, *Masters of Political Thought,* Vol. II, pp. 83-84.
21. G.H. Sabine, op. cit., p. 352.
22. J.W. Allen, op. cit., p. 444.

had given such a concept in his *The Prince.* Machiavelli protrayed his ideal prince as an over-lord over his subjects. His prince was not bound by any considerations whatsoever except sentiments for the love of the state. But Bodin gave sovereignty a different twist. He did not make his sovereign an unlimited authority. He bound him with certain limitations which were in the nature of making. The sovereign should be more responsive to the public opinion. Whereas Machiavelli could not shatter absolutism of medieval ages Bodin surpassed him by attaching public sentiments with sovereignty. He stressed that the people had as share in sovereignty which was absolutely a modern concept. He also surpassed Machiavelli in modernism in so far as his ideas about the respect of international treaties is concerned. Machiavelli remained practically medieval when he said that for a sovereign treaties were simply papers of no importance and that he should not care for them at all and should act in a fashion which suited his convenience. In so far as Bodin was concerned he believed that treaties executed by a sovereign, with the neighbouring states, were sacred documents. Every state and sovereign is bound to honour such documents once executed. This subsequently became the basis of international law for conducting the business of the state credit, for which does not go to Machiavelli but only to Bodin.

2. Distinction between State and Government. Bodin clearly differentiated and distinguished between the state and the government. Before him none, not even Machiavelli, had thought of separating the two. This was due to their still began wedded to Medievalism in which the king was state. Bodin went a step ahead of Machiavelli in this regard.

3. Natural Law as Scientific Political Theory. Bodin revised traditional concept of natural law which was a check on the authority of the sovereign. For the first time, Bodin gave it a scientific character. According to Sabine, "So successful was it that natural law became in the estimation of seventeenth and eighteenth centuries, the valid scientific form of political theory." The conception of natural law, as expounded by Bodin, was subsequently developed by Grotius and Locke in their political philosophies.

4. Scientific Political Theory. According to Dunning, "Bodin brought back political theory to the form and method from which it has gone far astray with Aristotle, and gave it again the externals, at least, of a science."

5. Ethics and Politics. Machiavelli maintained that morality had no place in the framework of the state. He divorced ethics from politics. This was no doubt a great achievement but who can deny that an immoral state can have only immoral citizens, who are not citizens at all. Like a modern thinker Bodin realised that religion and morality have their own place in social and political set up and their complete divorce from each other will be ruinous to all. He surpassed Machiavelli when he said that both should be separated from each other but not divorced.

6. Means and Ends. Bodin can claim to be more original than Machiavelli when he says that power is not an end in itself but on the other hand Machiavelli maintained that means justify the end and the principles of morality are based on consideration for achieving ends. We realised that means which are basic for achieving ends, are attached more importance than the ends. If the foundations are not properly laid the superstructure is bound to be wrong. Bodin was therefore more modern when he said that power was simply a means to an end and not an end itself.

7. Right to Protection. Bodin had more modern outlook than Machiavelli in his idea about the protection of private property and advised his Prince that he should not confiscate the property of his subjects. But for him property was the handmaid of sovereign's will who could confiscate it, it need be. But Bodin made it a fundamental right, which is quite a modern idea. He believed that family's right to hold property and sovereign's right to seize that were opposite to each other. The sovereign should not seize property which every family has legitimate right to own.

APPRECIATIONS

We may conclude that Bodin was more modern in his thinking than Machiavelli and deserved higher place than what has usually been assigned to him today. He was responsible for preaching religious tolerance in those days of intolerance. Credit goes to him for giving political science a new outlook both in method and approach, which was once given by Aristotle. Following are some appreciations:

1. Murry. "He was a scholar who strove to be a thinker; a lawyer who was interested in the origin of legal rules as the rulers in themselves; and a man of the world who brought all the resources of shrewd common sense to the investigation of political problems; a sociologist who neither dealt in names nor played with words."

2. Maxey. "Jean Bodin belongs to immortals. In an age of bigotry and fanaticism he walked by the steady light of reason; in an age of distraction and dissension he exalted unity and order; in an age of irrational creeds he was a believer in none, but an unrelenting foe of intolerence; in an age of intellectual sterility he was an enlightened and independent thinker animated by the true spirit of philosophy."

3. Sabine. "Despite many confusions in his thought Bodin's political philosophy was a work of no light influence."

4. Allen. "Bodin's claim to special honour rests primarily on the fact that almost alone in the 16th century he made an honest effort to construct a comparative theory of political society."

QUESTIONS FOR EXERCISE

1. "Bodin does not solve the problem of sovereignty. But in a sense, it is precisely the failure which makes his theory interesting and illuminating." Jones. Discuss.
2. "I say first mark of sovereign prince is the power of giving laws to all the people in general or to each one is particular—with out consent of any besides himself." Comment.
3. Bodin's statement of the principle of sovereignty is generally agreed to be the most important part of his political philosophy. Discuss.
4. "Bodin's statement of the principles of sovereignty is generally agreed to be the most important of his political philosophies." Explain and discuss.
5. "Sovereignty is the supreme power over citizens and subjects unrestrained by law." Comment.
6. "As a prince is bound by no laws of his predecessors, much less he is bound by his own laws." Comment.
7. "It has been said of Bodin that he eliminated the mandate of God which theory of Divine Rights offered as a foundation of king's authority but that he did not fill the gap with the natural explanation." How far do you agree with this statement? Give reasons for your answer.
8. "The principal mark of sovereign majority and absolute power is the right to impose laws generally on the subjects regardless of their consent." (Bodin). Comment.
9. "Sovereignty of Bodin is a recognised and unlimited authority to make law." Discuss.
10. "Bodin had created to be medieval without being modern." Explain this statement, and bring out the defects of his theory of sovereignty.
11. "Sovereignty is unrestrained by law." (Bodin). Comment.
12. "The forerunner of Monstequieu, Bodin was also successor of Aristotle and also of Machiavelli." Discuss.
13. "Bodin's political philosophy was a singular mixture of the old and the new as all philosophical thought in the 16th century was." Discuss.

21
Hugo Grotius (1583-1645 A.D.)

Hugo Grotius was the son of an eminent lawyer in Holland. He showed himself as an intellectual giant from his early age. In the age of sixteen he got the degree of doctor of laws from Leydon University and started practice of law. At the age of 30, he was appointed a magistrate in Rotterdam and took part in the controversy of Arminianism and Gornarism. Prince Maurice of Orange sided with Gomarism and charged Grotius for sedition and sentenced him to life imprisonment. From jail, he made a dramatic escape, thanks to the courage and ingenuity of his wife. He spent the remaining days of his life in exile and poverty. It was during his exile that he wrote his famous book about international law "*The law of war and peace.*"

Though Grotius was a versatile genius and cultivated many fields of learning like history, classics, poetry, drama and theology but his fame rests on his achievement in the field of international jurisprudence and on his monumental work,*The law of war and peace,* which is unanimously regarded as the first comprehensive authoritative commentary on the practices that prevailed in the sphere of international relations during those days. It laid the foundation of modern law of nations.

Grotius was profoundly influenced by the unstable conditions of his times. He witnessed gun powder plot of England of 1605, assassination of Henry IV of France, in 1610 thirty years war of Europe in which Catholic league and Protestant confederation mercilessly fought with one another. He believed in peace and religious toleration. He desired peace in the interest of Christianity and the comity of European nations. So he wrote his most important treatise "*De Jure Beeli Pacis.*"

PRECURSORS OF GROTIUS

Spanish Jurist Surcze wrote before Hugo Grotius, Protestant writer Wincler reduced the law of nature into a well defined code of 21 articles. Melanchthom held that the contents of the law of nature were to be found in right reason. Grotius credit to the formation of the International law is due to the fact he coordinated and codified what existed before him. To quote Hearn

Shaw, *De Jure Belli Pacis* "summed up the accepted wisdom of the ancients and applied it to the unprecedent conditions of Renaissence and reformation world. It epitomised all that had been written by Stoic philosophers, Roman lawyers, Scholastic theologians and Justinian Jesuits concerning the law of nature and the law of Nations and combined it into a solid foundation for an incalculably valuable superstructure of international morality and customs."

CONTENTS OF DE JURE BELLI PACIS

De Jure Belli Pacis represents the creation of liberal mind against the inhumanities of 36 years war. Shaw said, "I saw prevailing throughout Christian world, a licence in making war, recourse being heart to arm for slight reasons or for no reason and when human laws were lost; just as men are henceforth authorised to commit all crimes without restraint...he set out, to discover a philosophy that would provide a standard for the conduct of war in terms of social and earthly objectives."

'*De Jure Belli Pacis*' contains a dedication to Louis XIII of France, a Prolegomena and three books. In book I Grotius treats war in general and maintains that war can be just. Book II deals with just grounds of war. Book III is the most important of all the three, discusses the laws of war embodying amoral and customary limits which the belligerants must not cross. His political philosophy, however, is to be found mainly in book I. It is based on the law of nature, the law of nations and the doctrine of sovereignty.

If Bodin laid the foundation of national sovereignty, Hugo Grotius laid the foundation of the international sovereignty. If Bodin propounded the sovereignty as the indispensable foundation of peace and progress in a well ordered state, Hugo Grotius formulated the concept of international order of which all the independent nations are members. He held that people of world form a community with a common law in force in regard to war and conduct of war. His great book, '*The war and peace*' was designed to prove his thesis, in which he became the founder of international law and international jurisprudence. He could not stop war but regulated the struggle between nations. He laid the foundation of international morality and of international law.

CONTRIBUTION TO POLITICAL THOUGHT

Grotius saw a necessary ingredient of social existence. Following the footsteps of Aristotle that man by nature is a social animal. He believed that man and society are so interlinked that one cannot exist without the other. According to him people need some common regulatory measures. There should be some system of law and justice in their common relations. For a higher type of human society there is greater need of law and justice because human society is the product of reason. Grotius believed that wherever there is social life there is reason and natural law.

Definition of Jus Naturale

Grotius classified all law as *Jus Naturale,* i.e. based on reason and volition, i.e., based on will. He called the law of nature *Jus Naturale*. He defined it as "the dictate of right reason," indicating that any act, from its argument and disargument with the rational nature, has in it moral turpitude or moral necessity.

Grotius conceded that there is a body of universal law, the law of nature or right reason which is equally applied to all people and is absolute as supreme reason itself. He believed that the law of nature is unchangeable. He formulated his conception of the law of nature on the basis of right and justice embodied in the essential, universal and unchangeable human nature. He rejected the idea that all law, justice and rights have their basis in utility or expediency. Human nature and reason constitute the original foundation of all laws. Civil law is rooted in the law of nature. There were certain principles of universal recognition. Representing the necessary deduction from the principles of nature, they are under the category of law of nature. Representing the deliberate choice of all men they belong to the law of nations.

Defining natural law Grotius said "The law of nature is, a dictate of right reason which point out that an act according to it is or is not in conformity with rational nature, has in it a quality of moral baseness or moral necessity and that in consequence such an act is either forbidden or enjoyed by the author of nature, i.e. God."

Distinctions of Just Naturale

Regarding distinction with voluntary laws, Grotius says, "The distinction between these kinds of law is not to the drawn from the testimonies themselves....but from the character of the nature. For whatever cannot be deducted from certain principles by a sure process of reasoning and yet it is clearly observed everywhere, must have its origin in the free will of man...." The volitional law is not based upon absolute reason but upon universal consent rendered by unbroken custom and testimony of those who are skilled in it. An institution of universal acceptance is national law if it satisfies reason, otherwise it represents Jus Gentium. Grotius distinguished even Jus Naturale as (1) pure law of nature representing state of nature prior to the formation of society and (2) law of nature after the formation of society but prior to civil law. The criterion for recognition of natural law is conscience of normal individual. It is found among best minds and practice of most civilised nations. In short this criteria was "common dictates of conscience," the basis of his theory of international law.

Characteristics of Jus Naturale

1. The natural law is the dictate of right reason, agreeing with rational nature and as such with God.

2. Natural law is permanent, eternal, universal, authoritative and absolute reason itself and is unchangeable.

3. The sanction of natural law is to be found in rational nature. It is based on ideal of peace and harmony all over the world.

Jus Gentium

According to Grotius as against law of nature which represents the dictates of reason there is Jus Voluntarium, a body of positive commands which were dictates of will. He defined Jus Gentium as the "law governing the intercourse between the nations." He took it as a human and national law. It consent is what has been accepted as obligatory by the consent of all or many nations. All mankind, or at least the great part of it constitute society of people for which the rule of general law is indispensable. According to Hearn Shaw, *Jus Gentium* or law of nations was to Grotius, a code of percepts distinct from the Just Naturale and of lower authority yet immensely valuable. It provided a body of international custom which could supplement the universal morality of the law of nature.

Father of International Law

Thus, Grotius was the first to create a comprehensive and systematic treatise on international law. Therefore he is regarded as the father of international law. The central theme of Grotius was the totality of relations between the states. He distinguished just wars from unjust wars. He rejected the idea that states have absolute right to make war. The will of states was not to be the only source of international law. The basis of international law is the nature of man which is endowed with goodness, altruism and morality. Grotius refuted the conception of reason of state. He propounded the theory of qualified neutrality by which nations carrying on a just war was to be bound.

The Jus Gentium included the practices which civilized nations follow in their dealings with one another. According to Dunning, "Its content is what has been accepted as obligatory by the consent of all or many nations. What is included under it is proved by constant usage and the testimony of the learned. Just as the occasion of civil law is the welfare of the aggregate which consists of many individuals for such a body or right, the occasion of International law is that aggregate which included all or many nations. According to Grotius law of nations is based on the consent of nations.

Grotius wanted to lay down rules of justice which would be binding on man. He wanted to apply those rules, under the name of natural law to the mutual relations of nations. He held that the rights common to all were derived from natural law which is the dictate of right reason. It indicates that any act has in it a moral turpitude or moral necessity from its agreement and disagreement with its rational nature.

According to Sabine, Grotius's importance in the history of jurisprudence rests not upon a theory of the state or upon any thing that he had to say upon international law, but upon his conception of a law regulating the relations between sovereign states....Grotius's contribution to the special subject of international law is beyond the limits of a history of political theory. His importance lay in the philosophical principles upon which he sought to found his special subjects and which he set out specially in the prolegomena to his great work. He brought international law into prominence.

Political Sovereignty

To Grotius political sovereignty is human in origin. It is vested in people who may delegate it conditionally or unconditionally. After delegating it, they cannot take it back. Sovereignty means supreme political power. By political power Grotius means that moral faculty of governing a state under which are include functions of general and of special character, of public or of primary interest and functions performed either by sovereign immediately or by persons commissioned by him. The sovereign must obey Natural law, divine law, constitutional law and the law of nations. But not civil law or human law is binding upon him. As command of a sovereign against divine or natural law it must not be obeyed, but the punishment for disobedience must be endured without resistence to a legitimate sovereign.

Sovereignty and International Law

Grotius believed that a sovereign is totally independent of other sovereigns. Each sovereign state is on terms of complete equality with other sovereign states, legally and diplomatically. The natural relations between nations can be of three kinds, i.e. of peace, of a war and of neutrality. To Grotius, "war is an armed conflict carried on under conditions, fixed by morality and custom between the public forces of respective states." He held that superfluous cruelty must be avoided even among the combatant forces.

Grotius held that the sovereignty of state is not incompatible with compliance of international law. Just as an individual submits to the sovereignty of his state and to its law for his own good so a sovereign state should submit to international law for his own good because it represents the will of community of nations.

The greatest positive contribution of Grotius to political science was his foundation of a scheme of rights and duties applicable to the relations of nation and nation.

Appreciations

1. Brierly. "Few books have won so great a reputation as the "De Jure Bells Pacis" but to regard its author as founder of international law is to exaggerate its originality and to do less than justice to the writers who proceeded him, neither Grotius nor any other single writer can properly be said to have founded the system."

2. Starkes. "Grotius had an abiding influence in the history of international law. He was continually relied upon as a work of reference and authority in the decisions of courts and in the text books of later writings of standing."

3. Jackson. "His work has remained a living force,....essence of his thought has passed into the conscience of civilised world."

In his conception of natural law Grotius introduced an ideal or normative element. He provided a scientific method. As Sabine says, "the references which Grotius made to Mathematics are significant". He gave the concept of equality of nations which laid the basis of certain provisions of League of Nations, League Assembly, U.N. Charter and the procedure of U.N. Assembly etc.

QUESTIONS FOR EXERCISE

1. Grotius is known as father of International Law.
2. "The law of nature is dictate or right reason." (Grotius). Explain.
3. How far is it correct to say that Grotius was the father of modern science of International law. Discuss his view in this connection.
4. "While on the side the work of Grotius promoted the cause of absolute monarchy, on the other side, it was a source of much aid and comfort to the advocates of limited government." (Dunning). Explain.

22

Seventeenth Century Political Thought

According to Maxey, "Few theories have served political society more usefully than much belaboured dogma of divine right of kings. In Bible, Lord Jehovah himself states "By me kings regin and princes decree justice." St. Peter and St. Paul said, "The powers that he ordained of God; whosoever therefore resist power, resist the ordinance of God." This gave rise to "Divine Origin Theory" of kings.

According to Maxey Robert Filmer was the most artful and effective conversationalist on the royal side of the struggle. Absolute monarchy was supported by King James I of England as well as by Sir Robert Filmer. Thomas Hobbes also supported absolute monarchy.

As thesis gives rise to anti thesis, so the theory of divine right of kings gave rise to the conceptions of the rights of man. In Greece, the individual existed primarily as an ingredient of his family and his city. In Roman world the individual existed for the advantage and use of state. Individual rights depended upon the social status of the person claiming them, but he had no rights whatever as a human being. As such Napoleon Bonaparte once remarked, obedience is the destiny of men but dispute of parliament and king brought into existence the famous petition of rights in 1628.

War of American independence was the logical corollary of petition of rights and Bill of rights which claimed, "no taxation without representation". Stuart Kings and Filmer lost ground as democratic ideas gained prominence.

Voices of freedom were raised by Milton in Aeropagitica and the Tenure of Kings and Magistrates. Thus in 17th century "for the first time according to Maxey, almost in twelve dismal centuries men began to explore the essence of things...to arrive at ultimate truth and reality."

In 17th century, England took lead in the sphere of political speculation. The development of political speculation in Rome and in England has been more or less on similar ancient lines. In both cases after political institutions have ripened and were functioning well political speculation involving abstract principles of political philosophy entered into consciousness of political theorists about the power of king and parliament.

Englishmen developed strong monarchy, a council for checking tyranny of parliament for legislation and taxation and an organisation of fiscal and judicial administration. The controversy between the king and the parliament resulted into armed conflict and brought into existence thinkers like Filmer, Hobbes, Locke and Milton etc.

SIR THOMAS MORE (1478-1535 A.D.)

Sir Thomas More was born in 1478 in a judge's family. He was educated at the House of Arch of Canterbury. He studied law in London and became a member of parliament. He held the post of a member of Privy Council, treasurer of the Exchequer, Speaker of House of Commons and finally Lord Chancellor. In 1532, due to his differences with king Henry VIII, he was forced to resign and was beheaded in 1535 on the charge of treason due to his stubbornness.

Utopia

More wrote a famous book—*Utopia,* which means in Greek, no where or "knowing in trifles". In this book a Portuguese wanderer tells about an island's administration. More attacked the criminal justice of England, other institutions and also the Government. He held that the institution of private property is the root cause of all evils. To get rid of these evil, he advocated communism. He said, "As long as there is any property....I cannot think, a nation can be governed either justly or happily." These views were unrealistic.

Utopia is an island in which every man or woman is obtained to learn a trade. Everyone has to labour six hours a day. The family is the basic unit. Each is trained in the art of agriculture, youths who show aptitude for arts or sciences are excused from manual labour. The condemnation of war and military glory and a remarkable theory of religious toleration are other important features of Utopia. More's common wealth is republic with ultra-democratic institutions. Utopia is unrealistic and imaginary.

RICHARD HOOKER

Richard Hooker was the most noteworthy philosopher of the puritan revolutionary period in England. He was primarily a theologian. He aimed at refuting the attacks of the priestly theoreticians on the policy of Angilcan church. He applied same principles both to secular and ecclesiastical governments. He made the examination of the origin, nature and obligation of law in general. His was carried an important influence on later political thought. According to Hearn Shaw, he insisted that the law of reason which governed the thought of men, and the law of conduct which bound them into political societies, was equally divine in origin and binding in character with the special laws of religion revealed in the Bible.

Hooker believed that men originally lived in a state of nature in which there was no organized authority. As the thought was full of violence and anarchy prevailed everywhere, so men being social animal, established and organized political authority by formal contract. Based on popular consent Hooker's theory of government proved to be very useful to future theorists, who had leaning towards democracy. He also expressed his views on law of nations. He agreed that if it is good for the individual to avoid anarchy and adopt civil society, so it is good for nations to do so. According to Gettell, "His work contained either explicitly or secretly, germs of most of the leading ideas of 18th century."

JOHN MILTON (1608-1674 A.D.)

Next to Shakespeare John Milton is the greatest literary giant of England. Literary fame of Milton eclipsed his fame as political thinker. However, he stood for liberty and opposed king's absolute power.

John Milton was born in 1608. He got his early education at Cambridge. His youthful and effeminate appearance won him the title of "The Lady of Christ's." He wrote famous poems even when he was a student. He was a lover of freedom and he wrote *Aeropagitica* a speech for the liberty of unlicensed printing. He wrote "*The Tenure of Kings and Magistrates*" to defend execution of the king Charles I. He was made Secretary during republican regime. However the restoration of kingship of Charles II forced him to retire from active politics. He passed his life in writing poems and died in 1674 at the age of 65. He wrote "*Paradise lost*" famous all over the world.

In *Aeropagitica*, Milton pleaded that the censorship and suppression discourage all scholarship. These are useless. Intelligent and fair administration of laws is impossible due to them. Milton said, "One who kills a man kills a reasonable creature, God's image; but who destroys a good book, kills the reason itself, kills the image of God. Many men live a burden to the earth; but a good book is the precious life blood of a master spirit."

Milton published the tenure of Kings and Magistrates a few days after the execution of Charles I. He set out to prove, "That it is lawful and hath been held so through all ages, for any one who have the power to call to account a tyrant, or wicked king and, after due conviction, to depose and put him to death...." He added "No man who knows can be so stupid today to deny that all men were naturally born free, being the image and resemblance of God himself and were by privilege alone all creatures, born to command and not to obey....the power of king and magistrates is nothing else but what only is derivative, transferred and committed to them from the people under the common good of all." He added to say, "King has as good a right to his crown and dignity, as any man to his inheritance, is to make subject no better than King's slave his chattell, or his possession that may be bought or sold."

He refuted divine origin theory by saying that to say that kings are accountable to none but God, is overturning all lord and governments. For if they may refuse to give account, then all convents made with them at coronation, all oaths are in vain, and were mockeries; and laws which they swear to keep are made to no purpose". Perhaps his arguments are still good against tyrants and dictators. Milton was against absolute power of Kings. He stood for popular sovereignty and status, "the right of choosing, yea of changing their Government is the grant of God himself to the people."

Liberty was the first and the controlling passion of Milton's philosophy. He wrote "Give me liberty to know, to utter, to argue freely according to consciousness above all liberty."

JAMES HARRINGTON (1611-1677 A.D.)

James Harrington was born in England in 1611. He died in 1677. He has an important place in the history of political philosophy. His book "*The common wealth of Oceana,*" is his greatest contribution to political philosophy. He put forward a suggestive plan of government to replace the monarchy. According to Gettell, "he prefaced his plan of model common wealth by a sketch of seven principal republican constitutions of history." '*The commonwealth of oceana*' was written in the form of Utopia. It was dedicated to Cromwell because he hoped that Cromwell will put principles into effect.

Political Thought

Harrington believed that the basic principle of Government is balance of forces. A government may be either the empire of laws and not of men or the empire of men and not of laws. The end of the state is public interest and secondly, private interest. Governments may be either foreign or national, based on wealth or intellectual distinction. A government can be stable by delegating power to land owning class. Monarchy, Aristocracy or Democracy is natural as land may be in the hands of one, few or many. The relation between property and political power represents the balance of dominion. The distribution of power must correspond to the distribution of property. The Government must consist of a senate of natural aristocracy, a council and a magistracy. There should be a system of rotation in Government, a system of ballot and also one for limitation of land. Both Milton and Harrington maintained the doctrine of popular sovereignty. Both were aristocratic in their outlook.

Harrington's influence was profound in America. According to G.P. Gooch, "The constitutions of Carolina, New Jersy and Pennsylvania reflected his thought and a century later his authority was fully quoted in the discussion which followed the elaboration of American constitution." His works formed the political Bible of Otis. John Adams and Jefferson's copy is preserved in the Congress, translated into French. Harrington's name is linked with many of his ideas. His name is quoted among three great revolutionaries of modern world.

ROBERT FILMER

Robert Filmer was a supporter of absolute sovereign power. His political philosophy was influenced by Hobbes and Bodin. He agreed with Bodin that there must be a single, absolute power in every state. He said, "Government originated in an enlargement of family, the kin being father and people his children and by obeying king the people can preserve true religion." Filmer opined that the king was the source of law and parliament was just an advisory body. His conception that state is natural and of organic growth is a valuable contribution. He wrote only one book '*Patriarchs*'. It was the best statement of theory of monarchy adopted by many Torries after the restoration. It was answered by Sydney and Locke who discarded his views.

BENEDICT SPINOZA

Spinoza was born in 1634, at Amsterdom. Highly educated and an accomplished linguist, he studied science and optics and was greatly influenced by Hobbes, Grotius and Machiavelli. He wrote *Tractatus Theologico Politicus, Tractatus Politicus* and *Ethics* etc.

Political Views

Like Hobbes, Spinoza held that the chief motive of human action is self-interest. To him, the state was not a necessary evil but a positive good. It was created to promote general happiness. It came into existence through a voluntary contract with which the powers of individual were combined. Their natural right to do what led to their separate advantage was resigned in favour of a ruling power which employed the natural right of whole community. For the fullest employment of freedom men entered into a contract and are bound by it.

According to Spinoza, it was foolish to expect a man to keep contract when the violation of it does him less harm than good. He suggested organic unity of state and conceived its sovereignty resting upon the common reason and on general mind of its members. He favoured republican form of Government He desired individual liberty and stated that the power of state is limited by natural rights of men. He favoured the federation of states to diminish war among states.

Rousseau borrowed his theory of general will from Spinoza. Locke was greatly influenced by Spinoza. According to Maxey "No cult of political pragmatism bears his name, but his utilitarian concept of the state gradually permeated the thought of the world and later thought of the genius of such theorists as Bentham and Mill was evolved into a dynamic system of political philosophy."

QUESTIONS FOR EXERCISE

1. Write a short note on Sir Thomas More and his Utopia.
2. Write a short note on Richard Hooker.
3. Write a short note on political ideas of John Milton.
4. Write a short note on Harrington and his book Oceana.
5. Estimate the importance of Harrington's Oceana in the history of political thought.
6. Wrote short note on Robert Filmer and Benedict Spinoza.
7. Write a short note on Benedict Spinoza.

23

Thomas Hobbes (1588-1679 A.D.)

Thomas Hobbes was born in England in 1588, at Malmesbury in the year of Spanish Armada. It is said that his mother gave birth to twin, himself and fear. But Jones says that "certainly Hobbes' conduct in life did not show him to be so fearsome, as he (biographer) would have believe us to be." Although it is true that he fled England when the clouds of civil war began to gather, this was an act of prudent man than of coward.

Hobbes was also the prey of broken home. His father was a wicked man who deserted his wife and children when Hobbes was still a child. He received his early education in Wilshire and joined Oxford at the age of fifteen. He graduated at the age of nineteen. He was not at all satisfied with the university education and found it barren and pointless. In Ointhian, he condemned universities for their frequency and insignificant speech.

On leaving Oxford, he became tutor to the heir of William Cavendish who later on became Earl of Devonshire. His connection with their powerful family brought him into contact with the most important personalities of the period such as Ben Johnson Bacon, Clarendon and Galileo etc. According to Jones, "His life long connection with this powerful and distinguished family was certainly one of the greatest factor....without which he would have died as unglorious as Milton."

During civil war, Hobbes had to go to France because he had seen the fate of Laud and Stafford. In Paris, he joined the royalist group and remained there for eleven years. He wrote his greatest book *Leviathan* in 1651. *Leviathan* made him popular both with royalist and Papacy. So he had to go to England and was allowed to live, on accepting, that he would keep himself out of politics.

In 1660, Charles II was restored to monarchy, who remarked when he saw him coming, here comes the bear baited. Hobbes soon won royal favour for a short period but later on his political activity was banned He spent his last 20 years in writing books on history, physics, law and literature. At the age of 85, he translated Odyssey and died at the age of 92 in 1679.

By those who knew him intimately, Hobbes is described as a man of singular attraction. Handsome, witty, generous, loyal, epicurean in taste and mode of life and a profound thinker. But puritan clergy held him as a personification of evil, atheist, libertine, monarchist, supporter of human rights and a Satan incarnate.

POLITICAL PHILOSOPHY OF HOBBES

Hobbes's political writings were prompted by the civil wars and were intended by him to exert influence upon the side of the king. He was a great critic of the upholders of the constitutional rule based on popular consent in the 17th century. Here his writings were designed to support an absolute monarchy. He was attached to the royalist party. He sincerely believed that monarchy was the most stable and orderly kind of government. Yet his books could not arouse the sympathy of the Stuarts or of the revolutionists and constitutionalists. His political philosophy had too wide a sweep to make good propaganda. But its drastic logic affected the whole later history of moral and political thought. In the nineteenth century, his ideas were included in the philosophical radicalism of the utilitarians and in John Austin's theory of legal sovereignty.

Hobbes was the first modern political thinker who tried to bring political theory into close connection with a thoroughly modern system of thought, and he "strove to make this system broad enough to account, on scientific principles, for all the facts of nature, including human behaviour both in its individual and social aspects."[1] Though his ideas which mostly suited to his own time have become obsolete now, yet he said something which can be rightly described as a science of politics. It served as an integral part of his whole conception of the natural world. He maintained it with an extraordinary clearness. His philosophy illustrates the remark of Bacon that "Truth emerges more easily from error than from confusion." Due to the clarity and pungency of his style, Hobbes is regarded as the greatest writer on political philosophy that the English speaking people have ever produced.

Scientific Materialism

The political philosophy of Hobbes is a part of his general philosophy called scientific materialism. He borrowed it from the system of motion of Galileo and Newton. Galileo suggested that the physical world is a purely mechanical system in which all that happens can be explained with geometrical precision by the displacement of bodies relative to one another. Likewise, Hobbes conceived that all knowledge is of one piece and mechanics gives the pattern. Motion is the completely pervasive fact in nature. To this Hobbes related his analysis of human nature.

1. Sabine, G.H., *A History of Political Theory* (Third ed., George G. Harrap & Co. Ltd., London, 1957), p. 388.

Analysis of Human Behaviour

Sensation, feeling, imagination, memory, reason, and thought play a dominant role in shaping human behaviour. Human behaviour is a mode of motion, a mechanical system, which can be explained with all exactness by analyzing the above factors. Social behaviour, upon which the art of government rests, is merely a special type of human behaviour which is exhibited when men act with reference to one another. Thus, the science of politics is built upon psychology. Hobbes proposed to show not what the government is, but what it must demonstrably be in order to control successfully beings whose motivation is that of the human machine.

Utilitarianism

While discussing his political philosophy Hobbes's first problem was, to state the principle of human behaviour, and to formulate the conditions upon which a stable society is possible. According to materialistic principles reality consists in the motion of bodies, which is "transmitted through the sense organs to the central nervous system, where it appears as sensation."[2] The perception of external bodies, causes an inward motion to the sense organs of the living organism which calls forth an outward reaction from the brain or heart. Every outward reaction of the sense organ is not to be called sense but only that "which at several times is by vehemence made stronger and more predominant than others." As the vital motion is always connected with the heart rather than the brain, is heightened or repressed, two primitive types of feeling appear appetite or desire and aversion. Some appetites or aversions are born with man; others are acquired in due course of time. The object of a man's appetite is called 'good', that of his aversion, 'evil'. He did not believe that anything is inherently good or evil. Goodness or badness of a thing depends upon human feelings towards it. It is, therefore, subjective. It may also differ from man to man. An object may attract one man and repel another. Men try to pursue in life what appears good to them. Thus, Hobbes's whole conception was more or less utilitarian in the sense that a man considers the utility and goodness of his action before he decides to act upon it. Man, not only pursues the object of his attraction, he also tries to defend it jealously against others who obstruct his effort of obtaining it. Further, if two men desire the same object which they both cannot enjoy, their equality of ability and hope of achieving the object makes them enemies. Power means the acquirement of present means to attain some future good. Hobbes recognized three principal causes of conflict between men, i.e., competition, diffidence and glory.

---

2. *Ibid.*, p. 392.

STATE OF NATURE

Hobbes described state of Nature by his idea of selfish nature of man. The only basis of human action is a perpetual desire for power because man is essentially selfish and egoistic. Men are by nature, equal in powers, both of body and mind. No man is so strong as to be safe against the attack of others. Men are also equal in their desire of safety, glory and gain. Passions of acquisition and self-preservation create mutual distrust and state of war. The means of security being precarious, no moderation of desire can place a limit to the struggle for existence. The desire for security is for all practical purposes inseparable from the desire for power, the present means of obtaining apparent future goods, because every degree of security requires to be still further secured. Hobbes explained:

"I put for a general inclination of all mankind, a perpetual and restless desire of power after power, that ceaseth only in death. And the cause of this, is not always that a man hopes for a more intensive delight, than he has already attained to; or that he cannot be content with a more moderate power; but because he cannot assure the power and means to live well, which he hath present, without the acquisition of more."[3]

SELFISH HUMAN NATURE

Hobbes, thus, described the individual as a completely self-centred and power-seeking animal. He has an endless need for power of every sort, riches, position, reputation, honour—all that may forfend the inevitable destruction which must in the end overtake all men. The means for attaining power may be either tangible, what Hobbes called 'gain', or intangible, what he called 'glory'. The value of both is the same. As such, every individual, is an absolutely solitary individual. Contrasting men with bees and ants, Hobbes said, "Men are continually in competition for honour and dignity, which these creatures are not; consequently amongst men there ariseth on that ground, envy and hatred and finally war."[4] Therefore men will always live in a condition of perpetual fear of competition and war. Hobbes further argued that since knowledge comes from the senses and different senses cannot see the same world, a man and his world must be one and different from the world of other men. Different individuals have absolutely separate worlds, separate pleasures, truths, goods, and they belong to no order, moral or politic. Frequently portrayed as the great absolutist, Hobbes was thus the greatest individualist in the history of political thought. To quote Wayper "His is an extreme doctrine of individualism embracing everything. He is a

3. *Leviathan*, XI.
4. *Ibid.*, XI.

Nominalist of the School of Occam, and his individualism is quite unqualified— more so, indeed, than that of any other writer."[5]

Life Before Society

In the state of Nature, each human being is actuated only by considerations that touch his own security or power. Other human beings are of consequence to him only as they affect this. Since individuals are roughly equal in strength and cunning, none can be secure, and so long as there is no civil power to regulate their behaviour, their condition is a "war of every man against every man." In such a condition, there can be no distinction between right or wrong, or just or unjust, for any conception of right and wrong or just and unjust presupposes a common standard of conduct, a common law to judge the case and a common superior to adjudge things. It is also inconsistent with any kind of civilization. Hobbes remarked: "In such condition, there is no place for industry; because the fruit thereof is uncertain; and consequently no culture of the earth; no navigation, nor use of the commodities that may be imported by sea; no commodious building; no instruments of moving, and removing, such things as required much force; no knowledge of the face of the earth; no account of time; no arts; no letters; no society; and which is the worst of all, continual fear, and danger of violent death; and the life of man, solitary, poor, nasty, brutish, and short."[6] Man's vain glory or pride unfits him for success in such a condition, but the condition itself is the result not of his defects but of his very nature. The state of Nature, as Hobbes described it, is "the ill condition which man by mere nature is actually place in." And the problem of Hobbes was how to extricate him from a position which the very principle of the universe, motion, has apparently designed for him.

This is only the one half of the picture of human nature, as discussed by Hobbes. And if, on the basis of Hobbes's description of this part of human nature, we once hold that man is completely self-centred and egoistic or savage and anti-social, it is not possible for him to set up a government. It is, therefore, necessary to analyze the second principle in human nature, which is reason. If the first principle—desire—hurries man on to take for himself what other men want and so embroils him with other men, the second principle—reason—teaches him to "fly a contranatural dissolution." Reason does not add a new motive but a regulative power, or foresight, by which the pursuit of security becomes more effective without ceasing to follow the general rule of self-preservation.

---

5. Wayper, C.L., *Political Thought* (The English Universities Press Ltd., London, 1958), p. 52.
6. *Leviathan,* XI.

Thus the human nature as described by Hobbes is neither so reasonable nor so unreasonable as he at first assumed it to be. Being actuated by the consideration of self-preservation, the reason, decides in favour of a civilized and social life. The transition is, however, made by the Laws of Nature, the "conditions of society or of human peace." The Laws of Nature are a set of rules according to which an ideally reasonable being will pursue his own advantage, if he is perfectly conscious of all the circumstances in which he is acting and is quite unswayed by momentary impulse and prejudice. The Laws of Nature state hypothetical conditions upon which the fundamental traits of human being allow a state government to be founded. They do not state values but they determine casually and rationally what can be given value in legal and moral systems. Hobbes explained:

"Therefore, the Law of Nature....is the dictate of right reason, conversant about those things which are either to be done or omitted for the constant preservation of life and members, as much as in us lies."[7]

"A Law of Nature is a precept, of a general rule, found out by reason, by which a man is forbidden to do that which is destructive of his life, or taketh away the means of preserving the same; and to omit that by which he thinketh it may be best preserved."[8]

NATURAL LAWS

Important Laws

Reason teaches men to obey Natural Laws, which are nineteen in number of which following four are most important:

1. The first Law of Nature holds that every man should seek peace and preserve it, and if he cannot obtain it, he should "use all helps and advantages of war."

2. The second Law of Nature lays down that a man must be willing, along with others and in the interest of peace and self-preservation, to forswear his right to all things, be content with as much liberty as would allow others over himself and transfer some of his rights by a contract.

3. The third Law of Nature enjoins that "men perform their covenants made."

4. According to the fourth Law of Nature, the man to whom the rights are transferred caused no injury to the one who makes that transfer.

There are the most important Laws of Nature. Other Laws of Nature point to the advisability of an individual accommodating himself to the

7. *De Civc,* II, 1.

8. *Leviathan,* XIV.

rest, cultivating complaisance, spirit of freedom, sense of equity and avoiding the spirit of revenge, cruelty, pride and avarice.

Characteristics of Natural Law

There are two characteristics of Natural Laws :

1. They are not the principles of an Eternal Justice or of a Perfect Morality, as understood by the Stoics, of which actual law is the imperfect reflection. They are merely "counsels of prudence." Hobbes remarked that "there are no such things as moral rights, no clash between a man's duty and a man's interest, but only an appeal from man drunk to man sober only a difference between bad and good calculation.[9]

2. Hobbes's Natural Laws do not imply that there is such a thing as common good. They are merely the postulates by which Hobbes's rational construction of society is to take place. They are at once the principles or rules of perfect prudence and of social morality. Therefore they make possible the step from the psychological motives of individual action to the precepts and values of civilized law and morality.

CONCEPTION OF SOCIETY

Laws, of Nature serve as the sound basis of society and later on of government. The prime condition of society is mutual trust and the keeping of covenants. Without it there can be no certainty of performance. But there must be a reasonable presumption that other persons will meet you on the same ground. Hobbes was conscious of the fact that the egoistic element in human nature would make any covenant or society impossible. He, therefore, worked out a plan for the Laws of Nature. The setting up of the Laws of Nature is a way of redressing those competitive and ruthless qualities of human nature which are inconsistent with mutual confidence. However, Hobbes was a utilitarian and an individualist in his thinking. According to him all human behaviour is motivated by individual self-interest, and society is essentially a means to this end. The power of the state and the authority of the law are justified so far as they contribute to the security of individual human beings. There is no rational ground of obedience and respect for authority except the anticipation that these will yield a large individual advantage than their opposites. Social well-being as such is replaced by a sum of separate self-interests.

According to Hobbes, Society is an 'artificial' body, a collective term of the fact that human beings find it individually advantageous to exchange goods and services. But the will of the representative, who is to act as the sovereign, cannot be the common will of all, because there is no such thing. His representative will is a substitute for the conflicting individual wills.

---

9. *Ibid.*

This substitution is the only way in which many men can find unity. In the words of Hobbes "A multitude of men are made one person when they are by one man, or one person, represented; so that it be done with the consent of everyone of that multitude in particular. For it is the unity of the representer, not the unity of the represented, that makes the person one. And it is the representer that beareth the person, and but one person: and unity cannot otherwise be understood in multitude."

Although Hobbes's analysis of human nature is defective, there is a logical consistency in his ideas and conclusions. He considered man's nature as antisocial. Hence, it is unreasonable to expect men to agree spontaneously to respect one another's rights. The performance of covenants may be reasonably expected only if there is an effective government which will punish non-performance. To quote Hobbes,

"Covenants, without sword, are but words, and of no strength to secure a man at all."[10] "The bonds of words are too weak to bridle men's ambition, avarice, anger, and other passions, without the fear of some coercive power."[11] All the Laws of Nature, such as, justice, equity, modesty, mercy etc., are helpless to teach men to live in co-operation with mutual understanding without the force of power to cause them to be observed. Hence coercive power is needed to apply necessary sanctions to curb man's innately unsocial inclinations. Apparently Hobbes meant that reason provides a sufficient ground for mutual accord but is too weak to offset the avarice of men in the mass. In substance his theory amounted to "identifying government with force; at least, the force must always be present in the background whether it has to be applied or not."[12] Hobbes's thought on this point becomes further clear when we consider his statement that "the agreement of *other* creatures is natural; that of men is by covenant only, which is artificial: and, therefore, it is no wonder if there be somewhat else required, besides covenant, to make their agreement constant and lasting; which is a common power, to keep them in awe, and to direct their actions to the common benefit."[13]

THE ORIGIN OF COMMONWEALTH

In the second part of *Leviathan,* Hobbes created a commonwealth by giving a new orientation to the old idea of the social contract. Before him the social contract represented as governmental contract, a contract between the ruler and ruled. He built his commonwealth on the following idea:

10. *Leviathan,* XVII.
11. *Ibid.,* XIV.
12. Sabine, G.H., *op. cit.,* p. 398.
13. *Leviathan,* XVII. (Italicized word mine).

"The only way to erect such a common power, as may be able to defend them from the invasion of foreigners and the injuries of one another, and thereby to secure them in such sort as that, by their own industry, and by the fruits of the earth, they may nourish themselves and live contentedly; is, to confer all their power and strength upon one man, or upon one assembly of men, that may reduce all their wills, by plurality of voices unto one will; which is as much as to say, to appoint one man, or assembly of men, to bear their person; and everyone to own and acknowledge himself to be author of whatsoever he that so breath their person, shall act or cause to be acted in those things which concern the common peace and safety; and therein to submit their wills, everyone to his will, and their judgements, to his judgement."[14]

Hobbes further explained:

"I authorize and give up my right of governing myself to this man, or to this assembly of men, on this condition, that thou give up thy right to him, and authorize all his actions in like manner." This done, "the multitude so united in one person, is called a *commonwealth,* in Latin *civitas.*[15]

The underlying idea of all Hobbes's arguments is that a mere multitude cannot have right and cannot act authoritatively. Only individual man can do this. Any collective body is merely artificial. Someone must act in the name of the whole group. And a corporation is not really a collective body at all but one person, whose supreme will is so be received for the will of all its members. On this analogy society is a mere fiction. As George H. Sabine remarks, "Hobbes's thought on this point can be states, perhaps more accurately, by using the legal conception of a corporation instead of contract, as he did in *De Cive.*"[16] Sabine assumed that Hobbes's commonwealth is, more or less, based on the legal conception of a corporation, and not on the idea of a perfect contract which entails an agreement on the part of the people who compose a corporation, or who are part and parcel of it. To admit this assumption means to conclude that Hobbes's conception of political commonwealth was not at all individualistic in essence, and the members have no say in making of a corporation or of a political commonwealth. Such a confusion does arise when we examine the attributes and powers of Hobbes's sovereign. However, it is not adequate to say, as Sabine remarks, that the idea of contract or of voluntary agreement amongst people themselves is not clear in Hobbes's commonwealth. Hobbes was quite emphatic on this point when he stated: "The attaining to this sovereign power is by two ways. One, by natural force; as when a man maketh his children to submit themselves and their children to his

14. *Ibid.*
15. *Ibid.*
16. Sabine, G.H, *op. cit.*, p. 398.

government....The other, is when men agree amongst themselves to submit to someone, or assembly of men, voluntarily, on confidence to be protected by him against all others. This latter may be called a political commonwealth, or a commonwealth by *institution*; and the former, a commonwealth by acquisition."[17]

HOBBES'S LEVIATHAN

Characteristics of sovereign however, for Hobbes, there is no choice except between absolute power an complete anarchy, between an omnipotent sovereign and no society of whatsoever kind. According to him, social body has no existence except through its constituted authorities, and its members have no rights except by delegation. All social and political authority must accordingly be vested in the sovereign. The characteristics of Hobbes's *Leviathan* are unmistakable. He is the sole source of laws, and he is, of course, the sole interpreter of laws. He is not subject to civil laws, although he remains bound by them so long as he does not repeal them. Hobbes did not recognize the utility of the traditional medieval idea that the king should be *sub lege*, subject to the condition that he should obey the law. Nor did he recognise the use of a law that cannot be changed by the sovereign without the consent of the people. He wrote that "I could never see in any author, what a fundamental law signifieth." Sovereign is the creator of Right and Justice. The Law of Nature cannot be pleaded against him, for the purpose of the Law of Nature is the creation of sovereign, who alone can interpret it The Law of God can also not be pleaded against him, because it is through him that the Law of God can be approached. Hobbes wrote that "there is no covenant with God, but by mediation of somebody that representeth God's person; which none doth but God's lieutenant, who hath the sovereignty under God."[18] Further, the sovereign is the sole judge of what opinions and doctrines are averse, and what are conducive to peace and tranquillity. He has the final right of judging things; that is to say, of hearing and deciding all controversies which may arise concerning law, either civil or natural, or concerning fact. "For," he wrote, "without the decision of controversies, there is no protection of one subject against the injuries of another: the laws concerning *meum* and *tuum* are in vain: and to every man remaineth, from the natural and necessary appetite of his own conservation, the right of protecting himself by his private strength, which is the condition of war, and contrary to the end for which every commonwealth is instituted."[19] Sovereign has also the right of making war and peace with other nations and commonwealths; that is to say, of judging when it is for the public good, and how great forces are to be assembled, armed

17. *Leviathan*, XVII.
18. *Ibid.*, XVIII.
19. *Ibid.*

and paid for that end; and to levy money upon the subjects, to defray the expenses thereof. These are some of the rights which the Sovereign of Hobbes enjoys and which are the marks by which a man may discern in what man, or assembly of men, the sovereign power is placed and "resideth."

Utilitarian Government

There is also another side of his theory of sovereignty to which Hobbes was not blind at all. For controversial purposes he stressed the point that resistance to authority can never the justified, since justification would require the approval of authority itself. It equally follows, however, that resistance will, in fact, occur wherever government fails to protect— the condition for subjects' submission. If the protection is not guaranteed by the sovereign to the people, the latter may then be thrown back upon their individual resources for self-protection and may rightly give their obedience to a new sovereign who can protect them. Hobbes justified any government, only on the utilitarian ground. The later thinkers had no difficulty in accepting this point of view. Sabine is right when he remarks, "What limits the sovereign is not the law of nature but the power of his subjects. Hobbes's sovereign is faced by a condition and not a theory, but there can be no limitation of the civil law in its own field. Bodin's conception of a constitutional law limited the competence of the sovereign has disappeared entirely."[20]

It is wrong to say that Leviathan is a person who can tolerate no liberty. There is liberty under him. It is that which man enjoys in the silence of the laws. Leviathan has no passion for undue interference. "For the use of laws is not to bind the people from all voluntary actions; but to direct and keep them in such a motion, as not to hurt themselves by their own impetuous desires, rashness or indiscretion; as hedges are set, not to stop travellers, but to keep them in their way." Men can enjoy sufficient liberty "to buy and sell and otherwise contract with one another; to choose their own abode, their own diet, their own trade of life, and institute their children as they themselves think fit; and the like."[21] Though not an early exponent of *laissez-faire,* Hobbes convinced that the distressed "ought not to be left to the charity of private persons" — they were Leviathan's responsibility. He also held that "there ought to be such laws as may encourage all manner of arts, such as, navigation, agriculture, fishing, and all manner of manufacture which requires labour." But, Hobbes believed, Leviathan was not to interfere in the matters of intellect and conscience as these were beyond his reach. Also Leviathan cannot force "men to believe". "Thought is free". Hobbes was an implacable enemy of all authority in philosophy, belief and opinion. And the justification for the

---

20. Sabine, G.H. : *op. cit.,* p. 6.
21. *Leviathan,* XXI.

existence of the "secret-thought police top be found in 20th century totalitarian states is not to be sought in him."[22]

INDIVIDUALISM

Hobbes's political philosophy was individualistic in essence in spite of the fact that he propounded a theory of an absolute sovereign. He was as much the product of the circumstances of his time as Machiavelli. Hence it would be wrong to expect from him the doctrine of a perfect democracy or of a perfect individualism of the 20th century. Although the despot, the hero, the divinely-appointed ruler—or whatever else Hobbes may choose to call him will not invariably have wisdom or foresight, at least it will always be in his interest to keep the rival folly, the innate lawlessness of the many-headed multitude, in check. The besetting sin of democracy is anarchy. The best check yet discovered upon anarchy is the strong arm and, when necessary, the sharp and sword of the ruler who is ultimately responsible only to himself. It is true that the motive power must commonly, if not always, be looked for from below: but the wild forces of nature, which furnish the raw material of the statesman, will in the ordinary course of things spring from the multitude and the soil. At the lowest estimate, Vaughan rightly remarks, "the second element is as necessary to the final product, the welfare and progress of mankind, as the first. And if, on the strictest construction, the rulers can claim no more than the second place, that is the worst of reasons for asserting that he has no place at all. Judged by a purely ideal standard, both may be evils; certainly, both carry many evils in their train. But in this imperfect world, both are necessary evils; and the one without the other would be ten times more evil yet.[23] But looking from the viewpoint of the spirit of political commonwealth another remark of Vaughan that "the state of Leviathan is a state avowedly founded upon slavery; founded therefore upon a principle which is the very negation of all justice"[24] does not hold much truth. Also his remark— "The 'Society' called together by the 'covenant' is seen, directly we examine it, to be no society at all. All life is gathered in the 'one man' at the head of it; the rest of the body is a dead weight, a mere unprofitable mass"[25] — does not sound very convincing. If we closely examine the liberty of subjects and the condition of revolution against the sovereign, discussed by Hobbes in Chapter XVIII of *Leviathan*, his viewpoint becomes crystal clear. Further, Hobbes's discussion of the characteristics of political commonwealth in Chapter XVII of *Leviathan* also clearly indicates that the voluntary consent of the people remains fundamental in the making of a corporation or of an institution. The idea of

---

22. Wayper, C. L. : *op. cit.*, p.59
23. Vaughan, C.E., *History of Political Philosophy* (Manchester University Press, England, 1925), p. 53.
24. *Ibid.*, p. 51.
25. *Ibid.*, p. 54.

self-preservation which actuates men to agree to the authority of a sovereign serves as a positive limitation to the unbridled passions and authority of the sovereign. Men, according to Hobbes, were so egocentric and so jealous of their freedom that they remained at war against one another in the state of Nature. But there cannot be reduced to the state of slavery under any circumstances. They submit to the authority of sovereign purely on the utilitarian ground. As society which is based on a utilitarian principle cannot be regarded as a society of mere slaves or of 'unprofitable mass' as Vaughan wrongly remarks.

Social Contract and Leviathan's Sovereign Authority

Natural Laws remind that Leviathan's authority is legitimate only because of the consent of each individual. Men can be forced to obey a *de facto* sovereign power, but they have no moral obligation to do so in the sense that they have a moral obligation to obey the Leviathan that they have authorized to act for them. Hobbes doctrine of social contract was an attempt to answer the question, "Why do men obey the state?" Hobbes remarked, "This is how I can best explain my idea of the state," and his advice is legitimate since his is an analytical and not a historical problem. Hobbes's doctrine of social contract ought to be understood in a logical and not in a chronological sense. It was mainly concerned with the origin of the state, not in time but in reason. Over the above, for Hobbes as for Burke, "politics ought to be adjusted, not to pure human reasoning, but to human nature: of which the reason is but a part, and by no means the greatest part." Given such an individual as the one with whom Hobbes starts, no other contract than this is conceivable. Admitting the fact that man's nature is constant, only such a contract as this, Wayper rightly remarks, "can ensure that the natural result of man's nature, namely chaos, will not also be constant. The reflection of a lantern can be changed by the insertion of a lens through which its rays must pass without any alteration being made to the lantern itself, and the chaos which is the normal result of a man's quest for Felicity in a world in which he is not alone can be changed into peace without any alternation in man himself—but only by insertion between man and the screen of the world of the artificial lens, which is Leviathan."[26]

THEORY OF SOCIAL CONTRACT

With the passage of time man wanted to discard the life of constant fear. His social self began to assert himself. He wanted an atmosphere in which his life and property were secure. According to A. Hecker, "This state of nature eventually proved to be either impossible or undesirable to maintain. Therefore at as specific time the inhabitants of a natural state eventually proved to be either impossible or undesirable to maintain.

26. Wayper, C.L., *op. cit.*, p. 62.

Therefore, at a specific time the inhabitants of a natural state came together and consequently agreed to set up social and political institutions. This agreement is called a social contract or a covenant of sometimes a social compact. It marks the beginning of a social and political authority." Hobbes himself says, "The only way to erect such a common power as may be able to defend them (i.e. men) from the invasion of foreigners, and injuries of one another....is to confer all their power and strength upon one man or upon assembly of men they may reduce all their wills....which is as much as to say to appoint one man or assembly of men to leave their person....This is more than consent or concord, it is real unity of them all, in one and supreme power."

To remove constant fear men thought of surrendering their right to a Lord Protector to whom they wanted to be the custodian of their rights, duties and social justice. Men declared, "I authorise and declare and give up my right of governing myself to this man or to this assembly of men, on this condition that thou give thy right to him and authorise all his actions in like manner. This done the multitude so united in one person is called commonwealth."

The assembly of persons and their social instinct was the basis of social contract and also the origin of the state. It motivated them to come out of the brutish and nasty state of nature to the civilized society, with a social order.

Characteristics of Sovereign

According to Hobbes, the person to whom rights were surrendered was the sovereign: a great Leviathan before whom all were to bow. He was the preserver of peace, hope for prosperity, development and security. To quote Hobbes, "By this authority, given to him by every particular man in the commonwealth, he has the use of so much power and strength conferred on him, that by error thereof, he is enabled to form wills of them all, to peace at home and mutual aid against their enemies abroad. And in this consists the essence of common wealth and he shall think expedient, for the peace and common defense." The sovereign of Hobbes has the following salient characteristics:

1. Above Laws. Sovereign shall not be party to the contract and shall remain above all laws.

2. Custodian of Rights. He shall accordingly retain all the rights which he used to enjoy in the state of nature. Since all have surrendered their rights willingly to the sovereign, the sovereign was the custodian of their rights. None should challenge sovereign on grounds of infringing his rights.

3. Beyond Constitutional Checks. The sovereign, according to Hobbes, had no constitutional checks, whatsoever, "For before the constitution of sovereign power, all men had right to all things...this property being necessary to peace, depending on sovereign power, is the act of that power, in order to achieve the public peace."

4. Sole Interpreter of Law. He was the sole interpreter of law and his actions could not be prejudicial to social interests.

5. Beyond Breach of Trust. He could not be charged with breach of contract because he was not a party to the contract.

6. Symbol of National Unity. He was the symbol of national unity and as such any challenge to his authority was irrational. According to A. Hecker, "All the citizens have agreed to regard sovereign an extension to their personalities and as the repository of their rights. This means that loyalty is to be rendered exclusively to the state. There is no room left over for associations in society which might compete with the state for the allegiance of the citizens. The sovereign must demand complete obedience to his laws. There is no allowance for individuals who take a light heated view of the political authority. Similarly, associations, which by their very existence, divide the loyalties of citizens, are dangerous to commonwealth."

7. Final Authority to Contracts. No contract can be quoted against the sovereign. He was the final authority to approve all contracts. There could be no contract against him. Hobbes maintained that the obedience to authority was universal. The minority should not disobey the commands of a sovereign on the grounds that it was not party to the contract. To quote Saxo Commins, "And whether he be in the congregation or not, he either must submit to their decrees, or be left to the conditions of war, he was in before; whereas he might without injustice be destroyed by man whatsoever."

8. Sovereignty. Hobbes could not reconcile himself to the idea of limited sovereignty. Sovereignty must be indivisible and inalienable. The right of choosing his own ministers and magistrates was valid in the hands of the absolute and inalienable sovereign. He was, however, in no way bound by the advice of is ministers or magistrates.

9. Ultimate Authority. The sovereign was the ultimate authority for "making war and peace with other nations and commonwealth, that is to say of judging when it is for the public good and how great forces are to be assembled: armed and paid for that end: and to levy money upon the subjects, to defray the expense thereof."

10. Absolute Dictator. Hobbes that thus created his absolute indivisible and inalienable sovereign. His sovereign was the dictator. He was one of the most undemocratic persons. After having been elected in a most democratic way he tried to stress that his subjects, magistrates and ministers might shine in his absence but they cannot find a place in his presence. As

Robert N. Linscott puts it, "As in the presence of the master, the servants are equal any without and honour at all, so are the subjects in the presence of the sovereign. And though they shine some more some less, when they are out of his sight, yet in his presence, they shine no more than the stars in the presence of the sun."

Criticism

1. Authoritarianism. The concrete proposal which emerged from the theory of social contract was the creation of an omnipotent sovereign with unlimited authority. But Hobbes has failed to understand that a sovereign with such absolute powers was bound to collapse in actual practice. Howsoever genius he might be a person cannot be an expert in state affairs. He must have certain advisers, helpers and must depend upon them. Concentration of power is bound to result in frustration at one stage or the other.

2. Neglect of Minority. Hobbes has given no place to the minorities. which must be kept satisfied for smooth working of state administration.

3. No Value of Public Opinion. The sovereign of Hobbes has left no room for the majorities to express their disapproval of the actions of the authority to whom they have surrendered their rights. It cannot be expected that sovereign must always be justified. He is also liable to commit mistakes. Hobbes has provided for no channels to point them out.

4. One Party Contract. The contract of Hobbes is one party contract which can hardly be a valid one. There was *prima facie* no difficulty for Hobbes if he had made sovereign a party to the contract with some extraordinary powers.

5. Contradiction in Divine Authority and Social Contract. Hobbes' sovereign derives his authority from God. He is accountable to none for his actions. He is the deputy of God on earth. But it is strange that a divine authority derives powers from the brute subjects of state of nature. This hardly appears sound and reasonable.

6. Uncivilized Rule Over Civilized. The sovereign did not surrender his rights. Under arrangements those who did not surrender their rights remained in the state of nature and thus uncivilized while those who surrendered rights became members of civilized state. In other words, the sovereign remained uncivilized while the subjects became civilized. It is an uncivilized person who shall be governing a civilized nation. History still will have to trace such an example.

7. Contract After Death of Sovereign. Hobbes has made the position of his sovereign quite unsafe. The contract was executed with a person and is valid for that person. What would happen to the society when the sovereign dies ? Will that be the end of sovereignty ? How the gap would be covered is not clear ? The sovereign's contract with the subjects is for ever. But how can a generation bind posterity for ever?

8. Government by Force. Hobbes's sovereign wants to command over his subjects by force and not by their natural willingness. T.H. Green subsequently stressed that it was will and not force that mattered in governing the people.

Thus Hobbes has tried to create an omnipotent sovereign but he has failed to give it a rational basis. His concept of sovereignty is 'pernicious and impossible.' His theory leads to mere despotism. It proposes no checks against oppressive and tyrannical sovereign. He has miserably failed to create any bond between one another. "The only cement provided is that which binds each of them, singly and separately, by sheer terror to the tyrant who stands above them all." Therefore, it has been rightly said that "Hobbesianism, in fact stood for atheism, materialism, despotism or for many other such isms, that the fancy of the age had suggested. His Leviathan is condemned as a rebel's catchism, and also as the nearest of all the ethical theories." Hobbes went to the extreme ends. Even the Stuarts were not very much satisfied with him whose cause he wanted to support. Sabine concluded, "Hobbes's principles were at least as contrary to the pretensions of Stuarts whom he meant to support as to those of revolutionists whom he meant to refute and more contrary to both than either royalist or Parliamentarian was to other. The friends of kings might well feel that Hobbe's friendship was as dangerous as Cromwell's enmity."

Hobbes was a great political thinker of his age, who believed that the state came into being as a result of social contract executed between the individual and the sovereign. According to him before man came in the state he was living in the state of nature in which the hands of all were against all and hands of one against all. In the state of nature neither his life, nor property nor anything else was secure. He, therefore, surrendered his everything to his most powerful and strong sovereign to secure his life and property. As already discussed, Hobbes also created a very powerful and almighty sovereign, who was supreme in all matters and the subjects had ordinarily no right to challenge his authority. This has created a very serious problem as to whether subjects or any individual had any right to resist the authority of the sovereign. Hobbes came to the conclusion that under certain circumstances he had such a right.

NATURAL RIGHTS AND NATURAL LAWS

Hobbes have given his ideas about most of the important political problems like the liberty of the individuals and their rights etc. In all walks of life he tried to tighten the grip of sovereign over his subjects. He strongly pleaded that the church was a department of state. He was more individualist than Plato who absolutely subjected his citizens to the sovereign.

What are Natural Rights?

Hobbes maintained that in the state of nature and even prior to that there were certain rights which were very dear and precious to man. Man struggled for their preservance, he had a strong desire to retain them. These rights were at stake when he thought of joining the civil state and subjected himself to the authority of sovereign in order to retain his rights. For their sake he gave up all his rights except those of life and property. He could give up everything but not these rights. He reserved with himself the right to disobey the sovereign if at any stage he felt that such of his rights were being snatched. Natural rights were such rights which were kept with himself even after joining the state of nature.

Natural Rights and Natural Laws

Hobbes clearly distinguished between natural rights and natural laws. The natural rights of men were based on their selfish views. If strictly and closely followed, these were the basis of war. On the other hand, natural laws would positively lead to peace and avoid war. With natural rights men could struggle to preserve what they had with them. On the basis of natural laws men gave up some of their rights in order to have sure realisation of rights of all. According to Hobbes the natural laws are "Immutable and eternal."

LIBERTY AND RIGHTS OF INDIVIDUALS

Hobbes stressed that the men would not honour the covenants enjoined upon them on account of the dictates or right reasons embodied in the natural laws. He pleaded the use of force as an essential element for the preservation of these dictates. The covenants without swords were mere words on papers. In the words of Sabine, "The law of nature really meant for Hobbes a set of rules, according to which an ideally reasonable being would pursue his own advantage, if he were perfectly conscious of all the circumstances in which he was acting and was quite unswayed by momentary impulses and prejudices. Since he assumed that men do not act in this way, the laws of nature state hypothetical conditions upon which the fundamental traits of human beings allow a stable government to be joined. They do not state values but they determine casually and rationally what can be given value in legal and moral systems."

Hitherto, common view of Milton and Levellers were based on the most democratic idea and stood for the freedom of the individual as a member of the social community. Hobbes tried to distinguish between the liberty of the individual as a member of the society and state and the freedom of the state as an agency to regulate the rights of the members of the society. He was of the view that the liberty of the state, i.e., of commonwealth was unqualified and absolute and that there were no checks upon that. But the freedom of individual depended on the factor upto which the state could allow that. The freedom of individual was thus a relative and not an absolute term. In the words of A. Hacker, "Freedom for Hobbes, is the sphere of that reason, is the creation of the state; it does not exist independently of it. Just as justice must grow out of law, so liberty must grow out of political power."

There were no checks on the liberty of the commonwealth. Individual freedom consisted in what state did not forbid and permitted to do e.g. the purchase and sale of goods, freedom of movement and so on. Examples of such rights were the rights of self defence and preservation. In the state of nature the rights of men depended on their mights. In the civilized states their rights depended upon mutual consent of the sovereign and having legal sanction behind them. Liberty of the individual, however, was not at the cost of the sovereign. There are no limitations on his absolute character and nature of the sovereign. Except the right of self preservation the sovereign could disallow, check or refuse any freedom. No individual could prefer his rights against the state. In his *Leviathan* Hobbes said, "The liberty of subject lieth therefore only in those things which in regulating their action, the sovereign hath permitted; such as is the liberty to buy and sell, and otherwise contract with one another; to choose their own abode, their own diet, their own trade of life and institute their children as they themselves think fit, and the like."

Hobbes's ideas about individual freedom depended on the will and desire of his sovereign. His individual had far more liberties than the individual of Plato who had stooped too low to regulate the affairs of mankind. Here Hobbes has shown a sense of more practicability than Plato who thought that the state could effectively and efficiently regulate all aspects of human behaviour. The individual should be left to regulate some behaviours of his life though neither at the cost of state nor that of the sovereign but at his own cost. Hobbes agreed with Aristotle that the unity is desirable. It could be achieved by vesting extensive powers in the hands of sovereign, who was the symbol of unity. At the same time too much of unity and denial of basic liberties to the individuals would positively weaken the state.

Believing in absolutism Hobbes in many ways was an individualist. His political philosophy depended on the individual nature of man. He gave his individuals freedom to disobey the sovereign when his life and property was at stake. One could refuse to serve in army if he was sure that his life was in danger. In a passage in his*Leviathan* Hobbes says that

"The obligation of the subjects to the sovereign is understood to have lasted as long and no longer than the power latent, by which he is able to protect them."

SECULARISM

Hobbes believed in absolute sovereignty. He did not believe in the spiritual authority of the church and its right to equate itself with the sovereign. His conception overlordship of sovereign, both temporal and spiritual, left no ground for the church to exert its influence. The church had no power whatsoever. It was an assembly of persons believing in some particular religious doctrines. If they assembled without the permission of the sovereign or the sovereign did not refuse permission that was his goodwill. Thus the church is a department of the state and not at par or above the state and the sovereign. Hobbes condemned ideas of both world religion, state and the sovereign. The church always tried to superimpose itself and sought for establishing his own authority over temporal lords but there is no spiritual government. There could not be a world church. Each church is confined to its own state. The sovereign is both temporal and spiritual authority. His authority is derived from God. He is the deputy of God on earth. Being representative of God there is no need to separate spiritual authority of church from that of the state. Hobbe's philosophy had no place for church state. To quote Maxey, "He was so devastatingly critical of the theological absurdities of the time, so cogently insistent upon the supremacy of temporal authority, so skeptical of supernaturalism in all its forms and pretenses, and so savagely disparaging to the Roman Church in particular, that his name became anathema to the pious of all creeds."

CRITICISM OF HOBBES

According to Hobbes, the men came out from the state of nature as a result of a contract which gave birth to the state. Before man came in state he was living in the state of nature which was nasty, brutish and savage. Men were fighting and quarrelling with other fellow beings so as to gain glory and honour. Men came out of the state of nature by asserting their social instinct and surrendering there rights to a sovereign. The state of nature was thus converted into a civilized state. Hobbes' theory of social contract has been criticised on many grounds of which many are valid and convincing. Main points of criticism levelled against him are the following:

1. Social Contract was Defective. Hobbes has brought out his state on the basis of social contract. A contract could not only be concluded between the two parties. In Hobbes' contract, the sovereign was not a party to the contract. As such, it remained only one party contract which technically cannot be called a contract.

2. Contract was Sudden. According to Hobbes human beings were nasty, savage and brutish. Their selfish habits were natural to them. They were wedded to this selfishness since times immemorial. But all of a sudden they threw away this selfishness and asserted their social feelings. By a magic stroke they became realistic and ready to surrender all their rights and authority to the sovereign. How could they become social and why did they leave their unsocial character is not clear.

3. Rule of Uncivilized. The sovereign did not surrender his rights. He thus remained in the state of nature in which the people were uncivilized. Yet he was to rule over the persons who had left the state of nature and had become the members of civilized state. It is astonishing that an uncivilized person should govern the civilized people.

4. Invalid Contract. A contract can be concluded between two civilized parties who understand their duties and responsibilities for the execution of the terms of contract. Social contract was between a civilized and an uncivilized party which cannot be considered as valid contract. "A contract again, implies at least two persons as parties, but the people were not a 'person' capable of acting as a party to a contract with the sovereign before they were united in subjection to him, up to that time they were merely an aggregate of isolated persons."

5. Locke's Criticism. Locke has criticised Hobbes by saying, "When men, quitting the state of nature entered into society, they agreed that all of them but one should be under the restraint of laws; but that he should still have all the liberty of state of nature, increased with power and made licentious by impunity. This is to think that men are so foolish that they take care to avoid what mischief may be done to them by polecats and foxed, but are content nay, think it safety, to be devoured by lions."

6. No Irrevocable Contract. Hobbes maintained that social contract is irrevocable. This is wrong. Every contract is for a specific period and how could savage people agree to perpetual subordination.

7. Wrong Estimate of Human Nature. Hobbes maintained that social contract is irrevocable. This is wrong. Every contract is for a specific period and how could savage people agree to perpetual subordination.

8. Wrong Estimate of Human Nature. Hobbes has either not understood human nature or has tried to adjust that to suit his requirements. At one time men were disunited and isolated individuals having no concern with each other and at other time they were united and realised needs and necessities of others like civilized citizens. They were most willing to cooperate with each other. Hobbes thus made men savage animals and civilized creatures at one and the same time. What he thought of man and his nature is not clear.

9. Individual was Never the Basis of Growth. Historically, Hobbes is not correct when he makes an individual the basic unit for the growth of civilized community. Nowhere and at no stage of history for individual has been the basis of development. Either family or clan has been considered as a basic unit of the growth of the state.

10. Wrong Notion About Replacement of Sovereign. Hobbes has tried to establish that if the sovereign was challenged and dethroned, the alternative would be anarchy. History is an evidence that the death of a monarch does not result in anarchy. In the middle ages the church replaced the temporal authority. In the modern ages the constitutional machinery is strong enough to make alternative arrangements for substituting a sovereign authority.

11. Undue Importance to Force. Forgetting that 'herd instinct' is stronger than force, for unity and peaceful living, Hobbes believed that the force of sovereign is the only uniting factor. On certain occasions force is repulsing rather than a uniting factor.

12. Underestimate of the Value of Individual. In his social contract Hobbes assigned only negative functions to the state which is improper and undesirable. It becomes still more intolerable when we find that Hobbes considered people as a flock of cattle brutely driven by Leviathan sovereign.

13. Excessive Power for the Sovereign. Hobbes gave his sovereign excessive powers with no checks. He forgot that sovereign is a human being with inherited weaknesses. He forgot that 'power corrupts and absolute power corrupts absolutely.'

WAS HOBBES AN INDIVIDUALIST?

The above criticisms do not mean that Hobbes' theory and political philosophy was faulty. It was the result of his political philosophy that nation's attention was diverted from the theory of 'Divine Origin' of the state to a new trend in political thought. By calling 'human being' as the pivot of his philosophy, he gave due place to the individual in the political set-up. He was perhaps the first English philosopher who pleaded and stood for more freedom for individuals than had been pleaded so far. Vaughan has wrongly said, "Hobbes with all his genius contributed nothing to the theory of state....As state in the development of political philosophy *Leviathan* is worth nothing."

Though *prima facie* individualism has no place in Hobbes' philosophy yet that is not absolutely missing. It has rightly been considered by some of the political thinkers that he was more individualist than even Plato. The greatest element of individualism in him was the treatment of individuals. He believed that they are equal in knowledge and development. He stood for absolute rule because as an individualist he did not believe in the idea of privileged classes. The absence of privileged class could be made good by the institution of absolute monarchy. Hobbes monarchy was not anti-individualist but pro-individualist. Unlike Plato and Aristotle, he did not assign morals as well as political function to the sovereign and the state. His state stands for public safety. He does not ask the state to perform the functions of looking after the well being of the individuals. He gives the individual sufficient scope for their development.

THEORY OF SOVEREIGNTY

Hobbes thus defines sovereign: "By his authority given to him by every particular man in the commonwealth, he has the right of so much power and strength conferred on him, and by that terror thereof, he is enabled to form the wills of them all to place at home and mutual aid against their enemies abroad." And it consists the essence of commonwealth which is one person, of whose acts a multitude by mutual convents one with one another have made themselves, everyone the another or the end he may use the strength and means of them all as he shall think expedient, for their peace and common defence. Hobbes said, "Every order of the ruler, however contrary to the law of God and nature must be accepted, simply because it is his order, as perfectly lawful and just." Thus Hobbes holds that subjects have no right to resist or interfere with the orders of the sovereign. The sovereign possesses unlimited power and unfettered discretion.

Attributes of Sovereignty

1. The sovereign is the source of all positive law and sole law making authority.

2. The sovereign has unlimited power and unfettered jurisdiction and discretion.

3. Subjects have no right to threaten, resist, to punish or depose him.

4. The sovereign has the power to create judicature.

5. He is source of justice.

6. Sovereign cannot do injustice. For he that does anything by authority from another, does therein no injury to him by whose authority he acts. It is true that those having sovereign power may commit inequity, but no injustice, or injury in the proper significance.

7. The sovereign has power to declare war and conduct treaty.

8. Sovereign is indivisible, inseparable and incommunicable.

Specific Functions of Sovereign

1. The Exercise of Final Judgement as to the Expressions of Opinions and Doctrines. Hobbes did not permit freedom of speech without the strict supervision of supreme authority. To quote him, "It is annexed in the sovereignty to be judge of opinion and doctrines are averse and what conducting to peace...right belongs to him that has sovereign power, to be judge or constitute all judges of opinions and doctrines as a thing necessary to peace, thereby to prevent discord and civil war.

2. Control Over Property of His Subjects. Hobbes said, "The whole power of prescribing the rules whereby everyman may know what good he may enjoy, and what actions he may do, without being molested by any of his fellow subjects, and this it is, men call property."

3. Right of Judgement in the Disputes of His Subject. "For without the decision of controversies, there is no protection of one subject against the injuries of another and to every man remains the right of protecting himself by this private strength, which is the condition of war and contrary to the end for which, every commonwealth is instituted."

4. Sole Power of Declaring War and Making Peace. Sovereign has absolute control of the resources of the subjects in carrying the policy so chosen. It is the right of sovereign to decide how great forces are to be assembled, armed and paid for the end; and to levy money upon the subjects; to defray the expenses thereof.

5. Sole Source of Official Authority. In counsellors and magistrates, of honours, wealth and previleges conferred for service to the state, and of gradation of dignity among the recipients of such awards, Sovereign is the sole source of official authority.

Thus in Hobbes' thinking sovereign power is absolute and unshared. Sovereign has the sole right to use force against individuals. He has overwelming power to terrorise individuals to do the comman good. He is the essence of unity of the commonwealth. He is the source of law and its interpretations. Hobbes' views on sovereignty are different from that of Bodin.

Authority to Make Law

Hobbes believed that only the sovereign has authority to make law binding on all subjects. Laws regulate the behaviour of individuals and they must be obeyed by all. Laws are command of sovereign but sovereign himself is not bound by the commands of law, because he is above law. The king can do no wrong. The laws should be enforced by coercion, if necessary. Laws are command of sovereign and must be enforced by punishments. Thus Hobbes was the forerunner of Austin. His conception is still accepted in English system of courts.

Hobbes was of the view that the interpretation of law by sovereign as communicated by his magistrates is binding on the subjects. Divine law must supersede civil law but it is the sovereign alone who can interpret divine law, for otherwise every law would pass for divine law. Sovereign's will and judgement is the law of God, the law of nature the law of nations and the civil law to a subject.

Absolute Monarchy

Thus Hobbes supported absolute monarchy. Some writers have remarked that Hobbes has surpassed all the writers in glorifying the power of sovereign and sovereignty under him has reached highest climax. In ancient and medieval age state and its ruler were subordinate to church. Even the propounders of divine origin theory have made the monarch responsible to God and have placed many limitations on his power. But Hobbes discarded even those limitations on the sovereign. Bodin did not give power to king to go against the law of nature and did not give the monarch control over private property which Hobbes has given. So far views about sovereignty and law are concerned. Hobbes is nearer to Bodin. He has supported absolute power to sovereign but in case of conflict such as the command of sovereign to individual to take his own life, it cannot be commanded by the sovereign. The fundamental right of self defence is inalienable. So long as man is man or an individual is alive, he had the natural propensity to defend himself. If a sovereign cannot protect the lives and the property of the subject then he is no longer sovereign. Hobbes said, "Where there is no common powers there is no law, where there is no law, no justice." Again, "Leviathan cannot oblige men to believe (for) thought is free." Thus Hobbes' thought about sovereign power is in favour of its absoluteness though his philosophy has still some tinge of individualism.

Individualism

The political philosophy of Hobbes starts with individualism but ends in a sort of collectivism, although his collectivism is different from that of Rousseau and Hegel. Hobbes starts with individualism because in the state of nature man used to lead a lonely life. The state of natural life on an individual was solitary, brutish, poor and nasty. Hobbes' philosophy is quite contrary to that of Bodin who considers family as basic unit and thinks that the state came into existence for the protection of family. Even Machiavelli stated that the king should honour women so as not to meddle in family life of subjects. Thus Machiavelli, Bodin and other thinkers assumed some sort of corporate life and desired its protection but Hobbes assumed that individuals lonely and nasty life brought state into existence for the protection of individual.

Feudalism was collectivist but merchant way of life was based on the basis of individualism and self-interest. Being influenced by a merchant's outlook Hobbes supported individual and self-interest. He concluded that every individual safeguards his own self-interest ignoring even the family ties. In the state of nature there was war of every individual against the other and so to protect their individual lives and self interest each individual entered into social contract as an individual and brought the state into existence.

Collectivism

Upto this extent Hobbes remained individualistic, but he became collectivist because his sovereign power represents the will of all individuals within the commonwealth. The authority of sovereign is not totalitarian because thoughts and beliefs are outside the power of the state. The state exists for the sake of individual individual does not exist for the state. The sovereign should be disobeyed, if he orders individual to take his life. Sovereign is not a social, cultural or intellectual entity. Thus political philosophy of Hobbes leans more towards individualistic outlook than collectivistic outlook or to totalitarian society. He starts as an individualist but ends as an absolutist.

Criticism of Hobbes's Theory

1. Neglect of Good Side of Man. Hobbes considers man as bad and declares him selfish, solitary and quarrelsome but neglects good side of man's nature, i.e. his love for peace and co-operation etc.

2. Contract Based on Force. The cardinal qualities of Hobbes' state of nature are force and fraud but with such virtue, social contract based on reasoning and natural sacrifice cannot be possible as he imagines.

3. Fraud in Sovereign. The Hobbesian sovereign is representative of people but if it is expected that force and fraud are basic features of human nature, how can it be expected that sovereign will play force and fraud with the people and he will be the true representative.

4. Locke's Criticism. Locke rediculed the social contract of Hobbes saying "When men quiting the state of nature entered into society, they agreed that all of them but one should be under the restraint of law....this is to think that men are so foolish that they take care to avoid what mischief may be done by tigers and foxes but are content, may think it safety, to be devoured by lions."

5. Wrong Concept of Human Nature. Hobbes based his theory on unsound grounds. He considers man not as a social animal but a quarrelsome animal leading a solitary life. As the creation of a human being and his child nourishment cannot be possible without corporate life, the conception of solitary, bruish and nasty life falls to ground. It seems Hobbes uses his concept of the life as it suits him.

6. Contract Not Historical. Historically, man was able to survive when he sought safety in groups against dangerous animals and no social contract was entered for sovereignty as such a conception is not historical but fiction.

7. Pernicious Theory. According to Vaughan, "Hobbes theory of sovereignty is pernicious and impossible. Pernicious because it leads to despotism, it gives the subject, no defence against oppressive and tyrannical rule of a despot and reduces the whole herd to slavery....the sole union is common terror."

8. Green's Criticism. Hobbes believes that man obeys the command of sovereign because the sovereign possesses the power to use force against those who disobey, but Green holds that individual obeys the sovereign not due to fear but as it is natural for man to obey.

9. Criticism of Leviathan. According to Murray, "Hobbes' biographer could find a solitary supporter, while his assailants were countless. Hobbesianism in fact stood for atheism, materialism, despotism or for many other isms that the fancy of age has suggested. His *Leviathan* is condemned as a rebel's catchism, and as the meanest of all ethical theories. According to Vaughan, "Hobbes with all his genius contributed nothing to theory of the state....as a state in the development of political philosophy '*Levithan*' is worth nothing." He adds, "So far as the vital development of political thought is concerned '*Leviathan*' has remained and deserves to remain, without influence, with fruit, fantastic hybrid." According to Sabine, "Hobbes principles were at least contrary to the pretensions....whom he meant to support as to those of revelation whom he meant to refuse and more contrary to both than either royalist or parliamentarian was to the other. The friends of king might feel that Hobbes' friendship was as dangerous as Cromwell's enmity.

10. Rousseau's Criticism. According to Rousseau, Hobbes's theory lead to tyranny. He provides no basis for civil society. His ideas are fruitless. According to him, 'The man's renouncement of the freedom is inconsistent with man's nature. To strip his will of all freedom is to strip his actions of all moral. His common wealth by contract is no society at all. All life gathers in one man (sovereign) a mere unprofitable man.

IMPORTANCE OF HOBBES

Thomas Hobbes was one of those political philosophers who, by their writings and preachings, played a great role in the social and political life of the people of their times. He stirred the then existing order. He created a sense of great dissatisfaction in many of the then existing institutions. He stood for secularism. The church could not reconcile itself to the philosophy of Hobbes, which so elevated the state and sovereign that the Church became merely a department of the state. The unqualified low position assigned to the church was a source of constant criticism by church fathers. Similarly, the believers of Divine Rights of kings could not support Hobbes in the theory of social contract as it made the monarch a bye product of contract and not a descent of God on earth. On the same line, the followers of parliamentary system of government could not adjust themselves to the ideas of Hobbes which virtually left very little ground for the parliament and much within the purview of monarch. Hobbes could not make much headway for quite some time. His philosophy was not followed till the times of Bentham and Austin. But today the significance of his philosophy has been fully realised. The following points show the importance of Hobbes in the history of political thought:

1. Subordination of Church to State. He was the first political philosopher of the middle ages who ventured to subordinate church and religion to the state.

2. Secularism. Machiavelli separated religion and morals from politics but Hobbes subordinated both to politics. He thus stood for secularism which even today is considered as the best basis for stability of government.

3. Theory of Sovereignty. He was the first political thinker who declared sovereignty as the indivisible and inalienable personality. In this respect he even surpassed Machiavelli who could not dare say that the natural law and divine law would find their expression through a sovereign. His theory of sovereignty is the basis of all definitions given by the political thinkers today. He was the first political philosopher who stood for unlimited sovereignty. Before him, Filmer preached unlimited and unfettered sovereignty but the basis of his sovereignty was not social contract but divine origin which did not make any scope for individualism and was thus unacceptable to the people of his times. J.W. Gough has said, "In the long run his chief contribution to the political theory was his clarification of the principle of sovereignty and the relation of sovereignty to law."

4. Synthesis of Absolute Sovereignty and Individualism. His another contribution to the political philosophy was the beauty with which he synthesised absolute sovereignty and individualism. Both were combined together and made dependent upon each other.

5. Equality of Man. It was in his philosophy, for the first time, that the masses were taken into consideration for the formation of the state and the human equality was brought to the front. In his political philosophy all men were considered equal in talent and development.

6. Synthesis of Elected and Absolute Authority. Hobbes skilfully combined the elected element with the unlimited and absolute authority of the sovereign. He very efficiently made community an agency for the creation of Leviathan. He pleaded absolutism when in the form of 'Theory of Divine Rights of King' that theory had lost ground through out the world.

7. Rejection of Divine origin and Divine Right Theory. God has nothing to do with the origin of the state. Hobbes did not believe that there was any mystery in the creation of the state. The state was a contrivance of man. Hobbes gave a serious set back to the theory of Divine Rights of Kings and the theory of Divine Origin of the State.

8. State as Conciliator of Interests. Credit goes to Hobbes for giving the idea that the state was conciliator of interests. This was otherwise difficult to solve. In this regard Bentham borrowed from him.

9. Realism and Utility. Realism and utility is another contribution of Hobbes. He was clear in his mind that the people left the state of nature and joined civil society, only because they wanted to gain something out of that. Unless the state proved useful and was capable of discharging its obligations it has no right to demand obedience from the citizens. He thus gave the concept of utility and portrayed utilitarian approach to the people.

10. Materialism. It was for the first time that Hobbes gave the idea that matter alone was everything and he based his philosophy on this basic conception. This idea was further developed by Marx, while developing his theory about materialistic interpretation of history.

11. Fictitious Corporation. Credit goes to Hobbes for contributing to the theory of fictitious corporation. He gave the idea that the multitudes cannot act. An individual alone can act in the name of the people. According to him, "Consequently to say that a body of men acts collectively really means that some individual acts in the name of the whole group as its accredited agent and representative."

12. Scientific Legislation. Hobbes proved a guiding genius for the scientific legislation. He clearly said that in all matters of legislation relating to human affairs man made law and not the natural law mattered. Thus Hobbes gave the concept of positive law.

13. Theory of Social Contract. Hobbes said that the sovereign is the creature of a contract signed between the individuals. On the one hand he introduced the idea that the individuals were competent and capable of signing in a contract. On the other hand, he made it amply clear that the sovereign was creature or product of the contract which of course was a novel idea in those days. As A. Hacker said, "But it is Hobbes who has created a theory which embraces a psychology, a sociology and a political science, which integrates these into a coherent theoretical framework."

APPRECIATION OF HOBBES

Following are some estimates of Hobbes by scholars:

(i) ***Sabine.*** "Hobbes' is probably the greatest writer on political philosophy that the English speaking people have produced."

(ii) ***Gettell.*** "The first comprehensive work in political philosophy by an Englishman was by Thomas Hobbes. Indeed his personality played a vital role in shaping his views on the concept of government."

(iii) ***Dunning.*** "Hobbes works placed him at once in the front rank of political thinkers and his theory became, from the moment of its appearance, the centre of animated controversy and enormous influence throughout the western Europe."

(iv) *Wayper.* "It is not accident that J. Bentham borrowed heavily from him here as he did from Hobbes' ideas on felicity. Succeeding generations have usually disagreed with him, but it is no exaggeration to say that they have found in him a mine well worth their while to work for the riches of the ore that it yields."

(v) *Maxey.* "Altogether we are forced to conclude that the debonair and versatile tutor who spent the major part of his life imparting rudimentary learning to succeeding generations of Cavendish heirs was one of the great English race, one whose name will endure as long as men tremble their minds about political matters."

(vi) *A. Hacker.* "Locke, Bentham and Mill are in essential agreement with Hobbes. Burke, Hegel and Marx follow the earlier definition. Rousseau and Tocqueville attempt to reconcile the two and the dialectic of freedom (as preached by Hobbes) will go on so long as political philosophers continue to talk."

(vii) *Oakeshott.* "And he conceived this system was such an imaginative power, that in spite of its relatively simple character, it bears comparison even to the grand and stable creation of Hegel."

(viii) *J.E. Greene.* "He firmly established the sovereignty of national state. Moreover, he declared that the power of the state and the authority of the law are justified only because they contribute with security of individual human beings, and that there is no sense life ground of obedience and respect for authority except the anticipation that these will yield a larger individual than would their absence. It is this over-tone of individualism which makes Hobbe's philosophy one of the most revolutionary theories of the age."

QUESTIONS FOR EXERCISE

1. "The only way to erect such a common power....is to confer all their power and strength upon one men or upon one assembly of men, that may reduce all their wills by plurality of voice into one will." Comment.
2. "Convents without sword, are but words and on no strength to secure a man at all." Comment.
3. "The law of nature and civil law serve each other and are of equal extent." Comment.
4. "A convent not to defend myself from force by force is always void.." Hobbes. Comment.

5. "His work is the first statement of complete sovereignty in the history of political thought." Discuss with reference to Hobbes.
6. "If a sovereign commands a man to kill himself....yet hath that man liberty to disobey." (Hobbes). Comment.
7. "Where there is no common power, there is no law; where no law, no justice." (Hobbes). Comment.
8. "I authorise and give up my right of governing myself, to this man or to this assembly of men, on this condition that thou give up thy right to him and authorise him in all actions in like manner." (Hobbes). Comment.
9. "The Leviathan is the greatest perhaps the sole masterpiece of political philosophy written in English Language." (Oakeshott).
10. "The liberty of subjects lieth only in those things which regulate their actions the sovereign has permitted." (Hobbes), Comment.
11. "The law of nature and civil law contain each other, and are of equal extent." (Hobbes). Comment.
12. "The greatest liberty of subjects consists in the silence." Comment.
13. "It is this clear cut individualism which makes Hobbes' philosophy the most revolutionary theory of the ages." (Sabine). Elucidate and examine.
14. "The truth is that there is very profound contradiction in Hobbes thoughts; the spirit in which Hobbes conceives the state purpose really runs counter to the extreme naturalism of the position from which he begins." (W.T. Jones). Comment.
15. "Hobbes' thought served the ends of a middle class liberalism, a cause with which the philosopher would have had little sympathy." Comment.
16. "Hobbes theories and conceptions are not only defective but also undesirable." Discuss.
17. "Hobbes submerged his subjects in the personalities of his sovereign but claimed to preach individualism". Discuss.
18. "While Hobbes theory of sovereignty resulted in absolutism it was nevertheless based on the doctrine that all men are naturally equal and upon a belief in the desirability of large number of individual freedom." Explain and discuss.
19. "Hobbes starts as an individualist but ends as an absolutist." Discuss fully this statement.
20. "Law in general is not counsel but command." Comment.

21. "These dictators of reason men use to call by the name of laws but improperly for they are but conclusions or theorems concerning conduct to the conservation and defence of themselves." Comment.

22. "Law is the word that by right bringeth command over others." (Hobbes). Comment.

23. Hobbes starts as individualist, but ends as an absolutist. Discuss fully.

24. "Where there is not common power, there is no law; where there is no law, no justice." Comment.

25. "The defence of monarchical absolutism formed a very superficial part of this (Hobbes') effective political philosophy and thought the civil wars occasional his thinking and writing, they account only in small degree for the importance of what he had to say." (Sabine).

26. "With two exceptions, Hobbes with all his genius contributed nothing to the theory of state." (Vaughan). Explain.

27. "The fatal defect of Hobbes' is that his ideas are not fruitful." (Vaughan). Discuss.

24

John Locke (1632-1704 A.D.)

Born at Wrington in Somersetshire in 1632, Locke was the greatest figure in the history of English political thought. He came of Puritan parents. For fourteen years he was educated in his own family circle—a little pocket of peace in a restive country soon to be plunged into civil war. He was educated at Westminster and Oxford. Judging from some of his observations in a later essay entitled *Thoughts on Education*, he was most unhappy at school, forming a poor opinion not merely of Westminster but of public schools in general. Even at Oxford, where he went in 1652 and stayed for thirty years, he was not very happy. Governed by Independents and crowded and Presbyterians, Oxford was becoming a hot-bed of fanaticism and heresy-hunting; and although Locke was favourable to Puritanism, he found a great deal less liberty in the new regime than he had expected. Nevertheless, advocates of genuine religious liberty, Owen and Godwin inspired in Locke that devotion to the idea of *Toleration* upon which he was later to write with such eloquence.

Early Influences

Recounting his early career to his patroness, Lady Masham, Locke later confessed that he was far from being a model student. Nevertheless, he studied in his own way, read widely, including the works of Descartes and Hobbes. The writings of Descartes awakened his interest in philosophy. His friendship with Robert Boyle aroused his enthusiasm for the natural sciences. He became a student of medicine. He was appointed physician to Lord Ashley. He was later appointed confidential secretary to Lord Shaftesbury, the founder of the Whig party. This association influenced Locke's life. It gave him direct experience of practical, political affairs.

COMPARISON WITH HOBBES

Both studied at Oxford, for which both had little use. Both on leaving the University formed connections which influenced his whole life. Both wrote against a background of hectic political life and finally of revolution. Both sought refuge and safety abroad, and both peacefully completed their life in

England. Both were an acknowledged political figure. However, their conclusions regarding the ultimate goal of human life and the theory of state were widely divergent. About their differences C.L. Wayper wrote, "Hobbes is roused the wrath and resentment of Englishmen; Locke won their enthusiastic regard. His was the perfect justification for their perfect revolution-typically English alike in its lack of bloodshed, its respect for property,and its refusal to push matters to their logical conclusions." Locks emerged as a public figure. On Ashley's influence (afterwards famous as Earl of Shaftesbury) he was appointed Secretary to the Council of Trade and plantations in 1673.

Locke's immersion in public life proved beneficial to him and to his philosophy. At Exeter House, he met persons of every sort. He could select at will those with whom he wished to form lasting associations. Like many others who are surrounded by a throng of people, he enjoyed best the company of a small group of intimates. Out of a little 'study circle' at Exeter House in 1671 developed the greatest enterprise of Locke's life. Five or six friends' had assembled at Locke's invitations, to discuss the 'principles of morality and religion'. They were soon baffled by 'difficulties that arose on every side'. Locke suggested that, as a prelude to such discussion, the members should think out for themselves the limits of man's capacity for knowledge. At first he believed it possible to jot down on 'a single sheet of paper' what these limits were; but he soon found the task more arduous than he could have dreamt possible. Thus 'what was begun by change was continued by entreaty, written by incoherent parcels, and after long intervals of neglect resumed again as humour and occasions permitted.' Twenty years were to pass before the great *Essay Concerning Human Understanding* was finally completed, but such were its small beginnings.

Essay Concerning Human Understanding

Locke finished the *Essay*, contributed articles to Le Clerc's *Bibliotheque Universelle* (these latter were his first publications) and, thus at the age of fifty-four embarked upon the career of authorship for which he had been so long preparing. The next two years were occupied in consolidating his fame. He had a large number of manuscripts ready for the press, which were issued one after another to an eager receptive public; the *Letters on Toleration*, the two *Treatises on Civil Government* (published anonymously), and the *Essay Concerning Human Understanding* itself. After that Locke, partly from inclination and partly on account of his indifferent health decided to retire to the country. This was to prove the most pleasant exile of all that he had experienced. His hosts, Sir Francis and Lady Masham, were the embodiments of hospitality and of human understanding. Thus Locke spent the last years of his life at the little village of Oates, conveniently situated in the heart of Essex twenty miles out of London.

John Locke was the apostle of the Revolution of 1688, the most moderate and the most successful of all revolutions. Its aims were modest, but they were exactly achieved, and no subsequent revolution has hitherto been found necessary in England. Locke faithfully embodied its spirit. Most of his works appeared within a year of 1688. His chief work in theoretical philosophy, the *Essay Concerning Human Understanding,* was finished in 1687 and published in 1690.

This is the most important book, upon which his fame most securely rests. At the same time, his influence on the philosophy of politics was so great and so lasting that as Betrand Russell said, "He must be treated as the founder of philosophical liberalism as mush as of empiricism in theory of knowledge."[1] Locke completed his work in theoretical philosophy at the time when the government of his country fell in the hands of men who shared his political opinions. Both in practice and in theory, his views were held, for many years to come by the most vigorous and influential politicians and philosophers. With the developments due to Montesquieu his political doctrines were embedded in the American Constitution, these may be seen at work whenever there is as dispute between President and Congress. The British Constitution was based upon Locke's doctrines until about fifty years ago, and so was that which the French adopted in 1871. The intimate connection between his theory of knowledge and his politics is fully evident not only in France, but also in England.

Lack of dogmatism is a characteristic of Locke, which descended from him to the whole Liberal movement. From his predecessors he took over the concept of man's existence, the existence of God, and the truth of mathematics. But he differs, from his forerunners, because truth is hard to ascertain, and a rational man will hold his opinions with some measure of doubt. This temper of mind is connected with religious toleration, the success of parliamentary democracy, *laissez-faire,* and the whole system of liberal maxims. Although Locke was a deeply religious man, a devout believer in Christianity who accepted revelation as a sources of knowledge, he nevertheless hedged round professed revelations with rational safeguards. On one occasion he said: "Revaluation must be judged by reason." What Locke meant by 'reason' is to be gathered from his whole book in which there is a chapter called 'Of Reason'. This is mainly concerned to prove that reason does not consist of syllogistic reasoning. It is summed up in the sentence: "God has not been so sparing to men to make them barely two-legged creatures, and left it to Aristotle to make them rational." Reason, as Locke used the term, consists of two parts : first, an inquiry as to what things we know with certainly; second, an investigation of propositions which it is wise to accept in practice, although they have only probability and not certainty in their favour. "The grounds of probability", he said, "are two-conformity with our own experience, or the testimony of others' experience."

1. Russel, B., *A History of Western Philosophy* (George Allen & Unwin Ltd., London, 1947, 2nd impression), p. 628.

FOUNDER OF EMPIRICISM

Locke has been regarded as the founder of empiricism which means that all our knowledge is derived from experience. Locke's first book in the *Essay* is concerned in arguing, as against Plato, Descartes and the scholastics, that there are no innate ideas or principles. Locke launched a frontal attack upon a-*priori* thinking in general. If truth is native to our minds, he said, observation and experimental enquiry will lead us nowhere; at best they can merely confirm our knowledge, never add to it. It is doubtful whether, taking the word confirmation literally, they can even confirm such knowledge; because an indubitable 'inner' conviction of the kind furnished by Descartes's *Cogito*, for instance, needs no additional evidence in its favour. In Locke's opinion, however, we arrive at knowledge by a method which is the reverse of that of the spider, who spins its web out of its own bowels. We do not nurture ideas from within, we acquire them from without. There are no 'innate ideas'. All our ideas (i.e., all our knowledge) are acquired through and in sensation. In the second book, Locke set to work to show, in detail, how experience gives rise to various kinds of ideas. Having rejected innate ideas, he said: "Let us then suppose the mind to be, as we say, white paper void of all characters, without any ideas; how comes it to be furnished? Whence comes it by that vast store, which the busy and boundless fancy of man has painted on it with an almost endless variety? Whence has it all the materials of reason and knowledge? To this I answer in one word, from experience : in that all our knowledge is founded, and from that it ultimately derives itself."[2]

Our ideas are derived from two sources : (1) sensation, and (2) perception of the operation of our own mind, which may be called 'internal sense'. Since we can only think by mean of ideas, and sine all ideas come from experience, it is evident that none of our knowledge can antedate experience.

Perception, he said, "the first step and degree towards knowledge, and the inlet of all the materials of it." This may seem almost a truism to a modern man. But in Locke's day the mind was supposed to know all sorts of things a-*priori*, and the complete dependence of knowledge upon perception was a new and revolutionary doctrine.

To 'know', in Locke's view, is to perceive a relation between ideas. Ideas, according to him, are of two kinds. These are: first, simple ideas, derived either immediately in sensation, or by a kind of 'inner' experience called reflection; second, there are complex ideas, which are no more than combinations of the first. The mind or spirit of man originally resembles an empty tablet: experience is that which writes upon it. Before we admit sensation, we cannot engage in thinking : 'There is nothing in the intellect which was not previously in the senses.'

---

2. *Essay Concerning Human Understanding*, Book II, Chap., I, Sec. 2

That which causes an idea to be produced in our mind is in Locke's terminology, the 'quality' of the external object. Here Locke introduced a distinction which has played an important role in all later philosophical thought. Qualities, such as, solidity, extension, form, number, etc. are all constant qualities : to whatever alterations the body or object is subjects, these qualities suffer no changes. Such qualities Locke called 'primary'. They are to be distinguished from what he called 'secondary' qualities, which though not to be found in the object itself, are the result of the impact of some power in the primary qualities upon our sense organs. Such secondary qualities are colours, odours, sounds, tastes, etc. : qualities occasioned by the object but *produced* as a result of something which we, as observers, contribute. Without human sense organs, colours and sounds, odours and tastes would simply not exist.

Granted that we know all things through sensation, or that all our knowledge purely depends upon perception it does not follow at all that our perception of things or our experience of the external world is always identical. The experience or the knowledge about a thing varies from time to time and from person to person. This poses a problem of a great importance to both a psychologist and a student of ethics. Our knowledge regarding the constant qualities, which Locke called 'primary' qualities, of an object may be alike,but our experience in the form of an inner sensation or feeling cannot be the same. Her Locke introduced his ethical doctrines with which his later political ideas are closely connected.

ETHICAL DOCTRINES

Like Bentham, Locke was a man filled with kindly feeling, who yet held that everybody (including himself) must always be moved, in action, solely be desire for his own happiness or pleasure. A few quotations will clarify this point :

"Things are good or evil only in relation to pleasure or pain. That we call 'good' which is apt to cause to increase pleasure, or diminish pain, in us."

"What is it moves desire? I answer, happiness, and that alone."

"Happiness, in its full extent, is the utmost pleasure we are capable of."

"The necessity of pursuing true happiness (is) the foundation of all liberty."

"The preference of vice to virtue (is) a manifest wrong judgement."

"The government of our passions (is) the right improvement of liberty."[3]

Locke said that liberty depends upon the necessity of pursuing true happiness and upon the government of our passions. This opinion he derived from his doctrine that private and public interests are identical in the long run, though not necessarily so over short periods. It follows that in a community

3. Refer to Book II, Chap. XX.

of citizens who are all both pious and prudent, they wiil all act in a manner to promote the general good. There will be no need of human laws to restrain them, since divine laws will suffice. The hitherto virtuous man who is tempted to become a highwayman will say to himself : "I might escape the human magistrate, but I could not escape punishment at the hands of the Divine Magistrate," He will accordingly renounce his nefarious schemes, and live as virtuously as if he were sure of being caught by the police. Legal liberty, therefore, is completely possible only where both prudence and piety are universal; elsewhere, "the restraints imposed by the criminal law are indispensable." Locke repeatedly stated that morals, like mathematics, is a demonstrable science, subject to ascertainable, universal laws, but he did not develop this idea so fully as could be wished.

These universal laws are the Divine Law and the Natural Law. The Divine Law is God's will for man's behaviour, which is made available to man both by divine relation and by the use of his own reason, and which is, above all, to be looked for in the New Testament. The Natural Law is also an eternal law, the criterion of good and evil, discoverable by reasoning and commanding men to carry out the will of God.

It is typical of the contradictory nature of Locke's theory of morals that, having said that men are incapable of desiring anything but pleasure, be maintained that they ought to act so as to produce the greatest amount of public or general happiness, and contended that criterion of the goodness and the badness of their actions is their result expressed in terms of public happiness.

CONCEPTION OF HUMAN NATURE

Locke's view of human nature is not so profound and as consistent as that of Hobbes. However, his problem was the same as that of Hobbes: Why do men wish to form civil society, and how can they do so? Locke's answer to that problem was very different from that of Hobbes. It was essentially a justification of the Glorious Revolution of 1688 a revolution which Hobbes would have regarded as anarchic and deplorable in the extreme. And in order to put forward his answer to that question and advance his justification of the Revolution, Locke made use, of the state of nature and of the social contract as devices which helped him to clarify his ideas. This was also done by Hobbes and so many other thinkers of 17th century to which the feudal contract was still a lively memory and commercial contract comparatively new and very appealing.

Filmer's Theory

Locke's two *Treatises on Civil Government* are different both in object and in value. "The first is a detailed and tiresome response to the historic

4. Laski, H.J., *Political Thought in England* (Oxford University Press, Great Britain, Reprint 1955), p. 29.

imagination of Sir Robert Filmer."[4] It is a reply to Sir Robert Filmer's *Patriarcha: Or The Natural Power of Kings,* which was published in 1680, but written under Charles I. The king, according to Filmer, is perfectly free from all human control, and cannot be bound by the acts of his predecessors, or even by his own, for "impossible it is in nature that a man should give a law unto himself." *Patriarcha* begins by combating the "common opinion" that "mankind is naturally endowed and born with freedom from all subjection, and at liberty to choose what form of government it please, and the power which any one man hath over others was first bestowed according to the discretion of the multitude." "This tenet," he wrote, "was first hatched in the schools." But the truth, according to Filmer, is quite different. It is, that originally God bestowed the kingly power upon Adam, from whom it descended to his heirs, and ultimately reached the various monarchs of modern times. He advances his arguments in his *Patriarcha*, "Kings now either are, or are to be reputed, the next heirs to those first progenitors who were at first the natural parents of the whole people." Our first parent, it seems, did not adequately appreciate his privilege as universal monarch, for "the desire of liberty was the first cause of the fall of Adam." The desire of liberty is a sentiment which Sir Rober Filmer regarded as impious. According to him, political power derives, not from any contract, nor yet from any consideration of the public good, but entirely from the authority of a father over his children. His view was : that the source of regal authority is subjection of children to parent; that the patriarchs in Genesis were monarchs; that kings are the heirs of Adam, or the least are to be regarded as such; the natural rights of a king are the same as those of a father; and that, by nature, some are never free of paternal power, even when the son is adult and the parent is in his dotage.

Locke's Reputation of Filmer

Locke's first *Treatise on Civil Government* was written to disapprove the doctrine of royal prerogative based upon the divine right. It followed the method of Sydney in refuting point by point the arguments of Filmer's *Patriarcha*. Locke pointed out that, if parental power is what is concerned, the mother's power should be equal to the father's. He laid stress on the injustice of primogeniture, which is unavoidable if inheritance is to be the basis of monarchy. He showed the absurdity of supposing that actual monarchs are, in any real sense, the heirs of Adam. Adam can have only one heir, but no one knows who he is. Would Filmer maintain, he asked, that, if the true heir could be discovered, all existing monarchs should lay their crowns at his feet? If Filmer's basis for monarchy were accepted, all kings, except at most one, would be usurpers, and would have no right to demand the obedience of their *de facto* subjects. Moreover, parental power, he stated, is temporary, and extends not to life or property.

THE STATE OF NATURE

Locke's second *Treatise on Civil Government* is a comprehensive and systematic discussion of the origin, nature and province of government. He acknowledged his indebtedness to Hooker from whom he derived his main ideas. In his individualistic point of view and in his dependence upon the social contract theory he agreed with Hobbes. But he rejected almost every premise of Hobbes's philosophy. To Hobbes the State of Nature and preceding political organization had been a stage of war. Neither peace nor reason could prevail where every man was his neighbour's enemy : and the establishment of absolute power, with the consequent surrender by men of all their natural liberties, was the only means of escape from so brutal a regime. Locke denied such a state of affairs in the State of Nature, although he, like Hobbes, considered 'State of Nature' antecedent to all human government. According to Locke, in this state there is a 'law of nature', but the law of nature consists of divine commands and it not imposed by any human legislator. It is not clear how for the State of Nature was, for Locke, a mere illustrative hypothesis, and how far he supposed it to have had a historical existence; but he tended to think of it as a stage that had actually occurred. Men emerged from the State of Nature by means of a social contract which instituted civil government. This Locke regarded as more or less historical.

LAW OF NATURE

What Locke had to state about the State of Nature and the Law of Nature was not original, but a repetition of medieval scholastic doctrines. St. Thomas Ecquina said: "Every law framed by man bears the character of a law exactly to that extent to which it is derived from the law of nature. But if on any point it is in conflict with the law of nature, it at once ceases to be law; it is mere perversion of law."[5] Throughout the Middle Ages, the Law of Nature was held to condemn 'usury', i.e., lending money at interest. Church property was almost entirely in land, and landowners have always been borrowers rather than lends. But when Protestantism arose, its support came chiefly from the rich middle class, who were lenders rather than borrowers. Accordingly, first Calvin, then other Protestants, and finally the Catholic Church, sanctioned 'usury'. Thus, Natural Law came to be differently conceived, but no one doubted its existence.

Many doctrines which survived the belief in Natural Law owe their origin to it; for example, *laissez-faire* and the right of man. These doctrines are connected. Both have their origins in puritanism. Two quotations given by Tawney will be sufficient to illustrate this. A committee of the House of Commons in 1604 stated:

"All free subjects are born inheritable, as to their land, and also as to the free exercise of their industry, in those trades whereto they apply themselves and whereby they are to live."

---

5. Quoted by Tawney in *Religion and the Rise of Capitalism.*

And in 1636 Joseph Lee wrote:

"It is an undeniable maxim that every one by the light of nature and reason will do that which makes for his greatest advantage.... The advancement of private persons will be the advantage of the public."[6]

Thus in theory of Government Locke, resembles most of the men who have won fame for their ideas, and in this there is little that is original. As a rule, the man who first thinks of a new idea is so much ahead of his time that everyone thinks him silly, so that he remains obscure and is soon forgotten. Then, gradually, the world becomes ready for the idea, and the man who proclaims it at the fortunate moment gets all the credit.

In regard to the State of Nature, Locke was less logical than Hobbes, who regarded it as one in which there was war of all against all, and life was nasty, brutish and short. But Hobbes was known as an atheist. Locke considered the State of Nature a happy state in which the conduct of men was governed by a body of rules. The belief in a happy State of Nature in the remote past is derived partly from the Biblical narrative of the age of the patriarchs, partly from the classical myth of the golden age. The general belief in the badness of the remote past only came with the doctrines of evolution. Locke defined the State of Nature in the following words: "Men living together according to reason, without a common Superior on earth, with authority to judge between them, is properly the state of nature. "The State of Nature has a Law of Nature to govern it, which obliges everyone, and reason, which is that law, teaches all mankind who will but consult it, that being all equal and independent, no one ought to harm another in his life, health, liberty or possessions; for men being all the workmanship of one omnipotent and infinitely wise Maker; all the servants of one Sovereign Master, sent into the world by His order and about His business; they are His property, Whose workmanship they are made to last during His, not one another's, pleasure. "And that all men may be restrained from invading other's rights and from doing hurt to one another, and the Law of Nature be observed, which will the peace and preservation of all mankind, the execution of the Law of Nature is in that state put into every man's hands, whereby everyone has a right to punish the transgressors of that law to such a degree as may hinder its violation."[7] Unlike Hobbes such a description, was of an imagined community of virtuous anarchists, who need no police or law-courts because they always obey 'reason', which is the same as 'natural law', which in turn, consists of those laws of conduct that are held to have divine origin. Its arbiter is reason. In the natural state, reason shows us that men are equal. From this quality are born men's natural rights which Locke, like the Independents in the Puritan revolution identifies with life, liberty and property.

6. Quoted by N Russell in *History of Western Philosophy*, p. 649.

7. Lock, *Civil Government*, *Book* II, Chap. II

Obviously enough, for Locke, the instinct of self-preservation was the deepest of all human impulses. By Liberty, Locke meant the right of the individual to follow his own bent. Law is clearly a means to the realization of freedom in the same way that the rule of the road will, by its common acceptance, save its observers from accident. It promotes the initiative of men by defining in terms which by their very statement obtain acknowledgment of the conditions upon which individual caprice may have its play. Locke derived the conception of the right to property from some sort of primitive anarchism in which a man was supposed to defend his property by every possible means with which he had associated his labour, or from a primitive communism which became transmuted into individual ownership whenever he mingled his labour with some object.

In contrast to the argument of Hobbes the State of Nature, which Locke described, was thus pre-eminently social in character. It was one of "peace, goodwill, mutual assistance and preservation." Locke defended it on the ground that the Law of Nature provides a complete equipment of human rights and duties. But such a state of Nature was in no way a civil state. There was no common superior to enforce the law of Nature. Each man protected his own interests as best as he could, and his right to his own and his duty to respect what was another's were as complete as ever they could become under government. But as the reason of men worked differently in the absence of common standard of justice there was bound to be an inconvenient variety in the conceptions of justice. The result was uncertainly and chaos. It was here that the social contract emerged. But just as Locke's natural state implies a natural man utterly distinct from Hobbes's gloomy picture, so does Locke's social contract represent rather the triumph of reason than of hard necessity. Everything that is ever right or wrong so eternally; positive law adds nothing to the ethical quality of different kinds of conduct, but merely provides an apparatus for effective enforcement. Against Hobbes, Locke tires to set up the proposition that moral rights and duties are intrinsic, that morality makes law, and not law morality, and that governments have to give effect to what is naturally right prior to its enactment.

THE SOCIAL CONTRACT

According to Locke, civil society came into existence from the consent of its members. He defined civil power as the right of making laws with penalties for the regulating and preserving of property, and of employing the force of community in the execution of such laws, all this only for the good of public. "Power came into existence by consent because men entered into a contract, to get rid of the incremonials of the state of nature and the state of nature changed into a political state."

Locke states that the sovereign power thus created by the contract is vested in the community as a whole and not in any one single person. The contract must be unanimous and irrevocable because after having once made it, the people cannot go back to the original state. The contract however must respect natural rights i.e. rights to life, liberty and property of man and also with the law of nature.

Features of Contract

Gettell says, "The contract was specific and limited, not general as Hobbes had said." According to a writer contract is single, because to Locke man is social by nature; but according to C.E. Vaughan it may be inferred that the contract was double.

1. The contract is of each with all.

2. Each individual agrees to aid to the community as a whole.

3. As body politic is formed by means of contract, each individual gives up his personal right to interpret and administer the law of nature in return for a guarantee that their natural rights of life, liberty and property will be preserved.

4. The sovereign power in vested not in a single man or organ but community as a whole.

5. Contract is unanimous and based on the consent of people.

6. By contract no one accepted any restriction on his freedom of action.

7. The contract is irrevocable as men cannot return back to the state of nature.

8. Men surrender their personal right to interpret and administer the law of nature but they do not surrender the natural rights of life, liberty and property.

9. The civil community or authority is bound to respect the right of life, liberty and property i.e. natural rights of men and had to abide by the law of nature itself.

Criticisms

The theory of social contract put forth by Locke has been put to following criticisms:

1. Protection of Propertied Class. That natural man had some property and authority. He wanted that a good government should protect those rights. Thus Locke stood for the protection of propertied class. This philosophy cannot be justified on the basis of equality and common principles of justice.

2. Misunderstanding of Human Nature. Like Hobbes, Locke misunderstood the nature of man. Man was not nasty, brutish and uncivilised as Hobbes conceived him. Man was also never gentle, self-realising and responsible to the extent to which Locke thought of. At no stage of human history man has acted as restrained person in the absence of any authority. Locke is thus a victim of miscalculation of man's nature and his basic instincts.

3. Society of Government. It is doubtful whether Locke created a society or a government. Government is an agency which has executive, legislative and judicial powers. In the case of Locke, it has only limited legislative functions which were assigned to the supreme authority and that too of only on interpreting the laws. It is doubtful whether Locke created a sovereign or only a judge and thus whether the state came into being at all.

4. Social Contract not a Fact. As expounded by Locke, the theory of social contract postulates the individuals who was given indivisible rights and also the legislature which was the only organ of the government. This is not correct.

5. Sacrifice of Legal Sovereign. Locke's main task was to bring a man from pre-civil state to a civil state and thus to create a legal sovereign. In his defence of revolution he failed in this main task as well. He rather sacrificed his legal sovereign at the alter of popular sovereign.

6. Majority not Tyrannous. As Sabine has pointed out, "If an individual's rights are really indefensible, it is no better for his to be deprived of them by a majority than by a single tyrant; apparently it occurs to Locke that majority could be tyrannous. In general it cannot be said that the principle of majority rule has any such obvious validity as Locke imputed to it."

CONCEPT OF PRIVATE PROPERTY

Private property is an age of old institution. It is the subject matter of many controversial theories both in political as well as economic fields. No serious political philosopher could afford to ignore discussion on this subject. About the growth of this age old institution it has beer said "Plato believed that property obscured men's reasoning powers and he therefore denied it to the Guardians. Aristotle approved of property, but he said that any class which became too wealthy would constitute a threat to political stability. St. Thomas refused to assert that property is sanctioned by natural laws and claimed that it is an addition enacted by human legislators. And Hobbes allowed his citizens to own property but be gave the sovereign the power to regulate the way in which it was employed. All the theorists have in short expressed reservation about property."

Support of Private Property

Locke believed that the institution of private property is essential for the development of mankind. Man is an enterpreneural animal. He has right to own private property. Commonwealth came into being `o protect his natural rights of life, liberty and property, of them all the right to property was most sacred and valuable one. Locke did not agree with Aristotle about the notion of private property. He did agree with Rousseau when he said, "that property ownership has become concentrated in too few hands and hence can no longer enter a claim to legitimacy." Locke believed that private property must be preserved if the citizens should live happily. Private property is always a source of joy.

Justification of Private Property

1. Religious Ground. Locke believed that ownership of private property was justified on different grounds. God did not commit himself on public or private ownership of earth resources. Locke said, "The appropriate means for making use of the resources which God gas given to men is for individuals to develop them so that they can actually sustain life." According to Locke therefore on religious grounds it is not unjustified to own or hold private property.

2. Property a Result of Labour. Another justification for the retention of private property is that men have mixed labour in that. Locke said, "Every man has a property in his own persons; thus nobody has any right but to himself. The labour of his body and the works of his hands we may say are properly his. Whatsoever then he removes out of the state that nature bath provided and left it in, he hath mixed his labour with and joined it to something that is the own, and thereby makes it his property" Men put in their labour by way of tilling and sowing the land. It is their labour which makes the lands into private property. To quote Locke, "As much as man tills, plants, improves, cultivates and can use the product of so much is his property." Quoting in support of his own argument, he says, "Thought the water running in the fountain be every one's yet who can doubt that in pitcher it is his only who draws it out."

3. Socially Sanctioned. Possession of private property has social approval and sanction from times past. It has social sanction and recognition. "Property is legitimate because men who must live in its midst have consented to its existence...Rousseau will insist that consent must been active process, one renewed each day in men's lives; while Burke will claim that genuine consent is found in the established customs which men unconsciously develop over generations and centuries. Furthermore, Locke defended property through consent only part of the way; he has also said that property is sanctioned by God and earned by men."

4. Social Product. Locke also justified the retention of private property on the grounds that it emerged in the society and continues to exist even today whether we like that or not. He said "You shall see that some man will begin presently to enlarge his possession." The very fact that property has got social approval throughout these ages is sufficient to indicate that it is an unobjectionable institution. It is natural to bulk of society as every one has a desire to increase one's possessions. This sense of ownership elevates self-confidence among all. Locke adopted a middle course between medievalism and modernism. Sabine has said, "Apparently he was generalizing from the example of colonists in new land like America, but it is probable that he was influenced also by strong sense of the superior productivity of private agricultural economy as compared with communal tillage of more primitive systems."

5. Historical Grounds. Another justification of private property is based on historical grounds. According to Locke history is a witness that only those have suffered under tyrannies who did not own property. Liberty of those people was snatched who were without private property. Once the institution of private property is encouraged, that is sure guarantee for all kinds of liberties. Maxey says, "Guarantee every man freedom of property, and according to the Lockeian theory, there would be little cause to worry about his other liberties, he would be amply able to look out himself." Locke was of the view that possession or private property is essential particularly for middle classes he, however, suggests a degree of social control over private property.

LOCKE'S INDIVIDUALISM

1. Definite Status of the Individuals. Locke did not agree that the individual has no standing what so ever and that he is only an insignificant and subordinate organ of the society. He believe that the individual has definite standing. According to Vaughan, "Everything in Locke's system revolved around the individual, everything is disposed so as to ensure the sovereignty of individual." That state is the best where the interests of the individuals are best protected. It is the foremost duty of the state to preserve, protect and honour the inborn and natural rights of the mankind. Locke says, "Men agreed to join and unite into a community for their comfortable, safe and peaceful living, one amongst another, in a secure enjoyment of properties and greater securities against anything that were not before it."

2. Govt. Exists for Individuals. The sole intention of Locke was to subordinate government to the community. According to Sabine, "Government is indispensable and its right therefore in a sense in indivisible, but it is also derivative in the sense that it exists for the well being of the nations." Locke emphasised that the government exists only for the welfare of the individuals. According to Dunning, "There is in this conception nothing that absolute and uncontrollable sovereignty which was the soul of Hobbe's system." Maxey says "it was not his concern to exalt its political authority but to describe its limitation."

3. Division of Powers for Individuals Freedom. To uphold his individualism, Locke attempted on the theory of division of powers which he believed was essential for preserving individuals and freedoms.

4. Right of People of Revolt. Lock's individualism is amply expressed in his ideas about the rights of the people to revolt against their sovereign. The people have power, not the right, to remove a government whose policies they find are curtailing their rights. The people have certain basic minimum rights. No authority in the state has any right to snatch these rights from him. A state should bestow and not snatch rights. Locke said "The legislative being only of judiciary power to act for certain ends, there remains still in the people a supreme power to remove or alter the legislative when they find the legislative contrary to the trust reposed in them. And the community perpetually retains a supreme power saving themselves from the attempts and designs of anybody even of their legislators whenever they shall be so foolish or so wicked as to lay and carry on designs against the liberation and properties of the subjects."

5. Authority of People to Dissolve Legislature. Law making agency should not betrary the trust reposed in it. As soon as there is such betrayal, the legislature was defunct for all purposes. In Locke's own words, "Government is dissolved when the legislature is so transformed as to bring the law making power into the hands of other than those to which it was entrusted by the community and its organisation or when either legislature or executive acts contrary to its trusts." As to the doubt whether the legislature has betrayed the confidence of the people or not, Locke felt that the society as a whole should decide in this regard. This decision is final, unchallengeable and indisputable. Since society is to be influenced by the decision of this agency, it is the best judge to decide about the nature and character of legislature. Locke believed that the people have ultimate authority to decide whether dissolving conditions have come or not.

6. Preservation of Natural Rights. Locke's love for individualism is also clearly reflected when he assumed that the individuals is everything and that state is a means to achieve certain ends. It is the supreme duty of the state to preserve natural rights of men. Revolution is justified when such rights were flouted, disregarded or disrespected.

STATE AND SOVEREIGNTY

Locke wrote in Book II : "Men being, as has been said, by nature all free, equal, and independent, no one can be put out of this estate and subjected to the political power of another without his own consent, which is done by agreeing with other men, to join and unite into a community for their comfortable, safe, and peaceable living, one amongst another, in as secure enjoyment of their properties, and a greater security against any that are not of it. This any number of men may do, because it inquires not the freedom of the the rest; they are left, as they were, in the liberty of the state of Nature: when any number of men have so consented to make one community or government, they are thereby presently incorporated and make one body politic, wherein the majority have a right to act and conclude the rest."[8] As such, it was a contract with the community as a whole which resulted in the establishment of that common political superior—the state—which was supposed to enforce the law of Nature and punish infractions of it.

Locke's state, thus, is not a sovereign state: The word 'sovereignty' does not occur throughout the treatise, the state has power only for the protection

8. Lock, *Civil Government,* Book II, Chap.VIII.

of natural law. Its province ends when it passes beyond those boundaries. The power given up was not vested in the single man or organ but in the community as a whole. Even the sovereignty of the political community or state is not absolute. It has only the power to protect natural law. Such as contract involved the necessity of majority rule. Each man surrendered to community his right to execute natural law: The minority must be bound by the will of the majority, who might use force if necessary. The consent of individuals to membership in the political community might be expressed or tacit. Thus, the effect of the original contract was made binding upon the descendants of its founders. However, the government remains responsible to the people; its power is limited both by moral law and by the constitutional traditions and conventions inherent in the history of the realm. Government is indispensable and its right is therefore in a sense indivisible, but it is also derivative in the sense that in exists for the well-being of the nation.[9] Both government and society exit to preserve the individual's rites, and the indivisibility of such rights is a limitation on the authority of both.

Locke regarded the original contract as the first step to the drawing up of a trust. People, having formed a society, must then institute a government. They do not do this by making a contract but by drawing up a trust which creates government as "only a fiduciary power to act for certain ends." If there is a miscarriage of power by those in authority, the government will be dissolved and the power will revert to the society. Locke concluded his *Treatise on Civil Government* with the following remark:

"The power that every individual gave the society when he entered into it can never revert to the individuals again, as long as the society lasts, but will always remain in the community: because without this there can be no community, no commonwealth, which is contrary to the original agreement, so also when the society hath placed the legislative in any assembly of men, to continue in them and their successors, with direction and authority for providing such successors, the legislative can never revert to the people whilst that government last; because, having provided a legislative with power to continue for ever, they have given up their political power to the legislative, and cannot resume it. But if they have set limits to the duration of their legislative, and made this supreme power in any person or assembly only temporary: or else, when by the miscarriages of those in authority, it is forfeited; upon the forfeiture of their rules, or at the determination of the time set, it reverts to the society, and the people have a right to act as supreme, and continue the legislative in themselves or place it in a new form, or new hands, as they think good."[10]

9. Refer to Lock's *Civil Government,* Book II, Chapt. IX

10. Lock, *Civil Government,* Book II, Chap.. XIX.

THE CONCEPT OF GOVERNMENT

Locke recognized the distinction between state and government. Indeed, at times he approximated a secondary contract by which government was created after establishment of civil society. The distinction is made in the light of what is to follow. For Locke "was above all anxious to leave supreme power in a community whose single will, as manifested by majority verdict, could not be challenged by any lesser organ than itself."[11] Government must be there if political society is to endure; but its form and substance are dependent upon popular institution. And his 'right to revolution', a development of the earlier theory of resistance, became one of the most influential parts of his doctrine. A government which begins in force can be justified, only by its recognition and support of the moral rights inherent in persons and commodities. The moral order is permanent and self-perpetuating, governments are only factors in the moral order.

Classification of Government

In dividing governments into monarchies, aristocracies and democracies Locke followed the great Aristotelean traditions considering the location of legislative authority as the fundamental test. He viewed the executive and the judiciary as clearly dependent upon the law-making body. He did not explicitly develop the theory of separation of powers. He was willing to have a king if the king were divested of his law-making power and if his right to rule were acknowledged to depend upon popular consent. However, Locke did completely dislike kingship. His *Letters* show that he disliked the Cromwellian system and the republicanism which Harrington and Milton had based upon it. He was ready to have a kingship provided it fulfilled the condition, mentioned above. Admitting that monarchy, from its likeness to the family, is the most primitive type of government, he denied Hobbes's assertion that it is the best. It seems to degenerate always into the hands of lesser men who betray the contract they were appointed to observe. In the same way, Locke did not consider aristocracy much better off since it emphasizes generally the interest of a group against the superior interest of the community as a whole. According to Locke democracy alone proffers adequate safeguards of an enduring good rule; a democracy, that is to say, which is in the hands of delegates controlled by popular election. Although, in a democracy, the legislature is the most supreme organ of the government, it must be removable by the community. Like the English House of Commons, the legislative is to be elected from time to time by popular vote. The condition that the legislative should be removable by the people condemns the part allowed by the British Constitution in Locke's day to King and Lords as part of legislative power. In all wellframed governments, Locke said, the legislative and executive are separate. If the Executive fails to summon the

11. Laski, H.J., *Political Thought in England* (Oxford University Press, 1955), p. 33

legislative at the proper times is at war with the people, and may be removed by force. This is obviously a view suggested by what happened under Charles I. From 1628 to 1640 he tried to govern without Parliament; this sort of thing, Locke felt, must he prevented by civil war if necessary.

Rights of People Against the Government

The question of the rights of the people against the government, is a very difficult one. It is too readily assumed by democrats that, when the government represents are majority, it has a right to coerce the minority. Up to a point, this may be considered true, since coercion is the essence of every government. But this sort of divine right of majorities, may become almost as tyrannical as the divine right of kings. In his *Essays on Government* Locke said little on this subject but he considered it at some length in his *Letters on Toleration*, where he argued that no believer in God should be penalized on account of his religious opinions. The state should deal only with the preservation of social order, not with the souls of men. The Church is a voluntary society, without the right of coercion. Locke favoured toleration in religion. The state should suppress opinions only when they are subversive of public peace. But Locke was against Catholics, Mohammedans and atheists. He argued that Catholics owed allegiance to a foreign power; Mohammedans' morals were incompatible with English civilization; and atheists lacked a sanction for good conduct. Their Locke's conception of toleration in religion was limited and biased. The same defect appears in his theory of popular consent. As soon as he accepted the right of the majority to coerce the minority he paved the way for the tyrannical rule of majorities, no mater half-heartedly or whole-heartedly, or either for the perpetuation of civil society or in the public interest. There is no guarantee that the choice of the majority is always good and pious and in the interest of the community as a whole, while the minority is always wrong and its every action threatens the very basis of society. Locke's silence on this puzzling but important subject makes his individualism or his theory of popular consent as ambiguous and idealistic as that of Green in the nineteenth century.

FUNCTIONS OF GOVERNMENT

Locke believed that body politic and commonwealth came into being for the welfare of the individuals and the community. He, therefore, assigned following functions to the Government:

1. To Fix Standards of Ethics. The government should attempt to create standards by which the individuals should be in a position to decide as to what was right or wrong. The law of nature which all followed in the state of nature was clear and rational yet selfish interest make man blind to proper understanding. These also influence his judgement of deciding as to what is right or wrong.

2. Impartial Authority to Decide Disputes. The government should provide its subjects with an impartial authority to decide the disputes arising out of social misunderstanding in the community. This is essential because men were usually partial towards themselves. They usually carry their interests rather too-off. To quote Locke, "For everyone in that state being its judge and executioner of the law of nature, men being partial to themselves, passion and revenge is very apt to carry them too far, and with much heat in their own case, as well as negligence and unconcurredness to make them to remiss in other men's."

3. To Safeguard People's Interests. Locke believed that it was the duty of the state to safeguard the interests of its individual and subjects against undue intervention from outside agencies. He goes to the extent of saying that the state has a right to declare war if it feels that the life and property of its subjects is at stake. The state should not hesitate to sacrifice anything when it felt that the rights of the individuals were being challenged. Laski says, "Locke may not possess the clarity and ruthless logic of Hobbes, nor the genius for compressing into phrase the experience of a life time which makes Burke the first of English political thinker. Hobbes, after all, worked with an impossible psychology and sought no more than the prescription against disorders. Burke wrote rather text book for cautious administrator than a guide for the liberal statesman. But Locke said that the main problem of the state is the conquest of freedom and it was for its definition in terms of individual good that he above all strove."

Constitutional Government

As regards his concept of constitutional government it is worthwhile to note that Locke was perhaps the first thinker who realised that unless rule of man against man was based on consent it had not legal justification. His stress for constitutional government was more in the days when he was expounding his philosophy.

Limitations on the Authority of Government

Locke did not agree with Hobbes that the Government has absolute power and authority. He was of the opinion that the government was bound by the following limitations:

1. No Right to Destroy. The Government could not have a right to destroy, enslave or impoverish the subjects.

2. Through Known Laws. The government should govern not by unknown laws but the laws which have been promulgated and are known to judiciary.

3. Property. The government has no authority to take rightly earned property of any of his subjects without their consent because it does not stand for snatching the property but for preserving that.

4. Legislation as Trust. The legislation was trust for the nation and hence that could not be transferred to any other authority.

5. Natural Rights. The Government could not abrogate the natural rights of the individuals.

6. Promoting Ability. On the other hand it should function for promoting utility.

7. Laws of Nature. The legislature must act according to the laws of nature.

Separation of Powers

Legislature had a supreme authority and place in Locke's philosophy. The executive and judiciary were subordinate to legislature. Legislature and executive must be separated from each other both in functions and personnel. The executive may issue ordinances when legislature is not is session. In this connection it is worthwhile to remember that Locke picked up the thread after Polybius. From Locke Montesquieu picked up the idea and made it the basis of his theory of separation of powers. It was indirectly the influence of Locke on the constitution makers of U.S.A. which is based on the doctrine of separation of powers.

Religious Tolerance

Locke believed in religious tolerance except in the case of those who had foreign allegiance or had a code of peculiar morality. The church should not interfere in the affairs of the state. The state should not interfere in the religious affairs of the individuals except when peace and tranquillity of the state was in danger. The church and the state are separate organisations and should be treated as such. According to Locke, tolerance is essential for human and national development. Locke also pleaded it on grounds of fair-play and public policy. Religious intolerance was bound to put a ban and premium on human intellect and limit human understanding.

LOCKE AND BENTHAM

Locke was the true progenitor of Benthamism, and his work can hardly be understood, save in this context. Just as in his ethical inquiries it was always the happiness of the individual that he sought, so in his politics it was the happiness of the subject he had in view. "That which is for the public welfare," he said, "is God's will"; and therein we find the root of that utilitarianism which, as Maine pointed out, is the real parent of all nineteenth-century change, with Locke, as with the Benthamites, his clear sense of what utilitarianism demanded led to an over-emphasis on human rationalism. No one can read the second *Treatise* without perceiving that Locke looked upon the state as a machine, which can be built and taken to pieces in a very simple fashion. Herein, undoubtedly, he, to quote Laske, "over-simplified the problem; and that made him miss some of the cardinal points, a true psychology of the state must seize. His very contractualism, indeed, is part of this affection for the rational. It resulted in his failure to perceive how complex is the mass of motives embedded in the political act. The significance of hard instinct and the vast primitive deeps of the unconscious were alike hidden from him."[12] Our age is one of organization, and its conflicts are between organisations, not between separate individuals. The state of Nature, as Locke stated, still exists as between states. A new international Social Contract is indispensable before we can properly enjoy the promised benefits of governments. Here Bertrand Russell correctly remarks that if "once an international government has been created, much of Locke's political philosophy will again become applicable, thought not the part of it that deals with private property."[13]

HOBBES AND LOCKE

Similarities

1. Products of Time. Both were the products of their times. If Hobbes was the child of civil wars, Locke was that of Glorious Revolution.

2. Social Contract. Both believed that the state was the result of a contract and that the sovereign was created out of that.

3. State of Nature. Both have pleaded that before the people joined the state they were living in the state of nature and it is from there that they joined political state.

4. Final Contract. Both also believed that contract once signed will be final and could not be revoked.

5. Contract by Consent. Consent was the basis of the state, according to them both. The contract was signed by people with their own accord and will.

6. Rational Law of Nature. Both of them also believed that the law of nature was based on reason.

7. State Above Individual. Both agreed that the state should remain above individual.

8. Rights of Individuals. Both were of the view that the state should protect the rights of the individuals.

Dissimilarities

1. Different Concepts of Human Nature. Hobbes believed that in the state of nature the people were nasty, selfish and brutish. Locke believe that in the state of nature the people were selfless, loving and good.

2. War or Peace. Hobbes was of the view that the state of nature was a state of war. According to Locke the state of nature was essentially that of peace and goodwill.

---

13. Russell, B., *op. cit.*, p. 665.

12. Laski, H. J., *Political Thought in England*, p. 47

3. Nature of Social Contract. For Hobbes social contract was total and people surrendered their rights to the sovereign. For Locke social contract was partial and the people gave the sovereign only the right of interpretation.

4. Supremacy of Community. Hobbes did not believe in the supremacy of community. Locke believed in supremacy of community.

5. Right to Rebel. Hobbes did not give any right to the people to rebel or disobey the state. Locke gave the people the right to rebel or disobey the state.

6. Rationality of Contract. Hobbe's idea of contract has not much rationality. Locke's idea has much rationality than that of Hobbes.

7. Despotism v/s Individualism. Hobbe's approach to the problem was despotic. Locke has been called as the champion of 19th century liberalism and individualism.

8. Private Property. Hobbes did not favour individual's right to private property. Locke was of the view that the individual had every right to hold private property.

CONTRIBUTION TO POLITICAL THOUGHT

Criticism

Political Philosophy of Locke is full of certain anomalies. These have entered his philosophy for having certain pre-conceived notions about certain basic principles of life. Anomalies and difficulties have mainly emerged because Locke has failed to make up his mind as to the direction in which he was to move. This uncertainty resulted in practical difficulty. Locke could not decide as to what were the principles and what then were derivatives. He based the superstructure of his philosophy on these basic notions. Thus the difficulties were bound to arise e.g., he loved private property and wanted to preserve the fruits of Glorious Revolution.

1. Wrong Idea of National State. It is wrong to believe that at any stage man was by himself very innocent and law abiding. If this conception is compared with realities of life, one is forced to conclude that mankind has virtually much retrogressed both morally and intellectually.

2. Private Property. Locke laid so much stress on the institution of private property that he pleaded that it ought to be preserved at all costs. He felt that the society stood to preserve and not to snatch private property but in fact one finds that "primitive man is on his (Locke's) lips, but the portrait he paints is that of civil man."

3. Concept of Sovereignty and Individuals. Locke's conception of sovereignty, if pressed to its logical conclusion, makes state a corporate body. He believed that the individual was ultimate and sovereign. Sovereignty was thus aggregate of individuals and not the supreme power which was the characteristic of sovereignty. Sovereignty became a limited liability company. It is very strange that Locke placed individual even before the state. The individuals have no doubt, a place in the state and play an important role in democracies, but to believe that they were above the state was something which was undesirable. According to Sabine, "The individualism of all social theory between Locke and J.S. Mill depended less on logic than on its agreement with interests of the class that mainly produced it."

4. No Need to Create Civil Society. Forthly, Locke has taken many things for granted in his philosophy e.g. the moral and intellectual values of mankind without the coercive powers of the state. But if in actual practice the moral tone of the people of pre-civil society was so high as Locke assumed, then there was very little need the necessity for the creation of political organisation and civil societies.

5. Minorities have no Right to Revolt. Locke allowed the people the right to revolt. This is unwarranted because history is an evidence that revolutions are carried out by minorities and not by majorities. A minority has no right to upset social order and thus harm the progress of the majority.

6. Hedonism Against Revolution. Locke based his theory on pleasure and pain principle. These are closely associated with the ideas of preservation, welfare and well being of the people. This is against the reality of revolution.

7. No Philosophical Justification. Locke failed to give a philosophical justification for his political theories. According to Sabine, "It is exceedingly difficult to understand exactly what Locke believe to be the philosophical justification for his theory of natural rights, or in other words to see how he meant to unite his political theory with his general philosophical justification for his theory of natural rights, or in other words to see how he meant to unite his political theory with his general philosophical position."

8. Conflict of Tolerance and Intolerance. Locke proposed the theory of tolerance for religious purposes and also of intolerance. "The curious result in his social philosophy was a theory markedly tolerant and critical in defending religious freedom and capable of being highly dogmatic in defending rights of property."

9. Wrong Notion of Social Contract. In a lengthy statement Wayper has criticised Locke about his notion of social contract. According to him, "It is clear too, that his social contract has become little better than a force. If consent then be the hall-mark of democracy, Mussolini's Italy and Nazi Germany and Bolshevick Russia must be regarded as being much more democratic than those countries in which governments have perforce to reconcile themselves to persistent, vigorous and often widespread opposition."

10. Corporate Community v/s Individualism. Locke failed to reconcile his ideas about corporate character of the community on the one hand and his ideas about individualism on the other. From medieval traditions he borrowed the former whereas his love for individual gave birth to latter. This inconsistency has continued throughout his philosophy.

11. Mechanical Theory to State and Society. Locke has been criticised for this mechanistic views about state and society. His idea that the individual could destroy and create the state at all was not sound to reason and needed careful consideration.

12. No Source and Code of Law of Nature. Though according to Locke's philosophy law of nature is perfect yet he has not given its source and has not tried to modify that.

13. No Ground for Civil Society. Locke has been criticised for not providing and solid grounds which forced the people to leave the state of nature and in its stead joint political or civil society.

Appreciations

In spite of the above anomalies and ambiguities in his philosophy Locke has his own place among political philosophers. According to Maxey 'Laying hold of abstruse and important concepts that had been floating around in the back eddies of European political thought for many generations, he wove them into a coercive kinetic body of doctrine that has grouped the political consciousness of Europe and America for two tremendous centuries."

1. First Utilitarian. Locke was rather the first utilitarian when he said that "happiness and misery are the two great springs of human action."

2. Natural Rights. Locke emphasised doctrine of natural rights and stressed that the state stood for the preservation of these rights. According to him, "Commonwealth came into being for upholding these natural rights. The most distinctive contribution to political theory is doctrine of natural rights."

3. Separation of Powers. Locke was the first modern thinker and philosopher who developed the idea of 'Separation of Powers' as an essential ingredient for the preservation of individual liberty. Subsequently this theory was developed to its logical conclusions by Montesquieu.

4. Popular Sovereignty. Locke's another contribution to political philosophy was his idea about popular sovereignty which has a preference even over political sovereignty.

5. Fore-runner of Individualism. In Locke's setup, everything revolved round the individual who was even before the state. This conception of individualism is much more ahead of the modern individualism. Locke can claim to have a place as the fore-runner of modern individualism.

6. Distinction of State, Government and Society. Locke's another contribution to the political philosophy is that for the first time he distinguished between state, government and society. He also said that society came prior to state and this idea is accepted even today.

7. Supremacy of Community. Locke gave the idea of supremacy of community. This idea was subsequently developed by Rousseau in his theory of general will. Rousseau simply widened the channel dug by Locke.

8. Father of Liberalism. Locke was the champion of individualism and liberalism of 18th century. Thus he gave the basis of liberal state. Prof. Wayper believed that he was the father of liberalism.

9. Set Back to Divine Rights. Locke gave a very serious set back to the theory of Divine Rights of Kings.

10. Right to Revolt. For Locke individuals had a right to revolt against the state if the state failed to achieve the ends for which it was created. According to Gettell, "Because of its influence on Jefferson and others, Locke's theory of revolt must be considered one of the most important parts of his doctrine." Sabine says "His sincerity, his profound moral convictions, his genuine belief in liberty and in the dignity of human nature united with his moderation and good sense, made him the ideal spokesman of the middle class revolution." To conclude with Maxey, "He was an unfailing arsenal of ideas and arguments whence 18th century smashers of autocracy drew most deadly intellectual munitions; his were the theories and ideals by which 19th century makers of constitutional monarchy and democracy ought to shape popular institutions."

11. Influence on Political Institutions. Locke had tremendous influence on political institutions of his own time and also on that of posterity. French freely borrowed from his ideas. The Dutch also took much from him. Montesquieu and Rousseau were indebted to him for their subsequent philosophic ideas. The impression of Locke on the American Declaration of Independence is quite clear. The influence of his two treatises on government was the only motivating force for American Revolution. According to Maxey the reformists of 18th & 19th centuries were influenced by Locke. He says that "the shaping head was that of Walpole, Jefferson, Gambelta or Cavour, the voice was invariably the voice of Locke."

12. Estimates. Following are some estimates of Locke:

(i) *Jones.* "What is important and valuable about his theory is that he recognises that man is a moral being."

(ii) *Wayper.* "He laid down the essential theses of liberalism that the people is the source of all political power, that the state must be resisted if it steps beyond its powers and authority."

(iii) *Gettell.* "Because of its influence on Jefferson anothers Locke's theory of revolt must be considered one of the most important part of his doctrine."

(iv) *Maxey.* "His were the theories or ideals by which 19th century makers of constitutional democracy sought to shape popular institutions."

(v) *Harold Laske*. "If Hobbe's theory of sovereignty is today one of the commonplace of jurisprudence, ethically and politically, we occupy ourselves with erecting about it a system of limitations each one of which is in some sort due to Locke's perception."

(vi) *Dunning*. "The most distinctive contribution of Locke to political theory is the doctrine of natural rights."

(vii) *Sabine*. "As he combined diverse elements from the past, so from his political philosophy emerged diverse theories in the centuries that followed him."

In spite of the above contributions there is no denial that Locke has given nothing original to political philosophy. His only contribution was his commonsense with which he regulated and channelised the already existing ideas. Sabine has rightly said, "The chief mark of his genius was neither learning, nor logic but incomparable commonsense by which he gathered together the chief convictions, in politics, morals and education; that the experience of the past had generated in the more enlightened minds of his generation."

QUESTIONS FOR EXERCISE

1. "The great and chief end therefore, of men writing into commonwealth and putting themselves under Government is the preservation of their property." Comment.
2. "Men living together according to reason without a common superior on earth with authority to judge between them, is properly the state of nature." Comment.
3. "The great and chief end therefore, of men uniting into commonwealth, and of putting themselves under Government is the preservation of their property." Comment.
4. "Whether then he moves out of the state that nature has provided and left it, he has mixed his labour with it, and joined to its something that is his own, thereby make it his property." Comment.
5. "The reason why men enter into society is the preservation of their property." (Locke). Comment.
6. "The Supreme power cannot take from anyone any part of his property without his own consent." (Locke). Comment.
7. "The great and chief end, therefore, of men uniting into commonwealth and putting themselves under government is the preservation of their property." (Locke). Comment.
8. "Everything in Locke's system revolves around the individual, everything is disposed so as to ensure the sovereignty of the individual." (Vaughan). Discuss.

9. "Examine critically John Locke's theory of natural rights and trace its influence on political thought in the eighteenth century."
10. According to John Locke, "Absolute monarchy is indeed inconsistent with civil society and so can be no form of civil government at all." What are the arguments which Locke advances in support of this assertion.
11. "Men living together according to reason, without a common superior on earth with authority to judge between them is properly the state of nature." Comment.
12. "The legislative being only a judiciary power to act for certain ends, there remains still in the people's supreme power to remove or alter the legislative, when they find the legislative act contrary to the trust reposed in them." Comment.
13. "The liberty of men in society is to be under no other legislative power but that established by consent in the commonwealth, not under the dominion of any will or restraint of any law but what that legislative shall elect according to the trust put in it." Comment.
14. "The state therefore is, at the most, no more than a limited liability company; the real sovereignty resides in the individual." (Locke). Comment.
15. "Locke makes government depend not merely on institution, but always on consent of the governed and regards all rulers as liable to be displaced if they govern tyrannically." Elucidate. What method does he provide to get rid of a corrupt government?
16. "The greatest weakness of Locke's political philosophy in all its branches was that he never got back to first principles." (Sabine). Discuss.

25
Baron De-Montesquieu (1689-1755 A.D.)

Montesquieu was born on 1st January 1689 in France at Bordex in an aristocratic and noble family. In the beginning, he studied at home, and, later on, at Juilly in a school for 11 years. He studied law. In 1714, he was admitted to the grade of counsellor.

Up to the age of 27, he was known as Baron de La Brade at De, but after the death of his uncle, he inherited his title and judicial office and worked as chief magistrate of Bordex for 13 years.

He was interested in Literature and History. He wrote his first book, the Persian Letters in 1721 in which he criticised political, social and religious institutions of France. In 1728, he started for extensive tour and visited Austria, Hungary, Venice, Rome, Switzerland, the Rhine, Holland and England. In England, he stayed for 18 months. The English conception of liberty and English system of Government had a deep impact upon him. He devoted rest of his life in literary pursuits and died in 1755. By his study of Constitution of England, he propounded his theory of separation of Power.

INFLUENCES

Montesquieu, Charles Louis de Secondat, was the son of a distinguished French lawyer steeped on legal traditions from his very birth. He was a true French literateur of the mid-eighteenth century. He reacted against the absolutism and general conditions prevailing in the age of Louis XIV. He was in active touch with the intellectual movement of his time. He loathed the atmosphere of the degenerate French court, and found in study, 'the sovereign remedy against all his disappointments'. He gave a number of historical references to substantiate his conclusion. There is a marked tendency in his writings to correlate political philosophy with physical sciences. His mind was moulded not only by wide study, but also by an extensive travelling. The study of Roman history of contemporary English institutions determined the purpose as well as the content of Montesquieu's political philosophy. These two sources gave him the conception of liberty which forms the central theme of his speculation. He studied the histories of Rome, France, England, Egypt, Persia, India, China and Japan, which left their deep impressions on the cultivated mind of the philosopher. But Montesquieu did not draw his views primarily from history, but used history to illustrate and verify them.

Writings

The *Persian Letters* of Montesquieu embodies a brilliant satire on the existing social, political and religious institutions in France. His *Considerations on the Greatness and Decay of the Romans* shows the great political insight and catholicity of view of Montesquieu.

Two Strains

Within the soul of Montesquieu there were two men, the political philosopher and the practical reformer. The political philosopher, as Voltaire and Helvetius were not slow to detect was essentially conservative; reverent of the past; keenly alive to the organic unity of national life in all its varied expressions; averse to innovation, firm in the conviction, the fruit of long study and reflection, that without religion there can be no healthy national existence, and than the established form of religion is not more but less easily altered than that of any other object of which men have given their loyalty and devotion.[1] The practical reformer was a true child of his age and country, eager for reform; impatient of abuses, especially when they cut athwart his instincts of humanity; and in matters of a religious observance, critical, sceptical and, at moments, not a little contemptuous and satirical. The two strains are not easy to reconcile. But the one is no less characteristic than the other; the one needs to be no less carefully reckoned with than the other.

There is one point, however, in which the two strains meet and mingle. If any case presents itself in which the abuse, so far from being of old growth, was a recent innovation, it is evident that then both the conservative and reforming instincts of the author would be enlisted under the same banner; his whole nature would at once rise in rebellion. He would put forth all his powers to warn his countrymen of the danger and to combat it with every weapon at his command.

Hence there is the deep undertone of uneasiness, the exasperation of the thinker who sees his most cherished distinctions trampled under foot; the anguish of the patriot who watches his country driven to ruin by a dissolute monarch and a gang of policemen who sacrificed everything to the alleged convenience of the moment, content, like their master, with the coward's maxim; 'After us, the deluge.' Unless this be borne in mind, some of the most striking pages of *Esprit des lois* will remain an indecipherable riddle.[2]

1. See *Esprit des lois*, xxiv, 1-3.
2. *Ibid.*, viii, 6-9; ix, 6-7. x, 9.

IMPACT OF ARISTOTLE

In the formulation of ideas, Montesquieu's indebtedness to Aristotle is obvious. The method of treatment of both is empirical and based on observation. Aristotle shows his distaste for idealism; Montesquieu discards the contemporary ideals of the sovereignty of the people, natural rights, etc. Aristotle hints at the separation of powers, Montesquieu develops the theory. Both dilate on the influence of geography on the form of government. Both classify governments on the basis of law. Both uphold monarchy as the best form of government.

METHOD

Montesquieu was the first thinker of the 18th century who bade farewell to the traditional method of treating a problem. As a traditional thinker, he did not like to idealise the things. On the other hand, he adopted scientific methods for the study of problems which faced him. Like his contemporaries he did not depend on the observation of others. He depended on actual observations based on historical evidences, he was more Aristotelean than Platonic. To quote Dunning, "Methods employed by Montesquieu in the solution of his problems were of Aristotle and not of Plato, of Bodin and not of Hobbes or Locke." He did not believe in the perfection of human institutions. Because of his deep faith in employing historical rather than empirical or idealistic way, he has been called the father of modern historical research. He did not believe that customs and institutions of mankind come from above. They have natural growth and differ from man to man and society to society. He employed historical method for the study of these institutions. According to Jones, "And he set himself the tremendous dual task of (1) determining what these basic underlying uniformities are and (2) what the factors are which produce the actual observed diversity. Finally also he wanted to show (3) how these differences are in fact produced, so that it would be possible for statesmen and legislators to control them in the interest to mankind, each different type of government as complete as exemplification of ideal as is possible for its to be."

SPIRIT OF LAWS

Mintesquieu criticized the social, religious and political institutions of France in order to reform them and not so much in a hostile spirit of destructive criticism. He was more concerned with the real spirit of liberty and harmonious working of political institutions than with the political dogmas of the age like the Rights of Man, Sovereignty of People and Natural Equality of Men etc. He wanted to reform political life in France by infusing in it the British sense of liberty and by introducing into the French constitution the principle of separation of powers, characteristic of the British constitution. His *Spirit of Laws* represented an effort in this direction. To him, climate and geography, as also economic conditions, had a great hand in moulding the character and the national institutions of a country. All the philosophers of the 18th century demanded a constitutional type of government. They wanted religious toleration, civil freedom and a rational system of jurisprudence. They did not condemn a limited monarchy. They feared the demons and stuck to their rights and privileges including the sacred rights of property.

The unity and diversity are harmoniously reconciled in the universe. In the human world, behaviour patterns are fixed to some extent, because man is also a physical being. In the human world, there is both uniformity and diversity of behaviour pattern. Uniformity is provided by the universal law of self-preservation and natural impulses and diversity by the variety in customs, conventions, moral codes and institutions arising out of differences in environment, climate, soil and genius of a people and so on.

Importance of Laws

According to Montesquieu "Laws, in the widest possible connotation, are any necessary relations arising from a thing's nature. In this sense all beings have their laws : the Deity His laws, the material world its laws, the intelligences superior to men their laws, the beasts their laws, man his laws..." Though man has his laws, yet because of the exercise of free will and because of defective human intelligence, "the intellectual world is far from being so well-governed as the physical." Man is a free agent, but is subject to ignorance, error and impetuous passions. Montesquieu said, "Such a being might every instant forget his creator; God has, therefore, reminded him of his duty by the laws of religion. Such a being is liable every moment to forget himself; philosophy has provided against this by the laws of morality. Formed to live in society, he might forget his fellow-creatures; legislators have therefore by political and civil laws confined him to his duty." Before those laws were made, man was guided by the laws of Nature. The first law of Nature enjoined on him the necessity of self-preservation, peace and security. Other laws point out the advisability of satisfaction of human wants, the necessity of leading a life in association with his fellow-beings. Social contract develops human intelligence. It develops a rational desire to live in society. Life in society necessitates positive laws.

Two Kinds of Relation

It follows that if there are any laws which the political life of man follows, any generalizations to be drawn from his actions as a civic being, they are to be discovered solely by a study of the relations in which he stands to his outward surroundings and to his fellow-men : including, those relations, which, just because they are the most intimate and deep-reaching, are roughly described as constituting his intrinsic nature. On the one hand, it includes that relation to his fellows which we have in mind when we say that he is essentially a moral being, with a sense of duty and responsibility both to other men and to God; on the other, those evident relations, both to other men and to the world without, which spring from his primary instinct of self-preservation, his innate desire to secure his own welfare and happiness.

Each of these two main kinds of relation carries with it far-reaching consequences. On the one had, if man is by nature a moral being, a being bound to his kind by ties from which there is no escape and no release, and if those ties of duty are further strengthened by innumerable promptings of self-interest, then there in no need to ask when and how civil society had its origin. There is no need to look for that origin in any 'covenant' such as has been supposed to constitute the obligation which binds men to civil society, in any 'contract' from a previous 'state of nature'. The real state of nature, for man, is civil society. There was no need of any contract or covenant to draw him thither. For this reason the individualist theory of the state must be rejected without ceremony. Man is what he is by relation to his fellows. The naked, isolated individual is an abstraction, and a false abstraction, if there ever was one.[3]

Knowledge of Relations

'All knowledge is knowledge of relations.' It would be accepted by all schools of thinkers: by materialists as well as idealist; by disciples of Bentham, as well as disciples of Rousseau or disciples of Mazzini. To this eighteenth century, however, it was a dangerous heresy. And Montesquieu, if not the first to proclaim it, was at least the first to give it currency in the field of politics. He was the first to grasp it as a general truth; the first to apply it to the whole range of political discussion. What Vice had been dimly groping after is set in the clearest light by Montesquieu. What is implied throughout the *Scienza nuova* is explicitly asserted and worked out in *L'Esprit des Lois.*

Positive Laws

Hence the idea of relations is placed in the very forefront of his treatise. His opening sentence defines *Law* as 'the sum of relations which necessarily flow from the nature of a given object'. Montesquieu did not care for abstract notion of things. To him 'all knowledge was knowledge of relations.' Human positive laws were not merely the dictate of reason or a command of sovereign lawgiver. The laws represent a body of rules to regulate the life of a nation in accordance with the spirit and genius of that nation. Hence, a study of social rules is important because the positive laws of a people must have national social customs as their basis. Law is related to social environment. There is no universal positive law, because a number of influences determine its course. It is a rule of action based on social relationships and social experiences. It is rooted in society. It varies with the different types and structures of society.

---

3. Compare Burke , *Appeal from the New to the Old Whigs : Works,* I, pp. 522-25.

Developing his conception of positive laws, Montesquieu tells us that man in the State of Nature was as timid creature. He was not an intelligent creature as Locke thought, nor a wilful brute as Hobbes conceived. With the formation of societies and increase of knowledge man lost his timidity and sought for dominion over others. He inaugurated a state of war. There began a conflict between individuals and societies. This gave rise to positive laws which are of the types corresponding to three sets of relations : (1) law of nations corresponding to the relations between nation and nation, (2) positive law corresponding to the relation between ruler and ruled, and (3) civil laws governing the relation between individual citizens. The law of nations is common to all, but positive and civil laws differs from society to society. The positive laws must be related to the character of a people. The civil laws must be related to topography, climate, size of population, religion of a people, and so on. Further, these three laws must be related to one another. In the spirit of laws. Montesquieu repudiated social contract theory. The state, according to him, was the product of environment. It was organism and not conventional in nature. The laws of Nature taught the man the desirability of peace and security, and of living in society in a friendly spirit.

Types of Government

In his *Spirit of Laws* Montesquieu analyzes the different types of government and examines the characteristics of each different type. He does not overtly accept the traditional classification of governments into monarchy, aristocracy and democracy. He merely asserted that governments are of three types: monarchy, which represents the rule of one man with law; despotism, rule of one man without law; and republic, which would be further classified into aristocracy and democracy. Despotism differs from monarchy in being arbitrary and capricious, while the latter is a constitutional government according to forms of law and require the continuance of 'intermediate powers', such as, the nobility or communes, between the monarch and the people. His republic represented an idealized type of government in a country where the moral and intellectual attainments and standards of the people were very high. The essence of republic lay not in whether the government was in the hands of a few or many, but whether the government was animated by 'virtue' or not. Thus, to each of these forms of government Montesquieu attached a 'principle', or motive force in the character of subjects from which its power is derived and which is necessary to its continuance and functioning. Popular government, whether republic or democracy, depends upon the civil virtue or public spirit of the people. Monarchy depends upon the sense of honour of a military class and despotism depends upon the fear or slavishness of its subjects.

Government and Law

Montesquieu saw a definite relation between the nature of government and the constitutional law of a country. Montesquieu said, "for monarchy the most important laws relative to its nature are those which insure the pre-eminence of the privileged classes, especially the nobility." While dealing with the relations of laws and institutions to he basic principles of various forms of government, Montesquieu makes a number of pertinent observations. Education and legislation must correspond in character to the principles of a particular government. In a democracy, the laws must aim at promoting the love of equality and the practice of frugality. In a monarchy the main object of the laws should be to protect the privileges of the nobility.

Government, Religion and Size of a State

Montesquieu finds out relationship between various types of government and different religious and size of a state.

1. Religion and Government. According to him, certain religions had a definite affinity for certain forms of government. Protestantism goes well with a republican form of government, Roman Catholicism with a monarchical form, while Mohammedanism and despotism are well suited to each other.

2. Size of State and Form of Government. The size of a state also provides a basis for the classification of government. A republican form of government is possible only in a state of small size, monarchy suits the moderate-sized state, while a big country or an empire must have a despotic government. Change of size is attended with change in the type of government. Montesquieu was against the policy of expansion and aggrandizement. He decried international rivalry and pleaded for international justice. To prevent small states from being absorbed by the bigger ones, he favoured the principle of federation.

Influence of Physical Environment on National Life

Like Bodin Montesquieu also discussed the influence of physical environment on the social, economic, religious and political institutions of a country.

1. Climate. Climate influences character and institutions. Heat produces a spirit of monasticism and indolence, cold energy and drunkenness. People of cold country are restless and irritable in spirit. Then against from different wants in different climates arise different ways of living which result in different kinds of laws. According to Montesquieu, there is a direct relation between climate and liberty. He illustrates this theory by reference to England. English climate promotes irritability with a tendency to suicide. This irritability makes it impossible for Englishmen to tolerate personal despotism. English constitution is primarily the result of English climate. Montesquieu traces the extreme conservatism and the general backwardness of the laws, customs, manners and religions of the Asiatic countries to warm climate. Hot climate breeds despotism and slavery of both domestic (of women) and civil kind. The cold climate, as of Europe, makes for the virtues of strength, self-reliance and frankness and these virtues produce political and civil liberty.

2. Geography. Geography, too, plays an important part in the growth of national institutions. You will have liberty in the hills which are difficult of cultivation as well as conquest, and despotism in the plains which are more easily cultivable and conquerable. Again, the larger the area of a country, the smaller the chance of constitutional government and political liberty there. Then again continental people are more open to attack and, therefore, more liable to despotism than an isolated nation.

Thus Montesquieu made many observations about many things at different times. His conclusions were mostly episodic and had little dependence on what he alleged to be the evidence. Montesquieu oscillates between two tendencies inherent in the confused principles from which he started. On the one hand, he was inclined to assume that human law is rational and that accordingly there is a good reason, for any usage that is widely and permanently established. Such an attitude agreed with his general conservative inclination and with the theory that physical causes, such as climate, act directly on mental and moral capacities. Carried to its logical conclusion, however, it would have meant a complete moral relativism, and this was certainly never Montesquieu's position. On the other hand, he perhaps usually thought of climate and certain institutions (like slavery and polygamy) as adverse conditions which have to be compensate by legislation to produce a good moral result. This way of interpreting political evolution implies that the moral ideas at least of legislators are independent of social causation and that the causal influence of climate and the like is effective mainly as it enters into their calculations. Such a view cuts under a sociological theory of politics and repeats the exaggerated ideas about the influence of rulers which Machiavelli had made current. However, Montesquieu was less guilty on this score than his contemporaries.

It is difficult, therefore, to attach any importance to Montesquieu's celebrated dictum that laws must be adopted to the circumstances in which a nation lives. The statement that Montesquieu really envisaged and used an inductive and comparative method of study social institutions must be taken with extreme qualification. Probably few important political theorists were more addicted to hasty generalizations or less inclined to distinguish between exact inference and the impulsion of prior convictions. He was indeed a man of wide reading, but his knowledge was inexact, judged not by the scholarly standards of a later time but in terms of the sources at his disposal. His curious erudition was largely used to illustrate beliefs that would have been exactly the same of he had never heard of Persia. Even of political affairs in Europe, which lay under his eyes, Montesquieu was not so profound an observer as Machiavelli, Bodin, or even Harrington, who made no such pretensions to universal knowledge. What saves him from the charge of being an amateur was not his scientific achievement, but his whole-souled enthusiasm for liberty. He was a moralist, writes Sabine, "for whom the eternal verities had begun to wear thin but who lacked the constructive power to get on without them."[4]

Montesquieu's importance lay in spreading and strengthening the belief in British institutions as the means of political liberty. His dwelling in England freed him from the preconception that political liberty depends upon a superior virtue known only to the Romans and realized only in a city-state. It gave support to his rooted dislike for despotism and suggested a way in which the evil effect of absolutism in France might perhaps be remedied. He ascribed liberty in England to the separation of the legislative, executive and judicial powers, and to the balancing of these powers against each other. He set these doctrines as dogmas of liberal constitution-making. The extent of Montesquieu's influence in this respect is beyond doubt. It may be read at large in the bills of right of American and French Constitutions.

Classification of Laws

Montesquieu was of the opinion that the whole universe, including God himself, is governed by laws. Religious laws reminded man about laws of God whereas legislatures reminded him about his social obligations. Montesquieu believed that in the state of nature man was timid and neither so intelligent as Locke conceived him to be, nor as brutish as Hobbes imagined him. As knowledge increased, man lost his timidity and equality and sought domination over others. This tendency resulted in a state of war. The conflict was that of the individuals against the society. This gave rise of "Positive Laws". According to Montesquieu positive laws were created by man himself and thus could not be applied to all communities under all circumstances. They were not rigid and always subject to change as the customs and manners of the society changed. These laws had three sets of relations i.e., law of nation, of the relation of nation with nation, political law between the ruler and the subjects and civil law that of individual and the society. He believed that law of Nation was applicable to all the states whereas political and civil laws differ from nation to nation. Political laws have a definite relation with the character of the people. The civil laws depend on the climate, religion and social customs of the people.

In the state of nature each man believed in certain types of laws: (i) peace and security; (ii) abandoning fear; (iii) law of association.

Montesquieu defined laws, "as the necessary relations arising from the nature of things." In actual practice the process of laws was very complicated because the men were self-willed. To quote him, "As a sensible creature he (man) is subject to a thousand impetious passions. Such as being might at

4. Sabine, G.H., *op. cit*,., p. 471.

every instant forget his creator. God, has, therefore, reminded him of his duty by the laws of religion....he might forget his fellow creatures, legislators have, therefore by political and civil laws confined him to his duty." He classified laws as under:

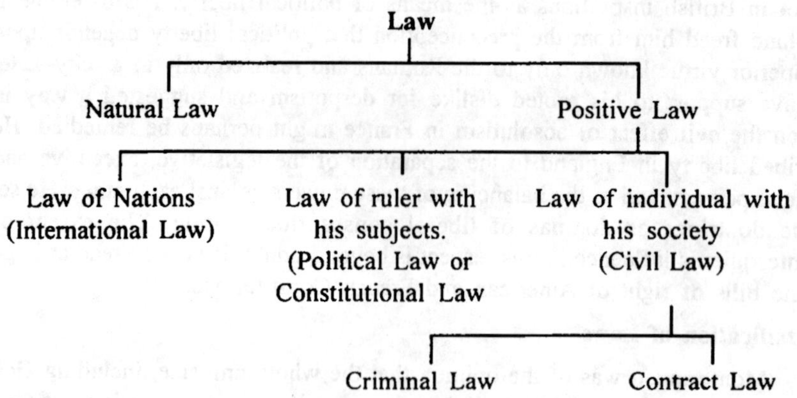

Criticism of Theory of Laws

According to Sabine, "Of all the French political philosophers in the 18th century (other than Rousseau) the most important was Montesquieu. Of them all he had perhaps the clearest conception of complexities of a social philosophy, and yet he too was guilty of extreme oversimplification." His political philosophy, however, suffers from the following defects:

1. Confusion. Montesquieu however, suffers from certain confusions in the treatment of law, which have arisen because of his developing a sociological theory of government and law and denouncing despotism for the sake of freedom. This confusion existed throughout his philosophy.

2. No Originality. His ideas about 'law' lack originality. He only systematised the ideas already given by Aristotle, Machiavelli and Bodin.

3. Republic Depends on Democracy. Montesquieu tried to establish that democracy was sub-type of republican form of government but democracy was not dependent on republic. Today republics have become an off-shoot of democracies. It is democracy Vs. socialism that matters much and not republic Vs. socialism or republic Vs. monarchy which draws our attention.

4. Despotism not at Par with Republic. Montesquieu tried to put despotism at par with republic which is not correct. Whereas in the former form of government people has no say, in the latter case the people are given full opportunity to express their views. To conclude with Maxey, "Montesquieu was often mistaken in his views, often in error in his deduction; but these were petty faults resulting from the inadequacy of his information or the fallibility of his judgment in particular cases."

CONCEPT OF LIBERTY

Montesquieu was mainly concerned with the concept of liberty. It was due to his love for liberty that we find a marked different in his conception of human nature. In this regard he was rather a progressive conservative and radical democrat. He was more concerned with real political liberty of mankind than the political dogmas. He wanted complete separation of powers in order to save liberty of people. He was much influenced by the English political system which, he felt, was very much conducive to individual liberty. He believed that people have given different definitions to the term liberty and have also tried to adjust the word and its meanings so as to suit their convenience.

Montesquieu borrowed his ideas of liberty from John Locke, although he rejected the abstract Lockean notion of natural right and natural justice promoting liberty. To him, political liberty meant a relation between the state and the subjects. It meant 'the right of doing all that the laws permit'. If an individuals violated law, he could not retain liberty because then everybody would violate law and there would be liberty for none. Political liberty, is to be gained by conforming to laws and not by violating them. It means freedom of action in accordance with and under the protection of the laws. It follows naturally that if in a state an individual or a body of individuals are above the laws, there can be no liberty. In a despotism, liberty is not secure because of the reasoned caprice of an individual ruler. Montesquieu does not define civil liberty clearly. His chief aim was to discover a governmental organization that would best secure political liberty because of its system of checks and balances.

Separation of Powers for Liberty

In the separation of the three powers of government — executive, legislative and judicial, Montesquieu found the best guarantee for liberty. He was of the opinion that if the legislative power is united with the executive power in the hands of one person or of one body of officials, there can be no liberty. Nor can there be any liberty if the power to judge is not separated from the legislative and executive powers. Again, there would be an end of everything, were the same man or the same body, whether of nobles or of the people, to exercise those three powers, that of enacting laws, that of executing the public resolutions, and that of trying the causes of individuals. The separation of powers ensured liberty by imposing a healthy check on the despotism of the governmental officials. In England the controversies between the crown and the courts of common law and between the crown and parliament had given concrete importance to the separation of powers. Harrington had considered it to be essential to free government. Locke had given it a subsidiary place in his theory of parliamentary priority. But Montesquieu developed the doctrine of the separation of powers into a system of legal checks and balances between the parts of a constitution. He, however, did not really contemplate an absolute separation of the three powers: the legislative ought to meet at the call of the executive; the executive retains a veto on legislation; and the legislature ought to exercise extraordinary judicial powers. The separation of powers, as Montesquieu described it, was crossed by a contradictory principle—the greater power of the legislature—which in effect made it a dogma supplemented by an undefined privilege of making exceptions.

Montesquieu's theory of liberty shows traces of the rationalizing spirit of the eighteenth century; but whereas his contemporaries, as also Locke, defended liberty, political and civil, on the score of natural right, Montesquieu cared little for the dogma of 'natural rights'. According to him, not the 'rights of man,' but the separation of powers was the panacea for liberty. For him all laws and institutions were relative, while his rationalistic friends drew from 'nature' rules of universal validity.

Liberty was writ large on the *L'Esprit des Lois,* but he was no democrat. He did not believe in popular sovereignty. He was a sort of 'French Whig' and his whiggism considerably influenced political theory in the 19th century.

Civil and Political Liberty

Montesquieu, defined liberty "as the right of doing whatever the laws permit," He also tried to distinguish between civil and political liberty.

1. Civil Liberty. According to Montesquieu civil liberty was the product of mutual relations of men. It was closely associated with the law of nature. It was the outcome of customs and manners of a civil society. The main object of these laws was to give the people a sense of security or real security against the unlawful citizenships.

2. Political Liberty. According to Montesquieu, "The political liberty of the subjects is a tranquillity of mind arising from the opinion each person has of his safety." Pre-requisite of political liberty is that the government be so constituted that one man need not be afraid of the other. Political liberty means the capability of doing things which law permitted. It could be achieved by obeying the laws and not in their violation. He agreed with Cicero that "We are slave on laws in order to enjoy liberty." He was however, of the opinion that liberty was always an outcome of customs of the people and not the constitution. Liberty was proper administration of justice which should be on sound principles and not on the whims of the rulers. There should not be indiscreet utterances as these were likely to destroy peace and security of the state. Montesquieu condemned slavery.

Theories of different writers idea about the theory of separation of powers which is generally associated with the name of Montesquieu, is not original. Plato in his *The Laws* gave the idea of a mixed state, which was used by Polybius while discussing the stability of Roman Government. The idea held ground in medieval constitutionalists. Controversies about superiorities of position between the monarch and common law gave importance to this theory. Harrington pleaded this theory while discussing his individualism. Locke, of course, gave it a subsidiary position.

According to Sidgewick, "Separation of fundamental powers of government and balanced distribution of them among different organs, differently appointed bodies or individuals, as that by natural play of the whole of organisation, any tendency to oppression on the part of any one organ of government may be checked by another." According to Hearnshah, "If the legislative power is united with the executive power is in the hands of one person or one body of officials there can be no liberty nor can there be any liberty if the power to judge is not separated from legislative and executive powers." Prof. Laski says, "Independence of judiciary from the executive is essential to the freedom. In that sense, the doctrine of separation of powers enshrines a permanent truth for it is obvious that if executive could shape judicial decision in accordance with its own desire, it would be unlimited master of the state." According to Sabine, "So far as Montesquieu modified the ancient doctrine it was by making the separation of powers into a system of legal checks and balances between the parts of a constitution."

Criticism of Theory of Separation of Powers

1. Unreasonable Source of Inspiration. Montesquieu derived his inspiration from England where had felt that there was complete separation of powers. But his source of inspiration was not based on reasonable grounds. In England before Glorious Revolution there was complete concentration of powers. Even after that the question of separation of powers did not arise at all because democracy there worked on the basis of concentration rather than separation of powers. In democracies the executive and legislature must go hand in hand and even the least conflict among these organs is bound to result in deadlocks.

2. Deadlock in Practice. If the theory of separation of powers, as enunciated by Montesquieu, is put into actual operation; that would result in deadlock in administration. In modern complex government all administrative departments are independent and their working cannot be separated without harming the society. If all the three departments of the same government function separately then this type of separation of powers would neither be conducive to office efficiency nor shall that be in the national interest.

3. Water Tight Division Impossible. In modern administrative set up complete water tight division approach in more or less impossible. Even in U.S.A. where an attempt has been made in this regard by introducing a system of checks and balances, it has not been found very much of administrative convenience. Many a time U.S. people have thought of even amending their constitution. In the words of Gettel, "Government consists of a group of organs with differentiated functions but with a common task and purpose, and their harmonious cooperation is essential to success. A strict line of separation cannot be drawn between the several departments."

4. Closely Knitted Powers. In modern governments each department performs certain functions which are primarily not of its concern e.g. executive performs legislative functions whereas the legislature is obliged to discharge such duties which are properly the responsibility of executive and judicial departments. Even if an attempt is made for separation of these departments that is bound to fail. In fact these functions are very closely knitted with each other.

5. All the Three are not Equally Important. The theory pre supposed that all the three departments are equally important but judiciary comes in the picture after the legislature has laboured hard to give the nation requisite laws. If the legislature becomes inactive, the judiciary will not come into picture at all. Therefore the presumption that all the three departments are equally important does not arise.

6. Hasty and Superficial. According to Sabine, "His love of political liberty, the sole enthusiasm of an otherwise chilly temperament, was in the best tradition of the eighteenth century but he united his theory to a hasty and superficial analysis of the constitutional principles of liberty."

Appreciation of the Theory

In spite of the above mentioned criticisms there is no denial that the theory of separation of powers was accepted in principle by many thinkers. According to Sabine, "Perhaps its greatest use had been as a make shift against extreme centralisation and as a reminder that no political organisation will work unless it can assume comity and fair dealing between its various parts." Maxey has said, "The authors of the American constitution were familiar with Montesquieu and adopted his doctrine as to the separation of powers with copy book of literalness, but did not equally value his concept of the governing principles underlying republican government.

MONTESQUIEU AND ARISTOTLE

Montesquieu has been called Aristotle of 18th century. He closely followed Aristotle in following respects:

1. Realist and Practical. Like Aristotle he was a realist and had practical approach to many problems.

2. Historical Method. Like Aristotle he followed historical method for the study of the subject before him.

3. Influence of Physical Environment. He followed Aristotle when he felt the necessity and influence which physical environment played in shaping the political institutions.

4. Laws the Product of Collective Wisdom. Montesquieu borrowed from Aristotle the idea that laws were products of collective wisdom of society and that they should suit the circumstances.

5. No Government Absolutely Bad. Both of them agreed that no form of government was absolutely good or bad but that it was only relatively good or bad. The governments change not in form but sometimes due to circumstances they change their shape and thus every change is not in kind but in degree only.

6. Political Institutions Based on Public Will are Permanent. Credit goes to them for giving the idea that the political institutions once established on sound reasons and will of the people remain basically the same. Local conditions might bring about a change to some extent but the fundamentals always remain unchanged.

7. Moderates. Both of them are not extremists but only moderates. In the words of Dunning, "Aristotle and Bodin, while close to him in many respects are widely different in the contention which they devoted to the general theory of the state, in its nature and origin and to the fundamental principles of public law, topics treated perfunctorily by Montesquieu." Laski has said, "His belief that the present is to be explained by its necessary will justifies us to say that at least in respect to method, he can be said as Aristotle of method."

CONTRIBUTION TO POLITICAL THOUGHT

Montesquieu has contributed following to the political thought:

1. Practical and Realist. Montesquieu was a realist in his approach to the problems before him. He believed more in practice than in theory. He justly realised that the states can work not on theories but must be practical both in national and international relations.

2. Individualism. Montesquieu gave the concept of individual liberty or individualism. Though living in quite adverse circumstances in which conditions were unfavourable he revolted against common slavish philosophy of his times. He valued liberty and followed that to the end. His whole political philosophy revolved round the word 'Liberty'. According to Sabine, "His love of political liberty, the sole enthusiasm of an otherwise chilly temperament, was in the best traditions of the eighteenth century, but he united his theory to a hasty and superficial analysis of the constitutional principles of liberty."

3. Methodology. Montesquieu made significant contribution in the field of methodology. In the words of Jones, "But the fact remains that his major contribution lies not in the field of theory, but in the field of method." He succeeded in bringing about a revolution in the field of method.

4. Widened the Scope of Political Science. Montesquieu widened the scope of political science by saying that physical environments influence political institutions.

5. Placed Political Science on Solid Footing. Montesquieu freed political science form all sorts of dogmas and placed it on solid footing of investigation.

6. Theory of Separation of Powers. Montesquieu is remembered for his theory of separation of powers. This theory was not but Montesquieu developed his ideas to their logical conclusions. His influence on the contemporary and subsequent political philosophy was immense. Even today it is accepted in principle that subject to the administrative convenience all the three organs of government should be separated from each other.

According to Sabine, "Montesquieu himself believed to possible to imitate English government in France might perhaps be remedied to that Montesquieu himself believed it possible to imitate English government in France is probably not true, but certainly the famous eleventh book of the Spirit of Law in which he ascribed liberty in English to the separation of legislative, executive and judicial powers and to the balancing to these powers against each other, set up these doctrines as dogmas of liberal constitution making. The extent of Montesquieu's influence in this respect in unquestionable and may be read large in the bills of rights of American and French constitutions." Sabine has also stressed the importance of this theory when he says that the theory was preserved and honoured till Bentham attacked it. To quote his words, "This theory of the constitution was preserved, partly under the last man to take seriously rigid separation of legal powers, believed that Revolution had resulted in the balancing of interests and orders. It was not until Bentham's criticism of Blackstone in the '*Fragments of Government*' (1776) that the separation of powers was effectively attacked."

7. Treatment of Laws. Montesquieu's contribution lies in his able treatment of laws. He believed that laws could not be separated from social environments and physical conditions. The impact of climate and physical environments is always writ large on the political and social laws. Sabine has said, "Climate, soil, occupations, form of government, commerce, religion, customs are all relevant conditions in determining what in a particular case reason (or) law will set up...obviously what Montesquieu was suggesting was as sociological study by as comparative method of institutions and the incidence upon them of institutions and non-institutional physical conditions."

CRITICISMS OF MONTESQUIEU'S THOUGHT

In spite of all his valuable contribution there is no denying that Montesquieu committed errors in following respects:

1. Over—Simplification. It has rightly been said that Montesquieu did not properly understand the complexities of the problems and hence oversimplified them. It has also been said of him that "Of all the French political philosophers in the 18th century (other than Reusseau) the must important was Montesquieu. Of them all he had perhaps the clearest conception of complexities of philosophy, and yet he too is guilty of extreme oversimplification."

2. Absence of Universalism. Montesquieu has written not with a view to the conditions of world at large but with special reference to the conditions prevailing in France at that time thought incidentally similar conditions prevailed in many other European countries. It has rightly been said that Montesquieu's '*Spirit of the Law*' did not meet the fate of Bodin's '*Republic*' due to any universalism in it but only due to its superior style.

3. Wrong Generalisation about the Influence of Climate. According to Montesquieu climate influences a form of Government and he has tried to generalise that. According to him hot climate suits dictatorship but cold climate is favourable for democracy. Though climate might effect a form of government, but this generalisation is in no way justified.

4. Hasty Decisions. Montesquieu has been charged with taking hasty decisions. This did not justify a philosopher of his deep study and knowledge.

Appreciation

Montesquieu was the spiritual father of philosophers like Blackstone, Gibbon, Bentham, Washington and Jefferson. Fathers of the American constitution liberally borrowed from his philosophy. His writings found a via media in the ideas of reactionaries and liberals, Sabine Says, "His writings gave aid and comfort both to reactionaries who hoped for the restoration of parliaments, the estates, and the provincial assemblies and to liberals who looked to an imitation of the English government." His ideas were read with interest and care by Louis XVI, Catherine the great and also Frederick, the Great. Vaughan says, "Whole life of a nation is woven of one piece, and therefore, it is impossible to make sweeping changes in one direction without laying the train for a thousand changes, unforeseen and perhaps undesired in all other directions also, that in this vast issue of relations one stand is perpetually liable to run athwart the others, one relation to find itself in conflict, more or less deadly with the others, and therefore that there is constant need for adjusting the one to the others; these are perhaps from his fundamental principles." While discussing the contribution of Montesquieu's political philosophy Dr. J.E. Greene has said, "At a time when thinkers were beginning to question the autocratic rule of the kings and church officials, Montesquieu raised a courageous lamp of inquiry and suggested changes with luminous logic."

QUESTIONS FOR EXERCISE

1. "Laws in their most general significance are the necessary relation arising from nature of things". Comment.
2. "Law is settled reason of the community." Comment.
3. "Most significant of the political contribution of Montesquieu in his conception of liberty which pervades his spirit of laws." Explain and summarize briefly the leading ideas of "Espiritials Lois".
4. "If it is true that the temper of the mind and the passions of the heart are extremely different in different climates the laws ought to be so in relation both in variety of those passions and to the variety of those tempers." (Montesquieu). Illustrate and examine.
5. "Laws in their most general signification are the necessary relations arising out of the nature of things." Discuss.
6. "The first of all empire is the empire of climate." (Montesquieu). Discuss.
7. A law means "the necessary relations arising from the nature of things." (Montesquieu). Discuss.
8. "Laws in their general signification, are the necessary relations arising from the nature of things." Discuss.
9. "Political liberty, mentions Montesquieu, does not consist in an unlimited freedom to do what one pleased." Do you agree with this position? What reasons does Montesquieu advance in support of it?
10. Critically examine Montesquieu's theory of separation of powers. What in your opinion Montesquieu desired to establish by (i) an absolute or (ii) a limited separation of powers?
11. "Power should be check to power." (Montesquieu). Comment.
12. "Law is the necessary relations springing from the nature of things." Discuss.
13. "Montesquieu was Aristotle of 18th Century". Discuss.
14. "Montesquieu is throughout guilty of over simplification and hasty generalisation. In political writings he was an elegant amateur." Explain this verdict on Monstesquieu.

26
Jean Jacques Rousseau
(1712-1770 A.D.)

Jean Jacques Rousseau was born in 1712, in Geneva of parents of French protestants ancestry, in a middle class family. His father was a watch-maker but became a dance master and went to Constantipole leaving his mother who urged him to come again. After this reunion Rousseau was born, ill and weak and her mother dies. Issac, the father of Rousseau brought him up without giving him proper education, but forced him to read about erotic romances all night, which, according to Rousseau, "Gave me wonderful romantic impressions of life."

At the age of ten his father entrusted Rousseau to his uncle's care and left Geneva. Upto the age of 13, Rousseau had to work as an apprentice under a cruel engraver. When 16, Rousseau left home and led a life of vagabond for 20 years wandering at different places. In 1742, he tried many trades but met with no success. He was very much disappointed but with the help of his friend, he got a post in the French Embassy at Vienna. But he was soon dismissed. He again came to Paris and opened a hotel. Here Cauasser, a servant in hotel became his real and lasting friend.

In the year of 1742, the Acadamy of Dizon announced a prize for the best essay on the subject, "Has the progress of science and arts contributed to corrupt or purify morals?" Rousseau presented his thesis that the progress of sciences and arts tended to degrade the human morality. He wrote an essay which depicted an early state of society in which all men lived under conditions of simplicity and innocence and traced the present evils of society to the thirst of knowledge and to the addition of artificialities of civilization. He won the prize which made a great sensation. It was the first ramble of revolution. In 1753, Rousseau wrote another essay on "What is the origin of inequality among men and is it authorized by natural laws ?"

Later on in 1755-1761 Rousseau wrote many of his important books. In 1762, he left Paris and led a life of vagabond for 16 years. This was a period of gloom, failing health, broken spirit, haunting terrors, paralysing illusions and of accumulating despair according to Hearnshaw.

Rousseau's Writings

1. *Two essays written for Acadamy.*

2. *Contract Social or The Principles of Political Right* — published in 1762 is most famous.

3. *Emile* dealing with education.

4. *Confessions.*

5. The Dialogues.

6. *The Reveries* — Published between 1762-1770.

Rousseau's books rebelled against the rational thinking of his age. He brought out the problems and conflicts inherent in civilised societies.

Bonald declared that he wished "to make constant the inconstant, to order disorder." Lamennais wrote that his work was "a sacrilegious declaration of war against society and against God." He is also regarded, as the extreme absolutist, the precursor of nineteenth-century German idealism. Constant said of him that "he is the most terrible ally of despotism in all its forms." Duguit remarked that "J. J. Rousseau is the father of Jacobian despotism, of Caesarian dictatorship, and the inspire of the absolutist doctrines of Kant and of Hegel." As such, he is both extreme individualist and extreme absolutist. "A stern asserter of the State on the one hand," Vaughan stated, "a fiery champion of the individual on the other, the could never bring himself wholly to sacrifice the one ideal to the other."

It is, however, surprising and rare in the history of political philosophy that the source of influential theory can be so precisely traced to individual personality as in the case of Rousseau. Indeed, there is none so fine, brilliant, the lucid a master of the finest prose, as Rousseau was, since Plato in the whole history of political thought. We dare not believe that he could not adequately express what he wanted to say. But he "had the dangerous gifts of epigram and paradox, and the greatest of writers if he indulges them too frequently is open to misunderstanding."[1]

ROUSSEAU'S PRINCIPLES

1. Each man by giving all to the society makes it absolute. Though authority is absolute but individuals still possess equal rights.

2. None is loser but every body is gainer.

3. The individual makes surrender to entity to which every individual is constituent part and "over whose activities he has the same degree of control as any other member of the community."

1. Wayper, C. L., Political Thought (English University Press Ltd., London, 1958), p. 138

4. The civil state brings out a tremendous change in man. Rousseau defends everything on moral principles and right, supplements appetite and makes his a reasonable being and a man. He showed that as men produced culture and civilisation they also suffered decline as human beings. Man's own creation overpowered and enslaved him. Men were born free but they entered into a life or bondage that was created by themselves by law, custom and social set up.

SOURCES OF INFLUENCE

Rousseau drew his inspiration from following sources for expounding his political philosophy :

1. Communism. Rousseau's was living at a time when it was being felt that political was meaningless without economic equality. He was influenced by these communistic tendencies of his times.

2. Family Life. Rousseau's personal life was not happy. He was neither faithful towards his family nor his children. His teachers were not very much sympathetic towards him, with the result that he became indifferent to actual life, which is reflected in his philosophy.

3. Hobbes and Locke. In his basic philosophy of *'Social Contract'* which he made the basis of the state, Rousseau was influenced by Hobbes and Locke, who had preceded him in this regard.

4. Plato. Influence of Plato on Rousseau was immense. According to Sabine, "The writer who did most to realise Rousseau from his individualism was Plato." He was Platonic in his conception about human nature. He was so much in love with the reasonability of human nature that in the very opening paragraph of his *Social Contract* he said, "Men is born free and everywhere he is in chains."

5. Montesquieu. In constitutionalism, Rousseau was influencedby Montesquieu who made him democratic rather than despotic.

6. Humble Life. One also finds the influence of Rousseau's humble life in his writings and philosophy. He realised the problems and difficulties of the life of an ordinary man and enunciated his philosophy to suit the multitudes. In the words of Maxey, "A further source of his power was his lowly origin and his humble, mendicant way of life. He was not merely the people's advocate, he was bone of their bone and flesh of their flesh."

7. Geneva. Last but not least was his love for Geneva which was the centre of democracy and hence he developed a love for democratic institutions.

Rousseau very bitterly attacked the prevalent notions about reason. Contrary to them he pleaded that reason was not developed through science but by love for labour and family life. Rousseau distinguished between reason and intelligence. He, however, condemned reason, intelligence and science where they deprived man of faith and reverence. He felt the necessity of reason in day today life as it promoted intelligence and knowledge.

CONCEPT OF HUMAN NATURE

According to A. Hacker, "Aristotle believed in the wickedness of human nature. St. Augustine and St. Thomas affirmed the doctrine of original sin, and Machiavelli stated that men in general are, ungrateful valuable, dissembles, anxious to avoid danger, and covetous of gain....Rousseau has observed the men and the same perversities as have the theorists who precede him. The wicked behaviour of mankind has hardly escaped his eyes, yet this he says is a superficial view of man in society." According to Rousseau man by birth had no evil tendencies. It was the result of wrong social actions which made him evil.

1. Self Love. Rousseau believed that man by nature has only two instinct, of them one is 'self love.' "His first preference always is to attend to his own presentation, his first cares are those which he owes to himself."

2. Sympathy. Man's second instinct is that of sympathy or instinct of mutual aid. These instincts, Rousseau believed, always make our struggle for existence easier and do us more good than harm.

3. Conscience. There was every possibility of the clashing of both these instincts at one time or the other. As a result of clash another instinct called 'conscience' emerges. This conscience is something above education and reason. It resolves conflict between the first tow instincts. Reasoning comes only when the complexities of problems come to the front. Sentiments attached with those instincts do not successfully motivate the actions of man in proper direction.

4. Pride. A problem which is bound to crop is that if man was good by nature and gifted with the sentiments of love and sympathy then what makes him bad? Rousseau's simple answer that self love went astray to become 'pride' and the pride made man begin to feel ashamed or honoured over being deprived or getting something in competitions. This pride was the root cause of many evils. In his *'Meaning of Rousseau'*, Wright has said that if we can give up pride, we cease from all comparison with other men and simply go about our destiny. "We can renounce a lot of imaginary desires and hold fast to the true things, needful castaway a world of illusion and disorder our own self. We can be meek, and inherit our soul. In a world, we can return to nature. This is all the famous phrase means."

5. Freedom of Choose. Rousseau also believed that in addition to above instincts nature has also gifted mankind with another instinct namely the freedom to choose his own path which distinguished a man from an animal. This freedom was essential for the perfection of mankind.

STATE OF NATURE

1. Peaceful Ignorance— Rousseau believed that in the state of nature all lived as isolated and had neither ties of obligation nor duties. Man did not know how to deliver a speech and had no cares for dress. He was free self contented and unknown to social good, evil or fear. He was not even afraid of death. He had no fear of loss of property or family because he had neither property nor family. Man was in peaceful ignorance. Rousseau ridiculed Hobbes by saying that "Above all, let us not conclude, with Hobbes, that because man has no idea of goodness, he must be naturally wicked; that he is vicious because the does not know virtues; that he always refuses to do his fellow creatures services which he does not think they have right to demand; or that by virtue of the right he truly claims everything he needs, he foolishly imagines himself the sole proprietor of the whole universe."

2. Group Life. Man could not lead a solitary life for long. His social instinct compelled him to live in groups. Social institutions began to develop gradually. Instinct of self-love began to shape itself into pride and man began to think in terms of having private property. "The first man, having enclosed a piece of ground, he thought himself of saying 'This is mine' and found other people simple enough to believe him, was the first real founder of civil society."

3. Property. Institution of private property, which entered the society, disturbed the whole atmosphere of pre-civil state. To quote Rousseau himself, "It came as a serpent and bit all. It brought misery, sorrow and evil in the minds of men who were otherwise good and noble." "So long as men remained content with their rustic huts...and confined themselves to such arts as did not require several hands, they lived free, healthy, and happy lives so long as their nature allowed, and as they continued to enjoy the pleasures of mutual and independent intercourse. But from the moment one man began to stand in need of the help of another; from the moment it appeared advantageous to any one to have provisions for two, equality disappeared, property was introduced; work became indispensable, and the vast forests became smiling fields; which men had to water with the sweat of his brows, and where slavery and misery were soon seen to germinate and grow up with the crops."

According to A. Hacker, "For a social system based on private property sets an egoistic standard for success, and it complies this standard in all individuals. Men, came to feel that they must own property, be superior to other man, in a word, be successful,....Not only men came to judge themselves as success or failures by social standard, they also became compulsive about the way they were viewed by those who lived around them."

The private property created a problem and the society was divided between the rich and the poor. It also resulted in the division of labour. Thus the whole social set-up was disturbed. Rousseau said, "From these first distinctions arose on the one side vanity and contempt and on the other shame and envy; and the fermentation caused by these new heavens ended by producing combinations fatal to innocence and happiness." He concluded his discussion on the subject by saying that, "In short, all men fall prey to frailties of their own age."

Soon after the serpent in the form of private property, entered the society the peaceful atmosphere and order was disturbed. Men began to feel the necessity of bringing about the old order of calmness and happy life. This problem was solved by the creation of a social or a political association to which all the members of the society agreed. A reconciliation between the individuals on the one hand and society on the other was to be arrived at by way of contract. Rousseau agreed with Locke that individual's consent was necessary for binding him in contract. The contract was concluded in the following order, according to Rousseau, "Each of us puts his person and all his power in common under supreme direction of the general will, and in our corporate capacity, we receive each member as an individual part of the whole. At once in place of the individual personality of each contracting party, this act of associating creates a moral and collective body composed of as many members as the Assembly contains votes and receiving from his act its unity, its comman identity, its life and its will. Yet each person in the state, possessing equal and inalienable position of the sovereignty of the whole, gains back under state protection the rights he has given up."

Individual Merged in the State

Like Plato and Hobbes, Rousseau also tried to completely merge individual in the state. He maintained that this system of equality made all to surrender their rights. The individuals who had by now become selfish and self-centred were not willing to subordinate themselves to any individual. Rousseau solved this problem by saying that the contract was concluded between the individuals and the society or the community. His contact was a double sided one. As part of sovereignty, his individual was bound to other individuals. As a part of the state he was bound to the sovereign. In order that social contract may not prove an empty formula it concludes the tacit understanding that whosoever refuses to obey the general will shall be compelled to obedience by the whole body of citizens.

FORMATION OF POLITICAL SOCIETY

The natural state, as conceived by Rousseau, is a state of substantial equality. No baneful distinction could be found among the individuals who pursue in isolation the placid routine of satisfying their physical needs. But the deadly seeds of a different order were ready to germinate. With no necessary ground for it in his description of the savage state, Rousseau assumed that as the human race became increasingly numerous; divergences of soil, climate and season caused differences in manner of life among men. Men began to take into account the difference between objects and to make comparisons. They acquired the ideas of beauty and merit, which soon gave rise to feelings of preference. In consequence of often seeing each other they could not do without seeing each other constantly. A tender and pleasant feeling insinuated itself into their souls, and the least opposition turned it into an impetuous fury: with love arose jealousy; discord triumphed, and human blood was sacrificed to the greatest of all passions.

As ideas and feelings succeeded one another, and heart and head were brought into play, men continued to lay aside their original wildness; their private connections became more intimate as their limits extended. Their life became gradually complicated. They could no more enjoy peaceful living. Intercourse of individuals and families became common through the ideas of competition and preference. "From the moment one man began to stand in need of the help another; from the moment it appeared advantageous to any one man to have enough provisions for two, equality and peace disappeared, property was introduced, work became indispensable, and vast forests became smiling fields, which man had to water with the sweat of his brow, and where slavery and misery were soon to germinate and grow up with the crops.[2] Although evils follow in their train, this primitive stage is not, according to Rousseau, intolerable state. Looked upon as a mean between the indolence of the savage state and the too intense activity of the later phase, it appears to him the happiest period in the life of humanity— "the least subject to revolutions, the best for man."[3] While Rousseau described the savage state, he was disposed to consider it as the happiest and best, and when he moved on to the tribal and early social state, this in turn appealed to him as preferable. But, according to him, evil arose with the progress of civilization. The division of labour that followed the development of the arts, metallurgy and agriculture and the rise of private property created distinctions between the rich and the poor and ultimately broke down the happy natural condition of mankind and necessitated the establishment of civil society.

Political society, according to Rousseau, is created with a view to safeguarding the individual against the corrupting influences of society. In the political writings, *Contract Social* (1762) and also *Constitution for Corsica* (1765), the "state is all in all". While in the social and moral writings of Rousseau it seems at first sight to be either disparaged or wholly disregarded. On closer inspection, however, this first impression needs to be corrected. The state which Rousseau disparaged in the

---

2. Contract Social (1762).
3. Dunning, W.A. : *Political Theories* (From Rousseau to Spencer). The Macmillan Co., New York (1920), p. 9.

Discourse on Inequality (1754) and in *Emile* (1762) is not the ideal state of the *Contract Social*, but the actual state, as known to us from experience and history. What excited Rousseau's suspicion in these writings is not the state, but society of any sort, quite apart from the civic ties by which, in fact, it is held together. His ideal, alike in the *Discourse* and in *Emile*, is, no doubt, individual freedom: freedom, however, not in the sense of immunity from the control of the state, but in that of withdrawal from all the oppressions and all corruptions of society. In both treatises alike, it is not the state, but society, which is the enemy. Rousseau's conclusion is : "It is our business to make every individual member absolutely independent of his fellow- members and absolutely dependent on the state. It is only by the force of the state that the liberty of its members can be secured."[4] And if Rousseau had really been the individualist as some critics suppose, it is certain that he might easily have woven them into a theory more or less closely resembling that of Locke. But it was equally open to him to turn them in exactly the opposite direction; to argue that the reason without which the primitive instincts of 'conscience' are no more than blank forms, so far from being inherent in the natural growth of the individual, does on fact come to him only in and through the state. C.E. Vaughan rightly remarks : "Regarding *Discourse* and *Emile,* it can be said that the state of nature is glorified in the one. The ideal of the other was, or was taken to be, an isolation of the individual almost as complete as that attributed to the state of nature. And hasty readers jumped to the conclusion that the man who thus mistrusted society must look with still deeper suspicion upon the very existence of the state; that, at the very least, he must desire to restrict its action within the narrowest limits possible; the must be a sworn foe to entrusting it with any powers beyond the protection of individual life and individual property."[5]

THE SOCIAL CONTRACT

Theory of State

In his *Contract Social* Rousseau presented a theory of the state. In the development from the state of nature, there comes a time when individuals can no longer maintain themselves in primitive independence. It then becomes necessary to self-preservation that they should unite to form a society— a political society. Rousseau admitted that "the problem is to find a form of association which will defend and protect with the whole common force the person and goods of each associate, and in which each, while uniting himself with all, may still obey himself alone, and remain as free as before. This is the fundamental problem of which the social contract provides the solution." In the first chapter

---

4. *Contrat Social*, II, xii.

5. Vaughan, C.E. : *Du Contrat Social on Principles Du Droit Politique* (Published by Manchester University Press, 1947), Introduction, p. xviii.

of his book, *Contract Social* he also remarked : "Man is born free and everywhere he is in chains. One who believes himself the master of the rest is only more of a slave than they. How does that change come about? I do not know. What can render it legitimate (*legitime*)? That question I think I can answer."[6] The liberty and equality that characterize the state of nature are gone in the civil state Rousseau justified their disappearance, in his usual way, by proving that they subsisted as fully after, as before, the institution of government. Authority of man over man can have no rational basis, he held, save agreement and consent. And there is but one species of agreement conceivable in which liberty is retained while authority is instituted. This single species is the pact through which a multitude of individuals become a collective unity— a society.

Criticism of other Theories of State

Rousseau's thought seems to reject the prevalent notions regarding the origin of the state. He rejected the view that family is the basis of the state. The state, he argued, is not an outgrowth of the family; for it lacks the natural basis, the tie of natural affection upon which the family rests. Also, he rejected the force theory. According to him, it is not founded upon the 'right of the stronger', nor, more specifically, upon the 'right of slavery', the right of the conqueror to enslave those he has subdued in battle, for such claims are the negation of all Right. And even if this were not so, they could give rise to nothing more than an 'aggression'; they could never produce that organic union which is essential even to the most rudimentary forms of what we recognize as the state.[7] Hence the only alternative left, is to base political society upon 'convention' or 'contract'; and that is the solution adopted by "the soundest of those who have written of such matters: above all, by two thinkers so different as Hobbes and Locke." Rousseau's thought shows the very strong influence of both Hobbes and Locke. It is the latter, however, whom he followed to the end. From the ingenious reasoning by which Hobbes made absolute monarchy a logical corollary of the social contract, Rousseau turned down with strong denunciation. But the Hobbesian precision in defining the terms of the contract obviously appealed to him. His own treatment of the subject is but the substance of Locke developed by the method of Hobbes.

Social Contract

Political society was created through social pact, since only by agreement and consent could authority be justified and liberty retained. Rousseau held that each individual gave up his natural rights to the community as a whole. Or the contract consists in 'the total alienation of each associate, together with all his rights, to the whole community; for, in the first place, as each gives himself absolutely, the conditions are the same for all; and this being

---

6. *Contrat Social*, I, i.

7. *Ibid.*, I, vi.

so, no one has any interest in making them burdensome to others." The alienation is to be without reserve : "If individuals retained certain rights, as there would be no common superior to decide between them and the public, each, being on one point his own judge, would ask to be so on all; the state of nature would thus continue, and the association would necessarily become inoperative or tyrannical." Each person, according to Rousseau, in the state possessed and equal and unalienable portion of the sovereignty of the whole and gained back, under the protection of the state, the rights he had given up.

The contract of Rousseau was social and not governmental. To him, as to Hobbes, it was the total surrender of the whole community, to a community itself. It was Rousseau's belief that the conditions essential for the formation of a specific code of right and wrong, however, rudimentary, are to be found only in that ordered development of society which we call the state. The state is not something external to the individual, but of the very essence of his being. It is the condition without which liberty would be only another name for bondage to his most selfish and most destructive passions. According to Rousseau, there could be no conflict between authority vested in the people as a whole and their liberty as individuals. Viewed in this way, the social contract is not a contract which men make with their future ruler. The government is their mere agent. To make a contract with it would not only give it a dignity to which it ought not to pretend, it would place men under the rule of some individuals or groups, which would be nothing but slavery. Such a contract would defeat the ends for which men come together, those ends being the fulfilment of their nature, which slavery would make impossible. Therefore their problem is to create a society "in such a way that each, when united to his fellows, renders obedience to his own will, and remains as free as he was before." And the sovereign "cannot impose upon its subjects any fetters that are useless to the community, nor can it even wish to do so." It should be observed here that the 'sovereign' means, in Rousseau, not the monarch or the government, but the community in its collective and legislative capacity.

The social contract can be stated in the following words: "Each of us puts his person and all his power in common under the supreme direction of the general will, and, in our corporate capacity, we receive each member as an indivisible part of the whole." This act of association creates a moral and collective body, which is called the 'state' when passive, the 'sovereign' when active, and a 'power' in relation to other bodies like itself. Rousseau was convinced that the community, the state, is something essentially different from the sum of the individuals who compose it. It has a being, a life, of its own which is not identical with that of its members, taken severally. It is not an aggregate, but a corporate unity. It is an organization, to the life of which every member contributes, unconsciously as well as consciously. The idea of the state as an organism dominates the whole of the*Contrat Social.*

What did Rousseau mean by his assertion that, with the passage from the natural to the civil state, the sense of justice and duty is first awakened in the mind of man; that "his actions receive thereby a moral character which was wanting to them before"; that "from a stupid and limited animal, he now for the first time becomes a reasoning being and a man;"[8] in a word, that, apart from the state, no distinctively moral life is possible for man? He surely did not mean that as a member of the state, man suddenly finds himself possession of qualities of which in his previous condition he had given no sign, no promise, whatever. Such a view would, in itself, be wholly irrational. The instinct of justice according to Rousseau is present in man's heart; but this instinct should develop into a conscious sense of duty. This is possible only under the fostering guidance of the state.

THEORY OF GENERAL WILL

The state, according to Rousseau, which is created through the social contract is not an arbitrary state. It is established to maintain an atmosphere in which individuals can enjoy their liberty in the best possible way. It has to work through a 'general will'. The general will is no abstract idea. It is a living principle of action : a principle to be kept alive only by the sleepless devotion, the watchful jealously, of all the individuals concerned. It is this devotion, this jealousy, which alone can "hold the state true, to the end for which it was founded—that is, the common good of all" : that common good, the necessity of obedience to which is "the one fundamental law of the state, the one law which flows directly and immediately from the social contract."

The conception of the 'general will' plays a very important part in Rousseau's system. In this connection, it is argued that the sovereign need give no guarantees to its subjects, for, it is formed of the individuals who compose it, it can have no interest contrary to theirs. "The sovereign, merely by virtue of what it is, is always what it should be."

CHARACTERISTICS OF GENERAL WILL

1. Definition of General Will. Rousseau was of the opinion that men grew sick of the anarchy which the serpent of private property brought in the society. Hence they thought of creating a sovereign through social contract. The contract was concluded by a pact between the individuals and the community consisting of the individuals who formed the society. The individuals surrendered all their powers and rights to the community as a whole and bowed before the General Will, which was the sovereign in the ultimate analysis.

2. Actual Will and Real Will. In order to properly understand the theory of 'General Will' it is necessary to understand the terms Actual Will

8. *Contrat Social.* I, viii.

and Real Will. From 'Actual Will' Rousseau understood the will which was selfish and irrational and thought of the good of the individual alone. It conceives of the individual alone. It has no concern with the welfare of the society. On the other hand, Rousseau believed that 'Real Will' was something higher, nobler and supreme. It was concerned more about the well being of all than that of one individual. It was more social than anti-social, more collective than individualistic. In other words, the real will was a channel for promoting the well being of the individuals and society because when it thought of the society it *ipso facto* thought about the welfare of the individuals. Real will was permanent and not transitory. It did not take into consideration only the momentary aspects of life but also its permanent aspects. Real will was based on reason and criticism.

3. Real Will and General Will. According to Rousseau 'General Will' was the sum total of all the 'real wills' of the individuals which were based on reason and farsightedness of the individuals. It was will of all the individuals for collective welfare. It was common consciousness. Rousseau has defined General Will as "The public person, so formed by the union of all other persons is called by its members, state when passive, sovereign when active."

4. Nobler Than Real Wills. According to Rousseau General Will was not the sum total of good and bad will of the individuals by a method of plus and minus but was something nobler. It was the product of deliberation, discussions and consciousness. General Will is concerned with general good but it might not be willed by the majority of the members of the society.

5. Everybody Free in General Will. Rousseau believed that in General Will none was slave or under subordination to anyone else. Every body was free. To quote Rousseau, "If the state is a moral person whose life is in the union of its members, and if the most important of its care is the care of its own preservation, then it must have a universal and compelling force in order to dispose part as may be advantageous to the whole."

6. General Will and Will of All. Rousseau tried to distinguish between the General Will and the will of all. General Will considered about the good of the community as a whole whereas will of all was only majority will and considered about the welfare of a few only. The will of all could become General Will of peculiar interests, which have selfish ends and are taken away from it. In Rousseau's own words, "There is often a considerable difference between General Will and will of all, the former aims at the common interest, the latter aims at private interest and is only a sum of particular wills. But if we take away from these wills the various particular interests which conflict with each other what remains as the sum of difference is General Will."

7. Salient Features of General Will. General Will has the following particular features according to Rousseau:

(i) ***Unity.*** General will is rational. It is not self-contradictory. It thus gives unity in the sense that it is indivisible because once divided it cannot be called 'General Will' but only sectional will.

(ii) ***Permanent.*** As General Will is based on reason, wisdom and experience and thought about the good of all, it is not to do away with the time but is permanent. It cannot be altered. It is pure. Even though it may be dominated by other wills for sometime yet in the ultimate analysis this will dominate.

(iii) ***Right Will.*** It is will which takes into consideration not only the political and social but also moral conditions. As such it is right will based on right reasonings and presumptions.

(iv) ***Inalienable.*** Rousseau's sovereign is 'General Will' and not any human being. The sovereign cannot give up the sovereignty. He cannot pass that on to any other individual because sovereignty was vested in the community as a whole. Community could not pass on the sovereign authority to any other individual or organisations but to the General Will. Thus sovereignty and General Will are inseparable and hence inalienable. For Rousseau alienating General will is just killing it.

(v) ***Unrepresentative.*** According to Rousseau people have no right to delegate their authority or representing themselves by anybody else. He believed in theory of direct democracy through General Will.

(vi) ***Rational.*** Rousseau based his theory of General Will on 'rationalism' and not on force. For him will is not force but the very basis of sustaining state.

(vii) ***Disinterested.*** According to Rousseau General Will is disinterested because it is not concerned with the individual but with the community as whole. It is disinterested because it promotes public spiritedness. Thus General Will is not interested in any section of society but took into consideration will of society as a whole. Rousseau, however, made it clear that perfect unanimity cannot be achieved and differences of opinion are bound to exist. General Will is a corporate will functioning through people as a whole.

(viii) ***Unenforceable.*** General Will is not executive. Since General Will is impersonal it cannot be loaded with the responsibility of enforcing law. It is sovereign in nature and character. As such government is only an agency of General Will. General Will cannot be executive as well as legislative body.

Criticism of General Will

Theory of General Will as expounded by Rousseau has been put to severe criticism:

1. Confused. Theory of General will is confused. It boils down to striking the balance of real will and actual will. It tries to give it an arithmetical touch. Even if Rousseau's notion is accepted, General Will is a dynamic process and not arithmetical one.

2. No Difference in General Will and Will of All. Rousseau has tried to distinguish between 'General Will' and 'Will of All' which, in practice is impossible to achieve.

3. Unanimous and not Majority Will. Rousseau's conception of General Will is more or less a unanimous will and not a majority will. Unanimous will and decisions are possible only in the animal and not in human society.

4. Wills Cannot be Divided. Rousseau has divided the will of an individual into integral parts namely essential and non-essential wills. According to him, essential will is rational and represents sum total of essential wills. However, individuals and their wills are corporate. It is impossible to distinguish and divide the wills.

5. No Reconciliation of General Will and Justice. Rousseau believes that general will is one which coincides with justice. But by this criteria he creates more confusion. Justice is an equally abstract conception and reconciling the two is not only impossible but undesirable.

6. General Will cannot be Reconciled with Freedom. According to Rousseau whosoever refused to obey the 'General Will' will be made to obey it and thus set free. By setting free this way is in the other words to use force for obeying commands. Rousseau has tried to reconcile individual freedom with the authority of the General will or freedom with force but has failed to do so.

7. What if not Majority Will. Rousseau has reduced his theory of 'General Will' to nothingness when he says that General Will is not majority will. If it is not majority will then what is it?

8. Distinction in General Will and Individual Good. Rousseau believed that General Will is something else than the individual good. This means that there is something above the individual which may be called the 'state'. Rousseau has thus tried to distinguish between the individual and the state. In actual practice, however, the state consists of individuals and their interests are inseparable.

9. General Will Impossible in Nation States. The notion of General Will as expounded by Rousseau, may to some extent be possible in case where the community is small and the individuals have personal contacts with each other. But it is impossible to follow this conception and put it into actual practice in case of nation states of today. It is more or less impossible to ascertain General Will on the lines suggested by Rousseau.

10. Direct Representation not Possible in his State. Rousseau believed that in General Will there should only be direct and not indirect representation. This again is not practicable in modern nation states. The system of direct representation can only be practicable in small states. No nation state in the world has found it possible to adopt direct democracy as a method for realising the will of the people. Hence in actual practice this theory is bound to collapse, particularly in big states.

11. Impractical on Human Grounds. The conception of General Will is not practicable on human grounds. In normal times men are selfish and consider their own interests above everything else. It is only in national crises and grave emergencies that they think of common good. To think of men giving up their selfish ends for collective ends is something against human nature. It is an attempt to mould human nature which is very difficult, if not impossible.

12. Practical Failure. Rousseau has also failed to guide the community as to how it can be applied in actual practice and also how to achieve it.

13. Against Social Contract Theory. Rousseau's theory of General Will is against his Social Contract theory. According to C.E.M. Joad, "It seems to follow that a strict adherence to the doctrine of General Will would in practice entail frequent revolt against most governments." Wayper says, "For if the General Will is supreme, the Social Contract is unnecessary and meaningless, and, if the Social Contract is necessary and significant, the General Will cannot be supreme." Colhan has said, "Theoretically, the sovereignty of the General Will represents an attempt to justify philosophically the law. Its effects on liberty in the state will depend on the way in which the General Will principle is elaborated." Cole says, "The freedom which is realised in the General Will, we are told, is the freedom of the state as a whole, but the state exists to secure individual freedom for its members. A free state may be tyrannical, a despot may allow his subjects every freedom. What guarantee is there that the state, in freeing itself, will not enslave its members."

The above criticism does not mean that Rousseau's concept of General Will has no worth at all. It has the following features in its favour:

1. Will, not Force, is the Basis of State. The greatest value of the theory is that it preached that 'will not force is the basis of the state.' It has made the community realise the worth of human co-operation.

2. Basis of Democracy. The theory of General Will is the basis of true democracy in the true sense.

3. Concept of General Good. The theory advances the conception of general good and puts social interests before individual interests which aim at creating an ideal state with ideal citizens.

4. Corporate Character of State. The theory has preached corporate character of state. It has tried to recognize and reorganise society apart from the citizens as individuals.

5. Theory of National State. Rousseau also is primarily responsible for promoting the theory of nation state. According to Dunning, "Through these concepts a way was opened by which the unity and solidarity of a population became necessary presupposition of a scientific politics. Rousseau thus contributed largely to promote the theory of national state."

It is thus difficult to agree with the critics that Rousseau would have not done more justice to the subjects had he not enunciated his theory of General Will. To conclude with Bosanquet, "The General Will seems to be, in the last resort, the ineradicable impulse of an intelligent being to a good extending beyond itself, in so far as that impulse takes the form of a common good, though this impulse mastered and created in a degree, yet if it were extinct human life would have ceased."

CONTRIBUTION TO POLITICAL THOUGHT

1. Theory of General Will. Rousseau is one of those political philosophers of 18th century whose influence has been immense in his own times and has been gradually increasing in our days. Politically he belonged to philosophical school of thought and was thus responsible for giving new ideas and thoughts. He was one of the most controversial figures of his age. Lord Morley once remarked, "Would it not have been better for the world if Rousseau had not been born?" Sabine estimated the value of Rousseau by saying that "Rousseau's political philosophy was so vague that it can hardly be said to point in any specific direction." But Hearnshaw has estimated his importance by saying that "From numerous and varied sources we get an impression of a man of high originality and undoubted genius; an intense individualist impatient at any sort of restraint....sensitive to noble impulse, full of fury against tyranny and injustice, capable of copious weeping on any convenient occasion. He loved the human race, although he quarrelled with every specimen of it with which he was brought into but the most transient contact." According to Dunning Rousseau was suggestive. His theory of General Will became one of the springboards for subsequent political philosophers who were interested in asserting the rights of men and believed in individualism. According to Cole, "As new generations and new classes of men come to study his works, his conceptions, often hazy and undeveloped, but nearly always of lasting value, will assuredly form the basis of a new political philosophy, in which they will be taken up and formed." Jones has assessed the value of his doctrine of General Will when he says that "the notion of the General Will is not only the most central concept of Rousseau's theory, it is also the most original, the most interesting and historically the most important contribution which he made to the political theory."

It has been said that history of General Will and his writings became too thought provoking throughout the 18th century that Rousseau was quoted to excite men. His writings became the Bible for political thinkers. No revolutionary could afford missing him in thoughts, actions and words.

2. Forerunner of English and German Idealism. After Aristotle, Rousseau preached that man was a political animal. This was against the political philosophy preached by Machiavelli and Hobbes, who believed that man was egoistic and aggressive and that his impulses should be checked. Rousseau said good bye to the traditional theories of the middle ages. It has been said by Cole that, "He is, in fact, the great forerunner of English and German idealism."

3. Nationalism. Rousseau did not believe in the idea of nation state, as he saw that free citizenship was rather impossible in those days. He, however, contributed to the philosophy of his age by saying that there must he national solidarity and unity. Though himself not a nationalist he stood for nationalism. According to Sabine, "Without himself being a nationalist Rousseau helped to revive the ancient ideal of citizenship in such a form that national sentiment could appropriate it."

4. National State. It has been said of Rousseau that his philosophy preached unity, solidarity and national integration. Like Bodin and Hobbes he was responsible for giving the nation the conception of nationalism and nation state.

5. Sovereign v/s Government Law. Rousseau distinguished between state and government and also between the sovereign laws and governmental decrees. He believed that sovereign law is based on fundamental rights and constitution and has thus value and standing. Government law is temporary in nature and reason and thus based on immediate needs of the people.

6. Political People as Ultimate Authority. Rousseau contributed to political philosophy by saying that, "The political people were the ultimate authority and source for giving all political authorities and that government was simply as agency to execute the directives given by this sovereign authority."

CONTRADICTIONS IN ROUSSEAU'S POLITICAL PHILOSOPHY

Rousseau's political philosophy suffers from following contradictions:

1. Private Property. In *Discourse on the Origin of Inequality* and '*Emile*' Rousseau has condemned private property whereas in his subsequent discussions he has made it obligatory on the state to defend private property.

2. Democracy and Absolutism. Rousseau tried to plead for democracy and give maximum rights to the people but in actual practice he has become most absolutist. Duguit has said that "J.J. Rousseau is the father of Jacobin despotism, of Caesarian dictatorship and the inspirer of the absolutistic doctrines of Kant and Hegel."

3. Confused Nationalism. Rousseau tried to be a nationalist but here also he is victim of confusion.

4. Confused Democrat. Rousseau has tried to be democrat but it has rightly been said that his sovereign was more powerful than even that of Hobbes and in fact absolute than most powerful dictators.

INFLUENCE OF ROUSSEAU'S POLITICAL PHILOSOPHY

Rousseau's political philosophy had following influence on his age:

1. French Revolution. His concepts of liberty and equality were responsible for French Revolution of 1789. His political philosophy was not only a source of inspiration but a guiding force for the French people after the Revolution and at least till the rise of Napoleon.

2. U.S. Practice. The impact of Rousseau's theories on U.S. practice is evident. Jefferson's government in 19th century was influenced by Rousseau's ideas. The theory of Social Contract found its due place in the Declaration of Independence and Bill of Rights in U.S. Constitution.

3. Inspiration to Bentham. In England Rousseau was responsible for inspiring Bentham by giving him the idea of the greatest good of the greatest number.

4. Inspiration to All Political Philosophers. The Individualists and Collectivists, the Monists and the Pluralists all find their solace in the political philosophy of Rousseau. These rival group followers quote from his writings. He has in fact become a source of inspiration not only for Anarchists, Federalists, Syndicalists but also to many others.

5. Passage from Medieval to Modern State. Ernest Rays has rightly said about Rousseau, "In political thought he represents the passage from a traditional theory rooted in the middle ages to the modern philosophy of the state.....he was in fact the great fore runner of the German and English Idealism."

6. Appreciations. Following are some appreciations of Rousseau's political philosophy:

(i) *Maxey*. "The concept of General Will is the crux of Rousseau's System and probably his most important contribution to political thought."

(ii) *Prof. Hearnshaw*. "He displays the people as the ultimate source of political authority.....he stressed the view that state is social organisation.....it is a common conscience and General Will; he maintains the doctrine that true basis of political obligation is consent; he proclaims the possibility of ultimate reconciliation of freedom and authority....He takes a high place among political idealists."

(iii) *Dr. J.E. Greens.* "The philosophy of Rousseau was a mixture of Lao Tse's return to nature, Buddha's compassion for the poor; Isáiah's search for social justice, St. Augustine's progress from licentiousness to love and Locke's blue print for a better world. In addition.....Rousseau brought to his work the imagination of a poet and the sympathy of a gentle soul."

HOBBES, LOCKE AND ROUSSEAU COMPARED

1. Sovereignty. Hobbes and Rousseau maintained that sovereignty is absolute but to Locke, it was limited. Hobbes was of the opinion that sovereignty may be vested in one, few or the many but once it is vested, it could not be recalled. Rousseau held that sovereignty is vested in the whole people.

2. Natural Man and State of Nature. To Hobbes natural man was selfish and the state of nature was a period of constant welfare. Rousseau believed that the natural man was good and there was happiness in the state of nature. Locke occupied a middle position on these points.

3. Government. Hobbes said that a change in government meant a dissolution of state. Locke held that the people had a right to choose the government and change it if they do not like it. To Rousseau, the government was merely the agent which executed the popular will.

4. Nature of Law. According to Hobbes in natural state there were no civil laws and the actions of men were controlled by natural laws. Locke maintained that in the state of nature, natural laws were the embodiment of the morality. These laws were based on reason. Human behaviour was controlled by them. Rousseau held that a law is a revolution of the whole people for the whole people, touching a matter that concerns all. The law must relate to general interest and must emanate from the people as a whole.

5. Natural Rights. Hobbes said that in the state of nature, might was the only right. Thus the rights of men were based on the power of the individual concerned. Locke drew a brighter picture. He maintained that in the state of nature everybody had a right to life, right to property and right to liberty, he maintained that rights were inborn. Rousseau held that the rights of liberty, equality and property were rights of the citizen and are not innate. However, he maintained that in the state of nature man was free to enjoy all his natural rights.

6. Social Contract. Hobbes said that in the state of nature man's life was solitary, poor and brutish. There was a constant warfare. Later on man discovered that peace was more useful. Hence he agreed that everyman ought to endeavour to peace as far as he has the hope of obtaining it and he must be content with so much liberty against other men, as he would allow other men against himself. On this basis, men agreed to establish a sovereign to whom all authority was transferred. Locke said that the state was established by a social contract. The duty of the state was to define and enforce the natural laws. The sovereign's authority was limited and man surrendered to him some of his natural rights and not all of them.

Rousseau maintained that political society came into being on the basis of a social contract to which each and all members assented. It was to provide its members with both the freedom of the state of nature and the advantages of civil order.

QUESTIONS FOR EXERCISE

1. "Beginning as an architect in revolt against all social coercion, Rousseau came in time to a conclusion which made the state everything and the individual nothing." (Kingsley Martin). Examine this estimate of Rousseau's Political thought.

2. "For Hobbes political unity lies in a will which is actual but not general, for Locke it lies in a will which is general, but not actual, for Rousseau it lies in a will which is at once actual and general." Discuss.

3. "The real objection to the term (General Will) is that in so far as it is will, it is not general, and in so far as it is general it is not will." (Hobhouse) Which of these statements in your view, is the more fundamental concept of the General Will?

4. "Rousseau's concept of General Will has been characterised as more absolute than absolutism of Hobbesian Leviathan and more democratic than the democracy of Locke." Is this remark tenable? Give reasons for your answer.

5. "The dictatorship is both the logical and also the historical consequence of the democratic theory of the General Will." (Colhan). Discuss.

6. "Rousseau's theory of General will is a strange mixture of utopian idealism and plain common sense." Discuss.

7. "There is often a considerable difference between the General Will and will of all." (Rousseau). Comment.

27
David Hume (1741-1778 A.D.)

David Hume was born in a Scotish family in 1711. After completing his early education, he studied law but devoted himself to literary pursuits. He did business but did not succeed. He failed in all professions and being frustrated, he went to France. He lived in France for a few years and wrote *'Treatise on Human Nature'* at the age of 26. At the time of its publication only a few people purchased it, few read it and none understood it but now it is regarded as his masterpiece. He was a philosopher, scholar and thinker. He died in 1778.

Works

1. *Treatise on Human Nature*
2. *Essays : Moral and Political*
3. *History of England*
4. *Enquiry into Principles of Morals*
5. *Political Discourses*
6. *A Natural History of Religion*
7. *The Original Contract*

POLITICAL PHILOSOPHY

David Hume was one of the most important empiricist philosopher in the history of Western Philosophy. To him the only reality was human sensation or what a man can see, hear, feel, taste or smell. Each particular sensation created a sense impression but sense impression did not disappear but retained in memory. These retained images become ideas. The truth or falsity of an idea depended on how clearly it resembled the sensation that has given rise to it. Thus sensations are in human life reality and all others are secondary or derivatives of it.

Human conduct is guided by emotions. A man does what his emotions tell him to do. Reason and intelligence are dependent upon sensation. Hume remarks, "Reason is and ought only to be slave of passions". By passions, he means emotions or sense experiences. Reason and intelligence depend on information supplied by sensations because empirical truth of realistic world depends upon sensations. Hume discarded the old belief that reason guides. He stated, Reason follows passion.

About Hume's Political philosophy Gettel observes, "He was opposed to popular government. His writings contained many acute observations of the political issues of his days. He recognised with Harrigton that government authority tends to accompany the distribution of property." He realised the growing democracy that was making the house of commons the real centre of power. He saw the futility of the parties and the necessity of a free press in popular government. N.K. Smith remarks, "His general philosophy is of course beyond our scope. Hume agreed that natural law or any other value system could not claim scientific validity because it could not be demonstrated that values were either true or facts."

J.Y.T. Greig said, "In metaphysics, theory of knowledge, economics, ethics and religion, and in politics, so far as it concerns Americans, he deserves rather to be dubbed a radical, he depended not upon authority, but upon his own reasonings. He accepted no scheme of things, because he established and defended the Fathers : he disintegrated and destroyed many settled notions by an acid logic of his own."

With Montesquieu David Hume is ranked as one of the two most enlightened men of the eighteenth century. In 1714, he brought out a collection of miscellaneous papers entitled *Essays : Moral and Political* which gave him both fame and money. The French translation of his Essays soon gave him the vast reputation of a political theorist.

The political philosophy of David Hume is contained in his several works like *Treatise on Human Nature, Essays : Moral and Political, History of England, Political Discourse, of the Original Contract* and *A Natural History of Religion.* Among his works, his *Treatise on Human Nature* is the most important. When Hume found that his Treatise of Human Nature failed due more to its form than its matter, he republished it in a popular form under the name *Enquiry Concerning Human Understanding.* However, the general tenor of his style shows that in turning to the writings of history, he forsook philosophy and political theory, made onslaughts upon religion and brought reactionism in politics. Hence, in his conversation with Adam Smith, he said, "Here am I, who have written on all sorts of subjects that are calculated to excite hostility. But I have no enemies except all the Whigs, all the Tories, and all the Christians."

Attack on Rationalism

The works of Hume reveal his peculiar position of being both a rejecter of the 'reason' and its acceptor by assigning it as secondary place in his political theory. Thus, he should be treated both as a child and a critic of the Enlightenment. The general notion of Hume's being a critic of the Enlightenment draws its sustenance from the anti-rational feature having so weighty a place that the 'secondary' role of reason is hardly visible to a reader of his political theory. The premises of Hume's vehement assault upon the doctrines of natural law and natural rights signify his refutation of the concept of reason. He emphatically rejects the view of natural law theorists that the norms of moral action exist in an *a-priori* form, that they can be discovered by reason, and that the passions of men, would divert them from the ways to a proper study of human behaviour. A study of Hume's ideas leaves an impression of his being a thinker of the anti-rationalist school. However, a deeper study of his political philosophy shows that he assigns a secondary place to reason by adding that 'reason is the slave of passions.' Though the use of reason is 'limited, it may be employed to show logical relationship even though it cannot demonstrate the existence or values of natural law. "Human values are determined by passion or feeling. Reason may be helpful in directing action towards the attainment of values, but its role is secondary. It is an instrument."

HUME V/S HOBBES

What seems to take Hume very close to the psychological system of Hobbes is his view that 'passions' move men. However, Hume's treatment of the passions is fundamentally different from that of Hobbes. To him passions are of two kinds : instinctive and secondary and the experience alone can demonstrate how they can be satisfied. Secondary passions such as desires are based upon experience involving pain and pleasure. There are no *a-priori* truths; it is the experience that tells us what is pleasant and painful. Thus, Hume tells us that social scientists should study human behaviour in these terms instead of concerning themselves with the hypothetical laws of nature. He distinguished between 'calm' and 'violent' passions and adding that it is the force of reason that becomes the very source of distinction between the two. Calm passions are directed by reason capable of understanding and enlightened self-interest; violent passions demand immediate gratification. "The practical political significance of this distinction is that the community must be guided by a minority of persons whose reasons is improved by education and who possess sufficient wealth not to be tempted to succumb to the desire to serve as selfish and short range interest. Justice is achieved when the community functions along the lines of enlightened self interest." Such as turn in the system of Hume indicates both his attack on the rationalist premises of the natural law school and his rudimentary contribution to the school of utilitarianism drawing sustenance from this observation of McDonald that the whole trust of Hume's social thought was to find a basis for distinguishing between justified and unjustified institutions.

REFUTATION OF SOCIAL CONTRACTUALISM

1. Impractical. Hume appears as one of the most distinctive critics of his times. He vehemently attacks the theories of divine origin and social contract on the origin and nature of state. In his work on the Original Contract, he firmly points out that both are purely speculative and hypothetical in as much as they are rational, devoid of factual foundations and absurd in their practical consequences. In this view, the divine origin theory is preposterous, since it makes the position of God ridiculous. It makes him as much responsible for bestowing authority upon an un-speakable tyrant as upon a wise and benevolent ruler and further holds that a constable no less than a king "acts by divine commission and processes an indivisible right."

2. Against History. More furious is Hume's attack on the theory of social contract. He maintains that this theory is false both historically and philosophically. A thing like social contract could not have taken place among the primitive people, because they did not have enough reason and intelligence to think of regular contract and stick to it after its creation. History does not furnish any examine of an original contract, nor can the consent of the parties perpetually bind their descendants. He argues that there is no avoidance of any formal contract between the ruler and the ruled playing any part in the building up of governmental organisations. It is foolish to say that contemporary rulers have no authority save by the consent of their subjects, or that their subjects are freed from the duty of obedience whenever they choose to hold their rulers derelict in their contractual obligations. It is absurd and without foundation to postulate a contractual relationship between the ruler and the ruled in the absence of any specific and recorded agreement to which reference might readily be made.

3. Philosophically Wrong. Hume continues that the social contract theory is wrong from the philosophical point of view as well. In his view, men are born in the state and they obey it habitually. But voluntary consent given at the time of social contract indirectly implies the power to withdraw from the state. In the primitive societies, no contract could be made, because the people were in as state of savagery. They had neither reason nor intelligence enough to understand the terms of a thing like social contract, it is impossible for the savage beings of Hobbes, or the social beings of Locke, or the noble savages or Rousseau to change their nature so radically and then to submit themselves to an authority of which they had no previous experience at all. Hume thus concluded that virtually all governments were founded without any pretense of open and voluntary consent of the people. Barker remarks: "Locke and Rousseau, if in different ways and different degrees, accepted the idea of the social contract, Hume, more historically minded, and more conservative in this convictions, was its critic."

NATURE OF STATE : SOCIETAL EVOLUTION

Having thus refuted the theories of divine origin and social contract, Hume expounds his own theory which strikingly anticipates the modern historical and sociological schools of political thought. In his view, the state is a growth and not a make and in its growth several factors (including the consent) have played their part. Hence, Hume propounds a theory of societal evolution. He believes that the governmental institutions grew more casually and more imperfectly where the superiority of courage and genius became more visible, where unanimity and concept were more requisite and where the pernicious effects of chaos and anarchy were more seriously felt. It is possible that the first descendants of one man over multitude had begun during a state of war, "The long continuance of that state," he further said, "and incident common among savage tribes, ensured the people into submission and if the chieftain possessed as much equity as prudence and value, he became, even during peace, the arbiter of all differences, and could gradually, by a mixture of force and consent, establish his authority."

ROLE OF POPULAR CONSENT

Although Hume so furiously denounces the social contract theory, he still recognises that consent might have played its part in the societal evolution of state and wishes that it might emerge as a paramount factor in the life of modern state. The people must consent to their authority to obey not by way of a religious duty or a mystic contract but as the only was where society can exist and advance from lower to higher forms of civilisation. Hume says: "But as human society is in perpetual flux, one man every hour going out of the world, another coming into it, it is necessary, in order to preserve stability in government, that the new breed should conform themselves to the established constitution, and nearly follow the path which their fathers treading in the footsteps of theirs, had marked out to them. Some innovations must necessarily have place in every human institution, and it is happy where the enlightened genius of the age gives these a direction of the side of reason, liberty and justice."

POLITICAL OBLIGATION

Hume's utilitarianism finds a vague expression in his general theory of political obligation. While dismissing the theories of divine origin and social contract, he recognises that people obey the state, because it suits them to do so and not because they ordinarily reason about it. He holds that, in the last analysis, a sense of the advantage to the individual of peace and order in social life, becomes the reason for the general submission to established political authority. It follows that utility is the ultimate end while duty is the proximate motive of an individual's obedience to government. Ever since the formation of early political societies each exertion of authority in the chieftain must have been particular and called forth by the present exigencies of the case. In Hume's words : "The sensible utility resulting from this interposition, made these exertions become daily more frequency; and their frequently gradually produce a habitual, and if you please to call it so, a voluntary, and therefore precarious, acquiescence in the people."

UTILITARIANISM

Hume's theory of utilitarianism becomes more apparent in his vehement criticism directed against the system of natural law, natural or rational religion, rational ethics and the contractual and consensus theory of politics. The fictitious character of a rational is apparent from the indemonstrable existence of God. Opposing the rationalistic school and its philosophy based on the conception of law of nature, he insists that morality is based on expediency and, therefore, vitally related to positive law. He believes that utility is the touch stone of institutions and reason is an inert principle, because passions, arising from a sense of pleasure of fear from pain, motivate human actions. However, Hume dose not stick to the single factor of human pleasure or pain like his successors as Bentham. Rather, he believes that human nature is not so simple as to have only as single propensity. His view of human nature thus excludes the excessive amount of calculation and foresight that contemporary moralists of all schools were accustomed to impute to it. He clearly points out that men are to very calculating in pushing either their self-interest or anything else: they are only foresighted when this feelings and impulses are not directly engaged, but impulse interferes with self-interest as often as with benevolence.

VALUE OF CUSTOMS

Hume denies that there eternal verities rooted in human nature that lay down the standards of social life. Then needs of people living in a society have generally been fulfilled by social conventions based on common interest and not on any thing like promise, faith or rational truth. Naturally, the people have a right to change their social customs and conventions whenever these outlive their usefulness and to mould them to perceive a stable social life in accord with their propensities and interests. If so, the basis of political authority is neither faith in divine origin, nor belief in some primitive contract, but it should be traced in a set of conventional rules that discriminated a legitimate government from as instrument of usurpation or force. The nature of these rules of purely non-rational on account of the fact that they derive their strength from the fact of their utility and not from some rational or natural agency.

Preference for Monarchy

Hume's preference for monarchy is based on following four reasons:

1. Like James Harrington, he fears the correspondence between wealth and political power and thus detests both the republican and aristocratic governments. Except monarchy, he suggests, all other governments have 'sources of degeneracy' and they are most ruinous to their provinces.

2. Hume's peculiar definition of 'liberty' leads him to prefer this form of government. To his way of thinking the essence of liberty is not so much freedom as order, security and justice and it is only monarchical government

where property so safe, arts and culture flourish, trade and industry prosper, and order and justice are firmly grounded. His reasoning so that only this government is more stable, continuous and congenial to steady advancement in the essentials or true liberty.

3. The cause of the origin of government is war with the neighboring communities, with its natural sequel of civil strife over the spoils of war within the community itself. As military camps are the true makers of cities, all governments were monarchies in the beginning.

4. The excellence of monarchical system is supported by the organisation of the family. As in a family the rule of single head prevails and which entails peace and prosperity, so in the society the rule of a single monarch is most preferable.

Defender of Monarchy

Thus Hume appears as the most powerful defender of the merits and excellence of monarchy in the eighteenth century. He admires the constitutional systems of England and France. His great admiration for monarchy is evident from his own statement which says, "Though all kinds of government can be improved upon in modern times, yet monarchical government seems to have made the greatest advance to perfection. It may now be affirmed to civilised monarchies, what was formerly said of republic alone, that they are a government of law, not of men. They are found susceptible for order, method and constancy to a surprising degree. Property is there secure, industry is encouraged; the arts flourish; and the prince lives among his subjects like a father among his children."

Conservatism

In the following respects, Hume took to the side of conservation:

1. He deserted the growing trends of representative government. He greatly feared that the new changes taking place after the Glorious Revolution of 1688 were disturbing the delicate balance between the monarchical and republican elements of the English Constitution and affecting the marked differences of interest between the various classes of English society.

2. As a corollary to the above, Hume criticised the growing party system. The germs of party politics bred national animosity and its evils were often transmitted to the posterity. The deferences between the people were never bridged and so national unity suffered.

3. Hume denied that the people could bring radical innovations or make violent revolutions in their social and political systems.

4. Hume defended in the existing social and political system of England and detested any change in it going to the detriment of the powerful class

CRITICAL ESTIMATE

1. Destructive Critic. The writings of Hume show that he was more a destructive critic than a constructive theorist. He launched a massive attack against the principles of religion and natural law and thus incurred the charge of skepticism.

2. Vacillation from the Poles of Whiggism to Toryism. Hume's preference for monarchy, and his frank disapproval of republican system made him a defender of conservatism. By criticising the growing role of party system and by ignoring the achievements of democratic trends, he definitely showed his love for old things and this was distinctly due to his theory of utilitarianism. His idea that people should not destroy the old order but conserve it and improve it by means of gradual reforms did not appeal to the people. As a result, no school of political thought or no resplendent body of political doctrine is associated with his name. Like Montesquieu, his own ideas became a factor of ruining what he desired to preserve.

Influence of Hume

However, Hume's ideas prepared the way for Adam Smith, Burke, Bentham, Spencer, Henry Maine and others. He was destined to exert a great influence in the period of reaction and reconstruction following the French revolution and to prepare the ground for much of the political thought characteristic of the nineteenth century industrialism. He certainly corrected much of the political thought of his predecessors and contemporaries, particularly by rejecting the theory of natural rights, natural law and religious superstition. That is why, Gettel calls, him as 'one of the most powerful dissolvents of the eighteenth century.' Laski rightly says that Hume was always critical and suggestive.

Hume is generally regarded as the thinker of conservatism. But behind the facade of his conservatism we may study his empiricist enthusiasm. It may be said that while he put a brake on the tradition of rationalist enthusiasm, he gave stimulus to the age of empiricist enthusiasm that precursed the utilitarianism of Bentham. In the words of Sheldon S. Woten, "Hume was something more than the Enlightenment incarnates, for his significance is that he turned against the Enlightenment of its own weapons. And herein lies his importance as a conservative thinker.

QUESTIONS FOR EXERCISE

1. "Reason is and ought only to be the slave of the passions and can never pretend to any other office than to serve and obey them." Hume. Discuss.
2. What place would you give to David Hume in the history of political philosophy ? What are the main tenets of his theory?

28

Edmund Burke (1729-1796 A.D.)

According to Hallowell, "Perhaps the most eloquent spokesman for the conservative reaction to the age of enlightenment was Edmund Burke, whom someone has called not inappropriately the prophet of political commonsense". Edmund Burke was born in Dublin in 1729. He entered Trinity College, Dublin in 1741. He took his degree in 1748 and studied law in London. He got fame by the publication of some essays in 1765. He became private secretary to William Hamilton when he was appointed secretary for Ireland. He gave up his job in 1765 and became private Secretary to the Prime Minister Lord Rockingham. At the age of 36, he became a member of House of Commons and became one of the leaders of Whig party. He remained a member of parliament from 1765 to 1794 i.e. about 29 years. He was a great orator and parliamentarian. He fought for sanity and liberalism in the treatment for American colonies. His epic impeachment of Warren Hastings for high crimes and misdemeanours in India and his thunderous barrage against the French revolution made him famous. He died due to the shock of sudden death of his son in 1797 at the age of 68 years. He was a great conservative orator. Burke was the greatest orator and parliamentarian which England has ever produced. He was a philosophical politician whose ideas are to be found in speeches.

WORKS BY EDMUND BURKE

1. *Reflection on the Revolution in France* (1790).
2. *Theory on the Causes of the Present Discourses* (1770).
3. *Speeches on conciliation with America* (1795).
4. *Appeal from New to the old Whig* (1791).
5. *A Vindication of Natural Society* (1756).
6. *Speech on American Taxation* (1774).
7. *Thoughts on French Affairs* (1791).
8. *Letter on Residue Peace* (1795).
9. *Speeches on Impeachment of W. Hastings.*

A Man of Political Action

Edmund Burke was not of the type of an armchair thinker. Like Machiavelli, he was primarily a man of political action. He did not set forth explicitly the principles on which his conception of state rests. He did not give an elaborate analysis of human nature that Hobbes thought necessary to base his political theory. He did not propounded a moral and social principle which Bentham made use of to establish his idea of 'greatest good of the greatest number.' Nevertheless, he developed certain principles during the course of his dealing with some concrete contemporary political issues.

Like Aristotle, Burke always tried to avoid the extremes and preferred to choose the middle way. He was neither a radical nor a conservative in his approach to the problems of the day. His was a realistic mind in which theory illumines practice and practice tampers theory. He lived and worked during the period when political issues were the uppermost in the minds of the British statesmen. These were the French Revolution, the American war of independence, the colonial policy of the British Government and the behaviour of the British administrators in India. Burke reflected over these issues seriously with an open mind he gave vent to his ideas which served as the main currents of his political philosophy.

Burke was one of the most eminent of those political thinkers who have devoted their main energies to the actual conduct of affairs. He first attracted public attention by a work entitled *A Vindication of Natural Society* (1756), a brilliant satire on Bolingbroke's recently published works devoted to a vindication of natural religion, wherein he showed how the arguments, by means of which Bolingbroke had tried to reduce Christianity to deism, would, if applied to politics, reduce ordered society to chaos. In 1759 he became secretary to a prominent member of Parliament, W.G. Hamilton, who shortly afterwards (1761) was appointed secretary for Ireland. Burke's tour in Ireland made him believe that the troubles condition of Ireland was due largely to the penal religious laws, to the commercial disabilities of the Irish, to the factiousness of its parliaments, to the corruption of its administration and to the absenteeism of its landlords. Throughout his public life he never ceased to advocate reforms calculated to remove these evils.

A new and important stage in Burke's career opened in 1765 when he was appointed private secretary to the Marquis of Rockingham, the official chief of the Whig Party, who had just been summoned by George III to form a ministry. A seat in Parliament was also found for him by the end of the year. His political beliefs had become somewhat fixed by this time. He had acquired a profound admiration for the British Constitution, as determined by the revolution of 1688-89. He firmly believed in the government of the country by the landed aristocracy, of which class the Marquis of Rockingham was a splendid exemplar; he burned with a zeal for justice, a hatred for oppression and enthusiasm for good administration and a devotion to religion. His immense intellectual power and his torrential eloquence provided him with a unique position in the House of Commons and in the councils of his party. For a quarter of a century (1765-90) he remained the formulator and interpreter of Whig policy to the world.

DEFENCE OF CABINET SYSTEM OF GOVERNMENT

Burke had an opportunity to apply his notions and principles to many political problems of first importance. He defended forcefully the party or cabinet system of government against the system of administration by the monarch and the 'king's friends', which George III was trying to reintroduce. The king was determined not merely to reign but to rule. This meant completely reorienting the direction of Government. Since the settlement of 1688 the king had chosen for his ministers men acceptable to Parliament. Now an effort was made to choose only 'king's men' as ministers and to bend Parliament to the king's will as transmitted through his ministers. This was to be done by persuasion, bribery, or any other means available. Unfortunately, parliament was only too willing to be won over to the king's cause and was prepared to use the same high-handed methods in its dealings with the people that the king used towards it.

This was the situation which Burke had to fight against on entering Parliament. He believed that the government should exist for the whole people; but he did not hold, that the way to accomplish this was by putting the final power in the people's hands. He rather maintained that the people's representatives in Parliament should do, what they think is best. Hence his objection to the attempts of the 'king's men' to rule was not that they were taking the direction of affairs from its rightful owners, the people, but that men of king's favour would not, and could not, rule for the best interests of the country as a whole.

Burke made his defence in his *Observations on the Present State of the Nation* (1769) and in his *Thoughts on the Causes of the Present Discontents* (1770) with a masterly thoroughness which makes these works classics in English political philosophy.

Another great question that engaged Burke's attention was the controversy regarding taxation and representation, which had broken out early in George III's reign between the American colonies and the mother country. Burke made two important speeches on this problem. The first was on *American Taxation* (April 1774) and the second was on *Conciliation with America* (March,1775). These two speeches, together with his *Letter to the Sheriffs of Bristol on the Affairs of America* (1777), constitute in Lord Morley's opinion the most admirable of all his utterances.

On America

Burke detected injustice and oppression in America as well as in England. He also recognized incompetence, bungling and stupidity when he saw them. Refusing to discuss the abstract rights of either the one side or the other, Burke pleaded for a conciliatory policy in the interests of peace and prosperity. "The question with me is, not whether you have a right to render your people miserable, but whether it is not your interest to make them happy. It is not what a lawyer tells me I may do; but what humanity, reason and justice tell me I ought to do." And again, he argued on the actual declaration of war between the mother country and the colonies: "Lawyers, I know, cannot make the distinction for which I contend, because they have their strict rules to go by. But legislators ought to do what lawyers cannot; for they have no other rules to go by, but the great principles of reason and equity, and the general sense of mankind."[1]

Burke attached the utmost value to constitutional practice; but he interpreted practice in a liberal and generous sense. He made an appeal to constitutional usage, 'to the ancient policy and practice of the empire', which provided a 'sure ground' for a stable administration of the mother country in the colonies. He appealed: "Leave the Americans as they anciently stood....Let the memory of all actions, in contradiction to that good old mode, on both sides, be extinguished for ever. Be content to bind America by laws of trade; you have always done it....Do not burden them by taxes; you were not used to do so from the beginning. Let this be your reason for not taxing...."[2]

In the field of politics the first thing which struck Burke was the enormous complexity of the needs and interests at stake. Each fresh question that presents itself has its own peculiarities, and nobody can rightly decide about it unless he takes into account all its peculiarities and crucial conditions and circumstances. Burke asked the statesmen of his time not to act on abstract principles. Though the general principles must be there; but these principles must not be drawn from 'the school', but from experience. They ought to be modified to suit the circumstances of a particular case. A statesmen "has to look not only before and after, but also, with no less vigilance, to the right hand and the left. Touch the existing system of parliamentary representation, and you run more than a risk of upsetting the balance of the whole constitution. Employ high-handed methods in America and you will soon come to tolerate them in your own country...."[3] In his speeches, Burke never forgot the immediate issues, though he also invariably saw beyond them. Thus in the course of his attacks on the British administration he laid the basis for a sound colonial policy.

---

1. 'Letter to the Sheriffs', Works, Vol. I, London, Bohn's Edition (1861), p. 208.
2. 'American Taxation', *Ibid.* pp. 173-74.
3. 'Conciliation with America', *ibid.*, p. 184.

THE PRINCIPLE OF RESPONSIBLE RULE IN INDIA

Burke had great concern with the problem of the Government of India. Closely connected with it was the problem of the corruption of British politics by the over-wealthy 'nabobs' who returned from the East to buy up the pocket boroughs of the homeland. Burke's attack on the corrupt British rule in India came to a head in the famous and long-drawn-out impeachment proceedings against Warren Hastings. To understand this phase of Burke's thought it is necessary to have some knowledge of an earlier episode — the debts of the Nabob of Arcot.

Before the British rule in India was finally established, the direction of policies of the country continued to be in the hands of a private stock company with its head office in London. The directors of the company had to depend upon the company's servants in India for the real management of affairs there. And the company's servants had neither the knowledge of administration nor the character. As they were corrupt persons, they busied themselves in extorting huge fortunes from the unhappy country (India). The directors did their best to regulate their practices and forbade their employees to accept gifts from the Indian rulers. Unfortunately, it was easy to circumvent this prohibition by lending money to the princes at exorbitant interest rates. As the persons involved were often only penniless adventurers, the money was seldom paid to the creditors. As a result, enormous obligations were contracted in one way or another, which in the long run had to be fulfilled by the native population.

The debts of the Nabob of Arcot were contracted in this way. When the matter was brought to the notice of British Parliament, it ordered the company to institute the investigation. But before this was completed, the British Government changed its mind and closed the whole matter, authorizing the company to have payment in full. It was at this point that Burke condemned the affairs of the Nabob of Arcot. Censuring the company's administration in India, he said: "Fraud, injustice, oppression, peculation, engendered in India, are crimes of the same blood, family, and caste with those that are born and bred in England...." Arguing his point, he further stated .... "the Nabob of Arcot and his creditors are not adversaries, but collusive parties, and that the whole transaction is under a false colour and false names....It is, therefore, not from treasuries and mines, but from the food of your unpaid armies, from the blood withheld from the veins and whipped out of the backs of the most miserable of men, that we are to pamper extortion, usury, and peculation, under false names of debtors and creditors of state."[4] He finally asked the Parliament to examine into the conduct of those who "have no conduct to account for" and

4. 'Speech of the Nabob of Arcot's Debts', quoted from *Masters of Political Thought* by W.T. Jones, Vol. 2, London, G.G. Harrap & Co. (1964), pp. 342-43.

to do all possible things within its power for "the relief of our distressed fellow-citizens in India."[5]

In 1781 Burke was appointed a member of select committee to investigate the administration of justice in India. He was not happy with the state of affairs in India. It was at his investigation that Warren Hastings, the Governor General of India, was later impeached in 1787. He condemned the administration of Hastings as systematically conducted in defiance of morality and public law. Impeaching Warren Hastings of crimes and misdemeanours he said: "I impeach him in the name of the Commons' House of Parliament, whose trust he has betrayed....I impeach him in the name of the people of India, whose rights he has trodden under foot, and whose country he has turned into a desert...."[6] Burke challenged Hastings' claim that it was impossible to apply Western standards of authority and legality to government in the East. He appealed to the concept of the Law of Nature, the moral principles rooted in the universal order of things, to which all conditions and races of men were subject. Finally, he predicted that the rapacious rule of the company and its administrators and the loss of honesty and far-sighted intelligence would result in bitter resentment of the people amounting to the instability of the British Empire.

The impeachment dragged on for more than seven years and ended with Hastings' acquittal (April, 1795) on all charges. It resulted in an authoritative statement of the principle of responsible rule in imperial affairs and did much to impress all succeeding Indian administrators with a sense of their responsibilities.

REPUDIATION OF FRENCH REVOLUTIONARY PRINCIPLES

From the first Burke had looked upon the French Revolution with the deepest suspicion his judgment was confirmed by the execution of the king and queen. If the French chose to destroy themselves, that was undoubtedly their own affair. But, this could not be accomplished without serious repercussions in every country in Europe. And this was the fear which made Burke criticize vehemently the very principles of the French Revolution.

Burke's hostility to the dominant principles of the Revolution was directed against both their general character, and their specific content. He detested and spurned the method of precise mathematical formulation of human rights and social arrangements. The rigor of exact logic has no controlling place in the ultimate explanation of political life. The reduction of governmental science to the brief formulas of a written constitution appeared supreme foolishness to Burke. He observed that "from Magna Carta to the Declaration of Rights, it

---

5. *Ibid.*
6. 'Warren Hastings', *Works*, Vol. VIII.

has been the uniform policy of our Constitution to claim and assert our liberties as an *entailed inheritance* derived to us from our forefathers, and to be transmitted to our posterity — as an estate specially belonging to the people of this kingdom, without any reference whatever to any other more general or prior right...[7] He regarded the Declaration of the Rights of Man as "a sort of institute and digest of anarchy" — "such a pedantic abuse of elementary principles as would have disgraced boys at school."[8] He refuted the claim that man has any abstract rights and that the institution of society should be subverted by violent methods just for the achievement of these rights. He had a great respect for the established social and political institutions and world order. An attempt to overthrow social and political order will breed confusion and ultimately result in an anarchy. He argued: "The institutions of policy, the goods of fortune, the gifts of Providence, are handed down to us, and from us, in the same course and order. Our political system is placed in a just correspondence and symmetry with the order of the world, and with the mode of existence ...."[9] As a conservative Burke tried to uphold the inviolability of the civil institutions on the principle upon which Nature teaches us "to revere individual men : on account of their age, on account of those from whom they are descended." And he argued that "All your sophistries cannot produce anything better adapted to preserve a rational and manly freedom than the course we have pursued...."[10] He was not against the *real* rights of man, but he denied the false claims of right. He said: "....I do not mean to injure those which are real, and are such as their pretended rights would totally destroy. If civil society be made for the advantage of man, all the advantages for which it is made become his right. It is an institution of beneficence; and law itself is only beneficence acting by a rule."[11]

Burke admitted that "Government is a contrivance of human wisdom to provide for human wants," after the institution of society has superseded man's abstract rights. The provision for their wants is a matter that requires a careful consideration of means, and the organization of such means is the constitution of a state; but the matter of rights derivable from abstract reasoning about pre-social conditions no longer has importance.[12] Burke called the philosophy of the leaders of French Revolution a barbarous philosophy. He refuted their mechanistic theory that state is a purely artificial contrivance deliberately created by some formal contract or convention, which operates and functions like a machine and which can be arbitrarily reformed or reconstructed at the

7. Jones, W.T. *op. cit.*, p. 348.
8. *Works*, Vol. III, p. 221.
9. Jones, W.T., op. cit., pp. 348-49.
10. *Ibid.*, p. 349.
11. *Ibid.*, p. 351.
12. *Works*, Vol. III, pp. 310-11.

will of its creators, without any regard to historical law and established traditions of a people. He said, "On the principles of this mechanic philosophy, our institutions can never be embodied, if I may use the expression, in persons, so as to create in us love, veneration, admiration, or attachment. But that sort of reason which banishes the affections is incapable of filling their place...." He regarded the state as a product of long evolution, which has brought with it experience and wisdom of the past. He said, "The science of constructing a commonwealth, or renovating it, or reforming it, is like every other experimental science, not to be taught *a priori*."[13]

Burke discoursed both on the agreement that constitutes civil society and that which expresses the relation between monarch and subjects. But in neither case Burke gave such definitions to the contract as to justify the conclusions drawn from it by the revolutionists. The clarity with which Hobbes and Rousseau propounded the theory of social contract and set forth its terms, parties and the content of the social pact, had no attraction for Burke. He built up his argument around a vague outline of the contract and placed it with a dazzling rhetoric: "Society is indeed a contract ...... but the state ought not to be considered as nothing better than a partnership agreement in a trade of pepper and coffee. ....It is a partnership in all science, a partnership in all art, a partnership in every vertue and in all perfection. As the ends of such a partnership cannot be obtained in many generations, it becomes a partnership not only between those who are living, but between those who are dead and those who are to be born. Each contract of each particular state is a clause in the great primeval contract of eternal society....according to a fixed compact sanctioned by the inviolable oath which holds all physical and all moral natures each in their appointed place....[14]

Burke opposed the very essence of the fundamental dogmas of the revolutionaries, which were: that sovereignty resides constantly and inalienably in the people; that the people have a right to change the government at their will; that the will's will is reflected through the majority opinion; that the assignment of precisely equal weight to every individual's judgment is a requirement of political justice; that a constitution must be written and accepted by popular vote. With a vein of a conservative Burke rejected all these dogmas. He maintained that political society and government might have found their origin in the agreement of individual men and that the will of the people might be the ultimate source of political authority, but in the actual life and action of a state it would be wrong to regard the individual will as a predominant factor. The individual, once born in an established society, is under obligation to respect the institutions of that society. Duties rest upon men irrespective of

13. Jones, W.T., *op. cit.*, pp. 348-49.
14. *Ibid.*, p. 355.

their formal consent. They originate and grow from conditions and relations in which volition and choice have no part. The relation of a parent and child is not a voluntary one. So the political and social circumstances amid which a man is born are not his choice; yet they impose duties upon him. "No man or number of men have a right....to free themselves from that primary engagement....The place of every man determines his duty."[15]

Burke said that the people undoubtedly enjoy liberty to bring about a change in the government, but the liberty aimed at by the revolutionists was only a caricature of real freedom. It was only a licence, a kind of anarchy which would degenerate into the vilest of tyrannies. Burke's real thesis against the Revolution was that, however noble their aims, disaster could be the only outcome of a sudden and violent overthrow of existing institutions and of age-old traditions by a group of visionary and impractical idealists without any political experience.

AGAINST THE DOGMA OF POPULAR SOVEREIGNTY

Against the dogma of popular sovereignty, Burke's argument was that in a well-established and well-ordered state the individual will or a number of such wills are not the residence of sovereignty. The state that follows nature is necessarily aristocratic. Nature itself reflects a kind of aristocracy in its order of things. A natural aristocracy is to be seen in every "large body rightly constituted." In a nation, it is seen in "the class of those who by birth, wealth or intellect have a particular fitness for public functions."[16]

About the theory of constitution, Burke had nothing positive to offer beyond the appreciation of the British Constitution. According to him, constitution is not made; it grows or develops in response to the needs of time, and its evolution reflects the wisdom and experience of the people. Burke regarded the British Constitution, with its checks and balances, as the best. "The whole scheme of our mixed constitution is to prevent any one of its principles from being carried as far as, taken by itself and theoretically, it would go."[17]

Burke was also against the dogma that to obtain political justice every individual's judgment must be recognized of equal value. According to him, judgments are made by men of superior intelligence after a great thought and deep reflection. To make a government, he thought, requires no great prudence. To give freedom is still more easy. But "to form a *free government*, that is, to temper together these opposite elements of liberty and restraint in one consistent work, requires much thought....and combining mind."[18] Thus

15. *Works*, Vol IV, p. 167.
16. *Ibid.*, pp. 174-75.
17. *Ibid.*, p. 207.
18. Jones, W.T., *op. cit.*, p. 358.

political justice resides in conducting the affairs of the state in a well-balanced manner and in making wise judgments and decisions regarding its policies.

POLITICAL PHILOSOPHY

Main Features

Edmund Burke was a great orator and a very learned person. With all his wisdom, he was more a coiner of some happy political maxims than propounder of a regular system of political philosophy. In fact, he was a practical statesman and a realistic to know the things. That is why he opposed French revolution because he knew that French revolution may end in anarchy. But he supported American revolution because he thought that revolutionaries of America will be able to furrow the ship of the states on sound lines. Thus his significance as a political philosopher lies in his influence on the importance of the actually existing institutions and evolutionary nature of any reforms to be made in them. His main features of political philosophy may be summarised as below:

1. He avoided abstract speculations and denounced the metaphysical treatment of political affairs.

2. He appealed to history and experience as the only satisfactory guide in administrative affairs.

3. He laid emphasis upon expediency.

4. He favoured empirical nature of art of government. In shaping his political philosophy was influenced by empiricism. The basis of American Revolution, French revolution, Rule of the East India Company in India and Ambition of George III etc. were critically appraised.

Historical Method

Burke followed historical method in his studies as well as in solution of political problems. As historically state is a growth and not a social contract, so he refuted the theory of social contract and stated "social contract is a chaff and rags, purely blue shreds of paper about rights of man". According to Burke as quoted by **Murray** "the state is not a man made machine but an eminently complicated organism which the efforts of individual have certainly helped to shape, but whose evolution and destiny cannot be wholly understood by any individual."

Burke believed that the way in which state evolves and develops is largely determined by forces which no individual can fully comprehend, and that when men make changes they should do with restraint and caution since the consequences of their actions cannot be foreseen and may conflict with most fundamental interests of the community as a whole.

Burke held that man is a political animal and on account of constant contract, state has become a necessity for a man.'The state protects all natural rights of man and now man cannot live without the state. He stated "Society is partnership in all sciences, a partnership in all Arts. partnership in every virtue and in all perfection. He did not make distinction between state and society "Society is indeed a contract ... but state ought to be considered something better than partnership, agreement in a trade of pepper and coffee, calico or tobacco or some other such low concern to be taken up for little temporary interest and to be dissolved by the fancies of the parties. It is not to be looked upon with reverence, because it is not a partnership in things subservient only to the gross animal existence of a temporary and perishable nature. It is a partnership in all science, co-partnership in arts, a partnership in every virtue, in all perfection."

Theory of State

1. No Social Contract. He did not agree with social contract philosopher that the state was the result of a contract. He criticised it as chaffs and rags'.

2. Evolution of State. He believed that the state is complicated process, men helped in the evolution and growth of state but it was not possible for them to retreat the course. He says, "The state is no a man made machine but an immensely complicated organism which the efforts of individuals have certainly helped to shape. But those evolutions and destiny cannot be wholly understood by any individual." He believed that the way in which a state evolves and develops "is largely determined by force which no individual can fully comprehend, and that when they make such changes they should do so with restraint and caution, since the consequences of their actions cannot be foreseen and may conflict with the most fundamental interests of the community as a whole."

3. Need of the State. Man must now live in the state because the state is responsible for protecting the life, liberty and rights of the people. Burke said "It is to be looked upon with reverence, because it is not a partnership in things subservient only to the gross animal existence of temporary and perishable nature. It is a partnership in arts, a partnership in every virtue and in all perfection. As the end of such a partnership cannot be obtained in any generations, if becomes partnership not only between those who are living but between those who are dead and those who are to be born."

4. Religion and the State. Burke believed that the basis of the growth of state were the religious sentiments of the people. The state should promote religion. The state is more like an organism rather than an organisation. It had organic growth. Due to this organic growth old institutions give place to newer ones.

5. Contempt for Natural Law. In his 'Vindication of Natural Society' Burke showed his contempt for the national law.

6. Partnership. Burke's state was a partnership in which the people come for the pursuit of knowledge. It had no mechanical but only biological growth.

Natural Rights

Burke did not agree with Locke that men had natural rights and that they possessed them even before they joined the state. Rights are recognised by the state and granted by the civil laws only "to be a people, and to have to those rights are things incompatible. The one supposes the presence and the other the absence of a state of civil society. Men cannot enjoy the rights of civil society and of a civil state together."

Natural rights were abstract and hence could not be followed. The conception of equality of men is something not understandable. Burke believed only in the conception of regulated liberty.

3. American Revolution. Burke believed that the conception of upholding abstract rights was mainly responsible for many troubles. The problems could not be solved on the basis of abstract rights but on the basis of experience. He said, "The question will be, not whether you have a right to render your people miserable, but whether it is not your interest to make them happy." He preferred experience, expediency and utility over abstract thinking, right and philosophy. Burke was willing to throw away dogmas. Dogmas must go hand in hand with experience when experience did not corroborate expendiency, reason, justice and humanity.

4. Human Rights. Burke believed that men had rights only in the state. He did not agree that anyone ever enjoyed rights prior to the existence of the state. He distinguished between the civil and political rights. Whereas civil rights should be given to all, political rights should be given only to those who are capable of enjoying and exercising them.

5. Conservation Reforms. Burke was a conservative reformer. He believed in reforms and not in radical changes. As a Whig he believed that evolutionary changes were more stable than revolutionary ones. That was the reason why he could not pled for American Revolution. About French Revolution he said, "I should, therefore, suspend congratulations on the new liberty of France, until I am informed how it had been combined with Government, with public force, with the discipline and obedience of the armies, with the collection of an effective and well distributed revenue, with morality and religion, with solidarity and property, with peace and order, with civil and social manners."

6. Time Honoured Institutions. As a conservative reforms, Burke believed that the existing institutions had come to stay after long experience of mankind. Any change in them should be brought with great care, consciousness and by preserving all old time honoured traditions. According to him, "The disposition to preserve and the ability to impose, taken together would be my standard of statesmanship." He further said that, "If I cannot reform with equity, I will not reform at all." Property is a time honoured institution and it must be preserved. As a political reformer, Burke combined in himself devotion to liberty with respect for authority; hope for the future with reverence for the past.

7. Democracy. As a conservative, Burke could not reconcile himself to the idea of democracy. He believed that in democracy people frequently switched over to changes and thus did not honour traditions.

Political Conservatism

Burke's political philosophy is full of such instances which reflect his political conservatism. These are as follows. '

1. Evolution of State. The state is not the product of social contract but merely a growth. According to John, "The contract he has in his mind always involved those slowly evolved, habitual, intimate living ties between the members and classes of body politic which are so clearly not the product of any explicit act of contract between man and man or class and class that they have derived our sociologist to lift society above the categories of class and plug it deep in the categories of biology."

2. English Constitution. He always defended the English Constitution and believed that it was working well and as such pleaded that the rotten boroughs and pocket constituencies should not be abolished.

3. Rights of Men. He did not believe in the notion of rights of men.

4. Equal Rights. He did not like to preach the idea of equal political rights.

5. Revolution. He was always opposed to revolution.

6. Democracy. He was opposed to democracy because there people radically switched from one idea to another. Though the name of Burke has rightly been associated with conservatism, Murray writes, "Burke as a conservative reformer was equally opposed to Jacobitism and Jacobinism." Hearnshaw said, " He was always reformer and never a revolutionary, always a conservative and never a Tory."

7. George III. As a conservative, Burke so believed that George III was responsible for all unrest in the British colonies because he was trying to concentrate powers around himself and was thus trying to do away with the traditional powers vested in the hands of Parliament. According to Ivor, Burke gave to the philosophy of conservatism perhaps the fullest and the most eloquent expression the world has ever heard."

8. English Constitution. Burke was all praise for English Constitution. To him English Constitution was very satisfactory. It was an ideal constitution. Traditions surround all the institutions of this constitution. These could not be altered without disturbing the whole system. Burke said, "Our constitution stands on a nice equipoise with steep precipices and deep waters upon all sides of it. In removing it from a dangerous leaning towards one side there may be a risk of over setting it on other. Every project of a material change in an government, so complicated as ours is a matter full of difficulties, in which a considerate man will not be too ready to decide, a prudent man too ready to undertake, or an honest man too ready to promise."

BURKE'S INFLUENCE ON ENGLISH POLITICS

Burke has been described as 'one of the greatest men and, Bacon excepted, the greatest thinker who ever devoted himself to the practice of English politics. However, he was a prophet of the school of conservatism. To Burke, the instructions of history are not to be taken as the raw materials for an inductive examination of things, it is to be used as an authentic evidence for providing the wisdom of the past that should never be under-mined. As Barker says: "God operates and man, under His guidance, co-operates. Holding this view, Burke can believe at one and the same time in the immortality of the state and the experimentalism of politics. He can hold at one and the same time, that he cannot escape from the past, and that we can and must escape from the head of the metaphysical theories of politics which could cast life unalterably and irrevocably in one hard iron mould. The immortal state and the experimentalism of the politics by which the state is guided and governed—this is the paradox, the seeming paradox with which Burke seeks to confront the votaries of revolution....The past is not a dead hand, but a moving finger of guidance. If we respect the past, and the present in which the past lives, we are essentially and fundamentally free."[19]

Burke used the forces of religion, property and traditions to strengthen the premises of his theory of prescriptive institutions. For instance, he refuted all standards of empiricism when he said, "There is no room on earth, I believe, more willing than I am to lay it down as a fundamental of the Constitution that the Church of England should be united and even identified with it." This point is clearly evident from the interpretation of MacCunn: "Burke's political religion has its deep roots in three convictions. The first is that civil society rests on spiritual foundations, being indeed nothing less than a product of divine will; the second that this is a fact of significance so profound that the recognition of it is of vital moment, both for the corporate life of the state and for the lives of the each and all of its members; and the third, that whilst all forms of religion within the nation may play their part in

19. Barker, *op. cit.*, pp. 231-32.

bearing witness to religion, this is peculiarly the function of the established Church in which the 'conservation' of the 'State' finds its appropriate symbol, expression and support."[20]

One finds a line of contradiction in Burke's attack on the basic philosophy of the French revolutionaries and his own basic philosophy of eulogising the principles of his English Constitution. A deeper examination of the political philosophy of Burke, brings home that while he refutes his predecessors like Locke as well as his contemporaries involved in the revolution of France clamouring for the defence and preservation of their 'natural rights', he, at the same time, struggles for the 'natural rights' of his own people with the shrewd tongue of a parliamentarian. It is thus pointed out by Hearnshaw: "The inherent primeval rights of the individual—the right to life, the right to liberty, the right to property—were in the same case. Burke did not and could not as a good Whig definitely denounce them. Nay he even appealed to them now and again, when it suited to do as, for example, in his defence of the people of India against the tyranny of Warren Hastings. But as a rule he ignored them to be employed as weapons to rebut the claims of the French monarchy. The only rights to be commonly admitted as valid were rights based on the civil laws of the state, provided that civil laws accorded with the precepts of the eternal law of God."[21]

Burke's famous statement that state is not like a partnership in some low concern but a partnership in all sciences, arts, virtues and perfections, and among those who are not only dead and living but also among those of the coming generations, personifies the idea of an organic state having a sanctified character. As Hearnshaw once again says: "If one asks what is the meaning of this sonorous passage, the answer is that as it stands it has none. It is a resounding nonsense. In particular, the concluding sentence respecting primeval contracts and 'inviolable oaths' is the emptiest verbiage...The way is made clear for the entry of the new (yet immemorial only) idea of society as an organism; of the state as arising from the will of God rather than from the will of man; of community as an entity claiming priority to each and all of its members."[22]

Finally, Burke's ideas on representative democracy covering the areas of political party are 'hopelessly idealistic' and his consideration on the nature of representation are nothing else than a shrewd version of the excellence of the aristocratic form of government. Hence Thomas Paine accused Burke of making dead men more important than the living ones, of advocating rulers accountable to nobody because they are ruled by prescription, and of treating

20. J. MacCunn, *op. cit.*, p. 122.

21. Hearnshaw, *op. cit.*, p. 94.

22. *Ibid.*, p. 93.

the mass of men as contemptible fools. It may be pointed out that what Burke really desired went against much what his times demanded and this may be taken as another weakness in the empiricism of Burke. It is thus said: "Burke's ideas on representation are more medieval than modern. To him men are important as members of the class to which they belong; representation should be based on this principle."[23] Similarly, McDonald says: "Burke's conception of representation, or rather his conception of the priority of delegation over representation, rested on the aristocratic premise not only overly idealistic for its own day but largely irrelevant to his own non-aristocratic age."[24]

In a strict sense, Burke was not a political philosopher like Plato, Aristotle, Hobbes, Rousseau and Montesquieu. His political ideas were a product of occasion and not of academic speculation. He did not write books on the subject of politics; it is mainly the collection of his speeches, letters and addresses wherein the material of his political theory is available.[25] Still Burke occupies a very important place in the history of modern political thought.

Burke is said to have started a new tradition. Statesmen like Canning and Disraeli, men of letters like Wordsworth, Coleridge and Southey, and philosophers like Paine and Mackintosh followed the ideas of Burke in different directions. The reaction which he led against the French Revolution was the beginning of a shift which carried the prevailing social philosophy from attack to defence and therefore to a knew emphasis on the value of stability and the power of custom on which stability depends. Laski well concludes that it "is easy to praise Burke and easier to miss the greatness of his effort" and that there "is hardly a greater figure in the history of political thought in England."[26] Fredrick A. Dreyer observes:" If the question we ask is whether Burke made a major contribution to the development of political theory, the answer must be that he did not. He wrote and speculated within the framework of natural rights individualism: there is nothing in the text of his writings to suggest that he rebelled against the orthodoxiecs of his time or that he anticipated the novelties of the nineteenth century speculation. To picture Burke as a profound and original thinker is to misread the principles that he

23. M. Judd Harmon, *op. cit.,* p. 333.
24. McDonald, *op. cit.,* p. 256.
25. Dr. Margaret Sapher thus observes: "Despite an approach that suggests later historical school, Burke wrote not as a scientific historian but as the inspired and indignant prophet of conservatism and aristocracy.' *Readings in Recent Political Philosophy,* p. 46.
26. Laski: *Political Thought in England,* p. 182. Coker admires Burke thus: "He upheld the values of rank and social privilege in insuring the preservation of good manners, heroic enterprise, orderly living, respectful subservience of the humble to their betters and generous guardianship of the common by the noble." *Recent Political Thought,* p. 8.

actually asserted. It is, moreover, to thrust upon him a status which he laid no claim to."[27]

To conclude Burke was a representative thinker of the conservative school having his sympathy with the interest of the rising capitalist class. As Macperson puts it, "Everyone sees that Burke had always been a defender of a tradition, inherited social order of subordination of ranks. What has not generally been seen is that the traditional order which he cherished was not simply an hierarchical order but a capitalist one. His case against the French principles was the same as his case against the Speenhamland principle: both would destroy traditional society by destroying the prerequisite condition of a capitalist accumulation, that is, a submissive wage-earning class."[28] To quote Andrew Hacker: "Burke's political theory uses as its model a society which is old and established. A nation which has but recently come into existence, or one in the process of accelerated social change, poorly suited to follow the precepts Burke lays downs. Except for a few sheltered corners of the globe, hardly any societies have experienced— or will in the future experience— the luxury of gradual and cautious development. Burke's prescriptions are not meant for a recently emancipated colony in Africa or an Asian nation undergoing the tremors of sudden industrialisation. The importance of his theory, then, lies in its values: the principles of tradition and authority, class and civility, are enduring and of wide application. Even in an age characterised by democracy and industrialisation Burke's ideas are recurrent. While old ruling classes may be replaced by new elites, it is interesting to note that these elites strive to achieve the qualities of the class they have supplanted. Even the commissars of a Soviet state eventually begin to talk of history, stability and tradition; and they seek to perpetuate the social order through their property and children."[29]

CRITICISM OF BURKE'S POLITICAL THOUGHT

1. No Systematic Writings. Burke was one of the most illuminous parliamentary figure of 18th century England. He has not presented his political philosophy in a systematic way as Hobbes could do in his *Leviathan* or Machiavelli in his The Prince. Sabine said, "It is perhaps stretching a point to say that Burke had a political philosophy at all. His ideas are scattered through his speeches and pamphlets, all called out by the stress of events, though they have the consistency that is the stamp of a powerful intelligence and settled moral convictions. Certainly he had no philosophy other than his reactions to the events in which he took part and little knowledge of the history of philosophy."

---

27. Dreyer, *op. cit.*, p. 83.
28. C.B. Macpherson: *Burke*, p. 61.
29. Hacker: *Political Theory, Philosophy, Ideology, Science,* p. 381.

2. Contradiction. Burke has been charged for contradictions in his ideas. He stood to preserve traditions and ancient institutions. He wanted to stick to the spirit of law but in actual practice he contradicted himself. When he discussed the colonial problems he wanted to discuss not the spirit but the letters of the laws and traditions. In his conservatism he went to the extent of relating Rotten boroughs which was not illogical. Outdated institutions are burden on nation and without any use and utility. A progressive nation must dispense with outdated institutions. Burke was not agreeable to this.

3. Conservatism. His dictum of 'disposition to preserve and an ability to improve taken together would be my standard of statement and also his ideas about 'expendiency' are nothing but indications of political immobility. Even in the French Revolution he wanted to see the preservation of old institutions. He hesitated to congratulate the revolutionaries unless he was assured that old institutions would be preserved. In the words of Ivor Brown, 'So eager was Burke to see in society a natural organic growth that the notion of artificially stimulating that growth was utterly repulsive to him.'

4. Unjustified Praise for English Constitution. Burke's praise for English Constitution was unjustified. He quite well understood old English institutions but failed to appreciate that their continuation could result in a revolution of the French type, most of them being outdated. He failed to realise that the period of privileges was over and that those must give place to equality and the reasons.

CONTRIBUTION OF BURKE

The above criticism does not mean that there was nothing of significance about Burke. Maxey said that he was "....one of the ever luminous orbs in the galaxy of the political thought." His contribution to the political philosophy was many sided. It can be summed up as follows.

1. Conservatism. Burke has contributed to the political philosophy, the theory of conservatism. In his hands conservatism got a systematic touch. Sabine has said, "The point is not, of course, that before. Burke, there was no conservatism, but it is almost true to say that there was no conservative philosophy."

2. Expediency. Burke stood for 'expediency' rather than adhering to theoretical aspects of the laws. He realised that the genius behind the latters should be honoured and followed. He wanted to avoid political speculations. He wanted to give them a realistic touch. He stood for 'expediency' rather than dogmas. This expendiency is cherished even today.

3. Historical Method. Like Montesquieu and Rousseau, Burke applied historical method for the study of political institutions. Burke realised that the application of principles should be according to circumstances. Maxey has said that "History was bunk, reason despised, and facts were mere obstacles to be swept aside. Vision and rhapsodies were the things. Wishes were elevated as ideals, and the attainment of such ideals was sought with small regard, for either sense or morality.

4. Contradiction of the Inherited Rights. Burke contradicted the theory that men had any inherited rights. He believed that if God gave anything to men that was 'duty' and not 'rights'. He repudiated the theory of 'natural rights'. He stood for 'civil rights' which made the state a real living body responsible for the protection of civil rights of the subjects.

5. Value of Stability and Power of Customs. About Burke, Maxey says, "the real reaction which he led against the French Revolution was the beginning of a shift which carried the prevailing social philosophy from attack to defence and therefore to a new emphasis on the value of stability and the power of customs on which stability depends."

6. Influence on Contemporary Political Thought. Burke's political philosophy had wide effect on the contemporary political thought as noted by the following:

(i) *Sabine*— "Hegel whose philosophy embodied systematically all of Burke's scattered principles, was typically the advocate of a new political order in Germany...with Burke the destruction of the pseudo-science of natural law was the occasion, as it was with Kant for setting up a rational faith in which the warmth of reverence did duty for the assurance of truth."

(ii) *Hearnshaw*. "The most conspicuous general features of his political outpourings are first his avoidance of abstract political speculations and his denunciation of the metaphysical treatment of practical affairs; secondly, his insistence on the empirical nature of the art of government; thirdly, his appeal to history and experience as the only satisfactory guides in administrative matters; frothly, his emphasis on consideration of expendiency rather than on arguments based on rights, indubitable problems of policy; and finally, the essential moderation of all his opinions even when he expressed those opinions with extreme immoderation of language."

(iii) *Gettell*. "His insistence on the value of studying actual institutions and on the evolutionary nature of successful reforms was another influence of his philosophy."

(iv) *Laski*. "There is hardly any figure in the history of political thought in England looking out of the relentless logic of Hobbes, the acuteness of Hume, moral insight of Green, he has a large part of the faculties of each. He brought to the political philosophy of his generation a sense of direction, lofty, vigour of purpose and full knowledge of its complexity, such as no other statesman has possessed."

QUESTIONS FOR EXERCISE

1. How do you reconcile Burke's attitude towards the French revolution with his views on the American continent.
2. Examine Burke's view on British Constitution.
3. Burke sponsored the cause of the American revolution but criticised the position of the revolutionaries to France. Do you find any inconsistency in this. Illustrate your answer with examples.
4. Estimate critically the political ideas of Burke. Why is he regarded as father of modern conservatism.
5. Analyse the elements in Burke's thought which made him "the founder of self-conscious conservatism."
6. "The state ought not to be considered as nothing better than a partnership agreement in trade of pepper or calico or tobacco or other such low concern." Burke. Discuss.
7. "Burke indeed was never a democrat, that is the real root of his philosophy?" Laski. Discuss.
8. "The declaration of rights of man is a sort of institute and digest of anarchy." Burke. Comment.
9. "Englishmen know that a religion is the basis of civil society and of all good and of all comfort." Burke. Discuss.
10. "A disposition to preserve and ability to improve taken together would be my standard of a state." Burke. Explain.
11. "Burke is rightly regarded as the founder of self-conscious conservatism." Explain.
12. "Burke's political philosophy is a curious blending of liberalism and conservatism." Explain this statement.

BIBLIOGRAPHY

Abbot, F.F., *Roman Political Institutions.*

Abbot, F.F., *Society and Politics in Rome.*

Adams, A.M., *Plato, Moral and Political Ideals.*

Adams, G.B., *Civilization During the Middle Ages.*

Addington, R., *Voltaire.*

Annie Besant., *Fabian Essays.*

Aquinas, T., *Summa Theologia.*

Armstrong, E., *Political Aspects of the French Wars of Religion.*

Arnold, W.T., *The Roman System of Provincial Administration.*

Austin, J., *The Province of Jurisprudence Determined.*

Bagehot, W., *Physics and Politics.*

Bird, H.M., *Rise Of Huguenots in France.*

Barnes, H.E., *Sociology and Political Theory.*

Barnes, J.S., *Universal Aspect of Fascism.*

Barker, E., *Plato and His Predecessor*

Barker, E., *Politics of Aristotle.*

Barker, E., *Political Thought of Plato and Aristotle.*

Barker, E., *Social Contract.*

Barker, E., *Political Thought in England from 1848 to 1914.*

Bancour, J.P., *Foundation of Sovereignty.*

Benthem, J., *The Principles of Morals and Legislation;*

Benthem, J., *Fragments on Government.*

Blackstone, W., *Commentaries on the Laws of England.*

Bosanquet, B., *The Philosophical Theory of State.*

Bolingbroke, *Works.*

Bowle, *The History of Western Political Thought.*

Booth, A.J., *Saint Simon and Saint-Simonism.*

Bryce, J., *Studies in History and Jurisprudence.*

Bryce, J., *Holy Roman Empire.*

Brown, I., *English Political Theory.*

Burns, C.D., *Political Ideals.*

Burns, C.D., *International Politics.*

Calvin, J., *The Institutes of the Christian Religion.*

Carlyle, R.W. and A.J., *History of Medieval Political Theory.*

Cokker, F.W., *Readings in Political Philosophy.*

Cole, G.D.H., *Guild Socialism.*

Cole, G.D.H., *Social Theory.*

Cole, G.D.H., *The World of Labour.*

Cole, G.D.H., *What Marx Really Meant.*

Comte, A., *Positive Polity.*

Davidson, W.L, *The Utilitarians.*

Davidson, W.L, *Aristotle and Ancient Educational Ideals.*

Doyle, Phyllis, *A History of Political Theories.*

Dunning, W.A., *A History of Political Theories, Vol. I, II, III & IV.*

Duff, R.A., *Spinoza's Political Theory and Ethical Philosophy.*

Emerton, *Introduction to the Middle Ages.*

Emerton, *Mediaeval Europe.*

Engels, F., *Socialism Utopian and Scientific.*

Figgis, J.N, *From Gerson to Grotius.*

Figgis, J.N, *Modern State.*

Figgis, J.N, *The Divine Right of Kings.*

Filmer, R., *Observation Concerning the Origin of Govt. Patriarcha.*

Finer, *The Theory and Practice of Modern Government.*

Fisher, G.P., *A History of Europe.*

Fisher, G.P., *History of the Reformation.*

Fowler, W., *City States of Greeks and Romans.*

Freeman, E.A., *History of Federal Government.*

Garner, *Political Science and Government.*

Gettell, R.G., *Political Science.*

Gettell, R.G., *History of Political Thought.*

Gierke, O.F., *Political Theories of the Middle Ages* (Maitland's Trans.)

Giddings, F.H., *Studies in the Theory of Human Society.*

Godwin, W., *The Political Justice.*

Gooch, G.P., *Political Thought in England from Bacon to Halifax.*

Gooch, G.P., *Studies of Modern History.*

Gooch, G.P., *English Democratic Ideas.*

Grant, A., *The Ethics of Aristotle.*

Green, T.M., *Principles of Political Obligation.*

Hearnshaw, F.G.C., *The Social and Political Ideas of Middle Ages.*

Hearnshaw, F.G.C., *The Social and Political Thinkers of the Revolutionary Era.*

Hegel, G.W.F., *The Philosophy of Right.*

Hegel, G.W.F., *The Philosophy of History.*

Hobbes, T., *Leviathan* (edited by Rhys).

Hobhouse, L.T., *The Metaphysical Theory of State.*

Hobson, S.G., *National Guilds.*

Hobson, J.A., *Imperialism.*

Hyndman, H., *England for All.*

Joad, C.E.M., *Modern Political Theories.*

Jowett, B., *The Dialogues of Plato.*

Jowett, B., *The Politics of Aristotle.*

Knox, J., *Appellations.*

Laski, H.J., *Political Thought in England from Locke to Bentham.*

Laski, H.J., *A Grammer of Politics.*

Laski, H.J., *Foundation of Sovereignty and Other Essays.*

Laski, H.J., *Political Ideas of James I* (An Essay in the Political Science, Vol. XXXIV).

Laski, H.J., *Communism.*

Leckey, W., *England in the Eighteenth Century.*

Lindsay, A.D., *The State in Political Theory.*

Locke, J., *The Two Treatises on Civil Government* (Ed. by W.S. Carpenter).

Lord, A.R., *Principles of Politics.*

Lord, A.R., *Social Contract.*

Luther, M., *Letter to German Nobility.*

Luther, M., *How Far Obedience Is Due to Secular Authority.*

Luther, M., *Good Works.*

Mabbot, J.D., *The State and the Citizen.*

Macaulay., *Machiavelli* (Essays).

MacCunn, J., *The Political Philosophy of Burke.*

MacDonald, R., *Syndicalism.*

Machiavelli., *The Prince.*

MacIver, R.M., *Community.*

Marx, K., *The Capital.*

Maxey, C.C., *The Political Philosophies.*

Merriam, C.E., *History of Sovereignty Since Rousseau.*

Mill, James, *Essay on Government.*

Morley, J., *Machiavelli.*

Murray, J.M., *The History of Political Science.*

Nettleship, R.L. *Lectures on Plato's Republic.*

Paine, T., *The Rights of Man.*

Pease, E., *A History of Fabian Society.*

Pollock, Sir F., *The History of Law of Nature.*

Pollock, Sir F., *The History of the Science of Politics.*

Pufendorf., *The Law of Nature and of Nations.*

Reeves, J.S., *Jeremy Bentham and American Jurisprudence.*

Sabine, G.H., *A History of Political Theory.*

Se'ddilot, R., *A Bird's Eye View of World History.*

Sidgewick, H., *The Development of European Polity.*

Spencer, H., *Social Studies.*

Spencer, H., *Man Versus State.*

Stalin, J.V., *An Essay On Historical and Dialectical Materialism.*

Stalin, J.V., *Leninism.*

Symonds, *Renaissance in Italy.*

Taylor, H.O., *The Medieval Mind.*

Taylor, H.O., *Thought and Expression in the Sixteenth Century.*

Vaughan, C.E., *Political Writings of J.J. Rousseau.*

Vaughan, R.W.B., *Life and Labours of St. Thomas Aquinas.*

Walker, T.A., *History of Law of Nations.*

Wallas, G., *Fabian Essays.*

Wallas, G., *The Great Society.*

Wallas, G., *Human Nature in Politics.*

Wicksteed, P.H., *Dante and Aquinas.*

Willoughby, W.W., *Political Theories of the Ancient World.*

Willoughby, W.W., *The Nature of State.*

Woodbridge., *Philosophy of Hobbes.*

Zimmern, A.W., *The Greek Commonwealth.*